Community Health Education and Promotion

A Guide to Program Design and Evaluation

SECOND EDITION

Consulting Editor

Mary Ellen Wurzbach, RN, MSN, FNP, PhD
TRISS Professor
College of Nursing
University of Wisconsin—Oshkosh
Oshkosh, Wisconsin

JONES AND BARTLETT PUBLISHERS
Sudbury, Massachusetts
BOSTON   TORONTO   LONDON   SINGAPORE

World Headquarters

Jones and Bartlett Publishers
40 Tall Pine Drive
Sudbury, MA 01776
978-443-5000
info@jbpub.com
www.jbpub.com

Jones and Bartlett Publishers
Canada
2406 Nikanna Road
Mississauga, ON L5C 2W6
CANADA

Jones and Bartlett Publishers
International
Barb House, Barb Mews
London W6 7PA
UK

Copyright © 2004 by Jones and Bartlett Publishers, Inc.
Originally published by Aspen Publishers, © 2002.

LIBRARY OF CONGRESS CATALOGING-IN-PUBLICATION DATA
Wurzbach, Mary Ellen.
Community health education and promotion : a guide to program design and evaluation
/ Mary Ellen Wurzbach.—2nd ed.
p. cm.
Previosuly published in 1997 by Aspen Reference Group.
Includes index.
ISBN 0-7637-2596-X
1. Health education. 2. Community health services. 3. Health promotion. I. Title

RA440.5 .C626 2002
362.1'2—dc21
2001055992
CIP

PRODUCTION CREDITS
Publisher: Michael Brown
Associate Editor: Chambers Moore
Production Manager: Amy Rose
Associate Production Editor: Renée Sekerak
Production Assistant: Jenny L. McIsaac
Associate Marketing Manager: Joy Stark-Vancs
Manufacturing Buyer: Amy Bacus
Printing and Binding: The P. A. Hutchison Company
Cover Printing: The P. A. Hutchison Company

Printed in the United States of America
07 06 05   10 9 8 7 6 5 4 3 2

Contents

*For a detailed listing of chapter contents,
please see the first page of each chapter.*

Preface v

Chapter 1   Development of Health Education and Promotion 1

Chapter 2   Personnel Management 43

Chapter 3   Community Assessment and Mobilization 73

Chapter 4   Culturally Competent Health Promotion 195

Chapter 5   Developing Successful Programs 281

Chapter 6   Creating and Tailoring Effective Materials 441

Chapter 7   Publicizing Your Program 547

Chapter 8   Program Evaluation 581

Chapter 9   Adapting to Diverse Audiences in Different Settings 603

Appendixes 625

   Appendix A—Professional Organizations for the Health Educator 627

   Appendix B—The Internet and Other Resources 633

   Appendix C—*Healthy People 2010*: Summary of Goals and Objectives 641

Index 653

Preface

Welcome to the second edition of *Community Health Education and Promotion: A Guide to Program Design and Evaluation.* The previous edition was published in 1997 by the Aspen Reference Group. The purpose of this edition is to provide more practical guidance for the student of community health, health education, or health promotion about the design, development, and evaluation of programs in the community.

We live in an environment of constant change and numerous lifestyle choices, many of which could be hazardous to the health of the individual and community. We also live in an age of managed care and capitation, which focus new attention on the value of health education and promotion. Economic benefits for patients, providers, and payors now flow from motivating and empowering individuals to take responsibility for their own well-being. In addition, health education and promotion are the essence of community health practice and the way to prevent the effect of health hazards on both the individual and the community.

The federal government's *Healthy People 2000* and *Healthy People 2010* outline the national health objectives for the previous and the coming decade, emphasizing risk reduction and preventive care services. Worksites, schools, neighborhoods—all are challenged to adapt these objectives, establish local goals, and implement programs to pursue them.

Leading these efforts are the health educators. These men and women help citizens build the bridge between health information and health practice. They are the front-line soldiers in the battle against AIDS, cancer, heart disease, violence, and drug abuse.

Adding to the complexity of the health educator's job is the multicultural environment in which we live. Our society is divided by ethnicity, gender, sexual orientation, socioeconomic status, and age. Successful health promotion relies on a thorough knowledge of and respect for an audience's unique characteristics.

To support community health educators in their endeavors, the Aspens Reference Group designed *Community Health Education and Promotion: A Guide to Program Design and Evaluation.* It is a practical reference tool that guides the health educator through the planning, implementation, promotion, and evaluation stages of program development, with special attention paid to populations bound by shared risks, exposures, and behaviors.

In choosing materials for the manual, we kept in mind that health education programs exist in a variety of settings, including schools, worksites, and state and local health departments. Materials were gathered through a wide-ranging survey of health promotion organizations, both public and private, and an extensive review of the related literature. Our editorial board was instrumental in this manuscript development process.

Community Health Education and Promotion begins with useful definitions, followed by an exploration of legal and ethical issues pertinent to the health educator. Successive chapters address personnel management; funding programs; assessing and mobilizing the community; designing, implementing, and marketing programs; culturally competent program development and promotion; creating effective materials; program evaluation; and health education in different settings.

The text has changed considerably from the first edition. There is a new emphasis on program planning, Internet resources, and marketing of community health programs. Health promotion strategies and programs that have worked abound. *Healthy People 2010* is introduced as an update of the national health guidelines *Healthy People 2000*. Cogent advice about how to keep your mission alive is emphasized. The research aspects of community health are integrated (focus groups, in-depth interviews, and surveys). Sample program materials are provided in abundance and many of the materials emphasize cultural competence. Tips on screening, hiring, and evaluating communication consultants and contractors, a section on evaluation pitfalls, and sections on adapting health promotion materials to the audience add depth to the text.

Appendixes include a list of professional organizations for the health educator and two new appendixes, one about the Internet and its resources, and *Healthy People 2010*—Summary of Goals and Objectives. As a new feature, we have developed an Instructor's Manual to accompany the text. It contains class outlines, curriculum guides, and numerous easily adaptable classroom activities for the classroom instructor, all based on critical learning objectives.

The framework for the book is based on the Nursing Process—sometimes known as the Problem Solving Approach, which includes assessment, planning, implementation, and evaluation. This allows for systematic resolution of community health problems including those of health promotion and education.

We have formatted the manual for quick, easy reference. Throughout, the format emphasizes sample forms, charts, and worksheets that cover a full range of the health educator's responsibilities. All chapters are prefaced by a detailed table of contents. A complete index lets you locate specific items and cross-reference subjects of interest.

The primary audience for the text is graduate level students of community health nursing, community management, health education, or public health, as well as many of the health sciences. It also has great value for the practitioner, educator, or administrator already employed in the community health setting.

The unique features of this text include diverse resources that can be adapted to the reader's agency, practical advice from experts in the field, and resources essential to the design, development, and evaluation of community health programs. Whether the interest is community assessment, culturally competent educational materials, or formative and summative evaluation, this text offers the necessary resources for success.

1

Development of Health Education and Promotion

Definitions

Health Education and Promotion
Terminology 4

Criteria and Recommendations

Criteria for the Development of Health
Promotion and Health Education
Programs 9

Ethical and Legal Considerations

Ethical and Legal Issues in Health
Promotion and Education 11
Code of Ethics for the Health Education
Profession 15

Healthy People 2000

An Introduction to *Healthy
People 2000* 18

Summary List of Risk Reduction
Objectives from *Healthy
People 2000* 20
Healthy People 2000 Priority Areas and
Their Responsible Governmental
Agencies 25

Healthy Communities 2000

Healthy Communities 2000: An Introduction
to the Model Standards 26

Healthy People 2010

Proposed Healthy People Framework—Vision
of 2010: Healthy People in Healthy
Communities 28
Initiative To Eliminate Racial and Ethnic
Disparities in Health 29
Healthy People 2010 Overview: Goals,
Objectives, and Leading Health
Indicators 39

1

Development of Health Education and Promotion

OBJECTIVES

At the completion of this chapter, the reader will

- appreciate health education and promotion as it relates to optimal health
- be able to define health education and promotion terminology
- understand and appreciate the ethical and legal issues in health promotion and education
- understand both *Healthy People 2000* and *Healthy People 2010*

INTRODUCTION

Chapter 1 begins with the definitions of common health education and promotion terms and with criteria for the development of health promotion and education programs. A practical guide to ethical and legal aspects of health promotion and education and the Code of Ethics for the Health Education Profession (AAHE) follows. Historical analysis of *Healthy People 2000* and *Healthy Communities 2000*, plus a current synopsis of *Healthy People 2010*, concludes the chapter.

The glossary of terms, criteria for the development of programs, and Code of Ethics, which are essential and difficult-to-acquire references for the student of community health, are all made available in this chapter. Ethical issues will become paramount in the coming century with the emphasis on national health promotion designed to improve the health of the population, particularly if the value of individualism competes with the value of community. The developmental review of *Healthy People 2000* and *2010,* with the discussion of the national objectives that have been met, is an invaluable tool and the standard for our national policy on health promotion. The chapter contents provide a succinct overview of necessary health promotion and education background information, which will serve as a practical introduction to the practice of community health.

HEALTH EDUCATION AND PROMOTION TERMINOLOGY

CONTEXTUAL, PRIMARY HEALTH EDUCATION, COMMUNITY SETTINGS, AND EDUCATIONAL SETTINGS DEFINITIONS*

Certified Health Education Specialist (CHES)

An individual who has met required health education training qualifications, successfully passed a competency-based examination administered by the National Commission for Health Education Credentialing, Inc., and satisfies the continuing education requirement to maintain the national credential.

Community

A collective body of individuals identified by geography, common interests, concerns, characteristics, or values.

Community Capacity

Combined assets that influence a community's commitment, resources, and skills used to solve problems and strengthen the quality of life for its citizens.

Community Health Education

A theory-driven process that promotes health and prevents disease within populations.

Community Organization

The process by which communities mobilize to identify common problems or goals, mobilize resources, and in other ways, develop and implement strategies for reaching the goals they have collectively set.

*Source: This article is reprinted with permission from the *Journal of Health Education,* September 21, 2001, pp. 12–14. The *Journal of Health Education* is a publication of the American Alliance for Health, Physical Education, Recreation and Dance, 1900 Association Drive, Reston, Virginia 22091.

Complementary and Alternative Health Practices

These practices generally include natural substances, physical manipulations, and self-care modalities. These approaches often incorporate aspects of interventions derived from traditional practices. The approach in Western societies has been to select specific approaches from these systems and apply them to health maintenance, health enhancement, or disease management. Such approaches can be used to complement conventional allopathic care (complementary therapy), or as an alternative to conventional approaches (alternative therapy). Many of these complementary and alternative approaches have not been validated through experiential research, but those that have, such as acupuncture for pain, are being integrated into conventional health practices (integrative medicine).

Comprehensive School Health Education

The part of the coordinated school health program that includes the development, delivery, and evaluation of planned, sequential, and developmentally appropriate instruction, learning experiences, and other activities designed to protect, promote, and enhance the health literacy, attitudes, skills, and well-being of students, pre-kindergarten through grade 12. The content is derived from the National Health Education Standards and guidelines that are available in some states.

Coordinated School Health Program

An organized set of policies, procedures, and activities designed to protect, promote, and improve the health and well-being of students and staff, thus improving a student's ability to learn. It includes, but is not limited to, comprehensive school health education; school health services; a healthy school environment; school counseling; psychological and social services; physical education; school nutrition services; family and community involvement in school health; and school-site health promotion for staff.

Cultural Competence

The ability of an individual to understand and respect values, attitudes, beliefs, and mores that differ across cultures, and to consider and respond appropriately to these differences in planning, implementing, and evaluating health education and promotion programs and interventions.

Determinants of Health

Biological, environmental, behavioral, organizational, political, and social factors that contribute to the health status of individuals, groups, and communities.

Disease Prevention

The process of reducing risks and alleviating disease to promote, preserve, and restore health and minimize suffering and distress.

Evidence-Based Health Education

The systematic selection, implementation, and evaluation of strategies, programs, and policies with evidence from the scientific literature that they have demonstrated effectiveness in accomplishing intended outcomes.

Health Advocacy

The processes by which the actions of individuals or groups attempt to bring about social and/or organizational change on behalf of a particular health goal, program, interest, or population.

Health Education

Any combination of planned learning experiences based on sound theories that provide individuals, groups, and communities the opportunity to acquire information and the skills needed to make quality health decisions.

Health Education and Health Promotion Outcomes

Measurable changes in or reinforcement of health knowledge, attitudes or beliefs, personal behaviors, and/or skills of individuals or populations; changes in social norms and actions; and organizational practices and public policies that are attributable to health education and health promotion interventions.

Health Education Field

A practice that uses multidisciplinary theories and behavioral and organizational change principles to plan, implement, and evaluate interventions that enable individuals, groups, and communities to achieve personal, environmental, and social health.

Health Educator

A professionally prepared individual who serves in a variety of roles and is specifically trained to use appropriate educational strategies and methods to facilitate the development of policies, procedures, interventions, and systems conducive to the health of individuals, groups, and communities.

Health Informatics

The systematic application of information and technology to research, theory, practice, and learning applied to health.

Health Information

The content of communications derived from credible sources related to individual, group, and community health issues and concerns.

Health Literacy

> The capacity of an individual to obtain, interpret, and understand basic health information and services and the competence to use such information and services in ways that are health enhancing.

Health Outcome

> Measurable change in or reinforcement of factors related to health status or quality of life attributable to a series of events, planned or unplanned.

Health Promotion

> Any planned combination of educational, political, environmental, regulatory, or organizational mechanisms that support actions and conditions of living conducive to the health of individuals, groups, and communities.

Health Protection

> Any planned intervention or services designed to provide individuals and communities with resistance to health threats, often by modifying policy or the environment to decrease potentially harmful interactions.

Healthy Lifestyle

> Patterns of behavior that maximize one's quality of life and decrease one's susceptibility to negative health outcomes.

Non-Governmental Organization (NGO)

> A voluntary, task-oriented organization not officially connected to a local, state, national, or international government.

Post-Secondary or College Health Program

> A coordinated and planned set of policies, procedures, activities, programs, and services designed to enhance, protect, promote, and improve the health and well-being of students, faculty, and staff of colleges, universities, and other institutions of higher education.

Prevention

> Actions and interventions designed to identify risks and reduce susceptibility or exposure to health threats prior to disease onset (primary prevention), detect and treat disease in early stages to prevent progress or recurrence (secondary prevention), and alleviate the effects of disease and injury (tertiary prevention).

Professional Development

Planned learning activities designed to maintain and enhance one's competence in health education following a previously attained level of professional preparation.

Professional Preparation

An undergraduate or graduate course of study that includes career-related experiences offered through an accredited college or university, which is designed to prepare individuals to practice competently in the health education field.

Population-Based Health Education

Health education interventions designed to promote health and prevent disease within groups and communities rather than focusing on individuals.

Risk Reduction

Actions that can successfully decrease the probability that individuals, groups, or communities will experience disease or debilitating health conditions.

School Health Coordinator

A certificated or licensed professional at the state, district, or school level who is responsible for managing, coordinating, implementing, and evaluating all school health policies, activities, and resources.

School-Site Health Promotion for Staff

A planned set of policies, programs, strategies, and activities designed to protect, promote, maintain, and improve the health and well-being of all school personnel.

Social Marketing

The consumer-driven application of commercial marketing techniques to the analysis, planning, implementation, and evaluation of programs designed to influence positive health behaviors within intended audiences.

Wellness

An approach to health that focuses on balancing the many aspects, or dimensions, of a person's life through increasing the adoption of health enhancing conditions and behaviors rather than attempting to minimize conditions of illness.

Worksite Health Promotion

A combination of educational, organizational, and environmental activities designed to improve the health and safety of employees and their families.

CRITERIA FOR THE DEVELOPMENT OF HEALTH PROMOTION AND HEALTH EDUCATION PROGRAMS*

To meet the growing demand of organizations and agencies desiring to sponsor health promotion/disease prevention programs for employees and beneficiaries, an ad hoc work group of the American Public Health Association has developed a set of criteria intended to serve as a guideline for establishing the feasibility and/or the appropriateness of such programs in a variety of settings prior to a decision to implement. They reflect the kinds of issues that should be considered during the process leading to allocation of resources or the setting of health promotion program priorities. Each of the five criteria suggests a number of issues or questions that should be addressed during the decision-making process.

Criterion No. 1. A health promotion program should address one or more risk factors that are carefully defined, measurable, modifiable, and prevalent among members of the chosen target group—factors that represent a threat to health status and/or the quality of life.

An important issue under this criterion is the determination of whether a risk factor in a particular population group is indeed a problem and if it indeed warrants change. Another consideration is the prevalence of a risk factor relative to other factors.

Criterion No. 2. A health promotion program should reflect a consideration of the special characteristics, needs, and preferences of its target group(s).

It is important to determine the appropriateness of a particular intervention to its target group and whether the selected intervention reflects the priorities and preferences of the group. Access to the proposed program in the form of location, affordability, time of day, and language used can help dispel the perception by the target group of a program being "done to" rather than "offered with." Another issue is consideration of behavioral change principles in conjunction with the needs and preferences of the group. A final consideration would be whether there are strong positive or negative public attitudes toward the intervention (such as with sex education or birth control programs).

Criterion No. 3. Health promotion programs should include interventions that will clearly and effectively reduce a targeted risk factor and are appropriate for a particular setting. It is important to determine to what extent modification of a specific personal or environmental risk factor will alter the prospective health status of those to whom the intervention is directed. Some scientific rationale for the choice of program content is needed.

The nature of the proposed intervention should be examined and its critical elements identified. Another consideration would be to determine whether any part of the program should be implemented under special circumstances or sequential steps, and attention should be given to what would happen if only part of the intervention is carried out.

Criterion No. 4. A health promotion program should identify and implement interventions that make optimum use of available resources.

---

*Source: State of New York Department of Health. Abstracted from *American Journal of Public Health*, Vol. 77, No. 1, pages 89–92, American Public Health Association, Washington, D.C., © January 1987.

Required levels of organizational resources, including personnel, should be determined in order to implement and sustain the program. Monetary and nonmonetary costs, benefits, and other effects should be estimated as well as whether special funding will be needed. Many times, existing community resources might be used as part of the program initiative and can have an impact on program effectiveness.

Criterion No. 5. From the outset, a health promotion program should be organized, planned, and implemented in such a way that its operation and effects can be evaluated.

If possible, baseline measures of prevalence and incidence of the identified risk factors in members of the target group should be determined. Careful records should be kept in an objective manner throughout the program in order to measure participation. A good form of evaluation could involve a control group with different levels of exposure to the intervention. Many times there are individuals or organizations with competency in program evaluation who are able to assist with the evaluation tasks. An effective evaluation should be planned at the outset of a program.

NOTES:

ETHICAL AND LEGAL ISSUES IN HEALTH PROMOTION AND EDUCATION*

Health education has been occurring for a long time. The Bible contains many stories and parables concerning health and cleanliness. Other religious and historical writings refer to the need for proper behavior, clean environment, and methods to prevent illness. Consequently, one of the major factors involved in the advance of civilization from the dawn of history to the present is people learning and practicing positive health behavior. A next step is to begin to demand services that result in improved health status. Yet another step is to demand that others practice good health behaviors.

Questions begin to arise about whether certain practices of health education are morally, ethically, and legally appropriate for today's society, in which an individual's rights are emphasized. For example, should a person be forced to participate in a treatment in order to protect groups of people? Should patients with acquired immune deficiency syndrome (AIDS) be provided expensive treatment at government expense, when the needs of children without the disease are neglected by the government because of the cost? Should the parents of all children attending public schools be required to have their children immunized against childhood diseases and those affecting expectant mothers? Or should they be educated to want to do this? Should children be immunized against mild childhood diseases in which the disease itself may be less traumatic than the shot? What about a society that goes to the limit to protect and preserve all human life, whether genetically inferior or aged, and then educates its young to zero population growth and reinforces this by providing birth control and abortions? What about the ethnic overtones of a public health program that involves testing for sickle cell anemia but that does not provide affordable educational programs or genetic counseling for those affected? Or, for that matter, is it proper for those not formally trained in the profession to take on the duties of and claim to be health educators? Is it ethical for individuals who believe that homosexuality is a form of deviant behavior to work with AIDS patients?

The Nature of Ethics

Ethical issues involve opinions about what is good or bad. Laws assume there is a single correct behavior, whereas ethics deal with beliefs, values, and preferences of individuals or groups.

Ethics, by definition, is concerned with debatable and controversial issues. In a sense, ethical decisions are intensely personal. Even if one concurs with someone else's beliefs, the decision to concur is individual.

Decisions that affect groups of people are most ethical when they produce the following:

- autonomy in decision making (self-responsibility)
- justice (fair and impartial)
- no harm to members of the group (nonmaleficence)
- sense of community as a value (responsibility for others)

---

*Source: Donald J. Breckon et al., *Community Health Education: Settings, Roles, and Skills for the 21st Century*, ed. 3, Aspen Publishers, Inc., © 1994.

Individual behavior can be considered ethical or good if it:

- increases trust among people
- promotes integrity and honest relationships
- dissolves barriers between people
- increases cooperative attitudes
- enhances self-respect
- does not exploit others
- allows individuals to move toward mutual respect

Areas of Responsibility

The Public

Ethical and legal concerns dealing with the public vary from overall commitments to do public good to concerns with fairness and equality for each individual.

The Profession

The National Commission for Health Education Credentialing has determined that Certified Health Education Specialists have seven areas of responsibility. Working with individuals, groups, and organizations, they are responsible for the following:

1. assessing individual and community needs for health education
2. planning effective health education programs
3. implementing health education programs
4. evaluating effectiveness of health education programs
5. coordinating provision of health education services
6. acting as resources in health education
7. communicating health and health education needs, concerns, and resources

With adequate preparation, the individual will be theoretically ready to face these responsibilities and always do the "right thing." But what is the right thing?

Determining proper ethical responses is not easy. Codes of ethics recommend that health educators maintain their competence through continuing education; through active membership in professional organizations; through review of research, programs, materials, and products; and through leadership in economic, legislative, and cooperative endeavors.

Some of the ethical issues involved in the day-to-day functioning of health educators include those that violate moral and legal standards, those that help some individuals but are unfair to others, those that do not involve the people who are affected, those that do not communicate possible positive and negative outcomes of a course of action (informed consent), and those that use coercion rather than choice.

Colleagues

The relationships among people working in the same profession may be crucial to the success or failure of its activities. Complaints in several health-related professions relate to the lack of honesty, the failure to develop mutual respect, and the tendency of some individuals to take advantage of clients, situations, and peers for personal gain. Peer review may be needed as a mechanism to control behavior of individuals within the profession of health education.

Students

The quality of preparation of those who enter the field of health education is imperative to its success. Ethical concerns of this preparation involve mutual respect between teacher and student and teacher responsiveness to student interests, opinions, and desires. Every effort needs to be made to develop potential within individual students for high-quality contributions to the public's health and to create a culturally diversified profession.

Employers

Employers have a moral and legal right to expect their employees to be truthful. Health educators, after all, are attempting to help people change and develop a higher quality of life. Consequently, it is important that health educators be straightforward with their employees about their qualifications, expertise, experience, and abilities. They should act within the boundaries of their competence, accepting responsibility and accountability for their acts, which they should commit by exercising their best judgment. Failure to do so may not only result in their being fired from their jobs but also do damage to clients and the profession.

Research and Evaluation

Research implies discovery of ideas, causation factors, and consequences. Evaluation is used to change, promote, and develop better programs and activities. Ethical concerns for health educators in these areas include protecting individual rights, accurately representing information, ensuring privacy, avoiding discrimination, and maintaining accountability and confidentiality.

Liability Issues

Educators have generally been considered a low-risk group for lawsuits, and that is certainly true of health educators as well. Society is becoming more litigious, however, and health educators are well advised to ascertain their liability insurance coverage. Some employers have such coverage for all their employees, and some professional organizations offer optional group liability insurance coverage. Home owner insurance policies often have options for liability insurance also.

The most basic responsibility of any professional is to do no harm. Certainly, that concept applies to health educators as well as to others. One implication of this concept is the need to ensure that clients are making the decisions voluntarily and are well informed about those decisions. Educators must not be induced to make decisions for clients or to pressure clients for the preferred behavior. It goes without saying that in most noneducational interventions, signed consent forms should be used. When in doubt, legal advice should be obtained, especially when developing new programs.

A more abstract issue relates to whether or not a health service professional should have done more than he or she did. Legal issues often arise over acts of omission, in addition to acts of commission. Again, the standards of practice will be the basis of comparison. If a matter goes to court, other health educators may be called to testify about the professional conduct expected of a health educator in a given situation.

If, however, a client experiences a problem he or she perceives as related to something the health educator failed to do, the burden of proof is generally on the claimant to establish that the health educator did not follow normal standards of practice. Stated differently, the claimant must demonstrate that the health educator did not conduct himself or herself as "a reasonably prudent health educator" would have in the same situation.

Most of the ethical and legal issues stemming from health education practices, especially some newer challenges involving health promotion, are yet to be tested in the courts.

Health educators need to do their work without fear of litigation because to do otherwise is counterproductive. It must again be emphasized that seldom are health educators named in liability suits, and even less frequently are judgments rendered against them. However, all health service professionals must be conscious of the possibility of a lawsuit and must always conduct themselves according to the standards of their profession. However, even health educators who follow the standards should carry liability insurance, because in a lawsuit, the court determines whether or not the standards were followed.

If health education programs expand as expected because of improved federal and state financing over the next several years, then legal suits from displeased clients will surely follow. This will be especially true if large amounts of money are involved.

NOTES:

Code of Ethics for the Health Education Profession

PREAMBLE

The Health Education profession is dedicated to excellence in the practice of promoting individual, family, organizational, and community health. Guided by common ideals, Health Educators are responsible for upholding the integrity and ethics of the profession as they face the daily challenges of making decisions. By acknowledging the value of diversity in society and embracing a cross-cultural approach, Health Educators support the worth, dignity, potential, and uniqueness of all people.

The Code of Ethics provides a framework of shared values within which Health Education is practiced. The Code of Ethics is grounded in fundamental ethical principles that underlie all health care services; respect for autonomy, promotion of social justice, active promotion of good, and avoidance of harm. The responsibility of each Health Educator is to aspire to the highest possible standards of conduct and to encourage the ethical behavior of all those with whom they work.

Regardless of job title, professional affiliation, work setting, or population served, Health Educators abide by these guidelines when making professional decisions.

ARTICLE I—RESPONSIBILITY TO THE PUBLIC

A Health Educator's ultimate responsibility is to educate people for the purpose of promoting, maintaining, and improving individual, family, and community health. When a conflict of issues arises among individuals, groups, organizations, agencies, or institutions, health educators must consider all issues and give priority to those that promote wellness and quality of living through principles of self-determination and freedom of choice for the individual.

Section 1. Health Educators support the right of individuals to make informed decisions regarding health, as long as such decisions pose no threat to the health of others.

Section 2. Health Educators encourage actions and social policies that support and facilitate the best balance of benefits over harm for all affected parties.

Section 3. Health Educators accurately communicate the potential benefits and consequences of the services and programs with which they are associated.

Section 4. Health Educators accept the responsibility to act on issues that can adversely affect the health of individuals, families, and communities.

Section 5. Health Educators are truthful about their qualifications and the limitations of their expertise and provide services consistent with their competencies.

Section 6. Health Educators protect the privacy and dignity of individuals.

Section 7. Health Educators actively involve individuals, groups, and communities in the entire educational process so that all aspects of the process are clearly understood by those who may be affected.

Section 8. Health Educators respect and acknowledge the rights of others to hold diverse values, attitudes, and opinions.

Section 9. Health Educators provide services equitably to all people.

ARTICLE II—RESPONSIBILITY TO THE PROFESSION

Health Educators are responsible for their professional behavior, for the reputation of their profession, and for promoting ethical conduct among their colleagues.

Section 1. Health Educators maintain, improve, and expand their professional competence through

continues

Code of Ethics for the Health Education Profession continued

continued study and education; membership, participation, and leadership in professional organizations; and involvement in issues related to the health of the public.

Section 2. Health Educators model and encourage nondiscriminatory standards of behavior in their interactions with others.

Section 3. Health Educators encourage and accept responsible critical discourse to protect and enhance the profession.

Section 4. Health Educators contribute to the development of the profession by sharing the processes and outcomes of their work.

Section 5. Health Educators are aware of possible professional conflicts of interest, exercise integrity in conflict situations, and do not manipulate or violate the rights of others.

Section 6. Health Educators give appropriate recognition to others for their professional contributions and achievements.

ARTICLE III—RESPONSIBILITY TO EMPLOYERS

Health Educators recognize the boundaries of their professional competence and are accountable for their professional activities and actions.

Section 1. Health Educators accurately represent their qualifications and the qualifications of others whom they recommend.

Section 2. Health Educators use appropriate standards, theories, and guidelines as criteria when carrying out their professional responsibilities.

Section 3. Health Educators accurately represent potential service and program outcomes to employers.

Section 4. Health Educators anticipate and disclose competing commitments, conflicts of interest, and endorsement of products.

Section 5. Health Educators openly communicate to employers expectations of job-related assignments that conflict with their professional ethics.

Section 6. Health Educators maintain competence in their areas of professional practice.

ARTICLE IV—RESPONSIBILITY IN THE DELIVERY OF HEALTH EDUCATION

Health Educators promote integrity in the delivery of health education. They respect the rights, dignity, confidentiality, and worth of all people by adapting strategies and methods to meet the needs of diverse populations and communities.

Section 1. Health Educators are sensitive to social and cultural diversity and are in accord with the law, when planning and implementing programs.

Section 2. Health Educators are informed of the latest advances in theory, research, and practice, and use strategies and methods that are grounded in and contribute to development of professional standards, theories, guidelines, statistics, and experience.

Section 3. Health Educators are committed to rigorous evaluation of both program effectiveness and the methods used to achieve results.

Section 4. Health Educators empower individuals to adopt healthy lifestyles through informed choice rather than by coercion or intimidation.

Section 5. Health Educators communicate the potential outcomes of proposed services, strategies, and pending decisions to all individuals who will be affected.

ARTICLE V—RESPONSIBILITY IN RESEARCH AND EVALUATION

Health Educators contribute to the health of the population and to the profession through research and evaluation activities. When planning and conducting research or evaluation, health educators do so in accordance with federal and state laws and regulations, organizational and institutional policies, and professional standards.

Section 1. Health Educators support principles and practices of research and evaluation that do no harm to individuals, groups, society, or the environment.

Section 2. Health Educators ensure that participation in research is voluntary and is based upon the informed consent of the participants.

continues

Code of Ethics for the Health Education Profession continued

Section 3. Health Educators respect the privacy, rights, and dignity of research participants, and honor commitments made to those participants.

Section 4. Health Educators treat all information obtained from participants as confidential unless otherwise required by law.

Section 5. Health Educators take credit, including authorship, only for work they have actually performed and give credit to the contributions of others.

Section 6. Health Educators who serve as research or evaluation consultants discuss their results only with those to whom they are providing service, unless maintaining such confidentiality would jeopardize the health or safety of others.

Section 7. Health Educators report the results of their research and evaluation objectively, accurately, and in a timely fashion.

ARTICLE VI—RESPONSIBILITY IN PROFESSIONAL PREPARATION

Those involved in the preparation and training of Health Educators have an obligation to accord learners the same respect and treatment given other groups by providing quality education that benefits the profession and the public.

Section 1. Health Educators select students for professional preparation programs based upon equal opportunity for all, and the individual's academic performance, abilities, and potential contribution to the profession and the public's health.

Section 2. Health Educators strive to make the educational environment and culture conducive to the health of all involved, and free from sexual harassment and all forms of discrimination.

Section 3. Health Educators involved in professional preparation and professional development engage in careful preparation; present material that is accurate, up-to-date, and timely; provide reasonable and timely feedback; state clear and reasonable expectations; and conduct fair assessments and evaluations of learners.

Section 4. Health Educators provide objective and accurate counseling to learners about career opportunities, development, and advancement, and assist learners to secure professional employment.

Section 5. Health Educators provide adequate supervision and meaningful opportunities for the professional development of learners.

Source: This article is reprinted with permission from the *Journal of Health Education*, September 21, 2001, pp. 12–14. The *Journal of Health Education* is a publication of the American Alliance for Health, Physical Education, Recreation and Dance, 1900 Association Drive, Reston, Virginia 22091.

AN INTRODUCTION TO *HEALTHY PEOPLE 2000**

Healthy People 2000, the national prevention initiative to improve the health of all Americans, was the product of unprecedented cooperation among government, voluntary and professional organizations, business, and individuals. The cornerstone of this effort was a set of national health promotion and disease prevention objectives for the year 2000. Development and publication of the objectives were coordinated by the U.S. Public Health Service (PHS).

Healthy People 2000 set three broad public health goals for the 1990s:

1. Increase the span of healthy life for Americans.
2. Reduce health disparities among Americans.
3. Achieve access to preventive services for all Americans.

To help meet these goals, 300 specific objectives were set in 22 separate priority areas. Quantifiable targets were set for improvements in health status, risk reduction, and service delivery. Organized under the broad approaches of health promotion, health protection, and preventive services, the national objectives provided direction for the ten-year drive to improve health. Individuals, organizations, and communities were challenged to change personal behaviors and the environments that support good health.

The year 2000 health objectives succeeded the 1990 health objectives that were set in 1980 following publication of *Healthy People: The Surgeon General's Report on Health Promotion and Disease Prevention.* Several themes distinguished *Healthy People 2000* from past efforts, reflecting the progress and experience of ten years as well as the expanded science base. A greater emphasis was placed on health outcomes other than premature mortality, reflecting a new appreciation for the prevention of illness and disability that impair quality of life. Furthermore, while significant improvements had been made in the nation's health over the past decade, gains had not been universal. Many of the objectives specified improving the health of groups of people who bore a disproportionate burden of suffering compared to the total population. This emphasis was especially critical since many of the groups with poorer health were also experiencing a faster rate of growth than the population as a whole.

Midcourse Review of the Year 2000 Objectives

In 1995 the PHS reviewed the nation's progress on its disease prevention and health promotion objectives. The review showed that of the 300 objectives:

- 50 percent were moving toward the target
- 18 percent were moving away from the target
- 3 percent showed no change
- 29 percent had insufficient data

This snapshot of progress gave cause for optimism about reaching a majority of the year 2000 targets. The assessment also illustrated the challenge of having periodic information with which to make evaluations.

---

*Source: U.S. Department of Health and Human Services, Public Health Service, Office of Disease Prevention and Health Promotion.

In addition, the PHS proposed revisions to the nation's health promotion and disease prevention framework. Made available for public comment in October 1994, the revisions included changes to targets to make them more challenging, new special population subobjectives, language modifications for clarification and for compatibility with data sources, and objectives incorporating new science, information, and data. Revisions made by the lead PHS agencies were subject to the same criteria used in the original drafting of the objectives and public comment. The *Healthy People 2000 Midcourse Review and 1995 Revisions*, published by the PHS in 1995, helped strengthen the nation's health promotion and disease prevention agenda and maintained its relevance to emerging health issues.

Special Populations

The second goal of *Healthy People 2000* specified the elimination of health status disparities that had been linked to racial and ethnic identity, as well as to economic status and gender of various population groups. Specific population targets were set for adolescents, American Indian/Alaska Natives, Asian and Pacific Islander Americans, African Americans, Hispanic Americans, older Americans, people with disabilities, people with low incomes, and women. As a part of the 1995 revisions, 120 special population targets were added to focus more attention on the needs of population groups that had the highest risk for premature death, disease, or disability. In each case new targets were added only if the group had demonstrated higher risk or was more vulnerable to the subject disease or condition than the population as a whole, or if the group had a different trend.

Special efforts are underway to identify gaps in current health statistics and to improve data collection for specific populations. Efforts such as the National Center for Health Statistics Minority Health Grants, the Office of Minority Health Programmatic Database, and the Surgeon General's Workshop on Hispanic/Latino Health have focused on data improvements for specific populations. *Healthy People 2000* specific population progress reviews documented data issues, barriers, and strategies to achieving the objectives, as well as implementation efforts underway to reach the specific population targets. Overcoming these barriers required solutions that included supplements to national data sources through state data systems and model standards approaches. It also demanded the continued commitment of states, communities, and the PHS.

Summary List of Risk Reduction Objectives from *Healthy People 2000*

PHYSICAL ACTIVITY AND FITNESS RISK REDUCTION OBJECTIVES

- Increase to at least 30 percent the proportion of people aged six and older who engage regularly, preferably daily, in light to moderate physical activity for at least 30 minutes per day.
- Increase to at least 20 percent the proportion of people aged 18 and older, and to at least 75 percent the proportion of children and adolescents aged 6 through 17, who engage in vigorous physical activity that promotes the development and maintenance of cardiorespiratory fitness three or more days per week for 20 or more minutes per occasion.
- Reduce to no more than 15 percent the proportion of people aged six and older who engage in no leisure-time physical activity.
- Increase to at least 40 percent the proportion of people aged six and older who regularly perform physical activities that enhance and maintain muscular strength, muscular endurance, and flexibility.
- Increase to at least 50 percent the proportion of overweight people aged 12 and older who have adopted sound dietary practices combined with regular physical activity to attain an appropriate body weight.

NUTRITION RISK REDUCTION OBJECTIVES

- Reduce dietary fat intake to an average of 30 percent of calories or less and average saturated fat intake to less than 10 percent of calories among people aged two and older.
- Increase complex carbohydrate and fiber-containing foods in the diets of adults to five or more daily servings for vegetables (including legumes) and fruits, and to six or more daily servings for grain products.
- Increase to at least 50 percent the proportion of overweight people aged 12 and older who have

adopted sound dietary practices combined with regular physical activity to attain an appropriate body weight.
- Increase calcium intake so at least 50 percent of youths aged 12 through 24 and 50 percent of pregnant and lactating women consume three or more servings daily of foods rich in calcium, and at least 50 percent of people aged 25 and older consume two or more servings daily.
- Decrease salt and sodium intake so at least 65 percent of home meal preparers prepare foods without adding salt, at least 80 percent of people avoid using salt at the table, and at least 40 percent of adults regularly purchase foods modified or lower in sodium.
- Reduce iron deficiency to less than three percent among children aged one through four and among women of childbearing age.
- Increase to at least 75 percent the proportion of mothers who breastfeed their babies in the early postpartum period and to at least 50 percent the proportion who continue breastfeeding until their babies are five to six months old.
- Increase to at least 75 percent the proportion of parents and caregivers who use feeding practices that prevent baby-bottle tooth decay.
- Increase to at least 85 percent the proportion of people aged 18 and older who use food labels to make nutritious food selections.

TOBACCO RISK REDUCTION OBJECTIVES

- Reduce cigarette smoking to a prevalence of no more than 15 percent among people aged 20 and older.
- Reduce the initiation of smoking by children and youths so that no more than 15 percent have become regular smokers by age 20.
- Increase to at least 50 percent the proportion of cigarette smokers aged 18 and older who stopped smoking cigarettes for at least one day during the preceding year.

continues

- Increase smoking cessation during pregnancy so that at least 60 percent of women who are cigarette smokers at the time they become pregnant quit smoking early in pregnancy and maintain abstinence for the remainder of their pregnancy.
- Reduce to no more than 20 percent the proportion of children aged six and younger who are regularly exposed to tobacco smoke at home.
- Reduce smokeless tobacco use by males aged 12 through 24 to a prevalence of no more than four percent.

ALCOHOL AND OTHER DRUGS RISK REDUCTION OBJECTIVES

- Increase by at least one year the average age of first use of cigarettes, alcohol, and marijuana by adolescents aged 7 through 17.
- Reduce the proportion of young people who have used alcohol, marijuana, and cocaine in the past months.
- Reduce the proportion of high school seniors and college students engaging in recent occasions of heavy drinking of alcoholic beverages to no more than 28 percent of high school seniors and 32 percent of college students.
- Reduce alcohol consumption by people aged 14 and older to an annual average of no more than 2 gallons of ethanol per person.
- Increase the proportion of high school seniors who perceive social disapproval associated with the heavy use of alcohol, occasional use of marijuana, and experimentation with cocaine.
- Increase the proportion of high school seniors who associate risk of physical or psychological harm with the heavy use of alcohol, regular use of marijuana, and experimentation with cocaine.
- Reduce to no more than three percent the proportion of male high school seniors who use anabolic steroids.

FAMILY PLANNING RISK REDUCTION OBJECTIVES

- Reduce the proportion of adolescents who have engaged in sexual intercourse to no more than 15 percent by age 15 and no more than 40 percent by age 17.
- Increase to at least 40 percent the proportion of once sexually active adolescents aged 17 and younger who have abstained from sexual activity for the previous three months.
- Increase to at least 90 percent the proportion of sexually active, unmarried people aged 19 and younger who use contraception, especially combined method contraception that both effectively prevents pregnancy and provides barrier protection against disease.
- Increase the effectiveness with which family planning methods are used, as measured by a decrease to no more than five percent in the proportion of couples experiencing pregnancy despite use of a contraceptive method.

MENTAL HEALTH AND MENTAL DISORDERS RISK REDUCTION OBJECTIVES

- Increase to at least 30 percent the proportion of people aged 18 and older with severe, persistent mental disorders who use community support programs.
- Increase to at least 45 percent the proportion of people with major depressive disorders who obtain treatment.
- Increase to at least 20 percent the proportion of people aged 18 and older who seek help in coping with personal and emotional problems.
- Decrease to no more than five percent the proportion of people aged 18 and older who report experiencing significant levels of stress who do not take steps to reduce or control their stress.

continues

Risk Reduction Objectives continued

VIOLENT AND ABUSIVE BEHAVIOR RISK REDUCTION OBJECTIVES

- Reduce by 20 percent the incidence of physical fighting among adolescents aged 14 through 17.
- Reduce by 20 percent the incidence of weapon carrying by adolescents aged 14 through 17.
- Reduce by 20 percent the proportion of people who possess weapons that are inappropriately stored and therefore dangerously available.

EDUCATIONAL AND COMMUNITY-BASED PROGRAMS RISK REDUCTION OBJECTIVE

- Increase the high school graduation rate to at least 90 percent, thereby reducing risks for multiple problem behaviors and poor mental and physical health.

UNINTENTIONAL INJURIES RISK REDUCTION OBJECTIVES

- Increase use of occupant protection systems, such as safety belts, inflatable safety restraints, and child safety seats, to at least 85 percent of motor vehicle occupants.
- Increase use of helmets to at least 80 percent of motorcyclists and at least 50 percent of bicyclists.

OCCUPATIONAL SAFETY AND HEALTH RISK REDUCTION OBJECTIVES

- Increase to at least 75 percent the proportion of worksites with 50 or more employees that mandate employee use of occupant protection systems, such as seat belts, during all work-related motor vehicle travel.
- Reduce to no more than 15 percent the proportion of workers exposed to average daily noise levels that exceed 85 dBA.
- Eliminate exposures that result in workers having blood lead concentrations greater than 25 μg/dL of whole blood.
- Increase hepatitis B immunization levels to 90 percent among occupationally exposed workers.

ENVIRONMENTAL HEALTH RISK REDUCTION OBJECTIVES

- Reduce human exposure to criteria air pollutants, as measured by an increase to at least 85 percent in the proportion of people who live in counties that have not exceeded any Environmental Protection Agency standard for air quality in the previous 12 months.
- Increase to at least 40 percent the proportion of homes that have been tested for radon concentrations and that have either been found to pose minimal risk or have been modified to reduce risk to health.
- Reduce human exposure to toxic agents by confining total pounds of toxic agents released into the air, water, and soil each year.
- Reduce human exposure to solid waste-related water, air, and soil contamination, as measured by a reduction in average pounds of municipal solid waste produced per person each day to no more than 3.6 pounds.
- Increase to at least 85 percent the proportion of people who receive a supply of drinking water that meets the safe drinking water standards established by the Environmental Protection Agency.
- Reduce potential risk to human health from surface water, as measured by a decrease to no more than 15 percent in the proportion of assessed rivers, lakes, and estuaries that do not support beneficial uses, such as fishing and swimming.

FOOD AND DRUG SAFETY RISK REDUCTION OBJECTIVE

- Increase to at least 75 percent the proportion of households in which principal food preparers routinely refrain from leaving perishable food out of the refrigerator for over two hours and wash cutting boards and utensils with soap after contact with raw meat and poultry.

ORAL HEALTH RISK REDUCTION OBJECTIVES

- Increase to at least 50 percent the proportion of children who have received protective sealants

continues

on the occlusal (chewing) surfaces of permanent molar teeth.

- Increase to at least 75 percent the proportion of people served by community water systems providing optimal levels of fluoride.
- Increase use of professionally or self-administered topical or systemic (dietary) fluorides to at least 85 percent of people not receiving optimally fluoridated public water.
- Increase to at least 75 percent the proportion of parents and caregivers who use feeding practices that prevent baby-bottle tooth decay.

MATERNAL AND INFANT HEALTH RISK REDUCTION OBJECTIVES

- Reduce low birth weight to an incidence of no more than 5 percent of live births and very low birth weight to no more than 1 percent of live births.
- Increase to at least 85 percent the proportion of mothers who achieve the minimum recommended weight gain during their pregnancies.
- Reduce severe complications of pregnancy to no more than 15 per 100 deliveries.
- Reduce the Caesarean delivery rate to no more than 15 per 100 deliveries.
- Increase to at least 75 percent the proportion of mothers who breastfeed their babies in the early postpartum period and to at least 50 percent the proportion who continue breastfeeding until their babies are five to six months old.
- Increase abstinence from tobacco use by pregnant women at least 90 percent and increase abstinence from alcohol, cocaine, and marijuana by pregnant women by at least 20 percent.

HEART DISEASE AND STROKE RISK REDUCTION OBJECTIVES

- Increase to at least 50 percent the proportion of people with high blood pressure whose blood pressure is under control.
- Increase to at least 90 percent the proportion of people with high blood pressure who are taking action to help control their blood pressure.

- Reduce the mean serum cholesterol level among adults to no more than 200 mg/dL.
- Reduce the prevalence of blood cholesterol levels of 240 mg/dL or greater to no more than 20 percent among adults.
- Increase to at least 60 percent the proportion of adults with high blood cholesterol who are aware of their condition and are taking action to reduce their blood cholesterol to recommended levels.
- Reduce dietary fat intake to an average of 30 percent of calories or less and average saturated fat intake to less than 10 percent of calories among people aged two and older.
- Reduce overweight to a prevalence of no more than 20 percent among people aged 20 and older and no more than 15 percent among adolescents aged 12 through 19.
- Increase to at least 30 percent the proportion of people aged six and older who engage regularly, preferably daily, in light to moderate physical activity for at least 30 minutes per day.
- Reduce cigarette smoking to a prevalence of no more than 15 percent among people aged 20 and older.

CANCER RISK REDUCTION OBJECTIVES

- Reduce cigarette smoking to a prevalence of no more than 15 percent among people aged 20 and older.
- Reduce dietary fat intake to an average of 30 percent of calories or less and average saturated fat intake to less than 10 percent of calories among people aged two and older.
- Increase complex carbohydrates and fiber-containing foods in the diets of adults to five or more daily servings for vegetables (including legumes) and fruits and to six or more daily servings for grain products.
- Increase to at least 60 percent the proportion of people of all ages who limit sun exposure, use sunscreens and protective clothing when exposed to sunlight, and avoid artificial sources of ultraviolet light (e.g., sun lamps, tanning booths).

continues

Risk Reduction Objectives continued

DIABETES AND CHRONIC DISABLING CONDITIONS RISK REDUCTION OBJECTIVES

- Reduce overweight to a prevalence of no more than 20 percent among people aged 20 and older and no more than 15 percent among adolescents aged 12 through 19.
- Increase to at least 30 percent the proportion of people aged six and older who engage regularly, preferably daily, in light to moderate physical activity for at least 30 minutes per day.

HIV INFECTION RISK REDUCTION OBJECTIVES

- Reduce the proportion of adolescents who have engaged in sexual intercourse to no more than 15 percent by age 15 and no more than 40 percent by age 17.
- Increase to at least 50 percent the proportion of sexually active, unmarried people who used a condom at last sexual intercourse.
- Increase to at least 50 percent the estimated proportion of all intravenous drug abusers who are in drug abuse treatment programs.
- Increase to at least 50 percent the estimated proportion of intravenous drug abusers not in treatment who use only uncontaminated drug paraphernalia ("works").
- Reduce to no more than one per 250,000 units of blood and blood components the risk of transfusion-transmitted HIV infection.

SEXUALLY TRANSMITTED DISEASES RISK REDUCTION OBJECTIVES

- Reduce the proportion of adolescents who have engaged in sexual intercourse to no more than 15 percent by age 15 and no more than 40 percent by age 17.

- Increase to at least 50 percent the proportion of sexually active, unmarried people who used a condom at last sexual intercourse.

IMMUNIZATION AND INFECTIOUS DISEASES RISK REDUCTION OBJECTIVES

- Increase immunization levels as follows:
  - basic immunization series among children under age two: at least 90 percent
  - basic immunization series among children in licensed child-care facilities and kindergarten through postsecondary education institutions: at least 95 percent
  - pneumococcal pneumonia and influenza immunization among institutionalized chronically ill or older people: at least 80 percent
  - pneumococcal pneumonia and influenza immunization among noninstitutionalized, high-risk populations, as defined by the Immunization Practices Advisory Committee: at least 60 percent
  - hepatitis B immunization among high-risk populations, including infants of surface antigen-positive mothers, to at least 90 percent; occupationally exposed workers to at least 90 percent; IV-drug users in drug treatment programs to at least 50 percent; and homosexual men to at least 50 percent
- Reduce postexposure rabies treatments to no more than 9,000 per year.

CLINICAL PREVENTIVE SERVICES RISK REDUCTION OBJECTIVE

- Increase to at least 50 percent the proportion of people who have received, as a minimum within the appropriate interval, all of the screening and immunization services and at least one of the counseling services appropriate for their age and gender as recommended by the U.S. Preventive Services Task Force.

Source: From *Healthy People 2000: National Health Promotion Disease Prevention Objectives*, U.S. Department of Health and Human Services, Public Health Service, DHHS Publication (PHS) #90-50212, Washington, D.C.

Healthy People 2000 Priority Areas and Their Responsible Governmental Agencies

1. Physical activity and fitness—President's Council on Physical Fitness and Sports
2. Nutrition—Food and Drug Administration; National Institutes of Health
3. Tobacco—Centers for Disease Control
4. Alcohol and other drugs—Alcohol, Drug Abuse, and Mental Health Administration
5. Family planning—Office of Population Affairs
6. Mental health—Alcohol, Drug Abuse, and Mental Health Administration
7. Violent and abusive behavior—Centers for Disease Control
8. Educational and community-based programs—Centers for Disease Control; Health Resources and Services Administration
9. Unintentional injuries—Centers for Disease Control
10. Occupational safety and health—Centers for Disease Control
11. Environmental health—Centers for Disease Control; National Institutes of Health
12. Food and drug safety—Food and Drug Administration
13. Oral health—Centers for Disease Control; National Institutes of Health
14. Maternal and infant health—Health Resources and Services Administration
15. Heart disease and stroke—National Institutes of Health
16. Cancer—National Institutes of Health
17. Diabetes and chronic disabling conditions—Centers for Disease Control; National Institutes of Health
18. HIV infection—National AIDS Program Office
19. Sexually transmitted diseases—Centers for Disease Control
20. Immunization and infectious diseases—Centers for Disease Control
21. Clinical preventive services—Centers for Disease Control; Health Resources and Services Administration
22. Surveillance and data systems—Centers for Disease Control

NOTES:

Source: From *Healthy People 2000: National Health Promotion Disease Prevention Objectives*, U.S. Department of Health and Human Services, Public Health Service, DHHS Publication (PHS) #90-50212, Washington, D.C.

HEALTHY COMMUNITIES 2000: AN INTRODUCTION TO THE MODEL STANDARDS*

Healthy Communities 2000: Model Standards put the objectives of *Healthy People 2000* into practice and encouraged communities to establish achievable community health targets. It covered the priority areas and age groups used in *Healthy People 2000* and included all of the national objectives. Community leaders could adapt the national targets according to local needs and could establish objectives based on their own situations using the fill-in-the-blank approach used in *Healthy Communities 2000: Model Standards.*

Communities were encouraged to use the objectives spelled out in *Healthy People 2000* as a guide for action by state and local communities. At the same time, Model Standards recognized the need for communities to select and develop objectives and individual targets based on their own situations. *Healthy Communities 2000: Model Standards* served as a guidebook and a process for planning community public health services as the following concepts and steps for using Model Standards illustrate.

Model Standards Principles

The concepts listed below provided a foundation for using *Healthy Communities 2000: Model Standards* in state and local communities.

Emphasis on Health Outcomes. A focus on health outcomes is essential for ensuring that the public's health is protected. Making progress in attacking major health problems depends on establishing an understandable set of health status objectives that are measurable and realistic with accompanying local process objectives for their achievement.

Flexibility. Model Standards is a flexible planning tool that allows communities to establish and quantify objectives and develop strategies based on their own situations. To accomplish this, Model Standards uses a fill-in-the blanks approach to allow communities to establish objectives that take into account current health status and available resources.

Focus on the Entire Community. Disease prevention is a shared partnership of the public and private sectors. Cooperation among major community groups and organizations creates the foundation for communities to establish and achieve the goals and objectives suggested by *Healthy Communities 2000: Model Standards.*

Government as Residual Guarantor. Government is the "residual guarantor" of health services whether they are provided directly or through community agencies. Every locale and population should be served by a unit of government that takes a leadership role in ensuring the public's health. This concept has become known as AGPALL (A Governmental Presence at the Local Level).

The Importance of Negotiation. Negotiation is the principal way to maintain local flexibility and promote agreement among agencies and individuals who have an interest in and responsibility to protect the public's health. This negotiation is critically important in defining agencies' responsibilities at the local level, negotiating responsibilities between state and local government health agencies, and determining the expected level of achievement.

---

*Source: From *Healthy Communities 2000: Model Standards*, 3rd edition. Copyright 1991 by the American Public Health Association. Adapted with permission.

Standards and Guidelines. The terms *standards* and *guidelines* are incorporated into the title of Model Standards. These concepts are integral to Model Standards. *Standards* implies uniform objectives to ensure equity and social justice, and *guidelines* emphasizes local discretion for decision making.

Accessibility of Services. Access to community preventive health services for all Americans is a major public health issue. *Healthy Communities 2000: Model Standards* is designed to help communities tailor special population targets to ensure services for those most in need.

Emphasis on Programs. Model Standards focuses on programs rather than professional practice standards because professional practice standards are usually set by the specialty practice organization(s). Public health professional roles, occupied by persons of a given discipline, are diverse and rapidly evolving. The roles of public health nurses, sanitarians, health educators, and others frequently cut across many different program areas. Respective professional groups are therefore encouraged to commit themselves to the development of such standards based on the Model Standards.

Steps for Putting Model Standards to Use

- Assess and determine the role of one's health agency.
- Assess the lead health agency's organizational capacity.
- Develop an agency plan to build the necessary organizational capacity.
- Assess the community's organizational and power structures.
- Organize the community to build a stronger constituency for public health and establish a partnership for public health.
- Assess the health needs and available community resources.
- Determine local priorities.
- Select outcome and process objectives that are compatible with local priorities and the *Healthy People 2000* objectives.
- Develop communitywide intervention strategies.
- Develop and implement a plan of action.
- Monitor and evaluate the effort on a continuing basis.

NOTES:

Proposed Healthy People Framework

VISION OF 2010: HEALTHY PEOPLE IN HEALTHY COMMUNITIES

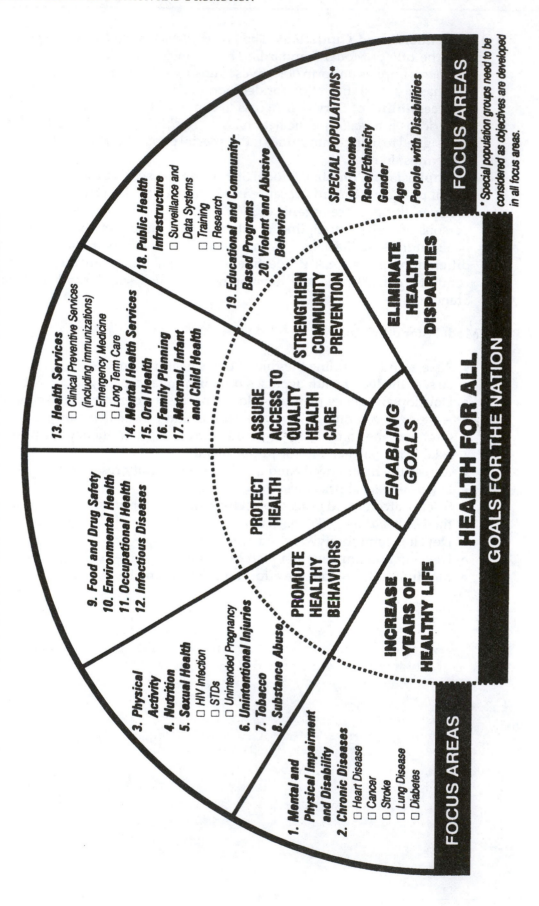

Source: *Developing Objectives for Healthy People 2010*, Office of Disease Prevention and Health Promotion, U.S. Department of Health and Human Services, September 1997.

INITIATIVE TO ELIMINATE RACIAL AND ETHNIC DISPARITIES IN HEALTH*

The President has committed the Nation to an ambitious goal by the year 2010: eliminate the disparities in six areas of health status experienced by racial and ethnic minority populations while continuing the progress we have made in improving the overall health of the American people. This goal will parallel the focus of *Healthy People 2010,* the Nation's health objectives for the 21st century, to be released by the President in the year 2000.

The Department of Health and Human Services has selected six focus areas in which racial and ethnic minorities experience serious disparities in health access and outcomes:

- Infant Mortality
- Cancer Screening and Management
- Cardiovascular Disease
- Diabetes
- HIV Infection/AIDS
- Immunizations

Goal 1—Eliminate Disparities in Infant Mortality Rates

Infant mortality is an important measure of a nation's health and a worldwide indicator of health status. Although infant mortality in the United States has declined steadily over the past several decades and is at a record low of 7.2 per 1,000 live births (1996 data), the United States still ranks 24th in infant mortality compared with other industrialized nations.

Infant mortality rates (IMRs) vary substantially among and within racial and ethnic groups. Infant death rates among blacks, American Indians and Alaska Natives, and Hispanics in 1995 or 1996 were all above the national average of 7.2 deaths per 1,000 live births. The greatest disparity exists for blacks, whose infant death rate (14.2 per 1,000 in 1996) is about twice that of white infants (6.0 per 1,000 in 1996). The overall American Indian rate (9.0 per 1,000 live births in 1995) does not reflect the diversity among Indian communities, some of which have infant mortality rates approaching twice the national rate. Similarly, the overall Hispanic rate (7.6 per 1,000 live births in 1995) does not reflect the diversity among this group, which had a rate of 8.9 per 1,000 live births among Puerto Ricans in 1995.

To achieve further reductions in infant mortality and morbidity, the public health community, health care providers, and individuals must focus on modifying the behaviors, lifestyles, and conditions that affect birth outcomes, such as smoking, substance abuse, poor nutrition, other psychosocial problems (e.g., stress, domestic violence), lack of prenatal care, medical problems, and chronic illness.

Women who receive prenatal care in the first trimester have better pregnancy outcomes than women who receive little or no prenatal care. For example, the likelihood of delivering a very low birthweight (VLBW) infant (less than 1,500 grams or 3 lb. 4 oz.) is 40 percent higher among women who receive late or no prenatal care compared with women entering prenatal care in the first trimester. Approximately 95 percent of VLBW infants are born preterm (less than 37 weeks gestation). The risk of

---

*Source: "The Initiative To Eliminate Racial and Ethnic Disparities in Health," U.S. Department of Health and Human Services Web site, March 1999.

early death for VLBW infants is about 65 times that of infants who weigh at least 1,500 grams.

In 1996, the proportion of pregnant women across the Nation receiving prenatal care in the first trimester reached 81.8 percent—a consistent improvement for the seventh consecutive year and up from 75.5 percent in 1989. Yet, one in five pregnant women, or three-quarters of a million women, still did *not* receive timely prenatal care; almost 47,000 women received *no* prenatal care at all. In addition, there are substantial racial disparities in the timely receipt of prenatal care. In 1996, 84 percent of white pregnant women, compared with approximately 71 percent of black and Hispanic pregnant women, received early prenatal care. Eliminating these disparities requires the removal of financial, educational, social, and logistical barriers to care.

Among the leading causes of death in infants, the racial and ethnic disparity (expressed as the ratio of the infant mortality rate for black infants to that for white infants, representing the greatest disparity) is greatest in the following: disorders relating to short gestation (preterm birth [PTB]) and unspecified low birthweight (4.1), respiratory distress syndrome (2.8), infections specific to the perinatal period and newborns affected by maternal complications of pregnancy (2.7), and sudden infant death syndrome (SIDS) (2.6). Overall, 13 percent of infants die for disorders relating to short gestation. A much higher incidence of PTBs occurs among black mothers than among white mothers (17.7 compared with 9.7 percent). Underlying factors, such as chronic hypertension and bacterial vaginosis, which have higher incidences among blacks, play a role in PTBs.

SIDS accounts for approximately 10 percent of all infant deaths in the first year of life. Minority populations are at greater risk for SIDS. In addition to the greater risk among blacks, the rates are three to four times as high for some American Indian and Alaska Native populations.

We will have a significant impact on infant mortality by increasing our efforts to address the racial disparities that exist in both PTB and SIDS rates. Racial and ethnic differences in PTBs and SIDS most likely reflect variations in the prevalance of risk factors, including socioeconomic and demographic factors, certain medical conditions, quality of and access to health care, and practices such as placing babies on their backs to sleep to prevent SIDS. We can work toward addressing all of these issues and measure their impact on reducing the rates of infant deaths due to PTB and SIDS.

Our goal is to continue progress in reducing overall infant mortality rates and to eventually eliminate disparities among groups. As a major step toward that end, we have set a near-term goal to reduce infant mortality among blacks (the group with the greatest disparity in terms of infant death rates) by at least 22 percent from the 1996 rate by the year 2000—or from 14.2 per 1,000 to 11.0 per 1,000 live births. We also will work to reduce infant mortality rates among American Indian and Alaska Natives, and Puerto Ricans, whose rates also are above the national average. In addition, we will continue to monitor progress in reducing the SIDS rates for all racial and ethnic groups as an indicator of our progress toward reducing the national infant mortality rate.

Near-Term Goal

Reduce infant mortality among blacks by at least 22 percent.

Goal 2—Eliminate Disparities in Cancer Screening and Management

Cancer is the second leading cause of death in the United States, accounting for more than 544,000 deaths each year. About 1.4 million new cases of cancer are expected to be diagnosed in 1997, and approximately 7.4 million Americans have or have had cancer. The chances of developing cancer in a lifetime are nearly 50 percent for men and nearly 40 percent for women. About half of those who develop the disease will die from it.

Many minority groups suffer disproportionately from cancer. Disparities exist in both mortality and incidence rates. For men and women combined, blacks have a cancer death rate about 35 percent higher than that for whites (171.6 vs. 127.0 per 100,000). The death rate for cancer for black men is about 50 percent higher than it is for white men (226.8 vs. 151.8 per 100,000). The death rate for lung cancer is about 27 percent higher for blacks than for whites (49.9 vs. 39.3 per 100,000). The prostate cancer mortality rate for black men is more than twice that of white men (55.5 vs. 23.8 per 100,000).

Paralleling the death rate, the incidence rate for lung cancer in black men is about 50 percent higher than in white men (110.7 vs. 72.6 per 100,000). Native Hawaiian men also have elevated rates of lung cancer compared with white men. Alaska Native men and women suffer disproportionately higher rates of cancers of the colon and rectum than do whites. Vietnamese women in the United States have a cervical cancer incidence rate more than five times greater than white women (47.3 vs. 8.7 per 100,000). Hispanic women also suffer elevated rates of cervical cancer.

Much can be done to reduce the burden of cancer in the United States through prevention. Lifestyles can be modified to greatly reduce an individual's risk for cancer. Tobacco use is responsible for nearly one-third of all cancer deaths. Evidence suggests that diet and nutrition may be related to 30 to 40 percent of cancer deaths. Additionally, many of the estimated 900,000 skin cancer cases diagnosed each year could be prevented by reducing sun exposure.

For some cancers that we do not yet know how to prevent, early detection can dramatically reduce the risk of death. Regular mammography screening and appropriate follow-up can reduce deaths from breast cancer by about 30 percent of women 50 years of age and older. Screening by Pap test for cervical cancer along with appropriate follow-up care can virtually eliminate the risk of developing this disease.

The purpose of goal 2 is to improve screening and management of cancer. Although colorectal cancer screening is now recommended, few data on screening rates exist. Screening for prostate cancer remains controversial, and for this cancer as well, few data on screening rates exist. Indeed, there is a significant need for public education about what is known, what is not known, and what is believed about prostate cancer screening and treatment. Breast and cervical cancers, however, have proven screening modalities for which screening data, both baseline and continuing, are available. For this reason, the strategy for achieving goal 2 focuses on breast and cervical cancers.

Despite the considerable gains in screening in the black community, the mortality rate from breast cancer for black women is greater than for white women. Some of the reasons for this disparity include the fact that many women have not yet had a mammogram or a Pap smear, many more are not screened regularly, and still others are screened but have limited follow-up and treatment services available to them. Hispanic, American Indian and Alaska Native, and Asian and Pacific Islander women also have low rates of screening and treatment, limited access to health facilities and physicians, and barriers related to language, culture, and negative provider attitudes, which negatively affect their health status. Eliminating these differences is critical and will be the focus of attention for the HHS initiative to help identify and understand approaches that have proven successful in some communities. Our focus on tracking breast and cervical cancer will serve as an indicator for assessing our overall efforts to reduce and eventually eliminate disparities in the prevention and management of all cancers.

Breast Cancer

Our goal for the year 2000 for breast cancer screening is to increase to at least 60 percent those women of all racial or ethnic groups, aged 50 and older, who have received a clinical breast exam and a mammogram within the preceding 2 years.

Near-Term Goal

Increase to at least 60 percent those women of all racial or ethnic groups, aged 50 and older, who have received a clinical breast exam and mammogram within the preceding two years.

Cervical Cancer

Our goal for the year 2000 for cervical cancer is to increase to at least 85 percent the proportion of all women aged 18 and older who have received a Pap test within the preceding 3 years.

Goal 3—Eliminate Disparities in Cardiovascular Disease

Cardiovascular disease, primarily coronary heart disease and stroke, kills nearly as many Americans as all other diseases combined and is among the leading causes of disability in the United States. Cardiovascular disease is the leading cause of death for all racial and ethnic groups. The impact of premature morbidity from cardiovascular disease on the ability of affected individuals to function independently or to participate fully in everyday life is devastating in terms of personal loss, pain, suffering, and effects on families and loved ones. The annual national economic impact of cardiovascular disease is estimated at $259 billion as measured in health care expenditures, medications, and lost productivity due to disability and death.

The major modifiable risk factors for cardiovascular disease are high blood pressure, high blood cholesterol, cigarette smoking, excessive body weight, and physical inactivity. The greatest potential for reducing coronary heart disease morbidity, disability, and mortality appears to be in prevention, by addressing these risk factors.

- Some people with *high blood pressure* have three to four times the risk of developing coronary heart disease and may have as much as seven times the risk of a stroke as do those with normal blood pressure. Clinical trials show that blood pressure reduction significantly reduces stroke mortality and can help to reduce deaths from coronary heart disease.

- Each 1 percent reduction in serum *cholesterol* level has been associated with a greater than 1 percent reduction in risk of coronary heart disease death.
- Prospective epidemiologic studies have documented a rapid and substantial reduction in coronary heart disease rates following *smoking* cessation. Reducing the proportion of youth who start to smoke and encouraging smoking cessation among current smokers are important preventive measures for reducing coronary heart disease incidence and mortality.
- A reduction in the proportion of Americans who are *overweight* and *physically inactive* can help lower coronary heart disease incidence and mortality. Risks of nonfatal myocardial infarction and coronary heart disease death increase with increasing levels of body mass index (BMI) (weight in kg divided by height in meter^2) and with weight gain. Risks are lowest in men and women with BMIs of 22 or less and increase with modest elevations of BMI. Persons who are physically active have one-half the risk of both coronary heart disease incidence and mortality compared to persons who are sedentary.

Major disparities exist among population groups, with a disproportionate burden of death and disability from cardiovascular disease in minority and low-income populations. The age-adjusted death rate for coronary heart disease for the total population declined by 20 percent from 1987 to 1995; for blacks, the overall decrease was only 13 percent. Compared with rates for whites, coronary heart disease mortality was 40 percent lower for Asian Americans but 40 percent higher for blacks in 1995. Stroke is the only leading cause of death for which mortality is higher for Asian-American males than for white males.

Disparities also exist in the prevalence of risk factors for cardiovascular disease. Racial and ethnic minorities have higher rates of hypertension, tend to develop hypertension at an earlier age, and are less likely to undergo treatment to control their high blood pressure. For example, from 1988 to 1994, 35 percent of black males ages 20 to 74 had hypertension compared with 25 percent of all men. When age differences are taken into account, Mexican-American men and women also have elevated blood pressure rates. Among adult women, the age-adjusted prevalence of overweight continues to be higher for black women (53 percent) and Mexican-American women (52 percent) than for white women (34 percent). Furthermore, the rates for regular screening for cholesterol show disparities for certain racial and ethnic minorities—only 50 percent of American Indians / Alaska Natives, 44 percent of Asian Americans, and 38 percent of Mexican-Americans have had their cholesterol checked within the past 2 years.

Our goal is to continue progress in reducing the overall death rates from heart disease and stroke and eventually to eliminate disparities among all racial and ethnic groups. To have the greatest impact toward that end, we have set near-term goals of reducing the heart disease and stroke mortality rates among blacks by 25 and 40 percent, respectively, from their 1995 level by the year 2000. Although age-adjusted death rates for cardiovascular disease among other minority groups are lower than the national average, there are subgroups within these populations that have high mortality rates from heart disease and stroke. We will develop strategies to reduce these mortality rates as well.

Near-Term Goals

- Reduce the heart disease mortality rate among blacks by 25 percent.
- Reduce the stroke mortality rate among blacks by 40 percent.

Goal 4—Eliminate Disparities in Diabetes

Diabetes, the seventh leading cause of death in the United States, is a serious public health problem affecting nearly 16 million Americans. The estimated total direct and indirect costs of diabetes for the United States in 1993 was $98 billion.

The prevalence of diabetes in blacks is approximately 70 percent higher than whites and the prevalence in Hispanics is nearly double that of whites. The prevalence rate of diabetes among American Indians and Alaska Natives is more than twice that for the total population and at least one tribe, the Pimas of Arizona, have the highest known prevalence of diabetes of any population in the world.

Cardiovascular disease is the leading cause of death among people with diabetes, accounting for over one-half of all deaths. Achieving mortality reduction among high-risk populations will require targeted efforts to reduce cardiovascular risk factors among these groups, which is a focus of our goal on eliminating disparities in cardiovascular disease. Individuals with diabetes, however, face not only a shortened life span, but also the probability of multiple acute and chronic complications, including end-stage renal disease (ESRD), blindness, and lower extremity amputations. All of these complications have the potential to be prevented.

- If uncontrolled hypertension among people with diabetes were reduced by half, about one-quarter of *ESRD* due to diabetes could be prevented.
- **Diabetic** *retinopathy* is the leading cause of new cases of blindness among people 20 to 44 years of age. Clinical trials have demonstrated that approximately 60 percent of diabetes-related blindness can be prevented with good blood glucose control or by early detection and laser photocoagulation treatment, which is widely available but underused.
- One half of all *lower extremity amputations* can be prevented through proper foot care and by reducing risk factors such as hyperglycemia (abnormally high blood sugar), cigarette smoking, and high blood pressure.

Preventive interventions should target high-risk groups. Rates for diabetes-related complications such as ESRD and amputations are higher among blacks and American Indians compared to the total population. Even among similarly insured populations, such as Medicare recipients, blacks are more likely than whites to be hospitalized for septicemia, debridement, and amputations—signs of poor diabetic control. Scientists are concerned that a number of people in these minority groups develop type 2 (noninsulin-dependent) diabetes in adolescence, and therefore face a lifetime of diabetes and its potential complications. Undiagnosed and poorly controlled diabetes increases the likelihood of serious complications; for every two persons who are aware of their illness, there is one person who remains undiagnosed.

Although the increasing burden of diabetes is alarming, the good news is that much of this major public health problem can be prevented with early detection, improved care, and diabetes self-management education. Diabetes presents both a challenge and an opportunity for public policy makers, health care providers, community leaders, and individuals with diabetes to apply prevention strategies known to make a significant impact. Recent studies in diabetes have confirmed that careful control of blood glucose levels is a strategy that works for preventing the complications of diabetes. The challenge is to make proper diabetes management part of daily clinical and public health practice.

Therefore, our goal is to monitor progress in reducing diabetes by reducing the overall rate of diabetic complications among all individuals with diabetes and eventually to eliminate disparities among groups. As a major step toward that end, we have set two near-term goals: (1) reducing the rate of ESRD from diabetes among blacks and American Indians/Alaska Natives by 65 percent from their 1995 levels by the year 2000, and (2) reducing lower extremity amputation rates from diabetes among blacks by 40 percent from their 1995 levels. Rates of diabetic complications among Hispanics are also high; however, current data do not permit us to monitor diabetic complications among this group. We will develop strategies to reduce diabetes-related complications among all minority groups and to improve data collection.

Near-Term Goals

- Reduce the rate of ESRD from diabetes among blacks and American Indians/Alaska Natives by 65 percent.
- Reduce lower extremity amputation rates from diabetes among blacks by 40 percent.

The rates of diabetes-related complications used as outcome measures are crude indicators of progress in eliminating disparities; however, they are the only outcome measures available consistently on a national basis. We also will monitor behavioral practices and health care access issues as indicators of success. Examples of these indicators include diabetes-specific preventive care such as self-monitoring of blood glucose levels, clinic visits, diabetic foot care, and dilated-eye exams.

Goal 5—Eliminate Disparities in HIV Infection/AIDS

HIV infection/AIDS is a leading cause of death for all persons 25 to 44 years of age. Between 650,000 and 900,000 Americans are estimated to be living with HIV infection. Approximately 62 percent (375,000) of the 604,200 adults and adolescents reported with AIDS in the United States have died from the disease.

AIDS has disproportionately affected minority populations. Racial and ethnic minorities constitute approximately 25 percent of the total U.S. population, yet they account for nearly 54 percent of all AIDS cases. While the epidemic is decreasing in some populations, the *number* of new AIDS cases among blacks is now greater than the number of new AIDS cases among whites.

There are several different HIV epidemics occurring simultaneously in the United States, each of which must address the specific population affected and their associated risk factors. For example, although the number of AIDS diagnoses among gay and bisexual men has decreased dramatically among white men since 1989, the number of AIDS diagnoses among black men who have sex with men have increased.

In addition, AIDS cases and new infections related to injecting drug use appear to be increasingly concentrated in minorities; of these cases, almost 75 percent were among minority populations (56 percent black and 20 percent Hispanic). Of cases reported among women and children, more than 75 percent are among racial and ethnic minorities.

During 1995 and 1996, AIDS death rates declined 23 percent for the total U.S. population while declining only 13 percent for blacks and 20 percent for Hispanics. Contributing factors for these mortality disparities include late identification of disease and lack of health insurance to pay for during therapies. The cost of efficacious treatment, between $10,000 and $12,000 per patient per year, is a major hurdle in the effort to ensure equitable access to available drug therapies.

Inadequate recognition of risk, detection of infection, and referral to follow-up care are major issues for high-risk populations. About one-third of persons who are at risk of HIV/AIDS have never been tested. Better prevention strategies are needed that are acceptable to the target community (i.e., they must be culturally and linguistically appropriate), and the capability of organizations serving at-risk populations to develop, implement, evaluate, and fund prevention and treatment programs must be improved. Efforts should include risk reduction counseling, street and community outreach, prevention case management services, and help for individuals at risk in gaining access to HIV testing, treatment, and related services.

At this moment, there are many causes for optimism in the fight against HIV/AIDS. HIV prevention efforts have contributed to slowing the spread of the disease. For the first 6 months of 1996, there was an overall decrease in deaths among persons with AIDS, attributed primarily to the effect of antiretroviral therapies on the survival of persons with HIV infection. The decrease in the growth of AIDS cases in minority populations, however, has not been so strong.

To enable HIV-infected persons to benefit from treatment advances, HIV counseling and testing programs in screening and health care settings must better facilitate early diagnosis of HIV infection and ensure that HIV-infected persons have access to care and treatment services. Continued emphasis on behavioral risk reduction and other prevention strategies targeted to these populations is still the most effective way to reduce HIV infections.

Although advances in prevention and treatment are improving the quality of life for individuals living with HIV/AIDS, not everyone is benefiting equally from this progress. Concerns regarding education about the benefits of knowing one's serostatus, access to counseling and testing, and referral and access to medical services, including efficacious therapies, will continue to guide the development and administration of federal initiatives to prevent HIV transmission and improve access to care for individuals living with HIV/AIDS.

Our goal is to continue progress in increasing the overall availability of early diagnosis of HIV infection and ensuring access to appropriate health services for all and to eventually eliminate disparities among groups. By the year 2000, the combined efforts of Medicaid, Medicare, and HRSA's Ryan White CARE Act will ensure early and equal access to life-enhancing health care and appropriate drug therapies for at least 75 percent of low-income persons living with HIV/AIDS. We will establish educational outreach to all major medical providers to promote the current standard of clinical care for all persons living with HIV/AIDS, including Medicaid-eligible women and children with HIV infection.

Near-Term Goal

Ensure early and equal access to life-enhancing health care and appropriate drug therapies for at least 75 percent of low-income persons living with HIV/AIDS.

Goal 6—Eliminate Disparities in Child and Adult Immunization Rates

The reduction in incidence of vaccine-preventable diseases is one of the most significant public health achievements of the past 100 years. This success is best illustrated by the global eradication of smallpox, achieved in 1977. The major factor in this success is the development and widespread use of vaccines, which are among the safest and most effective preventive measures. Billions of dollars are saved each year through the use of vaccines.

Childhood immunization rates are at an all-time high, with the most critical vaccine doses reflecting coverage rates of over 90 percent. The 1996 immunization coverage targets for all five vaccines (measles, mumps, and rubella [MMR]; polio; diphtheria, tetanus, and pertussis [DTP]; *Haemophilus influenza* type B [Hib]; and hepatitis b [Hep B]) were exceeded. Although immunization rates have been lower in minority populations compared with the white population, minority rates have been increasing at a more rapid rate, thus significantly narrowing the gap. For example, four of the five 1996 coverage targets were met for blacks. Current efforts must be sustained in order to achieve and maintain at least 90 percent coverage for all recommended vaccines in all populations.

Although coverage for preschool immunization is high in almost all states, pockets of need, or areas within each state and major city where substantial numbers of underimmunized children reside, continue to exist. These areas are of great concern because, particularly in large urban areas with traditionally underserved populations, there is a potential for outbreaks of vaccine-preventable diseases.

In addition to the very young, older adults are at increased risk for many vaccine-preventable diseases. Approximately 90 percent of all influenza-associated deaths in the United States occur in people aged 65 and older, the fastest growing age group of the population. Reduction of deaths in this age group has been hindered in part by relatively low vaccine utilization. Immunization is one of the most cost-effective strategies to prevent needless morbidity and mortality. Each year, however, an estimated 45,000 adults die of infections related to influenza, pneumococcal infections, and hepatitis B despite the availability of safe and effective vaccines to prevent these conditions and their complications. In addition, the overall cost to society for vaccine-preventable diseases exceeds $10 billion each year.

There is a disproportionate burden of these diseases in minority and underserved populations. Although vaccination levels against pneumococcal infections and influenza among people 65 years and over have increased slightly for blacks and Hispanics, the coverage in these groups remains substantially below the general population and the year 2000 targets.

Childhood Immunization

Our goal is to enhance current immunization efforts in order to achieve and maintain at least 90 percent coverage for all recommended vaccines in all populations and to eliminate remaining disparities among groups.

Near-Term Goal

Achieve and maintain at least 90 percent coverage for all recommended childhood vaccines in all populations.

Adult Immunization

Our goal is to increase pneumococcal and influenza immunizations among all adults aged 65 years and older to 60 percent and eventually to eliminate disparities among groups. To reach this goal by the year 2000, we need to nearly *double* the 1994 influenza immunization rates among blacks, Hispanics, and Asians and Pacific Islanders and *quadruple* the 1994 pneumococcal immunization rates among these groups.

Near-Term Goal

Increase pneumococcal and influenza immunizations among all adults aged 65 years and older to 60 percent.

HEALTHY PEOPLE 2010 OVERVIEW: GOALS, OBJECTIVES, AND LEADING HEALTH INDICATORS*

What Is *Healthy People 2010?*

Healthy People 2010 is the prevention agenda for the nation. It is a statement of national health objectives designed to identify the most significant preventable threats to health and to establish national goals to reduce these threats. *Healthy People 2010* offers a simple but powerful idea: provide the objectives in a format that enables diverse groups to combine their efforts and work as a team. It is a road map to better health for all and can be used by many different people, states, communities, professional organizations, and groups to improve health. *Healthy People 2010* builds on initiatives pursued over the past two decades.

The 1979 Surgeon General's reports, *Healthy People*, and *Healthy People 2000: National Health Promotion and Disease Prevention Objectives*, both established national health objectives and served as the basis for the development of state and community plans. Like its predecessors, *Healthy People 2010* was developed through a broad consultation process, built upon the best scientific information, and designed to measure programs over time.

Development of *Healthy People 2010* Objectives

The 28 focus areas of *Healthy People 2010* have been developed by leading federal agencies with the most relevant scientific expertise. The development process was informed by the Healthy People Consortium—an alliance of more than 350 national membership organizations and 250 state health, mental health, substance abuse, and environmental agencies. Additionally, through a series of regional and national meetings and an interactive Web site, more than 11,000 public comments on the draft objectives were received. Public comments are posted at www.health.gov/ hpcomments for people to use in their own health improvement efforts. The Secretary's Council on National Health Promotion and Disease Prevention Objectives for 2010 also provided leadership and advice in the development of national health objectives.

State and Community Health Objectives

Nearly all states, the District of Columbia, and Guam have developed their own Healthy People plans. Most states have built on the national objectives, but virtually all have tailored them to their specific needs. A 1993 National Association of County and City Health Officials survey showed that 70 percent of local health departments used at least some *Healthy People 2000* objectives. Many states, working with community coalitions, are now developing their own versions of *Healthy People 2010*. The Healthy People 2010 Toolkit, which provides examples of state and national experiences in setting and using objectives, is available on the Web.

---

*Source: Office of Disease Prevention and Health Promotion (ODPHP), U.S. Department of Health and Human Services. Online access: Healthy People 2010 http://www.health.gov/healthypeople, Office of Disease Prevention and Health Promotion http:// odphp.osophs.dhhs.gov.

Using Healthy People Objectives

Healthy People objectives have been specified by Congress as the measure for assessing the progress of the Indian Health Care Improvement Act, the Maternal and Child Health Block Grant, and the Preventive Health and Health Services Block Grant. Healthy People objectives also have been used in performance measurement activities. For example, the National Committee on Quality Assurance incorporated many Healthy People targets into its Health Plan Employer Data and Information Set 3.0, a set of standardized measures for health care purchasers and consumers to use in assessing performance of managed care organizations in the areas of immunizations, mammography screening, and other clinical preventive services.

Individuals, groups, and organizations are encouraged to integrate *Healthy People 2010* into current programs, special events, publications, and meetings. Businesses can use the framework, for example, to guide worksite health promotion activities as well as community-based initiatives. Schools, colleges, and civic and faith-based organizations can undertake activities to further the health of all members of their community. Health care providers can encourage their patients to pursue healthier lifestyles and to participate in community-based programs. By selecting from among the national objectives, individuals and organizations can build an agenda for community health improvement and can monitor results over time.

Goals

Healthy People 2010 is designed to achieve two overarching goals:

1. **Goal 1: Increase Quality and Years of Healthy Life**—The first goal of *Healthy People 2010* is to help individuals of all ages increase life expectancy and improve their quality of life.
2. **Goal 2: Eliminate Health Disparities**—The second goal of *Healthy People 2010* is to eliminate health disparities among different segments of the population.

Healthy People 2010 Focus Areas

- Access to quality healthy services
- Arthritis, osteoporosis, and chronic back conditions
- Cancer
- Chronic kidney disease
- Diabetes
- Disability and secondary conditions
- Educational and community-based programs
- Environmental health
- Family planning
- Food safety
- Health communication
- Heart disease and stroke
- HIV
- Immunization and infectious diseases
- Injury and violence prevention
- Maternal, infant, and child health
- Medical product safety
- Mental health and mental disorders
- Nutrition and overweight
- Occupational safety and health
- Oral health
- Physical activity and fitness
- Public health infrastructure
- Respiratory diseases
- Sexually transmitted diseases
- Substance abuse
- Tobacco use
- Vision and hearing

Each of the 28 focus area chapters also contain a concise goal statement. This statement frames the overall purpose of the focus area.

Examples of focus area goals are

- Cancer—Reduce the number of new cancer cases as well as the illness, disability, and death caused by cancer.
- Disability and Secondary Conditions—Promote the health of people with disabilities, prevent secondary conditions, and eliminate disparities between people with and without disabilities in the U.S. population.
- Food Safety—Reduce foodborne illnesses.

Leading Health Indicators

The Leading Health Indicators reflect the major public health concerns in the United States and were chosen based on their ability to motivate action, the availability of data to measure their progress, and their relevance as broad public health issues.

The Leading Health Indicators illuminate individual behaviors, physical and social environmental factors, and important health system issues that greatly affect the health of individuals and communities. Underlying each of these indicators is the significant influence of income and education.

The process of selecting the Leading Health Indicators mirrored the collaborative and extensive efforts undertaken to develop *Healthy People 2010*. The process was led by an interagency work group within the U.S. Department of Health and Human Services. Individuals and organizations provided comments at national and regional meetings or via mail and the Internet. A report by the Institute of Medicine, National Academy of Sciences, provided several scientific models on which to support a set of indicators. Focus groups were used to ensure that the indicators are meaningful and motivating to the public.

The Leading Health Indicators are

- physical activity
- overweight and obesity
- tobacco use
- substance abuse
- responsible sexual behavior
- mental health
- injury and violence
- environmental quality
- immunization
- access to health care

For each of the Leading Health Indicators, specific objectives derived from *Healthy People 2010* will be used to track progress. This small set of measures will provide a snapshot of the health of the nation. Tracking and communicating progress on the Leading Health Indicators through national- and state-level report cards will spotlight achievements and challenges in the next decade. The Leading Health Indicators serve as a link to the 418 objectives in *Healthy People 2010: Objectives for Improving Health* and can become the basic building blocks for community health initiatives.

For a listing of the 418 objectives in *Healthy People 2010*, see Appendix C.

2

Personnel Management

Personnel Management

Tools for Employee Selection 46
Sample Application for Employment 48
Interview Report 52
Recruiting and Retaining Volunteers 53
Establishing a Positive Work Climate 56

Working with Groups

Eight Tips for Effective Meetings 57
Sample Plan for the First Meeting with a
    Community Group 58

Checklist for a Good Group
    Leader 59
Group Process Evaluation Form 60

Fund-Raising

Locating and Applying for Health
    Promotion Funds 61
Proposal Development for
    Foundations 65
Proposal Development for State or
    Federal Agencies 68
Checklist for Grant Developers 72

Personnel Management

OBJECTIVES

At the completion of this chapter, the reader will

- know how to select employees for a community health agency
- understand how to recruit and retain volunteers in community programs
- understand how to establish a positive work climate
- know how to lead an effective meeting and how to be an effective group leader
- know about locating and applying for health promotion funds
- understand proposal development for grants from foundations
- understand proposal development for state or federal grants

---

INTRODUCTION

Chapter 2 provides essential advice and sample forms for the development of resources in community health. It contains guidance and tools for personnel management, group work, and fund-raising, all of which are succinctly, but completely addressed. Valuable forms and advice for hiring and retaining employees and volunteers are contained within the chapter. Tools for use in group work guide the student of community health. Grant application guidelines for the professional or student seeking to contact foundations, and state and federal governments for health promotion funding are summarized. The chapter concludes with an indispensable checklist for grant developers.

The content of this chapter is unique in that it provides invaluable advice and helpful hints for developing human and financial resources in community health. Tips about leading meetings, hiring and encouraging employees and volunteers, and successfully working with both individuals and groups are offered.

The community health professional or student looking for funding is also assisted with guidelines for submitting funding applications. The grantsmanship tips alone are those that could take a beginner years to discover. A wealth of experience and expertise with both personnel and financial resources is condensed into one practical chapter.

TOOLS FOR EMPLOYEE SELECTION*

The four basic tools used to select the right candidates for new positions are:

1. the application form
2. the reference check
3. skill testing
4. the personal interview

If these activities are appropriately completed in the order shown, a great deal of time can be saved.

The Application Form

The application form is used to collect the facts about the applicant. When properly structured, it may reveal more than the resume, especially for applicants who are selective about what they decide to report. It also lays the foundation for the other three methods of selection.

The Reference Check

Reference checks should be completed before time-consuming skill tests and interviews are scheduled. One major reason for this is that information reported by potential candidates must be verified for accuracy. Unfortunately, some people lie or "stretch the truth" when they fill out application blanks and submit resumes.

Managers should ask themselves whether they want to fill the position with someone who falsifies information or exaggerates the truth. No one wants to invite trouble, so if a problem is discovered during the initial stages of selection, managers can save time by screening out undesirable applicants before more time and energy are invested.

A second reason for doing reference checks at this point is so that the candidate's positive and negative characteristics can be identified. This helps to point out the skills that need to be tested and to focus the topics of discussion for the interview.

---

*Source: Rita Jackson, "Meeting the Challenges of Restructuring," *Hospital Food and Nutrition Focus*, Vol. 12, No. 1, Aspen Publishers, Inc., © September 1995.

While checking references, managers should try to speak personally with past immediate supervisors of all potential candidates. Managers at high levels may not be familiar with the day-to-day activities, achievements, or problems that have surfaced over the years, and unfortunately, performance evaluations do not always reflect true characteristics of employees.

Candidates for in-house transfer may have evaluations of their past performance available for review, but managers should remember that these evaluations do not always reflect true characteristics of employees, and their validity is highly dependent upon the competency of the person who completed them.

Not all reference checks will be positive, and it is very possible that applicants may have negative references that they do not deserve. While reviewing the answers to standardized questions that are asked during personal discussions with past immediate supervisors, managers should always be aware of possible personality conflicts and unfair judgments.

This is why managers must try to see the overall picture. One or two isolated incidents may not be important, but when a common theme of problems is seen it is worthy of consideration. The personal interview is an ideal forum for discussion of such problems with the candidate.

Skill Testing

Skill testing can range from the simple tasks of reading and writing to computer literacy. For dietitians and dietetic technicians, the performance of a nutritional assessment based on a case study is a useful exercise. For cooks and other food production personnel, managers can ask about common techniques or even require that candidates follow a standardized recipe to ascertain their skill level.

Managers should remember that if they are still unsure about a candidate, it is always possible to assign new employees on a trial basis. They should also consider the use of a probationary period, from two to three months, for all job reassignments.

The Personal Interview

Personal interviews enable managers to see aspects of an individual that cannot be seen on the application form or from reference checks.

When they are skillfully conducted, interviews provide important information. They help both the candidate and the interviewer to collaboratively determine if there is a good match.

Any anticipated problems based on data collected before this point should be openly discussed as the two persons try to predict the potential for success on the new job.

Sample Application for Employment

APPLICATION FOR EMPLOYMENT

Federal and state laws prohibit discrimination in employment practices on account of race, creed, color, national origin, ancestry, sex, age, marital status, veteran status, or handicap.

Last Name, First Name, MI	Date

Is any additional information relative to change of name, use of an assumed name, or nickname necessary to enable a check on your work record? Explain.

Present Address (Include Street, City, State, and ZIP Code)	Phone #

Last Previous Address (if at present address less than two years)

Are you over 17 years of age?	If under 18, do you have working papers?
Are you legally employable within the United States at the present time?	Have you ever been convicted of a crime? Give details.
Have you ever applied to this organization for a job before? If yes, when?	What brought you to this organization? ☐ newspaper ad ☐ friend/employee ☐ employment agency ☐ on my own ☐ school ☐ other source ☐ state employment service
Position Desired:	Salary Desired: $

Status (circle one): full/part time/summer	Earliest start date:

Work Experience—Account for all employment since high school or last ten years, whichever is less, with most recent experience first.

From Mo./Yr.	To Mo./Yr.	Employer Name, Address	Principal Duties	Salary Beg.	End	Supervisor's Name, Title, Tel. #	Reason for Leaving

Account for all unemployment since leaving school and between positions for the last ten years.

From Mo./Yr.	To Mo./Yr.	State what you were doing	Persons other than relatives who can confirm unemployment (give tel. #)

continues

Sample Application for Employment continued

Education Background

Name	Address	Course of Study	Graduate? If yes, state degree
High School:			
College/Tech/Bus Scl:		Major: Minor:	
Graduate School:		Major: Minor:	

Are you still in school? If yes, where?

How many courses are you currently taking?   Number of credits:

What is the course of study?

Special Skills (fill in only if job related):

Do you speak any foreign languages?   Read?   Write?

Personal Reference: Give the name, address, and telephone number of a personal reference other than a relative or employer.

Name	Address	Telephone #

Employee Responsibility to the organization. (Please read before signing.)

As a condition of my employment, I accept the principle that the welfare of the organization depends upon the conduct and honesty of the members of the staff and upon the trust and confidence of the public. Our customers rightly expect honesty, security, and confidentiality in their affairs. I therefore agree to the following:

1. I agree to give no unauthorized information relative to the accounts of the organization or its relation with others, and to discuss no matters of a confidential nature relating to the organization's affairs unless such discussion is in the necessary course of the organization's business and is in accordance with the organization's policy.
2. I also agree to inform the management of the organization, without delay, of any fraud, false entry, substantial error, embezzlement, or employee misconduct that I discover or know to have taken place in any records, property, or funds of the organization, and to report any transaction or matter that seems damaging to the organization.

I acknowledge and understand that any violation of this Agreement may result in the termination of my employment.

_____   _____   _____
Name   Signature   Date

continues

Sample Application for Employment continued

Please also read the following before signing. If you have any questions regarding this statement, please ask them of any interviewer before signing.

In the event of my employment with this organization, I will comply with all the rules and regulations as set forth in the organization's policy manual or other communications distributed to all staff members. I understand that such employment is conditioned upon a favorable health evaluation, which may include a physical examination by a physician selected by the organization and to which I hereby assent. I further agree to complete all necessary forms in that regard. Additionally, I authorize the organization to supply my employment record, in whole or in part, and in confidence, to any prospective employer, government agency, or other party with a legal and proper interest.

I certify that all statements made by me on this application are true and complete to the best of my knowledge and that I have withheld nothing that would, if disclosed, affect this application unfavorably. I understand this falsification could result in termination of my employment. In consideration of my employment, I agree to conform to the rules and regulations of the organization. I agree that my employment and compensation can be terminated, with or without cause, and with or without notice, at any time, at the option of either the organization or myself. This is not a contract of employment. Any individual who is hired may voluntarily leave employment upon proper notice and may be terminated by the employer at any time. Any oral or written statements to the contrary are hereby expressly disavowed and should not be relied upon by any prospective or existing employee. I further understand and agree that any employment will be at the sole discretion of the organization. If accepted for employment, I agree to have my fingerprints and photograph taken for the purposes of identification and the maintenance of internal security. I understand that past employers/educational institutions and/or the military will be contacted for references. For reference purposes,

you may ☐   you may not ☐   contact my present employer.

I hereby acknowledge that I have read the above statement and understand the same.

_____

Applicant's Signature

_____

Date

continues

Sample Application for Employment continued

For Personnel Use Only: Employment Form Checklist for Employment Processing				
Employee No.	Date of Hire	Department Name	Dept. No.	Job Code
Pay Grade	Title	Base Annual Sal	Hourly Sal	Wkly Sal
Review Date	Replace ☐	Req. No.	EEO Job Code	Monthly Sal
Status	New Pos. ☐	Referral Source	Ethnic Code	Handicap Code
Full Time ☐	Hours:	Social Security Number:	Marital Status	Sex Male ☐
Part Time ☐		Date of Birth: (mo, day, year) / /	Single ☐	Fem ☐
Per Diem ☐			Married ☐	Veteran Code
Summer ☐				

Identification Card Number: Date issued:

	yes	no		yes	no
I-9 Form			Employment Benefits Package		
Social Security Card			Hospitalization Card		
Proof of Birth Date			Surgical/Major Medical Card		
Proof of U.S. Citizenship			Life Insurance Card		
Diploma/Degree			Supplemental Life Insurance Card		
Transcript			Long-Term Disability Card		
City Tax Form			W4 Tax Form		

Emergency Notification Data:

Name(s)

Address

Relationship	Telephone Number with Area Code:

References Received (type, date, and by whom):

Processed by:

Date:

Source: Matthew J. DeLuca, *Nonprofit Personnel Forms & Guidelines*, Aspen Publishers, Inc., © 1994.

Interview Report

INTERVIEW REPORT

Rating Code:
Favorable–Unfavorable
1 2 3 4 5

Applicant Name: _____   For Position: _____

Interviewer Name: _____   Date: _____

Category	Rating	Comments
Appearance Greeting Self-Expression Responsiveness		
Work Experience 　relevance 　skill level 　process/result orientation 　motivation 　interpersonal skills 　initiative 　leadership 　growth and development 　teamwork		
Education 　sufficiency 　relevance 　intellectual development		
Background 　basic values and goals 　attitudes toward achievement 　self-image		
Present Activities and Interests 　management of time 　energy level 　maturity and judgment 　intellectual growth 　diversity of interests 　social skills 　language skills 　leadership 　basic values and goals		

Strengths: Weaknesses:

Summary and Recommendations:

Final Rating:

Source: Matthew J. DeLuca, *Nonprofit Personnel Forms & Guidelines*, Aspen Publishers, Inc., © 1994.

RECRUITING AND RETAINING VOLUNTEERS*

Volunteers help health organizations in two important ways: by performing jobs and by providing expert advice.

Volunteers should not be used to replace regular full-time employees. But they can perform special jobs—conducting surveys, distributing health promotion materials, and assisting at clinics. Volunteers from business and other professions can provide expertise, such as financial advice or advertising tips.

Volunteers can bring fresh ideas and new approaches to an organization.

Getting Started

Before you begin recruiting volunteers, you should:

- promote your organization
- conduct a needs analysis
- develop job descriptions

Promoting Your Organization

People want to know what kind of work your organization does and what image it has in the community before they consider volunteering their time and/or expertise. Preferably, a positive image of your organization is already established in the community as the result of its ongoing work and perhaps some promotion efforts. Any promotion, whether it is providing health education to the public or publicizing your organization's services, helps to attract volunteers. To promote your organization:

- create a speakers bureau of staff and volunteers to speak to community groups, such as Lions clubs, Business & Professional Women, garden clubs, high school and college groups, senior citizen clubs, and so forth
- prepare and submit news releases to newspapers and television and radio stations, and public service announcements to television and radio stations
- set up posters or displays at health fairs, shopping centers, schools, and so forth

Conducting a Needs Analysis

Take an in-depth look at your organization and those you need to serve to determine what kinds of programs you have and what your job needs are. Then decide what kinds of people you need for volunteer positions and what hours you need them.

Developing Job Descriptions

Develop descriptions for specific volunteer jobs with specific duties. Do not make all your volunteer positions "gopher" jobs (running errands). Some volunteers are happy doing this kind of work, while others want skilled work with more responsibility. Defining real jobs is very important: volunteers do not like to sit around doing nothing.

---

*Source: State of New York Department of Health, Albany, New York, © 1987.

Recruiting Volunteers

Now you are ready to begin your recruitment effort. The most effective methods of recruiting are person-to-person contact, newsletters, and using the media.

Person-to-Person Contact

Talk about volunteering wherever people gather in the community: club meetings, sporting events, churches, neighborhood coffee klatches, school meetings, health fairs. The most successful recruitment uses the "snowball" effect, which occurs when one person interested in volunteering speaks to another, and so on.

Newsletters

Contact the editors of newsletters for all the clubs and organizations in your community, including house organs of local businesses and industries. Ask them to include articles about your organization and the opportunities for volunteers.

Using the Media

Advertise your organization's opportunities for volunteers in news releases and public service announcements. For best results, develop personal contacts with editors, station managers, and public affairs directors, and seek their guidance in preparing professional materials for media use. Other ideas include the following:

- The media are always looking for good human interest stories with emotional appeal. If you have a service, event, special staff worker, or volunteer that fits in this category, try to get media coverage.
- Take out an ad in the weekly "shopper" in your area.
- Ask a supermarket to print a "volunteer message" on its paper bags.
- Obtain free space for posters on buses operated by public transportation agencies or public service space donated by companies that manage roadside billboards.

Emphasize Rewards

To sell people on the idea of volunteering for your organization, emphasize the rewards of volunteering.

For individuals, these rewards include:

- meeting new people
- becoming involved in the community
- being identified with a cause they believe in
- developing skills and experience useful in getting a job

For businesses and other professions, the rewards for having a representative volunteer with your organization include:

- contributions to the community
- more exposure in the community
- enhancement of their image
- exchange of in-kind services

Interviewing Volunteers

Prospective volunteers should be interviewed, just as you would interview a prospective employee. You have to make sure that the person is right for the job, and that the person's philosophy is consistent with that of your organization.

Supervising Volunteers

Volunteers should be treated the same as other staff. Be sure to:

- Give them their own work areas.
- Ask for their input and ideas.
- Provide training.
- Evaluate their performance.
- Provide feedback on performance.
- Be accessible to them.

How To Retain Volunteers

Keeping volunteers is simply a matter of keeping them happy. Include them in staff meetings and functions, and show your appreciation of their help by:

- saying "thank you" often
- noting their achievements in newsletters and news releases
- providing positive feedback
- inviting them to a coffee, lunch, or dinner in their honor
- recognizing their achievements or lengths of service with certificates, letters, pins, or plaques

Final Tips

- If your organization plans to use many volunteers, consider hiring a full-time volunteer coordinator.
- All the members of your staff should consider themselves volunteer recruiters; one person cannot do it alone.
- Occasionally, it becomes necessary to fire a volunteer, just as you would an employee who does not work out.
- When a volunteer resigns, always hold an exit interview to get the person's comments on the good and bad aspects of his or her volunteer work.

Establishing a Positive Work Climate

Work climate is the employee's perception of how well his or her basic needs are being met. If employees feel their basic needs are being met, they will view work more positively.

Climate influences staff performance. Because it reflects employees' perceptions of the positive and negative consequences of their actions, the work climate influences motivation. Basically, when employees feel their needs are likely to be met, they are more likely to take constructive action.

A number of factors influence the climate of a workplace. These factors include history, organizational structure, interpersonal qualities of members of the group, and management or supervisory behavior. Of any of these factors, management and supervisory behavior explain most of the variance in an employee's perception of work climate. Supervisors have the most influence on how their staff experience the workplace through their responses to the day-to-day needs of individuals in their organization.

There are a number of components of climate, each relating to underlying needs of the employee and behaviors of the supervisor. When supervisors respond positively to employees' underlying needs, the climate improves. When underlying needs are frustrated, the climate deteriorates. The following chart describes the climate components and the related supervisory practices.

CLIMATE COMPONENTS AND SUPERVISORY PRACTICES

Climate Component	Underlying Needs	Supervisory Practices
Clarity—the extent to which goals, expectations, and mission are clearly defined	Security, growth, and autonomy	Communicating expectations, sharing information, and providing feedback
Warmth—the extent to which sensitivity, support, and empathy are demonstrated toward the needs of employees	Intimacy, self-worth, and security	Sharing information and providing empathy and positive feedback
Openness—the extent to which employees feel free to express thoughts and opinions without fear of reprisal	Security and self-worth	Sharing information and providing feedback and empathy
Autonomy—the extent to which employees feel freedom to achieve goals according to strategies they define	Autonomy and self-worth	Communicating expectations, sharing information, focusing on monitoring results rather than process, and providing feedback based on results
Excellence—the extent to which high performance standards are expected	Self-worth and growth	Emphasizing results, setting clear expectations, and providing results-based feedback
Accountability—the extent to which employees feel they are responsible and accountable for performance	Security, self-worth, and growth	Providing feedback, monitoring results, and clarifying expectations
Leadership—the extent to which employees feel the authority system is competent to meet the organization's needs	Security and self-worth	Demonstrating comfort with the role, clarifying expectations, monitoring results, and providing feedback

Source: Adapted from Thomas D. Morton and Marsha K. Salus, *Supervising Child Protective Services Caseworkers*, U.S. Department of Health and Human Services, Administration for Children and Families, Administration on Children, Youth and Families, National Center on Child Abuse and Neglect, 1994.

Eight Tips for Effective Meetings

1. **Start and End on Time.** Each community has its own standards about what "on time" means. Some people may think "on time" means 15, 20, or even 30 minutes late. As a general rule, if most people have shown up, start without waiting for the rest.

2. **Take Turns.** Members should take turns hosting and leading meetings if there is no permanent leader selected.

3. **Clearly State the Purpose of the Meeting.** Tell people just how much you hope to get done.

4. **Stick to an Agenda.** Each meeting should have an agenda. If people want to discuss issues that are not on the agenda, put them on the agenda for the next meeting or include them in "new business" at the end of the meeting, as time permits.

5. **Assign Tasks and Set Timelines.** Move the group from talk to action by giving people responsibility for specific tasks, and giving them deadlines.

6. **Summarize Decisions Made.** A summary at the end of the meeting makes people feel good about what they have done and reminds them of tasks that have been assigned.

7. **Keep Minutes of the Meeting.** Minutes provide a permanent record of all the decisions that have been made. Minutes should be distributed to all group members in advance of each meeting.

8. **Give Praise.** Praise group members who have worked hard or who have finished tasks they were assigned. If people feel appreciated, they will continue to work hard.

NOTES:

Source: *Restoring Balance*, Health Promotion Resource Center, Stanford Center for Research in Disease Prevention (and the Indian Health Service), Stanford University, 1000 Welch Road, Palo Alto, California 94304-1885. Phone: (415) 723-0003. Fax: (415) 725-6906, © 1992.

Sample Plan for the First Meeting with a Community Group

Timeline	Plan
20 min.	1. State the purpose of the meeting.
	2. Introduce those who have helped to plan this meeting, and explain what the planning group has done so far.
	3. Tell people what is on the agenda (in this sample, it is items 5–10) so they know what to expect.
	4. Set the tone for the meeting by explaining that everyone is welcome to speak, and that each person's views will be respected.
20 min.	5. Have a speaker present the main topic for 15 to 20 minutes. (An outside "expert" is not necessary. Use someone from the community.)
30–45 min.	6. Break into groups of five to eight people for a discussion. This encourages everyone to share ideas. Each group should have the same task, for example, to share ideas on what is needed. Have one person in each group write down the ideas discussed.
	7. Bring the entire group back together and review the small groups' ideas.
30 min.	8. Write down the main themes from each small group so everyone can see them.
	9. Summarize the group reports so that people know what was accomplished. Tell the entire group how valuable their ideas will be in the next stage of the planning process.
10 min.	10. Decide who will follow up on the ideas from the meeting.
10 min.	11. Set the time and place of the next meeting.
	12. Thank people for coming.

NOTES:

Source: *Restoring Balance*, Health Promotion Resource Center, Stanford Center for Research in Disease Prevention (and the Indian Health Service), Stanford University, 1000 Welch Road, Palo Alto, California 94304-1885. Phone: (415) 723-0003. Fax: (415) 725-6906, © 1992.

Checklist for a Good Group Leader

You can use this checklist to see whether the group leader is doing a good job. If you are the leader, you can use it to check up on yourself. Check off each item you think the leader does well. The more checks, the better the leadership!

✔ A good leader does all these things. Does yours?

☐ Gives updates to the group about their progress and about what still needs work

☐ Speaks clearly and specifically (not in vague, general terms)

☐ Listens to all group members' ideas

☐ Makes new members feel part of the group

☐ Delegates tasks to group members

☐ Praises group members for taking on tasks

☐ Checks with group members to see if they have done tasks they agreed to do

☐ Praises group members for tasks completed

☐ Finishes tasks he or she agreed to do

☐ Helps to set goals and objectives

☐ Keeps the discussion focused on the main issue of concern to the group

☐ Solves problems with the group (asks questions, thinks of possible solutions)

☐ Is honest (gives accurate facts; doesn't lie or distort the truth)

NOTES:

Source: *Restoring Balance*, Health Promotion Resource Center, Stanford Center for Research in Disease Prevention (and the Indian Health Service), Stanford University, 1000 Welch Road, Palo Alto, California 94304-1885. Phone: (415) 723-0003. Fax: (415) 725-6906, © 1992.

Group Process Evaluation Form

Listed below are some characteristics of effective group behavior. Evaluate a group's behavior as well as your own behavior by using this checklist immediately after several group activities.
Rate whether members of the group did the following:

Yes	No	Sometimes	
____	____	____	Arranged the physical setting so as to be comfortable and so as to facilitate interaction
____	____	____	Clarified the purpose of the meeting and identified group goals
____	____	____	Helped initiate ideas and activities within the group
____	____	____	Solicited information and ideas from others
____	____	____	Called for alternate points of view
____	____	____	Helped others participate
____	____	____	Helped solve power and leadership struggles as they surfaced
____	____	____	Suggested procedures to help move the group toward a goal
____	____	____	Clarified and summarized issues
____	____	____	Helped the group reach consensus
____	____	____	Supported members of the group as needed
____	____	____	Helped to reconcile disagreement
____	____	____	Helped the group cope with tension
____	____	____	Expressed feedback honestly and openly
____	____	____	Received suggestions and disagreement without becoming defensive
____	____	____	Concluded discussion before members lost interest
____	____	____	Summarized the ideas expressed or the conclusion of the group
____	____	____	Gave positive recognition to the group for its accomplishment

Source: Donald J. Breckon et al., *Community Health Education: Settings, Roles, and Skills for the 21st Century*, ed. 3, Aspen Publishers, Inc., © 1994.

LOCATING AND APPLYING FOR HEALTH PROMOTION FUNDS*

Getting Started

Your organization needs funding for health promotion projects and you are the person responsible for finding it. How do you start? Where do you look? What will be required?

This guide will help you locate, apply for, and, hopefully, obtain the funding you need.

Since so many organizations compete for the same dollars, your first task is two-fold: (1) become familiar with public and private funding sources and (2) understand the application processes and requirements of those sources.

Before starting your funding search, ask yourself these questions:

- Why is the program needed?
- Who in the community supports the program?
- Is this an appropriate project for my organization?
- What public and private sector groups may supply funds?
- Are the health goals of the community and the funding source consistent with the objective of my proposed project?
- What makes my program special or unique?

Once you have documented that yours is a project that benefits your community, is one that your organization can effectively deliver, and does not duplicate efforts of another agency, you are ready for the next step.

Funding Options

It is important to explore all funding options available to your organization before deciding on a course of action. The options may include public or private sources of funding and grants or contracts. Keep in mind that some projects may require funding from more than one source.

Here are some definitions that will be useful:

- **Grants**—funding awarded for experimental, demonstration, or research projects in which success is uncertain. Most grants are awarded to nonprofit organizations.
- **Contracts**—money allocated to supply specified services to a funding agency. Contracts are usually awarded for programs that originate with the funding source.
- **Public funds**—money raised through taxes and administered by federal, state, and local governments
- **Private funds**—money raised and administered by private organizations, such as corporations, foundations, and charities. Often available as grants, private funds are awarded for new and/or experimental projects.

---

*Source: State of New York Department of Health, Albany, New York, © 1995.

Foundation Grants

Foundation grants can be difficult to find out about, and even more difficult to obtain. Typically, foundations have annual reports and funding guidelines available upon request. These documents should be studied and referred to when preparing a letter of intent or application.

Make sure your program is one that will be of interest to the funder. Follow the directions stated in the funding guidelines exactly. Many foundations specify what kind of projects will be funded. However, if they do not, call and ask questions. Most foundations will not fund projects requesting 100 percent funding. Therefore, it is important to seek multiple funding sources for your project.

Choosing the Right Foundation

Your first objective is to select the proper source of funding. Your local library may be able to refer you to a Foundation Center Library, or these publications can help:

- *The Foundation Directory*
- *National Directory of Corporate Giving*
- *Directory of Biomedical and Health Care Grants*

Corporate Grants

Corporate funding is even harder to secure than foundation funding. The key to obtaining this support is convincing the corporation that your program complements its business and that the corporation will get something positive out of the project (such as publicity, recognition, etc.). Types of corporate support include (1) outright gifts and grants, (2) matching gifts, and (3) gifts in kind. The most common approach to a corporate funder is through a telephone call to the company's corporate contributions or similar office. Corporate grants may require much less formal proposal preparation than a foundation grant.

Government Grants

Government grants are issued through a request for proposals (RFP) or requests for applications (RFA). An RFP solicits bids from contracts while an RFA solicits proposals for grants. Most grants go to nonprofit organizations. Rarely does funding go to applicants who submit unsolicited proposals (i.e., proposals that do not respond to a specific RFP or RFA). The main difference between grants and contracts is that grants allow more creativity and freedom in a particular project. A contract will have a specific set of deliverables and very little room for flexibility.

How Do You Find Out about Them?

Usually, if an organization has an idea for a program, it looks for a foundation. However, if the source is government funds, the idea often comes from a funding agency issuing an RFP or RFA. RFPs are issued to solicit bids for government contracts. Both nonprofit and for-profit groups bid on contracts. RFAs are issued to solicit proposals for grants. Most grants go to nonprofit organizations. Only on rare occasions is funding awarded to applicants who have submitted proposals without previous communication with the funder.

Federal RFPs and RFAs are published in the *Federal Register*. For further information, write or call the U.S. Government Printing Office, Washington, DC 20402, or call (202) 523-5240. This publication may also be available in your local public library.

State and local RFPs and RFAs appear in your state register. To obtain further information, write or call the state register office closest to you or check your public library.

Applying for a Government Grant

Once you have identified an appropriate RFA or RFP, the next step is to request any written material relating to the grant program, such as a program announcement and an application kit.

The program announcement usually contains the following information:

- purpose of the grant program
- eligibility criteria
- range and number of awards
- allowable costs
- evaluation criteria
- suggested outline for the proposal
- deadline dates
- program contacts

An application kit will usually include:

- grant application forms
- detailed instructions
- requirements for coordination with planning agencies

Proposal Preparation

Once you have selected one or more likely sources, you should submit a letter that outlines your project and credentials, describes your organization, and requests necessary forms, instructions, and, if possible, a face-to-face meeting.

After receiving the forms and instructions, you should be aware that proposal preparation is a time-consuming effort and that your submission must be accurate and thorough. The effort put into your organization's proposal will better prepare you for any questions that may arise or adjustments that might be requested.

Should you require assistance in preparing a proposal, you may want to contact a fund-raising consulting firm. Many firms that specialize in fund-raising for nonprofit groups are members of this organization. For a fee, they can supply feasibility studies, assist in planning, and help in writing the proposal.

The Proposal

The cover letter accompanying your proposal should contain a brief explanation of the project, its relevance to the foundation's or granting agency's interest, and your total funding requirement. Your personal and organizational credentials should also be established, along with an expression of enthusiasm and an offer to supply additional information as needed. The body of the proposal should contain these elements:

- **Abstract:** This is a summary of the entire proposal in a page or less. It should follow the same format as the proposal itself.
- **Background/Need:** This should include what your organization has done in the past, a brief background of the specific problem in your area, and data to support your claims.
- **Target Population:** This describes who will benefit from your project.
- **Goals/Objectives:** Goals are the prospective outcomes this project will help reach; the objectives are the specific accomplishments you will achieve.
- **Methods:** Methods are the specific activities you will conduct to meet your objectives. Include an approach, action plan, and timeline section.
- **Evaluation Plan:** Include both process and outcome measures to be used in evaluating the success of your project.
- **Management Plan:** Describe how your project will be managed, who the key staff members are, what their roles will be, and how activities will be coordinated. This is an important section that often is omitted.
- **Budget:** Itemize all expenses and provide a detailed justification for each, if possible.
- **Appendixes:** Include only relevant documentation, such as letters of support, data sources, resumes for key staff, and evaluation protocols.

Foundations and government agencies devote a lot of time and effort to developing background materials and application guidelines for those seeking funding. It is your responsibility to understand all background requirements and to faithfully follow all steps in the application process. Do not neglect to establish contact by telephone and/or letter with the individual responsible for your project area. That person can provide any needed assistance, and it is likely that he or she may need to call you to discuss project modifications or to monitor your progress.

A Final Note

When applying for funding, be aware that organizations that exhibit determination, perseverance, and a strong desire to succeed are most likely to receive funding from federal, state, and private foundation grant programs.

PROPOSAL DEVELOPMENT FOR FOUNDATIONS*

As the number of nonprofit organizations grows, so does the competition for foundation dollars. While the decision to award a grant to a nonprofit organization rests with the grant maker, the organization can take several steps to ensure the proposal is given serious consideration.

Uncovering Funding Sources

The first step in ensuring that your request does not end up in the grant maker's wastebasket is to look for foundations that support projects similar to yours. Your first source should be *The Foundation Directory*, published annually by The Foundation Center. This reference book provides a comprehensive listing of foundations by state. In addition to giving you the foundation's address and telephone number, it also provides information about the foundation's purpose and activities, giving limitations, previous grants, assets, and trustees. Because *The Foundation Directory*'s information is usually a few years old, it is a good idea to call each prospective funder for a copy of its most recent guidelines and annual report, if it publishes one.

When you receive the information from the foundation, read it carefully to make sure you have a thorough understanding of the grant maker's fund interests, deadlines, and application requirements. Many foundations are very explicit about what they will and will not fund. Read the material carefully and tailor your request accordingly. For example, if the guidelines clearly state that the foundation does not fund equipment purchases, do not send a proposal requesting underwriting for computer hardware. No matter how eloquently your proposal presents your organization's need, it will be turned down if it does not meet the grant maker's interests.

Organizing Your Proposal

The second key to successful grantsmanship is organization. Foundation staff receive countless requests in the mail each day; they want to be able to skim your proposal and easily discover the following:

- Does the proposal meet the foundation's guidelines?
- What is the proposal requesting?
- How much is being requested?
- What is the need the proposal meets?

If the person reading the proposal has to wade through massive amounts of paper and/or verbiage to find the answers to those questions, your proposal has lost points even before the substance has been evaluated.

---

*Source: Catherine P. Schwartz, "How To Develop a Winning Proposal: Staying One Step Ahead of Your Competition," *Nonprofit Financial Advisor*, Vol. 2:4, Aspen Publishers, Inc., © September 1995.

A well-organized proposal is composed of the following parts:

- **A one-page summary.** The summary explains the problem being addressed, your organization's solution to the problem, and what results will be achieved. It is best if you write this summary last, for you will have a clearer idea of what it is you are summarizing.
- **A section that describes in-depth the problem your proposal addresses.** Foundations, like individuals, give their money away to make a difference. The funds are used by organizations to address a need. In a successful grant proposal, you must explain what the problem is, the effect it is having on the community, and what will happen if it is not addressed successfully.
- **A project description.** How will your project be implemented? Who will implement it? What do you want to accomplish, and what methods will you put in place to ensure that the goals and objectives outlined in your proposal are met? These are all questions you must answer when you describe the project so that the funder understands both the project and its benefits, and so it can see that your organization has put some thought and time into developing the project.
- **A budget.** You will need to include a budget that specifically shows how the funder's money will be used, if funds from other sources will be used, if the project will be self-supporting at some point, and what portion of the money will be spent on overhead.
- **An historical overview.** Before a foundation decides to give your organization a grant, it will want to know your organization's history, what other groups or individuals support it financially, and what its track record is in doing similar projects. You should be able to describe this in three or four paragraphs—enough to give the funder a broad overview of your organization's work.
- **A cover letter.** The proposal should be sent with a cover letter, addressed to the appropriate person at the foundation. In the first paragraph, the cover letter should mention the amount you are requesting, the purpose of the grant, and the name of the organization requesting the grant. It should be signed by your organization's chief executive officer or board president. It is usually not signed by the development director.
- **Attachments.** Other attachments include a board of directors list, the Internal Revenue Service determination letter, and vitaes of key project personnel.

Writing the Proposal

The key to writing a good proposal is following the rules you learned back in high school English. Use clear, simple, unadorned language that communicates your organization's vision, the problem it wants to address, and its solution. Choice of correct spelling, words, paragraphs that have a topic sentence, and subsequent sentences that relate to the main idea and show a logical thought progression are crucial to good writing.

To see if you are doing a good job communicating your proposal's point, have someone who knows nothing about your organization read the proposal and take his or her comments into account as you polish your drafts. Remember, the foundation officer who reads your proposal knows nothing about your organization either.

Submitting the Proposal

Before submitting the proposal, you may want to call the foundation first. You may be lucky enough to get by the receptionist and speak to a program officer. The purpose of the call is to introduce your organization, explain that you are interested in submitting a proposal to the foundation, briefly describe the proposal, and request an appointment.

Do not be surprised if you are turned down. Many foundations will not meet with an organization until a proposal has been received. If that is the case, ask if you can submit the proposal and let the program officer know you will follow up in a few weeks.

In two to three weeks, call the program officer to see if the proposal has been received. If so, repeat your request for a meeting. You still may be told that he or she is not interested in meeting with you. Do not push—simply ask when you can expect a decision from the foundation regarding the proposal.

If your proposal is turned down, do not take it personally. It does not mean your proposal was bad. It could have been turned down for any number of reasons. If a reason is not outlined in the letter, give the program officer a call to find out why the proposal was turned down and if it would be appropriate to resubmit later. Do not argue with the program officer. Accept the foundation's decision and move on.

If you do receive a grant, remember to send a personalized thank you. Keep the funder informed about your progress and follow the funder's reporting requirements. Receiving a foundation grant is not the end of the process. In fact, it can be the beginning of a long-term partnership.

NOTES:

PROPOSAL DEVELOPMENT FOR STATE OR FEDERAL AGENCIES*

What Is a Proposal?

A proposal is a positive statement that sets forth a program or a set of activities. It requires two parties. It is a statement of what an individual or agency intends to do. It is made to another agency or institution and should be uniquely suited to that agency. It is written for presentation to another party in order to gain its acceptance.

Several types of proposals can be developed, the most common of which is a program proposal that offers a specific set of services to individual families, groups, or communities. A program proposal may be to provide training and consultation to agency staff and members of the community, or it may be to provide a number of other direct services. Technical assistance is a feature of many grant applications. Some planning proposals detail a set of planning and coordinating activities, which usually result in a program proposal. Similarly, there are research proposals to study a specific problem, evaluate a service, and so on.

Proposals can be solicited or unsolicited. A solicited proposal is prepared in response to a formal, written request for proposal, called an RFP. RFPs are prepared and sent to prospective agencies and operations. Similarly, program announcements and guidelines are described in various publications. The *Catalog of Federal Domestic Assistance* and the *Federal Register* are helpful in locating grant money and are available in most libraries. There are also grant-oriented newsletters, some of which are free. Potential grant writers need only request that their names be placed on an agency mailing list. A number of commercial organizations also prepare and sell subscriptions that describe currently available grant money. Although such subscriptions are expensive, they can pay for themselves quickly in terms of time saved and dollars garnered.

Unsolicited proposals are also received and reviewed regularly. It is important in both cases to ascertain if a project is a priority in the agency that is being solicited. A telephone call to the agency will usually result in the needed information.

Once one or more potential sources of grant money have been developed, the agency (or agencies) should be contacted for available guidelines and application forms. Further, prospective grant writers should telephone or visit a contact person in the agency and describe the essence of what will be proposed. Such first-hand information and advice are readily available, and staff members prefer to provide them before the project is fully developed, rather than after. Seeking and using such advice can save a lot of time and energy, but more important, it can increase the probability of a project being funded.

Each funding agency has its own application forms and guidelines. It is imperative that the forms be filled out completely and accurately. Writing a grant is more complicated than filling in the blanks, but ability and willingness to follow directions completely are an important part of the process.

---

*Source: Donald J. Breckon et al., *Community Health Education: Settings, Roles, and Skills for the 21st Century*, ed. 3, Aspen Publishers, Inc., © 1994.

What Should the Proposal Include?

Despite the dissimilarities and their importance, grants have a great deal in common. There are common elements in the proposal. They may have different names, be grouped differently, or be in different sequence. These items should be included in a proposal in some fashion. In unsolicited proposals, in which no formal guidelines or application forms are available, these proposal elements can be used as guidelines.

The narrative need not be long. It is not uncommon for agency guidelines to set a page limitation on the narrative, typically 10 or 15 pages of double-spaced typing. Such restrictions cause grant writers to revise the narrative until it is clear and succinct, permitting reviewers to evaluate it in a shorter period of time.

Letter of Transmittal

The letter of transmittal, or cover sheet, is the first page of a grant but may, in fact, be the last part of the application to be prepared. It provides, at minimum, the name and address of the organization submitting the proposal, a concise summary of the problem, and the proposed program. In an initial attempt to establish credibility, it often includes a statement of the organization's interest, capability, and experience in the area. It must contain the contact person's name, address, and telephone number and an authorized signature from a chief administrative officer. The authorized signature is necessary because the proposal is offering to use agency space, equipment, and staff to do specific tasks. Grant reviewers want to know that the agency is committed to such tasks. When funded, such a project has the effect of a contract.

Table of Contents

If the application is large, a table of contents usually follows the letter of transmittal. Use of headings in the body of the proposal facilitates development of a table of contents. Headings also make it easier for reviewers to follow the organization of the project and should be used even if a table of contents is not needed.

Introduction

An introductory statement that puts the proposal in context is appropriate. The statement may or may not include a description of the problem; the description can be a separate section. In either case, it is important to establish that there is a problem and that it has serious consequences to the citizenry. Documentation is usually necessary at this point and, even if not necessary, is helpful.

Applicant Agency Description

Funding agencies need to know if the organization is able to carry out the proposed project. Items to describe include organizational structure, past experience, qualifications of the staff, and budget.

Target Group

The target group should be described in detail and put in the context of the geographic area in which the program will take place. The number and kind of clients are valuable information. A description of the client group's involvement in the project planning process is also important.

Objectives

The specific objectives should be included in measurable form. Although behavioral objectives are not necessarily required, they lend themselves well to grant application specifications. A timetable for accomplishing the objectives should also be included.

Procedures

The procedures that will be used should be detailed. A logical, sequential timetable for the work plan is helpful. Specific methods and materials should be identified, with emphasis given to the innovative features of the program.

Evaluation

A plan for evaluation should also be included and is often a key part of the proposal. The tools and methodology to be used should be described in enough detail to ensure funding agencies that the results of the program will be summarized accurately.

Budget

A budget sheet is usually included in the application form. Because this varies from agency to agency, the forms of the grant agency should be used when possible. However, grant budgets do have some commonality. Usually they list salaries, by position. Salary schedules of the applicant agency should be used in calculations. Fringe benefits are ordinarily figured on a percentage of salary. They include employer contributions to Social Security, health insurance, unemployment compensation, workers' compensation, and so on. The figures vary from agency to agency and from year to year but are usually about 25 percent of the total salary costs.

If consultants are needed on technical projects, a realistic per diem fee should be used in a separate section of the budget. Consultants are not entitled to fringe benefits.

Supplies and materials should also be described in a separate section. They should be itemized by major types, such as office supplies, mail, telephone, duplication costs, and printing.

Equipment is usually itemized in a separate category, giving specifics such as model number and vendor.

Travel should be categorized as in country / out of country, in state / out of state; it can be divided by personnel or by program function. Reviewers usually want to know how travel allowances are going to be used.

Indirect costs include items such as utilities, space, procurement, and accounting staffs. Governmental funding agencies usually have a maximum allowable indirect rate. The rate is often negotiated; it may approach 50 percent of salaries and wages for the project.

Matching Funds

If matching funds are being used, they should be described. They represent the portion of the project cost that the institution is providing. In some instances, in-kind contributions have been used for this purpose. Institutions may agree to provide space, office furniture, and so on, and place a monetary value on that. In other instances, matching funds are required. In any case, the larger the amount of matching funds or in-kind contributions, the more attractive the application will be.

Assurances

When applying to government agencies, it is also necessary to provide assurance compliances. There are a number of such assurances and they change from time to time. They might include items such as treatment of human subjects, following affirmative action procedures when hiring, handicapped accessibility, and accounting practices. Again, funding agencies can readily provide copies of such required assurances.

Appendixes

As in other written documents, the appendixes are used to include material that, if included in the body of the proposal, would interrupt the flow. Vitae of key personnel in the project and supporting letters of other agencies are usually appended. Brochures, flowcharts, diagrams, and other supporting material may be included.

NOTES:

Checklist for Grant Developers

☐ Have you written or telephoned the funding source to gather additional information?

☐ Have you used the team approach involving clients, other relevant agencies, and other members of your own agency?

☐ Has a demonstrable need been established?

☐ Have you demonstrated familiarity with the relevant literature, research, programs, and so forth?

☐ Have you stressed innovative features?

☐ Does a cover page include the needed summary information, and is an authorized signature included?

☐ Has an individual outside your field read the proposal for clarity, organization, and so forth?

☐ Have the computations been double-checked for accuracy, and is the budget realistic and explained adequately?

☐ Have agency credibility and competency of project staff been established?

☐ Does the proposal have an attractive format?

☐ Have agency requirements been met in terms of deadlines, number of copies, and so forth?

☐ Are you prepared to negotiate the proposal or resubmit and/or implement the program as proposed if funding is denied?

NOTES:

Source: Donald J. Breckon et al., *Community Health Education: Settings, Roles, and Skills for the 21st Century*, ed. 3, Aspen Publishers, Inc., © 1994.

3

Community Assessment and Mobilization

Understanding Your Community

Healthy Communities: An Overview 76
Information You Need about Your
   Audience 78
Ways of Learning about the Audience 79
How the Public Perceives Health
   Messages 82

Defining Your Community

How To Define the Community 84
Community Profile Worksheet 85
Sample Dataset 87
Collecting Morbidity Data 93
Community Morbidity Data Worksheet ... 94
Contributors to the Leading Causes
   of Death 96
Demographic Data Worksheet 97
Calculating Rates To Compare Vital
   Statistics from One Area or Population
   to Another 99
The Five-Step Community Needs
   Assessment Process 100

Community Assessment

Data Sources for Your Community
   Assessment 101
Checklist for a Community
   Assessment 102

Fifty Community Health Indicators 103
Examples: Mapping a Community's
   Health Needs 105
Health Problems Analysis Sample 107
Health Problems Analysis
   Worksheet 108
Community Health Plan Sample 109
Tips for Running Health Assessment
   Programs 110
Identifying Priority Problems
   Worksheet 111
Worksheet for Understanding the Health
   Issue of Concern 112
Assessing Drug Abuse within and across
   Communities 113
Standard Data Request Form for Assessing
   Drug Abuse within and across
   Communities 114
Sample Worksheet for Identifying Who
   Needs AIDS Education in Your
   Community 115

Focus Groups

Focus Groups: An Overview 116
Guidelines to Key Aspects of Focus Group
   Methodology 118
Suggestions for Developing the Topic
   Guide 124
Sample Focus Group Moderator's Guide:
   Aging and Alzheimer's Disease 125

Sample Abbreviated Moderator's Guide
  for Focus Group with Children   127
Tips for Working with Young Children   128

Measuring Community Opinions

Community Opinion Data   129
Guidelines for Individual In-Depth
  Interviews   130
Communitywide Opinion Survey   132
Description of Respondent   133
Community Leader Opinion Survey   134
Which To Use—Focus Groups or
  Individual In-Depth Interviews?   135

Mobilizing Your Community

Involving the Community in the
  Program   136
Guidelines for Establishing Community
  Partnerships   138
Potential Community Partners   139
Checklist for Establishing Contacts and
  Developing Relationships   141
Sample Resource Inventory Survey   142
Follow-Up Contact Sheet   143

Building Coalitions

Developing Effective Coalitions:
  An Eight-Step Guide   144
Coalition Building Tips: Coalition
  Leadership   162
Coalition Building Tips: Coalition
  Membership   165
Coalition Building Tips: Engaging Residents
  in Coalition Building   167
Coalition Building Tips: Coalition Barriers
  and How To Overcome Them (Part I) . . .   171
Coalition Building Tips: Coalition Barriers
  and How To Overcome Them
  (Part II)   173
Coalition Building Tips: Building
  Partnerships between Schools and
  Communities   176
Community Coalitions: Developing a
  Public Relations Plan   179
Community Coalitions: Lobbying
  Strategies   182
Educate the Legislators   189
Find Common Goals with Policymakers . . .   189
Inventory of Collaborating Groups   190
How To Develop a Community Partnership
  To Reduce Children's Use of Tobacco . . .   191
Tips for Partnering with Local
  Churches   192

Community Assessment and Mobilization

INTRODUCTION

This chapter discusses understanding, defining, and assessing your community. In addition, practical suggestions are made for measuring community opinions through focus groups, individual interviews, and surveys. Decisions about choice of data collection methodology are made easier with a comparison and contrast of the different methods. Finally, the chapter concentrates on ways to build and mobilize coalitions for change in the community. Interspersed throughout the chapter are handy guides and forms to make the community educator's job easier. The step-by-step approach, if followed throughout the text, will ensure successful programs.

Frequently, community assessment is suggested as a beginning step in program development; but only one overall community assessment form, specific to a text, is provided, with little if any practical guidance. This chapter provides comprehensive expert advice about how to assess the community. Many unique tools for making the process easier, more precise, and more productive are offered. The advice is invaluable for both the novice and the more experienced professional. The chapter does not end there, however. It also includes critical information about how to mobilize coalitions to develop resources for a healthier community through public relations, lobbying, legislation, leadership, and engaging residents. Barriers to coalition building are discussed in detail. The combination of community assessment and community mobilization guidelines sets this chapter apart from those in other textbooks in that it is both theoretical and practical.

HEALTHY COMMUNITIES: AN OVERVIEW*

The Nature of Community

A community is more than a randomly selected group of people. Although they are usually thought of in geographic terms, communities also may be identified not by locality but by shared interests or characteristics, such as ethnicity, sexual orientation, or occupation. In other words, a community is a group of people sharing values and institutions (such as hospitals, schools, churches, and government).

Components of a community include locality, an interdependent social group, interpersonal relationships, and a culture that includes values, norms, and attachments to the community as a whole as well as its parts.

Examples of communities include cities or other governmental units, the Hispanic community, the gay community, alcoholics, smokers, the blue-collar community, the educational community, the senior citizen community, the arts community, the religious community, and others.

From a health education perspective, the shared values and institutions of a community are the key to developing health education strategies for risk reduction. An analysis of such shared values and institutions is critical when beginning to plan health education.

Community Structures

The view of the community as a system provides some insight into community organization for change. Change in one sector usually implies that adjustments or responses will eventually occur in other parts of the system.

Health education can occur in any of the systems (economic, political, educational, etc.) and will eventually permeate the whole if a program having a large impact is

---

*Source: Adapted from Donald J. Breckon et al., *Community Health Education: Settings, Roles, and Skills for the 21st Century*, ed. 3, Aspen Publishers, Inc., © 1994.

present. Interventions aimed at changing behavior of individuals are inadequate because the system is a more powerful and pervasive determinant of behavior and of health than decisions made by individuals operating in a supposed full-choice situation. Therefore, an understanding of the total community and its subsystems is required if a health educator is to be successful.

Settings

A variety of community agencies are appropriate settings for focused health education programs, including governmental units, voluntary health agencies, health care providers, and employers. However, regardless of the agency or institution that employs the health educator, and regardless of the specific target group of health education programs, the larger community and its political, economic, educational, religious, and health care systems all have to be analyzed, considered, and used.

The interdependence of people and the common elements that provide a sense of community are also the elements that usually must be affected to improve the health of people in that community.

Locus of Responsibility

A time-honored principle is that government is responsible to do for the people what the people cannot do for themselves. Thus, governmental units provide police protection, educational systems, clean air and water, safe food supply, and health care. The government is often considered the residual guarantor of health services, whether they are provided directly or through community agencies. It is therefore appropriate and natural for governmental units to be charged with the responsibility to establish standards for community health and to ensure that they are met.

However, not all programming comes from government. It must come from a variety of community agencies. Healthy communities will always have multiple interventions and overlapping programs. The problems and opportunities are too great to be left to government alone. Prevention is a shared responsibility of the public and private sectors. The two must coordinate their efforts to solve common problems so that the most efficient use of resources has the greatest impact on improving the health of the community.

Information You Need about Your Audience

- age, sex, ethnicity, income and education levels, places of work, and residence
- causative/preventive behaviors related to your topic
- related knowledge, attitudes, practices, values, and beliefs
- patterns of use of related services
- cultural habits, preferences, and sensitivities related to your topic
- barriers to behavioral change
- effective motivators (e.g., benefits of change, fear of consequences, incentives, or social support)

In some cases, critical information about your audience will not be available in existing data. At this point, you may decide to conduct new research of your own to fill these information gaps. Whenever possible, supplement national data with local population statistics. National data may not capture unique characteristics of your audience.

NOTES:

Source: *Clear and Simple: Developing Effective Print Materials for Low-Literate Readers*, NIH Publication #95-3594, U.S. Department of Health and Human Services, Public Health Service, National Institutes of Health, National Cancer Institute, December 1994.

WAYS OF LEARNING ABOUT THE AUDIENCE*

Several methods help reveal the lifestyles, health status, and other characteristics of an audience. These methods include literature reviews, observations, informal conversations, surveys (oral and written), in-depth interviews, focus groups, or a combination of these methods. Not every method is appropriate for every audience; for example, oral but not written surveys may be appropriate for persons with limited literacy skills, while focus groups may not be appropriate in particular cultures that traditionally do not share personal opinions/feelings in a small-group setting.

Literature reviews are often the initial fact-finding step. Community observations, informal conversations, and surveys are usually conducted next and may provide background information needed to develop questions for in-depth interviews or focus groups.

The choice of individuals to be interviewed or included in research depends greatly on the type of information needed. Are you looking for general information about the community, or specific and detailed information? Will information from community leaders (e.g., gatekeepers, ministers, politicians, program directors) be enough, or do you need information from other community members (e.g., teachers, physicians, nurses, other professionals, block club presidents, block club members, patients, men, women, moms, dads, grandmothers, grandfathers, children of the intended audience)? Each type of source may provide a different kind of information.

Each resource method is described briefly below.

Literature Reviews

Literature reviews are a good way to "do your homework" before going into the community. They are only a first step, though, and should not be an isolated method of learning about the community. In searching the literature on the intended audience, some topics to consider include:

- **community demographics**, including age, sex, income, education, employment, culture, ethnicity, religion, and other variables
- **social demographics**, including social and medical services available (or lacking)
- **lifestyles, health beliefs, and health behaviors** of the audience

The types of literature to review include medical and public health references, such as epidemiological and health intervention articles about the health problem(s) to be addressed, and behavioral and social science literature, especially culturally specific information.

Additional sources of information that may bring a broad national understanding to a more locally defined level include:

- local newspapers, magazines, and newsletters
- posted materials describing local interests and events

---

*Source: AMC Cancer Research Center, *Beyond the Brochure: Alternative Approaches to Effective Health Communication*, U.S. Department of Health and Human Services, Public Health Service, Centers for Disease Control and Prevention (CDC), Atlanta, Georgia 30333, 1994.

- census data
- maps
- government documents, reports, and statistics
- marketing data and survey data (national and local)
- personal interviews or meetings with community leaders

Observations

Community gathering places, businesses, worksites, and clinics are good places to begin to discover how audience members live day to day and good places to let audience members get to know you. When conducting observations, follow the guidelines the experts use: Visit the community at different times of day and night and on weekdays and weekends. Visit social gatherings, religious ceremonies, and other events. Always explain who you are and why you are there. Observe how people interact—children with adults, men with women, community members with health professionals. Record the observations and discuss them with a variety of community members.

Informal Conversations

Informal conversations are an unstructured way for health professionals and audience members to get acquainted and provide valuable insight into the nuances of a community. Discuss what goes on in the community on a daily basis and other issues that may be relevant to the project. Explain what you are doing and let conversations run their natural course. As in any relationship, trust takes time, and people may need to interact with you several times before feeling comfortable talking with you. Listen to what people have to say, paying careful attention to key comments or anecdotes. Wait to record observations until after leaving the community. Use a dictaphone on the way home or write down observations as soon as possible afterward.

Surveys

Surveys may include questions on community demographics as well as specific health issues. Written surveys may include pictures or may be read to respondents. Survey community members, community service agency representatives and local professionals, and/or others who may provide information about the audience. Remember to make the survey appropriate for the respondents (i.e., culturally appropriate, at the appropriate reading level).

In-Depth Interviews

In-depth interviews provide detailed information about the community from its members. This form of qualitative research is characterized by extensive probing and open-ended questions and is conducted one-on-one between a community member or respondent and a trained interviewer. Often, community members are trained to conduct the interviews, since other members of the community may be more likely to answer probing questions from someone they know or can relate to than from an "outsider." As the name implies, in-depth interviews are lengthy and detailed. From your informal conversations with community members, identify key people to interview who know about or have extensive experience in the primary issues of concern. Also interview public health and other professionals who have worked in the community.

Focus Groups

Like in-depth interviews, focus groups are characterized by extensive probing and open-ended questions. Unlike in-depth interviews, though, they rely on group interaction. Focus groups are the most widely used form of qualitative research. A skilled moderator guides a group of community members through increasingly focused issues related to the research topics (e.g., health beliefs and behaviors, barriers to health care, cultural influences, or review of health-related materials). The issues discussed in the focus group may have been gleaned from in-depth interviews. Group interaction and a skilled and sensitive moderator are integral parts of focus groups.

NOTES:

How the Public Perceives Health Messages

Thinking about how the public perceives health messages prior to message development can help ensure that the public will hear and heed the information educators want to convey. Factors affecting public acceptance of health messages include the following:

- **"Health risk" is an intangible concept.** Many people do not understand the concept of relative risk, and so personal decisions may be based on faulty reasoning. For example, the public tends to overestimate the risk of car and airplane accidents, homicides, and other events that most frequently make the news, and underestimate the risk of less newsworthy but more common health problems, such as strokes and diabetes.

- **The public responds to easy solutions.** The ability to act to reduce or eliminate an identified risk not only can lessen actual risk but can abate the fear, denial, or mistrust that may result from new health information. The public is more likely to respond to a call for action if the action is relatively simple (e.g., get a blood test to check for cholesterol) and less likely to act if the "price" of that action is higher, or the action is complicated (e.g., quitting smoking to reduce cancer risk). Therefore, when addressing a complex issue, there may be an intermediate action to recommend (calling for information, preparing to quit).

- **People want absolute answers.** Some people do not understand probabilities. They want concrete information they can use to make certain decisions. In the absence of firm answers from a scientist, the media will sometimes draw an inappropriate conclusion, providing the public with faulty but conclusive-sounding information that the public finds easier to accept and deal with. Therefore, educators must carefully and clearly present their information to both the public and the media.

- **The public may react unfavorably to fear.** Frightening information, which sometimes cannot be avoided, may result in personal denial, disproportionate levels of hysteria, anxiety, and feelings of helplessness. Worry and fear may be accentuated by faulty logic and misinterpretation, and compounded if there are no immediate actions an individual can take to ameliorate the risk.

- **The public doubts the verity of science.** The public knows that scientists can be wrong and recalls incidents such as the predicted swine flu epidemic. They may hesitate to believe a scientist's prediction.

- **The public has other priorities.** New health information may not be integrated as one of an individual's priorities. When the National Cancer Institute (NCI) conducted focus groups with retired shipyard workers, it found that a future threat of cancer from a long-ago exposure to asbestos paled in importance in comparison with group members' daily infirmities. Conversely, teenagers, many of whom may never have experienced poor health, may find it inconceivable that they will be susceptible to future illness. For many people, intangible health information cannot compete with more tangible daily problems.

- **Individuals do not feel personally susceptible.** The public has a strong tendency to underestimate personal risk. An NCI survey found that 54 percent of respondents believed that a serious illness "couldn't happen to them" and considered their risk as less than that of the general public, regardless of their actual risk.

- **The public holds contradictory beliefs.** Even though an individual may believe that "it can't happen to me," he or she can still believe that "everything causes cancer," and, therefore, there is no way to avoid cancer "when your time comes," and no need to alter personal behavior.

- **The public lacks a future orientation.** The majority of Americans say that it is better to live for the present than to worry about tomorrow. The public, especially lower socioeconomic groups, has trouble relating to the future concept, and

continues

How the Public Perceives Health Messages continued

many health risk messages foretell of outcomes far in the future. Focus group participants who were convened to help plan a cancer prevention program agreed that it would take an actual health scare, or seeing a health problem in a friend or loved one, to make them alter their own behavior.

- **The public personalizes new information.** New risk information is frequently described in terms of its effect on society (such as predicted morbidity and mortality rates). The individual needs to translate that information into personal risk to understand it; translation of information offers an opportunity for misinterpretation and misjudgment, especially because technical analyses may be incomprehensible to the public.

- **The public does not understand science.** Technical and medical terminology, the variables involved in calculating risk, and the fact that science is not static but evolves and changes over time are all poorly understood by the public. Therefore, individuals lack the basic tools required to understand and interpret some health information.

NOTES:

Source: *Making Health Communication Programs Work: A Planner's Guide*, NIH Publication #92-1493, U.S. Department of Health and Human Services, Public Health Service, National Institutes of Health, Office of Cancer Communications, National Cancer Institute, April 1992.

HOW TO DEFINE THE COMMUNITY*

A community may be defined by geographic boundaries, political boundaries, or demographic characteristics. Because data are often available for geographic or political units, defining a community by geography makes data collection easier. Also, selection of a political unit may increase the ability of the community to influence the use of government resources and policies to address priority health problems. Thus, a community can be a neighborhood, a township, a city, a county, or a district. Special settings, such as public housing complexes, can also be communities. Whatever the definition of the community may be, residents must have public health needs in common and the resources within the community to respond effectively to those needs. To ensure that these internal resources are present, the community unit may need to be larger than a high-risk population who may become a target of future interventions. Members of a community should also have a "sense of community." They should have a sense of identity, shared values, norms, communications, and helping patterns and should identify themselves as members of the same community.

When working to unite the community, one task may be to help community members increase their sense of the larger community. Educators will need to establish a general definition of community before they begin working to mobilize community members and form partnerships, adjusting the definition as appropriate. In essence, the community defines itself. The community begins to be defined when a group of citizens comes together to improve community health. During the process of defining the community, educators should develop a profile of the community to understand its makeup.

Developing a Community Profile

When completing a community profile, basic demographic information may help educators ensure that the makeup of the program's community group reflects the makeup of the community. This information may also help educators decide how best to approach the community and its health problems, as well as what some obstacles to communication may be.

For example, information about the average household income and size may help determine the economic status of the community and thus what its resources may be. Knowing the average educational level of residents may help educators gauge the level of their presentations and materials. Learning that the community has a large ethnic population may indicate the need to use non–English-language communication channels, such as foreign-language newspapers and radio stations.

Educators may want to add other items to the profile as well. Some communities identify the main employers in their community and then ensure that those organizations are represented in the health program's community group or at least kept informed about the program.

Most of the information for the community profile can be obtained from data collected by the Bureau of the Census. Census data are generally available by region, state, metropolitan areas, and smaller geographic areas. Educators should collect data so that they can make comparisons between the community and other areas such as the state or nation and thereby determine the relative status of the community.

---

*Source: *PATCH: Planned Approach to Community Health*, Centers for Disease Control and Prevention, National Center for Chronic Disease Prevention and Health Promotion, Division of Chronic Disease Control and Community Intervention, Atlanta, Georgia 30333, revised January 1995.

Community Profile Worksheet

Community: _____   Year of data: _____

Lead agency: _____   Date collected: _____

Contact person: _____

Address: _____

Telephone number: _____

Community type: Urban _____   Rural _____   Suburban _____   Other _____
Geographic size or description:

_____

_____

Total Population

Unemployment rate: Community _____
                  State _____

Per capita income: Community _____
                  State _____

Families below
poverty level (%): Community _____
                  State _____

Age Distribution in Years

Community			State		
<1:	%	No.	<1:	%	No.
1–14:	%	No.	1–14:	%	No.
15–24:	%	No.	15–24:	%	No.
25–64:	%	No.	25–64:	%	No.
≥65:	%	No.	≥65:	%	No.

Number of Households, by Household Size

Number of Persons in Household

Community	State
1:	1:
2:	2:
3:	3:
4–5:	4–5:
6+:	6+:

Total number of households:

Annual Household Income

	Community		State	
Less than $14,999:	%	No.	%	No.
$15,000 to $24,999:	%	No.	%	No.
$25,000 to $49,999:	%	No.	%	No.
$50,000+:	%	No.	%	No.

continues

Community Profile Worksheet continued

Marital Status

Single:	%	No.	Male:
			Female:
Married:	%	No.	Male:
			Female:
Separated:	%	No.	Male:
			Female:
Widowed:	%	No.	Male:
			Female:
Divorced:	%	No.	Male:
			Female:

Racial/Ethnic Composition

White:	%	No.	% Male:
			% Female:
Black:	%	No.	% Male:
			% Female:
Hispanic*	%	No.	% Male:
			% Female:
American Indian†	%	No.	% Male:
			% Female:
Asian‡	%	No.	% Male:
			% Female:

Total Percentages: Male:

Female:

Education

Number of persons currently enrolled:

	Community
Elementary school	_____
High school	_____
Technical school	_____
College	_____

Educational achievement (% of adults who completed):

	Community	State
Elementary school plus three years high school	_____	_____
High school	_____	_____
Technical school	_____	_____
College:		
1–3 years	_____	_____
4 years	_____	_____
≥5 years	_____	_____

NOTES:

*Includes both blacks and whites.
†Or Alaskan Native.
‡Or Pacific Islander.

Source: *PATCH: Planned Approach to Community Health*, Centers for Disease Control and Prevention, National Center for Chronic Disease Prevention and Health Promotion, Division of Chronic Disease Control and Community Intervention, Atlanta, Georgia 30333, revised January 1995.

Sample Dataset

The following tables can be used by a community to determine its present state of health. Formulas used to calculate the rates shown can be found following each dataset.

DEMOGRAPHICS OR POPULATION DATA

Description	Local Numbers	Local Rate/ Percent	State Number	State Rate/ Percent
Race—Ethnicity				
Total population				
Total Whites				
Total Blacks				
Total Asians				
Total Native Americans				
Total other				
Total Hispanics				
Total Mexicans				
Total Puerto Ricans / Hispanics				
Total Cubans				
Age Groups				
Ages 0 to 1				
Ages 0 to 2				
Ages 3 to 5				
Ages 0 to 4				
Ages 0 to 5				
Ages 6 to 13				
Ages 14 to 17				
Ages 6 to 17				
Ages 18 to 20				
Ages 45 to 64				
Ages 65 and over				
Ages under 18				

continues

Sample Dataset continued

Description	Local Numbers	Local Rate/ Percent	State Number	State Rate/ Percent
Ages under 20				
Ages under 21				
Women ages 10 to 17				
Women ages 15 to 17				
Women ages 15 to 44				
White women ages 15 to 44				
Black women ages 15 to 44				
Native American women ages 15 to 44				
Hispanic women ages 15 to 44				
Socioeconomic Data				
Per capita income				
Persons living below 50% poverty				
Persons living below 75% poverty				
Persons living below 100% poverty				
Persons living below 125% poverty				
Persons living below 185% poverty				
Persons living below 200% poverty				
Children under age 5 living below 100% poverty				
Children under age 18 living below 50% poverty				
Children under age 18 living below 75% poverty				
Children under age 18 living below 100% poverty				
Children under age 18 living below 125% poverty				
Children under age 18 living below 185% poverty				
Children under age 18 living below 200% poverty				
Total families				
Families living below poverty				
Single-parent families living below poverty				
Total persons age 25 and above				
Persons age 25 and above who have completed high school or above				

continues

Sample Dataset continued

FORMULAS FOR THE POPULATION DATA TABLE

Description	Formula	

Race—Ethnicity

Percent of Whites	$\dfrac{\text{Number of Whites}}{\text{Total Population}}$	$\times 100$
Percent of Blacks	$\dfrac{\text{Number of Blacks}}{\text{Total Population}}$	$\times 100$
Percent of Asians	$\dfrac{\text{Number of Asians}}{\text{Total Population}}$	$\times 100$
Percent of Native Americans	$\dfrac{\text{Number of Native Americans}}{\text{Total Population}}$	$\times 100$
Percent of other	$\dfrac{\text{Number of other}}{\text{Total Population}}$	$\times 100$
Percent of Hispanics	$\dfrac{\text{Number of Hispanics}}{\text{Total Population}}$	$\times 100$
Percent of Puerto Ricans/Hispanics	$\dfrac{\text{Number of Puerto Ricans/Hispanics}}{\text{Total Population}}$	$\times 100$
Percent of Cubans	$\dfrac{\text{Number of Cubans}}{\text{Total Population}}$	$\times 100$

Age Groups

Percent of children ages 0 to 1	$\dfrac{\text{Number of children ages 0 to 1}}{\text{Total Population}}$	$\times 100$
Percent of children ages 0 to 2	$\dfrac{\text{Number of children ages 0 to 2}}{\text{Total Population}}$	$\times 100$
Percent of children ages 3 to 5	$\dfrac{\text{Number of children ages 3 to 5}}{\text{Total Population}}$	$\times 100$
Percent of children ages 0 to 4	$\dfrac{\text{Number of children ages 0 to 4}}{\text{Total Population}}$	$\times 100$
Percent of children ages 0 to 5	$\dfrac{\text{Number of children ages 0 to 5}}{\text{Total Population}}$	$\times 100$
Percent of children ages 6 to 13	$\dfrac{\text{Number of children ages 6 to 13}}{\text{Total Population}}$	$\times 100$
Percent of children ages 14 to 17	$\dfrac{\text{Number of children ages 14 to 17}}{\text{Total Population}}$	$\times 100$

continues

Sample Dataset continued

Percent of children ages 6 to 17

$$\frac{\text{Number of children ages 6 to 17}}{\text{Total Population}} \times 100$$

Percent of children ages 18 to 20

$$\frac{\text{Number of children ages 18 to 20}}{\text{Total Population}} \times 100$$

Percent of persons ages 45 to 64

$$\frac{\text{Number of persons ages 45 to 64}}{\text{Total Population}} \times 100$$

Percent of persons age 65 and over

$$\frac{\text{Number of persons ages 65 and over}}{\text{Total Population}} \times 100$$

Percent of children under age 18

$$\frac{\text{Number of children under age 18}}{\text{Total Population}} \times 100$$

Percent of children under age 20

$$\frac{\text{Number of children under age 20}}{\text{Total Population}} \times 100$$

Percent of children under age 21

$$\frac{\text{Number of children under age 21}}{\text{Total Population}} \times 100$$

Percent of women ages 10 to 17

$$\frac{\text{Number of women ages 10 to 17}}{\text{Total Population}} \times 100$$

Percent of women ages 15 to 17

$$\frac{\text{Number of women ages 15 to 17}}{\text{Total Population}} \times 100$$

Percent of women ages 15 to 44

$$\frac{\text{Number of women ages 15 to 44}}{\text{Total Population}} \times 100$$

Percent of White women ages 15 to 44

$$\frac{\text{Number of White women ages 15 to 44}}{\text{Total Population}} \times 100$$

Percent of Black women ages 15 to 44

$$\frac{\text{Number of Black women ages 15 to 44}}{\text{Total Population}} \times 100$$

Percent of Asian women ages 15 to 44

$$\frac{\text{Number of Asian women ages 15 to 44}}{\text{Total Population}} \times 100$$

Percent of Native American women ages 15 to 44

$$\frac{\text{Number of Native American women ages 15 to 44}}{\text{Total Population}} \times 100$$

Percent of Hispanic women ages 15 to 44

$$\frac{\text{Number of Hispanic women ages 15 to 44}}{\text{Total Population}} \times 100$$

continues

Sample Dataset continued

Socioeconomic Data

Percent of persons living below 50% poverty	$\dfrac{\text{Number of persons living below 50\% poverty}}{\text{Total Population}} \times 100$
Percent of persons living below 75% poverty	$\dfrac{\text{Number of persons living below 75\% poverty}}{\text{Total Population}} \times 100$
Percent of persons living below 100% poverty	$\dfrac{\text{Number of persons living below 100\% poverty}}{\text{Total Population}} \times 100$
Percent of persons living below 125% poverty	$\dfrac{\text{Number of persons living below 125\% poverty}}{\text{Total Population}} \times 100$
Percent of persons living below 185% poverty	$\dfrac{\text{Number of persons living below 185\% poverty}}{\text{Total Population}} \times 100$
Percent of persons living below 200% poverty	$\dfrac{\text{Number of persons living below 200\% poverty}}{\text{Total Population}} \times 100$
Percent of children under 5 living below 100% poverty	$\dfrac{\text{Number of children under 5 living below 100\% poverty}}{\text{Total number of children under 5}} \times 100$
Percent of children under 18 living below 50% poverty	$\dfrac{\text{Number of children under 18 living below 50\% poverty}}{\text{Total number of children under 18}} \times 100$
Percent of children under 18 living below 75% poverty	$\dfrac{\text{Number of children under 18 living below 75\% poverty}}{\text{Total number of children under 18}} \times 100$
Percent of children under 18 living below 100% poverty	$\dfrac{\text{Number of children under 18 living below 100\% poverty}}{\text{Total number of children under 18}} \times 100$
Percent of children under 18 living below 125% poverty	$\dfrac{\text{Number of children under 18 living below 125\% poverty}}{\text{Total number of children under 18}} \times 100$
Percent of children under 18 living below 185% poverty	$\dfrac{\text{Number of children under 18 living below 185\% poverty}}{\text{Total number of children under 18}} \times 100$

continues

Sample Dataset continued

Percent of children under 18 living below 200% poverty	$\dfrac{\text{Number of children under 18 living below 200\% poverty}}{\text{Total number of children under 18}} \times 100$
Percent of families living below poverty	$\dfrac{\text{Number of families living below poverty}}{\text{Total number of families}} \times 100$
Percent of single-parent families living below poverty	$\dfrac{\text{Number of single parent families living below poverty}}{\text{Total number of single parent families}} \times 100$
Percent of persons age 25 and over who have completed high school or above	$\dfrac{\text{Number of persons age 25 and over who have completed high school or above}}{\text{Total number of persons age 25 and over who have completed high school or above}} \times 100$

Example: If a person wants to know the percent of women ages 15 to 44, the formula should be calculated as follows:

Number of women ages 15 to 44 = 4,016
Total population = 19,181

$$\frac{4,016 \times 100}{19,181} = 20.94\%$$

NOTES:

Source: C.A. Monahan et al. *Focus on Children Community Planning Manual: Needs Assessment and Health Planning for Children, Including Children with Special Health Care Needs*, Maternal and Child Health Bureau, Health Resources and Services Administration, Public Health Service, U.S. Department of Health and Human Services, 1996.

COLLECTING MORBIDITY DATA*

When making a comparison of mortality rates by race, sex, and age groups, you will need to aggregate three to five years of data unless your community is a large metropolitan area. If your community has data on additional populations within the community, such as Hispanics, Asian Americans, and Native Americans, prepare complete worksheets to record those data.

The morbidity data a community is able to collect vary. Communities can generally obtain hospital discharge data and display them for their community group. When you obtain or present hospitalization data, you should distinguish what discharge diagnoses are used. Most forms of hospitalization data may be tabulated by primary discharge diagnosis, any listed discharge diagnosis, or both. Reporting only primary diagnosis will often underrepresent the actual prevalence of a particular disease condition, whereas reporting any listed diagnosis may more accurately represent the disease burden associated with a disease condition.

As you coordinate data working groups, consult with the working group collecting opinion data to find out key priorities identified. As appropriate, be able to provide additional morbidity data concerning major priorities.

Explore the availability of mortality and morbidity data within your community and state and from your various partners. Some of the resources for community data include:

- **state and local health departments**—census data on births, deaths, and social conditions such as divorces
- **state and local social service departments**—variety of data including percentages of population on welfare and unemployment
- **state and local departments of highway safety**—data on traffic injuries and seat belt use
- **state and local police departments**—information on crime trends, high-crime areas, and driving under the influence of alcohol or drugs
- **boards of education**—information on percentage of population who have secondary degrees and undergraduate degrees (also in census data)
- **voluntary agencies**—data on causes of death and disability, and their risk factors
- **hospitals**—information on length of stays, major causes of hospitalizations, and description of hospitalized populations
- **major employers or chambers of commerce**—demographic information on work force, illness, and disability
- **colleges and universities**—information on morbidity trends and forecasts on population trends

*Source: *PATCH: Planned Approach to Community Health*, Centers for Disease Control and Prevention, National Center for Chronic Disease Prevention and Health Promotion, Division of Chronic Disease Control and Community Intervention, Atlanta, Georgia 30333, revised January 1995.

Community Morbidity Data Worksheet

Age < 1	Cause	Total*	Percent**
1.			
2.			
3.			
4.			
5.			
All other causes			

Age 1–14	Cause	Total*	Percent**
1.			
2.			
3.			
4.			
5.			
All other causes			

Age 15–24	Cause	Total*	Percent**
1.			
2.			
3.			
4.			
5.			
All other causes			

continues

Community Morbidity Data Worksheet continued

Age 25–44	Cause	Total*	Percent**
1.			
2.			
3.			
4.			
5.			
All other causes			

Age 45–64	Cause	Total*	Percent**
1.			
2.			
3.			
4.			
5.			
All other causes			

Age 65+	Cause	Total*	Percent**
1.			
2.			
3.			
4.			
5.			
All other causes			

*Total number of deaths from this cause.
**Number of deaths from this cause divided by total of all deaths in this age group.

Source: *PATCH: Planned Approach to Community Health*, Centers for Disease Control and Prevention, National Center for Chronic Disease Prevention and Health Promotion, Division of Chronic Disease Control and Community Intervention, Atlanta, Georgia 30333, revised January 1995.

Contributors to the Leading Causes of Death

		Heart Disease	Cancers	Stroke	Injuries (Nonvehicular)	Influenza/ Pneumonia	Injuries (Vehicular)	Diabetes	Cirrhosis	Suicide	Homicide
Behavioral Risk Factor	Tobacco use	•	•	•	•	•					
	High blood pressure	•		•							
	High blood cholesterol	•		P							
	Diet	•	•	P				•			
	Obesity	•	•					•			
	Lack of exercise	•	•	•				•			
	Stress	P		P	•			•		•	•
	Alcohol abuse	•	•	•	•		•		•	•	•
	Drug misuse	P	•	P	•		•			•	•
	Not using seatbelts						•				
	Handgun possession				•					•	•
Nonbehavioral Risk Factor	Biological factors	•	•	•		•		•	•	•	P
	Radiation		•								
	Workplace hazards		•		•		•				
	Environmental		•				•				
	Infectious agents	P	•			•			•		
	Home hazards				•						
	Auto/road design						•				
	Speed limits						•				
	Health care access	•	•	•	•	•	•	•	•	•	•

P = Possible

Source: *PATCH: Planned Approach to Community Health*, Centers for Disease Control and Prevention, National Center for Chronic Disease Prevention and Health Promotion, Division of Chronic Disease Control and Community Intervention, Atlanta, Georgia 30333, revised January 1995.

Demographic Data Worksheet

1. Age distribution

Age	Male %	Female %	Ethnic/Racial Composition	%	Completed Years of School	%
1–5 years			White		< 8 years	
6–18 years			Black		9–12 years	
19–64 years			Hispanic		> 13 years	
65–74 years			Asian			
75–84 years			American Indian			
> 85 years			Other			
Total population						

2. Family characteristics
   a. Average family size _____
   b. Families headed by female _____%

3. Socioeconomic data
   a. Area that is rural ____%, urban _____%, suburban _____%
   b. Major industries or sources of employment:

   _____

   _____

   _____

   _____

   c. Employment
       Population employed _____%, unemployed _____%

4. Annual median income
   a. for family of four $_____
   b. per capita income $_____

	%
Families living on incomes below the poverty index	
Female-headed households living on incomes below the poverty index	
Elderly (over 65) living on incomes below the poverty index	
Households on Aid to Families with Dependent Children (AFDC)	
Households on Supplemental Security Income (SSI) (elderly, blind, disabled)	
Medicaid eligible	

continues

Demographic Data Worksheet continued

5. Housing characteristics

	# or %
Total housing units (number)	
Homes without indoor water (percentage)	
Homes without electricity (percentage)	
Homes without cooking facilities (percentage)	
Homeless (estimated number)	

NOTES:

Source: Mildred Kaufman, *Nutrition in Public Health: A Handbook for Developing Programs and Services,* Aspen Publishers, Inc., © 1990 Mildred Kaufman.

Calculating Rates To Compare Vital Statistics from One Area or Population to Another

$$\text{Birth rate} = \frac{\text{\# of live births}}{\text{population of area}} \times 1000$$

$$\text{Fetal mortality rate} = \frac{\text{\# of fetal deaths}}{\text{\# of live births} + \text{\# of fetal deaths in area}} \times 1000$$

$$\text{Infant mortality rate} = \frac{\text{\# of infant deaths}}{\text{\# of live births in area}} \times 1000$$

$$\text{Death rate} = \frac{\text{\# of deaths}}{\text{population of area}} \times 1000$$

NOTES:

The Five-Step Community Needs Assessment Process

STEP 1—ENLIST PARTNERS FOR THE ASSESSMENT PROCESS

A community-based planning process begins with recruiting local stakeholders who represent a variety of community-based organizations and groups.

STEP 2—DEFINE AND ANALYZE THE COMMUNITY

The process of needs assessment begins with a definition of the "community" in terms of geography, demographics, economics, and politics.

STEP 3—DEVELOP A COMMUNITY HEALTH PROFILE

Health status indicators are identified and analyzed, with comparisons to state and national data and health norms such as those outlined in the federal government's landmark report, *Healthy People 2000.*

STEP 4—CONDUCT THE COMMUNITY ASSESSMENT

Beyond the profile of health status, the needs analysis process will collect community opinions and develop a local consensus on health issues, including development of a "scoreboard" of causal factors such as lifestyle, environment, human biology, and lack of health services.

STEP 5—MOBILIZE THE COMMUNITY

The final step in the process is the formation of a coalition for change, mobilization of community support to carry out selected interventions to raise health levels in priority areas, and communication of the strategies to the public and local agencies.

NOTES:

Source: Russell C. Coile, Jr., ed, "Community Needs Assessment: Provider Networks Plan for Health," *Russ Coile's Health Trends*, Vol. 7, No. 4, Aspen Publishers, Inc., © February 1995.

Data Sources for Your Community Assessment

Census Tracts

The U.S. Department of Commerce, Bureau of the Census, has census tract information and maps, as do regional planning commissions.

ZIP Codes

The U.S. Postal Service has ZIP code boundaries.

Vital Statistics

Each state department of health provides both birth and death records at the address level for specific research projects. This information is then geocoded to the census tract level.

Geocoding of records can be completed by mapping packages such as Atlas GIS or Map INFO. Or records can be outsourced to these same groups or other companies such as The SACHS Group, Inc., Evanston, Illinois.

Demographics

Demographics for 1990 can be obtained from the Census Bureau at the census tract level. However, for more recent estimates various companies such as Claritas/National Planning Data Corporation can provide these data at the census tract and ZIP code level.

Inpatient Discharge Data

Many states maintain a patient database that contains 100 percent of the discharges at the diagnosis-related group level. In some states all of the data may not be a matter of public record because of privacy concerns, but it may be possible to purchase the data or arrange to use the data in some form.

Personnel

- **Physicians:** Each state, as well as Medical Economics and the American Medical Association, provides listings that can be purchased of active physicians, by specialty, address, age, and so on.
- **Nurses and nurse practitioners:** Each state should be able to provide a listing of nurses and nurse practitioners by specialty, degree, number of unfilled positions, and office address.

Survey Data

Survey data can be obtained by conducting the surveys required or by sharing the results of another organization's survey, as in Dallas, where the Greater Dallas United Way conducted a 4,000 household telephone needs assessment survey.

Inventory of Primary Care Services and Community Services

This information can be obtained from local information and referral service inventories. If the local city or county does not have one, then the data should be sought from the state department of health, state department of human services, state department of aging, and specific administration agencies.

Medicaid Eligibles and AFDC

State departments of human services or health should be able to provide, at the ZIP code level, the number of Medicaid eligibles, Aid to Families with Dependent Children recipients, and food stamp program participants.

Source: Sue Pickens, Paul Boumbulian, and Michelle Tietz, "Community Assessment: Strengths, Assets & Management," *Inside Preventive Care*, Vol. 1, No. 6, Aspen Publishers, Inc., © September 1995.

Checklist for a Community Assessment

ASSET DEVELOPMENT

- [ ] Land
- [ ] Libraries
- [ ] Parks
- [ ] Police stations
- [ ] Fire stations

COMMUNITY ORGANIZATIONS

- [ ] Crime Watch
- [ ] Neighborhood Watch
- [ ] Women's clubs
- [ ] Optimist
- [ ] Kiwanis
- [ ] Lions
- [ ] Businesses
- [ ] Schools
- [ ] Colleges

GOVERNMENT ASSISTANCE

- [ ] Number of families receiving Aid to Families with Dependent Children
- [ ] Number of persons receiving public assistance
- [ ] Number of persons receiving Medicaid
- [ ] Number of persons receiving food stamps

HEALTH RISK VARIABLES

Population Variables

- [ ] Population
- [ ] Total population density
- [ ] Population age groups (0–4 years of age; 5–17 years of age; 18–64 years of age; 65 and older)

Ethnicity

- [ ] Percentage white
- [ ] Percentage African American
- [ ] Percentage Hispanic

Socioeconomic Data

- [ ] Percentage of persons below federal poverty guideline
- [ ] Total number of households
- [ ] Estimated per capita income
- [ ] Estimated average household income

- [ ] Percentage of households with incomes <$15,000
- [ ] Unemployment rate
- [ ] Occupational status
- [ ] Value of housing
- [ ] Educational level

Birth and Birth-Related Information

- [ ] Fertility rate
- [ ] Percentage of teen births
- [ ] Percentage of low birth weight
- [ ] Percentage of infant mortality

Age-Adjusted Death Rates

- [ ] Accident
- [ ] Cancer
- [ ] Cirrhosis
- [ ] Diabetes
- [ ] Heart disease
- [ ] Human immunodeficiency virus
- [ ] Homicide
- [ ] Pneumonia/flu
- [ ] Respiratory
- [ ] Stroke
- [ ] Suicides

Access to Primary Care

- [ ] Primary care physicians per population (family practice, general practice, pediatrics, internal medicine, and OB/Gyn)
- [ ] Primary care providers per population (nurse midwives, nurse practitioners, and physician assistants)

Inpatient Discharges per 1,000 Population

- [ ] Discharges per 1,000 population for each service area or the county as a whole excluding newborns
- [ ] Discharges per 1,000 population for each service area or the county as a whole for the top five discharges

SURVEY DATA

- [ ] Top five health concerns
- [ ] Insurance status
- [ ] Access to care

Source: Sue Pickens, Paul Boumbulian, and Michelle Tietz, "Community Assessment: Strengths, Assets & Management," *Inside Preventive Care*, Vol. 1, No. 6, Aspen Publishers, Inc., © September 1995.

Fifty Community Health Indicators

This list was compiled from several community health assessments. Indicators are not listed in order of importance.

1. incidence of low birth weight, as measured by percentage of total number of live-born infants weighing less than 2,500 grams at birth
2. births to adolescents (aged 10 to 17 years) as a percentage of total live births
3. prenatal care, as measured by the percentage of mothers delivering live infants who did not receive prenatal care during the first trimester
4. neonatal mortality rate
5. early childhood mortality rate
6. childhood poverty, as measured by the proportion of children less than 15 years of age living in families at or below the poverty level
7. percentage of people reporting good or excellent health, on a scale of 1 to 10
8. percentage of public participation in health activities at community or regional levels
9. percentage of population using preventive medical services
10. percentage of population using a primary care source for coordination of preventive and episodic health care
11. proportion of residents practicing health-promotion/disease-prevention activities
12. percentage of population without health insurance
13. percentage of population reporting hunger or using food banks
14. percentage of functionally illiterate adults
15. homeless rate
16. percentage of people who feel safe walking alone at night
17. percentage of people reporting being a victim of crime
18. percentage of people reporting fewer than five social contacts per week
19. percentage of residents registered to vote for municipal elections
20. perceived annoyance/urban stress index
21. number of days with air quality in the good range
22. percentage of children and adults who are overweight
23. percentage of children and adults who are physically fit
24. percentage of children and adults who "eat all their vegetables"
25. percentage of population that smokes tobacco
26. rate of condom use among the sexually active
27. percentage of sexually transmitted disease cases that are repeat cases
28. percentage of population with untreated tooth decay
29. percentage of population that had their blood cholesterol checked in the last five years
30. percentage of population reporting overall satisfaction with the way they live

continues

Fifty Community Health Indicators continued

31. rate of suicide attempts
32. prevalence of mental disorders among children, adolescents, adults, and the elderly
33. average age of reported first use of drugs
34. alcohol and other drug use rates and patterns by household
35. percentage of businesses providing employee assistance and stress-reduction programs
36. number of motor vehicle crashes
37. number of vehicle crashes due to drug and alcohol use
38. teen violent death rate
39. dropout rate
40. rate of work-related injuries
41. number of occupational skin disorders
42. alcohol-related death rate
43. homicide rate
44. assault rate
45. number of child abuse investigations
46. elder abuse rate
47. sexual assault rate
48. domestic violence rate
49. diabetes diagnosis rate
50. injury death rate

NOTES:

Source: Mark Scovill, "Using Data in the Community Health Assessment Process," *Inside Preventive Care*, Vol. 1, No. 12, Aspen Publishers, Inc., © March 1996.

Examples: Mapping a Community's Health Needs

The following map shows the percentage of a county's population between 100% and 185% of the federal poverty level and the estimated number of births that would have qualified for a prenatal care assistance program using federal criteria.

Erie County

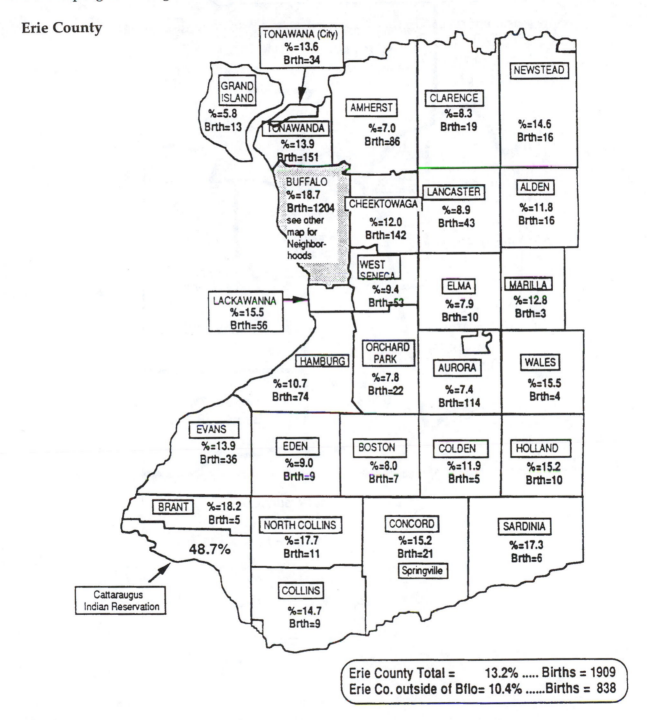

TONAWANA (City)
%=13.6
Brth=34

GRAND ISLAND
%=5.8
Brth=13

NEWSTEAD
%=14.6
Brth=16

AMHERST
%=7.0
Brth=86

CLARENCE
%=8.3
Brth=19

TONAWANDA
%=13.9
Brth=151

BUFFALO
%=18.7
Brth=1204
see other map for Neighborhoods

CHEEKTOWAGA
%=12.0
Brth=142

LANCASTER
%=8.9
Brth=43

ALDEN
%=11.8
Brth=16

WEST SENECA
%=9.4
Brth=53

ELMA
%=7.9
Brth=10

MARILLA
%=12.8
Brth=3

LACKAWANNA
%=15.5
Brth=56

ORCHARD PARK
%=7.8
Brth=22

AURORA
%=7.4
Brth=114

WALES
%=15.5
Brth=4

HAMBURG
%=10.7
Brth=74

EVANS
%=13.9
Brth=36

EDEN
%=9.0
Brth=9

BOSTON
%=8.0
Brth=7

COLDEN
%=11.9
Brth=5

HOLLAND
%=15.2
Brth=10

BRANT %=18.2
Brth=5

48.7%

NORTH COLLINS
%=17.7
Brth=11

CONCORD
%=15.2
Brth=21
Springville

SARDINIA
%=17.3
Brth=6

Cattaraugus Indian Reservation

COLLINS
%=14.7
Brth=9

Erie County Total =   13.2% ..... Births = 1909
Erie Co. outside of Bflo= 10.4% ......Births = 838

continues

Examples: Mapping a Community's Health Needs continued

Buffalo

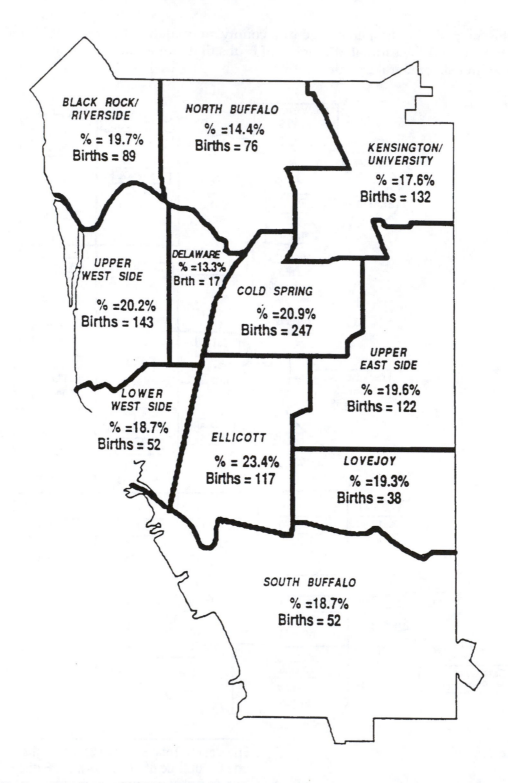

BLACK ROCK/
RIVERSIDE

% = 19.7%
Births = 89

NORTH BUFFALO

% =14.4%
Births = 76

KENSINGTON/
UNIVERSITY

% =17.6%
Births = 132

UPPER
WEST SIDE

% =20.2%
Births = 143

DELAWARE
% =13.3%
Brth = 17

COLD SPRING

% =20.9%
Births = 247

UPPER
EAST SIDE

% =19.6%
Births = 122

LOWER
WEST SIDE

% =18.7%
Births = 52

ELLICOTT

% = 23.4%
Births = 117

LOVEJOY

% =19.3%
Births = 38

SOUTH BUFFALO

% =18.7%
Births = 52

Source: Buffalo Prenatal-Perinatal Task Force, New York State Department of Health, 1990 Census.

Health Problems Analysis Sample

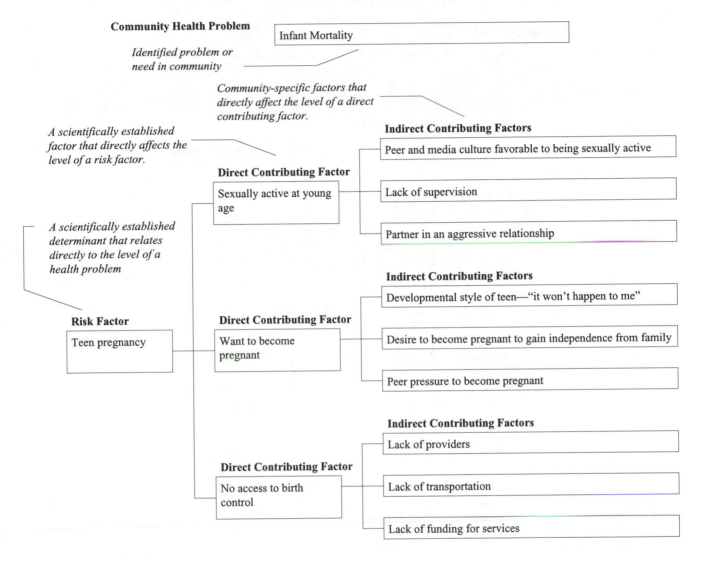

Community Health Problem

Identified problem or need in community

Infant Mortality

Community-specific factors that directly affect the level of a direct contributing factor.

Indirect Contributing Factors

A scientifically established factor that directly affects the level of a risk factor.

Direct Contributing Factor

Sexually active at young age

Peer and media culture favorable to being sexually active

Lack of supervision

Partner in an aggressive relationship

Indirect Contributing Factors

A scientifically established determinant that relates directly to the level of a health problem

Developmental style of teen—"it won't happen to me"

Risk Factor

Teen pregnancy

Direct Contributing Factor

Want to become pregnant

Desire to become pregnant to gain independence from family

Peer pressure to become pregnant

Indirect Contributing Factors

Lack of providers

Direct Contributing Factor

No access to birth control

Lack of transportation

Lack of funding for services

Source: Adapted from the National Association of County and City Health Officials, 1991, C.A. Monahan et al. *Focus on Children Community Planning Manual: Needs Assessment and Health Planning for Children, Including Children with Special Health Care Needs*, Maternal and Child Health Bureau, Health Resources and Services Administration, Public Health Service, U.S. Department of Health and Human Services, 1996.

Health Problems Analysis Worksheet

Community Health Problem

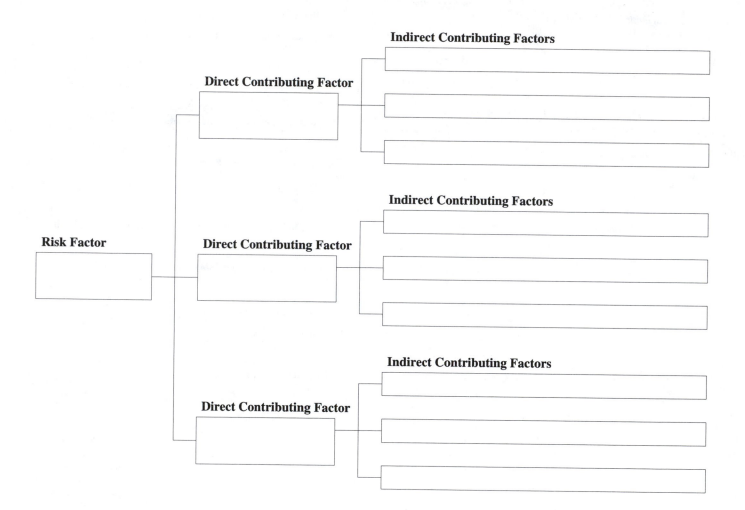

Source: Adapted from the National Association of County and City Health Officials, 1991, C.A. Monahan et al. *Focus on Children Community Planning Manual: Needs Assessment and Health Planning for Children, Including Children with Special Health Care Needs,* Maternal and Child Health Bureau, Health Resources and Services Administration, Public Health Service, U.S. Department of Health and Human Services, 1996.

Community Health Plan Sample

DESCRIPTION OF NEED/PROBLEM

Community has high incidence of babies born with low birth weight. Indirect contributing factors include the following:

- lack of access to prenatal health care
- lack of education & awareness about hazards of smoking, alcohol & drug usage, & not gaining enough weight
- prevalence of billboards advertising alcohol throughout community

DESIRED OBJECTIVES OR OUTCOME(S)

1. Educate teens about the health consequences of poor prenatal care.
2. Work with community groups to remove excessive alcohol advertising billboards.

SPECIFIC OBJECTIVES	ACTION STEPS	PERSON(S) RESPONSIBLE	TIMELINE		RESOURCES NEEDED	ACTION STEP BENCHMARKS
			Start	End		
By June 30, 1997, educate 36 pregnant teens about prenatal health hazards.	Develop workshops on prenatal hazards.	Health Department staff	Jan. 1997	June 1997	40 hrs. from researcher & access to health dept. info	• Course outline or syllabus • Folder of facts from Health Dept. sources
	Produce flyers & posters about prenatal hazards.	Health Department PR intern			20 hrs. from writer/designer, desktop publishing, & printing costs	• Flyers readable, useful, and in adequate number? • Eye-catching posters available for schools?
	Hold 3 information workshops at local high schools, with each attracting at least 12 teenage girls.	Two teachers who are members of CPG			Workshop location, instructor, & school cooperation	• Pregnant teens identified and invited? • All who attend receive materials?
By December 1, 1997, remove 10 billboards advertising alcohol from the community.	Link with church coalition that has spoken out against billboards.	Linkage subgroup of CPG	Jan. 1997	June 1997	Personal access to church coalition	• Has member of church coalition joined CPG? • Do members of subgroup of CPG attend coalition meetings?
	Find and talk to owners of billboards.	Member of local chamber of commerce	Mar. 1997	May 1997	30 hrs. research & telephone access	• Has a formal linkage been formed? • Names of billboard owners identified? • Interviews or phone calls made?
	Assemble group to attend April town meeting to bring issue up with town council member.	Subgroup	Feb. 1997	April 1997	Telephone access, transportation, & copies of health data	• Requests presented? With what result? • How many attend town meeting? • Is billboard issue presented effectively? • Does town council member sign on?

Source: C.A. Monahan et al. *Focus on Children Community Planning Manual: Needs Assessment and Health Planning for Children, Including Children with Special Health Care Needs*, Maternal and Child Health Bureau, Health Resources and Services Administration, Public Health Service, U.S. Department of Health and Human Services, 1996.

Tips for Running Health Assessment Programs

- **Offer individualized counseling to participants.** Rather than generalize, look at the individual, the individual's risk factors, and discuss viable interventions for that particular individual. Set up an action plan and short-term goals.

- **Be aggressive about existing risk factors.** Even if somebody has only one risk factor, that one risk factor must be addressed. Your program should be able to work with that individual on lowering that risk factor.

- **Make referrals to educational classes to help people learn about their risk factors.** Once that education is provided, patients are more receptive to aggressive management to reduce the risk factor.

- **Offer a soft, introductory course for people who are new to exercise.** Ohio State University's Center for Wellness and Prevention, for example, provides orientation sessions where exercise physiologists talk about exercise equipment, different methods of exercising, and the benefits of various kinds of exercise.

- **To sell your organization's leaders on the value of an assessment program, point out how it will build the organization's image.** Such a program speaks highly of your organization, and indicates that you're concerned about the overall health and well-being of your community.

- **Point out to organizational leaders that an assessment program is a low-cost way to bring new referrals into your system.** One-on-one contact, rather than direct mail or newspaper ads, will put new referrals into your system.

- **Contact third-party payers,** such as HMOs and managed care organizations. Some may pay for assessments at companies they insure. Once the assessment is done, work with the managed care payer to implement programs.

- **Make sure your program is comprehensive.** Make it an integrated program, and make sure you offer counseling, a vital part of the equation.

- **Be very competitive on pricing.** Your organization needs to also look at how the program generates indirect revenue, such as new patient referrals, rather than direct revenue.

- **Educate medical staff and other employees about the program,** what it means for the organization, and how it will benefit the community.

- **If you are using volunteers, take good care of them.** Ask the volunteer director in your organization to build a core of people who are willing to work at screening events. Send everyone a thank you note for volunteering.

NOTES:

Source: Steve Larose, ed., "Tips for Running Health Assessment Programs," *Inside Preventive Care*, Vol. 3, No. 1, Aspen Publishers, Inc., © April 1997.

Identifying Priority Problems Worksheet

Based on the analysis of the behavioral data, community mortality data, community opinion data, and other pertinent information, _____ (community) has identified the following community priority problems:

Rank	Problems
#1	
#2	
#3	
#4	
#5	

NOTES:

Source: *PATCH: Planned Approach to Community Health*, Centers for Disease Control and Prevention, National Center for Chronic Disease Prevention and Health Promotion, Division of Chronic Disease Control and Community Intervention, Atlanta, Georgia 30333, revised January 1995.

Worksheet for Understanding the Health Issue of Concern

What is the health issue of concern? _____

_____

Who has a need for change? _____

_____

_____

What is the effect of the health issue on the community? _____

_____

_____

_____

What causes the health issue of concern?

1. *Individual factors*

    Awareness and knowledge: _____

    _____

    _____

    Attitudes and beliefs: _____

    _____

    _____

    Skills and behavior: _____

    _____

    _____

2. *Factors outside the individual's control*

    Community factors: _____

    _____

    _____

    Regulations: _____

    _____

Source: *Restoring Balance,* Health Promotion Resource Center, Stanford Center for Research in Disease Prevention (and the Indian Health Service), Stanford University, 1000 Welch Road, Palo Alto, California 94304-1885. Phone: (415) 723-0003. Fax: (415) 725-6906, © 1992.

ASSESSING DRUG ABUSE WITHIN AND ACROSS COMMUNITIES*

Data about drugs used prior to entering treatment are generally collected from clients entering treatment programs. If information about the names and locations of drug abuse treatment programs is not currently available to network members, this information can be obtained from the State Alcohol and Drug Abuse Agency. A listing of treatment programs also is likely to be found in the Yellow Pages of local telephone directories and from directories obtainable from mayors' offices or chambers of commerce. Most publicly funded programs are required to collect and report admission data to the states, and the states report it to the federal government. Each state will have its own name for its client data system.

These data have limitations. Drug abusers entering treatment are not representative of drug abusers in the community. They represent individuals referred to drug treatment by criminal justice agencies because they were arrested or incarcerated, they are clients referred from other sources (e.g., family, church, school), or they can be self-referred clients. Usually they have been using drugs for a number of years prior to entering treatment, and their admission to treatment will not be a sign of the emergence of a new drug or new epidemic, but a sign that the client who began using drugs 10 or 15 years ago is now sufficiently impaired to the point of wanting and needing treatment.

Also, individual drug abuse treatment agencies may be structured to treat particular types of drug abusers, although client populations may change over time. In recent years, changes in insurance coverage and managed care have had an impact on these programs and the types of clients served. In addition, information is often reported only by publicly funded programs, and the types of clients who can afford private treatment will not be represented in the information submitted to the state agency. Try to obtain information from the private programs to supplement the information from the public programs.

In contacting drug abuse treatment programs to determine if client data are available, several things should be kept in mind.

- Information that would potentially make it possible to identify an individual client cannot be divulged under penalty of federal law, so programs cannot provide the information that might be desired except at aggregate or summary levels.
- Treatment programs are in the business of treating clients; not surprisingly, staff see treatment as their primary obligation. Often these staff do not see the potential benefits of research and are likely to feel that any attempt to obtain client data is another demand on their limited time.
- The task of treating drug abusers is very difficult and requires a considerable investment of time and resources.
- The HIV/AIDS epidemic has added considerable pressure on staff and programs, especially those programs that serve clients at high risk for this disease (e.g., injection drug users).
- Most treatment programs have limited resources and an ongoing need to identify and secure additional financial resources.
- The current emphasis on managed care has placed considerable pressure on treatment programs to reduce the length of services provided and reduce costs.

*Source: National Institute on Drug Abuse, National Institutes of Health, U.S. Department of Health and Human Services, 1996.

Standard Data Request Form for Assessing Drug Abuse within and across Communities

CHARACTERISTICS OF CLIENTS ADMITTED TO TREATMENT

From _____ to _____ , _____ (months/year)

Total number of treatment admissions, excluding alcohol only: _____

	Alcohol-in-combination (exclude alcohol only)	Cocaine	Heroin	Marijuana	Stimulant/ Methamphetamine
Total No: (Use to derive percentages)					
Gender:					
Male	%	%	%	%	%
Female	%	%	%	%	%
Race/Ethnicity:					
White	%	%	%	%	%
African American	%	%	%	%	%
Hispanic	%	%	%	%	%
Other 1. _____	%	%	%	%	%
Other 2. _____	%	%	%	%	%
Age at Admission:					
17 and under	%	%	%	%	%
18 to 25	%	%	%	%	%
26 to 34	%	%	%	%	%
35 and older	%	%	%	%	%
Route of Administration:					
Smoking	%	%	%	%	%
Sniffing	%	%	%	%	%
Intravenous	%	%	%	%	%
Other/multiple	%	%	%	%	%
Secondary Drug:					
Type of Drug	%	%	%	%	%
Tertiary Drug:					
Type of Drug	%	%	%	%	%

Source: National Institute on Drug Abuse, National Institutes of Health, U.S. Department of Health and Human Services, 1996.

Sample Worksheet for Identifying Who Needs AIDS Education in Your Community*

(1) Population Group	(2) Possible Preventive Actions	(3) Existing Programs in Your Community	(4) Needed Resources
Health professionals	Counseling patients on risk reduction; referring for needed services; providing school-based AIDS education		
Teachers	Providing school-based AIDS education		
Adolescents	Delaying onset of sexual intercourse; using condoms; staying off drugs		
Community leaders	Initiating prevention programs; allocating resources		
Parents	Educating children about AIDS		
IV drug users	Entering drug treatment programs; practicing safer sex; cleaning needles		
Men who have sex with other men	Practicing safer sex		
Elected officials	Passing legislation that encourages prevention; funding prevention programs		

*This is a process for surveying education needs; it is not a definitive list of all groups in need of education. Complete column 3 by contacting existing groups. In column 4, list estimated resources needed to develop preventive actions (column 2) that are *not* being addressed by existing programs (column 3).

Source: Nicholas Freudenberg, *Preventing AIDS: A Guide to Effective Education for the Prevention of HIV Infection*, American Public Health Association, Washington, D.C., © 1989.

FOCUS GROUPS: AN OVERVIEW*

Focus group interviews or discussions are a versatile, qualitative research technique that is useful in obtaining data about feelings and opinions of small groups of participants about a given problem, experience, service, or other phenomenon that is then transferred to a larger universe. They have been primarily used in the business world for market research to help businesses know their consumers, but are increasingly being used by health care researchers to advance education and learn about health.

Focus groups are relatively easy to use for learning about a consumer's ideas and opinions. They overcome some of the problems of surveys by gathering people together, allowing for an easy exchange of information. A wide range of information can be obtained using just a few individuals (three to four) or, more ideally, a larger number (10 to 12).

Focus Group Planning

To ensure success in convening a focus group, several items need to be considered. These are outlined below.

Purpose

The reason for convening the group should be well articulated.

Size and Composition of Groups

Groups can be any size. Ten to 12 participants is ideal. More need to be invited to compensate for no-shows. In addition, the type of person to be invited needs to be identified. Should the group consist of a cross section of the entire community or representatives from specific socioeconomic or cultural groups? The focus group must be homogeneous to ensure effectiveness.

Setting

The setting needs to be nonthreatening, comfortable, and accessible to people with disabilities. Off-site settings may be more nonthreatening, but focus groups can be held on-site for convenience and lower cost. It is also valuable to provide some type of food as an incentive for people to participate.

Time

Sessions should be held at times convenient for participants. The maximum time allotted should be about two hours, which allows time for the participants to eat and socialize in addition to the actual discussion.

Invitations

How the consumers are invited influences their willingness to participate. One successful method is for nurses to invite participants and then have the agency follow up with a telephone call or confirmation letter.

---

*Source: Adapted from Donna Ambler Peters, "Improving Quality Requires Consumer Input: Using Focus Groups," *Journal of Nursing Care Quality,* Vol. 7:2, Aspen Publishers, Inc., © 1993.

Transportation

Providing transportation is probably necessary for at least some of the participants, especially for those with limited mobility (such as those who use wheelchairs) or low income. Possible methods include the nurse bringing the client in, reimbursing for use of public transportation, and hiring taxi cabs.

Group Leader

The group leader should be a neutral, yet respected figure, be familiar with the health issue being explored, and be skilled in group process. The leader should also be familiar with the culture of the focus group participants.

The role of the group leader is extremely important. It is the responsibility of this person to create the nonthreatening, positive, supportive climate that will encourage participants to contribute openly and honestly. The leader clearly articulates the purpose of the meeting, covers predetermined topics and questions, and facilitates the group interaction. This facilitation can take the form of encouraging participation, injecting probing comments, presenting questions in an unbiased way, asking transitional questions, determining how group members feel about ideas or feelings expressed by others, and summarizing.

Recording

To get the most information from these gatherings, documentation of the proceedings should be retained. This can be done by having a nonparticipant be a recorder or by using a mechanical tape recorder at the session. If a tape recorder is used, it is a good idea to tell participants that the session is being recorded and ask them to sign consent forms.

Budget

Focus groups can be held at a reasonable cost. Costs might include the facilitator, food, transportation for participants, and room rental if the focus group is held off-site.

Focus Group Benefits

Focus groups are a useful method for learning consumers' attitudes and feelings about quality, but they can also bring other benefits to both the consumer and the institution. For example, at one site it was discovered, when calling discharged consumers who were being considered as potential participants, that there was a group of patients that needed care again. These consumers were reregistered for service, and agency administration began planning for more routine follow-up on this type of client. Other focus group benefits include the following:

- Teaching and learning take place at many levels.
- They are a marketing tool. The group participants become more informed about health care and the agencies providing that care. In addition, agency strengths that are identified in the groups can be used in marketing to others in the community.
- They are a social experience. People have a reason to get out and be with other people with similar experiences in an enjoyable, informal setting.
- They can serve as a support group session for some persons.

GUIDELINES TO KEY ASPECTS OF FOCUS GROUP METHODOLOGY*

Traditional focus group sessions are 1- to 2-hour structured discussions among 6 to 10 participants. They are led by a trained moderator working from a list of topic areas and questions (referred to as a moderator's guide or topic guide). People chosen to participate in the group meet certain criteria designed to ensure that they have the requisite target audience characteristics.

Focus group sessions are usually most productive when they are composed of homogenous groups. Participants are often divided into different groups based on demographic characteristics such as gender, age, and socioeconomic status. The reasons for such divisions are twofold: (1) people are more likely to speak openly in front of other people whom they perceive to be like themselves, and (2) any real or perceived hierarchy among group members will impact group dynamics. For example, if nurses and physicians are combined in one group, it is unlikely that much useful information will be obtained from the nurses. Many will defer to the physicians because physicians are viewed as more expert. If the nurses do participate, they will likely provide socially acceptable responses, describing what they are supposed to do as nurses. If they do something differently, they are unlikely to talk about it in front of physicians and so many valuable insights may be lost.

Most researchers think carefully about topic matter before combining men and women in a group consisting of patients or members of the public, in part because there are many health topics that each gender will discuss more openly if members of the other gender are not present. Similarly, consumers with divergent socioeconomic status typically are not combined in one group. People with higher education often are more articulate than their counterparts with lower education, causing those with lower education to shut down. Additionally, people tend to use language differently when they are among members of their own group, whatever group that happens to be, in part as a way of signaling group identity. This phenomenon is perhaps most pronounced with teenagers but occurs with other groups as well. If one goal of conducting the groups is to learn how to talk to them or how to reference particular behaviors or products, mixing group members may thwart that goal because people may not use their normal word choices or speech patterns.

In addition to natural differences in conversational style, some demographic characteristics, particularly age and socioeconomic status, often lead to lifestyle differences. Depending on the subject matter, these differences may not only make it difficult for participants to relate to each other, but may in turn lead to differences in behavioral determinants and perceived benefits of and barriers to particular behaviors. For example, consider behaviors such as changing food preparation methods or increasing physical activity. In general, retirees can fit such changes into their schedules much more easily than middle-aged people with full-time jobs and children. But retirees may have many health-related barriers to such changes that most younger people do not have. Differences in socioeconomic status can have a similar effect; among low-income people, product price (for example, for particular foods) is often the number one barrier, but among high-income people, price is much less of an issue.

---

*Source: Michael Siegel and Lynne Doner, *Marketing Public Health: Strategies To Promote Social Change*, Aspen Publishers, Inc., © 1998.

In general, discussion is more honest if participants do not know each other. However, in some instances it is nearly impossible to convene a group in which no one knows anyone else. This problem often occurs when groups of professionals are assembled, particularly in smaller geographic areas. For example, health care professionals are likely to know each other or to have worked at the same places. Principals and teachers often know each other as do business or community leaders.

Designing the Study

Step 1: Determine what you need to know and set research objectives. For example, determine what decisions will be made as a result of the study and outline the research report as a way of coming to agreement on what information the study will provide. This process also helps identify any areas of miscommunication between researchers and program managers and keeps research costs down by separating nice-to-know areas of inquiry from need-to-know questions.

There are two other important things to keep in mind during this process. First, there is a 2-hour window, at most, in which to discuss all of the topics. That may sound like a long time, but consider this: if the group has 10 participants, each of them has 10 to 11 minutes to talk (the moderator will spend a certain amount of time asking questions). Granted, every person will not respond to every question, but if you were doing an in-depth interview instead of a focus group, how many topics would you expect to cover in 10 to 15 minutes?

Second, remember that these are called *focus* groups for a reason. Make sure that the discussion is, in fact, focused, and not a 2-hour omnibus study. If there are many topics to cover, prioritize them or break them into separate studies.

Step 2: Prepare proposed study design. The study design should spell out the research objectives, the total number of groups that will be conducted, the cities in which they will be conducted (and why they were selected), and the composition of each group or set of groups (recruiting specifications). It should also present a rough timeline and budget.

It is best to conduct groups in multiples of two. For example, if the audience of interest is black men aged 25 to 34 who have a family history of high blood pressure, the study should include at least two groups with this audience in each location. Conducting two of each type of group helps to ensure that (1) comments from one anomalous group are not given more credence than they should be given and (2) if something disastrous happens (such as an uncontrollable participant or only three people show up for the group), there will be another group's input to use.

Consider conducting groups with doers (those who already engage in the desired behavior) and nondoers (the target audience). This approach can help you identify the determinants of doers' behavior and then find out to what extent these determinants and values can be tapped in the target audience.

Also consider the ideal size of the focus groups. In some situations, mini-groups or triads are preferable to full focus groups. For example, if the topic is such that much in-depth discussion will be required, sometimes mini-groups (four to five participants) are more productive. Mini-groups can also be useful for projects at the other end of the spectrum; when there is a lot of ground to cover, and all participants would not have a chance to talk in a larger group. Triads can be a useful technique with children, many of whom are uncomfortable talking in a larger group of children they do not know.

Step 3: Prepare data collection instruments. The first task is to draft a recruitment screener based on the group composition criteria. The recruitment screener is a short questionnaire designed to determine whether people are eligible for the group and, if so, whether they are willing to participate. In addition to questions to ensure participants meet the criteria for inclusion, recruitment screeners usually contain two questions used to exclude participants who might be more expert than others in the group. One question asks about occupation and disqualifies anyone who works in advertising, marketing, or market research (because they know too much about focus groups) or any occupation that would make them "expert" compared with the other group members. For example, nutritionists are usually excluded from groups discussing dietary behaviors, and health care professionals are excluded from consumer groups discussing health behaviors, particularly treatment issues. The other question is whether they have participated in a focus group before, and if so, how long ago it was held, to avoid getting "professional" focus group attendees. The increasing popularity of the methodology has made it much more difficult to identify people who have never participated in a focus group.

The next task is to draft a topic guide. Some topic guides include questions developed for other studies, but often much of a new guide must be developed from scratch (see box "Suggestions for Developing the Topic Guide"). Remember that the guide is just that—a guide. People may agonize over every word in a topic guide, but the words that come out of the moderator's mouth may be quite different from those on the page.

Conducting the Group

Step 4: Arrange logistical details, including a moderator and a facility in which to convene the group. Traditionally, focus group guidebooks recommended contracting with a professional moderator (unless, of course, staff members have such skills). However, recent trends have been toward greater community participation in the focus group process. There are a number of reasons for this trend; two pragmatic ones are quality of data and cost. As Krueger and King (1998) note, there are many situations in which an outside researcher may be unlikely or unable to collect the in-depth inside information that a community member volunteer can collect. Additionally, volunteers can help conduct a study when resources are scarce. (Professional moderators in major metropolitan areas often charge $1,000 or more per group; specialized moderators, such as those who are an ethnic minority or who work with children, can command much higher rates.)

Krueger and King (1998) outline the following additional situations in which a volunteer moderator is appropriate or when the required research is not complex or does not demand highly technical skills; when the process of research is more important than its product (i.e., the study can encourage people to think in new ways about a situation); and when the program or situation to be studied is not highly political. When none of these conditions is true, Krueger and King recommend using professionals.

When deciding whether to use a professional or a volunteer, be aware that moderating a focus group is not as simple as running a meeting. The moderator must perform a delicate balancing act of being detached in the sense that he or she asks questions but does not offer opinions while being able to persuade group members to open up. Moderating focus groups also requires substantial background in group dynamics and skill at handling a range of personality types. Additionally, an outside moderator's distance from the program is often a plus. Someone on the program staff is vested in how the groups turn out, particularly when ideas are being tested, and may have difficulty remaining unbiased and may unintentionally lead the group in the "right" direction.

If a professional moderator is used, the best way to identify a good one is to ask colleagues for recommendations. When you have identified two or three candidates, ask them for tapes (all will have audiotapes; many have videotapes as well) to get a feel for how they run groups. Generally speaking, it is a good idea to match the gender and ethnicity of the moderator to the gender and ethnicity of the group. Most moderators will not have as much health knowledge as program staff, but it is best if they have moderated groups on health topics with similar audiences in the past. In particular, if you are conducting focus groups with children, it is important that you use a moderator who specializes in working with children.

Moderators can have varying amounts of responsibility; most can draft the recruitment screener and topic guide, conduct the groups, and prepare a report. However, many moderators' reports are analytically weak; ask for examples of their reports before contracting out this critical aspect of the project. Moderators usually charge per group and may charge separately for writing a guide and report.

The easiest (but usually most expensive) way to conduct focus groups is to contract with a commercial focus group facility. These facilities feature rooms of an appropriate size, built-in audiotaping capabilities (with microphones located unobtrusively on the ceiling), and viewing rooms separated from the focus group room by a one-way mirror. Using your recruitment screener, commercial facilities can recruit most groups of consumers and professionals, unless the participants are very difficult to find in the general population (for example, if you need people recently diagnosed with asthma or women who use the services of a breast cancer clinic). However, it is important to monitor the quality of a facility's recruiting. In addition to checking references, one way to do so is to readminister the screener to participants when they show up to ensure that they are qualified for the group.

When contracting with a vendor, the vendor will need the dates and times of the groups, the number of people to recruit for each, and whether videotaping is desired (audiotaping is automatically included). A general rule of thumb is to recruit two more participants per group than needed; that way, if a few people do not show up, the group will still be large enough. In addition to recruiting the participants, the facility staff will send confirmation letters with directions and make reminder calls a day or two before the group. Commercial facilities typically want to be paid for the incentives (payment to participants) before the groups take place; the balance is due after the groups meet (usually within 30 days). Incentive costs vary widely, depending on the locality and the type of participants; the facility can recommend an appropriate amount.

Groups can be convened at commercial facilities even if the recruiting is handled separately. Alternatively, if there are no facilities available (often true in smaller cities) or the program cannot afford commercial facilities, a focus group can be held in a hotel meeting room, a school classroom, or an office conference room. If you choose to conduct the groups yourself, you will need to handle the recruiting, confirmation letters, and follow-up calls; obtain a room and make sure it is set up properly (round or oblong tables are best); make sure participants have access to the room (if the group takes place after-hours in an office building, for example); make tent cards for all participants; handle audiotaping; and disburse the incentives.

Step 5: Conduct the focus groups. With a commercial facility and an outside moderator, all you need to do is show up and watch. You do not have to attend every group, but it is a good idea to attend at least one or two. Be forewarned that good moderators cover the topics on the guide, but they will not use the exact words and they may jump from section to section if participants make comments that make natural segues (and if the topic order is not critical). The first group is usually a pilot test; expect to make revisions to the guide afterward. Some sections may run long, some may need more probing, instructions to exercises may need revising, and some questions may just not work.

If the goal of videotaping is to be able to edit the groups into a brief highlights video, the audio quality will be mediocre at best and will not withstand being projected into a large room, unless participants were individually miked. Also, videotaping for wider use raises a number of ethical issues; participants are usually told that their comments are confidential. If there are plans to replay the videotapes to larger groups, participants should be informed of how the tapes will be used and asked to sign written release forms.

If the focus groups are conducted someplace other than at a commercial facility, no more than one person should observe the groups (unless a camera is set up and linked to a monitor in another room). The observer should sit at the table and take notes. He or she should be introduced to the participants, and his or her role should be explained. It is not acceptable to have multiple people sitting in the room watching; the effect on group dynamics is too adverse. If you are taping the groups, use the best tape recorders you can find, test them before each group, make sure the moderators know how to use them, and always carry extra batteries and tapes. It is safest to use two tape recorders per group, particularly if participants are seated at an oblong or oval table. Positioning the recorders near each end ensures that all voices, even those of soft-spoken participants, are captured.

Analyzing the Results

Steps 6 and 7: Analyze data and prepare report. Often it is best to prepare a top line (highlights) summary within a few days of the final group. The final report usually takes 4 to 6 weeks, in part because it cannot be completed until transcripts are ready. There are a number of approaches to analyzing focus group data. Some people present the results of each group separately; that is inappropriate for many projects since the point of analysis is to look for trends across groups or to identify and categorize a range of issues. The approach that may work best is to make summary statements and then support them with illustrative verbatim comments (hence the need for the transcripts; going back to the tapes is usually far more expensive). The type of person making each comment is identified (e.g., Baltimore primary care physician).

The report itself should contain an introduction describing the program and the objectives of the research study; a methodology section outlining the number of groups, their composition, and when they took place; a section detailing the findings of the research; and a section discussing conclusions and recommendations. The report may also contain an executive summary at the beginning.

REFERENCE

Krueger, R.A. & King, J.A. (1998). *Involving Community Members in Focus Groups.* Thousand Oaks, CA: Sage.

Suggestions for Developing the Topic Guide

- Open by thanking participants and explaining the process (i.e., there are no right or wrong answers, the goal is to get their opinions, the conversation is being taped). Provide a general description of the topic they will discuss and, if they may be anxious or suspicious, the reason why you convened this particular group.
- Begin by asking participants to introduce themselves; then ask one or two warm-up questions that get them talking and ease them into the subject matter.
- Ask open-ended questions. The goal is to stimulate conversation, not tally responses. The transition from writing structured quantitative questionnaires to relatively free-flowing qualitative topic guides is a very difficult one for more researchers to make.
- Build in exercises. They keep the group from getting bored and are a useful way of obtaining and capturing different kinds of information.
  1. Laddering exercises can be used to get at core values. Participants are first asked to name the positive attributes they associate with a behavior. The moderator records each attribute on a flip chart and, as each one is named, asks why that is important. The moderator continues asking why each subsequent attribute is important until the participant can no longer answer. For example:
     – What are the advantages of going for a 20-minute walk each day? It makes me feel good.
     – And why does it make you feel good? Because I have more energy the rest of the day, and I know I'm doing something good for my health.
     – And why is it important to have more energy? Because I can get more work done and feel more in control.
     – And what's good about doing something good for your health? Well . . . I want to be around for my kids . . . and I feel like I should . . . and I never have any time. There's so many things I don't do, so it makes me feel good when I accomplish talking the walk.
     Now we have learned that the walk makes the person feel more in control, is motivated in part by a need to meet family obligations, and increases self-esteem by making the person feel good.
  2. Free association is another technique to identify the attributes people attach to particular products or behaviors: "I'm going to say a word (or phrase) and I want you to tell me what comes to mind. The word is . . . ."
  3. Participants can sort message concepts (provided on separate sheets of paper) from most compelling to least compelling (and then explain their rankings to you).
  4. Pictures can be used as stimuli in many different ways. For example, you can show participants a picture of someone engaging in the desired action and ask them to describe that person (another way of getting at values). You can also ask them to describe how they are different from and similar to the person pictured.
  Pictures of food can be extremely useful for exploring dietary knowledge. For example, show participants a variety of foods and ask them to group them into food groups, or ask them which ones are higher or lower in fat or fiber.
- Ask participants to recount a recent experience involving the behavior. Have them walk you through what happened and their perceptions of various aspects of the experience. For example, if you are trying to improve a health clinic, you might ask: Think about your last visit to the clinic. How did you make your appointment? (Probe for staff promptness and timeliness.) Was the appointment time that you wanted available? What happened when you arrived for your appointment? How were you treated by the front desk staff? What was the waiting room like? (Probes: What was good and bad about it?) How long did you have to wait to be seen? Was the wait longer or shorter than you expected? How was your experience with the nurse? Now tell me about the exam room. What was good and bad about it?
- Close the group by asking whether people have any additional comments about any of the topics discussed and then thank them for their participation.

Source: Michael Siegel and Lynne Doner, *Marketing Public Health: Strategies To Promote Social Change*, Aspen Publishers, Inc., © 1998.

Sample Focus Group Moderator's Guide: Aging and Alzheimer's Disease

WARM-UP AND EXPLANATION

Introduction

1. Thanks for coming.
2. Your presence is important.
3. Describe what a focus group is—like an opinion survey, but very general, broad questions.

Purpose

1. We will be discussing some issues related to health.
2. I'm interested in all of your ideas, comments, and suggestions.
3. There are no right or wrong answers.
4. *All* comments—both positive and negative—are welcome.
5. Please feel free to disagree with one another. We would like to have many points of view.

Procedure

1. Explain use of tape recorder (one-way mirror). All comments are confidential—used for research purposes only.
2. I want this to be a group discussion, so you needn't wait for me to call on you. Please speak one at a time so that the tape recorder can pick up everything.
3. We have a lot of ground to cover, so I may change the subject or move ahead. Please stop me if you want to add something.

Self-Introductions

1. Ask participants to introduce themselves. Tell the group your name and where you live.

FOCUS GROUP QUESTIONS

General Attitudes: Health and Aging

1. Is your health something that you actively think about? (If not, why not?)
2. When you think of health, what do you think about?

3. What about the health of your family? What issues or topics do you think about?
4. (45–54 and over 55 groups) Do you think about growing older, and the changes that might bring? What do you think about? (Probe re: health changes, independence, changes in lifestyle.)
5. What do you think other people/your parents feel about growing older? (Probe re: health changes, independence, changes in lifestyle.)

Relationship to Older Family Members

1. Do you have parents, other older relatives, or friends who are close to you?
2. What is your relationship with these older relatives/friends? (How much contact? Do you feel close to them? Responsible?)
3. Do you think about their health and well-being? What, specifically, do you think about? (Probe re: health concerns, independence, living situations.)

Knowledge of Alzheimer's Disease

(If Alzheimer's disease hasn't come up in the conversation)

1. Have you ever heard of Alzheimer's disease? What have you heard?
2. What do you think it is? Is it different from just getting old? (Probe for: age of onset, how many people it affects, cause(s), symptoms, prevention, how it is diagnosed, how it is treated, how quickly it progresses, is it contagious, what happens, new research they have heard about, what kind of care is required—at home, nursing homes, related costs.)
3. Is it (senility or Alzheimer's) an inevitable consequence of aging?
4. Where have you heard about Alzheimer's disease? (Probe for source.)
5. Do you have questions? What would you like to know about it? What else?

continues

Sample Focus Group Moderator's Guide continued

6. Do you ever have any thoughts or concerns about Alzheimer's disease? For yourself or for someone else? (Who?)
7. What kind of concerns?

Sources of Information (General)

1. If you wanted to find out more about Alzheimer's disease (had questions or concerns), how would you go about it? (Probe for: additional sources, e.g., family physician, friends, workplace source, where else in own community, library, or national agencies.)
2. Do you know of any agencies or organizations that deal especially with older people or Alzheimer's disease?

Facing Alzheimer's Disease

1. Now I want you to think about a particular situation where you are concerned about a friend or relative. You think they might have Alzheimer's disease. What would you do? (Probe: how would you interact with that individual, e.g., a parent; where would you turn for help [call, write, go]?)
2. In particular, what would you need to know to deal with the situation? Issues to probe for:
   • more information about what it is
   • diagnosis
   • consequences—what happens
   • treatment
   • physician referral or how to find one
   • research they've heard about
   • services—where to go, what kinds of services exist
   • financial burden

Sources of Information and Assistance When Facing Alzheimer's Disease

1. Would you be more likely to seek help in your own community or to contact a national organization?
2. What if your relative lived in another town? What would you do then?
3. Have you ever heard of the National Institute on Aging?

4. How have you heard of them/What have you heard? (If not: it is a part of the National Institutes of Health in Bethesda, Maryland, which is the federal agency responsible for medical research.)
5. Would you be likely to call or write to the National Institute on Aging? (Why or why not?)
6. Have you ever heard of the Alzheimer's Disease and Related Disorders Association (ADRDA)? (If not mentioned previously.) (If not, explain ADRDA and its chapters.)
7. How have you heard of it/What have you heard?
8. If you had questions, would you be more likely to contact a national organization or a local organization?
9. Would you prefer to be able to talk with someone (e.g., a hotline) or would you want written information? Or would you prefer to speak with someone in person? Why?

Attitudes toward Proposed Center

1. The National Institute on Aging is planning to establish a National Alzheimer's Disease Center. The Center will be a national source of information about Alzheimer's disease, including information about diagnosis, treatment, consequences, new research, and services available for its victims and their families. What do you think about this idea (the new center)? Do you think that it is a good idea or not? Why?
2. What kind of information would be most valuable for you, if you had to cope with someone who had Alzheimer's disease (diagnostic, treatment, medical referral, social services referral, support groups, respite care)? (Probe for meaning of respite care.)
3. What advice would you have for the Institute as they plan for this new center?

CLOSING

1. I will make sure that they know about your opinions.
2. Thank you very much for your contributions.

Source: *Making Health Communication Programs Work: A Planner's Guide*, NIH Publication #92-1493, U.S. Department of Health and Human Services, Public Health Service, National Institutes of Health, Office of Cancer Communications, National Cancer Institute, April 1992.

Sample Abbreviated Moderator's Guide for Focus Group with Children

1. **Introduction and Warm Up**
   - Introduce yourself and assistant or comoderator.
   - Ask the children their first names, what grade they are in, who their teacher is, and if they have siblings and their ages.

2. **Explanation of Purpose and Ground Rules**
   - Explain that you are here to learn what kinds of projects, games, and other school-type activities children like and do not like, and to learn what they know about drugs.
   - Explain your ground rules: only one person speaks at a time, raise your hand, no side conversations, encourage everyone to participate, say what you think or feel.
   - Explain that you are audiotaping the group to make sure you don't miss anything that is said and that it will not be shared with parents or teachers.

3. **General Questions of the Group**
   - What kinds of games/activities do you like to play at school? (not sports) (The moderator should probe to find out what kinds of learning activities the children like best, e.g., word games, puzzles, stories, coloring, videotapes, field trips.)

4. **Messages (Role Play and Group Discussion)**
   The following questions and in-depth probes might be included as appropriate for the age groups.

   Role Play:
   - How do you say no to someone who asks you to do something you don't want to do? For example, if _____ (a child from the group) is over at your house and suggests you throw a ball around inside, act out what you would say.

   Discussion:
   - What are some ways to stay healthy?
   - Does anyone know what a drug is? A medicine? Can you give an example?
   - Where have you heard the most about drugs? (family? school? other children? TV? neighborhood? nowhere?)
   - Why do you think some young people might begin to use beer, wine coolers, cigarettes, marijuana? (Name only drugs the children have already mentioned.)
   - What can happen when you use drugs?

5. **Materials Selection Activity**
   Set out materials in random order on a table away from the main group. Ask children, one at a time, to pick out the materials that they would like to read or play with. Make sure that none of the children can see what the others have selected. Record each child's selection on a tally form.

6. **Language Probe and Wrap Up**
   - If you wanted to tell other young people like you not to use drugs, what would you say?
   Summarize what you heard. Correct any misunderstandings the children may have mentioned. Give each child an opportunity to make one last statement about materials and messages he or she would like to see developed.

Source: Center for Substance Abuse, "Technical Assistance Bulletin: Conducting Focus Groups with Young Children Requires Special Considerations and Techniques," U.S. Department of Health and Human Services, Public Health Service, Substance Abuse and Mental Health Services Administration, Washington, D.C., September 1994. Materials contributed to CSAP by John Rosiak, Director of Substance Abuse Prevention, National Crime Prevention Council.

Tips for Working with Young Children

Using focus groups with young children can be challenging. However, when conducted correctly these groups provide valuable information for program planners. To get the most out of these groups, plan to do the following:

- Establish rapport by using a skilled moderator who is comfortable working with children.
- Draw out very shy children (even though you requested articulate, outgoing students) by seating them directly across from the facilitator for maximum eye contact.
- Control very talkative children who ramble on and on in an almost endless stream of imagination or who are so excited to have an adult listen intently that they try to dominate the group.
- Actively moderate the group by probing short answers and keeping the discussion flowing and on track. Groups with young children require a higher level of moderation.
- Cover more topics with children in a shorter time than with adults who have a longer attention span. Plan the moderator's guide accordingly, and intersperse discussion with activities. A stretch break also helps children.
- Engage the children in a variety of activities to confirm what they are verbally reporting.

- Pay special attention to language. Have a teacher who works with the grade level you are interviewing review your guide before you begin.
- Take special steps to ensure that children feel comfortable enough to speak freely. That means keeping interested observers out of the room and controlling the more dominant children. It also means using a space children will be comfortable in—for example, one with small tables and chairs, or a space to sit on the floor.
- Listen for "kid language" in the group that will give you vocabulary and logic for use in developing your final materials.
- Approach the analysis as objectively as possible. When analyzing the results, don't gloss over what the children said or didn't understand. Writing materials for children is like developing a new brochure for a different culture.
- Consider using comoderators with children's groups. This allows the moderators to monitor activities more closely, watch for nonverbal cues, and help keep the children's attention by switching speakers. If the children are from a particular racial or ethnic group, every effort should be made to see that at least one of the moderators is from that group.

NOTES:

Source: Center for Substance Abuse, "Technical Assistance Bulletin: Conducting Focus Groups with Young Children Requires Special Considerations and Techniques," U.S. Department of Health and Human Services, Public Health Service, Substance Abuse and Mental Health Services Administration, Washington, D.C., September 1994. Materials contributed to CSAP by John Rosiak, Director of Substance Abuse Prevention, National Crime Prevention Council.

COMMUNITY OPINION DATA*

Opinion information provides viewpoints from the community about health awareness, needs, and perceived health problems. A combination of quantitative and opinion data will help the community define problems and develop meaningful community goals and objectives. A comparison of quantitative information (mortality, morbidity, and behavioral data) with the opinion data will either substantiate or disprove the opinions of the community.

Knowing what the community or specific populations perceive to be their health needs is extremely important in planning programs to address those needs. Opinion information also reveals the community's level of awareness about health issues and its health problems and can help direct the design of press releases and educational information. It reflects community values and other qualitative factors not provided by the quantitative data. Also, the process of collecting opinion data provides an opportunity to inform more community members about the program and helps build community support for planning and carrying out health programs. It also helps identify sources of support and opposition within the community.

There are two types of surveys that can be done—one of community leaders and one of the community at large. Conducting a survey of the community at large can be a big task. For the survey to be representative, respondents should be randomly selected from the entire community. However, most community groups lack the time and resources to conduct this type of survey. Some communities collect communitywide data in malls, at health fairs, or by placing mail-in coupons in the newspaper. Although these data are not representative enough to weigh heavily in the decision-making process, they may be valuable by increasing the awareness of the community group and identifying issues that may need to be explored further when designing interventions later in the program process. They should be analyzed separately from the leader survey.

Identifying Opinion Leaders

Every community has "opinion leaders." They are people in positions of power who have the reputation for getting things done, who made key decisions on previous issues, who actively volunteer their time to help the community, or who are formal or informal neighborhood or community leaders. Whereas some opinion leaders are easy to identify because they hold official positions in the community, there are many other leaders who are not in positions of authority but are influential and knowledgeable about the community. Special efforts should be made to identify these unofficial informal leaders to obtain their opinions. The final list of interviewees should represent the sex, age, race, and affiliation groups that reflect the demographic makeup of the community. Many communities generate 100 to 150 names and complete 60 to 125 surveys.

*Source: *PATCH: Planned Approach to Community Health,* Centers for Disease Control and Prevention, National Center for Chronic Disease Prevention and Health Promotion, Division of Chronic Disease Control and Community Intervention, Atlanta, Georgia 30333, revised January 1995.

GUIDELINES FOR INDIVIDUAL IN-DEPTH INTERVIEWS*

In-Depth Interviews

With in-depth interviews, a trained interviewer talks with one research participant at a time. The interviews can take place over the telephone or in person. In-depth interviews are commonly used when a group setting is not feasible (for example, if appropriate participants are scattered across the country or state) or if it would have a chilling effect on discussion. For example, if the research participants are very young children, a one-on-one format is better suited to their attention span and tendency to become shy in groups of children they do not know.

The process of designing, conducting, and analyzing in-depth interview studies is similar to that used for focus groups. Minor differences are described below. For a detailed discussion of the approach to each step, please refer to the focus group section of this chapter.

Designing the Study

Step 1: Determine what you need to know and set research objectives. The average in-depth telephone interview lasts about half an hour; some run 45 minutes. Interviews conducted in person can run longer (up to about an hour), except with young children, in which case they should be kept to the length of a telephone interview. If you cannot adequately address all of the objectives in that amount of time, cut some objectives. As with focus group studies, determining what decisions will be made based on the study can help refine objectives. The conversation should focus on one subject as much as possible; too much bouncing around distracts respondents.

Step 2: Prepare proposed study design. The study design should spell out the research objectives, the total number of interviews to be conducted, the types of people to be interviewed, and how to obtain the names and phone numbers. It should also present a rough timeline and budget.

It is good practice to conduct at least 8 to 10 interviews with each subgroup. As with focus groups, consider conducting some interviews with doers (those who already engage in the desired behavior) and nondoers (the target audience). This approach can help you identify the determinants of doers' behavior and then find out to what extent these determinants and values can be tapped in the target audience.

In some instances, it may be desirable to set up the interviews as dyads, in which the interviewer talks to two people at once. For example, dyads can be useful for discussing some behaviors involving couples.

Step 3: Prepare data collection instruments. Some in-depth interviewing projects require a recruitment screener (for example, if participants will be recruited from the general population and then come to a central site for interviews). Most telephone in-depth interviews do not require a screener because they are conducted with people known to qualify. Recruitment screeners are discussed in more detail in the focus group section of this chapter.

*Source: Michael Siegel and Lynne Doner, *Marketing Public Health: Strategies To Promote Social Change*, Aspen Publishers, Inc., © 1998.

All interviewing projects require a topic guide, usually one similar to that used for focus groups. Obviously, if the interviews will be conducted by phone, some of the exercises described in the focus group section cannot take place. In-depth interviewing guides are more likely than topic guides to be administered verbatim; when preparing them, read them out loud to make sure they are written in conversational language. Sentences are usually too long and language too abstract the first time through.

Conducting the Interviews

Step 4: Arrange logistics. Vendors may be involved with in-depth interview projects that take place in person. Focus group facilities can also recruit in-depth interview participants for you and usually have interviewing rooms. Interview rooms are smaller, to provide a more intimate setting for the interview, but still provide audiotaping and other amenities (e.g., television monitors if needed).

A professional, staff member, or volunteer with some training can conduct interviews. Many focus group moderators also conduct in-depth interviews; other qualitative researchers specialize in interviews. If you contract out for the interviewing, the interviewer will most likely prepare the report (unless you want to read a lot of transcripts or listen to hours and hours of tapes). Asking for sample reports will help ensure that you hire someone who does quality work.

Step 5: Conduct the interviews. As with focus groups, if the interviews are being conducted in person at a commercial facility by an outside interviewer, all you must do is show up and watch. After the first two or three interviews, take a look at the guide, and revise it as needed.

If you do the interviewing, you have the option of taping telephone interviews, taking notes, or a combination of both. Taping allows the conversation to flow more naturally (although it is a good idea to take some notes in case something happens with the tape recorder). If you tape interviews, make sure to inform each interviewee that you are going to tape the conversation. Informed consent is particularly important with telephone interviews to avoid violating federal wiretapping laws. If you take notes, it is helpful to write in pencil and go over them the minute you put the phone down. You often can expand on them considerably.

Analyzing the Results

Steps 6 and 7: Analyze data and prepare report. In-depth interview reports can be organized much like focus group reports are. As with focus groups, the approach is usually to make summary statements of findings and then support them with illustrative verbatim comments. If more than one type of person was interviewed, identify the type of person making the comment.

The report should contain an introduction describing the program and the objectives of the research study; a methodology section outlining the number of interviews, their composition, and when they took place; a section detailing the findings of the research; and a section discussing conclusions and recommendations. The report may also contain an executive summary at the beginning.

Communitywide Opinion Survey

1. Where do you usually go for health information?
   ___ Friends
   ___ Health department
   ___ Magazines or other publications
   ___ Pharmacist
   ___ Private physician or health professional
   ___ TV or radio
   ___ Other _____

2. From the list below, choose three areas that you believe should receive more emphasis in the community than they do now. Rank them 1, 2, and 3, where 3 is the least emphasis.

   ___ Alcohol misuse   ___ Mental illness
   ___ Cigarette smoking   ___ Physical inactivity
   ___ Cost of medical services   ___ Poverty
   ___ Drug abuse   ___ Teen pregnancy
   ___ Drunk driving   ___ Traffic injuries
   ___ Environment   ___ Unemployment
   ___ Health problems of older adults   ___ Unhealthy diet and weight control
   ___ Heart disease   ___ Violence
   ___ Injuries (other than traffic injuries) ___ Other _____

3. Where do you go for health services, that is, nonemergency services?
   ___ Health department   ___ Private physician
   ___ Health maintenance organization   ___ Walk-in clinic
   ___ Hospital emergency department   ___ Other _____

4. Which specific health services and health education programs or activities are most needed in our community?

5. How could the existing health services be improved?

Source: *PATCH: Planned Approach to Community Health,* Centers for Disease Control and Prevention, National Center for Chronic Disease Prevention and Health Promotion, Division of Chronic Disease Control and Community Intervention, Atlanta, Georgia 30333, revised January 1995.

Description of Respondent

Respondent's name: _____

Record the following information for each respondent, without input from the respondent, if possible. To ensure confidentiality, separate this page from the rest of the survey before returning both to the working group chairperson or local coordinator.

1. Sex: _____ Female _____ Male

2. Race: _____ White _____ Black _____ Hispanic
   _____ Native American _____ Asian _____ Other

3. Languages Spoken: _____
   _____

4. Age: _____ <18 _____ 18–24 _____ 25–44 _____ 45–64 _____ 65+

5. Affiliation that resulted in respondent being selected:
   ____ Business person
   ____ Citizen activist
   ____ City/county official
   ____ Civic association member
   ____ Community outreach worker
   ____ Health professional (specify) _____
   ____ Law enforcement officer
   ____ Leader of organization of faith
   ____ Local celebrity
   ____ Media/news person
   ____ Neighborhood formal/informal leader
   ____ School board member/administrator/teacher
   ____ Social services provider
   ____ Voluntary health agency representative
   ____ Youth peer leader
   ____ Other _____

6. Member of community: _____ <3 _____ 3–9 _____ 10+ years

7. Geographic area: _____ Urban _____ Rural
   Neighborhood: _____

Source: *PATCH: Planned Approach to Community Health*, Centers for Disease Control and Prevention, National Center for Chronic Disease Prevention and Health Promotion, Division of Chronic Disease Control and Community Intervention, Atlanta, Georgia 30333, revised January 1995.

Community Leader Opinion Survey

1. What do you think the main health problems are in our community?

2. What do you think are the causes of these health problems?

3. How can these problems be reduced or eliminated in our community?

4. Which one of these problems do you consider to be the most important one in our community?

5. Can you suggest three other people I might talk with about the health problems in our community?

Thank you for your help. Right now I do not have any more questions, but may I contact you in the future if other issues come up?

Source: *PATCH: Planned Approach to Community Health*, Centers for Disease Control and Prevention, National Center for Chronic Disease Prevention and Health Promotion, Division of Chronic Disease Control and Community Intervention, Atlanta, Georgia 30333, revised January 1995.

Which To Use—Focus Groups or Individual In-Depth Interviews?

Issue To Consider	*Use Focus Groups When*	*Use Individual In-Depth Interviews When*
Group interaction	Interaction of respondents may stimulate a richer response or new and valuable thoughts	Group interaction is likely to be limited or nonproductive
Group/peer pressure	Group/peer pressure will be valuable in challenging the thinking of respondents and illuminating conflicting opinions	Group/peer pressure would inhibit responses and cloud the meaning of results
Sensitivity of subject matter	Subject matter is not so sensitive that respondents will temper responses or withhold information	Subject matter is so sensitive that respondents will be unwilling to talk openly in a group
Depth of individual responses	The topic is such that most respondents can say all that they know in less than 10 minutes	The topic is such that a greater depth of response per individual is desirable, as with complex subject matter and very knowledgeable respondents
Interviewer fatigue	It is desirable to have one interviewer conduct the research; several groups will not create interviewer fatigue or boredom	It is desirable to have numerous interviewers on the project. One interviewer would become fatigued or bored conducting the interviews
Stimulus materials	The volume of stimulus material is not extensive	A large amount of stimulus material must be evaluated
Continuity of information	A single subject area is being examined in depth and strings of behaviors are less relevant	It is necessary to understand how attitudes and behaviors link together on an individual basis
Experimentation with interviewer guide	Enough is known to establish a meaningful topic guide	It may be necessary to develop the interview guide by altering it after each of the initial interviews
Observation	It is possible and desirable for key decision makers to observe first-hand consumer information	First-hand consumer information is not critical or observation is not logistically possible
Logistics	An acceptable number of target respondents can be assembled in one location	Respondents are geographically dispersed or are not easily assembled for other reasons
Cost and timing	Quick turnaround is critical and funds are limited	Quick turnaround is not critical and budget will permit higher cost

Source: Reprinted with permission from M. Debus, *Handbook for Excellence in Focus Group Research,* © 1988, The Academy for Educational Development.

INVOLVING THE COMMUNITY IN THE PROGRAM*

Who knows a community better than its members?

Health educators sometimes develop strategies and materials without involving members of the intended audience in the process. The most frequently cited reason is that involving the community takes too much time. Involving others in the decision-making process may be more time consuming, but a program's success depends on it. Including community members in all phases of planning helps ensure the program's acceptance, relevance, and effectiveness.

Community members can make valuable contributions in the development of all components of the health education program, not just in the adaptation and development of materials. Members of the intended audience can be involved in:

- conducting the needs assessment
- choosing appropriate strategies to reach the intended audience
- developing the health messages
- identifying appropriate delivery channels (e.g., face-to-face, group, organizational, community, and mass media)
- identifying appropriate information sources (credible persons to deliver the information)
- identifying appropriate materials to use
- adapting or developing materials
- evaluating the program

Who Should Be Involved?

Determining who to involve and how to involve them are important decisions that need to be made before the planning begins. One way to involve community members in the program is to convene a program advisory group made up of selected community members. This group can provide guidance on every aspect of the program. Advisory group members should be selected carefully. They should be knowledgeable about community lifestyles, attitudes, health status, and resources. The group should include individuals who are well respected in the community and are able to provide expertise in various areas (e.g., health educators, ministers, teachers, community organizers, and patients or clients who may be involved in the program).

There are many other opportunities for community members to be involved in a program besides serving on an advisory group. Educators should select individuals who will provide relevant input to the program and who represent the program's intended audience. Other criteria for representation include, but are not limited to:

---

*Source: AMC Cancer Research Center, *Beyond the Brochure: Alternative Approaches to Effective Health Communication,* U.S. Department of Health and Human Services, Public Health Service, Centers for Disease Control and Prevention (CDC), Atlanta, Georgia 30333, 1994.

- income level
- educational level
- age
- marital status
- culture/ethnicity
- gender
- health behaviors
- access to health care
- personal experience with program topic
- personal experience with intended audience

Involving the Community in Materials Adaptation and Development

Once the needs assessment has been conducted and the advisory group and members of the intended audience have assisted in program planning, it is time to decide whether or not to adopt or adapt existing materials or to develop new materials. Including community members in this phase of the program development will help to ensure that the materials not only are appropriate and relevant for but are used by the intended audience.

Materials Adaptation

After existing health education materials have been collected from both local and national resources, members of the advisory group and the intended audience should be involved in reviewing and pretesting the materials to decide if they are appropriate for use. Community members can be helpful in reviewing all aspects of health education materials, including the text, narrative, captions, visuals, and format.

Developing Original Materials

There are many roles for advisory group and other community members to play when developing original health education materials, from concept development through materials development and pretesting. After the materials have been developed, audience members should be involved in reviewing and pretesting the content of the material.

NOTES:

Guidelines for Establishing Community Partnerships

ORGANIZE

1. Think about potential new partners to enhance your existing efforts and broaden the scope of your supporting organizations.
2. Send a letter asking partners if they would be part of your health promotion efforts; include a fact sheet, a contact number, and any other persuasive material you have.
3. Confirm participation of partners through follow-up telephone calls.

COORDINATE

4. Send information packet to participating partners.
5. Ask partners to use their own press office to create a media advisory and press release regarding whatever press event they intend to do.
6. Ask partners to include health promotion information in their existing advertising.
7. Get public service announcements and artwork from Ad Council if partners are willing to use it.
8. Use event checklist and contact sheets to help organize.

PROMOTE

9. Work closely with participant's partners' press offices, if relevant.
10. If partners will be involved in a press event, distribute a media advisory for local media to learn about the event.
11. Distribute a press release regarding partner involvement.
12. Make follow-up calls to press to confirm information.

FOLLOW-UP

13. Send thank you letters to partners.
14. Ask new partners to establish long-term health promotion efforts.
15. Clip articles that appear in paper.

NOTES:

Source: *Seven Days of Immunizations: National Infant Immunization Week*, U.S. Department of Health and Human Services, Public Health Service, Centers for Disease Control and Prevention (CDC), Atlanta, Georgia 30333, 1995.

Potential Community Partners

The list of groups and organizations below was generated for an immunization outreach program. These potential partners are a sampling of organizations that can help raise awareness and educate target audiences. Look in your community for additional groups.

MEDICAL GROUPS/ORGANIZATIONS/ASSOCIATIONS

- American Academy of Pediatricians (AAP)
- American Medical Association (AMA)
- American Nurses Association (ANA)
- Medical societies
- Nurse practitioner associations
- Visiting nurse associations
- Retired nurse associations
- Emergency department technicians
- Midwives
- Private pediatric practices
- Health maintenance organizations (HMOs)
- Hospitals
- Maternity wards
- Walk-in clinics
- American College of Gynecologists
- Medical colleges
- Schools of public health
- Pharmacists

GOVERNMENT AGENCIES/PROGRAMS

- Aid to Families with Dependent Children (AFDC)
- Americorps
- Child welfare agency
- Department of Agriculture, Extension Service
- Department of Education
- Department of Motor Vehicles
- Head Start
- Housing authority
- Immigration offices
- Maternal child health programs
- Refugee centers
- National Guard
- Postal service

- Tribal councils
- Tribal governments
- Women, Infants, and Children (WIC)
- Elected officials

COMMUNITY ORGANIZATIONS

- Junior League
- Rotary International
- Red Cross
- Kiwanis
- Lions
- Elks
- Healthy Mothers/Healthy Babies
- Religious organizations
- Places of worship
- Salvation Army
- Drug and Alcohol Resistance Education Programs (DARE)
- Alcoholics Anonymous (AA)
- Narcotics Anonymous (NA)
- Al-Anon
- Tenant community organizations
- United Way
- YMCA, YWCA
- Big Brothers/Big Sisters
- March of Dimes
- Homeless organizations
- Food banks
- Neighborhood watch
- Little League
- Minority organizations

EDUCATION-RELATED ORGANIZATIONS/GROUPS

- American Federation of Teachers (AFT)
- National Education Association (NEA)
- Adult education programs
- Board of education
- General equivalency degree (GED) classes
- Home school programs
- Fraternities/sororities
- Alumni organizations
- Preschools

continues

Potential Community Partners continued

- Day-care centers
- Recreation facilities/programs
- Trade schools
- High schools with day-care facilities
- Literacy volunteers
- Retired teachers

ADVOCACY ORGANIZATIONS

- Council de la Raza
- Children's Defense Fund
- National Association for the Advancement of Colored People (NAACP)
- Urban League
- American Association of Retired Persons (AARP)

BUSINESS ORGANIZATIONS/RETAIL OUTLETS

- Airlines
- Banks
- Beauty and barber shops
- Chambers of commerce
- Computer companies/stores
- Diaper companies

- Dairies
- Grocery stores
- Delicatessens/specialty/ethnic food stores
- Health clubs
- Ice cream/yogurt stores
- Insurance companies
- Laundromats
- Shopping malls
- Bowling alleys
- Maternity stores
- Movie theaters
- Phone companies
- Photo services: Fotomat, JC Penney, Sears
- Yellow pages
- Public transportation companies
- Billboard companies
- Video rental stores
- Toy stores
- Children's clothing stores
- Second-hand stores
- Fast food restaurants
- Pharmaceutical companies
- Service Corps of Retired Executives
- Utility companies
- Local sports teams

NOTES:

Source: *Seven Days of Immunizations: National Infant Immunization Week*, U.S. Department of Health and Human Services, Public Health Service, Centers for Disease Control and Prevention (CDC), Atlanta, Georgia 30333, 1995.

Checklist for Establishing Contacts and Developing Relationships

1. Have you assessed your own organization's level of commitment to the community, in terms of the following?
   - ☐ Motivation
   - ☐ Resources

2. In your exploration of the community, have you learned about the following?
   - ☐ Its physical layout
   - ☐ The routines and activities of the population, at different times of the day and week
   - ☐ The major institutions and businesses
   - ☐ The major gathering places

3. Have you developed the following?
   - ☐ A community profile
   - ☐ A community resource directory

4. Have you identified the following community contacts?
   - ☐ Political figures and government officials
   - ☐ Community and health service workers
   - ☐ Other professional and business leaders
   - ☐ Informal community leaders

5. Have you considered which method you will use to obtain the information you want? Check as many of the following as are appropriate.
   - ☐ Participant observation
   - ☐ Informal conversation
   - ☐ Interview
   - ☐ Case study/in-depth interview
   - ☐ Focus groups/survey

6. Have you sought out key individuals with whom you will work closely? If so, have you considered:
   - ☐ Their type of motivation
   - ☐ Their social and political status within the community
   - ☐ Their potential contribution

7. Are you prepared to approach all your community contacts in a way that can help you win their trust?
   - ☐ Yes
   - ☐ No

8. Can you give back to the community as much as (or more than) you take, in the following ways?
   - ☐ By keeping your contacts informed of progress
   - ☐ By offering to help people in their own community work
   - ☐ By giving recognition to those who help you

Source: Virginia M. Gonzalez et al., *Health Promotion in Diverse Cultural Communities*, Health Promotion Resource Center, Stanford Center for Research in Disease Prevention (and the Indian Health Service), Stanford University, 1000 Welch Road, Palo Alto, California 94304-1885. Phone: (415) 723-0003. Fax: (415) 725-6906, © 1992.

Sample Resource Inventory Survey

Name of organization: _____

Name of your contact: _____

Position in organization: _____

Address: _____

Phone number: _____

What services or programs do you provide in alcohol abuse prevention and treatment? _____

_____

_____

_____

_____

_____

_____

How often do you provide these services or programs? _____

_____

How much does your service or program cost? _____

Who uses your services and programs? _____

_____

How many people do you serve each year? _____

Do you have staff, facilities, or any other resources you could share with other groups interested in alcohol abuse prevention or treatment? _____

_____

_____

_____

What additional programs do you think our community needs to fight alcohol abuse? _____

_____

_____

Source: *Restoring Balance*, Health Promotion Resource Center, Stanford Center for Research in Disease Prevention (and the Indian Health Service), Stanford University, 1000 Welch Road, Palo Alto, California 94304-1885. Phone: (415) 723-0003. Fax: (415) 725-6906, © 1992.

Follow-Up Contact Sheet

Organization: _____

Contact name: _____

Address: _____

Phone: _____   Fax: _____

Initial call: Date   _____

                       Comments   _____

                                     _____

Follow-up call: Date   _____

                       Comments   _____

                                     _____

Organization: _____

Contact name: _____

Address: _____

Phone: _____   Fax: _____

Initial call: Date   _____

                       Comments   _____

                                     _____

Follow-up call: Date   _____

                       Comments   _____

                                     _____

Organization: _____

Contact name: _____

Address: _____

Phone: _____   Fax: _____

Initial call: Date   _____

                       Comments   _____

                                     _____

Follow-up call: Date   _____

                       Comments   _____

                                     _____

Source: *Seven Days of Immunizations: National Infant Immunization Week*, U.S. Department of Health and Human Services, Public Health Service, Centers for Disease Control and Prevention (CDC), Atlanta, Georgia 30333, 1995.

DEVELOPING EFFECTIVE COALITIONS: AN EIGHT-STEP GUIDE*

Health professionals attend numerous meetings and sometimes assume that they understand everything it takes for working groups to succeed. Often, however, groups fail or, perhaps worse, flounder. To avoid this type of experience, which only erodes faith in collaborative efforts, people need to sharpen the skills that are necessary to build and maintain coalitions. The following is an eight-step guide to building effective coalitions. It is written from the perspective of an organization considering initiating and leading a coalition, but can be helpful to anyone eager to strengthen a coalition in which he or she participates.

What Is a Coalition?

A coalition is a union of people and organizations working to influence outcomes on a specific problem. Coalitions are useful for accomplishing a broad range of goals that reach beyond the capacity of any individual member organization. These goals range from information sharing to coordination of services, from community education to advocacy for major environmental or policy (regulatory) changes. The word *coalition* is used herein in a generic sense to represent a broad variety of organizational forms. The approach is intended to be used by any collaborative group seeking to influence outcomes or goals.

Characteristics of Collaborative Organizations

- **Advisory committees** generally respond to organizations or programs by providing suggestions and technical assistance.
- **Commissions** usually consist of citizens appointed by official bodies.
- **Consortia and alliances** tend to be semiofficial, membership organizations. They typically have broad policy-oriented goals and may span large geographic areas. They usually consist of organizations and coalitions as opposed to individuals.
- **Networks** are generally loose-knit groups formed primarily for the purpose of resource and information sharing.
- **Task forces** most often come together to accomplish a specific series of activities often at the request of an overseeing body.

Coalition Glossary

- **Chairperson.** The chairperson primarily acts as spokesperson for the coalition. He or she may sign letters, testify in court, etc., on behalf of the coalition. The chairperson does not necessarily have to be from the lead agency. Frequently, the chairperson also acts as the facilitator.
- **Facilitator.** The facilitator is responsible for running the coalition's meetings. This person should be knowledgeable in group dynamics and comfortable with the task of including disparate members in group interactions, fostering group discussion,

---

*Source: Larry Cohen, Nancy Baer & Pam Satterwhite, *Developing Effective Coalitions: An Eight Step Guide*. For further information, please contact Larry Cohen, Prevention Institute, 265 29th Street, Oakland, California 94611, www.preventioninstitute.org. Edited and printed by the Children's Safety Network at the National Center for Education in Maternal and Child Health.

and resolving disagreements within the group. As with the chairperson, the facilitator does not necessarily have to be from the lead agency.

- **Individual member.** Individual members are those people who do not represent a specific organization within the coalition. They often join the coalition for reasons of personal or professional interest in the issue.
- **Lead agency.** The lead agency convenes the coalition and assumes significant responsibility for its operation. However, the lead agency does not control the coalition. The lead agency should recognize the amount of resources necessary to initiate and maintain the coalition and the importance of respecting the differences between the coalition's and the lead agency's perspectives.
- **Member organization.** Member organizations participate in coalition activities and send a designated representative to coalition meetings. In some coalitions, *member* is an official designation; some organizations may choose to become official members and others may participate on an ad hoc or informal basis.
- **Representatives.** Representatives are staff from member organizations who are selected to participate in the activities and meetings of the coalition. Ideally, these people have an interest in the problem, and their activities on the coalition constitute part of their regular job responsibilities.
- **Staffing.** Staffing refers to the support functions necessary to make the coalition work (e.g., planning meetings, preparing agendas). Staffing is typically a responsibility of the lead agency.
- **Steering committee.** A steering committee is a small subgroup of the coalition that takes primary responsibility for the coalition's overall direction. Typically, the steering committee will include the coalition chairperson and a representative from the lead agency. The steering committee may also include subcommittee chairpersons and representatives from other organizations that have a major commitment to the coalition's objectives. Steering committees sometimes plan meetings and may provide decision making between regular coalition meetings.
- **Turf.** Turf refers to the territory an organization feels is rightly its own. Turf may include geographic areas, specific issues, and funding sources. Frequently, "turf battles"—disagreements over who will work in a particular region or who will apply for a particular grant—arise in coalitions.

Advantages of Coalitions

Coalitions offer numerous potential advantages over working independently:

- Coalitions can conserve resources.
- Coalitions can reach more people within a community than a single organization can.
- Coalitions can accomplish objectives beyond the scope of any single organization.
- Coalitions have greater credibility than individual organizations. The broader purpose and breadth of coalitions give them more credibility than individual organizations. In addition, coalitions reduce suspicion of self-interest.
- Coalitions provide a forum for sharing information.
- Coalitions provide a range of advice and perspectives to the lead agency.
- Coalitions foster personal satisfaction and help members to understand their jobs in a broader perspective.

- Coalitions can foster cooperation among grassroots organizations, community members, and diverse sectors of a large organization. Coalitions build trust and consensus among people and organizations that have similar responsibilities and concerns within a community.

However, a coalition is not appropriate in every situation and is only one of a variety of tools for accomplishing organizational goals. A lead agency should consider carefully the responsibilities of developing and coordinating a coalition. The success of a coalition is usually uncertain. In addition, lead agencies tend to underestimate the requirements needed to keep coalitions functioning well, especially the commitment of substantial staffing resources. Coalitions also require significant commitment from the members, who frequently must weigh coalition membership against other important work. Potential results need to be measured against their costs, keeping in mind that results of coalition efforts often diverge from the initial expectations of the organizations that created them. Further, some tasks are inappropriate for coalitions because they may require quick responses that are unwieldy for coalitions or an intensity of focus that is difficult to attain with a large group.

Before initiating a coalition, it is important to determine if related groups already exist within the community. At times, it will be far more effective to participate in an already existing group with compatible goals than to form a new coalition.

> *TIP: People and organizations often define terms differently. It is important to define clearly the type of group that will be set up, including its mission, membership, and structure, and to make sure that all participants understand and agree with this definition.*

Eight Steps to Building an Effective Coalition

1. Analyze the program's objectives and determine whether to form a coalition.
2. Recruit the right people.
3. Devise a set of preliminary objectives and activities for the coalition.
4. Convene the coalition.
5. Anticipate the necessary resources.
6. Define elements of a successful coalition structure.
7. Maintain coalition vitality.
8. Make improvements through evaluation.

Step 1: Analyze the Program's Objectives and Determine Whether To Form a Coalition

Three different situations may cause an organization to consider forming a coalition: (1) The organization recognizes a community need or responds to community leaders' requests to facilitate an effort, (2) the organization recognizes that a coalition will help it fulfill its own goals, or (3) the process of building a coalition is required, for example, by a grant mandate or as the outcome of a conference. Recently, many grants have required organizations to establish coalitions. Consequently, the initiation of a coalition may be in response to the grantor rather than the result of recognizing it as the best solution to a problem. Therefore, the organization's objectives may be based on an assessment of data, may stem from an existing programmatic emphasis, or may be set by a funding mandate.

Sometimes a coalition is established spontaneously by the joint decision of a group of individuals and organizations, without a lead agency. These coalition organizers should approach the eight steps to effective coalition building as though they share the responsibility as the lead agency. Among them, they must assume the responsibilities delineated for the lead agency. Sometimes these shared efforts can capitalize on the energy of their beginnings and can achieve remarkable results.

A potential lead agency must assess its credibility in and capacity for providing neutral facilitation. On some issues, the organization may have the credibility and resources to provide the lead. In other situations, history, turf issues, or lack of resources might prevent the achievement of a cohesive effort. In these cases, the group should consider designating a different lead agency.

When deciding whether to form a coalition, first consider whether a coalition is the appropriate tool to serve the organization's needs. Then consider the resources needed from the lead agency and from coalition members. Finally, consider whether coalition efforts represent the best use of these resources. To answer these questions, it is important to examine the objectives and to determine specific strategies that could help achieve those objectives. The following steps should be undertaken.

Clarify the Objectives and Appropriate Activities. Often, policy advocacy requires the resources of several organizations within a community and may necessitate the formation of a coalition.

Take a broad, creative look at activities that can accomplish the objectives. In many prevention programs, efforts center primarily on education. Yet, individual and community education is not enough. A child can drown in minutes, even with an attentive caregiver nearby who knows that water is dangerous. A fence around a pool, however, is an effective safeguard that helps prevent such tragedies by physically separating the child from the danger. In this case, promoting an ordinance requiring proper pool fencing will be a more effective method of reducing childhood drownings than funneling all of the coalition's resources into individual and community education.

Critical questions to consider are the breadth of what the group may accomplish and the scope of the coalition's activities. For example, should the effort focus on car seats or on all childhood injuries? Will the coalition focus on a specific injury (e.g., sports-related injuries) or on a cross-cutting issue (e.g., improvement of data access)? The direction the coalition will ultimately take depends on the vision and interests of the lead agency and on the likelihood of success in meeting the identified objectives. The coalition's direction will also depend on the composition and interests of the membership (see step 3). For each approach, it will be important to have at least a general understanding of the roles of particular members in accomplishing the objectives. Different members may be better suited to different activities.

Assess Community Strengths and Weaknesses. How do the proposed approaches of the coalition fit into the context of the community's strengths and weaknesses? Look at the community in terms of potential barriers and supports. Is there a history of success or failure in dealing with similar problems in the community? Are there organizations that have similar objectives? Are there organizations (or even coalitions) that deal with closely related issues? Are there individuals or organizations that could be enlisted to provide support or overcome potential barriers? Are there organizations from other geographic regions with whom collaboration could occur? Are there individuals and organizations that may be opposed to the objectives or may view the coalition as competition for scarce resources?

Determine the costs and benefits to the lead agency. How great will the resource drain be? How much will the coalition's results coincide with the organization's overall goals? What will a coalition provide to the lead agency's program? Determine if adequate resources are available. If not, the objectives must be revised, or perhaps the coalition should not be created.

Step 2: Recruit the Right People

Membership Type. Determine the membership based on the coalition's goals. Most coalitions should have diverse membership. Of course, a coalition aimed at providing citizen input might consist only of citizens, a coalition designed to ensure that government departments coordinate their efforts effectively might consist only of those departments, and a coalition aimed at eliminating duplication of services might include only the service providers. Coalitions with less diverse membership may communicate and work more quickly because members' objectives may be more alike. These coalitions, however, may be weaker in their ability to comprehend other factors that contribute to the problems that lie beyond the purview of their member organizations.

Member Organizations. Start by identifying organizations that already work on the identified issue and look broadly for other organizations that should be involved. Consider those who have influence, those who will be supportive, and even those who may put obstacles in the coalition's path. Are there important citizen or client groups that should be included?

Individual Members. Many coalitions welcome individuals in their membership. Individual members may be community members, community leaders, or people who have directly experienced the problem. Unless there is a reason not to, it is a good idea to include individuals who are not affiliated with an organization, because they can perform functions that may differ from other coalition members. For example, individual members may be perceived by the media as having less of a vested interest and, therefore, more credibility. In addition, individual members can provide advice and outreach from a different, and perhaps more personal, perspective.

Decide whether to include or exclude potential competitors and adversaries, based on the sincerity of their commitment to the coalition's goals and whether they will be more of an impediment to the coalition if included or excluded.

Organization Representatives. Having identified key organizations, consider who will best represent each organization on the coalition. Agency directors are often effective at making policy decisions and establishing credibility as coalition representatives. They often have broad experience on certain coalition issues and a wide network of connections in the community. On the other hand, line staff are frequently more committed, enthusiastic, and available than top leaders and are often more in touch with the issues related to hands-on service delivery. It is important for agency directors to appoint these staff to represent their organization. In so doing, the directors validate the time employees spend doing coalition work. In addition, the directors will be more likely to provide latitude to their representatives when decisions need to be made by the coalition "on the spot."

Organization representatives with strong skills or interests should be recruited to serve on the coalition steering committee, asked to chair or facilitate, or given other positions of responsibility. In situations in which only top organizational leaders have the clout to play an effective role, recognize that their attendance may be irregular but that the coalition is receiving the benefit of key individuals.

Often, participation from both top leadership and line staff is essential to achieving coalition goals.

Membership Size. Consider the desired number of organizations and the diversity of membership when selecting organizations to approach about joining the coalition. A coalition developing a curriculum on boating safety may need fewer members than a coalition that is attempting to change community pool fencing ordinances, because writing curricula is a less complex task than influencing policy.

> *TIP: A group larger than 12–18 people requires more resources and will sometimes take longer to develop group identity and common purpose. Some coalition experts recommend calculating size based on organizational purpose. At times it is preferable to bring together a narrow group with more closely defined interests (e.g., service providers). This group would accomplish objectives quickly. Frequently, this type of beginning leads to broadening the coalition at a later and more appropriate time.*

Step 3: Devise a Set of Preliminary Objectives and Activities for the Coalition

In step 1, the lead agency's objectives were examined. It is important to meld these objectives with the objectives of other members. Defining coalition goals and objectives and how to implement them requires the inclusion of all coalition members in discussions. Therefore, the lead agency will need to broaden and modify its objectives. A written mission statement can be a useful tool to achieve clarity about coalition goals. However, it is important to avoid getting too bogged down in the semantics of the statement early in the coalition's life.

Melding the Objectives of the Member Groups. Some coalitions arise with a number of commonalities among the member organizations, minimizing the need to convince members of the benefits of the coalition. More typically, however, each member organization has its own goals, which may vary widely from those of other member organizations. It is important to create options that mutually satisfy the lead organization's objectives as well as the goals of other coalition members, to propose mutually productive activities, and to structure both objectives and activities in such a way that all coalition members feel included in the decision-making process. The coalition's original objectives must be kept in the forefront of all planning while ensuring that a balance is struck between those objectives and the concerns and interests of each member group.

Until trust is established, avoid issues and activities that will set up turf struggles or exacerbate existing turf issues between coalition member agencies. More importantly, the coalition should be careful not to become another competitor to its member agencies, but rather should play a complementary role.

> *TIP: It is not always possible to avoid turf struggles. However, a coalition should try to avoid exacerbating these areas of overlap and competition. At times, a coalition can be a constructive meeting place for openly discussing problem areas,*

establishing ground rules, and resolving turf issues. Formal and informal opportunities to understand the difference in agency history, mandates, and funding issues may soften turf struggles.

Coalition Goals and Objectives. While dealing with long-term objectives over time, set some objectives that can be addressed by all member organizations more immediately. However, always keep the long-range objectives clearly in mind. Far too often the effectiveness of a coalition decreases as the breadth of its agenda increases.

There can be advantages in dealing with a myriad of issues since approaches to different types of injuries may be related to one another. Regardless of the breadth of issues, keep the original coalition objectives foremost in all planning, lest members lose interest or enthusiasm.

In some cases, coalition objectives may be at cross-purposes with those of an individual organization, and one or another organization may elect not to participate in the coalition. It is important to find out why groups decline to participate. When forced to choose between groups, encourage the coalition to select objectives that put the needs of the community's citizens first. This is appropriate at all times and cannot fail to win respect.

Coalition Activities. Develop a variety of well-defined activities that meet the needs of participating organizations and use the skills of coalition representatives. Identify some activities that will result in short-term successes, such as a press release announcing the organization's formation and purpose, or a report outlining the group's initial findings. These products increase members' motivation and pride while enhancing coalition visibility and credibility.

Initial successes can be achieved without massive effort. For example, information sharing is typically part of initial coalition meetings as members get to know one another. Record descriptions of the types of services provided by each of the coalition's member organizations and distribute this information in an easy-to-read format, such as a chart. This creatively fulfills the need for a simple inventory of member services.

Bear in mind that what keeps a coalition going is the commitment of the individual representatives and the support of the organizations they represent. Generally, the more directly coalition activities relate to the specific objectives of the participating organizations, and the more each member is able to enjoy and be proud of its individual participation and contributions, the more the coalition will accomplish and the more it will flourish.

TIP: Select activities that members will experience as successful—activities in which they have something unique to contribute. Make objectives compelling. Be sensitive to the fact that coalition work is not the main job of coalition members and keep assignments simple and achievable. Keep reminding people that it is all right to say no or to set limits.

In some cases, broad goals can be accomplished best by joint activities with other coalitions, rather than by a single coalition. While regular meetings of all of the coalitions in one broad group would prove unwieldy to the members, it is in everyone's interest to work cooperatively on a specific issue. At times, coalitions find it valuable to send representatives to one another's meetings and to have reports regularly included on one another's agendas.

TIP: It may be helpful for staff of lead agencies to communicate on a regular basis, clarifying objectives and assisting one another with strategies.

Step 4: Convene the Coalition

Coalitions are typically initiated in one of three ways: (1) through a meeting, (2) at a conference, or (3) at a workshop.

TIP: The notion that members of a coalition will self-select at a conference or workshop and form a viable coalition is wishful thinking. Workshops or conferences can sometimes be used to initiate a coalition. However, they will require more resources than a single meeting and will not produce the carefully selected membership that a planned meeting will. As a result, the likelihood that members will participate on a consistent basis is slim. The rare exceptions to this rule might occur when (1) distance is such that people can receive approval to attend a conference workshop but not a meeting or (2) a political mandate leads to a highly visible event where coalition organizers can capitalize on the energy of the situation to create a coalition. In any case, identifying potential coalition members at workshops and conferences may prove valuable.

To convene the coalition for the first time, hold a meeting of potential members. At this meeting, the lead agency should clearly define the purpose of the coalition, and members should specify their expectations. In addition, the invited organizations and their representatives should have a chance to introduce themselves, state what they see as their role on the coalition, and consider what their organization's interest is in participating in the coalition. Potential members should be given an opportunity to define what they perceive as the purpose and goals of the coalition and to recommend others who they think should be involved.

To succeed, the lead agency should arrive at the first meeting with a strong proposal for the coalition's structure, including its mission and membership. Although many components of a coalition's structure are negotiable, the lead agency should be clear about the particular elements that are not. While being specific about how the coalition will operate, the lead agency should also explain where there is room for modification based on member input. Further, the lead agency should ensure that all participating organizations understand and agree with the definition they give to the coalition.

Of course, not all potential members will find the coalition worth their time and energy. Two determinants will be the specific activities the coalition chooses to undertake and the worth of the coalition as seen by the management of the member organizations. Therefore, once coalition activities are clarified, it is important to reconsider membership. Any well-designed coalition will be broad based and may have different organizations participating in different activities. Nevertheless, the decision by an organization not to participate in the coalition may be an appropriate one from its perspective.

Step 5: Anticipate the Necessary Resources

Effective coalitions generally require minimal financial outlay for materials and supplies but require substantial time commitments from people. The ability to allocate considerable staffing is one of the most important considerations for organizations providing coalition leadership.

Occasionally, the coalition can call upon its members for operational tasks. However, the lead agency generally provides the majority of staff time. Lead agencies may benefit by reallocating some of their staff time to coordinate coalition activities, because their investment is often repaid by the successes achieved by the coalition.

While staff time may be provided by many coalition members, it is important for the lead agency not to be too optimistic and to allocate a significant amount of its own staff time to the coalition. Preparation for coalition meetings requires substantial staff effort. To ensure meeting attendance and success, extensive work must be done prior to the meetings, including agenda preparation and written and telephone contact with the representatives. A coalition succeeds when staffing is adequate to handle the detail work.

It is important to recognize that coalition members' time is the most valuable contribution they can make. When this resource is discussed during coalition meetings, commitments are sometimes made in response to the enthusiasm of the meeting and seem less realistic when members return to their regular jobs. At other times, coalition members will fulfill their commitments but may resent the extra work. Both situations can have a long-term destructive impact on the coalition. Periodic discussions about resources, support, and time limitations of the members can minimize potential problems. Also, it is important to reevaluate the objectives and activities in order to monitor which are achievable, given the coalition's staffing and resources, and which may change over time. The more the coalition's objectives complement those of its members' agencies, the less member time will seem like "extra" work.

TIP: Estimate how much of the staff work will be the responsibility of the lead agency and how much to realistically expect of members. Anticipate that members will not always fulfill their commitments. Be appreciative of what is done, rather than "moralistic" when people cannot accomplish everything they planned.

Staff Demands on the Lead Agency.   The lead agency should expect extensive staff demands in the following areas:

- **Clerical:** mailings, typing minutes and agendas, making reminder calls, photo-copying
- **Meetings:** planning agendas, taking minutes, locating and preparing the meeting site, planning facilitation, coordinating with the coalition's chairperson or steering committee, providing refreshments
- **Membership:** recruitment, orientation, ongoing contact, support, encouragement
- **Research and fact gathering:** data collection, process and outcome evaluation
- **Public relations and public information:** development of materials, press releases, linkage to local reporters
- **Coordination of activities:** special coalition events, media campaigns, joint projects
- **Fund-raising:** raising money and other resources

TIP: When calculating the needed resources, estimate the number of hours per month required for each of these categories, and then multiply this total by two.

Financial Resources. Financial concerns can be distracting, particularly to a new coalition. Although it may be costly to establish and maintain a coalition, particularly in terms of staff time, the cost of achieving overall results should be less than if the lead agency attempted to accomplish these same objectives on its own. Frequently, coalitions spend thousands of dollars of personnel time in order to raise much smaller amounts of cash. While raising small amounts of money may provide members with a sense of accomplishment, these efforts must be minimized. Further, careful attention should be paid to minimizing financial obligations for members. For example, a conference held at a community site with volunteer speakers may be planned for a nominal cost. Additionally, five possible sources for supplementing coalition resources, whether in the form of cash or donated services, are the media, foundations, local service clubs, students and trainees, and volunteers:

- **Media** can be encouraged to provide information that reinforces coalition efforts. They also may be interested in printing and disseminating information on the materials produced by the coalition. A visibility campaign, using mass media (television, radio, newspaper) will help raise the coalition's profile and may help to promote the coalition to funders.
- **Foundations** usually give small amounts of seed money to coalitions because they value the opportunity to encourage cooperation and see it as a way to provide broad services at minimal cost.
- **Local service clubs** such as Soroptimists or Rotary like to contribute to broad-based community efforts. Also, they frequently have established links with some coalition members.
- **Students and trainees** frequently seek skills in coalition building and may be interested in a traineeship program. Linkage with a university or community college can be a cost-effective way to increase staffing.
- **Volunteers** are often pleased to contribute many resources and are anxious to learn the skills related to coalition building that will serve their own charitable impulses and careers.

Step 6: Define Elements of a Successful Coalition Structure

The technical details of the coalition's structure are vital to achieving success. As with other coalition considerations, it is important to have well-developed ideas as well as the flexibility to allow for input and modifications by coalition members. Structural issues to consider are: (1) coalition life expectancy; (2) meeting location, frequency, and length; (3) membership parameters; (4) decision-making processes; (5) meeting agendas; and (6) participation between meetings. There are no set rules about how a coalition should be structured, but each of the following six elements should be focused on thoughtfully.

Coalition Life Expectancy. The coalition's goals should dictate its longevity. Although an open-ended time frame may seem attractive to the lead agency, member organizations and their representatives often prefer coalitions with a specific life expectancy. The disadvantage of this approach is that some members may become dissatisfied if a decision is made to maintain the coalition after the specified time. Generally, it is best to meet two or three times to clarify potential coalition objectives, and then determine duration.

Meeting Location, Frequency, and Length. Attention to meeting location, time of day, comfort of the site (size of room, lighting, chairs, ventilation, etc.), and regularly scheduled dates can contribute to enhanced member participation. In addition, a time for refreshments prior to meetings, during breaks, or after the meeting provides an opportunity for less formal conversation and builds group cohesion and morale.

To promote an atmosphere of equal contribution, consider holding coalition meetings on neutral territory, such as the local library. Rotating the meeting to different members' sites can add interest, although at times meetings are delayed when people get lost or confused by varying locations.

Other than an ad hoc emergency situation—such as a legislative deadline—coalitions should not meet more frequently than once a month. In some cases, attendance levels are more likely to be maintained by meeting once every two months. When coalitions meet less frequently, members are generally more willing to participate in subcommittees between general meetings. However, coalition commitment and continuity can suffer when meetings occur less than once a month. Groups separated by distance will meet less frequently (e.g., quarterly). If some members travel a great distance, longer but less frequent meetings make the travel time a better investment. Certain kinds of groups meet annually, with subcommittee meetings and conference calls in between, but their effectiveness can suffer unless members are highly motivated.

Remember, people's time is valuable; generally, meetings of one and one-half to two hours are best. Do not permit coalition meetings to run over the planned time.

TIP: Poll members to see which times and locations present the least conflict in terms of both personal and work commitments. Avoid meeting times that cause members to face traffic jams and sites where parking is difficult. The next time they receive a notice about a coalition meeting, they should think more about the content of the meeting than the traffic.

Membership Parameters. As step 2 points out, membership is critical. Coalition members must decide to what extent new members will be included. How defined should the membership be versus how open? In many cases, a compromise solution in which certain people are recruited and encouraged but no one is excluded is best. Open meetings lead to greater variability in attendance and a potentially unwieldy group, but this is generally of less concern than the danger of excluding, or creating the impression of excluding, important supporters. For example, conference organizers who invite only certain, specially selected people to attend may face significant backlash from others who feel that their participation in the conference would be valuable. A large group can be subdivided to maximize effectiveness.

TIP: New members add vitality to the coalition. Providing an orientation session for new members often reduces their need to interrupt coalition meetings to catch up with the topics.

Whether a broad cross section or a more narrowly defined group of members is chosen, it is worth analyzing the potential contributions of various disciplines (e.g., churches, business organizations, local government, school districts) in relation to the purpose and goals of the coalition.

It is also important to consider to what extent organizations should be asked to join and to become "official" members of the coalition. A general rule of thumb is not to seek official recognition (which typically means official action by the board of directors of a member organization) until the coalition has a clearly defined purpose or specific activities that would be strongly enhanced by this recognition. While official approval may add some prestige to the coalition, a more loosely formed coalition will initially minimize the need for bylaws and formal decision-making structures, which can prove cumbersome and pose an early barrier to cooperation.

More formalized membership procedures may become an issue when and if the coalition wishes to make public statements or endorse policy measures. Individuals who are official members (e.g., with their names on the coalition's letterhead) are likely to be concerned about making public statements. Although a deliberate decision-making process, involving considerable time, will be required to take a stand on an issue, the resulting statement will have more credibility if it has more supporters. Official membership works best when the coalition is small and the organizations are represented by "higher-ups" who can make decisions on the spot.

Because of the interorganizational nature of coalitions, public statements can become very complicated, particularly those statements that individual members cannot make without the approval of their board of directors. Even when individual members agree on a statement, the difficulty in obtaining board approval often impedes the possibility of making a public statement in a timely manner.

> *TIP: Sometimes, the positions of the coalition can be distanced from individual members. For example, a letter may state that the coalition's position represents the opinion of the majority of participating groups but does not necessarily reflect the position of any particular organizational member or group.*

Decision-Making Process. Good decision-making procedures are a key to coalition success. Establish a specific decision-making process before problems occur. It is important, however, that discussions on how decisions are made not become a barrier to coalition effectiveness. Sometimes coalitions become so involved in these kinds of discussions that they lose track of their fundamental purpose. It may be helpful to ask: Is this particular decision-making structure vital to the functioning of the coalition? Bear in mind that some members may find lengthy decision-making discussions distracting and, as a result, may decrease their attendance. Therefore, avoid discussions that are too detailed or cumbersome.

Decisions can be made by consensus. However, this process can become unmanageable. To avoid this, define consensus as an approach that the majority supports and others can live with. Health-based coalitions are usually happy to relinquish some of the detailed decision making in exchange for simplicity and reasonable results. On the other hand, tact must be exercised, especially on sensitive issues such as decisions related to money, policy, and turf. There will be cases in which consensus cannot be reached, and the group must either vote or accept no action on a certain issue. Sometimes having the group clarify in advance the kinds of issues that are sensitive (e.g., grants, turf, or legislation) will help to avoid problems later.

> *TIP: Coalitions often gravitate toward discussing their own internal workings and processes rather than resolving the community issue they came together to address.*

Avoid this "identity crisis." Though some coalition decisions require a group process to reach closure, the true purpose of the coalition must not get lost.

Meeting Structure. One of the most important ingredients for an effective coalition is a good meeting agenda. A clear agenda structure, which may be modified by those present at the beginning of the meeting, can reinforce the coalition's purpose and foster collaboration. To achieve such positive results, the agenda must be carefully planned and, ideally, should be distributed prior to the meeting.

A regular agenda format will help the coalition get focused, thereby giving members a sense of direction and momentum. Different formats will work better for some groups, but most agendas begin with agenda modification, a review of the previous meetings' minutes (if minutes are kept), and introductions, check-ins, or announcements. Many meetings conclude by evaluating the meeting, setting a date for the next meeting, and listing items for the next meeting's agenda.

The heart of the agenda will vary between groups depending upon their missions and the role of members identified in the structure of the coalition. A focus, for instance, on legislation would require a place on the agenda for updates on policy efforts, while a group that is concentrating on community outreach and education might have a section on the agenda for community action. Large, broad-based coalitions may have a variety of committees, and therefore a section for committee reports would be important. Inviting guest speakers or adding presentations by coalition members can enliven the meetings.

The lead agency, or whoever is responsible for developing the meeting's agenda, needs to discuss with the meeting facilitator how the agenda should be organized. They should anticipate which topics could generate controversy, who should lead the discussion on each item, which items require a decision, how much time should be allotted, and what would be the best process for each item (e.g., brainstorm, small group discussion, refer to committee, report only).

The agenda that is distributed to members prior to a meeting is often just an outline, with suggested times for each item. The facilitator will bring an annotated agenda indicating who will guide each section, what process will be used, and any other notes that will ensure that the meeting moves smoothly through the agenda in the allocated time. For long meetings, or meetings where the agenda is substantially altered from what was initially distributed, the facilitator may write a revised agenda on butcher paper taped to the wall. Bringing materials such as pens, butcher paper, audiovisual equipment, and tape is generally the lead agency's responsibility, but these materials may also be provided by staff at the meeting site.

Participation between Meetings. Successful coalitions generally have active planning groups or subcommittees, formal and informal, that carry out coalition activities. Based on time constraints, commitment, and relevance to their organization's own objectives, different members may show markedly different levels of involvement.

Unless coalition objectives are closely related to the objectives of the membership, it is not wise to expect more than a few hours of additional commitment between meetings. Often, members have less time available than what is realistically needed to make a coalition work. Be sensitive to the fact that coalition work is not the main job of coalition members. Some people volunteer far more than is appropriate both because of their enthusiasm at the time and because there may be group pressure for everyone to contribute. Keep reminding people that it is all right to say no. Remember that coalition members will not always fulfill their commitments. The more directly coalition activities are related to the specific objectives of the participating organizations, the more the coalition will accomplish and flourish.

It may be helpful to encourage the most active participants in the coalition to form a steering committee, which provides leadership by discussing long-range goals and the steps and strategies to achieve them. A steering committee often works well as an informal open body. For example, lunch meetings between coalition sessions can bring together key participants and allow them to provide their best input while increasing their buy-in. Members of a steering committee may be selected by the group as a whole or, in less formal situations, the lead agency may encourage members to attend the lunch meetings. It is important not to exclude anyone from participation. Coalitions are not just for fun, but when members enjoy working together, the coalition can achieve more of its objectives.

One of the main concerns organizations voice when participating in coalitions is that the coalition uses too much staff time, which is at a premium in this era of cutbacks in health and human services. Hence, the simpler the design of a coalition, the better. Further, encouraging members to participate in activities of their own choosing minimizes the possibility of some members overcommitting their time and burning out.

In all areas of coalition structure, the same rules apply: Minimize complications, maximize relevance, and encourage participation.

TIP: Nothing is better for coalition morale than healthy refreshments!

Step 7: Maintain Coalition Vitality

Coalition building is a craft, requiring broad vision and careful attention to detail. Leadership coalition building requires knowing not only how to create a coalition structure, but also how to recognize the warning signs of problems that may arise. The ability of coalition leaders to do both will greatly increase the coalition's chances for success. It is important for leaders to work hard at maintaining the vitality and enthusiasm of the coalition.

Warning signs may be difficult to recognize because even the most successful coalition has ebbs and flows. By dealing with potential problems as they emerge, however, the vitality of the coalition can be maintained.

TIP: A group attempting to coordinate services or embark on a joint advocacy effort should expect more pitfalls than a group formed solely for the purpose of information sharing, as the former tasks are more complex and demand more commitment.

Several activities that are important for maximizing coalition vitality are described below.

Addressing Coalition Difficulties. One clear indication that a coalition is having difficulties is a decline in membership. While earlier warning signs are less obvious, they might show up as repetitive meetings or meetings that consist primarily of announcements and reports; meetings that become bogged down in procedures; significant failures in follow-through; ongoing challenges of authority and/or battles between members; lack of member enthusiasm; or an unacceptable drain on lead agency resources as a result of attempts to bolster the coalition.

Coalition leaders must watch for warning signs, be aware of the conditions that can have a negative impact on coalition effectiveness, and constantly work to minimize the difficulties. The most common difficulties include: (1) poor group dynamics, including unnecessarily draining decision making and power dynamics, such as tension over leadership, decisions, or turf; (2) membership/participation concerns such as a difficult agency or member, changes in the needs of participating agencies, shifts in staff assignments, changes in available resources, or member burnout; (3) coalition emphasis on too many long-term goals without short-term objectives to generate short-term wins that add energy to the group; (4) ineffectiveness in achieving coalition activities due to inadequate planning or resources; or (5) changes affecting the coalition's mission, such as new legislation that has an impact on the objective reality of the issue the coalition was formed to address.

Although the lead agency will not always be able to overcome these challenges, effective management of the problem is an essential first step. The lead agency should identify and respond to significant problems, issues, or changes that appear to impede the coalition. It is the lead agency's responsibility to bring identified problems to the attention of coalition members and to encourage collaborative solutions. The most valuable source of information about negative coalition conditions is input from the coalition members themselves. Therefore, it is crucial to maintain open communication among the members so that problems surface quickly. Further, it is important to be flexible regarding how objectives will be met.

Sharing the Power and Leadership. Many coalition members will readily defer power to the lead agency to facilitate smooth functioning. However, if the coalition solidifies as an independent entity and develops a body of work that it performs or creates collectively, members will expect greater involvement in decision making. At this point, the coalition becomes a more independent group and requires less guidance from the lead agency.

Ironically, the characteristics that indicate a strong coalition—a heightened sense of collective identity and a high degree of interest in, and commitment to, work that is developed collaboratively—can also exacerbate tensions in defining the direction of the coalition. It is important to deal with these issues directly. Negotiating issues of a power imbalance in decision making, especially when a coalition has achieved this state of maturity, requires sensitivity and may require setting aside extra time to clarify.

Recruiting and Involving New Members. Membership changes are to be expected. Sometimes an organization's mandate will change; other times staff members simply have personal interests and priorities that draw them away from the coalition. It is worthwhile to develop new leadership and support periodically. Wide distribution of coalition minutes and information outside the coalition is one way to inform a broad group of potential members. Attention must be paid to ensure that new members are welcomed and oriented to fulfill vital functions of the coalition. They will add new energy and enthusiasm to the coalition's ongoing activities. It is important to attend to the ways that the coalition can be inclusive, since many people leave coalitions after one or two meetings because they feel that they have nothing special to offer. An invitation to join a subcommittee can be helpful.

Promote renewal by providing training and by bringing challenging, exciting new issues to the group. Coalition building and injury prevention each require their own set of skills, and some members will be more experienced than others. Every member will bring to the coalition his or her own perspective. Therefore, a broad framework, a common vocabulary, and a set of principles for preventing injury must be presented early in the coalition's formation. Remember, too, that new members will need to be brought up to speed. Further training, encouraging coalition members to attend conferences, and bringing in guest speakers can be helpful. This approach will ensure that members share the big picture of the problem as well as the underlying philosophy of the coalition. Everyone involved in the coalition, both lead agency staff and members, can and will benefit from training, consultation, and the opportunity to discuss what is and is not working.

Preventing Frustration and Exhaustion. Therefore, retreats, trainings, opportunities to discuss coalition building with others, and recognition of lead agency staff are all essential in preventing burnout. Because lead agency staff are a critical resource required for coalition effectiveness, it is important to provide them with support and encouragement. Lead agency staff and coalition members need exposure to new information on their chosen issue in order to stimulate creative ideas and to reinvigorate coalition efforts.

Celebrating and Sharing Successes. Maintaining morale and a sense that the coalition is playing a vital role in addressing the problem is essential. Too often, coalitions focus on problems and next steps without pausing to appreciate their accomplishments. Keys to boosting coalition morale include implementing effective activities that result in tangible products, giving coalition members credit for coalition successes, celebrating short-term successes with publicity or awards, reexamining objectives, and taking a brief respite from coalition meetings and activities.

Step 8: Make Improvements through Evaluation

Coalition evaluations can provide the assigned staff person, lead agency, and coalition members with important feedback. Components of coalitions that should be evaluated include objectives, activities, processes, and unanticipated events. By assessing the processes, outcomes, and impacts associated with coalition activities, staff can improve their outreach and coordination skills, and members can determine which strategies help the coalition achieve its ultimate goals most effectively. The results, if positive, can also help the coalition improve its reputation within the community and can be included in future resource development proposals. Further, when a coalition modifies its efforts to eliminate problems pinpointed by an evaluation, the coalition's credibility can improve significantly.

Coalitions can employ two basic types of evaluations: formative and summative evaluations. Formative evaluations focus specifically on the coalition's process objectives. For example, a coalition may want to encourage the media to promote bicycle safety. A formative evaluation would analyze the process by which the coalition attempted to achieve this goal. Questions in the formative evaluation might include: How many members actively monitored the local media on a regular basis? How many times did staff and members meet with local media representatives to encourage safe bicycling pictorials? How many times did the coalition submit press releases or letters to the editor? The results of formative evaluations help staff and members improve the functioning of the coalition.

Summative evaluations help coalition members to determine whether or not the coalition's strategies resulted in the desired consequences. Summative evaluations help assess both outcome and impact objectives. To evaluate outcome objectives in the example described above, a summative evaluation would include questions like the following: Did the local media organizations that the coalition contacted change their practices to include photos of safe bicycling? How many coalition-sponsored activities received coverage in the local press? To assess impact objectives, the summative evaluation might include a component that analyzed changes in parents' and children's attitudes and behaviors after reading coverage of coalition activities. Were parents, for example, influenced to purchase bicycle helmets after reading the coalition's articles? The answers to summative evaluation questions help coalition members make strategic decisions about strengthening promising interventions and discontinuing ineffective ones.

Evaluating coalition efforts is not simply a matter of evaluating the effect of the coalition's planned activities on injury prevention. What can be overlooked are the myriad effects a coalition can have, whether it achieves its stated goal or not. Because coalition building stimulates a variety of interventions and activities, evaluation results must be interpreted thoughtfully. Critical to any evaluation planning is the documentation of intended successes. Further, a coalition's visibility may increase public awareness and the community's perception of the problem.

Other spin-offs might include liaisons between agencies that previously had not worked together, increased rates of cross-referral, and improvements in the skills and morale of coalition participants. These effects can augment more formal evaluation results, thus enhancing the coalition's sense of effectiveness and legitimacy. Sometimes these results are difficult to judge. A new coalition may experience unequivocal success or failure, but usually not all of the outcomes could have been predicted at the initiation of the effort. Therefore, all facets of coalition life must be taken into account in a summation of efficacy.

Evaluation is an ongoing process throughout the life of a coalition. Every major coalition event should be evaluated. Surveys of coalition members will give lead agencies an idea of the level of involvement of each member. It is ideal to evaluate whether or not further collaboration between members may occur in addition to their participation in the coalition. This information may be especially useful for formative evaluations. Likewise, simple pre- and post-tests and satisfaction surveys work well for trainings, courses, and conferences. Content analysis of meeting agendas, minutes, and attendance lists will help determine if process, outcome, and impact objectives were met and will help identify unintended successes. Taking the time to evaluate the effectiveness of coalition efforts is a way of acknowledging that the skills and contributions of coalition members are important. Honest reflection also ensures that the coalition grows from its experiences, regardless of the programmatic outcome.

Evaluating a coalition can lead to changes in a coalition's approach. In addition, evaluation can increase a coalition's effectiveness and can ensure that the community and participants benefit from the coalition's activities. Coalition evaluation is an emerging field, and more work needs to be done. However, the availability of evaluation tools is increasing, and current evaluation efforts are strengthening the ongoing work of coalitions.

Conclusion

Coalitions do not last forever. Sometime a coalition can be repaired, and sometimes the effort to do so is not justified. Be ready to dissolve a coalition if it does not achieve satisfactory goals or if it is no longer effective. Sometimes it is best to walk away with a handshake and a smile. At other times, a celebration at the conclusion of a successful campaign is a great way to acknowledge the relationships forged during the life of the coalition.

Remember, virtually every carefully crafted coalition will have an impact.

An effort may fail, then partially succeed, then falter, and so on. Since mutual trust is built up over a period of time, coalition organizers should avoid getting so caught up in any one effort as to view it as "make or break." Every effort at cooperation among groups prepares the way for greater and more sustained efforts in the future.

Coalitions consist of people. Shared efforts leave participants with surprises, memories, and mutual respect.

NOTES:

COALITION BUILDING TIPS: COALITION LEADERSHIP*

Coalition Leadership

Coalition leadership requires attention to basic organizational functions—communication, clarity of roles, decision making, etc.—just as in other organizations. However, in some ways, coalitions are unusual forms of organization and raise special leadership issues.

Types of Leadership Structures

How leadership in coalitions is defined and how it functions vary enormously. Some coalitions have *paid staff*, who may be part-time or full-time and either from the local community or not. Large, well-funded coalitions often have a full-time director and look a great deal like a traditional human service agency. In other coalitions, leadership is *totally voluntary* and emerges solely from the membership. Other coalitions have some *combination of paid and volunteer leadership*.

Coalition Leadership Models Vary with Coalition Goals

Depending upon the goals of the coalition, a variety of these styles may prove to be effective. One coalition might be run by a specific charismatic leader, while another coalition's leadership might be shared among several different individuals. In this discussion, leadership issues apply to coalitions that have as their goals bringing together various components of the community to become more effective problem solvers and maximizing the use of resources in the community. Those goals require a commitment to community development, and thus a shared leadership model tends to be the most effective in achieving these goals. For coalitions that have a commitment to community development, not only is the involvement of existing leaders critical, but developing new leadership is also adopted as a goal.

Skills and Style

Critical skills and styles for coalition leaders include the following:

- **An inclusive, welcoming stance:** Coalition leaders should set the tone for welcoming new members and for bringing them into the coalition. Orienting new members and urging them into active roles are part of the welcoming.
- **Excellent, communication skills:** Both in verbal and written materials, coalition leaders need to take complex materials and make them understandable to all audiences.
- **Group facilitation skills:** Coalition leaders need to be able to guide both large and small meetings, with numerous participants and various agendas. Meetings should allow everyone to have their say and yet follow agendas, move through problem-solving processes, and ultimately make decisions.

---

*Source: © AHEC/Community Partners, 24 S. Prospect Street, Amherst, MA 01002, (413) 253-4283. Full sets of the Coalition Building Tip Sheets are available for $10. *From the Ground Up: A Workbook on Coalition Building and Community Development* is available for $30.

- **Conflict resolution skills:** It is helpful for coalition leaders to appreciate the benefits of conflict, because conflict is common in coalitions. Seeing conflict as an opportunity to be grappled with, rather than a horror to be avoided, is crucial to coalition leadership. Identifying the various self-interests, seeing the common ground, and helping to seek compromises are part of this activity.
- **Ability to share the spotlight:** Coalition leaders must leave their egos at the door and be able to share the glory and the spotlight with other coalition members and other entities in the community. This can be a complicated tightrope; being too modest can lead to the coalition remaining invisible, while being too forward may bring resentment.
- **Trust:** Coalition leaders must be able to engender trust in those with whom they work. They must be reliable, prompt, honest, and true to their word.
- **Energy and hope:** Coalition leaders must bring energy and hope to coalitions in both their styles and their skills.

One can easily see how hard it would be to find one individual with all the above traits. Thus, the advantages of a shared leadership model that calls upon many individuals' skills are obvious. Also clear are the risks of relying on a single leader to be the initiator of all coalition activity.

Specific Issues and Challenges of Coalition Leadership

Delegation

The role of coalitions as catalysts instead of doers is paralleled in the role of the coalition leaders. The leaders must also be catalysts for action instead of doers of the action. An excellent program manager and program developer who knows how to get things done can actually be less successful as a coalition leader, because he or she may not foster delegation and develop new leadership. Coalition leaders must support the active engagement of all members and seek support for themselves from others in the coalition.

Juggling Responsibilities, Roles, and Time

Coalitions, when they start to become effective, open more and more doors with each success. Balancing these various opportunities and obligations is critical. Numerous coalition leaders suffer from making too many commitments and spreading themselves, and the coalition, too thin.

Jealousy and Criticism

Coalition leaders often are the target of criticism and jealousy. Being central and visible figures, these negative reactions can occur quite separate from any inappropriate action being taken by the leader. Understanding that this is a natural part of group process is a necessary stance for the leader. Constructively dealing with criticism and jealousy by listening and responding nondefensively is necessary for the feelings to diminish.

Action Orientation

Many coalitions get bogged down in lengthy planning processes or in cautiously avoiding controversial issues. Coalition leaders must be able to move the coalition toward action and accomplishments, so that coalition members can keep a balance between the time that they put in and the benefits that they reap from the coalition's accomplishments. This drive for products must be carefully linked with a thoughtful coalition process.

Paid Staff

The use of paid coalition staff (rather than volunteer leadership) raises two important issues:

1. When coalitions have paid staff, a key issue is the differentiation of tasks to be performed by staff versus coalition members. As unpleasant tasks arise, do all eyes focus on the paid staff and does the staff person take on the task or try to delegate it? And if he or she tries to delegate the task, do coalition members help or do they leave it for the staff person? The ways these scenarios play out can decide the tone of the coalition.
2. Supervision and support for paid staff is a second key issue. The high-stress job of being a coalition staff person requires skilled supervision and support, which is rarely available. The supervision needs to come from one or more individuals with practical knowledge of coalitions, group process, and conflict resolution.

Developing Leaders

Coalitions vary in their commitment to developing new leadership with the coalitions and in communities. When leadership development is a stated goal, it creates new leadership issues. Specifically, one needs to decide if new leaders are going to be sought from professional ranks or from citizens. And then existing coalition leaders play a key role in modeling, mentoring, training, and encouraging new leaders.

NOTES:

COALITION BUILDING TIPS: COALITION MEMBERSHIP*

Below are a number of issues that help clarify the limitations and opportunities that are established by various definitions of coalition membership.

Inclusion, Exclusion

The group development literature informs us that inclusion and exclusion are key variables in the start-up of any group. Coalition start-ups are no exception. Initial coalition discussions about who should be invited, and who should not, are often among the coalition's first decisions. One often hears "Don't invite him; he's a troublemaker." "We don't want people from that town, because they're different from us." "Let's make sure we get the mayor and the chief of police; we need them." If one makes the assumption that the goal of the coalition is to mobilize as many resources from as many sectors of the community as possible to work on community issues, then one needs to make initial membership decisions that would create a sense of equal access to the coalition. Developing and maintaining the open-membership system requires a constant examination of coalition practices. Do new members get introduced when they arrive? Do they feel welcomed? How does one bring new members up-to-date on what's happening? If coalitions limit who can be members, who can be on steering committees, whose resources they are interested in tapping, then by definition they are excluding people from the community; such coalitions will not be able to tap into their capacities and resources to solve the community's problems. Often coalitions decide to start off small and try to increase their inclusiveness as time proceeds. The difficulty with this approach is that, when others come on board, they can feel that critical decisions were made without them. An inclusive approach requires addressing the issue at the start.

Money and Membership Issues

Many coalitions ask people who are members to show their support by paying a fee to cover coalition expenses. How the issue of money and membership is constructed will have a large impact on the coalition. If the coalition sets the fee as a membership fee, then it says a member is one who pays the fee. An alternate approach is to say that anyone who supports the mission of the coalition and signs up as a member is a member, and those who are able to provide financial support become sponsors of the coalition. This separates the issue of membership from financial support. By setting a fee as a membership criterion, one potentially eliminates low-income citizens, even if one establishes a scholarship or sliding-fee scale, since having to make requests for that can be a humiliating experience. Balancing the need to obtain financial support from members with the need not to exclude people based on fees is a key issue around membership in coalition activities.

Activity Level

Although membership can be claimed by those who sign up as members or those who send financial support, the key component of coalition membership is activity.

*Source: © AHEC/Community Partners, 24 S. Prospect Street, Amherst, MA 01002, (413) 253-4283. Full sets of the Coalition Building Tip Sheets are available for $10. *From the Ground Up: A Workbook on Coalition Building and Community Development* is available for $30.

Without coalition members providing their time and their efforts, there is no coalition. Thus, a key factor in the success of any coalition is the amount of energy and time invested by its members in the community. No matter how many people have paid their dues, if members do not sign up for activities and task forces, the projects that the coalition takes on will fail. Marian Wright Edelman of the Children's Defense Fund, in talking about developing teen pregnancy–prevention coalitions, says that it is necessary to distinguish between the talkers and the actors. Often at the beginning of the coalition, one sees more of the talkers and only later do the actors emerge. Thus, another important factor in assessing membership in a coalition is to examine the activity level.

Multisectoral, Multicultural Coalitions

How well the coalition membership represents the various sectors and subcultures of a community is another key variable in membership. For membership to be truly representative, efforts have to be made to reach those who don't easily come to coalition activities. The hardest-to-reach individuals tend to be those at the very top of the power structure (the heads of corporations, police chiefs, superintendents of schools) and those at the very bottom of the power scale (the disenfranchised, the citizens). Specific efforts involving individual, personalized outreach need to be focused on those groups not well represented, so the coalition can be both multisectoral and multicultural. Getting these hard-to-reach individuals into the room is only the first step; the coalition will need to create a welcoming environment if the newcomers are to stay with the coalition. Without this, the strength of the membership will be weakened.

The Role of Citizens

Although coalitions proclaim themselves as empowering institutions, giving voice to the members of the community, they often fail at involving citizens in their efforts. Coalitions are often quite successful at engaging certain components of a community to interact in daytime meetings, in formal settings. But this modality has enormous barriers to involving citizens at the grassroots level, including time, money, language, family responsibilities, transportation, etc. There are no simple answers as to how best to engage citizens in coalition activities. Changing the meetings to evenings and providing interpreters and day care may be ways of enticing citizens to a meeting, but one is likely to lose many human service providers with after-work events. One should not assume that coalition building efforts and citizens' community-development activities can always be or need to be merged into one organization. Rather, one must seek the areas of overlapping interest of these initiatives. There needs to be an active exploration of how neighborhood organizations, community-development groups, citizens' action groups, and community coalitions can find common ground and ways of collaborating. This indeed may be the greatest future challenge for coalition membership.

The strength of a coalition is the sum of the capacities of its members. Seeking a broad representation of active members and maintaining an open door are critical to coalition success.

COALITION BUILDING TIPS: ENGAGING RESIDENTS IN COALITION BUILDING*

Many coalitions begin with institutional leaders and service providers at the table. Often at the outset or as the coalition evolves, the group decides that community residents need to be more directly involved in the development of community agendas and programs.

There are a myriad of reasons why the participation of diverse community members is important. Among these are

- insights of more people in defining the issues and priorities
- community ownership and investment in issues and solutions
- broader networks of people to inform and involve
- more energy with which to tackle projects

The benefits are clear, but deciding on the best approach to achieving this result is more elusive. Some coalitions seek to involve residents fully in the life and work of the coalition. Others focus on getting community members to participate on specific committees that work on community issues of interest to them, perhaps including them in an assessment process for selecting the issues.

A third approach, which is increasingly compelling, sees provider coalitions as facilitators, both for developing neighborhood/community coalitions (if they do not already exist) and for providing technical support to resident-driven groups. The provider coalitions can then build ongoing partnerships with these neighborhood coalitions to better apply the resources of each to community capacity building and problem solving. In most communities, this approach is more effective in yielding successful provider-resident collaborations. Through these partnerships, community residents can discover and exercise their power in naming the issues, defining the solutions, and becoming integrally involved in implementing these solutions.

Below are a number of issues to consider in designing typical coalition activities that will enhance the possibility to real community engagement—with related barriers to success and some potential strategies. These concerns and ideas cover an array of challenges, and not all will apply to a given coalition (particularly those that are neighborhood based). It is useful, however, to review them all (and others you may add) when planning to reach out to expand community participation.

The more socioeconomically diverse the audience, the more of these issues will apply. The ideas may be applied to provider coalitions, to their committees, and to neighborhood/community-based groups.

Access

Related Barriers to Success

Lack of transportation and mobility impediments are two common physical barriers to resident participation. Language can be an obstacle for those whose native

---

*Source: © AHEC/Community Partners, 24 S. Prospect Street, Amherst, MA 01002, (413) 253-4283. Full sets of the Coalition Building Tip Sheets are available for $10. *From the Ground Up: A Workbook on Coalition Building and Community Development* is available for $30.

language is other than English. When only certain people receive invitations to join, others may be denied access—whether by design or oversight.

Strategies

- Meet in central location.
- Offer rides.
- Meet in "barrier-free" buildings.
- Provide translators, bi-/multilingual publications.
- Have open membership with broad outreach.

Agenda

Related Barriers to Success

Meetings that are focused on institutional or special-interest concerns—or that are formal, lengthy, or disorganized—make it difficult to attract and retain community members.

Strategies

- Have clear agenda based on broad member input.
- Maintain action focus, based on group-set priorities.
- Keep meetings to reasonable length.

Scheduling

Related Barriers to Success

Finding a time when institutional, professional, and community members can and will commit to meeting regularly is among the most difficult challenges. Monday through Friday, 9 to 5, works well for some and excludes others. Evenings are hard for most people with families, and for those who work but do not live in the community.

Strategies

Potential strategies for this issue are elusive; successful ones are rare. Most coalitions, at some point, face the choice of whether to lean toward the professional (daytime) and do the best it can to attract community members, or to lean toward residents (evening) and try to keep professionals involved. Another option is to establish parallel groups (provider and neighborhood), with open memberships that maintain close communication and collaboration.

Cost

Related Barriers to Success

Out-of-pocket costs for participation, such as child care or transportation, can be a barrier to involving residents with low incomes. Lost wages due to missing work to participate in coalition activities is another.

Strategies

- Offer child care or reimburse for care if needed.
- Schedule short meetings before or after work.
- Offer rides or reimbursement.

"ISMs"

Related Barriers to Success

Professionalism in various forms can intimidate potential community members. Structural discrimination (racism, etc.) and tokenism are barriers to a diverse membership.

Strategies

- Avoid jargon and "alphabet soup."
- Value all types of input.
- Use a more informal meeting style.
- Welcome diversity.
- For outreach plan, don't ask one or two people to "represent" a sector.

Information

Related Barriers to Success

Unequal access to basic information about the group and its activities will impede the participation of neglected members. Inadequate background information about the group and its work can make it hard for new attenders to become full participants. Lack of knowledge about how the larger system works may inhibit the effective involvement of traditionally marginalized residents.

Strategies

- newsletter, other media
- orientation, "buddy system"
- training

Skills/Experience

Related Barriers to Success

Many potential members lack experience and related skills in being part of an ongoing problem-solving group. They often have little or no experience interacting with community leaders and decision makers, and lack training in how to deal with them effectively. Many have no role models to emulate in taking on these new experiences.

Strategies

- Seek out/nurture existing or natural leaders.
- Provide leadership training, mentoring.
- Promote visibility of positive role models, job shadowing.

Implications for Coalitions

A number of these strategies involve changes in how many coalitions conduct "business as usual." This requires that groups carefully assess the unseen impacts of their normal practices on the participation of community residents and make needed changes.

Other strategies call for outreach efforts, which must be well-planned, targeted, and ongoing to be effective. For most coalitions, it is unrealistic to undertake this significant outreach without the support of paid staff, at least part-time. For the resident members to be in a strong position to plan effectively and to negotiate from a position of strength with public officials and professionals, as many as possible should be representatives of specific community constituencies. Thus, an outreach strategy for any approach is to recruit initial resident participation through direct, personal requests for representation extended to diverse neighborhood and community organizations (both formal and informal).

NOTES:

COALITION BUILDING TIPS: COALITION BARRIERS AND HOW TO OVERCOME THEM (PART I)*

Anyone who has been in a coalition will say that the path to success is a rocky one, often marked by two steps forward and one step back. This shouldn't surprise us! Many forces in communities and community helping systems are opposed to coalition building and community development. The path of coalition progress is a dynamic one that is constantly changing with time. New obstacles (and opportunities) always keep arising. Below are some commonly encountered barriers to coalition success and some strategies to counteract them.

Barrier 1—Turf and Competition

A clear and explicit goal of coalitions is often to promote coordination, cooperation, and collaboration. But it comes as no surprise that turf, territoriality, and competition among coalition members are major barriers to coalition success. The capacity of one organization to feel competitive with another often amazes outsiders. This competition can be among health and human service agencies as they compete for clients and contracts, or it can be between the private and the public sector, between local and state government, or between local government and the community. A new request to provide a service might be issued by the state, and two or three agencies—all members of the same coalition—might begin to compete for that contract, seemingly undermining the coalition's goal of cooperation. One would hope that creating a coalition would reduce these turf battles, but they often escalate instead.

Strategies

Too often we expect self-sacrifice from individuals and organizations as they move toward coalition solutions. If we understand that personal and organizational self-interest is part of the reality and part of what motivates people, then we can look for strategies that take self-interest into account. It is also possible to minimize the impact of turf, territoriality, and self-interest by appealing to a larger good. The larger and common good that has most appeal is that of the *community* and *neighborhood*. This is why coalition building often focuses on geographic areas.

Barrier 2—Bad History

The most frequent comment that is heard when communities talk about building a new community coalition is, "Oh, we tried that once before here. It doesn't work." Most communities have had unsuccessful attempts at building cooperation and forming coalitions in their past. Most frequently, these attempts were ill-fated because they did not involve a carefully thought-out process, did not have enough resources to succeed, or were imposed from above as a mandate: "You WILL cooperate."

A history of conflict may exist between agencies and different components in communities, and one should never forget its impact. Too often we enter communities without knowledge of context, thinking that history starts when we put our foot in the

*Source: © AHEC/Community Partners, 24 S. Prospect Street, Amherst, MA 01002, (413) 253-4283. Full sets of the Coalition Building Tip Sheets are available for $10. *From the Ground Up: A Workbook on Coalition Building and Community Development* is available for $30.

door. We should never forget the power of history. All we have to do is talk to an agency director and hear, "We don't work with that other agency because 15 years ago they had a director who insulted our director at a public meeting" to realize how important it is.

Strategies

The first strategy is to learn the community's history. Determine what efforts occurred in the past to build cooperation and coalitions, and how they succeeded or failed. One can also collect a detailed history of conflict and cooperation among agencies in the community. Following that, the second key way to undo bad history is to create an open and fair process that allows everyone to participate, everyone to set the ground rules, and everyone to shape the coalition's agenda. In this way, some of the factors that led to conflict in the past can be avoided in this new round of coalition building.

Barrier 3—Failure To Act

One of the most lethal behaviors of coalitions is to engage in endless, long-term planning meetings that bog down a coalition before it ever acts. Many of us have sat on coalitions that aim to solve problems by involving a large number of important people with busy schedules, who sit around a room for more than a year thinking, planning, and doing needs assessments before anything happens. In most cases, this long planning process without action is unnecessary and can destroy a coalition before it starts. Administrators and bureaucrats are used to sitting in planning meetings, though the best of them have a limited tolerance. But citizens, citizens' groups, and those in the community who are committed to change are often quickly turned off by such an atmosphere. Coalitions at their heart are based on creating change and demonstrating the capacity to act. It is this capacity that attracts the kinds of members who make coalitions succeed. When coalitions fail to display a commitment to action, or display a fear of advocacy, they discourage the involvement of exactly the people who will make the coalition a success.

Strategies

Although a coalition must be able to engage in planning, it must also be able to produce some actions and results in its first weeks and months of existence. These are not opposing goals. One can be involved in a careful, long-term planning process, while at the same time acting on issues like creating a newsletter, circulating a petition at a coalition meeting, or holding a public session on a controversial topic. All of these can happen within the first months of a coalition's existence. Such actions show the members and the community that the coalition is committed to making something happen, as opposed to writing reports that sit on someone's shelf. In order to keep players in the coalition from the start, the coalition must be able to demonstrate a commitment to action and then it must indeed *act*. Both commitment to action and action itself must be sustained throughout the history of the coalition.

COALITION BUILDING TIPS: COALITION BARRIERS AND HOW TO OVERCOME THEM (PART II)*

Barrier 4—Dominance by Professionals

Although key professionals in communities are often important members of coalitions and can be especially helpful assets, they can also become barriers. This happens when professionals dominate the process. When members are professionals, the view of the community is generated only by professionals, and the control of the coalition is in the hands of professional agencies. Since many agencies view citizens and communities from a "deficits" point of view, they then bring this viewpoint to the coalition's work.

We see this kind of barrier in action, for example, when a group of adult service providers decides to deal with teen issues in the community by developing a teen center. In one actual situation, providers went about designing and opening a teen center without any input from the teens themselves. When no teens showed up in the first months, the professionals perceived the teens as being apathetic and blamed the teens for the problem. The providers did not recognize that only by consulting with teens, and letting them decide how best to set up the teen center, did they have any chance of success. This happens much too frequently—and not only with individual agencies, but with entire coalitions.

Strategies

Active attempts to recruit citizens are critical to coalition success. One should also respect the important role of "citizen helpers." These are people who have professional roles in communities, but who are also active citizens of the community, and therefore can wear both hats. Having citizen helpers does not eliminate the need to have citizen members who are not in a professional, formal helping role. Often, getting citizen input requires the coalition to actively go out in the community, talk to citizens, and test out new ideas before implementing them. Unless the coalition is constantly asking the community what it wants and then responding to it, it will be hard to overcome the dominance of both professionals and professional "deficit" models.

Barrier 5—Lack of a Common Vision

Increasingly, one sees examples of coalitions, often funded coalitions, where there is clear disharmony and disagreement around the coalition's goals. When these are funded coalitions, it is often the case that the original group formed the coalition because they were attracted by the dollars, not by a common vision. This does not automatically rule out a common vision, but certainly creates a barrier to that process. In these situations, it is often a matter of "Take the money and run," rather than "We are here to create a joint vision and joint changes for our community." The existence and failure of these coalitions because of a lack of common vision potentially threatens the success of the whole coalition movement.

---

*Source: © AHEC/Community Partners, 24 S. Prospect Street, Amherst, MA 01002, (413) 253-4283. Full sets of the Coalition Building Tip Sheets are available for $10. *From the Ground Up: A Workbook on Coalition Building and Community Development* is available for $30.

Strategies

Clearly, the most helpful strategy would be to develop a common vision before the onset of the coalition. Grassroots community coalitions typically have that; for example, the neighbors in the community all gather together to make sure that the community playgrounds are safe. Where the joint vision has not emerged at the start or dissolves quickly after the grant application is written, there needs to be a clear planning process that involves visioning, revisiting the mission, clarifying the goals, and articulating objectives and action plans. This will help the coalition see whether there are indeed shared tasks that members wish to work on together. If there are not, the coalition needs to be brave enough to dissolve it. If there are, the coalition can rewrite its mission statement and move forward. Coalitions are such vibrant and responsive institutions that this process of revisiting vision, mission, goals, and objectives needs to occur on a very regular basis (at least annually).

Barrier 6—Failure To Provide and Create Leadership

Coalitions have two leadership missions. One is to provide competent leadership for the coalition itself and for its tasks. The other is to create new leadership in all sectors of the community. Many coalitions struggle with one or both of these missions. There are coalitions where there is a lack of leadership—many lieutenants but no generals. The coalition then seems to flounder, not heading in any one direction or accomplishing any one task. Often coalitions that manage to exchange information but never move forward to action suffer from the above difficulty. On the flip side, some coalitions have a single dominant leader who does not delegate and who does everything him/herself. As with any other organization, the members or followers then feel powerless, excluded, and increasingly less involved. One of the problems of bringing on coalition staff can be that these paid individuals take on leadership roles. The members can then easily say, "Well I don't need to do that; we'll let our staff person do it." The creation of that kind of staff role implicitly undermines the creation of new leadership roles among the members.

Strategies

Coalitions must consciously foster the development of leadership among all their members for coalition tasks, and also seek out new individuals to take leadership roles in the community. Leadership must be seen as multifaceted and occurring in many ways—not just who runs the meeting or who chairs a task force, but also who volunteers to get people to come to a meeting, who sets up refreshments, or who is the lead person behind the scenes making things work. Each of these is a leadership role. Coalitions must regularly evaluate how their organizations are being led and how good a job they are doing at creating leaders.

Barrier 7—Poor Links to the Community

The majority of coalitions seem to have little success in establishing solid links to the community as a whole. When coalitions begin with gatherings of human service providers or educators, the meetings that are scheduled are often inaccessible to working citizens in terms of time, space, and the language and culture of the meetings.

When a group of providers talks about funding sources coming from the state, using a variety of acronyms and initials, ordinary citizens quickly understand that this is a world that they are not a part of; they may not return.

Strategies

Obvious strategies include not only making meetings more accessible in terms of language, time, space, and child care, but also having the agenda and process be citizen-driven. It has been suggested that most of the basic institutions in our communities have become unaccountable to their citizenry; that the clergy is separated from its congregation, the schools from parents and students, the health and human service system from clients and patients. Rebuilding these links, and the accountability of the systems to the citizens, is a critical piece of coalition work.

In some ways, the major strategy has to be an investment of funding into identifying and supporting and—if they are missing—creating citizen advocacy groups so that citizens can come to the table as representatives of constituencies like everyone else. In many communities, these citizen and neighborhood groups already exist. They should serve as equal partners. In other communities, funding and staffing may be needed to develop these groups and create that partnership.

NOTES:

COALITION BUILDING TIPS: BUILDING PARTNERSHIPS BETWEEN SCHOOLS AND COMMUNITIES*

More and more communities are working together to strengthen their schools. There is increasing recognition that if schools are supported in their mission to educate children, the community gains enormous benefits. These benefits include having well-educated children to address the needs of our changing society, better-equipped students to meet the challenges of obtaining higher education, increased employment opportunities, decreased poverty and truancy, and fewer risk behaviors such as smoking and drug and alcohol abuse. Below are some ideas on how to start a school-community partnership.

Create a Planning Team

A planning team comprised of equal numbers of parents, principals, or other school staff or officials, and representatives of community-based organizations should be formed. Members of health and human service agencies, houses of worship, service organizations, and businesses should also be considered when forming the planning team. In addition, the team should reflect the diversity of the community, both in terms of ethnicity and socioeconomic status.

Equal representation is important so that one group does not feel "outranked" by another group on the planning team. The planning team is responsible for determining who else should be at the table, assessing needs and resources, and planning activities to address the mutual needs of school and community.

Identify Local Needs and Resources

In order to determine the activities you want to work on together, it is essential to find out what is going on in your community. While it is important to find out community needs, it is equally important to determine your community's resources. And every community has resources, no matter how "impoverished" it might feel.

There are low-cost or free ways to get data to help the planning team identify needs. One can contact the local or county government office or library and request census data for the community. Census data can give poverty and educational statistics, among other items. One can also check with the local United Way office, public health office, or community action agency for data.

Choose Doable and Measurable Activities

It is important for planning team members and the extended community to achieve success. The best way to ensure success is to develop activities that are well defined and where the expected outcome is very clear. This process is linked to developing clear goals and strategies to meet those goals. For example, the planning team may have a goal to ensure that children have something to do after school. The creation of an after-school program utilizing retired citizens in the community as teachers is an

---

*Source: © AHEC/Community Partners, 24 S. Prospect Street, Amherst, MA 01002, (413) 253-4283. Full sets of the Coalition Building Tip Sheets are available for $10. *From the Ground Up: A Workbook on Coalition Building and Community Development* is available for $30.

example of a strategy to meet the goal. In addition, the planning team can then determine how to identify the retired citizens, what subject areas they want to teach, and where the after-school program should occur.

Involve Parents and Families

Thirty years of research has shown that parent and family involvement improves students' learning. This is true regardless of the child's grade in school, whether the family is rich or poor, or whether the parents finished high school. Therefore, critical to the success of building a school-community partnership is (1) determining how parents and other family members can be involved in their child's learning and (2) encouraging parents' participation in their child's school in a meaningful way. This includes parent and family involvement in hiring school administration staff, reviewing curricula, and shaping school policies.

Get Technical Assistance

Creating school-community partnerships is a complex and evolutionary process. It takes time to build and nurture the relationships necessary to making the school-community partnership effective. It can be helpful to identify sources of technical assistance in order to determine how the planning team will make decisions, resolve conflicts, and set goals and priorities. Team-building exercises are also instrumental to developing a strong planning team that will guide the development of the school-community partnership.

Put It in Writing

Once needs and resources have been identified and activities have been proposed, put them in writing. These written components become the basis for the community's action plan. Planned activities should have goals and deadlines so the community can stay on target to address the identified needs. Every member of the planning team should get a copy of the plan. It can be circulated to local decision-making authorities such as the school committee, parent-teacher organizations, and parent councils, as well as to local media. The plan can also be an important tool in raising awareness and obtaining funding to carry out the proposed activities.

Keep Up the Interest

It is important to sustain the interest and energy of the planning team, because no one has time to waste. Some suggestions:

- Start and end meetings on time.
- Be task oriented.
- Brainstorm tasks for people who want to participate but cannot attend meetings (e.g., type up a flyer for events, write an article for a newsletter).
- Have food and fun at your meetings.
- Meet in someone's home.
- Do a potluck supper.
- In general, keep the work enjoyable; if people—especially volunteers—don't enjoy what they are doing, they won't want to do it.

Evaluate Your Progress

Contrary to popular belief and practice, evaluation can be simple, cost-effective, and fun. It is an opportunity to assess how things are going, and it provides a way to make improvements during the course of one's work.

Celebrate Your Successes

It is important to document the coalition's accomplishments and celebrate them on at least an annual basis. This can be done at an annual meeting of the planning team, at an awards dinner, or at an open house. Make it fun and festive and share with each other and the greater community all that the coalition has accomplished. It is surprising how much a coalition can do!

NOTES:

COMMUNITY COALITIONS: DEVELOPING A PUBLIC RELATIONS PLAN*

Introduction

Coalitions need to be aware of the very different types of media with which they will be working. Coalition goals must be identified before the appropriate media are approached.

Most people think of the word *media* as meaning the press or news. Coalitions should have a press plan in place with goals and objectives that reflect crafting events, news stories, appearing at the city council meetings, meeting with reporters from the electronic and print media, meeting with the editorial board of newspapers, appearing on public awareness shows, and making presentations to community groups. Press coverage helps a coalition promote its goal as an issue and the coalition as an organization.

However, to promote the coalition and its messages, the advertising and public relations media must be targeted. The coalition needs a public relations plan by which to inform, persuade, and motivate its target audience. Advertising means public service announcements, advertisements in the print media, billboards, and so on. Again, appearances on public affairs shows, printed brochures, and coalition-sponsored events are all essential to gaining recognition of the coalition and its purpose.

Any coalition building a base of support in hopes of influencing public policy, filling service gaps, and creating linkages among multijurisdictional and multidisciplinary agencies must create a public perception of credibility, action, and political power. To create such an image with the citizenry, it is critical that every coalition work intimately with the local media. An image in the community should not happen by accident. Staff and the board of the coalition need to set media goals. Media need not be intimidating. **Coalition leaders need to know how to "work" the local media.**

When working with the media to create an image, advertising and public service announcements are only part of the equation. Public relations, although difficult to quantify, can have a powerful impact on a coalition's efforts by adding visibility and credibility to coalition activities.

Through news and feature stories, editorial board briefings, public affairs programs, speeches to local community groups, and so on, a coalition will become a local resource, extend coalition messages to the public, and motivate elected officials and the public to become involved and support coalition efforts. **The coalition needs a public relations plan.**

Suggested Strategies

The following steps should be taken by the staff of the coalition or by the public awareness/media task force or committee of the coalition.

Phase 1—Developing a Media Strategy

Know Your Organization. What is the coalition's mission? (Prepare the mission statement for release to the media.) Define the coalition's overall objectives for

---

*Courtesy of the Community Anti-Drug Coalitions of America, Alexandria, Virginia. Produced in collaboration with the American Bar Association.

at least the next 12 months and briefly describe how the coalition will accomplish them.

Know the Environment. Are there other similar coalitions in your community/region? What are they doing? Have you attempted partnering with them? Is there an easily understood difference in mission and approach?

Specify How Your Coalition Differs from Similar Coalitions. What information, knowledge, expertise, or notable personalities does your organization offer that others do not?

Know Your Audience. Who are you trying to reach through your communications? Is the audience parents, young adults, teens, children, public officials, police departments, teachers, health care professionals, or others? The audience will help determine the choice of media. In certain parts of the country, studies show that teens do not read billboards, for example.

Be Clear on What You Want Your Public Relations Effort To Accomplish. The goal may be to:

- *inform* (build awareness, knowledge in the community)
- *persuade* (have the community develop a conviction about your issue)
- *motivate* (act; become involved by talking to children or others; participate in community activities, etc.)

Phase 2—Program Elements

Conduct Research. Always localize data regarding program-related elements. Assign staff or volunteers, or approach a local college or university to establish baseline data and monitor any changes in the data. **Do not underestimate the importance of this monumental and ongoing task.** News on the national and state level must always be compared with such local statistics to be of much interest to your local media. News, trends, and human interest stories all will emanate from this baseline information and the future comparisons your coalition will be able to draw.

Develop a Press Plan. As a staff or committee, set a goal. For example, set a goal to have a coalition-related story appear once a week in the electronic media and twice each week in the print media. Reaching such a goal will require crafting events, stories, appearing at each city council meeting, and so on, in the beginning months of a coalition. However, once the coalition has met the exposure goal several times, the media will begin coming to the coalition for a local spin on national releases, reaction to a local program-related news event, and so on.

Develop not more than two clear, concise messages for each target audience. If you aim to reach parents, you might say, in all press interviews, "Talk to your kids about drugs now." This same rule applies to each media exposure. In any on-camera interview, be prepared with the two main messages you want the audience to receive. Weave those messages into each answer or comment you make. When the footage is edited, the chances will be greater that what you wanted to communicate will be on tape. Use the name of the coalition in practically every sentence to create name recognition.

Develop Media Tools. Develop a press kit that includes a fact sheet on the organization, a list of board or steering committee members, examples of the organization's work, possibly a brochure, a press release on the coalition, and current coalition events or activities. Tapes (videos and audios) can also be useful.

Develop an Ongoing Relationship with Local Media. Make personal visits to key individuals, and establish a personal relationship with newspaper editorial boards and public service directors of television stations. Establish a relationship early on with the key editors and reporters who cover program-related issues. Let them know why the coalition is in place and what the coalition plans to accomplish. Tell them you will be visiting them regularly with coalition progress reports and story ideas. Talk about data and events that interest them. Human interest stories are always solicited. Do not expect the media to be a "scrapbook" of the coalition. You must educate the media and meet their needs.

A variety of methods can be used to publicize the program:

- Place feature stories and by-lined/op-ed pieces in the local newspapers.
- Appear on local public affairs shows; give interviews (radio and television).
- Give small media briefings for key editors and reporters from newspapers, magazines, and broadcast outlets, focusing on news trends or creative approaches to the problems addressed by the coalition. In a substance abuse program, for example, talk to the press about the rise in the use of heroin and the reasons why needle usage is generally avoided during first use but seems to lead to eventual intravenous use.
- Do not overlook cable for relevant interviews or a possible public access show on program-related issues.
- Establish a speakers bureau to address schools, community groups, local businesses, and others regarding the coalition and program-related issues.

Make the coalition easily identifiable. Develop an umbrella theme, slogan, and logo for use in all coalition activities. To kick off its public relations efforts, the coalition may want to adopt a yearly or debut "signature" event that is synonymous with the coalition. Some communities sponsor annual street festivals or musical events, all-day anti-drug rallies for teens, and so on.

Phase 3—Program Evaluation

Review annually what has worked and what has not, and adjust the coalition's public relations plan accordingly. If possible, conduct focus group assessments composed of new organizations and the target audiences to assess the impact the public relations plan has had both in the community and for the coalition. The public relations plan should complement the coalition's total media/communications plan that distributes public service announcements and advertising to the various local media.

Summary

Keep in mind that reporters in most local markets are young people who move on to other media markets fairly regularly. In addition, the reporter covering drug, crime, and health issues changes often. The coalition must make the education of media an ongoing priority. You are not at the mercy of the media. They need and want your cooperation. Strike deals with media to temporarily embargo information, if needed. Agree to speak off the record to those with whom you have established a relationship. The point here is that the media are a tool to use when addressing program-related issues locally. Practice using that tool until you are comfortable. Instead of finding the media intimidating and scary, you will find them to be helpful and interested in the issues you address each day.

COMMUNITY COALITIONS: LOBBYING STRATEGIES*

Introduction

Lobbying, advocacy, and education play an integral role in shaping public policy at all levels of government. Many coalitions have been successful in advancing their organization's goals through the legislative process.

It would be naive to assume that financially powerful groups do not have an advantage over nonprofit organizations. Big contributors have tremendous sway with lawmakers, but money is not the only source of political muscle. Politicians respond to their constituents, especially to large groups of constituents. Coalitions can exercise a great deal of leverage with elected officials and become a strong political force because they represent so many parts of the community.

The reality is that much of what happens in a community is affected by government. Federal, state, and local government impact every major institution including health education coalitions. A group must make its voice heard so that governmental action will deal with program-related problems in a meaningful way. Policy is not formed in a vacuum. Groups that lobby for what they believe in will be heard, provided they are organized and armed with the tools to be effective.

This guide is largely devoted to lobbying practices at the federal level. The wide variation between the legislative process in state and local governments makes it extremely difficult to define specific lobbying strategies in these areas. However, the general advocacy principles outlined in this document are applicable to any level of government.

Phase 1—Know the Facts about Lobbying

Nonprofit, tax-exempt organizations have been given generous provisions to lobby under the 1976 lobby law. This law recognized lobbying as a proper function of nonprofit organizations. The subsequent 1990 Internal Revenue Service (IRS) regulations detail the amount of money that 501(c)(3) nonprofits can spend on lobbying. For a coalition to quality for these expenditures, it must elect to come under the conditions of the 1976 lobby law. This is a simple procedure that involves a vote by the coalition's board of directors and the filing of IRS Form 5768.

If a coalition does not elect to come under the 1976 lobby law, it will be subject to the vague "substantial" test. The IRS has never defined the amount of time or dollars covered under this rule, so it is difficult to know when the legal lobby limits have been exceeded.

What Is Lobbying?

Too often, groups are confused about what actually constitutes lobbying. Lobbying takes place when a coalition seeks to influence a local, state, or federal politician on a specific piece of legislation. In fact, most of a coalition's interaction with legislators

---

*Courtesy of the Community Anti-Drug Coalitions of America, Alexandria, Virginia. Produced in collaboration with the American Bar Association.

will be characterized as education or advocacy. It is not considered lobbying when a group meets with an elected representative to talk about the merits of the coalition or to highlight a new program. Remember, lobbying only takes place when a group tries to persuade a lawmaker to support or oppose a specific bill related to the coalition's cause.

Another important point to consider is that lobbying only takes place when there is an expenditure from the organization involved. For groups that have elected to come under the 1976 law, volunteers who work to influence legislation are not counted as a lobbying expenditure.

Is All Lobbying the Same?

All lobbying is not created equal, at least in the eyes of the IRS. *Direct lobbying* occurs when individuals attempt to influence legislation through communication with elected representatives or government officials. Communications with a coalition's members encouraging them to contact legislators on behalf of a certain bill falls under the category of direct lobbying. Nearly all of a coalition's lobbying efforts will be characterized as direct lobbying.

Grassroots lobbying occurs when a group communicates with the general public regarding a specific piece of legislation, takes a position on the legislation, and urges people to call or write their legislator to support their position. Grassroots lobbying does not take place when a coalition contacts its own members (this is direct lobbying).

Nonprofits are allowed to spend one-quarter of the amount they spend on direct lobbying for grassroots lobbying. Grassroots lobbying is going beyond the coalition's membership base to mobilize the community at large.

Can Grant Money Be Used To Lobby?

Many health promotion coalitions receive sizable grants from government agencies. These federal grants have restrictions that prohibit certain lobbying activities. However, there are ways that federally funded coalitions can participate in lobbying activities without jeopardizing their grant.

Remember, lobbying can occur only when there is an expenditure from the coalition. Several coalitions have used a volunteer staff person to coordinate public policy issues. Other coalitions have formed legislative committees to establish legislative priorities for the coalition. This committee is generally made up of coalition volunteers, so little or no staff time is involved. There is nothing in federal grants that prohibits a coalition from using moneys from other grants to pay staff who are working on lobbying activities.

Nonprofits can use foundation grants to lobby, provided that those grants are awarded for general purposes and are not earmarked funds. There are community foundation grants available that can be earmarked specifically for lobbying. Provisions against lobbying are a strong argument for developing diversified funding support for a coalition.

The coalition should be sure to check its grant(s) for any stipulations against lobbying before it becomes active in this area. There are no barriers that cannot be legally overcome if the coalition uses volunteers and board members wisely.

Phase 2—Preparation for Effective Lobbying

Step 1

> The first thing to keep in mind is that you elect legislators, and they should be expected to represent your interests. Elected representatives are interested in serving the needs of their constituents, and to do this they need your input.

Step 2

> You have expertise on issues of importance to most policy makers. Coalition leaders have firsthand experience in dealing with health problems at the grassroots level. Legislators are hungry for information from people who are working in the trenches. Politicians are eager to understand how policies will impact their constituents. Make your coalition a resource for your elected officials—you will be providing them with a valuable service.

Phase 3—Starting To Work with the Legislature

Step 1: Form a Legislative Committee

> Identify coalition members with political influence and connections with either party. Include current or previous state legislators (if they do not carry too much negative baggage with their peers). Involve people who know the legislative process.

Step 2: Identify Key Legislators

> You should know your senators and representatives in Congress; your governor, state senator, and legislators; and your local elected officials. Learn their office locations, addresses, and telephone numbers; how long they have served in office; and their committee assignments.

Step 3: Identify Key Committees

> Learn which committees and subcommittees are important to your cause. At each level of government, the coalition should be aware of the committees that address alcohol, tobacco, drugs, violence, and other relevant health issues. Know who the committee chairs are and what their position is on key legislation.

Step 4: Learn about the Legislative Process

> The coalition needs to understand the legislative process and know the key dates when members will introduce and vote on specific legislation. It must also know the appropriations cycle so it can be prepared in advance to generate grassroots support or opposition for a bill. The following chart is an example of the standard legislative process.

The Legislative Process

① Executive (president, governor) introduces legislation

② Legislation goes to committees of both houses for action

④ New legislation is voted on by both houses and sent back to the executive for approval or veto

③ Legislation travels to a conference committee made up of members from both houses to iron out differences in the two bills

The best way to understand how the legislature really functions is by talking to legislators or legislative staff. They will usually feel flattered that you are seeking their knowledge of the legislative process.

Do not take shortcuts in this area. There are very few windows of opportunity in the legislative process. How well your coalition is organized during these periods will often determine the fate of the bill.

Step 5: Stay Informed about the Issue

Make every effort to stay informed on program-related issues. Read state and local newspapers daily for program-related information. Subscribe to journals so you are familiar with the latest research in the field. Request to be placed on the mailing list of your senator, representative, state representative, and state delegate. If your coalition is lobbying on behalf of a certain legislative proposal, you will want to know the following facts:

- the details of the legislation you are supporting or opposing
- why the legislation is important to the community, and the impact it will have if passed (or not passed)
- how much the legislation will cost and how much money it will save in the long term (cost benefit)

Phase 4—The Nuts and Bolts of Lobbying

Now that the coalition is prepared to advocate for specific issues, the next question is where to start. A guiding principle to keep in mind is that the coalition's efforts need to be narrowly focused. Because lobbying will only be a small portion of a coalition's activities, the coalition should concentrate energy on the most critical issues.

The Legislative Committee's Role

The goal of the legislative committee is to determine the legislative priorities of the coalition. Keep the list small, with no more than five legislative items. List both state statute legislative priorities and local ordinance priorities. Have the coalition's board of directors ratify the legislative recommendations of the committee. Publish the legislative priorities in a booklet with a short paragraph of rationale for each legislative priority. In addition, the legislative committee should work to develop a grassroots network of other organizations and individuals that can be mobilized to respond to legislative initiatives.

Meeting with Policy Makers

Develop and cultivate a relationship with your local, state, and federal legislators. Lawmakers are always eager to meet with their constituents and to gain support.

It is always better to call than write a letter when making an appointment to meet with a legislator. A telephone call will allow you to offer a number of dates for the meeting. If you want to meet with your senators or member of Congress, you can call the office in the home district. Call the county courthouse to find the local address and telephone number of each member. All you have to know are the ZIP codes.

Members have periodic recesses around federal holidays that bring them back home. These breaks, called District Work Periods, are an ideal time for scheduling a meeting with members. Most state legislators have local delegations composed of senators and representatives within a given county or township. These delegations usually hold workshops to hear legislative priorities from various organizations. The workshops usually take place between Thanksgiving and Christmas. Contact the chair of the local delegation early in November to schedule the coalition at a workshop. City council and county commissions also have regularly scheduled workshops where coalitions can make a presentation on a specific issue. Call the city or county manager's office to request time at these workshops.

Another effective strategy is to invite policy makers to a special event, such as a legislative breakfast, sponsored by your coalition. This will give your legislator a better understanding of what your group does in the community. Having a lawmaker on hand at a coalition event will help attract the media.

If the coalition board or staff are visiting Washington, D.C., they should call *at least* a week in advance to arrange a congressional meeting. Be sure to reconfirm the meeting time the day before your arrival. Keep the size of the group small, ideally two or three people, or you will never get past the introductions. Do not expect more than 15 minutes for your presentation, so be prepared. Be brief in your remarks, but be sure to cover the essentials: who your coalition is (number of groups you represent), what you have accomplished (use anecdotes and facts), your group's position on any relevant legislation, and how you can support the member. Make sure your visiting delegation has met previously to discuss the objectives for the meeting.

Bring materials that describe the coalition (brochures, annual reports) when meeting with policy makers. Present your legislative priority brochure. If you plan to advocate for a particular bill, bring a fact sheet that outlines your coalition's position. Do not be offended if you are forced to meet with a legislative aide. Aides actually have a great deal of influence, and often they have a better understanding of your issue. Regardless of who you meet with, be sure to follow up with a thank you letter, restate any agreements you reached, and provide any information you promised.

Keep track of where the coalition's legislative issues are in committee. Schedule two or three volunteers or staff to testify at the state capitol on proposed bills. You will be surprised at the small number of people who appear to comment before committees.

The coalition should plan to make periodic appearances on the agendas of the city council, county commission, and board of education. Use these opportunities to update policy makers on the coalition's progress and policy needs. When important votes come up, be sure to have a large turnout from the coalition at the meeting.

Letter-Writing Campaigns

Politicians pay close attention to their constituent mail. Personal letters are considerably more convincing than hundreds of form letters. If you organize a letter-writing campaign, here are some guidelines to keep in mind:

- Give your coalition members talking points, but have them add personal stories. Mass-produced messages cannot replace a compelling human interest letter.
- Stick to one or two issues in the letter. Do not give the lawmaker a laundry list of requests.
- If you are writing about a specific bill, be sure to include the bill's number and title.
- Make sure your name and address are on the letter, since the envelope usually gets thrown away in the mailroom. Have board members write the letters on their office letterhead.
- Send out letters while the issue is still hot. Timing is critical when writing about a bill.

Telephone Calls

A telephone call is another good way to make an impression on legislators. Always identify yourself as a constituent when you call. Explain who your coalition is and why you are calling, and ask if the legislator would be willing to discuss the issue on the telephone. If you cannot get through to a legislator, leave a detailed message and ask for the legislator to return the call.

There are other circumstances where coalition members will need to call because there is not enough time to organize a letter-writing campaign. An important bill may be coming up for a vote in committee or before the full legislature, and you need to respond in a hurry. Ten to 50 calls from your coalition can really influence a legislator before the vote.

If you cannot reach the legislator, ask to speak to the aide who works on the issue. If that individual is busy, register support or opposition to the bill with the person answering the phone. Politicians keep a close count of the number of calls they receive on a bill. Any member of Congress can be reached by calling (202) 224-3121. This number will reach your member's office as quickly as calling the direct number. To communicate your coalition's views to the White House, call the White House Comment Line at (202) 456-7639. State legislatures have toll-free hotlines that are used to solicit comment on legislation.

Introducing Legislation

Once you have organized the lobbying effort, you may want to consider introducing legislation. The first step in this process is identifying an influential committee member or council member who will champion your cause. Do your homework to ensure that you recruit the best person for the job. Forging a close relationship with the legislative staff person is important for enacting the legislation. This person has the power to keep your bill high on the legislator's agenda. The staff person is also familiar with the intricacies of the legislative process, knows who the key players are, and can keep you updated on the progress of your bill.

Media support is another great way to generate public support for your coalition's initiative. The coalition should engage in an aggressive campaign of op-ed pieces, editorial board briefings, and press conferences to sell the bill.

Summary

Hopefully, this guide has debunked the myth that lobbying is only for experts. Coalitions have a great deal of political leverage that has remained virtually untapped. The broad membership of every coalition forms the nucleus of a powerful political constituency.

NOTES:

EDUCATE THE LEGISLATORS*

Don't allow legislators to ignore outreach work. Outreach workers need congressional and state legislators not only to validate the important work of outreach but also to provide funding so that the work can be continued.

- Talk to the press, and help them become better informed.
- Network with others in your community with similar policy goals, including your clients.
- Call and write to members of Congress and state legislators.
- Meet with members of Congress and state legislators.
- Invite legislative representatives to visit and go with them to meet others in the community. Ask local representatives to walk around their own district.
- Vote!

Try these specific strategies:

- "Feed" legislators by providing information and support—invite them to lunches and committee meetings. Provide them with facts for their speeches; volunteer to help pass out pamphlets. (Money is not a prerequisite for having influence.)
- Make voter registration available on an ongoing basis—in neighborhoods, at clinics, outside grocery stores, everywhere.
- Write thank you letters to legislators—including those who vote against the outreach program's needs.
- Be visible and participate in conferences and in the community.
- Regularly send evaluations and newsletters to local legislators.
- Provide opportunities for representatives to meet staff and encourage clients to share their stories of how the program's outreach services have benefited them.
- Start letter-writing campaigns.
- Build coalitions at the state level. Remember, there is power in numbers.

> "The government has noticed us, but even if they forget, we will still be here, supporting each other, taking care of each other, and feeding our communities."
>
> —Outreach Worker

FIND COMMON GOALS WITH POLICYMAKERS*

Outreach workers need to make cost-effective arguments based on prevention. They need to pose questions such as "Do we want people going to emergency rooms when it's not necessary?" For example, 19 percent of U.S. women are entitled to get mammograms through Medicare, but only 3 percent receive this screening. Preventive services are available, but people aren't accessing them. They are afraid of the system or they don't have time. Policymakers need to hear that their funding may be wasted because they are not funding outreach programs in the communities to make sure people have access to the services. This knowledge will help policymakers share outreach goals of increased access to services.

*Source: McCann T, Young BW, Hutten D, Hayes A, Wright B. 1996. *The Healthy Start Initiative: A Community-Driven Approach to Infant Mortality Reduction—Vol. IV. Community Outreach.* Arlington, VA: National Center for Education in Maternal and Child Health.

Inventory of Collaborating Groups

To collect information about community organizations with which you might collaborate, contact the Chamber of Commerce, public libraries, United Way, city and county planning agencies, local media, and community leaders.

	Recruit for community group	Request mailing list	Ask for letter of endorsement	Request newsletter	Request data	Collaborate on intervention	Recruit volunteers
Agricultural extension service							
Businesses, Chamber of Commerce							
Charitable organizations							
Civic groups							
Government officials (e.g., mayor, commissioner)							
Health agencies (e.g., health department, voluntaries)							
Health councils/coalitions							
Labor unions							
Public safety agencies (e.g., departments of police, fire)							
Medical facilities (e.g., hospitals)							
Medical societies							
Mental health services							
Older adult groups							
Professional associations							
Organizations of faith							
Public service (schools, colleges, and universities)							
Service groups							
Social service agencies							
Others							

Source: *PATCH: Planned Approach to Community Health*, Centers for Disease Control and Prevention, National Center for Chronic Disease Prevention and Health Promotion, Division of Chronic Disease Control and Community Intervention, Atlanta, Georgia 30333, revised January 1995.

How To Develop a Community Partnership To Reduce Children's Use of Tobacco

1. **Work with your local college health care administration program in the development of a questionnaire** about children's use of tobacco products. The questionnaire needs to be reliable and valid. Your local college can provide expertise to ensure that it is.

2. **Contact the CDC's Office on Smoking and Health** for publications, research data, and reports. Call Karen Siener, CDC project officer, at 770/488-5705 or access the office's Web page at http://www.cdc.gov/nccdphp/osh/tobacco.htm

3. **Form a local task force** comprised of community leaders interested in reducing children's access to and use of tobacco. This group needs to include individuals who can help get the cooperation of local school districts in the completion of the survey. Community leaders on the task force can suggest where to raise funds. They can also help with the effort to change public policy in your state.

4. **Once the survey is completed, use the results to attract media attention** for rapid dissemination of the findings. Use this publicity to attract support for a future educational initiative to deal with the problems uncovered by the study.

5. **Share the results of the study with public officials** so that appropriate public policy can be developed to deal with the community problem.

6. **Complete another study of the same school districts two years later** in order to determine if the educational initiative was a success. The survey results must be kept anonymous because if you mention which school district has which problem, you won't get schools' cooperation in the future.

NOTES:

Source: Bernard J. Healey, "How To Develop a Community Partnership To Reduce Children's Use of Tobacco," *Inside Preventive Care*, Vol. 3, No. 1, Aspen Publishers, Inc., © April 1997.

Tips for Partnering with Local Churches

Churches can play a leading role in improving the health of a community. Congregation members often see their church as an excellent place to hold screenings and educational programs. Physical, emotional, and spiritual health of community members can all be addressed through church-based programs.

Encouraging church leaders to play a pivotal role in community health improvement may prove challenging. Some churches may not believe they have the resources to get involved. Others may not see health care as part of their mission.

By following these important steps, health care providers can connect with interested congregations.

Start with the Basic Question of How the Church Sees Itself. Does it view itself as a "health place," with a mission in health? Did it previously have a health mission, which needs to be revitalized?

If leaders feel the church does have something to offer its membership related to health, then they are going to be interested in some of the concrete ways that can be exhibited and who can be partners in this endeavor.

Probe the Clergy's Mind Set. Through conversation with the church pastor, determine if he or she is open-minded and progressive. Find out if this is the best time for the church to engage in this work. Is the congregation involved in external community projects? Ask what kind of health ministry is taking place. If there is none, are church leaders considering any?

Forward-looking clergy who see their congregation as a health place will often say everything they do in the church is related to health. Less-proactive clergy will struggle to answer these questions.

The way in which questions are asked and answers are given will give a health care professional an idea of whether the church leadership has this perspective. And if they do not, are they willing to explore it? That is what you are looking for: Is this partnership to be mutually agreeable?

Look beyond Traditional Religious Ties. Many hospitals were founded by a church and continue that relationship today. However, health care professionals can reach out to other denominations to open a dialogue about improving community health.

Usually most health care institutions are looking at broad geographic coverage. They need to be in partnership in an ecumenical way. Usually, no one denomination is going to have a geographic area covered. If you are interested in reaching a diverse number of people in your community, you should be interested in partnerships with more than one denomination.

Contact Your Clergy Friends. Many health care providers already have relationships with some churches because clergy visit their institutions. So they may have clergy friends in the community already. Providers can reach out and have deeper conversations with these clergy.

Meet Church Leaders in Their Environment. Do not expect church leaders to come to your facility. Visit their churches, begin the conversation about partnering where clergy are most comfortable, and explore the environment of these community gathering places.

Contact the Regional Ecumenical Organization. Almost every area has an ecumenical council made up of various church leaders, so approaching it could be a timesaving step. Out of that, you are going to find those who are interested. Your organization's clergy friends may be able to arrange an invitation to speak before this group.

Discuss Access to Health Care and Appropriate Use of Resources. Access is something churches should be able to relate to, because church members often come to their clergy with questions about obtaining care.

Another prime issue to discuss is encouraging people to become more active partners in the management of their health. Obviously, health care institutions want to encourage this. It also is an issue churches have some investment in, because

continues

Tips for Partnering with Local Churches continued

they want their members to be healthy. The congregation is a voluntary organization, and the healthier its members are, the more likely it is that they will be involved in community service.

Focus on the Term *Health*. Referring to *health care* tends to narrow the discussion to just the physical aspects. Churches are also interested in emotional and spiritual well-being, so using the term *health* promotes a broader meaning.

Be Clear about the Resources You Can Commit. Be upfront about what kind of partnerships your organization is looking for. Specify if your organization will share financial resources, or if you are looking to just share human resources.

Offer To Begin a Partnership Slowly. A simple way to start is to offer a hypertension screening for church members.

Dedicate a Liaison to the Church. It is important that clergy have one consistent contact person within the health care organization. This liaison should have a "whole person" understanding of health and a passion for creating a healthier community.

NOTES:

Source: Adapted from an interview with Ann Solari-Twadell, in Steve Larose, "Eleven Tips for Partnering with Local Churches," *Inside Preventive Care*, Vol. 1, No. 7, Aspen Publishers, Inc., © October 1995.

4

Culturally Competent Health Promotion

Becoming Culturally Competent

Understanding Cultural Values and
  Beliefs 198
Culturally Competent Programs:
  Overview 201
How To Better Serve Multicultural
  Populations 203
Adapting Your Program for Different
  Cultures 206
Suggested Activities and References for
  Training in Cultural Sensitivity and
  Awareness 208
Understanding Diversity
  Worksheet 209

**Communicating Health Promotion
Cross-Culturally**

Culturally Sensitive Communication 210
Communication When the Patient Does
  Not Speak English 215
Strategies To Overcome Linguistic and
  Cultural Barriers 217

**Producing Culturally Sensitive Health
Promotion Materials**

Producing Materials for Special
  Audiences 220
Recommendations for Developing Health
  Education Materials in Other
  Languages 221

Recommended Procedure for Translation
  of Written Materials 223
Key Steps in the Translation Process 223
Procedural Model for Arranging Your
  Own Translations of Health Education
  Material 226
Translation Checklist 228
Procedural Guidelines for Checkers
  Receiving Translations 229
Procedural Guidelines for Health Staff
  Checking Translations 232

Assessing a Program's Cultural Competency

Guidelines for Assessing a Program's
  Cultural Competence 234
Cultural Competency Checklist for
  Organizations and Institutions 236
Checklist for Cross-Cultural Health
  Promotion 240
Promoting Cultural Diversity and Cultural
  Competency: Self-Assessment Checklist
  for Personnel Providing Services to
  Children with Special Health Needs
  and Their Families 241

African American Communities

African Americans: Relevant Sociocultural
  Issues 244
African Cultural Patterns in Parenting
  African American Children 246
Health Education for African American
  Parents 248

Asian and Pacific American Communities

Asian and Pacific Americans: Relevant
Sociocultural Issues   251

Hispanic and Latin American Communities

Hispanic and Latin Americans: Relevant
Sociocultural Issues   253
Natural Support Systems in Hispanic/Latino
Communities   255
Background Information Form   258
Developing Effective Messages and Materials
for Hispanic/Latino Audiences   259

Native American Communities

Native Americans: Relevant Sociocultural
Issues   266

American Indian/Alaska Native/Native
Hawaiian Tribal and Village HIV/AIDS
Education Policy Guidelines   268
Zuni Community Health Opinion
Survey   276

Older American Communities

Reaching Older Americans   277

Gay, Lesbian, and Bisexual Communities

Problems Facing AIDS Educators Working
with Gay or Bisexual Men, and Some
Possible Solutions   278
Subgroups of Gay and Bisexual Men and
Suggested Locations for Education
Programs   279
Tips for Gay and Lesbian Substance
Abuse Campaigns   280

Chapter 4

Culturally Competent Health Promotion

OBJECTIVES

At the completion of this chapter, the reader will

- be more culturally sensitive
- be able to assess the cultural competence of a community program
- be aware of the methods for translation of cross-cultural material
- understand the process of developing health messages in other languages
- understand relevant sociocultural issues for African Americans, Asian and Pacific Islanders, Hispanic and Latino Communities, Native American Communities, older Americans, and gay, lesbian, and bisexual persons

---

INTRODUCTION

This chapter provides invaluable advice about how to make community health programs culturally competent. Insight into the beliefs and values of African Americans, Hispanics and Latinos, Native Americans, Asian and Pacific Americans, older Americans, and gay, lesbian, and bisexual persons is highlighted in the text. The advice is both philosophical and practical with a variety of tools to make cultural competence a true option for the community health agency.

Diverse topics that are seldom addressed in community health books are made available to the student. The student will learn how to work with a translator, how to develop a relationship with people of color, and how to adapt or develop health education materials for those of numerous cultures. In addition, the means for assessing the agencies' cultural competence are detailed. Tips, tools, and handy guidelines abound in this unique chapter.

UNDERSTANDING CULTURAL VALUES AND BELIEFS*

One key to cross-cultural health promotion is an understanding of value systems in other cultures and their influence on health. Every culture has a value system that dictates behavior directly or indirectly in that it sets norms and teaches that those norms are right. Health beliefs and practices, in particular, reflect that value system.

Cultural Values

A value is a standard that people use to assess themselves and others. It is a widely held belief about what is worthwhile, desirable, or important for well-being. Educating clients from diverse backgrounds requires understanding one's own values as well as the values of other groups. Too often people interpret the behaviors of others as being negative or inferior because they do not understand the underlying value system of another culture. Values that one culture views as positive may be considered undesirable or threatening in another. It is important to realize that values commonly found in the United States may be repulsive to some other cultures. Simply exposing clients to a new idea or practice will not automatically result in adoption if that idea or practice conflicts with their values.

There is a natural tendency for people to be "culture bound," to assume that their values, customs, and behaviors are admirable, sensible, and right. Cross-cultural health promotion presents a special challenge because it requires the provider to work with clients without making judgments as to the superiority of one set of values over another. To enhance providers' understanding of cultural differences in values, the following list provides a general comparison of dominant Anglo-American values with values commonly found in some other, more tradition-bound, countries.

---

*Source: *Cross-Cultural Counseling: A Guide for Nutrition and Health Counselors*, U.S. Department of Agriculture/U.S. Department of Health and Human Services, Nutrition Education Committee for Maternal and Child Nutrition Publications, 1986. Reviewed and approved for reprinting, 1990.

Some Other Cultures' Values	Anglo-American Values
Fate	Personal Control over the Environment
Tradition	Change
Human Interaction Dominates	Time Dominates
Hierarchy/Rank/Status	Human Equality
Group Welfare	Individualism/Privacy
Birthright Inheritance	Self-Help
Cooperation	Competition
Past Orientation	Future Orientation
"Being" Orientation	Action/Goal/Work Orientation
Formality	Informality
Indirectness/Ritual/"Face"	Directness/Openness/Honesty
Idealism/Theory	Practicality/Efficiency
Spiritualism/Detachment	Materialism

Health Beliefs

Cultures vary in their beliefs of the cause, prevention, and treatment of illness. These beliefs dictate the practices used to maintain health. Health practices can be classified as (1) folk practices, (2) spiritual or psychic healing practices, and (3) conventional medical practices. Some cultures closely tie religious beliefs to state of health. When illness is viewed as a curse for sins, people may seek a cure through good deeds and forgiveness from a spiritual source rather than through medical care.

The value placed on "good health" is also variable. The Anglo-American culture emphasizes *duration* in life, whereas some other cultures place greater emphasis on the *quality* of life. From culture to culture, the perception of health will differ. Anglo-Americans believe thinness to be a desirable health goal, whereas other groups, such as Haitians, may consider thin people to be in poor health and fat people to be healthy and happy. Similarly, cleanliness is not closely associated with good health in some cultures. Natural body odors are acceptable and desirable, rather than offensive, in many cultures. Adoption of hygienic practices that have a positive effect on health, such as brushing the teeth, may need to be explained and promoted with clients.

Cultures do not uniformly categorize conditions as diseases or illnesses. A condition considered normal in one culture may be defined as a disease in another. For example, tuberculosis may be so common in a given culture that its symptoms are viewed as normal. Also, when no acute symptoms are present clients may be unwilling to seek health care. Children may not be brought in for care when they have skin eruptions or ear infections because the parents do not consider them ill. Preventive health checkups, such as dental or eye exams, may be avoided or considered unnecessary because no symptoms are present. Prenatal care may be delayed or avoided because childbearing is seen as a natural and personal process. For employed clients, seeking health care may mean time away from their jobs and lost income. For some cultures, such as Hispanic, it may also signify a lack of strength and control over their lives.

Clients may follow a specific process in seeking health care. They seek advice from family in choosing a healer or a course of treatment. Cultural healers often may be used instead of conventional medical care. The family supports and also frequently is involved in the treatment and cure. Western medicine too often makes the mistake of cutting off that support system by dealing with the client alone. Clients may need to consult with the support system before making a medical decision. Unconventional beliefs and practices must be respected. Many have survived for generations and are in fact effective. Health educators need to work with the client to develop an acceptable plan that builds on his or her beliefs in a positive way and involves the support group.

NOTES:

CULTURALLY COMPETENT PROGRAMS: OVERVIEW*

In order for prevention programs to be effective, they must acknowledge and respond appropriately to the culture of the service recipients that they are trying to reach. Programs that are applying for funding, or existing projects that are being evaluated, must be measured by how appropriately they address culture in their design and implementation. However, it is difficult to evaluate the cultural elements of a program because, unlike other areas of evaluation, there have been few guidelines offered to assess these elements.

The knowledge base on managing and evaluating programs and preparing grant applications continues to expand. Evaluators generally consider factors such as cost effectiveness, replicability, possibility of linkages with other programs, potential impact, and content quality when assessing a program's efficacy. While these considerations have become standard, the important aspects of culture are often omitted from the assessment process.

Why Consider Culture?

Culture provides people with a design for living and for interpreting their environment.

Culture has been defined as "the shared values, traditions, norms, customs, arts, history, folklore, and institutions of a group of people." Culture shapes how people see their world and structure their community and family life. A person's cultural affiliation often determines the person's values and attitudes about health issues; responses to messages; and even the use of alcohol, tobacco, and other drugs.

A cultural group consciously or unconsciously shares identifiable values, norms, symbols, and ways of living that are repeated and transmitted from one generation to another.

Race and ethnicity are often thought to be dominant elements of culture. But the definition of culture is actually broader than this. People often belong to one or more subgroups that affect the way they think and how they behave. Factors such as geographic location, lifestyle, and age are also important in shaping what people value and hold dear.

Organizations that provide information or services to diverse groups must understand the culture of the group that they are serving, and must design and manage culturally competent programs to address those groups.

What Are Culturally Competent Programs?

Cultural competence refers to a set of academic and interpersonal skills that allow individuals to increase their understanding and appreciation of cultural differences and similarities within, among, and between groups. This requires a willingness and

---

*Source: Center for Substance Abuse, "Technical Assistance Bulletin: Following Specific Guidelines Will Help You Assess Cultural Competence in Program Design, Application, and Management," U.S. Department of Health and Human Services, Public Health Service, Substance Abuse and Mental Health Services Administration, Washington, D.C., September 1994.

ability to draw on community-based values, traditions, and customs and to work with knowledgeable persons of and from the community in developing targeted interventions, communications, and other supports.

A culturally competent program is one that demonstrates sensitivity to and understanding of cultural differences in program design, implementation, and evaluation. Culturally competent programs:

- acknowledge culture as a predominant force in shaping behaviors, values, and institutions
- acknowledge and accept that cultural differences exist and have an impact on service delivery
- believe that diversity within cultures is as important as diversity between cultures
- respect the unique, culturally defined needs of various client populations
- recognize that concepts such as "family" and "community" are different for various cultures and even for subgroups within cultures
- understand that people from different racial and ethnic groups and other cultural subgroups are usually best served by persons who are a part of or in tune with their culture
- recognize that taking the best of both worlds enhances the capacity of all

NOTES:

HOW TO BETTER SERVE MULTICULTURAL POPULATIONS*

Specific recommendations to improve service to multicultural populations fall into three categories: provider training in the area of cultural competency, overcoming language barriers, and creating partnerships. The points within these three categories are outlined below. These groupings are not absolute, and it is important to realize that there may be some overlap between areas.

Train Providers in the Area of Cultural Competency

1. *Train health department staff in foreign language and interpretation skills.* Providers and support staff in local health departments need to have skill in relevant foreign languages, including technical language (e.g., immunization, reproductive health, etc.). Specific training in interpretation is also necessary. Good interpretation and translation require knowledge of the language, including technical language, and, perhaps even more importantly, the knowledge of the culture and the personal interpretation and understanding of health and illness.

2. *Train health professionals in the communities where they will serve.* The training of health professionals should be conducted in the areas in which the professionals will serve. By developing training programs in underserved and/or multicultural communities, health care providers will learn about diverse populations.

3. *Recruit more minorities into health professions.* Efforts must be expanded to recruit and retain representatives of racial, linguistic, and cultural minority groups.

4. *Educate health professionals about the cultural histories, norms, and values of those served.* Communication is more than language. Knowledge of the cultural history, values, and norms of a population are equally important. Knowing the health beliefs, preconceptions, and practices that affect health can improve communication and compliance.

5. *Investigate the creation of a clearinghouse for written materials.* A national clearinghouse for bilingual health education materials would be a useful resource for local health officials. If such clearinghouses already exist, information concerning their services must be provided to local health officials.

6. *Create lists of available training materials from a variety of sources.* A list of training materials and cultural competency curricula would be a useful training resource for public health officials and their staffs.

7. *Develop continuing education for health department staff.* As the United States' demographics change, the types of continuing education needed to ensure the cultural competency of public health officials also changes. Education of public health practitioners must adapt as needed. The health needs of groups change from one generation to another, and health departments need to be able to meet the evolving needs of diverse populations.

---

*Source: "1992 NACHO Multicultural Health Report," National Association of County and City Health Officials, Washington, D.C.

Overcome Language Barriers

1. *Train and use lay bilingual community members in health care settings.* Bilingual residents from the community are an untapped resource. By providing lay bilingual community members with training in technical language (e.g., in the areas of immunization, prenatal care, etc.), community members can become effective health educators, paraprofessionals, and assistants. In so doing, minority clients receive services from their peers, who are best able to assess their needs. Such training also helps to involve these groups in a wide range of health department efforts to improve the health of residents in the community.

Create Partnerships

1. *Use business/community resources.* Local businesses are an important link with minority communities and may act as a tremendous resource for interaction and information dissemination. These businesses should be integrated into the implementation of services for public health.
2. *Build broad-based coalitions involving representatives from education, law enforcement, housing, and so on.* Today the public health needs of diverse populations extend beyond the traditional medical model. Increasing numbers of participants in the public arena are being identified. To best meet the needs of increasingly diverse populations, coalitions need to be built that include those addressing the welfare of linguistic and cultural minorities, such as representatives from the educational system, law enforcement, housing, social services, and others. Community-based organizations are critical partners in these efforts. Local health departments can create or participate in existing coalitions.
3. *Maintain linkages with health professional schools.* To meet the growing needs of multicultural communities, local health departments must develop working relationships with health professional schools. Local health departments could provide the experience of serving linguistic and cultural minorities to students, thereby increasing the number of professionals who choose to serve these populations. Health departments can have an impact on professional schools by communicating their needs and by supporting the special needs of bilingual students who may need special services, for example, extended time on exams that are written in English.
4. *Facilitate longer and expanded projects to permit full program development.* Full development, implementation, and assessment of programs usually take longer than one year. Depending on the program, it can be unreasonable to provide one year of funding and then withdraw the funding due to lack of results. Developing a successful program takes time and it can be detrimental to evaluate a program too soon. Interim evaluation and assessment ensure that programs are doing what they intended to do; however, trends may take at least three years to establish.
5. *Facilitate community empowerment training by local health departments.* Public health departments work with the community to address health problems. By empowering the communities to develop a sense of ownership of public

health problems and solutions, local health departments promote the owner-ship of health interventions and services provided. Such training is likely to benefit communities in the long run.

6. *Reexamine and redefine broader minority health issues.* In anticipation of develop-ing shifts in demographics that make today's minorities tomorrow's majority, policy makers need to take into account that many so-called minority issues are, in fact, related not to race, language, or ethnicity but to the specific needs of the community, regardless of race.

7. *Conduct an interdisciplinary conference on multicultural issues including health and social sciences.* A national conference on health for linguistic and cultural minorities is greatly needed at this time. It should include interdisciplinary speakers representing not only medicine and public health, but social science such as anthropology and sociology. While there may be some concern over information being handed down from academic "ivory towers," a blend of academic and practical examples and concerns is likely to prove useful for local health officials.

8. *Include minority health issues in health systems reforms.* A health system in which health services are a right, not a privilege, for all residents would ensure health services for all populations. The Office of Minority Health (OMH) and other federal and national leaders could aggressively encourage incorporation of these issues in health care reform.

9. *Develop partnerships between local health departments and minority groups.* Repre-sentatives of minority groups targeted by local health departments should be included in programmatic and policy decisions affecting the services. Such participation increases the likelihood that services are appropriate.

10. *Use the Office of Minority Health to facilitate building bridges and teams among health providers.* Local health departments, which are often the primary source of care for linguistic and cultural minorities, would like the opportunity to enhance their relationship with OMH. This would provide a means to incor-porate more state-of-the-art programmatic designs into local health depart-ment services.

11. *Address health issues through economic development programs.* Economic develop-ment programs can address health in a variety of ways. They can directly develop clinics, pharmacies, home health services, or other direct providers of health and human services. The presence of these facilities can then attract other vendors to establish businesses in the area, thus leading to further economic development. Moreover, health departments need to participate in the decision-making process of economic development programs.

12. *Encourage mentoring programs.* Young people are an excellent resource. Mentoring programs within local health departments could develop the skills of young people and permit the participants to act as emissaries of the health department within their communities. Such programs may also serve to develop self-esteem in young people.

13. *Develop communication and exchanges nationally and internationally.* Changes in national economies and communities have developed the need for increasing information exchange not only nationally, but internationally as well. Shared borders and shared health problems and concerns make communicating essential for the health of the global community.

Adapting Your Program for Different Cultures

The following are some specific tips on how to adapt a program's activities for different cultures. Remember that members of your advisory group and other community contacts can help with this.

- Use a multilevel approach. Adapting a program involves more than making it culturally appropriate. It also means choosing different strategies that affect different levels of the problem such that the changes achieved are relevant to the community's health as well as to other aspects of community life (e.g., social, economic, or political conditions). Therefore, a multiplicity of efforts aimed at individual behavior change and effective community organization is essential for a successful community health promotion program.
- Do more than translate materials into different languages or dialects. Word-for-word translations often result in a product that is inappropriate for the target community, and that may even seem absurd. It is much better to create new materials from scratch. Focus groups can be used to help develop and refine these materials. For example, one smoking cessation program targeting a non–English-speaking community used focus groups to learn about that group's male smoking culture. The sessions were videotaped, and actual quotes from the focus groups were incorporated in the brochures. In another example, a nutrition education program adapted materials that discussed the use of different ethnic foods, giving advice on different ways to prepare these foods and adapt recipes. By preserving and blending in the ideas, words, concepts, and customs of that cultural group, you will have a more culturally appropriate and acceptable product, and one that emerges from the target population.
- Organize your health promotion activities around recreational or leisure activities, community celebrations, festivals, or even family events such as pregnancy or childbirth.
- Incorporate different types of music, art, and/or dance into health promotion activities. For example, rap music has been used to promote different health messages, such as in antidrug and antismoking campaigns. Organizing young people to do mural painting or become involved in theater groups has been used to provide alternatives to gang involvement or violence. Also, some communities have incorporated Latin salsa, "funk," and traditional Native American fancy dancing into fitness and weight-reduction programs for the appropriate ethnic groups.
- Try to personalize the delivery of your program. Many cultural groups prefer the personal, one-to-one or small group approach over the impersonal or mass media approach. Also, if possible, choose a community-based setting (such as a community cultural center) over an institutional one (such as a hospital). In your contact with people, train staff and volunteers to be warm and friendly with community people rather than impersonal or businesslike.
- Include different family members as much as possible into the delivery and dissemination of health information. For example, if elders are the primary source of health advice, train them first to educate others in the family or community. If you are offering classes, invite family members and significant others to attend with the person who has signed up. To encourage this, try to make arrangements for transportation and/or child care as needed. And offer a choice of program times, or select times that are appropriate for the target group (e.g., weekends or evenings for the employed, weekdays for the elderly, etc.). Recruit school children to help with program publicity and dissemination of information. They are often effective in bringing health topics to the attention of others in the family, and may provide the only access parents and elders have to health information, especially for those who are limited in English or reading skills. Also, invite parents to participate in programs targeted at youth. When addressing delicate or sensitive issues, such as men's or women's health issues, include activities that

continues

Adapting Your Program for Different Cultures continued

educate both sexes about these topics, first separately and then together in groups. For example, a cancer prevention program targeting women might also teach husbands about their wives' need for breast self-examination and Pap smears. Ideally, as they come to understand why and how these techniques are performed, some men may then offer positive support and positively encourage their wives to practice these preventive methods. Or at least, they may no longer block their wives' practice of these methods.

- Identify positive role models for different members of the community and try to use them to deliver your message and/or teach new behaviors. This is a popular strategy used in many media campaigns.

- Develop health education materials that use clear and simple language to reach people of all educational levels. Be aware of the different literacy levels in the community. Design materials that are usable by these different groups. Choose appropriate models that portray characteristics similar to those of the target group (e.g., in race, gender, age, clothing, hairstyles, etc.). Avoid caricatures or illustrations of different ethnic groups in stereotypical roles. Rather, show positive and active role models. Consider the use of different formats for materials, such as photo-strip booklets ("fotonovelas," in Spanish), comic books, videos, plays, and music.

Also, use appropriate cultural symbols and motifs when designing the graphics for print materials.

- Ask community members to choose a name for the program so that it has special meaning to them. One community education program held a contest to find a culturally appropriate name for its program. The advisory committee chose the winner, who was then awarded a prize. This not only helped to involve more people from the community, but also increased community awareness, support, and publicity for the program.

- Remember to link health promotion activities to other aspects of community life. In this way people can address other nonhealth concerns at the same time.

After you have done these things, always field test new ideas and/or materials. Try them out on different focus groups. Listen to people's comments and watch for their reactions. These groups not only tell you how suitable your ideas or materials are for the different cultural groups in the target community, but also can give you specific suggestions for their revision. In fact, you can expect to revise materials at least once, if not more. The focus groups can also tell you whether or not your program strategies and activities seem acceptable.

NOTES:

Source: Virginia M. Gonzalez et al., *Health Promotion in Diverse Cultural Communities*, Health Promotion Resource Center, Stanford Center for Research in Disease Prevention (and the Indian Health Service), Stanford University, 1000 Welch Road, Palo Alto, California 94304-1885. Phone: (415) 723-0003. Fax: (415) 725-6906, © 1992.

Suggested Activities and References for Training in Cultural Sensitivity and Awareness

ACTIVITIES FOR THE INDIVIDUAL

- Read about the different cultural groups. Consider reading novels as well as nonfiction books about different groups, or books written by ethnic authors.
- Keep informed about current political and economic issues (e.g., civil rights, affirmative action and immigration policies, budget cuts, and other changes in social and health programs). Note their impact on different ethnic or cultural groups.
- Pay attention to the media. Watch for incidents of racial and cultural stereotyping. Be aware of the stereotypes you have.
- Read cultural magazines and newspapers; listen to and watch cultural programming to learn more about different groups' customs, languages, or dialects; forms of entertainment, and so on.
- Attend cultural events.
- Take classes or workshops to learn another language, increase your understanding of cultural/ race relations or learn about the history of different groups.

ACTIVITIES FOR GROUPS

- Conduct inservice workshops for staff; incorporate exercises in cultural sensitivity and awareness.
- Meet periodically with staff to discuss cultural issues. Invite an expert consultant to facilitate this.
- Participate in cultural exchanges with community contacts and/or advisory group members (e.g., potlucks, socials, festivals, exhibits, etc.).
- Invite prominent community leaders or academics from different cultural groups to discuss relevant issues with staff, or encourage staff to attend lectures, workshops, or conferences in the community.
- Pair staff members with community people to work together on different program tasks and learn from each other about differences or similarities in their cultural traditions, values, and experiences.

NOTES:

Source: Virginia M. Gonzalez et al., *Health Promotion in Diverse Cultural Communities*, Health Promotion Resource Center, Stanford Center for Research in Disease Prevention (and the Indian Health Service), Stanford University, 1000 Welch Road, Palo Alto, California 94304-1885. Phone: (415) 723-0003. Fax: (415) 725-6906, © 1992.

Understanding Diversity Worksheet

Think about yourself. Describe each word as it relates to yourself. Describe the strength or benefit that each provides you. Jot down your ideas.

Descriptor   **Strength or benefit**

Gender:_____

Family
  My family has special customs that include: _____
_____

Age
  In my generation we _____
_____

Race
  I am _____
Nationality
  I am _____
  My nationality has special customs such as: _____
_____
_____

Life experiences
  A particular event that has affected my life is: _____
_____

Education
  My educational experience includes: _____
_____

Values
  Three things I value most in life are:
  1. _____
  2. _____
  3. _____
Beliefs
  I have very strong beliefs about: _____
_____
_____

NOTES:

Source: Deborah A. Straka, "Look for So Much More!" *Advanced Practice Nursing Quarterly*, Vol. 2, No. 2, Aspen Publishers, Inc., © Fall 1996.

CULTURALLY SENSITIVE COMMUNICATION*

Nonverbal Communication

Messages are communicated by facial expressions and body movements that are specific to each culture. You should be aware of variations in nonverbal communication to avoid misunderstandings or inappropriate movements that may unintentionally offend clients. Also, you should use caution in interpreting the client's facial expressions or body movements. Your interpretation might be quite different from the client's intent.

Silence

You may view silence as awkward or wasteful of time. However, some cultures are quite comfortable with periods of silence. Clients who view silence as a normal part of a conversation may not appreciate your efforts to fill the void with small talk. Some Native Americans, for example, consider a minute and a half to be the normal amount of time to wait to respond, while Arab friends may spend 30 minutes or more sitting together in silence. Conversely, some cultures consider it entirely appropriate to speak before the other person has finished talking; therefore, you should avoid mistaking this overlap as rude behavior on the part of the client. Being tolerant of natural pauses or interruptions in the communication process will help foster the client's respect.

Distance

The most comfortable physical distance between two people varies from culture to culture. The Anglo-American generally prefers to be about an arm's length away from another person. Hispanics usually prefer closer proximity than Anglo-Americans, in contrast to Asians, who tend to prefer greater distance. Giving the client options for space preference, such as saying, "Please have a seat wherever you like," can help you establish the proper distance for that client.

Eye Contact

The amount of eye contact that is comfortable varies with each culture. Many Anglo-Americans are brought up to look people straight in the eye. However, older African Americans may have been taught not to make eye contact with whites. Staring is considered impolite by some groups, including Native Americans and Asians. However, if you avoid eye contact or break eye contact too frequently, as you might to complete paperwork, it may be misinterpreted by the client as disinterest. Observing the client both when listening and speaking can offer clues to appropriate eye contact. Also, you can arrange seating to meet the situation such as by sitting next to the client, rather than across from him or her, to reduce direct eye contact.

---

*Source: *Cross-Cultural Counseling: A Guide for Nutrition and Health Counselors*, U.S. Department of Agriculture/U.S. Department of Health and Human Services, Nutrition Education Committee for Maternal and Child Nutrition Publications, 1986. Reviewed and approved for reprinting, 1990.

Emotional Expression

Expression of emotion among people of different cultures varies from very expressive, as with Hispanics, to total nonexpressiveness, as with Asians. People have a tendency to regard those who are more expressive as immature and those who are less expressive as unfeeling. Happiness and sorrow are emotions common to all people, but they may not be openly expressed, particularly to outsiders. Varying beliefs about the origin and treatment of pain will dictate different emotional behaviors in different cultures. Also, people of some cultures, such as Asian, may smile or laugh to mask other emotions.

Body Language

The position, gestures, and motion of the body can be interpreted differently depending on the culture. The use of hands is a common vehicle for nonverbal expression. A firm handshake may be a positive gesture of goodwill in the dominant Anglo-American culture, but some other cultures prefer only a light touch. For instance, a vigorous handshake may be viewed as a sign of aggression by some Native Americans. Touching or being touched by a stranger may be considered inappropriate or an intimacy signal, as is the case with many Asians, but entirely appropriate with many Hispanics. Standing with hands on hips may imply anger to some clients. Pointing or beckoning with a finger may appear disrespectful, particularly to Asians who use that gesture to call their dogs. Positioning of feet also can be misinterpreted. Pointing a foot toward someone or showing the bottom part of a shoe is considered disrespectful by Asian clients. Conservative use of body language is prudent when you are uncertain as to what is appropriate within a cultural group. Observing the client's actions and interactions with others may give you direction for acceptable body language. Being open with clients and asking general questions about body language can also help if you have doubts about appropriate behavior.

Oral Communication

How you speak is as important as what you say in cross-cultural health promotion. Your tone of voice should be positive, avoiding a condescending, disinterested, or unpleasant tone. The volume should be audible, but not so loud as to make your client feel uncomfortable. Often people mistakenly assume that a louder voice is clearer and therefore better understood. Articulation of each word is important, especially for the client whose native language is not English. You may even have to adjust your speech rate. Speech that is too rapid might not be understood, while speech that is too slow might actually bore the client. Clients who speak slowly may not need to be spoken to at that rate. You might ask "Am I speaking too fast?" and adjust your rate appropriately. Avoiding slang and technical jargon will also help your client understand.

You should not try to imitate an ethnic communication style that is not naturally your own. For example, using African American language and communication style, when you are not of African American heritage, may be misinterpreted as ridicule.

Formality

Anglo-Americans tend to be informal in their oral communication, but some other cultures prefer to keep a relationship more formal. You should not assume that a first-name basis is appropriate for client relationships. Many African Americans may view being addressed by a first name as too familiar and may infer disrespect. In Vietnamese and Chinese cultures people have three- or four-word names. The first word is the family name, the second word the middle name, and the last one or two words the given name. The given name is usually preferred along with the title of Mr. or Mrs. With any client, terms of endearment such as "honey," or potentially derogatory terms such as "boy" or "girl" when referring to adults, should be avoided. Asking the client how he or she prefers to be addressed is the easiest solution, or assume formality when in doubt.

Rapport

Establishing rapport with your client is important. You should use "small talk" to reflect genuine concern for the client. Too much chatting, too many questions, or being "too nice" may cause uneasiness or raise suspicion. An opening question such as "How may I help you?" can provide an opportunity for clients to express their problems. If a client is not responsive to an open-ended question, you might suggest several options for the client to choose from. Silence on the part of the client does not necessarily reflect disinterest, but rather may be a thoughtful reaction to a question. Demonstrating patience, respect, and awareness of the client's culture can greatly help to establish rapport.

Subject

The subject matter may influence the success of your health promotion program. Certain subjects may not be acceptable for discussion. For example, clients may be unwilling to discuss personal or family matters with an unfamiliar counselor because those matters are considered to be private. Also, asking about family or spouses is not considered appropriate in every culture. Religious beliefs may be a taboo subject; therefore, actions based on them may be sensitive or difficult to discuss. You may be able to phrase questions in ways that are culturally more appropriate and explain why it is necessary to ask certain questions. You can also say to the client, "Please tell me if you do not want to answer."

Overcoming the Language Barrier

English as a Second Language

If you have ever tried to master a foreign language, you can appreciate the problems facing the client for whom English is a second language. He or she may have difficulty expressing thoughts and concerns in English and will require more of your time and patience.

You will want to allow sufficient time for the client to formulate answers to questions. Use simple vocabulary, and speak slowly and clearly; try to find words the client understands. Repeating the same words in a louder voice will not increase comprehension unless the client is hard of hearing; becoming frustrated with yourself or the client will only aggravate the situation. Further, a loud voice may be interpreted as hostility or disrespect. Ignoring the client, or halting the conversation and turning to another activity, such as paperwork, is unproductive and will only serve to increase the client's feeling of isolation.

Generally, your client will understand English better than he or she speaks it because of the difficulty in finding the right words. Remember that fluency in spoken or written English does not correlate with intelligence. Also, some clients may not be able to read their native language. Some clients will be able to speak, but not read, English well—or vice versa. Do not automatically assume that the level of fluency in speaking reflects the appropriate reading level when you are choosing materials, whether in English or translated. It is wise to check for comprehension before distributing written materials to clients with questionable reading skills. For clients who do not read in any language, try using materials such as pictures, models, and actual objects.

The Non–English-Speaking Client

If you and the client do not speak the same language, direct communication may be difficult or impossible. In that case, an interpreter must be included in the health promotion process. Concepts that are foreign to either you or the client can be explained by the interpreter. Also, an interpreter may be able to establish rapport with the client, thus eliciting more information.

There are, however, limitations and drawbacks in using interpreters. It adds another step and, therefore, additional time in the process. In general, translations tend to be simplistic, not reflecting the nonverbal and emotional expression. Some words or concepts may be difficult to translate due to a lack of vocabulary or to the personal nature of the subject matter. For example, in Cambodia there is no direct translation for the word *anemia*, so the word must be explained to clients. You should be aware that interpreters may censor or translate information from the client into what they think you want to hear.

When interpreters are necessary, they should be carefully selected. Bilingual staff and community volunteers can be used when hiring qualified interpreters is not feasible. Adult family members or friends of the client are also possible choices. Children, however, should not be asked to translate because of the value many cultures place on adults as authority figures and the possible inappropriateness of some subject matter for children. Enlisting interpreters from the waiting room is not recommended because some ethnic groups, such as Puerto Ricans, consider it a breach of confidentiality to have a stranger interpret for them. Also, you should not assume that any Latin or Asian can interpret for all others of the same cultural root. Puerto Ricans and Mexicans do not speak identical languages nor do Cambodians and Vietnamese. Mistaking one group for another may offend clients because they take pride in their ethnic origins.

You can do several things to improve the interpretation process. To begin, you should instruct the interpreter on the goals and the purpose of your health promotion program. Then, to enhance nonverbal communication, seat the interpreter so as not to obstruct your visual contact with the client. Also, try addressing your client directly instead of directing your statements to the interpreter. You will want to avoid slang words, complex ideas, difficult abstractions, or lengthy speeches without pauses. Instead, use language and examples your interpreter can understand and translate. Instruct interpreters to use the client's own words instead of paraphrasing, and encourage them to ask for further explanation whenever a word or phrase is unclear.

Acquiring Accurate Information

All health educators are concerned about getting accurate information from clients, and this intensifies when the promotion is cross-cultural. Finding approaches that yield true information is easier once you are aware of some additional barriers to communication.

Possible Barriers

There are several reasons why a client may not provide you with correct information. Clients may not trust you because you are a stranger or you resemble in appearance or position someone with whom they had a bad experience in the past. Even when clients trust you, they may view the information you request as too personal or inappropriate. In some African cultures, writing down a medical case history is not customary. Those clients may feel uneasy about your use of such information and, therefore, be unwilling to discuss their past. Also, in some cultures where only the physician has medical authority, clients may be unwilling to provide health information to others. Be aware that in the United States, public polls, surveys, and interviews have conditioned people to freely provide information to strangers; however, this is not common practice in many countries.

Your personal characteristics, such as your age, sex, educational level, or ethnicity, may influence the accuracy of your client's response. Some groups, for example, may not be comfortable giving certain information to a health educator of the opposite sex, particularly in the situation of a male client from a patriarchal culture with a female health educator. Also, clients may tell you what they think you want to hear in an effort to please or appear acculturated to the "American way." When an interpreter is used, those same barriers can alter the information being translated.

Suggested Approaches

- Establish rapport and show a genuine concern for the client. This will build a level of trust that encourages more accurate responses.
- Ask questions in several different ways to cross-check on the information obtained.
- Adjust the style of interaction to complement differences in age between you and the client. If you are younger, try to adopt a more serious and respectful attitude toward elderly clients. Conversely, if you are older, you may need to make special efforts to create an informal atmosphere that allows young clients to open up and speak freely.
- Use open-ended questions rather than questions requiring only "yes" or "no" responses; this may increase the amount of information you obtain.

NOTES:

COMMUNICATION WHEN THE PATIENT DOES NOT SPEAK ENGLISH*

When the patient does not speak English and the professional is not fluent in the patient's language, the nonverbal aspects of communication become even more crucial. The professional must be especially attuned to the nonverbal communication of the patient to assess clues to the patient's condition. Emphasizing one's own nonverbal communication can help in reaching the patient. It is critical to be mindful of the cultural differences in nonverbal communication. Common gestures may be interpreted differently in different cultures. The degree of eye contact considered polite also varies from culture to culture. Indeed, the entire range of nonverbal communication used by an individual is culturally driven. Some cultures use wide expressive gestures and dramatic vocalization. Others stress self-containment and stoicism. The professional needs at least a rudimentary knowledge of different cultures to distinguish the true level of distress implied by communicatory behaviors. Otherwise, the contained, minimizing behavior of one patient may be taken to mean that the illness is less serious than the same illness of the patient who complains dramatically.

The professional should first assess how much English the patient can speak and understand, if any. Many people can respond appropriately to "How are you" but become quickly lost if further conversation is attempted. The professional who knows even a word or two of the patient's language should say them. This simple action conveys caring and helps ease the isolation the patient feels.

When one is confronted with persons who do not speak English, a common response is to speak louder, as if volume alone could make the person understand. Another unproductive response is to concentrate on tasks and to stop speaking to the person altogether. This serves only to frighten and isolate the patient. Instead, the professional should continue to speak to the patient in a normal tone of voice, even if nothing is understood.

Although many alternatives can be used with the non-English-speaking patient, the professional must be aware that vital information can easily be missed (see box "Communication with Non-English-Speaking Patients). Persons who accompany the patient may be bilingual and can be used as translators. Picture boards can also be made to cover the most common complaints and interventions. Dictionaries and small medical phrase books are available, if the patient can read. Hospital personnel who are bilingual may serve as interpreters. Most agencies keep lists of employees who speak other languages.

There are some cautions, however, when one is using interpreters. Merely being employed in a hospital does not mean that the interpreter will have an adequate vocabulary of medical terms to interpret correctly. An interpreter from a different social class than the patient may not provide complete and accurate translations in either direction. Patients may not feel comfortable with an interpreter of the opposite sex. Often, patients bring with them an interpreter who is a bilingual child within the family, but adults may be unwilling to discuss intimate medical concerns via their child.

---

*Source: Lembi Saarmann, "Communication: The Vital Connection," *Topics in Emergency Medicine*, Vol. 14:4, Aspen Publishers, Inc., © 1992.

Communication with Non–English-Speaking Patients

DO	DON'T
Assess patient's knowledge of English	Shout
Be careful with gestures: They don't always translate	Exaggerate words
Use demonstration	Stop talking
Use picture boards or drawings	Assume that patient's nonverbal communication has the same meaning in patient's culture as in yours
Use dictionaries and phrase books	Assume that every translator will be able and willing to give accurate translations
Try to find translators fluent in both languages and in medical terminology	Equate ability to speak or not speak English with intelligence

Source: Lembi Saarmann, "Communication: The Vital Connection," *Topics in Emergency Medicine*, Vol. 14:4, Aspen Publishers, Inc., © 1992.

Working with an Interpreter: Guidelines To Follow

For you
   Speak clearly in short, simple sentences.
   Avoid technical terminology and professional jargon.
   Look at and speak to the client rather than to the interpreter.
   Maintain your role in the exchange.
   Listen carefully to your client and watch for and respond to nonverbal cues.
   Use comments and questions such as "Tell me about . . ." and "Did I understand correctly . . .?" to elicit cultural information and avoid misinterpretation.
   Remember that sessions with an interpreter take longer. Communication is the goal, so it's worth the extra time.

For the interpreter
   Use the client's own words rather than paraphrasing so that the person for whom you are interpreting receives the richness of the client's context.
   Avoid inserting or omitting information.
   Have the client repeat the instructions or general content of the discussion to check understanding.

Source: Graves DE, Suitor CW. 1998. *Celebrating Diversity: Approaching Families through Their Food* (rev. ed.), Arlington, VA: National Center for Education in Maternal and Child Health.

Strategies To Overcome Linguistic and Cultural Barriers*

BILINGUAL/BICULTURAL PROVIDERS

Hiring bilingual staff who can communicate directly with patients without need of an interpreter is clearly the most efficient approach for dealing with language barriers. If providers speak the same language as their patients, and especially if they are of similar cultural backgrounds, many problems encountered by their monolingual colleagues can be avoided.

A common constraint to this approach is the lack of trained health care professionals who are bilingual/bicultural. Recruiting for bilingual positions can be problematic, even for widely spoken languages such as Spanish. However, there are creative ways to overcome this gap. For example, foreign-trained health care workers can be retrained and utilized in professional or paraprofessional roles. Special programs can assist them to become certified or licensed in their original profession, or can train them for other health care roles, such as physician assistant or community health worker. Another method of bridging the language and culture gap is to bring in traditional healers, such as shaman and herbalists, to work as partners with practitioners of modern medicine. To be truly effective in this role, the traditional healers must be credible, respected members of their communities, and understand both cultures and health belief systems. Yet another approach to overcoming the language barrier is to encourage students of medicine and other health care sciences to study another language while in college, especially if they plan to work in communities with large non-English-speaking populations.

One area of concern in employing bilingual providers and other staff is that their language skills have rarely been evaluated. Few sites currently make an effort to assess language abilities of their bilingual staff, leaving to chance the quality of bilingual services provided. The need for an assessment of a non-native speaker's linguistic skills is clear—self-assessment of fluency is inadequate. Less obvious is whether an assessment is necessary for a native-speaking health care provider. While native speakers are generally proficient in the target language, problems can nonetheless arise. The dialect may be inappropriate, sociocultural differences may interfere with good communication, and medical terminology in the target language may be lacking depending on where the provider received medical training—in the United States or native country. Standardized evaluation tools of a provider's linguistic skills and cultural awareness would help to address this issue.

BILINGUAL/BICULTURAL COMMUNITY HEALTH WORKERS

By hiring staff who reflect the linguistic and cultural diversity of the community, community health worker programs connect mainstream health care institutions with communities that have often lacked access to adequate care. Community health workers improve the quality of health care services in several ways: facilitating access through outreach and health promotion activities; facilitating community participation in the health care system and educating providers about cultural relevance; and contributing to the continuity, coordination, and overall quality of care as members of a comprehensive health care team. It should be stressed that to be most effective, community health worker programs must provide training and ongoing support to their staff, who often work alone or in isolation from their colleagues and the mainstream agency.

---

*Written by Sherry Riddick. Major portions of this document were taken from her article "Improving Access for Limited English-Speaking Consumers: A Review of Strategies in Health Care Settings," which is to appear in an upcoming issue of the *Journal of Health Care for the Poor and Underserved*.

continues

Strategies To Overcome Linguistic and Cultural Barriers continued

EMPLOYEE LANGUAGE BANKS

The in-house language bank is one of the oldest strategies for dealing with language barriers in health institutions, especially hospitals. This strategy utilizes employees who speak other languages as volunteer interpreters when needed. One advantage is its apparent low cost since no extra staff need to be hired; another is that the language bank interpreter may be readily available and on-site for emergency requests.

However, problems with this approach are rampant unless the language bank program is carefully designed and organized. Usually no formal evaluation of language skills has occurred, with employees self-assessing their level of fluency. Also, few employees have received any training in medical interpreting skills, ethics, or vocabulary. This may lead to inappropriate, and even dangerous, situations. For example, a hospital housekeeper, in the United States for two years, fluent in her native language but barely speaking English, may be called upon to interpret for a patient being prepared for surgery. Or, an American-born nurse with two years of college French under her belt may be asked to interpret for a Creole-speaking Haitian refugee with a grade school education. In either situation, can we be sure that communication, let alone informed consent, has truly occurred?

Job conflicts can also arise when "volunteer" interpreters are called away from their regular duties. Supervisors and coworkers may blame the bilingual employee for time spent away from regular duties, leading to a negative work environment and resentment by the employee as well as colleagues and supervisors.

Some institutions are doing a good job of improving the quality of language banks by formalizing their structure: assigning a coordinator to assess language and interpretation skills of employees, maintaining updated lists of bilingual employees, providing interpreter training, and assessing the quality of service provided. These institutions have also found it useful to include interpretation as a listed job duty, to enlist the support and cooperation of supervisors, and to provide compensation for bilingual skills as a bonus or differential. Institutions with large numbers of limited-English-speaking patients may find the language bank an effective backup to other strategies when managed properly.

PROFESSIONAL INTERPRETERS

When bilingual providers are not available to care for monolingual patients, well-trained interpreters can do much to bridge the language and culture gaps. A variety of hiring approaches are currently used to obtain professional interpreter services:

1. Interpreters are hired as full-time or part-time regular employees—most common where need for a particular language is high.
2. Interpreters are hired as hourly, on-call employees or as independent contractors—most useful where demand for a particular language is intermittent. This also works best where most of demand is for pre-scheduled appointments, although emergency needs can be met when interpreters carry pagers and are accessible 24 hours a day.
3. In-person interpreter services are obtained through an outside agency. This agency may specialize in medical interpreting or provide a spectrum of interpretation specialties. Alternatively, an organization with another set of services (such as an immigrant social service agency) may decide to develop and market an interpretation service. Use of an outside agency works well where need is intermittent and diverse, and can also supplement an organization's regular interpretation staff.

continues

Strategies To Overcome Linguistic and Cultural Barriers continued

4. Telephone interpretation—also known as remote consecutive interpretation—can be obtained through outside agencies that specialize in this service. Often hospitals use such services for emergencies when it will take too long to get an interpreter in-person or for rare languages where a local interpreter is not available. Telephone interpretation may also be used for simple communications, such as setting up appointments, giving lab results, etc.—the many normal functions that are conducted by phone with English-speaking patients. More complex communications are best left to in-person interpretation services, where non-verbal cues are an important part of the communication process and accuracy of the interpretation is critical.

The cost of using professional interpreters is often cited as a barrier to using this strategy: what often is not examined is the cost of using untrained or ad hoc interpreters (family, friends, other patients). Potential liability costs, the cost of poorer health care due to inadequate communications, and undesired health outcomes may be more expensive than providing well-trained interpreters. Family, friends, and other individuals called upon as ad hoc interpreters may lack appropriate language skills and knowledge of medical terminology, leading to gross errors in communication. Also confidentiality is compromised, vital information may be censored, and internal family dynamics jeopardized, especially when children are used to interpret.

WRITTEN TRANSLATION MATERIALS

Materials that place English alongside the target language are sometimes used to communicate with non-English-speaking patients. Providers and patients then communicate by pointing to the appropriate phrase in their language. This method is obviously limited in usefulness and also requires patients to be literate in their native language. It is most often used in emergencies in the absence of a readily available interpreter, or for simple needs a hospital inpatient might have, such as indicating the need for a bedpan or a drink of water. It can also be useful for receptionists trying to identify the language of a patient before requesting an interpreter.

Translated forms, documents, and health education materials play a role in increasing access to service. Many agencies have developed a variety of translated materials. These can be useful with some populations if tailored to the reading level of the audience and adapted and tested for cultural appropriateness. Protocols for translating materials need to be standardized and clearinghouses developed to aid in the dissemination of appropriate and effective materials.

NOTES:

Producing Materials for Special Audiences

Although every target audience needs separate consideration to some extent, two kinds of audiences may require special message planning and materials development: ethnic minorities and patients.

ETHNIC MINORITIES

Interaction with target audience members and intermediaries familiar with them is especially important when targeting ethnic minorities. Remember the following:

- Use of a language may vary for different cultural groups (e.g., a word may have different meanings to different people).
- Differences in target groups extend beyond language to include diverse values and customs.
- Different kinds of channels may be credible and most capable of reaching minority audiences.
- Do not assume that "conventional wisdom," published research studies, or "common knowledge" will hold true for minority audiences. The degree of assimilation and mainstreaming is everchanging, so *current* information will be needed to choose the best channels and message strategies.
- Message appeals should be developed separately for each minority group, since perceived needs, values, and beliefs may differ among groups.

- Print materials should be simply written, reinforced with graphics, and pretested. People perceive graphics and illustrations in different ways, just as their language skills differ.
- Using bilingual materials will ensure that intermediaries and family members who are most comfortable with English can help the reader understand the content.
- Print materials should never be simply translated from English; concepts and appeals may differ by culture just as the words do.
- Audiovisual materials or interpersonal communication may be more successful for some messages and audiences.

PATIENTS

Patients and their families facing a disorder or disease may require different information in different formats at various points in the disease continuum. Remember the following:

- All patients are not alike, and they may have nothing in common except their illness. Therefore, their interests in information and ability to understand it may vary.
- Few patients and family members can handle everything they need to know at once, and they may find it particularly difficult to absorb information at the time of diagnosis.
- Patients' information needs may change as they emotionally adjust to their illness.

Source: *Making Health Communication Programs Work: A Planner's Guide,* NIH Publication #92-1493, U.S. Department of Health and Human Services, Public Health Service, National Institutes of Health, Office of Cancer Communications, National Cancer Institute, April 1992.

RECOMMENDATIONS FOR DEVELOPING HEALTH EDUCATION MATERIALS IN OTHER LANGUAGES*

Health care providers use a great deal of written information to communicate with patients. This material includes prescription and pre-op instructions, health education brochures, and managed care enrollment forms, member services materials, and health plan cards. Providers generally understand the futility of giving English language material to limited English proficient patients, but do so anyway assuming that the patients will find someone else to translate for them.

Increasingly, health care organizations are attempting to translate their commonly used written materials into several different languages, and how that process takes place can have implications for true patient comprehension.

Translation of written materials is mostly done on an ad hoc basis. Organizations needing materials translated often use in-house bilingual individuals who may have no background in translation; community-based ethnic organizations who do some translation but may similarly lack training or sufficient command of both languages; commercial translation services; and translated materials produced by other organizations. The process of translating material from English to the target language can be excessively mechanical—more like text re-processing—especially if organizations simply ship a collection of documents that may be unintelligible in English to be faithfully translated into another language without adaptation.

Ideally, written materials in other languages should reflect the dialectic and cultural nuances of the local target population. Documents that reflect an awareness of these details and the educational and literacy level of the target audience demand a more sensitive approach than mere text translation. There is no point in debating the best possible direct translation of "patient responsibility in a managed care environment" for Somali refugees who may only have been to a three-room clinic a few times in their life. In the best approach, materials should be developed from scratch *in the target language* based on discussions with focus groups, and should incorporate an appreciation of the cultural norms of the community. This process is especially important when the materials are to be used to motivate behavior change, as in health education and disease prevention. They can then be translated into English for review and reference purposes by the health care provider.

Given the difficulties of customized material development for most organizations, more could certainly be done to improve the availability and quality of traditional translations. One is the adoption of standards for translation. Some agencies and organizations have developed protocols for how written materials should be translated.

Also needed is the development, adoption, and dissemination of glossaries and dictionaries in a wide variety of languages. This would facilitate the work of both translators and interpreters, and standardize vocabulary used for medical terms, especially in the languages of more recent immigrant populations that may not have those concepts in their mother tongue.

The other task is to facilitate the more efficient sharing of already translated, commonly used written materials (such as basic disease prevention and health

---

*Source: Diversity Rx, Resources for Cross Cultural Health Care, Silver Spring, Maryland, www.DiversityRx.org

promotion brochures or pamphlets). Many organizations have tried or continue to collect and distribute a variety of these materials, and the Center for Applied Linguistics in Washington, D.C., sponsored two published collections of such information. The difficulty with currently available resources like these is that each effort is typically limited in focus or scope (i.e., just Spanish-language materials, or just materials on immunization); they are scattered around the country and difficult to track down; and the process of collecting, storing, copying, and disseminating written documents is time-consuming and expensive for the sponsoring organization. In addition, documents that rely on non-Roman script, adaptation, and customization of printed materials can be difficult for the client.

The Internet offers an attractive medium for a centralized database/repository of commonly used documents and glossaries. The costs of developing and enlarging the collection would not be dependent on storing and reproducing written documents, and the collection would be readily available for download and customization by anyone with a computer and appropriate software. It would also make ongoing review and updating easier—a necessary process to ensure that materials remain current with scientific and methodological advances. One such source has been developed by the NSW Department of Health in Australia, and the site receives heavy traffic from American users.

Summary Recommendations

- Promote original language development of health materials that incorporate community input and appropriate levels of medical and health care system terminology.
- Promote adoption of translation protocols (such as those developed by California and Minnesota state agencies) by community-based organizations, providers, provider organizations, and other agencies that produce or use translated materials.
- Support participation in translation certificate training programs for community-based interpreters/translators, especially from small language groups.
- Support consensus development, adoption, and dissemination of glossaries and dictionaries that attempt to standardize medical terminology, especially for small language groups.
- Support development of a centralized database of translated materials that include regular review and updating, ideally on the World Wide Web.

Center for Applied Linguistics
4646 40th Street NW
Washington, DC 20016-1859
202-362-0700
Web site: www.cal.org/crede/

NSW Department of Health Web site:
http://mhcs.health.nsw.gov.au

RECOMMENDED PROCEDURE FOR TRANSLATION OF WRITTEN MATERIALS*

The purpose of the following recommendations is to ensure the quality and accuracy of translated health education and promotional materials used by programs for family and community health. This will help ensure that the residents in the community who do not read and speak English well will have access to information that may improve their health and well-being.

The recommended translation procedure uses two translators. The first translator provides the original translation. The second translator provides a back translation to English. The back translation step is a method to review the translation for accuracy and appropriate tone and an opportunity to correct or edit the original. The services of paid, qualified translators should be utilized for the original translation. The back translation should also be done by a qualified translator, who is either paid or is a member of the program's staff. If a member of the program staff is used to provide the back translation, it is recommended that this work duty be included in that individual's job description.

It is also recommended that the advice of community members, consumers, or staff members who have knowledge of the cultural values of the group for which a translation is being prepared be sought to help ensure the material is understandable and sensitive to the values of that group or community. A field testing of the translated materials with the actual target audience is also recommended before the final printing of the materials.

Program directors are encouraged to set aside funds in their program budgets to pay for the translation of materials by qualified translators on a fee-for-service basis. Programs are encouraged to utilize translators who have established contracts with the department. The Translation Subcommittee maintains a listing of qualified translators and welcomes recommendations for additional qualified individuals.

Program Responsibilities

A designated staff member should be assigned responsibility for the completion of a given translation. That person will be responsible for preparing the material to be translated, working with the two translators through the actual translation process, field testing the translation, and producing the final printed materials.

KEY STEPS IN THE TRANSLATION PROCESS*

1. Preparation of Material: The material to be translated from English should be carefully selected or written to be at the *literacy level* of the target audience. The general rule for educational materials is to write them at a seventh-grade level. The program staff need to determine the literacy level that will be appropriate for the majority of individuals who will utilize the materials.

   A list of the *key messages* should be developed to guide the writing or editing of the English material.

   A *timeline* for the completion of the translation, utilizing interim dates for each step, should be developed (see the form, "Translation Checklist").

*Source: Adapted from the Translation Procedure of the Department of Public Health of the Commonwealth of Massachusetts for *Journey towards Cultural Competency: Lessons Learned*, National Maternal and Child Health Resource Center on Cultural Competency, Texas Department of Health, Austin, Texas.

2. Selection of Translators: The program staff member who is responsible for the particular translation should arrange to *meet with the two translators* at the outset. The translators should be provided information regarding the mission and scope of the program as well as the purpose of the material to be translated. The key health message(s) to be conveyed should be discussed as should key words in English, e.g., medical terms that may not be familiar. The literacy level of the target audience and the context in which the materials will be used should be explained. The translators should be encouraged to ask questions and present recommendations that they feel will make the translation understandable and culturally appropriate. The translation should convey the message in the intended tone and should use the natural speech patterns of the second language. Word-for-word translation is discouraged.

3. Initial Translation: The translator should read and understand the message(s) to be translated; prepare a *first draft* of the translated material; review the translation for accuracy and understandability; and edit the draft for typographical, spelling, or grammatical errors.

4. Back Translation: The draft translation should be given to the second translator who also reviews it for accuracy and understandability, spelling, grammar, appropriate tone, and literacy level. The second translator provides a *back translation* into English that is submitted to the responsible program person in writing. Suggestions of corrections or changes that may improve the translation are made to the program person.

   If there are *changes* to be made, the program person discusses the proposed changes with both translators, who then arrive at an agreement as to the final version. If agreement cannot be reached, the staff person makes the decision or seeks the advice of a neutral third party who has experience in reviewing translated materials. The assistance of the Translation Committee is available to provide resources for review of the draft document if there is difficulty in resolving differences of opinion regarding the best translation.

5. Final Review: A field test of the draft translation, through distribution to representatives of the target audience, is recommended. The draft is returned to the first translator for *final changes* and editing.

6. Final Production: A *final version* is typed or printed for reproduction. The Translation Subcommittee maintains a listing of resources for typing or typesetting in languages that do not use English script.

   The final version is reviewed by the original translator for typographical errors. Corrections are made.

   The document is sent for reproduction.

7. Post-Production: It is requested that copies of final versions of translated materials be sent to the Translation/Interpretation Committee to be included in a resource library for the division.

Timelines—Program staff should develop a realistic timeline for the completion of a translation, building in additional time for review and revisions. It usually takes longer than expected to complete a translation.

Selecting Translators—The Translation/Interpretation Committee has a listing of translators from which program staff should select. Suggestions for additional translators to supplement the list are welcome. Program staff should meet with both of the translators, if possible, to discuss the purpose of the material and the appropriate reading level of the material for the target population. Program staff should explain the key health messages and review English words, e.g., medical terms that are not familiar to the translators. Staff should encourage the translator to ask any questions he or she has about the translation at any time and also should review payment rates with the translator.

During the translation—The translator should follow these steps:

a. Read the entire document.
b. Prepare the first draft, aiming for full expression of the thoughts.
c. Read the draft aloud for style, rhythm, and flow.
d. Revise and proofread printed copy for errors.

After the initial translation is submitted—The translation should be given to the second translator to check style, grammar, and comprehension of the messages. The second translator should carefully review the literacy level of the translation and provide a back translation from the other language into English, either verbally, over the telephone, or in writing to the program staff person to make sure that the intended messages are clear.

If there are any changes in the translation, the program staff person should arrange a meeting with the two translators to discuss and negotiate these changes. If the translators cannot reach an agreement about the changes, the staff person will be responsible for making a final decision on the translation. The staff person should seek input from a neutral third person who speaks the language and has experience in translation review for a final resolution.

The Translation/Interpretation Committee suggests that the translated material be field tested with members of the target audience. Considerations for whether to field test include available program resources and staff, timeline for the translation, and the purpose and cost of the material.

After the final proof is ready—When the final version is ready for reproduction (i.e., a proof for Xeroxing or a camera-ready typeset proof for printing), one of the translators should do a final review of this proof for typographical or other errors.

NOTES:

Procedural Model for Arranging Your Own Translations of Health Education Material

Before you produce printed publications in other languages, you will need decisions on

- whether funds are available for the project
- whether written translations are the best way to provide information to your target group(s)
- who you are trying to reach and which languages will be needed
- how you will distribute the material once the translations are complete

It may be useful to seek advice at this stage from bilingual health staff and members of the appropriate ethnic communities or associations.

If it is considered that the information in the English original may be culturally sensitive, controversial, or of a complex nature, seek advice as above. If possible, arrange a briefing session with all translators before translation starts. In this case supply all translators with a copy of the English several days prior to the briefing session. If the translated material is to be published, you will need to decide at the beginning on the format and presentation.

When the content is finalized, write your text in clear, unambiguous English, avoiding medical or specialist health jargon.

- We recommend that you include the title, headings, and sub-headings in English and the other language, so that English-only health staff can find their way around the text even when it's in another language.
- Indicate to translators and typesetters by marking on the text any words that you want left in English only (e.g., titles of health staff, community health centers, addresses, phone numbers).

To quote effectively, translators and agencies need to know exact specifications: number of words, deadlines and layout requirements. Costs will be higher for urgent jobs, and for "camera ready" (print quality) work. You can ask for "copy" (photocopy) quality.

You will need to decide on

- page size, column width if a pamphlet, and how many folds
- cover, title design, and overall layout
- illustrations and how the text will fit around them
- page numbering

TRANSLATORS

Discuss rates of pay at the beginning of the project (see "Fees") for each task—e.g., translating, typesetting, proofreading.

TRANSLATION PROCEDURE

Nominate a contact person for translator inquiries, and prepare a job sheet, which you attach to each language version. It should remain attached to job documents at all times. In the job sheet include

- title of text
- name of translator (with contact details)
- name of checker (with contact details)
- language of translation
- date due for translation and date due for checking
- name and telephone number of the contact person
- instructions to translator and checker to keep a copy of the translation and keep the English text for future reference
- any layout specifications

Send out to each translator

- the job sheet
- the English text (two copies if using a checker)
- layout instructions as required

continues

Procedural Model for Arranging Your Own Translations continued

When using a checker, ask the translator to send translation and job sheet directly to the checker, together with a copy of the English text. The translator and checker should agree on changes. If there is a dispute between the translator and checker that cannot be resolved by discussion, seek a third (anonymous) opinion.

If possible, arrange for a further check by bilingual health workers, before arranging typesetting and printing.

TYPESETTING BY AN AGENCY

If you plan to have typesetting done by a multilingual typesetting agency, make sure the typesetter can demonstrate experience with multilingual work. When all languages are translated, and ready for typesetting, ask for estimates. This is especially important if you plan to include diagrams or illustrations.

When galley proofs or disks are received from the agency, send out to the translator (not checker) to proofread, together with the original copy, a return envelope, and the job sheet showing date due back. After proofreading, return to agency if corrections are needed.

When returned from agency, check that each correction has been made—if you are unable to do this, you may have to send the corrected proofs to the translator a second time. You will need to pay an additional proofreading fee.

TYPING

If translations are to be typed, select the typists; many translators have word processing facilities, so check with them first. Provide clear and complete layout instructions and typing paper if special paper is being used. Follow the same proofreading procedures as above.

When preparing final typewritten or typeset material for printers, do not fax or photocopy as this will affect the quality and sometimes the layout dimensions, resulting in your final version being of poor quality.

PUBLISHING/PRINTING

On final proofs, check all English headings, publication numbers, page numbers (if included), and ensure the language is clearly identified on the front cover in English.

Decide on size of print runs, paper weight, and obtain estimate from printer(s).

It may be useful to print each language on a different colored paper for easy identification by handlers and health workers.

Include the date of publication but do not include names of staff, to avoid outdated material being distributed to the public or having to be reprinted.

FEES

Fees will depend on the number of tasks undertaken by translators/typesetters. Fees are normally calculated on the number of words translated, checked, or typeset (English text). Fees are usually paid at completion of each stage of the process rather than at the end of the complete project. Fees will need to be negotiated with each translator.

Source: Procedural Model for Arranging Your Own Translations of Health Education Material, NSW Multicultural Health Communication Service, Sydney, Australia, July 1999.

Translation Checklist

PREPARING TO DO TRANSLATIONS

1. ____ Designate staff person to coordinate translation procedure.

STEPS IN THE TRANSLATION PROCESS

1. ____ Determine what materials need to be translated and their reading levels.
2. ____ Decide what language(s) to use.
3. ____ Assess literacy level of target group.
4. ____ Develop a list of key health messages to be included.
5. ____ Develop a timeline for translation completion.
6. ____ Choose translators from existing pool of qualified contractors.
7. ____ Review and assign health education material to translators (explain key messages and unfamiliar medical terms) and review translation process.
8. ____ Estimate cost. Current contract rates are $0.18 per translated word. The rate for editing already-translated material is $20.00 per hour.

Count the number of English words, add 20% of the total (the translated document will have more words), and multiply by 2 to include initial and back translations. Typesetting and printing will be an additional and separate cost.

Formula: Number of English words × 1.2 × $0.18 × 2 = Total Estimated Cost

9. ____ Obtain first draft from first translator and give to second translator.
10. ____ Obtain back translation (into English) from second translator.
11. ____ Negotiate any changes/discrepancies, if needed.
12. ____ Field test translated material for cultural appropriateness and make any changes.
13. ____ Have translator do a final review for typographical and other errors before printing.

NOTES:

Source: Colorado Department of Public Health and Environment Family and Community Health Services Division, *Journey towards Cultural Competency: Lessons Learned,* National Maternal and Child Health Resource Center on Cultural Competency, Texas Department of Health, Austin, Texas.

Procedural Guidelines for Checkers Receiving Translations

The task of the checker is to check that the translator has accurately transferred into the other language, in the same register, the meaning of all that the author wrote in English, and to report on any shortcomings of the translation. Health information should be understandable to the general public, and if you find that a translated text reads like medical information that the public would not understand, you should bring this to the attention of the project coordinator. It is not your role to change the level of language (register) or the translator's style.

Before you accept a checking assignment, it is important to agree on exactly what you are being asked to do, and the fee to be paid for the checking work. If at any stage you think that extra work is required, such as retranslation or extra typesetting or layout, inform the project coordinator and agree on any extra payment, before you do the work, to avoid any misunderstanding.

If, after you start checking, you find the translation is of a very low standard, contact your project coordinator immediately, for instructions on whether you should complete the checking.

The project coordinator will usually contact the original translator to discuss your report, so please provide a contact telephone number, and make yourself available to discuss proposed changes with the project coordinator, or with the original translator, depending on the circumstances. If you prefer not to talk to the translator, or to remain anonymous, you must inform the project coordinator at the beginning.

Following is a standard procedure for checkers to follow, consisting of seven steps. The first stage (Steps 1–3) involves careful perusal of the full text in the other language and then a meticulous comparison with the original English. The second stage (Steps 4–7) entails preparing a brief report in which details of your suggested corrections are provided. Both the English and language version should contain clearly marked details of errors or proposed corrections.

An example of how to prepare your report is provided at the end of this document.

- Step 1—Firstly, do not read the English version (put it aside to read later). Read the translation right through to assess the quality and suitability of the language version. By reading only the language version at first, you should gain a general impression of the ideas expressed in the other language, without your judgment being affected by what the English version says.
- Step 2—As you read, make a mental note of where you have to pause to get the meaning, or if any part of the translation is not possible to comprehend.
- Step 3—Now read the English version right through, and compare the translation with the English. If you think the translation is not a high enough standard to be published as health information for members of the public, please inform the project coordinator immediately to discuss whether you should continue the checking process.
- Step 4—Does the translated document convey the same meaning as the original English? Does it contain all, and only, the essential messages that were in the English original, and is it easy to follow? Are medical terms accurately translated into language that will be understood by the intended reader? Would the readers of the translated version, who only speak the other language, understand everything and be comfortable with the way it is expressed? Comment in your report (see Step 6).

Are there any mistranslations, additions or omissions, or unclear messages? Are there any serious mistakes that distort or cloud the meaning of any part of the text? Identify and mark any significant inaccuracies and write on your copy of the translation what you think it should say in your language. Also include brief explanatory comments in your report (see Step 6).

continues

Procedural Guidelines for Checkers Receiving Translations continued

Use the following symbols as you mark the language version.

Mistranslations—On the language version use wavy underlining to indicate any single words or phrases that you consider have been mistranslated, or where you consider the meaning is not clear. If there are several items, mark the section with a vertical wavy line in the margin. On the English version, use the same wavy underlining to indicate the corresponding words or phrases that you marked in the language version as mistranslated.

Omissions—If there is information that was in the English text but which the translator has unjustifiably left out in the target language

–indicate *in the language version* with ^ at the beginning and end ^ of where information (words or concepts) has been left out

–indicate if any headings or punctuation has been left out and provide details in your report

–underline on the English version the words or sections that the translator omitted to translate, and write 'omitted' in the margin

Additions—If any extra information has been added that was not in the English original, indicate with + and + at beginning and end of what has been added and give details in your report.

Grammatical, punctuation, and typographical errors—Please indicate and correct any grammatical errors, incorrect gender usage, mistakes in spelling, punctuation, script, accents, incorrect or inconsistent capitalization, or hyphenation.

–Underline with a straight line any grammatical mistakes, or incorrect word order.

–Indicate any missing punctuation or accents.

–Put a slash through spelling or typing mistakes [/] and correct in margin.

- Step 5—Are there any problems with general presentation, format and layout, font size, spacing, or alignment of text? Proofread carefully to make sure that all dates and times are correct, also the format of postal addresses, codes, etc., that titles and headings (including any in English) are consistent and complete. It is important to check that any English words or information included in the translated text has been spelled and inserted correctly. If there are mistakes, please make corrections on your copy and provide details in your report.
- Step 6—First part of checker's report: General comments
  Start your typewritten report in English (see sample at end) with general comments in one or two paragraphs on the quality of the translation. In these paragraphs say whether you think the translation is satisfactory overall. Comment, for example, if it has been translated "word for word" in a way that makes the meaning unclear. If you feel that the way the English original was written has led to problems for the translator, please make this clear. Remember that the project coordinator may not speak the language concerned, and is relying on you to explain why you consider the translation unsatisfactory. Suitability of language: Are the forms of address and genders used appropriate to the language concerned? If in your opinion there is anything in the translation that may not be culturally appropriate, or may offend some readers, please explain in your report.
- Step 7—Second part of checker's report: Essential corrections recommended
  Please provide comments and back translations where needed (see example below).
  Go through the corrections that you marked on the language and English versions in Step 4 and give each correction a number in the margin (in order, one for each correction). Insert the same numbers to correspond on the English version.

continues

Procedural Guidelines for Checkers Receiving Translations continued

Provide your comments as shown in the Example Report.

Column 1: Include the number of the correction concerned.

Column 2: Type in the relevant English word or phrase.

Column 3: Include back translation into English of the relevant word, phrase, or passage.

Column 4: Provide comments to explain the nature of the mistake.

EXAMPLE REPORT

Title of document:

General comments:

Marked on text	English source text (word or phrase)	Back translation into English of what was translated	Comments (type of mistake and why correction needed)
1	If asthma occurs suddenly and severely	Since asthma occurs suddenly	mistranslation
2	. . . like catching a cold or flu	0	omitted
3	AND SO ON . . .		

Source: Procedural Guidelines for Checkers Receiving Translations, NSW Multicultural Health Communication Service, Sydney, Australia, July 1999.

Procedural Guidelines for Health Staff Checking Translations

Health information written in English for the public should be clearly expressed in language that can be generally understood, and the same applies for information translated into other languages. For all translation projects intended to reach a wide audience, we recommend that health staff ask a qualified translator to check the quality of the translation. Translation is a complex process and even the best translator can inadvertently make mistakes, especially working to tight deadlines, or if the original English is unclear. Checking may add to project costs in the short term but in the long term often saves money, as any mistakes found can be corrected before funds have been spent on printing and distribution. It can also be used to ensure that a text, and any illustrations, are clearly laid out and appropriately presented to match the needs of the intended readers.

If the original English text was written in a medical register (in language at a level used by health professionals when discussing medical matters with each other), it will be translated into medical language. If checkers find that a translated text is written in medical jargon that will not be familiar to people who speak the other language, they can bring it to the attention of the project coordinator. In these circumstances it may well be that the English will need to be revised (then retranslated) to ensure it is understandable to average readers.

WHAT DO WE MEAN BY CHECKING?

Checking involves review by a qualified translator of a translation for the accurate, appropriate transfer of meaning from one language to another. It involves a lot more than just proofreading for spelling, accents (diacritics), and punctuation. The task of the checker is to check that the meaning of all that the author wrote in English has been clearly conveyed by the original translator in the other language in the same register (level of language), and to report any translation errors that they consider must be corrected.

WHAT IS THE CHECKER'S ROLE?

- Check that the meaning is clear; do not make changes to alter the translator's style.
- Check for overall accuracy—whether all the information in the English is included in the translation.
- Identify any mistranslations—whether there are serious mistakes that distort or cloud the meaning of any part of the text, or any inappropriate omissions or additions.
- Find and correct any grammatical or typographical errors.
- Provide a short report, typewritten in English with explanations in English, of comments and corrections (with examples in other language as needed).
- Comment, if requested, on the presentation of the text and illustrations in the language version—whether it is appropriate, or is of a different quality from the English version.
- Alert the project coordinator to anything that may be culturally unacceptable, or may even cause offense, and to suggest how it could be expressed more appropriately for the readership.

WHAT IS THE PROJECT COORDINATOR'S ROLE?

Supervise the checking process, contact checkers, negotiate tasks to be done, follow up on corrections suggested, negotiate fees, and arrange payments.

continues

Procedural Guidelines for Health Staff Checking Translations continued

STEPS TO FOLLOW AT THE START OF THE PROJECT

- Establish whether the translation is available on paper only, or if on disk, obtain the disk and details of software and hardware used by the translator in each language.
- Decide exactly what you want the checker to check (e.g., content only, or presentation as well, or any illustrations).
- Decide what further steps you will take once you have the checker's report.
- Do you have funds set aside to pay for changes, retranslation, or retypesetting?*
- Will you ask the checker to discuss corrections with the translator?
- Will you ask the checker or the original translator to retype, if the translation is on paper?
- Will you ask the checker or the original translator to make changes, if on disk?
- Count the number of words in the English text on which the translation is based (this is the usual basis on which fees are calculated for translation, checking, retranslating, and typesetting).

- Identify who wrote the English and how they can be contacted if necessary.
- Find out whether the translator was asked to leave some terms or titles in English.
- Calculate the checking fee per language.
- Factor in possible costs of retranslation or new typesetting or formatting.
- Locate checkers—contact a professional translator for each language asking if he or she has accreditation at the professional level into the language(s) concerned.
- Agree with the checker on procedures to follow, fees, and timetable.
- Establish that the checker is available to discuss proposed changes with the original translator and ask the checker for a contact telephone number.
- If checkers prefer to remain anonymous, they should inform the project coordinator before the work begins.
- Confirm details in writing—details of the job, fee to be paid, deadlines, and associated conditions. Contact the original translator to discuss the checker's report.

NOTES:

---

*The original translator should accept responsibility for mistakes and should not charge for retyping corrections. But if you ask the checker to retype and lay out part or all of the text because of a translator's errors, you should be prepared to pay the checker for the extra work.

Source: Procedural Guidelines for Health Staff Checking Translations, NSW Multicultural Health Communication Service, Sydney, Australia, July 1999.

GUIDELINES FOR ASSESSING A PROGRAM'S CULTURAL COMPETENCE*

A careful consideration of the following guidelines or indicators can help you in developing, implementing, and evaluating the cultural aspects of a health promotion program.

These guidelines or indicators have been designed to raise awareness and to stimulate thinking about the important role that culture plays in successful health promotion programs and activities. They should be expanded and tailored to your program or organization.

Organizations that are engaged in health promotion activities must often balance money, staff, and time. Following guidelines such as these may seem too expensive and time consuming. These problems may not be easy to solve and may require dedicated and creative solutions. But it is well worth the effort because a culturally competent program and organization will help to create strong and sound health promotion efforts.

Experience or Track Record of Involvement with the Target Audience

The sponsoring organization should have a documented history of positive programmatic involvement with the population or community to be served. The organization's staff, its board, and volunteers should have a history of involvement with the target population or community to be addressed that is verifiable by the general cultural group and by the specific community to be served.

Training and Staffing

The staff of the organization should have training in cultural sensitivity and in specific cultural patterns of the community proposed for services. Staff should be identified who are prepared to train and translate the community cultural patterns to other staff members.

There should be clear cultural objectives for staff and for staff development. These objectives can be demonstrated by a staff training plan that accomplishes the following:

- increases and/or maintains the cultural competency of staff members
- clearly articulates standards for cultural competency, including credibility in hiring practices, and calls for periodic evaluations and demonstrations of the cultural and community-specific experience of staff members

Emphasis should be placed on staffing the initiative with people who are familiar with, or who are themselves members of, the community to be served.

---

*Source: Center for Substance Abuse, "Technical Assistance Bulletin: Following Specific Guidelines Will Help You Assess Cultural Competence in Program Design, Application, and Management," U.S. Department of Health and Human Services, Public Health Service, Substance Abuse and Mental Health Services Administration, Washington, D.C., September 1994.

Community Representation

The community targeted to receive services should be a planned participant in all phases of program design. There should be an established mechanism to provide members of the target group with opportunities to influence and help shape the program's proposed activities and interventions. A community advisory council or board of directors of the organization (with legitimate and working agreements) with decision-making authority should be established to affect the course and direction of the proposed program. Members of the targeted cultural group should be represented on the advisory council and organizational board of directors. The procedures for making contributions or changes to the policies and procedures of the project should be described and made known to all parties.

Language

If an organization is providing services to a multilinguistic population, there should be multilinguistic resources, including use of skilled bilingual and bicultural translators whenever a significant percentage of the target community is more comfortable with a language other than English. There should be printed and audiovisual materials sufficient for the proposed program. If translations from standard English to another language are to be used, the translation should be done by individuals who know the nuances of the language as well as the formal structure. All translations should be carefully pretested with the target audience.

Materials

It should be demonstrated that audiovisual materials, public service announcements, training guides, print materials, and other materials to be used in the program are culturally appropriate or will be made culturally consistent with the community to be served. Pretesting with the target audience and gatekeepers should provide feedback from community representatives about the cultural appropriateness of the materials under development.

Evaluation

Program evaluation methods and instruments should be consistent with the cultural norms of the group or groups being served. There should be a rationale for the use of the evaluation instruments that are chosen. Include a discussion of the validity of the instruments in terms of the culture of the specific group or groups targeted for interventions. If the instruments have been imported from another project using a different cultural group, there should be adequate evaluation and/or revision of the instruments so that they are not demonstrably culturally specific to the target group(s). The evaluators should be sensitized to the culture and familiar with the culture whenever possible and practical.

Implementation

There should be objective evidence/indicators that the organization understands the cultural aspects of the community that will contribute to the program's success and knows how to recognize and avoid pitfalls.

Cultural Competency Checklist for Organizations and Institutions

I. GENERAL INFORMATION

Please √ the statement(s) that best describe your organization.

Policies are:

___ All created at state level
___ Some created at state level
___ Few or none created at state level

Procedures are:

___ All created at state level
___ Some created at state level
___ Few or none created at state level

II. DEMOGRAPHIC INFORMATION

Please indicate the percentage of individuals with the following characteristics who are served in your program compared to the percentage of individuals who reside in your state who are of the same age.

Population Characteristics

	White	Black	Hispanic	Haitian	Native American	Asian or Pacific Islander	Other
% Served by Program							
% Residing in State							

continues

Cultural Competency Checklist continued

III. POLICY/PROCEDURE INFORMATION

Please √ the correct answer.

Individuals from cultural groups have input into the development of policies.   —— Yes   —— No

Individuals from cultural groups have input into the development of procedures.   —— Yes   —— No

If answered no, please proceed to Section IV. If answered yes to either of the above questions, please complete the next section.

Please √ the appropriate area(s) that indicates the degree of input into a particular policy/procedure area by individuals from cultural groups and their frequency of review into the policy/procedural area.

Level of Authority and Review

	No Authority	Review/Make Recommendations	Modify Policy/ Procedure	Develop Policy/ Procedure	Review Annually
Policy procedure area					
All policies/procedures					
Eligibility policies/procedures					
Service policies/procedures					
Training policies/procedures					
Staff recruitment policies/ procedures					
Provider recruitment policies/ procedures					
Quality assurance policies/ procedures					
General administrative policies/ procedures					
Policies relating to cultural competence					

How are staff made aware of policies?

—— Inservice education

—— Routing of policy to each individual staff member

—— Posting of policy in local offices

—— Other (specify): ____

continues

Cultural Competency Checklist continued

IV. CASELOAD ASSIGNMENTS   Please √ all methods that apply.

___ Random Assignment   ___ Geography   ___ Cultural Background   ___ Level of Care
___ Other (specify): _____

V. RECRUITMENT/PROVIDER CONSIDERATIONS   Please √ Yes or No for each question.

___ Yes ___ No   If a position will serve culturally diverse groups, does the position description contain requirements for training and/or experience with cultural groups?

___ Yes ___ No   Does your program use certain recruitment methods to hire an individual with experience serving particular cultural groups?

___ Yes ___ No   Do you involve an individual(s) with a similar cultural background in selecting individuals to serve particular cultural groups?

___ Yes ___ No   Do you involve individuals from various cultural backgrounds in the development of inservice training programs or educational materials related to particular cultural groups?

VI. SERVICE PROVISION   Please √ services that are provided by your program for each individual group.

	White	Black	Hispanic	Haitian	Native American	Asian or Pacific Islander	Other
Translation							
Educational material							
Special outreach services for cultural groups							
Inservice training about cultural values							

continues

Cultural Competency Checklist *continued*

VII. PARENT/FAMILY INVOLVEMENT

Please √ Yes or No to the following questions.

Do you allow community representatives from various cultural groups to have input in your organization?   ___ Yes   ___ No

If yes, please answer the following questions. If no, proceed to Section VIII.

Are there clear roles and responsibilities for the community representatives concerning cultural competency issues?   ___ Yes   ___ No

Cultural competence responsibilities for community representatives include the following:

Training/skill building   ___ Yes   ___ No

Developing policy or procedures   ___ Yes   ___ No

Developing educational materials   ___ Yes   ___ No

Serving on advisory boards or councils   ___ Yes   ___ No

Doing quality assurance   ___ Yes   ___ No

Developing forms   ___ Yes   ___ No

Providing advice to families   ___ Yes   ___ No

VIII. ADDITIONAL INFORMATION

Please note any questions or concerns that you may have that were not addressed in this survey:

_____

_____

_____

_____

_____

_____

_____

Source: *Journey towards Cultural Competency: Lessons Learned*, National Maternal and Child Health Resource Center on Cultural Competency, Texas Department of Health, Austin, Texas.

Checklist for Cross-Cultural Health Promotion

PREPARING YOUR PROGRAM

☐ Understand your own cultural values and biases.

☐ Acquire basic knowledge of cultural values, health beliefs, and nutrition practices for client groups you routinely serve.

☐ Be respectful of, interested in, and understanding of other cultures without being judgmental.

ENHANCING COMMUNICATION

☐ Determine the level of fluency in English and arrange for an interpreter, if needed.

☐ Ask how the client prefers to be addressed.

☐ Allow the client to choose seating for comfortable personal space and eye contact.

☐ Avoid body language that may be offensive or misunderstood.

☐ Speak directly to the client, whether an interpreter is present or not.

☐ Choose a speech rate and style that promotes understanding and demonstrates respect for the client.

☐ Avoid slang, technical jargon, and complex sentences.

☐ Use open-ended questions or questions phrased in several ways to obtain information.

☐ Determine the client's reading ability before using written materials in the process.

PROMOTING POSITIVE CHANGE

☐ Build on cultural practices, reinforcing those that are positive and promoting change only in those that are harmful.

☐ Check for client understanding and acceptance of recommendations.

☐ Remember that not all seeds of knowledge fall into a fertile environment to produce change. Of those that do, some will take years to germinate. Be patient and provide support in a culturally appropriate environment to promote positive health behavior.

NOTES:

Source: *Cross-Cultural Counseling: A Guide for Nutrition and Health Counselors*, U.S. Department of Agriculture/U.S. Department of Health and Human Services, Nutrition Education Committee for Maternal and Child Nutrition Publications, 1986. Reviewed and approved for reprinting, 1990.

Promoting Cultural Diversity and Cultural Competency: Self-Assessment Checklist for Personnel Providing Services to Children with Special Health Needs and Their Families

This checklist was developed by HRSA's Maternal and Child Health Bureau/Children with Special Health Needs component of the National Center for Cultural Competence. It is for personnel providing health services and supports to children with special health needs and their families and is intended to heighten the awareness and sensitivity of personnel to the importance of cultural diversity and cultural competence in human service settings. The checklist provides concrete examples of the kinds of values and practices that foster such an environment. Directions: Select A, B, or C for each item listed below.

A = Things I do frequently   B = Things I do occasionally   C = Things I do rarely or never

Physical environment, materials, and resources

_____ 1. I display pictures, posters, and other materials that reflect the cultures and ethnic backgrounds of children and families served by my program or agency.

_____ 2. I ensure that magazines, brochures, and other printed materials in reception areas are of interest to and reflect the different cultures of children and families served by my program or agency.

_____ 3. When using videos, films, or other media resources for health education, treatment, or other interventions, I ensure they reflect the cultures of children and families served by my program or agency.

_____ 4. When using food during an assessment, I ensure that meals provided include foods that are unique to the cultural and ethnic backgrounds of children and families served by my program or agency.

_____ 5. I ensure that toys and other play accessories in reception areas and those that are used during assessment are representative of the various cultural and ethnic groups within the local community and the society in general.

Communication styles

_____ 6. For children who speak languages or dialects other than English, I attempt to learn and use key words in their language so that I am better able to communicate with them during assessment, treatment, or other interventions.

_____ 7. I attempt to determine any familial colloquialisms used by children and families that may impact on assessment, treatment, or other interventions.

_____ 8. I use visual aids, gestures, and physical prompts in my interactions with children who have limited English proficiency.

_____ 9. I use bilingual staff or trained volunteers to serve as interpreters during assessment, meetings, or other events for parents who would require this level of assistance.

_____ 10. When interacting with parents who have limited English proficiency, I always keep in mind that

_____ limitations in English proficiency are in no way a reflection of their level of intellectual functioning

_____ their limited ability to speak the language of the dominant culture has no bearing on their ability to communicate effectively in their language of origin

_____ they may or may not be literate in their language of origin or English

continues

Promoting Cultural Diversity and Cultural Competency continued

_____ 11. When possible, I ensure that all notices and communiqués to parents are written in their language of origin.

_____ 12. I understand that it may be necessary to use alternatives to written communications for some families, as word of mouth may be a preferred method of receiving information.

Values and attitudes

_____ 13. I avoid imposing values that may conflict or be inconsistent with those of cultures or ethnic groups other than my own.

_____ 14. In group therapy or treatment situations, I discourage children from using racial and ethnic slurs by helping them understand that certain words can hurt others.

_____ 15. I screen books, movies, and other media resources for negative cultural, ethnic, or racial stereotypes before sharing them with children and their parents served by my program or agency.

_____ 16. I intervene in an appropriate manner when I observe other staff or parents within my program or agency engaging in behaviors that show cultural insensitivity or prejudice.

_____ 17. I understand and accept that family is defined differently by different cultures (e.g., extended family members, fictive kin, godparents).

_____ 18. I recognize and accept that individuals from culturally diverse backgrounds may desire varying degrees of acculturation into the dominant culture.

_____ 19. I accept and respect that male-female roles in families may vary significantly among different cultures (e.g., who makes major decisions for the family, play, and social interactions expected of male and female children).

_____ 20. I understand that age and life cycle factors must be considered in interactions with individuals and families (e.g., high value placed on the decisions of elders or the role of the eldest male in families).

_____ 21. Even though my professional or moral viewpoints may differ, I accept the family / parents as the ultimate decision makers for services and supports for their children.

_____ 22. I recognize that the meaning or value of medical treatment and health education may vary greatly among cultures.

_____ 23. I accept that religion and other beliefs may influence how families respond to illnesses, disease, and death.

_____ 24. I recognize and accept that folk and religious beliefs may influence a family's reaction and approach to a child born with a disability or later diagnosed with a disability or special health care needs.

_____ 25. I understand that traditional approaches to disciplining children are influenced by culture.

_____ 26. I understand that families from different cultures will have different expectations of their children for acquiring toileting, dressing, feeding, and other self-help skills.

_____ 27. I accept and respect that customers and beliefs about food, its value, preparation, and use are different from culture to culture.

_____ 28. Before visiting or providing services in the home setting, I seek information on acceptable behaviors, courtesies, customs, and expectations that are unique to families of specific cultures and ethnic groups served by my program or agency.

continues

Promoting Cultural Diversity and Cultural Competency continued

____ 29. I seek information from family members or other key community informants, which will assist in service adaptation to respond to the needs and preferences of culturally and ethnically diverse children and families served by my program or agency.

____ 30. I advocate for the review of my program's or agency's mission statement, goals, policies, and procedures to ensure that they incorporate principles and practices that promote cultural diversity and cultural competence.

There is no answer key. However, if you frequently responded "C", you may not necessarily demonstrate values and engage in practices that promote a culturally diverse and culturally competent service delivery system for children and families.

NOTES:

Source: Tawara D. Goode, Georgetown University Child Development Center UAP. Adapted from "Promoting Cultural Competence and Cultural Diversity in Early Intervention and Early Childhood Settings" (Revised 1999).

AFRICAN AMERICANS: RELEVANT SOCIOCULTURAL ISSUES*

The sociohistorical relationship between African Americans and Anglo-Americans has left broad gaps in levels of trust and communication. Cultural differences, access to services, poverty, and level of education are only some of the barriers to effective medical treatment and health education. Sensitivity to some of these issues depends in part on understanding some basic sociocultural characteristics that influence health practices by African Americans.

For example, adverse environmental and economic factors can increase stress and lead to poor health. Many African Americans live in conditions of poverty that prevent their access to and utilization of conventional health care. It is important to recognize that many of these factors are caused by barriers to socioeconomic mobility. An awareness of the socioeconomic issues that affect minorities can assist the health educator in being sensitive to the needs of the client in terms of both physical and emotional support. In addition, health educators should be informed about the common diseases more prevalent in the African American population.

Family Relationships

African American culture is influenced in part by African heritage. The extended family and interdependent kinship ties are characteristic of both rural and urban communities. Health care is often viewed as a family responsibility, not just that of the individual and health care provider. The provider therefore can often solicit other family members as aides in caring for an ill African American. Interdependence and interchangeability of roles within a family setting are often present in African American families. Therefore, decision making within the family may rest with either a male or female as head of the household.

Religious Beliefs

Because religion is an important aspect in African American culture, members of the clergy are an integral part of the community. In many communities, they are trusted by and familiar with family members to such a degree that they can be helpful to health educators as liaisons between a family and a health practitioner or institution.

Because religion is such an integral part of the culture, illness may be viewed as punishment by God for sins. Therefore, the health educator should be alerted that feelings of guilt may be influential in the client's perception of an illness. In such instances, the health educator may want to consult with, or suggest that the client meet with, a member of the clergy in addition to health care providers. In some instances, religious beliefs and practices have been perceived as mental illness; for example, a client may report hearing or talking with God. This, however, might just be an expression of a client's religious belief.

---

*Source: *Cross-Cultural Counseling: A Guide for Nutrition and Health Counselors*, U.S. Department of Agriculture/U.S. Department of Health and Human Services, Nutrition Education Committee for Maternal and Child Nutrition Publications, 1986. Reviewed and approved for reprinting, 1990.

Much of African American folk medicine comprises elements from both Christian and traditional African tribal religions. Traditional healing practices include mystic (supernatural) phenomena, psychological support, and herbal remedies. Herbal practices are found in rural and urban areas. In urban centers, religious and folk medicine practitioners provide psychological and spiritual support.

In urban areas, African American spiritual advisors and folk medicine practitioners are often called on to relieve anxieties and fears. In this way, they perform the role of psychotherapists. Charms and other objects may be worn for protection or as a form of preventive medicine. For example, a small bag containing herbs or other elements may be worn to ward off evil spirits.

Clients who express belief in witchcraft should be taken seriously. It is helpful for the health educator to find out why the client feels he or she has been a victim of witchcraft, because this information can help the provider determine diagnosis or treatment of an illness. African American clients may be reluctant to talk about witchcraft or folk practices they have used. However, to provide appropriate treatment, it is important for the health care provider to ask specifically which healing practices have been used in order to determine openness to conventional health care.

Communication

The dialect used by some African Americans is an integral part of the culture. It has been influenced by English and African languages as well as by geographic location and social factors. The health terminology used by the health educator can be confusing or misunderstood by a client even though he or she speaks English. It is important for health educators to speak clearly and to explain terminology when discussing matters concerning medical treatment. A familiarity with lay medical terminology and its differences from scientific terminology can help avoid misunderstandings in communication and misinterpretation of symptoms the client describes. It also is important for the health educator not to try to adopt Black English unnaturally, because this may be viewed by an African American client as both patronizing and inappropriate.

NOTES:

AFRICAN CULTURAL PATTERNS IN PARENTING AFRICAN AMERICAN CHILDREN*

Cultural patterns are those patterns of values and lifestyles indicative of a race of people. African American culture has held a traditional value system and a common-sense approach to life regarding respect for elders, spontaneity, restraint, responsibility for other people and a sense of appropriateness, cooperation, and a sense of excellence.

Therefore, African American parents tend to stress the need for overachieving, mutual aid through kinship, and a strong belief in God. They also try to raise their children to live in a dominant, white society without becoming white people themselves. So, there are certain African culture patterns that African American parents use in parenting their children. These patterns are recognizable and are very common in African American families.

- Cooperation versus competition is often taught through compliance training that teaches obedience and conformity.
- Children are involved in daily work activities that require cooperation with other family members.
- Children are taught to comply with requests that do not offer immediate tangible rewards or that provide rewards that are shared.
- Children are taught a *care syndrome*, in which they are their brother's keeper.
- Children have more body contact (are breastfed longer than Anglo-American children, are held longer before and after waking, sleep with their mother longer, and learn to embrace their relatives). Thus, they grow up with a more human social network and expect to receive affection and comfort as well as give it.
- Children learn the responsibility of caring for younger children.
- Use of the extended family system provides children with male models through uncles, cousins, brothers, and others.
- Children learn the survival of the tribe (family) and oneness with nature.
- Children are taught oneness with the universe.
- Children are taught that there is a supreme being or a spiritual force that is greater than themselves.

Cultural Awareness in African American Families

When African Americans are not culturally aware and they begin to assimilate into Anglo-American culture, the family's good mental health begins to deteriorate. To maintain balance and family wholeness, African Americans must draw again the strength from their culture. Some experts argue that the more ignorant African Americans are of their own culture, the more problematic it becomes for them to live in a Anglo-American–dominant society.

---

*Source: *Training African American Parents for Success*, East End Neighborhood House, Cleveland, Ohio, © 1992.

African American cultural awareness is promoted in the following circumstances:

- African American children are taught the importance of exceeding white children's behavior and performance. Falling short would reflect unfavorably upon the group.
- African American children are given strict guidelines for public behavior, as loud, boisterous behavior could cause whites to generalize that *all* African Americans are that way.
- African American parents sacrifice to give their children what they themselves did not have, for example, college education.
- Material use of reinforcement, consultation, or talks and sensitivity to the child's feelings stimulate intellectual growth of younger children. This material child-rearing practice is important to African American child development.
- The preservation and transmission of racial heritage, celebrating African American history, is encouraged.
- An alternative frame of reference is provided through a parent's concept of growing up in white America and the parent's view of how to resolve the basic conflict between the European world view and the African world view.
- African American children learn about the duality of socialization between Anglo- and African American societies, such as speaking black vernacular in their immediate circle and standard English in other circles.
- Positive self-concept is promoted by displaying family pictures as well as pictures of famous African Americans or scenes depicting African American culture.
- Positive, stimulating experiences are provided for African American children.

NOTES:

HEALTH EDUCATION FOR AFRICAN AMERICAN PARENTS*

African Americans face difficult challenges in ensuring their families' optimum health. Conventional health care is not always an option, because many families are uninsured or underinsured. The traditional sources of health advice, experienced relatives, are often not available because of the demise of the extended family.

Some families live in environments that are toxic, such as polluted urban areas and lead-filled homes.

Budgetary restrictions, compounded with a lack of nutritional knowledge, also force parents to feed their families diets that result in a high incidence of cardiovascular disease, diabetes, obesity, and cancer.

Health professionals need to help parents believe in their abilities as health educators, advocates, and caregivers.

Central to physical and mental health for most African Americans is spirituality. Spirituality, or a belief in a supreme being, is the common strand that binds most African Americans. It affects how they view each other, social customs, health, and when and how they receive health care. Spirituality is central to parenting as it is the basis for family value systems.

Health Resources and Education

Paramount to achieving optimum family health is health information and awareness. Parents should be aware of basic first aid, signs of ill health, and when it is appropriate to seek professional advice. This information can be obtained through practical manuals on child care in the popular press. In addition, professional advice can be obtained free of charge in most areas from well-baby clinics, free clinics, emergency departments, and health departments. Parents also should become aware of health resources in their community.

Parents should be encouraged to develop relationships with experienced parents in their neighborhoods, schools, and churches. These parents can be invaluable sources of practical advice. Health educators should stress, however, that when in doubt, parents should seek professional advice.

Home Health Hazards

The leading cause of death and injury of children under 12 is home health hazards. Home health hazards are conditions in the home that could cause injury to all family members, but they are the most dangerous to children. They include, but are not limited to, lead paint poisoning; unsafe, slippery tubs and pools; stairs and windows; and small toys or other objects that can be ingested.

African American children in urban areas are at high risk for lead poisoning. Before 1970, lead paint was commonly used to paint houses, furniture, and food packages. The use of lead paint is now banned, yet many children are poisoned by eating paint that is peeling or chipped (on window sills, walls, or stair rails) and plaster that lead has leaked into from paint. If ingested undetected over long periods, lead can cause brain damage and, in rare cases, death.

---

*Source: *Training African American Parents for Success*, East End Neighborhood House, Cleveland, Ohio, © 1992.

All children under ten years of age should be tested for lead poisoning on a regular basis. As a precautionary measure, parents should inspect the exterior and interior of their homes for signs of possible lead paint contamination: old peeling paint on any surface, paint-covered windowsills and handrails, and exposed old plaster. Samples can be taken to the local health department to be checked for lead. Parents can also repaint all old painted furniture, especially cribs, with nontoxic paint.

While lead poison prevention is a major concern to many African American parents, health educators must also emphasize prevention of other home health hazards. Childproofing one's home can successfully prevent accidents and poisonings.

Human Sexuality

Sexuality begins at birth and ends at death. Children's ideas about human sexuality are constantly changing, based on external and internal forces.

Issues surrounding sexuality are often difficult for African Americans to discuss. Their parents often did not discuss sexuality issues, and many parents remain uninformed.

The key to teaching children about sexuality is for parents to become aware of their feelings, their sexuality, and how to discuss sexuality with their children. It is important that parents begin educating their children on sexuality early, beginning with teaching children the correct names for body parts and providing information when requested.

Nutrition

Historically, African American rites revolved around food. African American society is based on feasting, cooking, and raising food. Unfortunately, many African Americans have paid a high price for this lifestyle. More than two out of five African Americans have high blood pressure, their cancer rates are rising, and over one-third are overweight.

Economically disadvantaged African Americans must eat what is available at a low cost. This is not often fresh fruit, lean meat, and seafood. Health educators must encourage parents to provide low-cost nutritional alternatives to their families by adapting traditional foods to reduce salt and fat intake and by introducing new foods to their families. Simple changes in diet can include substituting herbs for meat in vegetable dishes, eating inexpensive raw vegetables such as carrots, and changing to a vegetable-based rather than a meat-based diet.

Health educators also could discuss practical assistance methods, such as growing a small garden, shopping at garden markets instead of traditional supermarkets, and developing budgeting clubs to buy items in bulk.

Making changes in nutritional habits is not easy for anyone. Further, health educators should be aware that some parents may resist change because of tradition. An easy method to encourage parents to buy into the process is to have them prepare favorite low-cost recipes, using nutritional modifications suggested by the health educator.

Chemical Dependency

Of the many challenges to the collective spirit of the African American family, chemical dependency is one of the most devastating. The pervasive use of alcohol and drugs and the glamorized lifestyle popularized by the media must be counteracted by strong prevention education by parents.

Parents can prevent drug use in their children by setting family values that emphasize drug-free behavior in all family members and by educating themselves and their children on the facts about drugs and alcohol. Preventing chemical dependency in children is important, but parents must also be aware of the signs of drug use in adult family members.

Stress

Mental well-being affects every individual's physical and emotional health. Stress is a significant part of each parent's life. When stress becomes unmanageable, parents must seek ways to lessen its effects on themselves and their families. Stress can be lessened by developing coping mechanisms, such as exercise. How parents identify and cope with stress and how they teach their children to cope with the stress are critical.

Spirituality

The essence of the African American experience is spirituality. The spirituality of African Americans affects every aspect of parenting.

Parents should provide spiritual education to their children that reflects their spiritual beliefs and use those beliefs as a basis for developing family values. Further, parents must prepare their children to live in a multifaith community. Children should be encouraged to learn about the traditions and rituals of other faiths, to see them as not wrong but just different. Children's awareness of their own spirituality and that of others gives them a world view that will prepare them for adulthood in the 21st century.

NOTES:

ASIAN AND PACIFIC AMERICANS: RELEVANT SOCIOCULTURAL ISSUES*

Among Asian and Pacific Americans are included those cultural groups that have migrated from China, Japan, Korea, and Southeast Asia, as well as Hawaii, the Philippines, Samoa, and Guam. Three general categories of Asian Americans have been identified. They represent varying degrees of acculturation and assimilation into Anglo-American culture related, to a great extent, to age at time of immigration and length of residence in the United States. Specific behavioral characteristics distinguish the three categories:

- *Category 1:* Individuals maintain traditional Asian values and behavior, which include obedience to parents, respect for authority, self-control of strong feelings, humility, praise of others, and blame of self for failure. Health- and illness-related practices manifest a balancing of Asian and Western traditions.
- *Category 2:* Individuals practice both traditional Asian and Western values and behaviors, which include a degree of respect for parents and authority, individual self-assertiveness, lack of self-effacement, and some expression of feelings. Health- and illness-related practices are predominantly Western but maintain some Asian characteristics. They are likely to be either immigrants who have been acculturated to some extent or children born in the United States of immigrants who have been exposed to both cultures.
- *Category 3:* Individuals have fully adopted Western values and behavior, which include development of individuality, openness of expression, assertiveness, independence, and self-confidence. Health- and illness-related practices approach those of middle-class Americans. This group is likely to be Asian Americans born in the United States whose parents or grandparents may also have been born in the United States.

New immigrants generally would fall into the first category. However, it is important to stress that these characteristics vary in degree according to individuals and groups, and only some of these may be present in any one culture.

Family Relationships

Family structure varies in Asian cultures. It is useful for practitioners to know whether a client is from an extended or nuclear family in order to better identify resources that are appropriate to the client in terms of family involvement in the health care and treatment process. Authority of the household can rest with the father, the mother, or both. This has implications for decision making in terms of health care, and the health educator should consult with the appropriate authority of the household when major decisions are to be made. For example, authority may rest with the father-mother pair, or decisions may be made by the father alone. In most of the cultures, a husband often will act as a spokesperson for his wife.

---

*Source: *Cross-Cultural Counseling: A Guide for Nutrition and Health Counselors,* U.S. Department of Agriculture/U.S. Department of Health and Human Services, Nutrition Education Committee for Maternal and Child Nutrition Publications, 1986. Reviewed and approved for reprinting, 1990.

Medical Beliefs and Practices

Asian and Pacific cultures are characterized by the yin-yang philosophy. Yin and yang represent opposites of each other, but are complementary in nature. A hot-cold classification of foods, as well as diseases, is generally categorized according to the balance of yin and yang, although specific classification of foods and/or diseases varies according to the particular culture. Yin diseases fall into a cold category, while yang diseases are considered hot. For example, cancer is representative of yin, a cold disease, whereas an ear infection is thought of as a hot disease, or yang. Yin illnesses would be treated by yang foods, and yang illnesses would be treated by yin foods.

NOTES:

HISPANIC AND LATIN AMERICANS: RELEVANT SOCIOCULTURAL ISSUES*

Hispanics constitute the second largest ethnic minority group in the United States. Generally, the following groups are referred to as Hispanics: Cubans, Mexican Americans or Chicanos, Mexican immigrants, Puerto Ricans, and South Americans. It must be emphasized that Hispanic cultures are diverse, with important cultural differences existing among these groups. Many of these differences are a result of extremely varied historical, social, economic, and political experiences.

Family Relationships

Identification with and unity of the family are highly valued and constitute the nucleus of Hispanic culture. Close kinship relationships characterize the family structure, which is a primary source of emotional, physical, and psychological support. Family structure may be either extended or nuclear. The nuclear family is composed of immediate members, that is, father, mother, and children. The extended family incorporates other relatives, such as the grandparents, aunts, uncles, and cousins.

Generally, authority in the Hispanic family rests with the eldest male. Most major decisions, therefore, will be made by either the father or the husband. In terms of health care, responsibility for care of an ill family member will rest with other family members. Usually, clients will have consulted with various family members before seeking outside care.

The Importance of Privacy

Modesty is highly valued. Health care professionals should take care to minimize situations in which a Hispanic client may feel compromised. In particular, communication between client and health educator should demonstrate respect for the client's needs in this area. Sensitivity to these cultural norms will help avoid embarrassment for parents and children. Interruptions of privacy during the program should always be avoided.

Religious Attitudes and Beliefs

Religious and fatalistic attitudes may influence a client's approach to an illness and its treatment. For example, the client may believe that illness is a result of punishment from God and that medical care cannot change the course or outcome of an illness. This has implications for the methods used for treatment as well as appropriate ways of communicating with the client about regimens. In terms of treatment, it is important to discuss what the client's reservations are and to identify what steps the client might be willing to take. Second, it may be useful to refer the client to a respected member of his or her religion, such as a priest, to discuss how management of a medical problem fits within the religion's framework.

---

*Source: *Cross-Cultural Counseling: A Guide for Nutrition and Health Counselors*, U.S. Department of Agriculture/U.S. Department of Health and Human Services, Nutrition Education Committee for Maternal and Child Nutrition Publications, 1986. Reviewed and approved for reprinting, 1990.

Folk medical beliefs, folk medical practitioners, and rituals are traditional Hispanic health practices. The hot-cold theory of disease organizes illnesses and cures into categories identified as either hot or cold. However, hot-cold categories vary among Hispanic groups. For example, Puerto Ricans have a "warm" classification in addition to hot and cold. Foods and herbs, as well as illnesses, are also classified in these categories. Unless the prescribed regimen fits the client's assessment of what treatment is appropriate, adherence to a regimen is likely to be minimal. Therefore, it is important for a health educator to identify the client's hypotheses about health problems and their treatment.

The *espiritista* (spiritualist) and/or *curandero* are some of the folk practitioners consulted when treatment is needed in many traditional Hispanic communities. They may be consulted before a conventional health practitioner. The health educator should ask the client whether he or she has consulted a folk practitioner and determine what folk remedies have been used.

One frequent reason for Hispanic clients' preference for traditional folk practitioners is distrust of conventional medicine and health care providers. Other factors in underutilization of conventional medical care are inadequate income, low level of education, and advanced age.

Communication

Communicating in English may be awkward or difficult for the client. It may change the client's expression of symptoms or may be misinterpreted. When language differences between Spanish-speaking clients and non–Spanish-speaking health educators exist, it is recommended that a bilingual interpreter be used. This may be a family member, a friend of the client, or a trusted individual within the community known by the client who is able to act as a liaison.

NOTES:

NATURAL SUPPORT SYSTEMS IN HISPANIC/LATINO COMMUNITIES*

What Are Natural Support Systems?

No comprehensive definition of natural support systems (NSSs) exists, but the term encompasses myriad formal and informal systems of care that help people in need. Broadly defined, NSSs are social structures that include family and friends as well as shopkeepers, vendors, folk healers, police, clergy, teachers, recreation volunteers, mutual help groups, community leaders, and social clubs.

Natural support systems are unique in that they are generally not recognized as part of a service provider system. Historically, prevention program elements have been compartmentalized and "professionalized" so that drug prevention programs are run by drug prevention professionals, education programs are run by educators, and health programs are run by medical professionals. NSSs, on the other hand, employ alternative sources of support by using the resources, earned authority, and respect of the community to influence people's physical, emotional, and spiritual health. For this reason, adding NSSs to existing prevention programs represents a more inclusive approach to service provision.

Rationale for Using Natural Support Systems

The human services field is leading the movement to more holistic approaches to health and mental services. Inspired in part by the public demand to make human services agencies more accountable and cost-effective, the field is pursuing greater coordination and collaboration among both formal and informal service providers. This new strategy also acknowledges the variety of interrelated factors that influence ATOD (alcohol, tobacco, and other drug) abuse and the social context in which it occurs.

Specifically, the psychological, spiritual, physical, and economic well-being that plays a critical role in guarding against the abuse of alcohol and other drugs is nourished by the community. Thus, an examination of this social and cultural context should yield important clues about which individuals might play key roles in successful prevention strategies. Support originating from within the community is particularly effective because of its cultural relevance, so productive ATOD prevention services need to capitalize on the strengths and resources available within each community.

Since NSSs and ATOD preventionists are natural partners in efforts to prevent and combat substance abuse, collaboration between them is critical to the success of any community-based program. This collaboration is particularly crucial for the Hispanic/Latino community, where NSSs often constitute the core of social, spiritual, and economic support.

*Source: *CSAP Implementation Guide: Hispanic/Latino Natural Support Systems*, U.S. Department of Health and Human Services, Public Health Service, Substance Abuse and Mental Health Services Administration, Center for Substance Abuse Prevention, DHHS Publication No. (SMA) 95-3033, Rockville, Maryland, 1995.

Strategies for Identifying and Accessing Natural Support Systems

Inventory the Community

Drive or walk around the area where your program participants reside with a person familiar with the community. Take note of the businesses, housing, churches, recreational facilities, and public transportation. Also, consider the qualitative aspects of the community:

- How noisy is it?
- Are the streets well lit?
- Are the streets patrolled?
- Do youth congregate around street corners, arcades, and liquor stores?

This inventory can reveal both the need for and impediments to prevention activities.

Think of the social, cultural, and economic characteristics of the particular Hispanic/Latino population you are serving. Is the population rural/urban, low/high income, low/high acculturation? Answers to these questions help you surmise the types of services the program participants use and the locations they frequent. For example, low-income urban Hispanics/Latinos are likely to use public transportation, laundromats, and check cashing services.

Below is a list of common Hispanic/Latino gathering places. How many exist in your community?

- Spanish markets and grocery stores (bodegas, tiendas, botánicas)
- music stores and concerts (salsa, mariachi, merengue, etc.)
- laundromats
- day labor pickup sites
- social clubs (billiard halls, dominoes tables, ice houses, coffee houses)
- health clinics and agencies and WIC (Women, Infant and Children) program offices
- travel agencies and places that arrange to send money to other countries, check lines in banks
- place of publication of Spanish language newspapers and magazines
- soccer games
- English language programs (Berlitz, Sanz)
- Spanish television, radio, newspaper, and consumer directories
- public squares
- ethnic and religious festivals
- street fairs and health fairs
- churches
- remedial and adult education programs
- advocacy agencies, other Hispanic/Latino community agencies (Legal Aid, La Raza)
- schools and day-care centers with high Hispanic/Latino enrollment

You can go to these places, observe who goes there, identify persons who seem to be informed, and ask about why people go there, what kinds of help they might receive, and from whom. After this information gathering, you can generate a list for future use that will include the kinds of help sought and potential helpers. This list will also help identify the community's informal leaders.

Informal community leaders, activists, and helpers exist in every Hispanic/Latino community. These women, men, and young people are residents who act as helping resources for individuals and families. Such people are outside the formal service provider network, but they are very important elements of the support system of a Hispanic/Latino family. Examples of some helpers are:

- women who live on the block or in the same building as the person or family that needs help (women who have a lot of information about how to get things done in the community)
- women or men who, on their own, are providing a temporary home, links to services for youth, or otherwise helping
- men who know how to effect change through the formal political system
- spiritualists (*espiritistas* or *santeros*) who work at home

Whether such people exist in your area, and who they are, can be determined by asking on the block or in the locations identified above. You could also ask clients who they seek help from in the community and for what needs, and how they are helped. Clients may refer to these informal helpers as *compadres* or *asistentes sociales*.

Obtain Information on Clients' Use of NSSs

Once you have established a solid relationship with a program participant, determine when and how to best obtain information about your client's natural support systems. You may wish to add a separate background information form, specifically designed to assess NSSs, to client files or revise your existing forms to include information such as that on the sample Background Information Form (see following page).

Document the Natural Support Systems

You may want to maintain a resource book or filing system of NSSs. Maintaining comprehensive written documentation on each system will guarantee continuity of resources despite staff or program changes.

NOTES:

Background Information Form

Hispanic/Latino subgroup (check more than one, if appropriate)

☐ Mexican   ☐ Cuban
☐ Puerto Rican   ☐ Salvadoran
☐ Dominican   ☐ Nicaraguan
☐ Honduran   ☐ Colombian
☐ Guatemalan   ☐ Other (specify): _____

Church membership/affiliation:

☐ Catholic   ☐ 7th Day Adventist
☐ Pentecostal   ☐ Jehovah's Witness
☐ Other (specify): _____

Use of folk healers:

☐ *Curandero*   ☐ *Espiritista*
☐ *Santero*   ☐ *Santiguador*

Household composition:

☐ Single   ☐ Married   ☐ Separated   ☐ Divorced

____ Number of children (Ages: ____, ____, ____, ____, ____)

____ Total number of persons living in home

(List occupants: _____)

____ Number of related persons living in home

(Specify relationship to you: _____)

Social clubs/recreation

☐ Dominoes   ☐ Sports (specify which): _____
☐ Bingo   ☐ Dance club
☐ YMCA   ☐ Other (specify): _____

Schools attending: _____

Schools children attend: _____

Number of adolescents not attending school: _____

Number of years of residence in the United States: _____

Source: *CSAP Implementation Guide: Hispanic/Latino Natural Support Systems*, U.S. Department of Health and Human Services, Public Health Service, Substance Abuse and Mental Health Services Administration, Center for Substance Abuse Prevention, DHHS Publication No. (SMA) 95-3033, Rockville, Maryland, 1995.

DEVELOPING EFFECTIVE MESSAGES AND MATERIALS FOR HISPANIC/LATINO AUDIENCES*

Define the Audience

When program planners simply target "the Hispanic/Latino community," their efforts may fail. Instead their research should make it possible to target specific segments of this community for prevention messages. Remember that the more specific the segment of the community targeted, the more successfully the target audience can be reached.

To develop a profile of the target audience, consider factors such as:

- Age and gender
- Geographic location
- Educational attainment
- Socioeconomic level
- Health status
- Religious practices
- Knowledge, attitudes, beliefs, and behaviors related to substance abuse
- Cultural norms and values
- Channels of communication
- Reasons for immigration and immigration status
- Degree of acculturation
- Intergenerational issues
- Literacy levels

There are many ways of segmenting the Hispanic/Latino community. For example, a substance abuse problem prevention program could be targeted to:

- Hispanic/Latino community leaders or Spanish-language news media
- Hispanic/Latino subgroups (e.g., recent, Mexican American immigrants, Cuban American adolescent males)
- Low-income Hispanic/Latino women, 18 to 25 years old, at risk for substance abuse
- Hispanic/Latino youth ages 9 to 13, and their families (an audience that has achieved even greater importance with today's rapidly changing youth culture)
- Spanish-speaking migrant farmworker populations

Develop a Relevant Message

To reach and have a significant impact on Hispanic/Latino audiences, develop an appropriate and culturally relevant message that is based on thorough knowledge and understanding of the audience and the community. Given the diversity of the Hispanic/Latino community, regional and local research is essential to the development of prevention messages.

---

*Source: *Technical Assistance Bulletin: Developing Effective Messages and Materials for Hispanic/Latino Audiences*, Center for Substance Abuse Prevention, U.S. Department of Health and Human Services, June 1997.

Work with Community Leaders

Community gatekeepers (e.g., health care providers, chamber of commerce members, public personalities, leaders in daily contact with the community) can help explain local conditions and issues, which can vary widely depending on local problems, perceptions, assets, and resources. They can also help develop messages and materials that will be successful in reaching specific segments of the Hispanic/Latino community. Research and direct consultation with members of the target audiences and with those who can reach and influence them are necessary to establish the content of messages and the form of materials.

Involve the Target Audience

Testing assumptions and ideas for specific prevention messages, formats, and languages to use by involving members of the target audience in discussions is essential. Obtain their reactions to ideas, sketches, scripts, and other materials in development. Coordinate with local projects and agencies that are producing materials for the Hispanic/Latino community. Close cooperation and an exchange of materials and experiences can improve understanding of the audience and result in more targeted and effective prevention messages and materials.

In addition to developing targeted and relevant messages that appeal to specific segments of the Hispanic/Latino community, producing prevention materials that express basic messages using global images and icons that have meaning for all Hispanics/Latinos is also important. Efforts to discover commonalties linking the daily life experiences of Hispanic/Latino people living in different geographical areas and under different local conditions may broaden the reach of prevention messages. Such efforts may also be cost-effective.

Lessons Learned from National Programs

The following recommendations reflect lessons learned from national campaigns and communication programs that have targeted Hispanics/Latinos:

- Always avoid stereotypes.
- Promote respect for elders and promote interest in disappearing traditions.
- Listen to and respect youth and promote this attitude among Hispanic/Latino parents.
- Facilitate sharing and discussion of experiences.
- Build on the strengths of the Hispanic/Latino community and its cultural values.
- Promote the importance of extended kinship (grandparents, uncles, aunts, cousins) in family relations. Also promote nonfamily forms of close integration between individuals, such as "compadrazgo" (a person who supports you as a friend; could be similar to a child's godparents) and friendship.
- Promote communal values and neighborly attitudes such as "barrio" (specific area in the community and/or neighborhood) fiestas and traditions; and in general support all forms of extended social networking that are central to Hispanic/Latino culture.
- Encourage general civic values, but also support all practices and events that promote ethnic cultural pride and higher self-esteem among Hispanics/Latinos.

- Praise and use as role models particular contemporary and historical heroes and figures who are of specific significance for each Hispanic/Latino subgroup.
- Highlight Hispanic/Latino contributions in the development of the American nation and in the emergence of world civilization.

Determine the Form Materials Should Take

Even if a message is developed and has a target population well motivated and interested in the type of material and information to be disseminated, this alone may not be sufficiently powerful to ensure success. Always keep in mind:

- **Form should not be considered secondary to content.** If the message is not presented in a form (style, vocabulary, voice, story line) that is clear and attractive, the content (concepts, values, perspective) of the materials may be misunderstood or simply disregarded. An appealing form enhances the content of messages.
- **Materials should be informative as well as appealing.** If materials are simply attractive and entertaining without being truly educational, they will not help to achieve program goals.
- **Modern culture is increasingly influenced by television and other visual media.** Visual images also offer a good opportunity to reverse stereotypes.
- **Identify appropriate visual images and cultural symbols.** During developmental stages and before launching visual materials, use working groups as well as focus groups to pretest the materials.
- **Good humor and jokes can be used successfully in visual images to communicate serious messages.** In fact, cartoons are often a powerful form for delivering prevention messages. But care must be taken to use humor in a way that is appropriate and sensitive to the cultural context.

Use Appropriate Language

Because Hispanics/Latinos constitute an essentially bilingual community, issues of linguistic competence and language use are of prime importance for those involved in prevention aimed at this sector of the U.S. population.

All English, All Spanish, or Bilingual?

There is no universal answer. Some communicators feel that all documents should be bilingual. Others argue that strategic market segmentation is a more effective strategy for distribution. Here are some guidelines:

- Adapt materials to better fit the needs and specificities of Hispanics/Latinos. Develop and write the text in both English and Spanish for bilingual materials. Do not rely on translations of the English text.
- Consider providing both English and Spanish texts in one document. Cut the length of written English materials by half so that there is room to write it in both languages.
- Look for alternatives to print materials; use oral messages in both languages whenever possible.

- Write messages in English clearly and simply for readers who are just learning the language.

Remember that the language level of new immigrants is usually unknown, which makes it difficult to know how best to target this population. Research in this area is needed to establish more realistic programs with regard to the use of Spanish and English in materials for Hispanics/Latinos.

Readability

What should be done if audience members speak mainly Spanish but do not read it? What if they read both English and Spanish but are truly literate in neither? Here are some strategies for enhancing readability:

- Use readability formulas, such as the SMOG formula or Gunning's Fog index.
- Develop materials at the appropriate literacy level of the audience.
- Make written materials as brief and clear as possible.
- Keep the use of technical jargon to a minimum.
- Accompany written material with good visual material. Ideally, the reader should be able to draw meaning from every picture.
- Explore images and symbols that communicate pan-Hispanic/Latino concepts. Some of these can be global cultural icons derived from nature, food, and celebrations.
- Use a type size large enough to be easily read.

Hispanic or Latino?

When is it appropriate to use which term, and when should both be used? For national materials, such as this bulletin, the combination "Hispanic/Latino" is probably the most appropriate and acceptable term. But realize that this practice may not be as effective at the local level. If materials are aimed at a local audience, carry out research locally to determine with which identity, which term, people feel more comfortable. Another viable way of referring to people is by the language they speak (e.g., Spanish-speaking people, Navajo-speaking people). A good working principle: Be as specific as possible to reach the majority of the target audience.

Colloquialisms

In general, many factors determine the different contexts in which either colloquialisms or formal Spanish may be used. If a targeted group constitutes a very wide audience (state and national levels), Spanish messages should be more formal and standard.

Although there seems to be no consensus on whether colloquialisms should be used, many professionals oppose their use, both in written and oral materials. Common voices are difficult to achieve given the wide variety of Spanish colloquialisms used among Hispanics/Latinos. Common wisdom suggests that it is best to approach each case separately without attempting to apply a formula mechanically. Ask members of the target group about specific local or regional dialect expressions that may be used in more informal conversations.

Examples of colloquialisms:

> Regional examples: "troka" (truck), "parkear" (parking), "carpeta" (carpet), "marketa" (market), "bueno bye" (good bye).

Reasons to use colloquialisms:

- Careful use of certain colloquialisms makes verbal messages more realistic and thus more credible.
- Certain colloquialisms, such as terms of endearment, may be more universal/or useful.
- Colloquialisms can be more freely used when they are part of a local message intended for a local audience.

Reasons to avoid using colloquialisms:

- Many Hispanic/Latino audiences consider colloquial language derogatory.
- Colloquialisms tend to stress differences among Hispanics/Latinos rather than emphasize linguistic and cultural commonalties.
- When using colloquialisms, be careful not to use them in a way that reinforces stereotypes sometimes used in the mainstream media to depict Hispanics/Latinos.

Plan Ways To Put Materials into the Community

To get messages across and to promote and distribute materials successfully, choose appropriate channels of communication and methods of outreach to the target audience. Strategies for planning successful outreach activities to Hispanic/Latino groups include the following:

- Plan and design the outreach process carefully, making sure local leaders and gatekeepers are involved.
- Promote and make good use of the positive family and communal values that are central to traditional Hispanic/Latino culture.
- Respect local and generational characteristics, but place special emphasis on promoting those basic historical and cultural foundations that unite all Hispanics/Latinos. Take advantage of the links that bind the individual to the family, the family to the community, and the community to the country.

Appropriate Methods of Outreach

Outreach methods and procedures should be tailored to cultural and generational differences. To ensure that messages get out to the Hispanic/Latino audience

- **Learn who the real leaders and gatekeepers of the community are,** gain their support, and get them to work collaboratively. Then, let local leaders and gatekeepers speak for and to their local communities.
- **Use creative strategies to involve local leaders and target audiences.** For example, in certain cases, men can be the channel for reaching women, other relatives, and peers.

- **Work with organizations/institutions with programs that focus on family in implementing the outreach process.** For example, clinics, day care centers, and women's organizations can be of great value for outreach purposes.
- **Consider seriously organizations used by the general population, such as churches and hospitals.** However, churches and hospitals are not always good intermediaries. It depends on local conditions that can vary greatly from one location or community to another.
- **Include viable intermediaries and gatekeepers such as teachers, pharmacies, recreation and civic associations,** fiestas, coaches, sport teams, corporate leaders, the media, health care providers, lay folk healers "curanderos," and Hispanic/Latino elected officials.
- **Use mass communication media, including television,** radio, VCRs, CDs, newspapers, and magazines.
- **Use community access television** and interactive technology as an outreach tool.
- **Work with "promotoras."** These are active members of a Hispanic/Latino community who work in close and direct contact with the target population in promoting values and preventive measures. "Promotoras" are lay people who receive instruction in the art and ways of promoting safe and successful attitudes toward the more immediate and pervasive health challenges and dangers faced by the Hispanic/Latino community. They work at the grassroots level and are probably the most effective type of intermediary. Several Latin American countries have successfully experimented with this type of intermediary action.

Media Channels for Reaching Hispanic/Latino Groups

Mass media channels offer many opportunities for reaching Hispanic/Latino audiences. For effective delivery of messages, consider the following:

- Videos in Spanish seem particularly viable. Recent studies indicate that most Hispanic/Latino households in the United States have VCRs. The U.S. market for videos in Spanish is also rapidly expanding.
- Novelas (soap operas) are of paramount importance in modern Hispanic/Latino culture. An effort should be made to incorporate implicit prevention messages in novelas.
- Talk shows are becoming popular among Hispanic/Latino audiences.

Because repetition of a message is essential for reinforcement, ensuring that the audience receives long-term exposure to materials assumes strategic importance. But the high cost of developing materials for distribution and of their repeated exposure through mass media, especially television, should be considered before deciding to reach Hispanic/Latino audiences through such channels. Distribution and marketing of Hispanic/Latino media materials have yet to be well defined and improved.

Evaluate the Effectiveness of Messages and Materials

The ability to pique the target population's interest is not proof that the materials are successful. To be effective, products not only must be appealing, but they must also be understood. Above all, they have to elicit some kind of action.

In testing whether the materials meet these objectives, methodologies based on social marketing approaches can be of great value:

1. Conduct preliminary formative research to determine the needs of the target population and the best means to reach this audience.
2. Develop and pretest the appropriate message and materials.
3. After disseminating and promoting the materials, conduct an evaluation to determine the results or outcomes of the prevention messages.

To assess the impact of the materials on people's daily lives and the value and relevancy of the materials to individuals and their families, ask:

- Who is using the material? Are they a part of the target group?
- How is the material being used? Is this the way it was intended to be used?
- Is the effort prompting the target audience to do anything different? If so, what? If not, why not?

Even when resources are limited, it is possible to incorporate into the evaluation plan collecting data, pretesting with focus groups, and monitoring implementation of program goals and objectives.

The evaluation methods and process selected depend not only on the resources available but also on cultural considerations. Care should be taken to build in appropriate resources for evaluation. But even greater care should be taken to select and apply evaluation methods and tools that are sensitive to cultural and other factors specific to the Hispanic/Latino community. For example, designing a survey instrument that requires written responses may not be useful or effective in evaluating the results of prevention messages with recent Hispanic/Latino immigrant groups with low levels of literacy. It may also indicate a lack of cultural sensitivity by the evaluator.

Evaluation results will enable the reassessment and refinement of ongoing health communication planning efforts to ensure that the substance abuse problem prevention messages and materials developed for Hispanic/Latino audiences are increasingly relevant and more effective.

NATIVE AMERICANS: RELEVANT SOCIOCULTURAL ISSUES*

Broad differences exist among the many subcultures of Native Americans. It is therefore extremely important for health educators to be aware of the cultural characteristics unique to the specific group and individual for whom they provide services. Presented here are some notes from the literature on Native American culture and health care. To help further identify these differences, health professionals may seek information about specific groups with whom they work by consulting their area's Indian Community Tribal Council or Indian health professionals.

As an example of the kinds of information available from such sources, the South Dakota United Indian Association provides information on cultural differences and has written a sensitivity packet for non-Indian health care providers. In one of its publications, the association describes the different lifestyles of traditional (reservation), contemporary (urban and reservation), and cosmopolitan Native Americans.

Traditional Native Americans maintain their culture and traditions within their communities through medicine men and religious practices. Their language and cultural practices are totally integrated into their daily activities. In comparison, the contemporary or bicultural Native American is usually found in urban centers. Some individuals are successful in becoming bicultural, while others are unable to cope with the "double standard" and exhibit mental and emotional instabilities, alcoholism, and drug abuse. Cosmopolitan Native Americans are integrated into Anglo-American culture, often intermarry with Anglos, and adopt Anglo identities. Currently, however, a growing number of cosmopolitan Native Americans are returning to their tribal identity.

The persistence of traditional healing practices is an important factor in Native American health care. Due to the coexistence of traditional and conventional health care systems, there is a need to collaborate whenever possible with traditional health care practitioners.

Some Cultural Characteristics

Although the definition of immediate family members will differ among tribes, the Indian family structure is characterized by an extended family unit with strong kinship ties. Both matriarchal and patriarchal systems function in certain tribes, with ownership passed on through the mother and also communal, that is, shared with others. Interdependency among individuals and responsibility to the tribe are highly valued, as are respect for an individual's rights and noninterference in another's personal life unless requested. Respect for elders is also a primary element of Native American culture.

A number of cultural characteristics of Native Americans may have a marked impact on the success of communication with and treatment of clients from this cultural group. For example, closeness to nature is characteristic of Native American cultures, and death is accepted as a part of the natural cycle. The concept of time is based on a continuum that focuses on the present rather than the future. There is a strong belief that many events cannot be altered by humans.

---

*Source: *Cross-Cultural Counseling: A Guide for Nutrition and Health Counselors*, U.S. Department of Agriculture/U.S. Department of Health and Human Services, Nutrition Education Committee for Maternal and Child Nutrition Publications, 1986. Reviewed and approved for reprinting, 1990.

Religious Beliefs and Tribal Healing Practices

Religion helps to maintain stability and gives a sense of cohesion to an individual's life; it is not separated from health care as it is in most Western cultures. The religion is based on belief in the almighty Mother Earth. "Bad" happenings are viewed as punishment, and "good" happenings viewed as reward. Religion is incorporated into daily activities and maintained by teaching and example. Religious and healing practices are interrelated in rituals, and illness is interpreted as a sign of disharmony with nature. Native Americans have a holistic concept of health care. Signs, symptoms, as well as causes are treated. Illness is considered to be caused by either natural or supernatural influences. Tribal rituals often involve the use of foods sacred to the particular tribe; for example, corn is considered curative by some groups. Cedar also may be important in religious healing rituals or in medicine bags.

Death rituals and taboos vary among groups, and attitudes vary about touching the body. Although tribal healing practices differ, they usually include:

- purification of the patient and the medicine man
- the Navajo practice of a Sign (ritual, chants, and sand painting lasting for various lengths of time)
- smoking religious tobacco
- gentle massage
- small sacrifices
- prayers

Other traditional approaches to health care are herbal remedies and bone setters. Some Indian groups take traditional medications, such as herbal teas, in large doses. Non-Indian medical care providers must be aware of the need to emphasize strongly the taking of prescribed medications according to directions.

Communication

Display of emotion is encouraged in some tribes but discouraged in others. Intense eye contact often is considered disrespectful; health educators often misinterpreted this as the client being inattentive or disinterested. Handshakes are an important symbolic gesture, although in some groups a vigorous handshake is sometimes viewed as a sign of aggressiveness.

Many Native Americans do not speak English; among these are the many rural elderly who live on reservations. When an interpreter is needed, a bilingual family member may be the most helpful person. Because public education is conducted primarily in English, children or grandchildren of elderly Native Americans in rural areas often are bilingual. However, misinterpretation can occur even with an interpreter. Some English words and concepts do not exist in Indian languages or are not easily translatable; the reverse is also true of some Indian words and concepts. Special care should be given to identify clearly the client's symptoms and to explain the illness. This requires more time and patience for both parties. If possible, health educators should meet the interpreter before seeing the client in order to discuss more fully the best ways to communicate medical terms and treatment.

AMERICAN INDIAN/ALASKA NATIVE/NATIVE HAWAIIAN TRIBAL AND VILLAGE HIV/AIDS EDUCATION POLICY GUIDELINES*

The Necessity of HIV/AIDS Education

Tribal programs and businesses are encouraged to support the physical, emotional, and spiritual well-being of community members and employees. The common goal is to make sure seronegative (does not have human immunodeficiency virus [HIV]) community members and employees remain seronegative. If policies help to prevent HIV infection, they have acted in the best interests of everyone. Each tribal program and business has a minimum responsibility to provide every community member and employee with basic education about HIV, for a number of reasons:

- As HIV continues to spread through the population, there will be increasing numbers of American Indian/Alaska Native/Native Hawaiian people with HIV infection. Many programs have already worked with HIV-infected people, sometimes without knowing it. There is every reason to believe that in the coming years many tribal programs will be working with HIV-infected people.
- Employers are in a similar position with staff. Supervisors and managers want employees to stay healthy, both because they are valued workers and because a healthy staff will minimize disruptions in activity.
- Tribal education efforts may be, for some people, one of the few sources of comprehensive information about HIV and acquired immune deficiency syndrome (AIDS). Other than the mass media or the often unreliable reports of others, community members and staff may have few other sources for accurate information and reliable advice.
- Supervisory staff should understand the nature of HIV transmission and its effects. They will be perceived, therefore, as credible and dependable sources of information. People will look to staff as HIV educators, even though staff may fail to recognize their role as such.
- A supportive environment, providing a safe and trusting environment, is needed to initiate and negotiate behavior change and should be made available by the tribe or agency.
- Programs will want to minimize the disruption that can occur when staff or community members react inappropriately to a known case of HIV infection. Some facilities, having failed to provide adequate education, have found themselves in crisis after receiving information about an HIV-infected person, because others, who are uninformed or misinformed, reacted hysterically or insensitively.
- Systematic education of all community members and employees about HIV minimizes potential legal liability. Educated employees and clients are less likely to behave in ways that may invite legal claims against programs and businesses.
- Programs and businesses will want to make sure that individuals are not mistreated because others perceive them to be HIV infected—even when they are not. Mistreatment based simply on perception of HIV-seropositive status is illegal. The less educated people are about HIV and AIDS, the more likely they are to assume incorrectly that, for example, "if you're gay, you must have AIDS."

---

*Courtesy of the National Native American AIDS Prevention Center, Oakland, California, © 1994.

- Finally, people who are seropositive deserve sound information about health maintenance. A program that has provided education to all community members and employees is more likely to meet those needs and goals.

The Nature of HIV/AIDS Education

Two fundamental principles guide the provision of HIV education for employees and community members. The first is that **mere exposure to information does not equal education**. Another way of saying the same thing is that **the goal of HIV education is behavior change**. Simply because programs have made brochures available, or arranged screening of videotapes, does not mean education leading to behavior change has taken place. The process of learning and changing is much more complex than that.

The second guiding principle is that **education should include roughly the same comprehensive content for everyone**, though, obviously, education for health, social service, and managerial staff may be more detailed. Everyone needs to know what HIV is, how it is transmitted, how it is not transmitted, and how individuals can protect themselves from infection in both their personal and professional lives. It is unreasonable to expect that all health, social service, and managerial staff can provide such education for people without having received training first. The educator will need to use his or her best judgment about what level of detail is appropriate for the audience or a particular person. In addition, educators should receive regularly updated training. The important measure for educational appropriateness is the person's needs and feelings, not the educator's.

The Behavioral Focus

If the focus of education is behavioral, rather than knowledge only, what kinds of behavior are targets for change?

The first target for change is **behavior that puts people at risk of HIV infection**. This includes sexual and injection equipment-sharing behaviors, pregnancy-related risks, and, to a much lesser degree, occupationally associated risk.

The second target for change is **behavior toward others who are already HIV infected, as well as groups of people perceived to be HIV infected**, which includes gay and bisexual men and lesbians, IV drug users, prostitutes, and, to an increasing degree, other communities of color.

In other words, the goals are to ensure that everyone who is currently seronegative stays that way, and that everyone who is seropositive, or perceived to be seropositive, is treated with respect and dignity, not hysteria or rejection.

In the long run, it will not be enough for people to know the information about risk reduction if people fail to act on it. Similarly, it will not be enough for staff to know they cannot get infected from casual contact, yet avoid people with AIDS, nevertheless, "just in case."

Educational Strategies

Experience and research are fairly clear in pointing out that some educational strategies and methods are more likely to support behavior change than others—though nothing guarantees it, for example:

- Current research indicates that the strongest motivator for change is **knowing someone with AIDS**. The significance is that if clients or staff do not know anyone, education must be personalized as much as possible and provided in a way individuals can understand and relate to emotionally. Quoting statistics is not likely to accomplish that task.
- Information is best presented in a way that is best understood by people. Many people simply do not comprehend the mechanics of retro viruses, the complexities of immunity, or the principles of epidemiology. That information needs to be worded so that it fits within people's world view and understanding.
- Education should acknowledge and respect the differences in audiences and clients. Approaches that work with men may not work with women, and styles effective for teenage audiences may not be successful for elders. HIV has affected a wide spectrum of communities and cultures, sometimes in very different ways. Gay or bisexual men and lesbians, heterosexual women, disabled people, and other groups deserve education that is sensitive to their needs and realities.
- Individual learning styles vary significantly. People will learn best when education is matched to personal learning styles. A single approach that emphasizes videotape education, for example, will not be effective for individuals who do not learn well from visual modes of instruction. Since programs are not always in a position to assess learning styles, a multifaceted approach that employs a variety of styles is best.
- Since the information about HIV/AIDS is sometimes complex, individuals will probably require repeated exposure to facts. This does not mean viewing the same videotape over and over again; it does mean presenting information in a variety of formats and settings.
- People are more likely to change their behavior if consequences—both positive and negative—are immediate and concrete. Even the possibility of death in the context of AIDS is puzzling and slightly unreal to many people. To tell a teenager, for example, that "if you are not careful today, you may get infected with a virus that may sometime over the next 15 years make you sick and some years after that kill you" is very abstract. "I won't have sex with you unless you wear a condom" is much more immediate and obvious than "one of us could be infected and infect the other, which could make us sick sometime in the future."
- People cannot change their behavior unless they are given detailed strategies for doing so:
  - If educators say, for example, "you should practice safer sex," without explaining how, they have neglected an essential ingredient in HIV and AIDS education. Even advising people to use condoms may be insufficient, since condoms are only effective if used every time, and properly. Even then, they cannot be said to be foolproof.
  - Similarly, it is inadequate merely to advise people to stop sharing drug injection equipment. Facts about the availability of sterile equipment, as well as detailed methods for cleaning one's "works" need to be shared.
  - What about the person who says, "I don't need to know that stuff!" He or she may be uncomfortable talking about safe sex or risk reduction, but discomfort alone is not reason enough for dropping the educational effort. The temptation to avoid the topic may also arise because the educator is uncomfortable. To get around the discomfort and still get important information across, the counselor may say,

"You may not need this information for yourself, but you might know someone—a friend, perhaps—for whom it could be helpful. You can take the information and pass it on to him, and help him out." With such an approach, the individual can learn what he or she needs to know and feel comfortable at the same time.

–Some educational strategies have placed the field of HIV education and counseling in a philosophical and ethical dilemma. For example, instructing people in the ways and means of safer needle use seems to contradict the widely and deeply held belief that abstinence is essential to recovery from alcohol and drug abuse. Health educators ask, "If we tell people how to get and clean their 'works,' aren't we approving continued drug use?" It is a difficult question to answer, because although abstinence may be the goal, a sizable percentage of people will fail in this effort. Many people expose themselves to HIV even after completing a treatment program for drug use. In relating critical information about risk reduction, health educators help people to protect themselves from HIV infection. In fact, instruction in safer needle use may work best in navigating through this dilemma.

- HIV is a topic often surrounded by strong emotions and firm beliefs. It is essential that people are given a chance to express those beliefs and emotions without embarrassment or shame. Behavior change itself is usually accompanied by fear or nervousness. Education therefore should avoid simply "lecturing at" people, and include interactive formats instead.

- Finally, educators need to be clear on their own values and attitudes about sexuality, sexual behavior, pregnancy and abortion, and IV drug use, being careful not to let those values undermine educational efforts. Many educators may not be completely comfortable with matters related to sexuality or specific behaviors. They need to acknowledge their own discomfort and beliefs when they get in the way of effective education.

Managerial Staff Education

Comprehensive education of managerial staff about HIV/AIDS should address several basic topic areas:

- the fundamentals of HIV and AIDS (i.e., what they are, how transmission occurs, discussion of fears related to casual contact)
- strategies for personal risk reduction and how to avoid transmission
- strategies for occupational risk reduction and how to avoid transmission
- HIV antibody testing
- the psychological and clinical realities associated with HIV infection or AIDS
- review of fundamental laws and statutes regarding confidentiality and access to services
- an orientation to existing policies and procedures relating to HIV/AIDS
- an overview of existing resources available for HIV-infected persons in the area and state

There are several logical formats or settings in which managerial staff HIV and AIDS education can take place:

- The information can be integrated into new employee orientation. New managerial staff may receive a packet that includes printed policy statements and basic background literature on AIDS. Or, they can watch an introductory video or attend a community workshop. At the very least, new managerial staff should be expected to read and "sign off" on any existing policies that relate to HIV; these policies should be the basis for discussion, presentations, and hands-on training.
- HIV training can be integrated into an ongoing inservice education calendar, conducted on-site for employees. For example, a three-hour inservice training for all managerial staff can touch on the basics of HIV. Additional training on specialized topics, for example, family issues and HIV, can be scheduled on an as-needed basis. Inservice training may be presented by an in-house staff person who has completed a training program or by external personnel.
- Staff expected to provide inservice education should attend a wide array of external training events and workshops on all aspects of HIV.
- If programs decide not to develop educational programs—or are not able to deliver them to staff—outside resources and resource people in the area should be contacted to provide education inservice.

Community and Employee Education

Community and employee education should cover basically the same topics as staff education, with slight variation. Comprehensive client/employee education addresses:

- the fundamentals of HIV and AIDS
- strategies for personal risk reduction, including not only the mechanics of risk reduction but communication and relationship concerns
- relevant community and program policies regarding HIV
- HIV antibody testing
- confidentiality rules and expectations
- an overview of HIV resources in the area, to include at least the telephone number of a local or state AIDS hotline, the national toll-free Indian AIDS Line, or the National AIDS Hotline

Educational opportunities for community members and employees are numerous in health and social service programs and through employment inservice training:

- Education can be part of an intake process. The easiest method is to give all new community members and employees a packet of written information. If there is time, a portion of the intake interview can be devoted to a discussion of HIV.
- HIV education can be integrated into individual client services with a primary provider or educator. When people raise personal issues about sexuality, relationships, IV drug use, or pregnancy, the opportunity is present not only to respond to the issues but to provide HIV information as well.
- Some groups are ideally suited for discussions about HIV. Sexuality groups, men's and women's groups, health classes, and even family sessions all offer appropriate occasions to provide education, either formally or informally.

- As with staff, community members and employees can be offered regular presentations on the basics of HIV and personal risk reduction. Programs and personnel can schedule lectures to ensure that each community member and employee attends at least one during the course of service or employment.
- Written materials should be readily available, as should videos that can be viewed at home or during a visit for services for any type of employee education program.
- Programs may make use of special community events by scheduling groups or events. For example, in some areas there are touring productions of plays by Native Americans that deal with the subject of AIDS. Hopefully, other special arts or community events devoted to the topic will become increasingly available.
- Finally, HIV education can be reinforced by making people aware of community-based HIV resources that can be helpful in the future. For example, community or area programs may choose to dispense condoms. Programs and businesses, in some instances, can make use of community resources, Native HIV/AIDS organizations, and state agencies, many of which may provide HIV education at little or no cost.

Risk Assessment

As an HIV education tool, risk assessment refers to a variety of structured and semistructured methods designed to determine an individual's risk history—a history of behaviors that may have involved exposure to or transmission of HIV. In some cases, risk assessment may refer to a structured interview with a person, reviewing sex and drug use practices over the past seven years or more. In other cases, risk assessment refers to written questionnaires about past and current behavior that can be interpreted by a health care worker or educator and used as the basis for discussion of risk reduction. In a few cases, risk assessment may involve a self-reporting and self-diagnostic instrument with which individuals can review their past and current behaviors and assess possible exposure privately, on their own.

Risk assessment presents potential benefits and drawbacks that should be examined carefully before use as a part of HIV education. Used correctly, as part of an overall risk reduction education strategy, it can:

- help pinpoint specific behaviors that put the person at continued risk of HIV infection, thereby allowing for risk reduction education that focuses specifically on those behaviors
- help heighten the person's sense of potential personal risk, as he or she reviews overall behavioral patterns
- build personal awareness of the need for behavior change to reduce future risk
- encourage self-examination to help the client determine whether or not to take the HIV antibody test
- eliminate at least some of the need to talk about "absolutely everything" with "absolutely everybody"

Without a proper perspective, however, an overreliance on risk assessment, or its untrained use, can be misleading or even counterproductive; for example:

- Staff may erroneously assume the accuracy of clients' past self-reported risk behavior. There are many understandable reasons why individual self-reporting might be unreliable as a source of information. For example, people may feel uneasy discussing their sexual and drug use behaviors out of embarrassment, guilt, fear, and so on.

- Staff may mistakenly exclude individuals from their educational efforts when, in fact, they may need information. One might assume, for example, that an individual who reports no high-risk behaviors needs minimal risk reduction education. Conversely, someone may report an episode of high-risk behavior and be provided intensive risk reduction information when the risk of exposure may have been minimal. **Everyone should receive the same general educational messages— tailored, of course, to individual needs and sensitivities—regardless of the extent of self-reported past risk behaviors.**

- Individuals with self-reported low-risk histories may place too much emphasis on past behavior. Sometimes such individuals will experience intense feelings of shame, remorse, or guilt about past behaviors that, on the whole, do not indicate a high risk of HIV infection. Those feelings are sometimes translated into undue worry that "I must be infected after what I did" and an unwarranted desire to get tested right away. The real issue in such cases may be unresolved feelings about past behaviors, not potential HIV infection, and such individuals should be encouraged to concentrate more on future risk reduction efforts than potential past exposure. One woman, for example, thought she had to get tested because of a relationship she had 15 years ago "with a man who I think was bisexual, because he looked kinda like he was." On further questioning, however, the woman realized that she still felt guilty about "cheating on my husband back then," and that there was no real reason for her to get the HIV antibody test.

- The educator may disregard the sensitive nature of what is being asked and expected of people. To inquire about the client's frequency of anal intercourse or same-gender sex is a delicate task for both the questioner and the respondent. Because of this, training in risk assessment emphasizes nonjudgmental approaches and stresses the importance of open-ended questions. Asking, for example, "Who do you have sex with—men, women, or both?" will generate more honest and useful answers than asking "Are you homosexual, heterosexual, or bisexual?" But even then, when such inquiry becomes too routine, the sensitivity and respect that such a process demands can be too easily ignored.

In light of the above, there are two ways risk assessment can be used in programs.

First, risk assessment can be used as a part of an intake process in appropriate programs. In those cases, risk assessment should be administered by a trained professional and used to promote one-on-one discussion about risk behaviors and risk reduction. "Trained professional" in this context means someone who has had specific, comprehensive training in risk assessment theory and technique, not someone who may have attended only a short presentation on the subject.

Second, programs might use risk assessment as a self-diagnostic tool by allowing individuals to fill out questionnaires and interpret the results on their own. In private, clients might be more honest with their responses. But again, some of the earlier problems might apply: Without proper follow-up education, risk assessment can leave the individual "hanging," and it may lead individuals to worry unnecessarily about past low-risk behaviors. When it is used as a personal instrument, risk assessment should have such warnings clearly stated as part of the questionnaire.

Again, risk assessment should not be considered as a technique or strategy separate from an overall risk reduction education process. It is not a device that provides easy solutions for educational dilemmas; it is one of a series of useful tools. As such, it requires skill and tact to successfully employ. In the absence of such demonstrable skills among current staff, programs should not emphasize risk assessment techniques too heavily. The decision to make such services available in the future may be made by providing for the risk assessment training of selected staff.

Educational Windows of Opportunity

As a program administrator recently stated, "No matter how much education you do, when it hits—when you get that first client who is known to be HIV infected—there's going to be a strong reaction. There's going to be a mini-crisis." Collective experience bears out the truth of that statement.

Such events should be seen as windows of opportunities for focused education, not as threats. They help to make the problem real rather than abstract. And over the course of the coming years, the nearly inevitable windows of opportunity can include:

- recognition of a person who is known to be HIV infected or who has a clinical diagnosis of AIDS
- awareness of a staff member with a similar diagnosis
- learning that a community member or employee has a family member or significant other who is HIV infected or who has AIDS
- discovery that a similar program, in a nearby area, has been working with a person or staff member who is HIV infected or who has AIDS

Tribal programs and businesses should not wait for such occasions before they take action. If anything, the message of this guide is that programs should anticipate the future and act accordingly. But when unforeseen events take place, programs can take advantage of the educational opportunities they provide. When emotions run high, and when beliefs and opinions rise to the surface, administrators and managers may be able to make significant strides in changing knowledge, attitudes, and behavior.

NOTES:

Zuni Community Health Opinion Survey

This survey will help the Indian Health Service and Zuni Tribe to plan and carry out health services that better meet Zunis' needs.

1. Ethnic group: ☐ Zuni   ☐ Navajo   ☐ Other Indian   ☐ Non-Indian

2. ☐ Male   ☐ Female

3. Age _____

4. Do you live on the Zuni Reservation?   ☐ Yes   ☐ No

5. Place of employment (*circle one*):

    A. School

    B. Hospital

    C. Tribal program

    D. Bureau of Indian Affairs

    E. Unemployed

    F. Self-employed (silversmith, etc.)

    G. Business (Halona, Malco, etc.)

    H. Other _____

6. Circle the five most important health problems in Zuni (in your opinion):

    A. Safe water supply

    B. Automobile accidents

    C. Other accidents

    D. Diabetes

    E. High blood pressure

    F. Kidney disease

    G. Alcohol and drug abuse

    H. Suicide

    I. Violence (physical beating, murder)

    J. Fetal alcohol syndrome

    K. Teen pregnancy

    L. Obesity and poor nutrition

    M. Ear infections (otitis media)

    N. Poor physical fitness

    O. Poor mental health

    P. Smoking

    Q. Sexually transmitted diseases (gonorrhea, herpes, and other venereal diseases)

    R. Cancer

    S. Unhealthy infants being born

    T. Pneumonia (and other lung diseases)

    U. Heart disease

    V. Poor dental health

    W. AIDS

    X. Poisoning

    Y. Child abuse/neglect

Source: *Restoring Balance*, Health Promotion Resource Center, Stanford Center for Research in Disease Prevention (and the Indian Health Service), Stanford University, 1000 Welch Road, Palo Alto, California 94304-1884. Phone: (415) 723-0003. Fax: (415) 725-6906, © 1992.

Reaching Older Americans

Health promotion programs can use a number of approaches to reach and serve the older Americans in the community.

Programs at senior centers or meal sites. In some communities, the senior center provides a focal point for the older adult community. By offering programs such as screening, immunizations, and health education at these locations, a health program can reach a large number of older adults in the community and advertise its existence and services.

Outreach efforts. Door-to-door visits by outreach workers can help to locate the isolated older adults. Another approach to reaching isolated older individuals, which was used in a rural area, was to get a list of individuals receiving Social Security checks. Contacting all providers of elder services in a local area and building a network of referrals is also important. Providers include meal sites, area agencies on aging, councils on aging, and so on.

Community involvement by staff of the health program. A great deal of outreach and advertisement can be accomplished in an informal way through staff involvement in various community activities, including serving on hospital, nursing home, or area agency on aging boards or conducting health education classes, for example. More formally, the health program could take part in or organize a local health fair or have a booth at a community gathering (harvest fair, spring fair, etc.).

Building a referral network. Referral networks should be built with other medical providers in the community, including physicians and hospitals, as well as providers of social services, such as meal sites, community service organizations, and home nursing and homemaker services.

Pamphlets and informational brochures. Pamphlets explaining the services offered by the health program are extremely useful for outreach purposes and can be distributed throughout the community to individuals and to other community organizations, agencies, and businesses with ties to the aging.

Public service announcements. Radio stations and newspapers will generally run public service ads free of charge. This can be a no-cost way of reaching a wide audience to advertise basic services or special programs.

Paid advertising. Health promotion programs could also use paid advertising to promote their services.

NOTES:

Source: Susan Koch Madden and Paul Campbell, *Guidebook on Geriatric Program Development in Community and Migrant Health Centers*, DHHS Publication #HRS-D-PC-91-2, U.S. Department of Health and Human Services, Public Health Service, Health Resources and Services Administration, Bureau of Health Care Delivery Assistance, July 1990.

Problems Facing AIDS Educators Working with Gay or Bisexual Men, and Some Possible Solutions

Problem	Possible Solutions
Problems Related to Personal Characteristics, Attitudes, or Feelings of Educators	
Discomfort talking about sex	Institute staff training.
	Recruit staff with expertise in sex education.
Negative attitudes toward gay men	Confront attitudes through peer discussion or support groups.
	Institute special training to sensitize staff or volunteers.
Perceptions by people of color, women, or gay/bisexual men of negative attitudes by white, male, or heterosexual staff or volunteers	Recruit people of color, women, and gay men as staff and volunteers.
	Institute training for staff and volunteers to overcome biases.
Need for support because of grief, loss, and the enormity of the epidemic	Develop informal peer support and structured groups in the organization.
	Encourage staff to use mental health services.
Staff perception of personal risk from AIDS	Confront attitudes through open discussions with peers.
	Institute training or support groups to deal with these feelings.
Unfamiliarity with language, culture, or values of gay men or subgroups of gay men	Build linkages with other groups already working with or familiar with gay community.
	Hire educators familiar with culture.
	Institute training on gay culture.
Problems Related to Knowledge, Attitudes, or Behavior of Learners	
Denial of risk or belief that AIDS is only a problem for others	Repeat information on risk.
	Use people with AIDS who are similar to audience as educators.
	Demonstrate specifically how people can reduce risk.
Unwillingness to change risky behavior	Concentrate on individuals or groups who are willing to change.
	Offer options for change (e.g., if you do not want to give up certain sex practices, learn how to make them safer).
	Reduce or minimize barriers to change (e.g., condom comfort workshops).

Source: Nicholas Freudenberg, *Preventing AIDS: A Guide to Effective Education for the Prevention of HIV Infection*, American Public Health Association, Washington, D.C., © 1989.

Subgroups of Gay and Bisexual Men and Suggested Locations for Education Programs

Group	Where To Reach
Gay men in mutually monogamous relationship for more than ten years	Not at risk through sexual behavior
Street youth, hustlers	Runaway centers, youth programs, juvenile detention centers, streets, schools, colleges, sex industry settings
Young men experimenting with sexual identity	Schools, colleges, street, community
Married gay or bisexual men	Bathhouses, general media, workplace programs
"Swingers"	Swinging clubs, swingers' media
Gay IV drug users	Drug programs, streets, correctional system
Street cruisers	Street, gay media, bathhouses, bars, sex industry settings
Gay men who know they are HIV positive	Health centers, test sites, or community programs for HIV-positive men or people with AIDS
Gay men with AIDS or AIDS-related complex (ARC)	Hospitals, health centers, or AIDS support organizations
Gay men of color	Community organizations, black, Latino, or gay media, churches, workplaces
Gay prisoners	Prisons, court system
Prisoners who have sex with other men	Prisons, correctional system

NOTES:

Source: Nicholas Freudenberg, *Preventing AIDS: A Guide to Effective Education for the Prevention of HIV Infection*, American Public Health Association, Washington, D.C., © 1989.

Tips for Gay and Lesbian Substance Abuse Campaigns

Here is some advice about how to develop a substance abuse campaign specifically for the gay and lesbian population.

- *Go slowly and do not appear to be judgmental.* Do not appear to be telling people what to do because this is a sensitive subject. Because a targeted substance abuse campaign is new in the gay community, you need to approach this subject carefully and begin educating people in a nonjudgmental way.
- *Collaborate with local and state officials.* Enlist the support of the county or state health department, and make contact with substance abuse agencies. Also try to win cooperation from bars and alcohol companies. Linkages and collaboration are more important than confrontation.
- *Seeking funding from private and public sources.* In some states, there are gay and lesbian foundations that distribute grants. Each state has an office on substance abuse services, and that's the best place to seek money.
- *Pay for advertising, because a paid ad is less likely to be bumped from a publication.* But stretch your grant dollars by reaching an agreement with newspapers and magazines. Negotiate sizeable discounts or ask the publication to provide a free ad for each one that you pay for.

Source: Steve Larose, "AIDS Prevention Project Raises Awareness about Alcohol and Drug Abuse," *Inside Preventive Care*, Vol. 3:11, Aspen Publishers, Inc., © 1998.

5

Developing Successful Programs

Behavior and Learning Theories

General Principles of Learning 284
General Principles of Adult
    Education 286

Core Competencies for Health Advisors

Core Roles and Competencies for
    Community Health Advisors 288

Planning Models

General Principles of Planning 292
PATCH Program Summary 298
The PATCH Process 300

Mission Statements, Goals, and Objectives

Sample Mission Statement: Sligo
    Community Wellness Center 302
Sample Mission Statement 303
How To Keep Your Mission Alive
    Everyday 304
Worksheet for Writing the
    Philosophy 306
Worksheet for Writing Objectives 307

Program Design and Planning Guidelines

Worksheet for Finding and Overcoming
    Obstacles 308

Worksheet for Planning Health Promotion
    Activities 309
Health Communications Program Plan:
    Outline 310
Checklist for Program Planning and
    Implementation 311

Program Implementation Guidelines

Types of Organizations and Activities To
    Consider in Health Communication
    Programs 312
Tips for Creating a Community
    Preventive Services Program 313
Narrow Your Focus for Intervention:
    "Ability" Factors 314
Preventing Teen Pregnancy 315
Principles for Successful Pregnancy
    Prevention Programs 324
Teen Pregnancy Factors at a Glance 325
Reproductive Pathways of Adolescent
    Women 326
Establishing a Steering Committee for an
    Adolescent Pregnancy Prevention
    Program 327
Taking the Pulse Worksheet 329
Formative Research for Interventions
    among Adolescents at High Risk for
    Gonorrhea and Other STDS 331
Major Program Components of the
    School/Community Sexual Risk
    Reduction Model 340

Guidelines for Establishing an
HIV/AIDS/STD Information
Hotline   341
Guidelines for Street and Community
Outreach for HIV/AIDS Prevention . . .   344
Tobacco Use Questionnaire   349
Ten Steps To Improve Smoking Cessation
Programs   350
Methods Used by Cessation Programs . . .   351
Sample State and Local Strategies for
Prevention and Cessation of Tobacco
Use   352
Developing a Tobacco-Free School
Policy   357
Tips for Establishing Falls Prevention
Programs   359
Tips for Establishing Injury Control
Programs   360
Information To Consider When Profiling a
Target Audience for Promoting Physical
Activity   361
Ideas for Action in the Community To
Promote a Physically Active
Lifestyle   364
Barriers To Being Active Quiz   365
Immunization Barriers and Strategies   367
Ways To Disseminate Immunization
Information without the Media   367

Program Marketing Guidelines

Social Marketing Overview   370
Social Marketing Tutorial   372
Guidelines for Developing Public Health
Frames   384

Special Events

How To Conduct Special Events:
The Basics   388
Special Event Planning Checklist   391
Planning a Health Fair   392
Organizational Strategies for Your Health
Fair   395
Health Fair Committee Planning Sheet . . .   398
Characteristics of a Good Screening
Test   399
Planning a Breakfast Event   400
Special Event Checklist   408

Strategies and Programs That Worked

Staten Island Community Nutrition
Program Helps Thousands Improve
Their Diet   410
Child Health Outreach and Enrollment
Initiative Gets High Marks in
Brooklyn   413
Community Collaboration Produces
Cancer Video for Immigrant
Population   416
Diabetes Sunday Program Helps Reach
the African American Community   419
Haircuts and Health Promotion   422
Nutrition: Strategies That Worked   423
Immunization Coalitions That Work:
Training for Public Health
Professionals   425
Recommendations for Community-Based
Efforts To Reduce Youth Violence in
Low-Income Urban Communities   436

Chapter 5

Developing Successful Programs

OBJECTIVES

At the completion of this chapter, the reader will

- understand general principles of learning
- understand the principles of adult education
- explain general principles for planning programs
- understand the PATCH process
- write a mission statement, goals, and objectives
- understand designing and planning health education programs
- be aware of the possible methods for implementation of a health education program
- be able to begin marketing a community health program
- understand how to plan special events
- be aware of health promotion strategies and programs that have been successful

INTRODUCTION

This chapter provides resources essential to the development of successful community health programs. Beginning with learning principles for adult education, all of the necessary steps in planning health education programs are addressed. These include planning models, mission statements, goals, objectives and design, planning, and implementation worksheets, outlines, or checklists. In addition, guidelines for marketing your program are a new feature of this chapter. Special event planning and examples of strategies and programs that have worked further enhance the chapter's practicality.

This chapter supplies guidelines and forms that would take years to accumulate if a student or professional were starting without assistance. Years of experts' experience are encapsulated in one concise document. The student of community health can call upon the expertise of many community health professionals who have learned through trial and error what works. This armchair consultant will add years of experience to both the student and health professional's repertoire.

GENERAL PRINCIPLES OF LEARNING*

There is no single theory or principle of learning that applies to all people in all situations. Rather, a series of principles and theories should be understood, so as to be able to use theories appropriate for given situations. It is generally understood that it is difficult to teach someone who does not want to learn. Attention should rather be focused on facilitating learning and on motivation. The probability that learning will occur is enhanced when the following principles are used:

- Learning is facilitated if several of the senses are used. People retain approximately 10 percent of what they read, 20 percent of what they hear, 30 percent of what they see, 50 percent of what they see and hear, 70 percent of what they say, and 90 percent of what they do and say. Methods that stimulate the widest variety of senses will generally be most effective.
- Learning is facilitated if the client is actively involved in the process rather than a passive recipient. Methods that engage and elicit responses from the learner are generally more effective than when the learner is passive. Discussion is basic, and other participative methods usually enhance learning.
- Learning is facilitated if the client is not distracted by discomfort or extraneous events. Attention to establishing an appropriate learning environment is an important step to take in facilitating learning.
- Learning is facilitated if the learner is ready to learn. Physical and emotional factors influence readiness. An assessment of readiness makes timing of learning possible and enhances learning.
- Learning is facilitated if that which is to be learned is relevant to the learner and if that relevance is perceived by the learner. Endeavoring to sense the readiness of the learning and making the connection to existing needs and interests of the client enhances learning.
- Learning is facilitated if repetition is used. Reviewing and reinforcing basic concepts several times in a variety of ways enhance learning.
- Learning is facilitated if the learning encounter is pleasant, if progress occurs that is recognizable by the client, and if that learning is recognized and encouraged. Frequent, positive feedback is important to enhancing learning.

---

*Source: Donald J. Breckon et al., *Community Health Education: Settings, Roles, and Skills for the 21st Century*, ed. 3, Aspen Publishers, Inc., © 1994.

- Learning is facilitated if material to be learned starts with what is known and proceeds to the unknown, while concurrently moving from simple to complex concepts. Material to be learned must be organized in ways that make sense to the learner.
- Learning is facilitated if application of concepts to several settings occurs, to facilitate generalization.
- Learning is facilitated if it is paced appropriately for the client. Self-pacing of a motivated learner is usually preferable. Attention to the learner's feeling that the pace is too fast or slow will usually enhance learning.

NOTES:

GENERAL PRINCIPLES OF ADULT EDUCATION*

Begin with a Needs Assessment of the Client or Clients

It is critical to interest and motivation that learners feel a need to learn, and that they make the decision to learn because they see a need for it. It is important to respect adult clients as self-directing humans.

An accompanying staff role is to expose learners to new possibilities, presenting what they need to learn in order to adequately confront current or future problems. Other significant staff roles are to assist learners to diagnose their learning needs and then to decide what is to be learned and how it is to be learned. Such a cooperative relationship requires trust, which leads to the second principle.

Establish a Learning Environment Characterized by Physical Comfort, Mutual Trust, and Freedom of Expression

Having an adequate physical environment is basic, yet often difficult to obtain in many agencies. Whenever possible, facilities should be available that have adequate lighting, heating, and ventilation; flexible seating; and adequate audiovisual capabilities. Whenever there are interruptions, distractions, noises, uncomfortable temperature or humidity, or inadequate lighting, attention is distracted from learning.

Of even more importance, however, is the development of an emotional climate that facilitates learning. This starts with the basics of establishing rapport and accepting and respecting each person as an individual of worth with his or her own feelings and ideas. It includes establishing an atmosphere of mutual responsibility whenever possible, so that clients and staff are learning from each other.

Involve the Client as Much as Possible in the Learning Process

Learners need to be assisted in setting their own learning goals and selecting learning experiences from those available to them. The educator should also help clients exploit the experience of both themselves and others while learning. The experience that adults bring to a learning encounter is another major difference between adults and children. Those who would teach adults effectively must learn to use these experiences effectively.

The client must also be involved in the learning process as much as possible so as to maximize learning. Active learning is preferable to passive learning. If students are involved in thinking, discussing, viewing, trying, and so on, learning is more likely to take place. The more of the five senses that can be involved in the learning, the more learning will occur.

---

*Source: Donald J. Breckon et al., *Community Health Education: Settings, Roles, and Skills for the 21st Century*, ed. 3, Aspen Publishers, Inc., © 1994.

Keep Learners Informed of Their Progress toward Goals

The educator can do this in part by facilitating self-evaluation on the part of the learners or by monitoring progress and reporting it as perceived by the staff. Such feedback is important. Pacing is also important. If teaching is faster or slower than individual readiness, learning will be inhibited.

Another role in this process is to assist learners in rediagnosis, that is, an assessment of what has already been learned and what yet needs to be learned. Thus, the process is cyclical and should ideally lead to lifelong learning.

NOTES:

CORE ROLES AND COMPETENCIES FOR COMMUNITY HEALTH ADVISORS*

We recommend the adoption of the following core roles and competencies by those working in the community health advisors (CHAs) field. We also recommend that practitioners and researchers further refine and validate these roles and competencies.

Recommendations

The following recommendations are based on data from three sources: (1) interviews and discussion groups conducted with CHAs, CHA supervisors, and program administrators; (2) a survey of CHAs and CHA supervisors; and (3) feedback and suggestions from the Core Roles and Competencies Working Group of the National Community Health Advisor Study's Advisory Council.

Recommend Roles of Community Health Advisors

The following roles were identified as encompassing the most important functions that CHAs carry out within their communities and within the health care system. Each role is followed by the functions that correspond to it. Not all CHAs play all the roles. The specific roles they play depend on the unique needs of the communities where they work. We recommend that these roles be used in concert with a community needs assessment when designing CHA programs. CHAs can use these roles to explain their work to those outside the field. The roles also can be used for policy development in the CHA field.

- **Bridging cultural mediation between communities and the health and social service systems**
  1. educating community members about how to use the health care and social service systems
  2. educating the health and social service systems about community needs and perspectives
     –changing the services that the system offers
     –changing the way in which services are offered
     –changing attitudes and behaviors
  3. information gathering
  4. interpretation and translation
- **Providing culturally appropriate and accessible health education and information**
  1. teaching concepts of health promotion and disease prevention
  2. helping to manage chronic illness
  3. training other CHAs

---

*Source: *Weaving the Future: The Final Report of the National Community Health Advisor Study,* A Policy Research Project of the University of Arizona funded by the Annie E. Casey Foundation, June 1998.

- **Assuring that people get the services they need**
  1. case-finding
  2. making referrals
  3. motivating and encouraging people to obtain care
  4. taking people to services
  5. providing follow-up
- **Providing information counseling and social support**
  1. providing individual support and informal counseling
  2. leading support groups
- **Advocating for individual and community needs**
  1. acting as spokespersons for clients
  2. acting as intermediaries between clients and the health and social service systems
  3. advocating for the needs and perspectives of communities
- **Providing direct service**
  1. providing clinical services
     - administering basic first aid
     - administering screening tests (i.e., heights and weights, vision, hearing, and dental screening, blood pressure, temperature, blood glucose)
  2. meeting basic needs (i.e., ensuring that people have the basic determinants of good health, such as food, adequate housing, clothing, and employment)
- **Building individual and community capacity**
  1. building individual capacity
  2. building community capacity
  3. assessing individual and community needs

Recommended Competencies of Community Health Advisors

These competencies include both the *qualities* and the *skills* that CHAs need in order to be effective. We define *qualities* as personal characteristics that can be enhanced but not taught, while *skills* are things that people know how to do because they have learned. Competencies do not correspond directly to roles; rather, many competencies are useful in playing a variety of roles.

Quality of Community Health Advisors

We recommend that the following list of qualities be used by program staff when recruiting and hiring CHAs.

- relationship with the community being served (i.e., a member of the community and/or processing shared experience with community members)
- personal strength and courage (i.e., healthy self-esteem and the ability to remain calm in the face of harassment)
- friendly/outgoing/sociable
- patient
- open-minded/non-judgmental
- motivated and capable of self-directed work
- caring
- empathetic

- committed/dedicated
- respectful
- honest
- open/eager to grow/change/learn
- dependable/responsible/reliable
- compassionate
- flexible/adaptable
- desire to help the community
- persistent
- creative/resourceful

Skills of Community Health Advisors

Capacity-building programs for CHAs should provide opportunities for developing and enhancing the following skills. Some basic level of competency in these areas should be a prerequisite for formal certification as a CHA. Each skills cluster is followed by the specific abilities that fall within that cluster.

- **Communication Skills**
  1. Ability to listen
  2. Ability to use language confidently and appropriately
  3. Ability to speak the language of the community being served
  4. Ability to document work
- **Interpersonal Skills**
  1. Friendliness and sociability
  2. Counseling skills
     –ability to develop rapport
     –maintain confidentiality
  3. Relationship-building skills
     –ability to gain or develop trust
     –ability to make people feel comfortable
     –ability to "meet people where they are"
  4. Ability to work as a team member
  5. Ability to work appropriately with diverse groups of people (i.e., cross-cultural sensitivity)
- **Teaching Skills**
  1. Ability to share information one-on-one
  2. Ability to use appropriate and effective educational techniques
  3. Ability to plan and conduct a class or presentation
  4. Ability to respond to questions about a variety of topics
  5. Ability to find requested information and bring it back to the client
- **Knowledge Base**
  1. Knowledge about the community
  2. Knowledge about specific health issues
  3. Knowledge of the health and social service systems
- **Service Coordination Skills**
  1. Ability to identify and access resources
  2. Ability to network and build coalitions
  3. Ability to make appropriate referrals

    4. Ability to provide follow-up
- **Advocacy Skills**
  1. Ability to speak up for communities and individuals and to withstand intimidation
  2. Ability to use language appropriately
  3. Ability to overcome barriers
- **Capacity-Building Skills**
  1. Empowerment skills
     –ability to help people identify their own problems
     –ability to work with clients to identify strengths and resources
  2. Leadership skills
     –ability to strategize
     –ability to motivate
     –ability to build relationships
     –ability to deliberate and interpret experience
     –ability to create an action program
     –ability to accept responsibility
- **Organizational Skills**
  1. Ability to set goals
  2. Ability to develop an action plan
  3. Ability to prioritize
  4. Ability to manage time wisely

Examples/Next Steps

The list of core roles can be used in concert with a community strengths and needs assessment when designing CHA programs. It also can be used to explain CHA work to those outside the field. Finally, it can be used for policy development in this field.

We recommend that program staff use the list of qualities when recruiting and hiring CHAs. We encourage supervisors, trainers, and co-workers to find ways to value and enhance these qualities.

Training programs for CHAs should provide opportunities to develop and enhance the skills we have identified. Some basic level of competency in these areas should be a prerequisite for formal certification as a CHA.

GENERAL PRINCIPLES OF PLANNING*

People have always schemed, designed, outlined, diagrammed, contemplated, conspired, or otherwise planned. Health educators, being no exception, have always planned programs to accomplish desirable ends.

Planning has become more sophisticated. Because much of the early planning failed to take into consideration a variety of important factors, it has become more systematized and, as a result, more effective. Various planning models have been developed and have enjoyed periods of popularity, but there is still no perfect model—and probably never will be—because of the accumulative nature of knowledge. Existing models are being revised continually to provide for perceived deficiencies. However, the similarities outnumber the differences. Several general principles of planning permeate all the models.

Principle 1: Plan the Process

It may seem like a play on words to suggest that the planning process needs to be carefully planned, but such is the case. A successful program begins as an idea that is shaped and molded through a process that is preplanned. Those who are in charge need to give thought to who should be involved, when the best time is to plan such a program, what data are needed, where the planning should occur, what resistance can be expected, and, generally, what will enhance the success of the project. Failure to take such factors into account can result in the inability to mount a good program that will meet existing needs.

A timetable needs to be developed. Many good planners use variations of the Program Evaluation and Review Techniques (PERT). To use PERT, it is necessary to state the goal of the planning process briefly and then list in sequence all the steps or activities needed to accomplish the goal. Target data for program implementation are established, and a timetable for each phase of the process is developed. The PERT process also recommends diagramming, so that planners can determine quickly what stage of the process they are in and whether they are on schedule. A typical PERT chart is shown below.

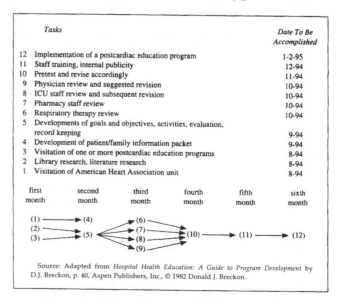

	Tasks	Date To Be Accomplished
12	Implementation of a postcardiac education program	1-2-95
11	Staff training, internal publicity	12-94
10	Pretest and revise accordingly	11-94
9	Physician review and suggested revision	10-94
8	ICU staff review and subsequent revision	10-94
7	Pharmacy staff review	10-94
6	Respiratory therapy review	10-94
5	Developments of goals and objectives, activities, evaluation, record keeping	9-94
4	Development of patient/family information packet	9-94
3	Visitation of one or more postcardiac education programs	8-94
2	Library research, literature research	8-94
1	Visitation of American Heart Association unit	8-94

first month	second month	third month	fourth month	fifth month	sixth month

Source: Adapted from *Hospital Health Education: A Guide to Program Development* by D.J. Breckon, p. 40, Aspen Publishers, Inc., © 1982 Donald J. Breckon.

*Source: Donald J. Breckon et al., *Community Health Education: Settings, Roles, and Skills for the 21st Century*, ed. 3, Aspen Publishers, Inc., © 1994.

Principle 2: Plan with People

Health educators have learned, through experience, the importance of involving clients in the planning process and the necessity of involving other principal parties to the problem or project.

Health educators, administrators, and others who are directly or indirectly affected should be involved in planning or should be consulted. Most notably, those who will be the recipients or consumers of the program and those who will be providing or delivering the service should be involved or at least consulted, preferably in the early planning stages. This action is necessary in order to develop a sense of ownership and concomitant pride. It is also necessary because those who are directly involved as participants are the ones most likely to understand the subtleties of problems and planning for this target group that are essential for success. Another reason for planning with people is the principle behind brainstorming: More ideas are likely to be generated and evaluated, with the best ones being selected for implementation. A planning committee is imperative for effective programming.

Principle 3: Plan with Data

Many programs have failed because the necessary data on which to base sound decisions were not sought. Data on diseases, disorders, and other vital statistics should be gathered and analyzed by age, sex, and ethnic or cultural origin. Data on existing programs should be gathered to avoid unneeded duplication of services and to facilitate joint programming. Data on previous programs should be gathered so that credit can be given and the new program can benefit from the experiences of the previous program. In recent years, data on existing social and environmental support systems for health programs have become important (e.g., smoking laws).

The planning committee may identify other needed data, but knowledge of the community's problems, people, and programs is important baseline information for health educators. Hospitals, health departments, social and marketing research organizations, and the National Center for Health Statistics are good sources of data. Most libraries contain U.S. Bureau of the Census data. Chambers of commerce often have data on services available.

A review of data offers a perspective of the context in which institutional or agency planning should occur. Such a review is most helpful if described briefly and discussed by the planning team for meaning. It is important to be able to condense and synthesize large amounts of data and still be able to discuss segments of the data in detail, if necessary, for ramifications for local planners. Another consideration is identifying both qualitative and quantitative data needs and sources.

Principle 4: Plan for Performance

Although some programs are planned on a one-time-only basis, the majority are or should be planned on an ongoing basis. Most of the problems addressed by health educators are never ultimately solved. Even diseases such as polio, tuberculosis, and syphilis still warrant attention, even though the tools for eradication exist. As new generations come along, new people are at risk and need to be educated. Health educators need to engage in long-range planning.

Staff time is usually the most expensive ingredient in the planning process. Cost-efficiency dictates that programs should be planned for permanence. Budget considerations should reflect a three-year projection. Similarly, staffing should reflect long-range commitment rather than expedient means. Program planners should develop job descriptions, policy statements, and promotional documents as if planning for permanence. Advisory committees should plan for staggered terms, a system of rotating chairs, and an ongoing budget. To fail to do so is to waste valuable planning time. A sense of continuity tied into the ability to do long-range planning is necessary to both cost-efficiency and cost-effectiveness.

Principle 5: Plan for Priorities

Because staff time is the most valuable resource expended in planning, it needs to be used wisely. Staff time should be spent developing programs that have the highest need and the greatest opportunity to make an impact. Even though a great need may be evident, the necessary resources or support may not be present to enable successful programming. In other instances, although an impact can be made, the same resources can carry greater impact in another aspect of community life.

Health educators should plan comprehensively, that is, be aware of most, if not all, of the needs and opportunities within a community or institution. A list of such needs should be kept and revised periodically. It should include the need to improve or expand existing programs as well as to add new programs. Prioritization of such a list can easily be transformed into either goals for the year or longer-range goals.

Planning for priorities implies an overall assessment of community needs and agency opportunities and a conscious decision on which programs to develop. It avoids letting others make the decision by simply demanding services.

Principle 6: Plan for Measurable Outcomes in Acceptable Formats

Healthy People 2000 goals are to (1) increase the span of healthy life for Americans, (2) reduce health disparities among Americans, and (3) achieve access to preventive services for all Americans.

Obviously, as goals, these are intentionally general and broad in scope. Objectives are more specific. *Healthy People 2000* uses three types of objectives: health status objectives, risk reduction objectives, and service and protection objectives.

To measure whether the three goals are being met, baseline data on the current health status of the targeted population need to be provided, along with the new health status objective. For example, Health Status Objective 18.1, regarding human immunodeficiency virus (HIV) infection, is "confine annual incidents of diagnosed AIDS [acquired immune deficiency syndrome] cases to no more than 98,000 cases. (Baseline: An estimated 44,000 to 50,000 cases in 1989)." Health Status Objective 18.2 reads "confine the prevalence of HIV infection to no more than 800 per 100,000 people. (Baseline: An estimated 400 per 100,000 in 1989.)"

Obviously, these objectives can be applied to various target groups and to the nation as a whole. It is one way that goal 2, to reduce health disparities among Americans, can be measured.

Yet, to reduce the incidence and prevalence of AIDS, risk reduction objectives need to be in place.

Risk Reduction Objective 18.3 for AIDS is as follows:

> Reduce the proportion of adolescents who have engaged in sexual intercourse to no more than 15 percent by age 15 and no more than 40 percent by age 17. (Baseline: 27 percent of girls and 33 percent of boys by age 15; 50 percent of girls and 66 percent of boys by age 17.)

Risk Reduction Objective 18.4 states the following:

> Increase to at least 50 percent the proportion of sexually active, unmarried people who used a condom at last sexual intercourse. (Baseline: 19 percent of sexually active, unmarried women aged 15 through 44 reported that their partners used a condom at last sexual intercourse in 1988.)

Healthy People 2000 also lists services and protection objectives. They are a way of measuring what services are provided and what impact they are having on protecting the public. For example, Services and Protection Objective 18.10 is as follows:

> Increase to at least 95 percent the proportion of schools that have age-appropriate HIV education curricula for students in 4th through 12th grade, preferably as part of quality school health education. (Baseline: 66 percent of school districts required HIV education but only five percent required HIV education in each year for 7th through 12th grade in 1989.)

Services and Protection Objective 18.13 states the following:

> Increase to at least 50 percent the proportion of family planning clinics, maternal and child health clinics, sexually transmitted disease clinics, tuberculosis clinics, drug treatment centers, and primary care clinics that screen, diagnose, treat, counsel, and provide (or refer for) partner notification services for HIV infection and bacterial sexually transmitted diseases, in 1989.

It is believed that most of the effort of health educators will focus on risk reduction objectives, so the Risk Reduction Objectives are reprinted in summary in Chapter 1 of this book. Readers may also wish to study the health status objectives and the services and protection objectives in *Healthy People 2000* on one or more topical areas. Certainly, students will want to use localized variations of the risk reduction objectives in class projects and must be able to write objectives in that format.

In addition, *Healthy People 2010* goals are to (1) increase quality and years of healthy life for all Americans and (2) eliminate health disparities among different segments of the population. There are 28 focus areas within these goals with a goal statement that frames the overall purpose of the focus area. There are also objectives related to meeting each of these goals. See further discussion of the *Healthy 2010* goals, focus areas, leading health indicators, and objectives in Chapter 1 and a list of all of the *Healthy People 2010* goals and objectives in Appendix C.

Principle 7: Plan for Evaluation

Evaluation should be built into the program design. It should be a continuous process in the sense that even the planning process is evaluated. Such questions as "Do we have the right people planning?" "Do we have the necessary data for planning?" "Is this the right time for planning this program?" should be discussed periodically by a team of planners.

Even outcome or impact evaluation needs to be planned early. A determination of when such evaluation should occur and who should do it is basic. Perhaps even more important is the question of what data should be gathered. Data are usually the very essence of evaluation. Recordkeeping systems and evaluation instruments need to be developed so that needed data are available for the evaluators' use.

NOTES:

PATCH

The Centers for Disease Control and Prevention staff have developed a planning model called PATCH (Planned Approach to Community Health). The model has been used successfully in a variety of settings, and the evaluation studies indicate that it is an effective model.

PATCH is essentially a networking model of planning, as advocated by the Healthy Communities 2000 project. Both vertical and horizontal networks are encouraged. Vertical networks include local, state, and national levels of government and nongovernmental agencies. Horizontal networks operate at local, state, and national levels as well, and they also cut across the broad spectrum of agencies concerned with the target population. A key concept is local ownership, but with a sense of partnership with and support by other organizations. PATCH and PRECEDE-PROCEED are compatible, according to Green and Kreuter. In fact, several of the concepts of PATCH were incorporated into the PROCEED model, so as to address the limitations of the PRECEDE model.

PATCH: Mobilizing Vertical and Horizontal Communications and Support among the National, Regional, and Community Levels

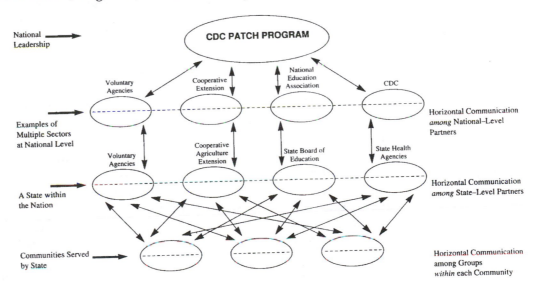

Conclusion

Other models exist and are being successfully utilized in planning and implementing programs. Yet other models will emerge in the next decade and become popular, and all will have elements that can be used by program planners. All represent tools that can help the health educator, if used appropriately, even if used on a "mix or match" basis. In academic research settings, or in funded projects where funding sources demand that the single model be used, more or less pure theoretical applications occur. In practice, however, intervention strategies are often selected based on perception of fit within the organization and acceptability to the community. Of course, what fits and what is acceptable is conditioned by familiarity, by personalities, and by organizational politics.

PATCH PROGRAM SUMMARY*

Definition and Goal of PATCH

PATCH, developed in the mid-1980s by the Centers for Disease Control and Prevention (CDC) in partnership with state and local health departments, is a process that many communities use to plan, conduct, and evaluate health promotion and disease prevention programs. The PATCH process helps a community establish a health promotion team, collect and use local data, set health priorities, and design and evaluate interventions. Adaptable to a variety of situations, the PATCH planning process can be used when a community wants to identify and address priority health problems or when the health priority or special population to be addressed has already been selected. It can also be adapted and used by existing organizational and planning structures in the community.

The goal of PATCH is to increase the capacity of communities to plan, implement, and evaluate comprehensive, community-based health promotion activities targeted toward priority health problems. The CDC promotes the use of PATCH in helping achieve the year 2000 national health objectives. These objectives aim to reduce the prevalence of modifiable risk factors for the leading causes of preventable disease, death, disability, and injury. Although these objectives are national in scope, achieving them depends on efforts to promote health and provide prevention services at the local level.

Elements Critical to PATCH

Five elements are considered critical to the success of any community health promotion process:

- *Community members participate in the process.* Fundamental to PATCH is active participation by a wide range of community members. These people analyze community data, set priorities, plan intervention activities, and make decisions on the health issues of their community.
- *Data guide the development of programs.* Many types of data can be used to describe a community's health status and needs. These data help community members select health priorities and develop and evaluate program activities.
- *Participants develop a comprehensive health promotion strategy.* Community members analyze the factors that contribute to an identified health problem. They review community policies, services, and resources and design an overall community health promotion strategy. Interventions, which may include educational programs, mass media campaigns, policy advocacy, and environmental modifications, are conducted in various settings, such as schools, health care facilities, community sites, and the workplace. Participants are encouraged to relate intervention goals to the appropriate year 2000 national health objectives.

*Source: *PATCH: Planned Approach to Community Health,* Centers for Disease Control and Prevention, National Center for Chronic Disease Prevention and Health Promotion, Division of Chronic Disease Control and Community Intervention, Atlanta, Georgia 30333, revised January 1995.

- *Evaluation emphasizes feedback and improvement.* Timely feedback is essential to the people involved in the program. Thorough evaluation can also lead to improvements in the program.
- *The community capacity for health promotion is increased.* The PATCH process can be repeated to address various health priorities. PATCH aims to increase the capacity of community members to address health issues by strengthening their community health planning and health promotion skills.

The first and last critical elements, related to community participation and capacity building, are essential to ensure community ownership. Although the local coordinator facilitates the program, the community directs the program and the program belongs to community members. Their decisions determine how the program progresses. All participants in the PATCH process share in its success.

NOTES:

THE PATCH PROCESS*

Although PATCH can be adapted to various health problems and communities, the phases of the process remain the same. Thus, once the mechanisms of the PATCH process are in place, only a few modifications are needed to address additional health issues. Phases can be repeated as new health priorities are identified, new target groups are selected, or new interventions are developed. The activities within phases may overlap as the process is carried out. Each of the five phases that constitute PATCH is described hereafter.

Phase I: Mobilizing the Community

Mobilizing the community is an ongoing process that starts in phase I as a community organizes to begin PATCH and continues throughout the PATCH process. In phase I, the community to be addressed is defined, participants are recruited from the community, and a demographic profile of the community is completed. By collecting this information, participants learn about the makeup of the community for which health interventions will be planned. Knowing the makeup of the community also helps ensure that the PATCH community group is representative of the community. The community group and steering committee are then organized and working groups are created. During this phase, the community is informed about PATCH so that support is gained, particularly from community leaders.

Phase II: Collecting and Organizing Data

Phase II begins when the community members form working groups to obtain and analyze data on mortality, morbidity, community opinion, and behaviors. These data, obtained from various sources, include quantitative data (e.g., vital statistics and survey) and qualitative data (e.g., opinions of community leaders). Community members may identify other sources of local data that should be collected as well. They analyze the data and determine the leading health problems in the community. The behavioral data are used during phase III to look at effects of behavior on the health priorities. During phase II, PATCH participants also identify ways to share the results of data analysis with the community.

Phase III: Choosing Health Priorities

During this phase, behavioral and any additional data collected are presented to the community group. This group analyzes the behavioral, social, economic, political, and environmental factors that affect the behaviors that put people at risk for disease, death, disability, and injury. Health priorities are identified. Community objectives related to the health priorities are set. The health priorities to be addressed initially are selected.

---

*Source: *PATCH: Planned Approach to Community Health,* Centers for Disease Control and Prevention, National Center for Chronic Disease Prevention and Health Promotion, Division of Chronic Disease Control and Community Intervention, Atlanta, Georgia 30333, revised January 1995.

Phase IV: Developing a Comprehensive Intervention Strategy

Using information generated during phases II and III, the community group chooses, designs, and conducts interventions during phase IV. To prevent duplication and to build on existing services, the community group identifies and assesses resources, policies, environmental measures, and programs already focused on the risk behavior and the target group. This group devises a comprehensive health promotion strategy, sets intervention objectives, and develops an intervention plan. This intervention plan includes strategies, a timetable, and a work plan for completing such tasks as recruiting and training volunteers, publicizing and conducting activities, evaluating the activities, and informing the community about results. Throughout, members of the target groups are involved in the process of planning interventions.

Phase V: Evaluating PATCH

Evaluation is an integral part of the PATCH process. It is ongoing and serves two purposes: to monitor and assess progress during each phase of the process and to monitor and assess PATCH intervention activities. The community sets criteria for determining success and identifies data to be collected. Feedback is provided to the community to encourage future participation and to planners for use in program improvement.

Using PATCH To Address a Specific Health Issue or Population

The phases just described outline the steps to identifying and reducing community health problems. When using the PATCH process to address a particular health issue of high priority, health educators should modify the steps in phases I–III accordingly. For example, they should make it clear to the community that they are mobilizing members to address a specific health issue and continue to recruit broad-based community membership for the community group while identifying and including community members or agencies that have a special interest in the specific health issue. Health educators should modify the forms and collect data for the specific health issue. Once the risk factors and target groups are selected, the PATCH process is the same for phases III–V when the health priority is not selected. Similarly, when using PATCH to address the health needs of a specific population, such as older adults, health educators should modify phases I–III as needed.

Resource Materials for PATCH

The CDC has a PATCH guide designed to help a local coordinator carry out PATCH in a community. The CDC also provides consultation on health education, health promotion, and community health planning issues to providers such as state health agencies, hospitals, and universities. For additional information, contact the Division of Chronic Disease Control and Community Intervention, National Center for Chronic Disease Prevention and Health Promotion, Centers for Disease Control and Prevention, Mailstop K-46, 4770 Buford Highway, N.E., Atlanta, Georgia 30341, or call 770-488-5426 or fax 770-488-5964.

Sample Mission Statement: Sligo Community Wellness Center

The Sligo Community Wellness Center, a dynamic ministry partnership of Adventist HealthCare MidAtlantic, the Sligo Seventh-Day Adventist Church, and the surrounding faith community, is committed to empowering men, women, and children of all backgrounds to enhance and maintain their health through the concept of holistic care. Therefore, the spiritual, intellectual, emotional, physical, and social dimensions of this larger community will be addressed through an active integration of the talents and resources of the partnership. Ongoing services provided may include health screening, counseling services, informative lectures, classes and other educational programs, activities and support, all of which are affordable and accessible.

Goals

The Wellness Center will:

1. use approaches that integrate the spiritual, intellectual, emotional, physical, and social dimensions of life
2. provide health education and support groups to encourage healthy life choices for all ages
3. be a personal, caring ministry, assisted by volunteers trained in methods consistent with the mission of the Center
4. listen to the needs of all voices in the community in planning the current and future directions of the Center
5. provide a visible, regularly staffed, and accessible resource facility
6. target audiences through maintaining an ongoing communication/public relations strategy
7. be a nonprofit, self-sustaining endeavor

NOTES:

Source: Steve Larose, "Adventist's Partnerships Spread the Gospel of Wellness," *Inside Preventive Care*, Vol. 1, No. 5, Aspen Publishers, Inc., © August 1995.

Sample Mission Statement

Healthy Valley 2000

We, the citizens of the Valley, are committed to a vision in which our community is a better place to live, work, raise a family, and enjoy life. This is what we are doing to make that vision a reality:

- We are taking responsibility for creating and developing a community that celebrates our rich cultural and spiritual diversity.
- We are working together to increase Valley pride.
- We are working together to identify and develop more effectively those things that make the Valley unique—our natural resources, our rivers, our historic buildings, and our people.
- We are working to develop a natural environment that is clean and aesthetically pleasing, makes full use of our green spaces and waterways, and is enjoyed by young and old alike.
- We are working together to build a vibrant, long-term Valley economy with decent jobs for all and a regional business outlook.
- We are working to bring top-notch health and wellness programs that nurture mind, body, and spirit to all Valley citizens.
- We are working together to develop Valley schools, and continuing education and training efforts that are second to none. We are working to integrate local schools so that we draw on the unique and complementary strengths of each.
- We are working together to ensure that our political system truly is by Valley people and for Valley people.
- We are listening to our youth, actively engaging them in all aspects of community life, and creating an environment that encourages them to reach their full potential.
- In all our work, we citizens, government officials, business, nonprofit, and religious leaders of all six Valley towns are working together to increase Valley cooperation and pride—realistically, consistently, and persistently.

We, the citizens of the Valley, want our actions to match our words, hopes, and dreams. That is why we are working together to make our vision a reality using our strengths and our abilities. This vision will constantly be revisited and revised to incorporate new input and ensure that it represents the collective vision of the community.

NOTES:

Source: Steve Larose, ed., "Connecticut Partnership Undertakes Large Scale Health Risk Assessment Program," *Inside Preventive Care*, Vol. 2, No. 11, Aspen Publishers, Inc., © February 1997.

HOW TO KEEP YOUR MISSION ALIVE EVERYDAY*

Excellent organizations know their mission. It's on the tip of everyone's tongue. Ask nearly anyone in a successful organization what their mission is and they will repeat it verbatim and give you reasons why they are the essential link in the chain to get the mission realized.

This kind of mission consciousness doesn't happen by accident. With the daily ups and downs of an organization and the distractions of life, it's hard to achieve a unified reason for being in an organization. Intentionality and meaningful repetition are the keys to achieving it.

To become a part of your organizational culture and part of the mind-set of the people who volunteer and work there, the mission needs to be seen everywhere and used often in decision making and marketing.

Visibility

The first step in making your mission alive in your organization is to make sure everyone knows what it is—and can easily find out what it is if they forget.

Have your mission statement drawn up in an attractive format; this can be done now with most word-processing programs, given their wide variety of fonts, backgrounds, and graphics. Mat and frame the mission statement, and place a copy of it in your reception area, staff lounge, and places where services are provided. Do this right: don't just copy the mission and have people tape it to the wall. And don't let the first time that staff members see the mission be the framed copy on the wall—make sure that they have seen and discussed it in advance (at time of hiring, if possible).

Put the mission statement in every document you print. It should be inside the front cover or in another prominent location in at least the following documents:

- your annual report
- all marketing and public relations materials
- your board manual
- your staff personnel policies
- your staff orientation manual (with heavy emphasis on why it is so important)
- your strategic plan

Using Your Mission

As a staff member, you have a responsibility to get the most good out of the limited resources that you have. It's ironic, then, that in the race to secure more resources to achieve more goals, people usually forget to use the mission itself as a resource.

The mission statement can be a management tool, a rallying cry, a staff motivator, a volunteer recruiter, and a fundraiser. Once you've gotten the mission statement right for your organization, your community, and the current environment, use it in these ways:

---

*Source: Peter Brinckerhoff, "Keep Your Mission Alive Everyday," *Strategic Governance*, Vol. 2, No. 4, Aspen Publishers, Inc., © September 1996.

Management Tool

The mission statement should be a regular part of staff discussions in questions such as: "Which of the three options that we have before us is most responsive to our mission?" or "Will this type of funding gain us dollars but distract us from our mission?" Use the mission statement as a backstop to make better management and policy decisions.

Rallying Cry and Staff Motivator

The mission statement can be used as a rallying cry and motivator for staff and volunteers in tough times.

Try this: when the going gets particularly tough, when morale is low, or if it seems like people have given up hope, ask your staff or board to list the good things that have happened in the last three weeks or months as a result of your organization being in business. Get personal, talking about the impact of your organization's services on individuals.

Then turn it around, and ask them what would have happened if you hadn't been around. Refocus on the mission statement as a higher calling, a cause worth working and sacrificing for. Note: you can't use this exercise every day, as it will lose its impact. Save it for when you really need it.

Volunteer Recruiter

Mission is key in volunteering. Remember the response when President Kennedy formed the Peace Corps? Or when the Red Cross needed help in south Florida after Hurricane Andrew in 1992? Remember the questions you ask when someone approaches you to serve on a board of a special committee? The key in all of these is the mission—what is being done. And mission should be a foremost topic when recruiting volunteers.

Fund-raiser

Here, as in volunteer recruiting, what good works you do and why you do them are paramount questions in a donor's mind. The crucial linchpin for the donor is not so much what you do as why you do it. Concern for the mission is what the donor shares with you, and that should be the first rationale for funding. Donors, especially large donors, like to see organizations that are focused on their mission, not just taking money for any purpose.

Worksheet for Writing the Philosophy

Questions for discussion

What are our community's values and beliefs about health? _____

_____

_____

_____

_____

_____

What is the purpose of our group? _____

_____

_____

_____

_____

_____

_____

What is our position on community involvement and responsibility for health? _____

_____

_____

_____

_____

_____

_____

What is our role in providing leadership? _____

_____

_____

_____

_____

_____

_____

Source: *Restoring Balance*, Health Promotion Resource Center, Stanford Center for Research in Disease Prevention (and the Indian Health Service), Stanford University, 1000 Welch Road, Palo Alto, California 94304-1885. Phone: (415) 723-0003. Fax: (415) 725-6906, © 1992.

Worksheet for Writing Objectives

Health Issue: _____

_____

Goal: _____

_____

_____

_____

_____

Objectives *(write the most important objectives first)*

1. _____

_____

_____

2. _____

_____

_____

3. _____

_____

_____

4. _____

_____

_____

5. _____

_____

_____

6. _____

_____

_____

7. _____

_____

_____

Source: *Restoring Balance*, Health Promotion Resource Center, Stanford Center for Research in Disease Prevention (and the Indian Health Service), Stanford University, 1000 Welch Road, Palo Alto, California 94304-1885. Phone: (415) 723-0003. Fax: (415) 725-6906, © 1992.

Worksheet for Finding and Overcoming Obstacles

Goal: _____

_____

_____

Forces working against reaching goal (barriers/obstacles/challenges): _____

_____

_____

_____

_____

_____

_____

Forces working for reaching goal (existing resources/strengths):_____

_____

_____

_____

_____

_____

_____

Approaches to overcome obstacles: _____

_____

_____

_____

_____

_____

_____

_____

_____

Source: *Restoring Balance*, Health Promotion Resource Center, Stanford Center for Research in Disease Prevention (and the Indian Health Service), Stanford University, 1000 Welch Road, Palo Alto, California 94304-1885. Phone: (415) 723-0003. Fax: (415) 725-6906, © 1992.

Worksheet for Planning Health Promotion Activities

What audience are we trying to reach? (List what you know about them.)

_____

_____

_____

_____

Where can we reach our audience? (Note specific settings, e.g., "Little Creek High School.")

☐ Home _____

☐ Work _____

☐ School _____

☐ Stores / restaurants, etc. _____

☐ Health care clinics / hospital _____

☐ Community organizations _____

☐ Churches _____

☐ Other _____

☐ Other _____

What health promotion approaches will work with our audience? (Summarize specific approaches.)

☐ Activities _____

_____

☐ Media _____

_____

☐ Policy _____

_____

NOTES:

Source: *Restoring Balance*, Health Promotion Resource Center, Stanford Center for Research in Disease Prevention (and the Indian Health Service), Stanford University, 1000 Welch Road, Palo Alto, California 94304-1885. Phone: (415) 723-0003. Fax: (415) 725-6906, © 1992.

Health Communications Program Plan: Outline

Title of Program: _____

Goal: _____

Objectives: _____

Sponsoring Agency: _____

_____

Contact Person: _____

Description of Need (why the program is being developed: _____

_____

_____

_____

Primary Target Audiences (in priority order) (Include age, gender, ethnic group, and other pertinent characteristics): _____

_____

_____

_____

_____

Key Strategies (list for each target audience):

_____

_____

_____

_____

Secondary Target Audiences (in priority order):

_____

_____

_____

_____

_____

Key Strategies: _____

_____

_____

_____

_____

Key Dates: _____

Estimated Costs: _____

Other Resources Required (e.g., staff, art shop, or computer time): _____

_____

_____

_____

_____

Potential Problems (scheduling conflicts, clearances, policies and approvals that you and other staff must address): _____

_____

_____

_____

_____

Methods of Evaluation (include formative, process, and summative [outcome] evaluation strategies): _____

_____

_____

_____

_____

NOTES:

Source: *Making Health Communication Programs Work: A Planner's Guide*, NIH Publication #92-1493, U.S. Department of Health and Human Services, Public Health Service, National Institutes of Health, Office of Cancer Communications, National Cancer Institute, April 1992.

Checklist for Program Planning and Implementation

1. Have you established a community advisory group with:
   - ☐ Representation of your targeted groups
   - ☐ The ability to provide valuable links with the community
   - ☐ Skills and resources that will be useful to the program

2. Have you identified community needs and concerns by way of:
   - ☐ Surveys/questionnaires
   - ☐ Focus groups
   - ☐ Public meetings or forums
   - ☐ Interested party analysis

3. Have you determined the community's priorities, taking into account:
   - ☐ Historical conditions
   - ☐ Traditional practices
   - ☐ Political and economic conditions

4. Have you developed program goals and objectives?
   - ☐ Yes
   - ☐ No

5. Have you decided on program strategies that:
   - ☐ Fit with the resources and needs of the community
   - ☐ Consider the beliefs, values, and practices of the community
   - ☐ Reflect field testing
   - ☐ Dispel health misconceptions
   - ☐ Change behavior
   - ☐ Change the environment

6. To implement your program, have you:
   - ☐ Prepared a timeline for program implementation
   - ☐ Listed people to be involved, and resources needed
   - ☐ Hired staff (preferably from the community)
   - ☐ Developed linkages with other community agencies, as appropriate
   - ☐ Planned to carry out an evaluation

7. Have you chosen appropriate methods and questions for:
   - ☐ Process evaluation
   - ☐ Outcome evaluation

Source: Virginia M. Gonzalez et al., *Health Promotion in Diverse Cultural Communities*, Health Promotion Resource Center, Stanford Center for Research in Disease Prevention (and the Indian Health Service), Stanford University, 1000 Welch Road, Palo Alto, California 94304-1885. Phone: (415) 723-0003. Fax: (415) 725-6906, © 1992.

Types of Organizations and Activities To Consider in Health Communication Programs

TYPES OF ORGANIZATIONS

- **Voluntary health associations**—such as the American Cancer Society, American Heart Association, American Lung Association, March of Dimes
- **Professional associations**—local medical societies and chapters of the American Academy of Family Physicians, American Academy of Pediatrics, American Nurses Association
- **Public health professionals**—local health officers/departments, school nurses, health teachers, university teachers/departments of public health
- **Health-related institutions**—hospitals, health maintenance organizations, medical schools, insurance companies, YMCAs and YWCAs, other fitness centers
- **Nonhealth industries**—television and radio stations, newspapers, employee assistance programs or personnel departments of major employers, labor unions
- **Nonhealth organizations**—PTAs, 4H Clubs, Boys Clubs, church groups, and other organizations concerned with youth and/or parents; fraternal organizations or other social/cultural groups related to the target audience; public libraries

SUGGESTED ACTIVITIES

Planning

- Join program development committee.
- Collect data to help target the program.
- Assess community health and other resources.
- Identify health and other organizations and media outlets in the community.
- Identify available, appropriate health communication materials.
- Help pretest materials.

Resource Development

- Recruit volunteers, organizations, and media to participate in the program and/or provide in-kind contributions (e.g., printing, collating, mailing services, public service space or time in media).
- Help raise funds.
- Contribute staff or volunteer time.

Program Implementation/Publicity and Promotion

- Provide conference rooms/space for program meetings and activities.
- Join program development committee.
- Organize or participate in attention-getting events (e.g., health fairs, press conferences).
- Prepare press releases.
- Prepare exhibits for public places (e.g., shopping malls, building lobbies, schools, public libraries).
- Distribute materials.
- Write letters.
- Publish articles in newsletters.
- Sponsor presentations.
- Offer individual counseling.
- Provide recognized, credible spokesperson.
- Provide media interview.

Tracking and Follow-Up

- Provide computer or manual services for program tracking.
- Identify and train other organizations interested in becoming involved.
- Follow-up by telephone with participants to ensure continued involvement.
- Serve on "thank you" committee.

Source: *Making Health Communication Programs Work: A Planner's Guide*, NIH Publication #92-1493, U.S. Department of Health and Human Services, Public Health Service, National Institutes of Health, Office of Cancer Communications, National Cancer Institute, April 1992.

Tips for Creating a Community Preventive Services Program

1. **Involve other social service agencies in the program.** Collaboration with all the social service agencies and health providers is vital.

2. **Ask a practicing local physician to head the program.** Use this provider to recruit others with face-to-face meetings, letters, and phone calls.

3. **Approach physicians first who you know will say yes.** Not only does that boost your self-confidence, but it allows you to say to other physicians that no one has turned you down so far.

4. **If a physician is reluctant, use it as an opportunity to explain the program further.** Once physicians see that the program reaches out to people who do not have access to preventive services, they may become much more interested in becoming involved.

5. **Conduct a needs assessment to show what percentage of the population does not have insurance.** Use the data to convince physicians and potential donors.

6. **Get hospitals and health systems involved.** Invite representatives of those organizations to sit on your program's board of directors. Talk about what you are doing at meetings where you know hospital officials will be.

7. **Involve schools and school nurses.** School nurses are an incredible resource. They are the ones who are in contact with at-risk people every day.

8. **Reach out to people where they live.** A lot of people in this income category may not have the resources to get to you, so you have to be prepared and willing to get to them.

9. **Give the program time to achieve successes.** Once those occur, take those successes and vocalize them in the community to increase the support outside your immediate network.

10. **Find dedicated and committed staff with experience in social services.**

NOTES:

Source: Steve Larose, ed., "New Hampshire Physicians Cooperate To Offer Preventive Services to Low-Income Residents," *Inside Preventive Care*, Vol. 2, No. 9, Aspen Publishers, Inc., © December 1996.

Narrow Your Focus for Intervention: "Ability" Factors

As you decide upon the one or more population segments you will target with intervention strategies, you might find it helpful to weigh and prioritize a number of criteria in relation to one another and to your program goals. As you try to decide which of several population segments or target populations you will try to reach first, ask yourself how each group passes the "ability" test.

The listed ability factors describe some of the variables you might want to consider before selecting one target audience over another. While each factor has its pros and cons, all may be important to your decision-making process. Certainly, no one factor alone is sufficient to determine the target audience. The relative importance of the ability factors will vary according to your situation; so feel free to add a few more "ability" categories of your own designing. Try drawing a matrix with your most likely target audience segments across the top, and the various ability factors down the side. Now rank each segment by each of the factors to determine which segment rates highest and is a likely target audience to achieve your program's goals.

"Ability" Factors

- **Impact-ability**
  How many people must you reach with a behavior-changing message or intervention strategy if you are going to make a difference? How large must the segment be to have a public health significance? How will each potential segment meet these criteria—how large is the population in this segment, and is it large enough to make a difference in the problem you are trying to address?

- **Benefit-ability**
  Who would benefit most from intervention? What physical, social, or emotional characteristics might distinguish one group of people as needing intervention or potentially benefiting

from it more than others (e.g., higher morbidity and mortality rates, at greater risk, or at a critical time when negative consequences might be avoided)?

- **Access-ability**
  How easily, affordably, or practically can you reach the population segment given your current resources? How readily accessible is this segment, considering your influence with this population? Is anyone else reaching this segment effectively and are they potential partners? Remember, there is no such thing as a hard-to-reach population, only populations that require more abundant or creative strategies to reach them.

- **Account-ability**
  To whom must your program remain accountable? And to what extent do those stakeholders determine the focus of the program (e.g., by job responsibilities, source of funding, policies mandated by the administration, specified program criteria)? Are you in a situation in which your target audience has been determined for you, to some extent, or do you have the freedom to choose any population segment within a defined geographic or political boundary?

- **Achieve-ability**
  What is most reasonable and feasible for you, given your particular situation? What practical, political, or financial constraints must you overcome if you choose to address one group of people versus another? And remember, constraints can be overcome with a little creativity and some innovative partnering. Have a can-do attitude as you approach this task.

- **Response-ability**
  Who is most ready, willing, and able to respond or to take the desired action? This factor ranks groups of people by their readiness to change, their stage of change, their lifestyle, or their competence in certain skills necessary for change.

Source: U.S. Department of Health and Human Services, Public Health Service, Centers for Disease Control and Prevention, National Center for Chronic Disease Prevention and Promotion, Division of Nutrition and Physical Activity, *Promoting Physical Activity: A Guide for Community Action*. Champaign, IL: Human Kinetics, 1999.

PREVENTING TEEN PREGNANCY*

The challenge of breaking the cycle of teen pregnancy patterns looms like an almost impossible task. For many, the tragedy of teen pregnancy within our society represents the failure of communities and government in addressing a fundamental social problem that sends hundreds of thousands of citizens into poverty each year.

The problems surrounding teen pregnancy are complex, and so are the solutions, according to a host of reports released during the last 18 months. Each of these reports paints a picture of a health problem that is staggering in its implications and epidemic in proportion.

One Million Pregnancies

Every year, one million American teenage girls get pregnant—that's 4 of every 10 girls; most of these pregnancies (8 of every 10) are unplanned. Most of these girls will never marry, or will live in single parenthood for at least 10 years before marriage. They will live in poverty, probably never work, and won't receive a basic high school education. More than likely, their children will grow up to be teenage moms living in poverty as well. Alarmingly, at least half of babies born to teenage women 15 to 17 years of age are fathered by men 20 years of age and older, despite the abundance of statutory rape laws (Guttmacher Institute, 1994; Kirby, 1997; Maynard, 1996; NOAPP, 1995).

Nationwide, teen pregnancies extract both an economic and physical toll. Of the teens who get pregnant, one in six will get pregnant again within one year. Most teens start having sex one year before they ever visit a contraceptive clinic, and the majority of unplanned pregnancies happen within six months from initial intercourse. One third to half of all teen pregnancies currently end in abortion, with middle-income and more affluent teens more often seeking abortion options than teens in lower-income categories. Teens also account for the majority of later-term abortions in the United States, according to a 1994 article in the *New England Journal of Medicine* (Morgan et al., 1995).

It can cost more than $100,000 to care for a preterm infant, and, in 1990, the United States disbursed $25 billion in Aid to Families with Dependent Children (AFDC) funds to teen moms. The total direct and indirect costs of adolescent pregnancy surpass $34 billion annually.

But there are glimmers of hope that current efforts now in place are reducing overall teen pregnancies. Information released late last year from the Centers for Disease Control and Prevention (CDC) demonstrated the first teen pregnancy rate declines since 1976. Still, rates hover at approximately one million pregnancies annually, a benchmark first noted in 1973. Federal health officials also reported that 37 states are currently experiencing sustained declines in teen pregnancies, and of those states, 10 noted declines of more than 10 percent. Yet, while birth rates for teens 15 to 19 years of age may have dropped, the birth rate for unmarried teens in that same age category grew.

"Almost all of the poor children in this country are living with one parent," said President Bill Clinton in addressing the issue in 1997. "It would be better if no teenager ever had a child out of wedlock; that it is not the right thing to do, and it is not a good thing for the children's future and the future of this country."

Welfare reform laws passed last year mandated that government ensure teen pregnancy prevention programs in 25 percent of communities nationwide. That number is currently approximately 30 percent, according to Donna Shalala, secretary of the U.S. Department of Health and Human Services (DHHS), the agency responsible for oversight. Additionally, the new laws provide $50 million a year in new funding for states to provide abstinence education activities, starting February 1998.

In remarks made during a January 1997 press conference during which the DHHS unveiled new programs to combat teen pregnancy, Shalala stressed that pregnancy prevention efforts were reaching out to girls starting at nine years of age. Increased governmental efforts are coming at a time when the age of initial sexual intercourse has dropped from an average of 16 years to between 14 and 15 years. Compounding that problem, the average onset age of menstruation has dropped from 14 years at the turn of the century to approximately 12.5 years (Kirby, 1997).

Battling the Rate

The United States has the highest teen pregnancy rate among industrialized nations, and although reporting variances may occur between nations, the rate is believed to be twice as high as next-in-line United Kingdom and 13 times higher than the pregnancy rate in Japan. Additionally, teens in the United States are twice as likely to abort their pregnancies as teens in other industrialized nations (Kirby, 1997; Maynard, 1996).

Some consider the high teen pregnancy rate a uniquely American phenomenon. Those who work within pregnancy prevention tend to lay blame on the unwillingness of adults to come together and work toward reducing teen pregnancies regardless of individual beliefs, said Sarah Brown, director of the National Campaign To Prevent Teen Pregnancy. Her comments are echoed by others in the field including Glori Feldt, president of Planned Parenthood Federation of America Inc.

Feldt was married by the time she was 15 and the mother of three children by age 20. Growing up in rural Texas, Feldt did what most of her peers did: she married early and started a family. Speaking at a Planned Parenthood conference last year in Los Angeles, Feldt railed against ideological obstacles within the teen pregnancy issue.

"We have the highest rate in the industrialized world. Is this because our kids are more sexually active? No. The difference is [other countries have] defined the problem as 'teen pregnancy,' and we have allowed the problem to be 'teen sex.' In other countries, it's a public health problem, and we define it as a moral problem," she told a group of Planned Parenthood supporters.

What both Brown and Feldt agree upon is that adults in the United States need a change of perspective.

"Ultimately," President Clinton indicated at a press conference about teen pregnancy, "what is needed is a revolution of the heart. We have to work to instill within every young man and woman a sense of personal responsibility, a sense of self-respect, and a sense of possibility. Having a child is the greatest responsibility anyone can assume. . . . And it's not the right choice for a teenager to make before she or he is ready."

That revolution may have already begun. As one Washington policy group has observed, the recent drop in the teen pregnancy rate may be directly tied to an increase in the number of teens choosing to abstain from sex. "Teen pregnancy is declining because more teens are choosing abstinence despite all of the federal government's efforts to promote the contrary. Statistics published by the Centers for Disease Control and Prevention show that the decrease in teen pregnancy rates is concurrent with the rising number of teens choosing to abstain from sex," said Gracie Hsu, a policy analyst with the Family Research Council.

In early May, the CDC announced that the number of teens choosing to abstain from sex is increasing. In a press conference held on May 1, DHHS secretary Shalala announced that the percentage of teens who have had sex has declined for the first time in two decades.

The 1995 National Survey of Family Growth, conducted by DHHS's National Center for Health Statistics, found that 50 percent of females 15 to 19 years of age have had intercourse, down from 55 percent of women in that same age category making that same indication in 1990. The statistics also indicated that before 1995, the percentage of teen girls who had had sex by 15 to 19 years of age has steadily increased from 29 percent in 1970, 36 percent in 1975, 47 percent in 1982, to 53 percent in 1988.

The findings are part of a study about childbearing and family planning among women 15 to 44 years of age scheduled for release at the end of May. Additional research sponsored by DHHS's National Institute of Child Health and Human Development indicated a similar trend for males, with 55 percent of never-married teen boys 15 to 19 years of age having had sex, down from 60 percent among that same group in 1990.

"We welcome the news that the long-term increase in teenage sexual activity may finally have stopped," Shalala said. "But this news should encourage us to do more, not lull us into doing less. We need to change the cultural messages that have been accepted too long. Continual increases in teen sexual activity are not inevitable, and we can take action together to protect the health and well-being of our young people."

Most adults in the United States want teens to abstain from sex, according to a new survey released in early May from the National Campaign as it was kicking off its official work to reduce teen pregnancies one third by the year 2005. Most Americans (95 percent) say it's important for teens to receive a strong abstinence message. And three of four persons surveyed in the National Campaign opinion poll said teens should have access to birth control if they are going to engage in sexual activity.

The National Campaign is intent on helping reduce the number of teen pregnancies each year. The National Campaign was founded last year with the goal of reducing teen pregnancy rates one third by the year 2005. Along with other groups, including the Association of Women's Health, Obstetric and Neonatal Nurses (AWHONN), the National Campaign recently encouraged teen pregnancy prevention advocates to put their support behind The Teenage Pregnancy Reduction Act of 1997, which, as of May, was scheduled to be introduced into the 105th Congress.

Authored by representatives Nita Lowey (D-NY) and Mike Castle (R-DE), cochairs of the National Campaign's advisory council, the act would provide $3.5 million in annual funding for three years for in-depth evaluation of promising teen pregnancy prevention programs; $10 million in one-time incentive grants to effective programs; and work toward the establishment of a national clearinghouse on effective prevention programs.

The introduction of their legislation coincided with the release of a critical report from the National Campaign, *No Easy Answers: Research Findings on Programs To Reduce Teen Pregnancy*, which works to dispel myths surrounding effective teen pregnancy prevention as well as herald successful model programs and their common characteristics.

"At a time when we are discussing making serious investments in teen pregnancy prevention programs, it's crucial that we understand which programs are effective and whether they can be replicated in other communities," said Rep. Castle, adding that the legislation will go a long way toward giving groups such as the National Campaign the information they need to seek out and promote model programs.

The overriding research findings arising from *No Easy Answers* indicate that teen pregnancy prevention programs need to be as multifaceted as the problem itself (Kirby, 1997).

"There are no simple or single approaches that will markedly reduce adolescent pregnancy," said report author Douglas Kirby, PhD, and director of research for ETR Associates. "Because some youths have sex while others do not, programs need to address both abstaining from or postponing sex using contraception," he said.

In just 100 pages, the report goes a long way to dispel some of the myths and trends that have clouded teen pregnancy prevention efforts in the past.

"This report confirms that there are no magic bullets for solving America's teen pregnancy crisis," said National Campaign president Isabel Sawhill, PhD. "The causes behind teen pregnancy are varied and pervasive; solutions require a comprehensive response from all sectors of society—parents and youth workers, religious leaders and politicians, entertainers and business leaders. We must help teens find reasons to delay early childbearing—adolescence must be seen by all as a time for education and skill-building, not pregnancy and parenthood."

Dispelling Myths

Among the *No Easy Answers* report's most critical findings are indications about the ineffectiveness of single-plank approaches or simple solutions to teen pregnancy problems. Included in the report's findings are facts that indicate:

- **Abstinence-only programs are unproven**—and even though they may be appropriate for very young teens, there is no published scientific research indicating they have actually reduced sexual activity. While the CDC has clearly stated that abstinence is the only strategy that will 100 percent effectively prevent teen pregnancies, more research needs to be done to determine the effectiveness of current abstinence-based programs.
- **Sex education does not increase sexual activity**—contrary to fears, research demonstrates that programs focusing on sexuality, including acquired immune deficiency syndrome (AIDS) and contraception education, do not increase teen sexual activity.
- **Contraception alone is not enough**—without adding other important educational and counseling components that address teens' motivations, research indicates that widespread access to contraception does not affect teen pregnancy birth rates. In fact, a 1995 study published in *Adolescence* indicated that despite the fact that condom usage doubled between 1980 and 1990, one third of all teens were still

practicing unsafe sex in 1990; and of those who got pregnant, 60 percent of their pregnancies were unplanned (Rodriguez & Moore, 1995).

- **Some sex education programs reduce unprotected sex**—Although modest in their impact, there are some programs that reduce unprotected sex among teens by delaying initiation of sex, increasing contraceptive usages, and reducing the number of sexual partners for some teens.
- **More and better research must be done**—Current analysis of research within teen pregnancy prevention is hampered by poor research methods, small sample sizes, lack of comparison groups and controlled studies, lack of long-term follow up, and little replication of findings.

Calling for more money to be "better spent," Kristin Moore, PhD, and chair of the National Campaign's Task Force on Effective Programs and Research, which produced the report, said, "This sound research review tells us that we must start taking teen pregnancy research as seriously as we do cancer research."

Assessing Health Risks

Health care providers stand in a unique niche and can play a significant role in helping combat teen pregnancy. Because of the respect afforded to them by their communities, and with their ability to provide education and counseling on family planning issues, health care providers can help link others in the effort to reduce teenage births.

"Nurses and doctors are deeply respected leaders in most communities and hence are natural leaders on this topic. They can bridge ideological divides where other groups can't," National Campaign Director Brown told *Lifelines* in a late-March interview after the release of the group's report.

Pregnant teens and teenage moms share greater health risks than their counterparts, according to research from the March of Dimes. Health care providers need to be aware that pregnant teens are at a greater risk for anemia, preeclampsia, delivering low-birth-weight infants, preterm delivery, and sexually transmitted diseases.

Because of the strong reputation nurses have always held for patient advocacy, nurses can play a key role in helping reduce teen pregnancy rates in their communities and nationwide. Efforts should be focused on encouraging young women and men to avoid risk-taking behaviors that tend to promote teen pregnancy, as well as caring for teens who are pregnant, advocates for reducing teen pregnancies say.

Additionally, the risks to the infant are just as substantial as those to the mother. When compared with the children of mothers 20 or 21 years of age, children of teenage mothers are more likely to be born prematurely and are 50 percent more likely to be low-birth-weight babies—or weigh less than five-and-one-half pounds at birth, which increases the likelihood for a variety of adverse conditions, including infant death, blindness, deafness, chronic respiratory problems, mental retardation, mental illness, and cerebral palsy (Maynard, 1996).

Teens who get pregnant may also have been victims of sexual abuse earlier in their lives, according to research published in the journal *Adolescence* (McCullough & Scherman, 1991). According to authors McCullough and Scherman, a 1986 study commissioned by the Illinois Department of Children and Family Services discovered that 60 percent of teens who had become pregnant during their adolescence had been forced to have an unwanted sexual experience during their childhood or early adolescence. One quarter of those teens reported that the abusers were close family members (McCullough & Scherman, 1991). Other more recent studies also have examined the link between adolescent pregnancy and sexual abuse, noting correlations from 40 to 60 percent of teens falling within this category.

Barriers to Prenatal Care

In addition to problems related to sexual abuse, health care providers need to know there are a host of reasons that keep pregnant adolescents from seeking prenatal care. According to research published in *Clinical Nursing Research,* more than half of all pregnant teens delay seeking prenatal care until their second and third trimesters, compounding the known relationships documented by the Children's Defense Fund between adolescent pregnancies and preterm labor, low birth weights, and handicapped infants.

In fact, according to the March of Dimes, in 1991, 11 percent of teen mothers received late or no prenatal care, compared with an overall average of 6 percent of all women pregnant during that same time period. The most common reasons teens give in not seeking prenatal care include concealment of the pregnancy, the cost of care, needing their own energy and time to deal with other personal problems, and long waits at health clinics (Lee & Grubbs, 1995).

For those teens who sought prenatal care, more than half indicated that they wanted to take adequate care of their baby (57.1 percent), they wanted to take care of themselves (34.2 percent), they were having problems with their pregnancy (28.7 percent), and when going for a family planning session they were told they were pregnant (5.7 percent), according to the study reported in *Clinical Nursing Research* (Lee & Grubbs, 1995).

When pressed further for information about how the teens learned they were pregnant, 67.5 percent indicated that they had missed a period, 43 percent felt "sick" and/or "nauseous," 16 percent had breast swelling or tenderness, and 13 percent also felt fatigued, according to the authors (Lee & Grubbs, 1995).

In wrapping up their research, the authors concluded that it's important for nurses and other health care professionals to help teens understand and recognize the signs and symptoms of pregnancy.

"Nurses and other health care personnel in clinical practice should provide information about the symptoms and signs of pregnancy, and about the importance of initiating early prenatal care, in all encounters with preadolescent and adolescent girls and their mothers, to increase the likelihood that teens will seek early prenatal care if they become pregnant," the authors urged.

Additional clinical implications arising from the *Clinical Nursing Research* report (Lee & Grubbs, 1995) include:

- Attempts should be made by health care providers to increase parental interest and concern about pregnant teens and prenatal care.
- Nurses should be involved in planning public and private educational and media programs.
- Nurses should stress the importance of prenatal care.
- Efforts should be made to involve parents and other adults in teen pregnancy prevention programs.

- Nurses should support and encourage public health education, especially education geared toward preventive care.
- Nurses should be involved in establishing school-based preventive health clinics that include pregnancy recognition, prenatal care, and pregnancy prevention at middle and high school levels.

It's also important for health care providers to recognize that parents may not be providing their children with adequate sexual education at an early enough age. In fact, in a survey of teens published in *Adolescence* (Rodriguez & Moore, 1995), only 52 percent reported that their parents had ever talked with them about sex; and when they did, it came later than adolescence. Only one in five indicated that their parents had discussed sex with them before 11 years of age (Rodriguez & Moore, 1995).

Programs That Make a Difference

There are literally hundreds, more likely thousands, of individual, community-oriented programs all working toward reducing teen pregnancy rates, says the National Campaign's Brown. Yet in compiling the group's most recent report, *No Easy Answers*, author Kirby (1997) could find only 80 programs that qualified under his group's research criteria and methodology that had sufficient follow-up to be considered for review.

"This shows you how much work we have to do," Brown says. "The research is weak." As a result, it's difficult, if not impossible, to predict whether a program that brings a certain degree of success in one community can be exported into another community, with similar results.

What has been documented, however, is fundamental, common characteristics of successful programs. Echoing the research trends that emerged in the National Campaign's most recent report, the DHHS focuses its activities and programs around five key principles inherent to successful community efforts:

- **Parental and adult involvement**—Mentors play a key role in encouraging teens to avoid early pregnancy and to stay in school.
- **Abstinence**—Personal responsibility is at the heart of all successful efforts.
- **Clear strategies for the future**—Teens need to see a clear pathway to college or jobs that give them hope and a reason to avoid pregnancy.
- **Community involvement**—All sectors have to find common ground and work together in shepherding teens, including parents, schools, businesses, media, health and human services providers, government, religious, and civic organizations.
- **Sustained commitment**—Efforts must remain committed to young persons over a long period of time.

Additionally, there are key elements of programs that fall within these five principal areas worth noting. When the Southern Regional Project on Infant Mortality and the Child Welfare League of America set out on a mission last year to hold a series of briefings and site visits, one of their first stops was at the South Carolina Legislature. More than 50 persons from the legislature and 70 people from advocacy and civic groups gathered during a two-hour legislative recess to take notes on what the presenters were identifying as components of successful programs that help prevent adolescent pregnancy. According to the Southern Regional Project and the Child Welfare League of America, those components include:

- age-appropriate family life education from grades K–12
- school-based or -linked health clinics
- community-based adolescent health clinics
- school drop-out prevention
- communitywide multimedia campaigns
- messages targeted at both girls and boys
- decision-making and communication skills development
- peer support
- adult mentors from similar backgrounds and communities
- individual counseling and case management for at-risk teens and their families
- mechanisms for family/parent involvement and support
- contraceptive services coupled with comprehensive health care
- community involvement and service opportunities for teens
- supervised after-school activities for teens, including adolescent centers
- development of "real life" options, including career counseling, job training, and college

In addition to these elements, common characteristics of successful teen prevention programs include broad community support and cooperation; age-appropriate sexual education with a focus on abstinence and/or the delay of sexual activity; and intensive, long-term programs that are developmental in nature and culturally appropriate.

Other programs include elements that focus on times and situations particularly inducing for teenage sexual behavior.

"It's 3 o'clock—Do you know where your children are?" That's a question Kristin Ditillo of the Campaign for Our Children finds herself asking time and again, particularly to parents and caregivers of vulnerable teens. After all, her group reports, most teens, when asked where and when they have had sex, say it was at their home just after school—typically between the hours of 3 PM and 6 PM.

So how can busy parents focus on their careers without calling home every 15 minutes within these three pivotal hours? "Encourage [teens] to get involved in after-school activities—busy teens don't have time to become parents," Ditillo says. "These activities also boost self-esteem, another key factor in preventing adolescent pregnancy."

Teens also need reasons beyond "just say no" when it comes to abstaining. When the Children's Aid Society launched an extensive seven-prong program in 10 New York City communities plus 17 other cities nationwide, the program's goal was to assist youth in avoiding unintended pregnancies as well as making responsible sexual decisions. Taking a multifaceted approach, the Children's Aid Society focused on these major components: career awareness, family and sex education, medical and mental health services, academic assessment and homework help, self-esteem programs through the performing arts, and sports activities. The Children's Aid Society's Harlem program also guarantees teens who graduate from high school or get their equivalency diploma admission to New York City's Hunter College. Preliminary findings, according to Children's Aid Society officials, indicate higher educational aspirations among teens in the program, lower alcohol consumption rates, less sexual activity, increased use of contraceptives within sexual activity, and better outcomes upon high school graduation.

Ultimately, when parents, teachers, community leaders, religious institutions, health care providers, school officials, and health and human services providers are all willing to step up to the challenge together to reduce teen pregnancy, there may be hope for continued reductions in teen pregnancy rates.

"We're really risking our future if we tolerate 1 million girls becoming pregnant in this country each year. There is no quick fix. And wouldn't constituencies across the board love it if we could say in five years that we're really starting to get a grip on this problem," Brown said.

REFERENCES

Alan Guttmacher Institute. (1994). *Sex and America's teenagers.* New York: Alan Guttmacher Institute: Author.

Kirby, D. (1997). *No easy answers: Research findings on programs to reduce teen pregnancy.* A research review commissioned by the National Campaign's Task Force on Effective Programs and Research. National Campaign to Prevent Teen Pregnancy. Washington, DC: National Campaign to Prevent Teen Pregnancy: Author.

Lee, S. & Grubbs. L. (1995). Pregnant teenagers' reasons for seeking or delaying prenatal care. *Clinical Nursing Research, 4*(2), 38.

March of Dimes. (1992). *Fact sheet: Facts you should know about teenage pregnancy.* White Plains, NY: March of Dimes Birth Defects Foundation: Author.

Maynard, R.A. (1996). *Kids having kids: A Robin Hood Foundation special report on the costs of adolescent childbearing.* New York, NY: The Robin Hood Foundation: Author.

McCullough, M. & Scherman, A. (1991). Adolescent pregnancy: contributing factors and strategies for prevention. *Adolescence, 26,* 809.

Morgan, C., Chapar, G.N., & Fisher, M. (1995). Psychosocial variables associated with teenage pregnancy. *Adolescence, 30*(118), 277.

National Organization on Adolescent Pregnancy, Parenting and Prevention (NOAPP). (1995). *Pregnancy, poverty, school and employment.* Bethesda, MD: Author.

Rodriguez, Jr., C., & Moore, N.B. (1995). Perceptions of pregnant/parenting teens: Reframing issues for an integrated approach to pregnancy problems. *Adolescence, 30,* 685.

Principles for Successful Pregnancy Prevention Programs

1. Acknowledge that teen sexual behavior is a complex issue that is often uncomfortable and difficult for adults to deal with.
2. Create strategies based on the latest research in teen pregnancy.
3. Start programs at early ages and provide interventions that reach young people through childhood, adolescence, and young adulthood.
4. Emphasize primary pregnancy prevention for both males and females.
5. Recognize that preventing first pregnancies requires different strategies than does reducing subsequent pregnancies.
6. Assess the effectiveness and quality of programs and build on existing foundations.
7. Ensure that programs are balanced, realistic, integrated, and multi-faceted.
8. Involve community members and teens in program planning, service delivery, and evaluation.
9. Collaborate with other community sectors, including business, religious organizations, and the media.
10. Set realistic goals based on available resources, definite time frames, and reachable objectives.
11. Realize that effective pregnancy prevention involves a sequential, though not necessarily linear, developmental process.
12. Recognize that long-term sustainability requires a significant investment of time, money, and committed individuals.
13. Recognize that effective pregnancy prevention efforts involve major changes and challenges and often require taking calculated risks.

Source: Brindis C., Davis L., *Mobilizing for Action*. (Communities Responding to the Challenge of Adolescent Pregnancy Prevention, v.1) Washington, DC: Advocates for Youth, © 1998.

Teen Pregnancy Factors at a Glance

- **Poverty.** Most teen parents are from low-income families. Many poor teens become parents because they are not motivated to delay pregnancy and parenthood.
- **School performance.** Poor academic performance is often a precursor to teen pregnancy. Many teens drop out of school before they become pregnant.
- **Family background.** Family history of early pregnancy, family dysfunction, and/or living in a single-parent household are associated with early childbearing.
- **Sexual abuse and victimization.** Teen pregnancy and childbearing are often linked to sexual abuse, sexual pressure, and sexual coercion.
- **Substance use.** Teen use of alcohol, drugs, and tobacco is associated with sexual risk taking.
- **Homelessness or in-state care.** Youth who experience behavioral problems, and those who are homeless, incarcerated, or in foster care have high rates of early pregnancy and childbearing.
- **Lack of knowledge and access to contraceptive services.** Teens often do not have the information, skills, or support systems to delay sexual activity, abstain from sexual intercourse, or use contraceptives effectively when they are sexually active.
- **Peer pressure.** Many teens feel pressured by their friends and peers to become sexually active.

Source: Reprinted with Permission. Brindis C, Davis C, *Mobilizing for Action*. [Communities Responding to the Challenge of Adolescent Pregnancy Prevention, v. 1] Washington, D.C.: Advocates for Youth, © 1998.

Reproductive Pathways of Adolescent Women

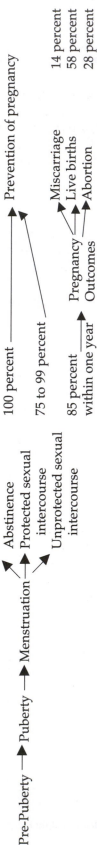

Pre-Puberty → Puberty → Menstruation →

- Abstinence
- Protected sexual intercourse
- Unprotected sexual intercourse

→ Prevention of pregnancy

100 percent

75 to 99 percent

85 percent within one year → Pregnancy Outcomes →

- Miscarriage — 14 percent
- Live births — 58 percent
- Abortion — 28 percent

A CONTINUUM OF COMMUNITY INTERVENTIONS IN ADOLESCENT REPRODUCTIVE HEALTH

Prior to Intercourse

The Question
How can we postpone sexual activity among young people?

Examples of Strategies
- STD/HIV prevention education for both males & females
- age-appropriate, skill-based, balanced, realistic sexuality education
- parent-child communication about sexuality
- life opportunities/youth development
- academics
- self-esteem enhancement
- communication skills
- teen-friendly, readily available contraceptive services

Among Sexually Active Teens

The Question
How can we encourage contraceptive use?

Examples of Strategies
- STD/HIV prevention education for both males & females
- age-appropriate, skill-based, balanced, realistic sexuality education
- parent-child communication about sexuality
- life opportunities/youth development
- academics
- self-esteem enhancement
- communication skills
- teen-friendly, readily available contraceptive services

Among Pregnant Teens

The Question
What services do pregnant teens need?

Examples of Strategies
- STD/HIV prevention education for both males & females
- age-appropriate, skill-based, balanced, realistic sexuality education
- parent-child communication about sexuality
- life opportunities/youth development
- academics
- self-esteem enhancement
- communication skills
- teen-friendly, readily available contraceptive services

Plus
- pregnancy options counseling
- prompt, safe, confidential abortion services
- prenatal care
- post-partum contraceptive services
- adoption services

Among Teen Parents

The Question
How can we ensure the best outcomes for young parents and the children they choose to raise?

Examples of Strategies
- STD/HIV prevention education for both males & females
- age-appropriate, skill-based, balanced, realistic sexuality education
- parent-child communication about sexuality
- life opportunities/youth development
- academics
- self-esteem enhancement
- communication skills
- teen-friendly, readily available contraceptive services

Plus
- parenting classes
- social services
- GED
- job/vocational training
- employment
- child care

Source: Reprinted with Permission. Brindis C, Davis C, *Mobilizing for Action*. [Communities Responding to the Challenge of Adolescent Pregnancy Prevention, v. 1] Washington, D.C.: Advocates for Youth, © 1998.

ESTABLISHING A STEERING COMMITTEE FOR AN ADOLESCENT PREGNANCY PREVENTION PROGRAM*

A planning committee is key in the initial stages of defining goals, developing organizational structure, and gaining community support. Experience in the field of pregnancy prevention suggests that a small planning group is best suited to these initial tasks, given the strong potential for conflict within pregnancy prevention coalitions. A small, inclusive planning committee can lay the groundwork by creating a mission statement, developing goals and objectives, and identifying potentially effective strategies. These strategies can later be adapted or changed, depending on the findings of the needs assessment, the interests and expertise of coalition members, and the resources available. However, the philosophy that initially drew the leadership together should be maintained.

Begin by organizing a working group of six to ten, but no more than 20, individuals who can analyze community health needs, assess local awareness of those needs, and determine the levels and sources of community support or opposition. If the initial group is too diverse in its approach to adolescent reproductive health, it may take too long to establish a mission and goals, or it may end with a mission so vague that effective pregnancy prevention goals cannot be established. The group should, at minimum, share basic philosophical beliefs about (1) abstinence, (2) sexual activity, and (3) adolescent access to reproductive health education and services. The group should also be willing to advocate for evaluated, research-based pregnancy prevention strategies. Finally, the initial group should be representative of the community; strongly committed to effort; willing to commit substantial time to the work; able to assist in reducing logistical barriers; and, willing to provide constructive feedback on program plan development and implementation.

The initial group should include at least one representative from each of the nine groups listed below who also share a basic philosophical approach to teenage pregnancy. (Note: Individuals may fit more than one category.)

- Teenagers can be valuable advocates, trainers, researchers, and media spokespersons. They should be involved in every stage of the coalition's work, from needs assessment and program planning to implementation and evaluation. Youth involvement is a key component in any adolescent pregnancy prevention program. Adolescents must be involved as more than token additions to the group.
- Parents are important and credible advocates for pregnancy prevention in the community. They help decide what services should be available to their children. They can speak out in many venues—schools, religious institutions, legislative hearings—and to the media.
- Health care and social service providers include professionals from family planning clinics, health departments, community-based clinics, health maintenance organizations, hospitals, private medical practices, social service agencies, foster

*Source: Reprinted with Permission. Brindis C, Davis C, *Mobilizing for Action*. [Communities Responding to the Challenge of Adolescent Pregnancy Prevention, v. 1] Washington, D.C.: Advocates for Youth, © 1998.

care agencies, child welfare organizations, and juvenile justice systems. These professionals can provide leadership for implementing controversial services, such as contraceptive access for teens, and can help coordinate services. High level administrators and health agency directors can be effective members of the initial group.

- Youth-serving or youth development organizations provide excellent settings for pregnancy prevention activities. Representatives should be included from youth-serving organizations (YSOs) that provide after-school or out-of-school care and recreation to youth. Usually non-governmental, YSOs are receptive to prevention strategies and open to working with youth who have multiple difficulties, such as school dropout, substance abuse, and family problems. YSOs often already operate prevention programs and can provide perspectives critical to the communitywide effort.

- Religious organizations can provide a moral and ethical voice to the debate on teen pregnancy prevention. Tapping into the strengths and resources of religious communities will encourage more creative, realistic, and productive responses to adolescent pregnancy prevention.

- Educational institutions, including schools, colleges, junior colleges, and vocational training centers, have experts that can contribute largely to pregnancy prevention activities. School personnel, including teachers, nurses, guidance counselors, and coaches, can offer expertise on training, service delivery, and evaluation. A university-based teaching hospital may be willing to link with a local school to create a school-based or school-linked health clinic. Intern programs offer a way to involve college students in service delivery. In addition, academic researchers and their students can provide important guidance, direction, and expertise in conducting needs assessments and program evaluation.

- Both philanthropic and business communities have joined with government agencies in public/private partnerships for pregnancy prevention. While foundations may provide start-up funds, the business community is a largely untapped resource for financial or material support, such as office space or equipment, as well as for endorsements. Business leaders can also open other doors as well as involve their employees in community efforts.

- The media can play a critical role in creating new norms around teen sexuality, pregnancy, and childbearing. The media should be included from the very start as media can create widespread support by launching public awareness campaigns for teens and families. Media can present teen perspectives, shape images regarding youth, and educate audiences, especially teens themselves, who learn much about sexuality from all forms of electronic and print media.

- Policy makers, elected officials, and government agencies can promote and strengthen pregnancy prevention efforts. Key decision makers, such as state governors, legislators, city and county officials, school board members, and their staff, can keep coalition members informed about pending legislation. Involving policy makers ensures both political commitment and a voicing of their concerns and opinions. Moreover, officials can help coordinate services, ensure funding, and collect relevant data. Coalitions can and should create long-term alliances between community leaders and policy makers.

The steering committee may use the questions on the "Taking the Pulse Worksheet" to assess community readiness—the willingness, openness, and capacity—to address teen pregnancy prevention and advance the agenda.

Taking the Pulse Worksheet

- Is the community aware of how teen pregnancy affects it?

  _____

  _____

  _____

- What is the magnitude of teen pregnancy and early childbearing in the community?

  _____

  _____

  _____

- Is there a nucleus of individuals concerned about the problem who are sufficiently motivated and committed to addressing teen pregnancy efforts?

  _____

  _____

  _____

- What kinds of synergy can be created and fostered around the issue of teen pregnancy?

  _____

  _____

  _____

- What resources and efforts are currently available upon which to build? Could additional new or existing resources be channeled into teen pregnancy prevention?

  _____

  _____

  _____

- How can the community mobilize its resources?

  _____

  _____

  _____

- Is the community sufficiently aware of how teen pregnancy affects young people? Can the issue be raised to a priority?

  _____

  _____

  _____

- How much "buy-in" exists from key stakeholders to develop and implement a strategic plan of action?

  _____

  _____

  _____

- What are the potential barriers to advancing an adolescent pregnancy prevention agenda?

  _____

  _____

  _____

continues

Taking the Pulse Worksheet continued

- How can common ground be developed so that the plan of action reflects the best research in the field, and also incorporates the diverse viewpoints found in the community?

_____

_____

_____

- How can community organizations work with researchers, policy makers, and the media to create a new social norm related to reducing adolescents' risk for early childbearing?

_____

_____

_____

- What potential pathways to prevention is the community ready to explore and test?

_____

_____

_____

- What is the community's vision for the situation of its teens next year? in five years? in ten years?

_____

_____

_____

Source: Reprinted with Permission. Brindis C, Davis C, *Mobilizing for Action*. [Communities Responding to the Challenge of Adolescent Pregnancy Prevention, v. 1] Washington, D.C.: Advocates for Youth, © 1998.

FORMATIVE RESEARCH FOR INTERVENTIONS AMONG ADOLESCENTS AT HIGH RISK FOR GONORRHEA AND OTHER STDs*

Introduction

Onondaga County statistics indicate that Syracuse, New York, has a high gonorrhea infection rate, especially among 15- to 19-year-old teenagers. In contrast to regional and national trends, local gonorrhea rates increased dramatically between 1992 and 1994, from 1,178 cases in 1992 to 1,661 cases in 1994.[1] The local infection rate for teenagers (age 15 to 19) during 1993–1994 was particularly high; one in 75 was infected per year. This corresponds to a rate of 1,350 per 100,000 teens, which is nearly twice the national norm. Although the local gonorrhea infection rate dropped by 28 percent in 1995, it remained higher than the 1993–1994 national norm of 733.3 per 100,000 teens. The local ratio for teen gonorrhea between males and females was 1:2 during the period of January 1993 to June 1995; nationally, the ratio was 1:1.6 for 1993–1994. More than 50 percent of all gonorrhea cases are concentrated in eight census tracts in low-income neighborhoods in the city of Syracuse.

The Onondaga County Health Department conducted a study to provide information for public health interventions regarding gonorrhea and other sexually transmitted diseases (STDs) in this high-risk population. Specifically, the study provides information to develop effective health education messages and establish accessible services for the teen population. The study questions included:

1. What is the extent of accurate knowledge among high-risk teens about the transmission and prevention of gonorrhea and other STDs?
2. What are teens' reported behaviors and beliefs that place them at increased risk of contracting an STD?
3. What barriers to access do high-risk teens face in obtaining health care for STD prevention and treatment?
4. What types of health education messages have the greatest potential for reaching this teen group?

Study Methods

During the study, six focus groups were conducted with adolescents and young adults and a brief self-administered survey was completed by focus group participants. The combination of two methods—focus groups and surveys—was chosen in order to provide triangulation of the data. Triangulation, a strategy that employs multiple methods to address a problem, is used in qualitative research to enhance validity.

*Source: Lillian R. Welych et al., "Formative Research for Interventions among Adolescents at High Risk for Gonorrhea and Other STDs," *Journal of Public Health Management and Practice*, Vol. 4:6, Aspen Publishers, Inc., © 1998.

Sample

Six focus groups were selected to reflect demographically the Syracuse adolescent population that was experiencing the highest incidence of gonorrhea. The participants in these groups were the same individuals who completed the self-administered survey. This target group at high risk for gonorrhea was identified through the results of the 1996–1997 Onondaga County Community Health Assessment. Therefore, the study participants do not represent the general adolescent population of the city of Syracuse. The participants were selected from the clients of community-based organizations and from among the incarcerated adolescent population. The criteria for participation were: (1) residence in one of the eight census tracts previously identified as having the highest incidence of gonorrhea, (2) age (between 15 and 19), and (3) voluntary consent to participate. No payment of any kind was given for participation in the study. The actual ages of the participants differed somewhat from the inclusion criteria. The youngest participant was 13 years old and the oldest was 28 years old. However, 87 percent of the participants were within the target age of 15 to 19 years of age.

The focus groups ranged in size from five to 16. (See Table 1 for focus group demographic characteristics.) Each focus group had an average of nine participants. Forty-six percent of the participants characterized themselves as African American, 28 percent as white, and 26 percent as "other" race/ethnicity. Of the total, 14 percent also characterized themselves as Hispanic. The sample was 56 percent male and 44 percent female. Most groups included both males and females, with two groups consisting of all males and one group consisting of all females. Because adolescent females had higher rates of gonorrhea than adolescent males in Onondaga County, it would have been preferable to have more female participants and additional female-only focus groups; however, considerable difficulty was encountered in identifying females at high risk for gonorrhea. For this reason, males in the sample outnumber females.

Table 1 Focus Group Characteristics

		Gender Breakdown	
Focus Group Name	**Age Range**	**Males**	**Females**
Group A: Parenting group from community-based organization (CBO)	18–29	1	8
Group B: Juvenile detention	13–16	11	0
Group C: Juvenile detention	13–16	6	10
Group D: County jail	16–18	13	0
Group E: Teen group from CBO	16–18, 23	5	4
Group F: Pregnant adolescent group	14–17	0	5
Total	13–29	36	27

Two facilitators conducted the focus groups, one asking prestructured focus group questions and the other serving as note taker and clarifying responses as needed. In addition, an observer was present to audiotape the sessions, which each lasted 1 to 1.5 hours. The facilitators and note takers were four public health educators from the staff of the Onondaga County Health Department. These health educators had been trained in the administration of focus groups, and three of them worked specifically in STD public health education.

An important issue that emerged in the first focus group was that the participants had specific questions for the health educators about STDs, human immunodeficiency virus (HIV), and general health. The health educator/facilitators in each focus group assured participants that they would answer all questions at the end of the focus group, which they did. This enabled the facilitators to listen actively to the ideas, concerns, and discussion during the focus group while providing accurate health information at the end of each session.

A brief, self-administered survey that included questions on demographics and behavior was given to participants at the end of the focus group. Of the 63 focus group participants, 61 filled out the survey at least partially.

Results

Exhibit 1 presents the range of responses elicited in five of the six focus groups. One of the six focus groups (see Table 1, Group E) differed significantly from the other five groups in that its participants' behavior placed them at lower risk for STDs. The responses of this low-risk group were analyzed separately and are described below. Table 2 presents the survey results of all focus group participants who completed at least part of the questionnaire.

The participants in Group E were members of a peer leadership program in a community-based agency. This program was designed to foster resilience in adolescents in order to protect them from substance abuse. They were low-risk adolescents with regard to health and social behaviors in that more than half reported currently not being sexually active and that nearly half had not yet initiated sexual activity. The sexually active members of this group reported fewer partners than participants in the other groups. They reported no drug taking activity and nearly no drinking with sexual activity. They were the only group of adolescents currently attending public high school and several were planning to attend college. They expressed interest and competence in seeking health information from the library, the internet, television, and other media sources. They were the only group to speak about the financial and personal responsibility involved in having a baby.

The following description of the results is organized according to the four research questions outlined. The data discussed in this section include responses from all of the focus groups and the survey results. In this section, where relevant, the responses from the low-risk group are also described.

1. What is the extent of accurate knowledge among high-risk teens about the transmission and prevention of gonorrhea and other STDs?

Participants in all groups demonstrated considerable knowledge regarding the transmission of HIV, acquired immunodeficiency syndrome (AIDS), and STDs, as well as STD symptoms. Their knowledge of condom use was excellent. However, participants were most concerned with those STDs that cannot be cured. For example,

Exhibit 1
NUMBER OF FOCUS GROUPS DISCUSSING SPECIFIC ISSUES

Health Concerns: "What are the teen health problems that concern you most?"
HIV/AIDS 5/5*
Pregnancy 3/5
Chronic diseases (diabetes, heart disease, lung cancer, skin cancer) 3/5
STDs 2/5
Violence 1/5

Sources of Health Information: "Whom do you turn to for help or advice?"
Health care provider (doctor or nurse) 5/5
Parents or family members 5/5
Clinics 4/5
Teachers 2/5

STD Attitudes and Perceptions: "What comes to your mind when you hear 'sexually transmitted diseases'?"
Teens need to worry about STDs 5/5
Birth control or oral contraceptives protect against STD 2/5
Withdrawal can protect against STD 2/5
Only worried about STDs that cannot be cured 2/5
Can tell if someone has an STD by smelling or touching a female's genitals (male response) 1/5
A male can tell if a woman has an STD by inserting some of his own earwax into her vagina; if she is infected, she will feel a burning sensation 1/5
Can use Vaseline or ointments with condoms 1/5
"A person with an STD can get a bad reputation, causing them misery" (female response) 1/5
"I would leave, beat, or kill [a partner] if I discovered that she had an STD and I did not" (male response) 1/5

STD knowledge: "What do you think happens to a person when they get an STD?"
Participants were aware of the following STDs:
HIV 5/5
gonorrhea 4/5
chlamydia 4/5
syphilis 3/5
"Need to get medical check-ups and treatment if you have a symptom" 5/5
Participants named the following symptoms and problems associated with STDs:

can get worse and cause more serious damage 3/5
burning with urination 2/5
sometimes no symptoms 2/5
won't be able to have kids 2/5
can pass it on to a baby if pregnant 2/5
sores that won't heal 1/5
Participants were aware that gonorrhea was a major problem 4/4
"Can get STD from anyone, cannot tell just by looking at a person" 4/5
"How is gonorrhea spread?"
Sexual intercourse 4/4
Unprotected sex 3/4
People who don't know that they are infected 2/4
Oral sex 1/4

Prevention/Risk Reduction Knowledge: "How can teens improve their chances of not getting an STD?"
Abstinence and safer sex 5/5
Participants expressed knowledge of the following:
what condoms are 5/5
how to use them 5/5
why to use them 5/5
where to buy them 5/5
where to obtain free condoms 5/5
that condoms need to be used every time 5/5
Sex with one person 2/5
Abstinence from drugs and alcohol 1/5
"What behaviors put you at risk for getting an STD?"
Having unprotected sex 5/5
Having sex with multiple partners 5/5
Using alcohol 5/5
Sex for drugs, money, clothing, sneakers 5/5
Using marijuana 2/5
Using other drugs—acid, mushrooms, and "woos" (crack and marijuana) 2/5
Rape in jail (male response) 1/5
"Where do you meet people who you might have sex with?"
City parks 5/5
Street corners, blocks 5/5
Parties, bars 5/5
Neighborhood stores 5/5
Schools 2/5
Malls 2/5
Abandoned houses 1/5

*denominator is the number of groups where question was asked

continues

Exhibit 1 continued

"Where does sex occur?"
  Houses, cars, and parks 5/5
  Motels 4/5
  "Labs," abandoned houses 2/5

Barriers to Prevention and Risk Reduction: "Are there any reasons that a teen would not use a condom when having sex?"
  Sex feels better without a condom 5/5
  Being drunk or high at the time 4/5
  Not having a condom with them at the time 3/5
  Would "take a chance" (have unprotected sex) if they think that the person has not "slept around" (male response) 3/5

Suggested Intervention: "Where is the ideal place for a clinic?"
  Downtown 4/5
  Each side of town 4/5
  "Do not want to go where everyone knows me" 3/5
"How can the clinic be made easier for you to use it?"
  Make it a general health clinic 3/5
  Ensure confidentiality 3/5
"How can we improve STD education to reach adolescents?"
  Educate early, by fifth or sixth grade 5/5
  Use fear tactics 4/5

all focus groups mentioned HIV/AIDS as a major concern, but only two of the five high-risk groups mentioned STDs as a concern.

Misinformation among the participants included the belief that nonbarrier birth control methods (such as oral contraceptives) provide protection against disease, that withdrawal (coitus interruptus) provides protection from infection, that Vaseline and ointments can be used with condoms, and that one could tell if a female partner had an STD by smelling or touching her genitals.

2. What are their reported behaviors and beliefs that place them at increased risk of contracting an STD?

Condom use: This is an area in which accurate knowledge was not congruent with reported behavior. The most important behavioral risk among the participants was having sex without a condom. Members of all focus groups mentioned this as a potential risk factor. One of the survey questions asked, "The last time you had sexual intercourse, did you or your partner use a condom?" Nearly half of the survey respondents reported not using a condom during their most recent sexual encounter. Among the reasons given by focus group participants for not using condoms were: sex feels better without a condom, partners in primary relationships are less likely to use condoms, not having a condom with them at the time of an opportunity to have sex, and the use of drugs and alcohol makes condom use less likely. Female focus group participants mentioned that carrying condoms might give the impression that they were "loose." In one group, the young men said that carrying condoms might give the impression that they are "only interested in sex."

Early sexual initiation: Among 54 survey respondents who answered the question regarding the age of first sexual intercourse, 20 (37%) were age 11 years or less, 26 (48%) were between the ages of 12–14, and 8 (15%) were age 15 or older. In contrast to the high-risk focus groups, four members of the low-risk group (all age 16) had not yet initiated sexual activity.

Multiple sexual partners: Among the 51 survey respondents who answered the question regarding numbers of partners in the previous six months: 21 (41%) had no partner or one partner, 8 (16%) had two partners, and 22 (43%) had three or more partners. In all of the focus group discussions, participants mentioned that having unprotected sex with multiple partners could place a person at risk for an STD.

Table 2 Self-Administered Survey of Focus Group Participants (n = 61)

	Percent	Number
Drink or drug last time?		
Partner, not I	4%	2
I, not partner	14%	7
Both	27%	13
Neither	55%	27
Sex with injectable drug user?		
Yes	6%	3
No	86%	45
Don't know	8%	4
Drugs for sex?		
Yes	5%	2
No	95%	42
Money for sex?		
Yes	11%	5
No	89%	40
Age at first intercourse (years)?		
11 or under	37%	20
12–14	48%	26
15–16	11%	6
17+	4%	2
Partners last six months?		
More than 6 people	10%	5
5–6 people	8%	4
3–4 people	25%	13
2 people	16%	8
1 person	27%	14
Frequency of condom use?		
Almost never or never	26%	14
Sometimes	36%	19
Every time	38%	20
Condom use last sex?		
Yes	49%	21
No	44%	19
Don't know	7%	3

Data source: OCHD, CD Program. Prepared by: OCHD, Bureau of Surveillance and Statistics.

In two of the focus groups, young women described a particularly high-risk behavior. This activity, called "running a lab" or "running a train," is group sex with one female and several males. The females who described this activity reported that it was consensual. They claimed young women go to an abandoned house and have sex with the men "one after another."

Drugs and alcohol: Of 49 survey participants who answered the question, "Were you or your partner using drugs or alcohol during the last time you had sex?" 24 (45%) answered that either one or both partner had used alcohol or drugs. In the focus groups, participants described that sexual activity often occurs in conjunction with drug use, especially alcohol and marijuana. When speaking of sex associated with drug and alcohol use, participants reported that they "hang out, use drugs, then sex happens."

Among the 52 survey respondents who answered the question, "Have you had sex with someone who had injected drugs?" only 3 (6%) answered yes. Although participants in three of the five high-risk focus groups mentioned injectable drugs, the majority of male participants in all groups spoke about alcohol and noninjectable drugs. Marijuana was the drug most often mentioned. Secondarily, participants reported adolescents taking phenycyclidine (PCP), lysergic acid diethylamide (LSD), mushrooms, and ecstasy. Crack cocaine, although mentioned, was said by participants to be not as frequently used by younger people. In two focus groups, participants discussed males having intercourse with females who were greatly intoxicated: "a person could get drunk and not know she's having sex."

Sex for drugs/sex for commodities: Of the survey respondents who answered questions about the exchange of sex for drugs or sex for money, only a scant minority answered yes. Two (5%) of 44 respondents reported exchanging sex for drugs, and five (11%) reported exchanging sex for money. These responses may have been biased by the preponderance of males in the sample.

In all of the focus groups, an unexpected finding emerged: the exchange of sex for commodities, such as meals at fast food restaurants, brand name clothing, and sneakers. This practice does not appear to be sex for survival, but rather sex for popular consumer items. The participants did not consider this exchange to be prostitution. When asked about prostitution, the participants defined it as sex for money and said it was primarily conducted by older women.

3. What barriers to access do high-risk teens face in obtaining health care for STD prevention and treatment?

The major concern regarding health care was confidentiality. Participants in all focus groups cited fears about the lack of confidentiality as a deterrent in seeking advice and treatment for STDs. In this regard, participants suggested creating a general adolescent health clinic rather than a clinic for STD treatment only so that merely entering the clinic would not be potentially stigmatizing. Also, participants stated that the clinic location and its hours of operation should be conducive to ensuring confidentiality. As an answer to this concern, focus group participants suggested locating a teen clinic either downtown or having a neighborhood clinic on each side of town. They said that adolescents do not want to go to clinics where everyone knows them, they do not want identification required as a prerequisite for treatment, they prefer the use of first names only or identification by number, and they do not want a requirement to reveal the names of their sexual contacts. Participants also recommended extending clinic hours to evenings and weekends and having a 24-hour telephone number for appointments.

The adolescents in the focus groups expressed serious concern with how they were perceived and treated by others, especially if they have an STD. One of the female focus group members said, "Having an [STD] can give you a bad reputation." Another female participant complained of physicians who were "rude and assume that you're sleeping around" if an adolescent has an STD. Therefore, the selection of both clinic staff and educators and their in-service education must emphasize the importance of a respectful attitude toward the client.

4. What types of health education messages have the greatest potential for reaching this group?

Sensation/pleasure: Participants in all focus groups stated that sex without a condom feels better. Several participants mentioned that the fit (too big, too small) of the condom was uncomfortable. Other concerns were that the male's penis would not remain erect with a condom on and that being "in a rush" to initiate intercourse made condom use difficult. These concerns primarily addressed the comfort, sensation, and pleasure of men during intercourse. Female comfort and sensation were not mentioned with regard to condoms, except by one participant who said that sex without condoms feels "closer" for females. Although most of the public health messages promoting condoms address protection from disease and pregnancy, the responses of focus group participants indicated that messages that address the potential for condoms to "feel good" or enhance sensation (such as ultra-thin condoms, water-based lubricants used with condoms, and the potential for condoms to enhance the experience for the female partner by delaying ejaculation) could reach this target group. While a focus on the sensory aspect of sex with condoms may be considered controversial, it could be considered part of health promotion with this high-risk group.

Healthy babies: Young women in one of the focus groups expressed a great deal of concern about the effect of STDs on the health of babies. This group consisted of pregnant or parenting teens. The concern with healthy babies was mentioned by female participants in one other focus group, but was not mentioned by any of the males. Given the high fertility rate among teens in the population and the high rate of gonorrhea infection among adolescent females, this concern could be the basis for STD education targeted toward this group.

Fear tactics: When asked what type of health messages would best reach high-risk teens, members of four of the focus groups suggested fear tactics such as: have teens share bad experiences, make a video depicting teens who have had an STD, have teens visit an STD clinic, publicize how many teens are infected or die, or show pictures of disease. Although the utilization of fear tactics runs contrary to most health education philosophy,[2] participants were adamant about the need for graphic, frightening depictions of the consequences of infection with STDs. When queried about what they would consider the most effective way to let teens know about STDs, all groups recommended early, comprehensive education by the fifth or sixth grade.

Discussion/Implications

Three troubling areas that this study highlighted are the interaction of STD risk with alcohol and drugs, the coercion or violence that may be involved with some of the teens' sexual activity, and the exchange of sex for commodities. One of the more heartening findings was the results of the low-risk group. Each of these four areas is addressed below.

1. Drugs and alcohol: A major portion of the adolescents' high-risk behavior occurred in conjunction with the use of alcohol and marijuana.

2. Violence/coercion: A number of the study's findings indicate that coercion and possibly violence are a part of sexual activity for at least some teens. Participants mentioned concerns with violence as a health problem, rape in jail as an STD risk, and sex with a female partner who is unconscious from intoxication. Female participants also reported that males would pressure them to have sex without a condom. A male participant reported that he would, "leave, beat or kill [a partner] if she had an STD and [he] did not." Also, the very early age of sexual initiation (over one third were less than age 11) implies that coercion is likely in the early sexual experience of adolescents in this group. Similar findings of early initiation are reported elsewhere.[3,4]

3. Sex for commodities: Although the adolescents did not consider the exchange of sex for consumer items to be prostitution, in all of the focus groups, participants described the practice of exchanging sex for consumer items. It is clear that the "consumer culture" of popular items advertised on television has a major impact on adolescents. The compelling desire for these status items leads adolescents to risk infection with STDs and HIV in order to obtain them.

4. Low-risk group: While it is commonplace in public health research to focus on poor health outcomes, one of the focus groups consisted of teens who were from the same geographical area as those at high risk but whose reported sexual experience and drug and alcohol risk behavior was quite low. This finding is an example of "positive deviance," in that some individuals in a population with poor health behaviors and outcomes appear to do especially well.[5,6] The adolescents in this low-risk group were attending school, many hoped to attend college, and seemed generally resourceful and confident. This group consisted of members of a peer leadership program established by a community-based agency, which had the goal of enhancing resilience in adolescents with regard to drugs and alcohol. The peer leadership program was a positive, goal-oriented program open to all adolescents interested in participating. The participants represented a variety of home environments, including single-parent homes and lower socioeconomic status families.

The Onondaga County Health Department has used the results of this study to obtain funding and develop interventions for adolescents at risk in Syracuse.

REFERENCES

1. Pirro, N.J., and Novick, L.F. *1996–1997 Community Health Assessment.* Syracuse, NY: Onondaga County Health Department, 1996.

2. Arkin, E.B. *Making Health Communication Programs Work.* Washington, D.C.: U.S. Department of Health and Human Services, NIH Publication No. 89-1493 (1989): 32.

3. Fang, X., et al. Similarity of Risk and Protective Behaviors among African-American Pre- and Early Adolescent Members of Naturally Occurring Friendship Groups. *Bulletin of the New York Academy of Medicine* 73, no. 2 (1996): 285–300.

4. Romer, D., et al. Social Influences on the Sexual Behavior of Youth at Risk for HIV Exposure. *American Journal of Public Health* 84, no. 6 (1994): 977–85.

5. Shekar, M., et al. Use of Positive-Negative Deviant Analyses To Improve Programme Targeting and Services: Example from the TamilNadu Integrated Nutrition Project. *International Journal of Epidemiology* 21, no. 4 (1992): 707–13.

6. Guldan, G.S., et al. Weaning Practices and Growth in Rural Sichuan Infants: A Positive Deviance Study. *Journal of Tropical Pediatrics* 39, no. 3 (1993): 168–75.

Major Program Components of the School/Community Sexual Risk Reduction Model

PROGRAM COMPONENTS	PROGRAM ELEMENTS
Enhance sexuality education	Teach courses for teachers, community members, and agency professionals on human sexuality and teaching methods Provide monthly inservice for training teachers on timely sexuality education topics and teacher newsletters Provide minicourses for parents, clergy, and community members on sexuality and talking to youths about sex Maintain a resource library with information about health and sexuality
Implement age-appropriate, comprehensive K–12 sexuality education	Educate youths in the following topic areas: knowledge of consequences of unplanned pregnancies; sexually transmitted diseases; importance of abstinence; understanding growth and development; skills in assertiveness, communication, problem solving, and decision making specific to sexuality; and knowledge and skills for effective contraceptive use Hold student focus groups to determine the level of sexuality education they are receiving and what they would like to have in their schools Conduct focus groups with teachers to document the level of sexuality education provided
Increase access to health services and contraceptives	Provide inservice training in assessment and revision of school nursing services Establish linkages with health care providers to increase access and decrease barriers to services (e.g., school-linked clinic) Establish linkages and pursue opportunities to conduct Early Prevention, Screening, Diagnosis, and Treatment screening and access to Medicaid-provided medical services for youths
Collaborate with school administrators	Meet regularly with administrative staff, parent advisory groups, health councils, and other groups involved in school health decisions Assess student knowledge, attitudes, and behavior related to sexual issues
Use the mass media to increase awareness and involvement	Provide bulletin boards, newsletters, and flyers Arrange for special events, speakers, forums, and speakers bureaus Develop public service announcements (radio, television, print) Solicit television, radio, and newspaper coverage of problem and the initiative
Provide peer support and education	Provide training for peer leaders in reproductive health, sexuality education, the provision of peer support and assistance, community health and education resources, and decision-making skills Facilitate peer support groups
Provide alternative activities for youths	Coordinate summer youth programs Staff after-school programs Establish mentoring and job opportunities
Establish community linkages	Participate in networking, interagency councils, and social agencies
Establish programs in religious organizations	Provide training and special programs

Source: Adrienne Paine-Andrews et al., "Replicating a Community Initiative for Preventing Adolescent Pregnancy: From South Carolina to Kansas," *Family and Community Health*, Vol. 19:1, Aspen Publishers, Inc., © 1996.

GUIDELINES FOR ESTABLISHING AN HIV/AIDS/STD INFORMATION HOTLINE*

Note: Many of the suggestions below can be applied to the development of information hotlines for other health issues.

Why Establish a Hotline?

A hotline can do the following:

- provide easy and immediate access for persons/populations who may not be reached by other methods, e.g., women at risk for human immunodeficiency virus (HIV) infection in rural communities
- provide an opportunity for a person to frame a question and have anonymous human contact
- provide information in a confidential manner, maintaining the privacy of the caller
- provide information in appropriate language level and style and permit discussion of issues caller does not understand
- afford the caller up-to-date, accurate information
- provide referrals for counseling and testing, treatment services, and various support systems
- serve as a monitoring mechanism for impact of public information activities, e.g., public service announcements that publicize the hotline number
- permit pre-screening of worried well to decrease unnecessary HIV testing

Quality Assurance

A quality assurance plan should be developed as part of the process of establishing a hotline. This plan should address the following minimum requirements:

- description of staff recruitment process and necessary qualifications for specialists
- information and timeliness for monitoring the specialists for accurate information dissemination, appropriateness of referrals, and proper call management skills
- performance appraisal based on whether persons are able to achieve standards, remedial activities for elevating performance, volunteers and paid staff judged according to the same expectations, and volunteers should understand that this is a job and conform to hours, vacation rules, confidentiality, etc.
- information on publicizing the hotline (in all languages the hotline offers) and methods for documenting calls
- explanation of data collection procedures and reporting forms, e.g., collection of information about callers—who is being reached and what they are asking
- description of management techniques for referral information, e.g., a regular review of database or written materials

Criteria for Establishing a Hotline

- The hotline should not impose any financial difficulties/barriers on prospective callers (e.g., should be free for the caller).

---

*Source: *Guidelines for Health Education and Risk Reduction Activities*, Centers for Disease Control and Prevention, Public Health Service, U.S. Department of Health and Human Services, 1995.

- Days and hours of operation should meet the needs of the target audience (e.g., not just during business hours, when employed callers could not be assured of privacy for calls).
- The Centers for Disease Control (CDC) National Sexually Transmitted Disease (STD) and the CDC National Acquired Immune Deficiency Syndrome (AIDS) Hotline numbers should be provided on a taped message for calls received after normal operating hours in order to provide access to callers having immediate needs.
- Physical space should accommodate future staff expansion and additional phone lines.
- Telecommunications equipment should be up-to-date and of sufficient capacity.
- Venues should be available for publicizing the hotline and should be appropriate for targeted audiences.
- Consideration should be given to phone lines that may be needed for special audiences, e.g., non-English-speaking people and people who are deaf or hard of hearing.

Also consider offering an auto-attendant system to operate during off-hours and weekends. Such a system can offer a menu of prerecorded messages for callers who do not need to speak with a counselor, but who want quick and anonymous access to information.

Staff Characteristics for Hotlines

Hotlines are staffed by information specialists who may be paid personnel or volunteers, depending upon available financial resources. If volunteers are used, the organization should commit at least one paid staff person for management purposes. A paid staff member is needed to ensure consistency and continuity of services because of the high turnover of staff commonly experienced among volunteers, the need to ensure quality services, and the need to maintain consistency in the implementation of policies and procedures. The manager should maintain and regularly update a comprehensive list of HIV/AIDS/STD services and organizations. A hard copy and/or computer-based list should be used by information specialists during work hours.

Information specialists provide information over the telephone; therefore, they require unique skills and abilities. They should always be prepared for the unexpected and act accordingly.

The successful information specialist should possess the following attributes:

- Be knowledgeable about HIV/AIDS/STDs.
- Understand the importance of anonymity and confidentiality.
- Have the ability to speak at various levels that are consistent with the language needs of the callers, e.g., physicians, lay persons who are or are not AIDS-knowledgeable.
- Exhibit active listening skills and be courteous, patient, understanding, and compassionate.
- Display a sensitive and nonjudgmental attitude when callers describe concerns, sexual activities, drug use, and/or symptoms.

- Refrain from giving advice during crisis-oriented calls, but appropriately refer to organizations adept in crisis intervention.
- Refer callers to appropriate resources in a timely, efficient manner by using proper call management skills.
- Demonstrate resourcefulness and ingenuity in providing referrals and finding answers to questions.

Once the information specialists have been recruited, they should be comprehensively trained to meet the challenges of their positions. Consider teaming new information specialists with more experienced staff until the new person is comfortable handling calls independently.

A training plan should address the following minimum requirements:

- Measurable goals and objectives for the training.
- Basic medical knowledge about HIV/AIDS/STD, including modes of transmission, disease-causing organisms, signs and symptoms, disease epidemiology, diagnostic methods, disease progression and complications, and treatment.
- Knowledge about common myths and misconceptions about HIV/AIDS/STD and correct information to dispel myths and misconceptions.
- Skills-building exercises in active listening and effective information dissemination (including crisis intervention).
- Interpersonal and multi-cultural communication skills-building.
- In-service training and updates on a continual basis to remain current on issues surrounding HIV/AIDS/STD.

For additional information, consult the training bulletins that the CDC National AIDS Hotline distributes to state health departments and others.

NOTES:

GUIDELINES FOR STREET AND COMMUNITY OUTREACH FOR HIV/AIDS PREVENTION*

Note: The following information focuses on efforts to reduce HIV/AIDS risk but can be useful in designing other types of outreach programs.

Street and community outreach can be described as an activity conducted outside a more traditional, institutional health care setting for the purposes of providing direct health education and risk reduction services or referrals. However, before conducting any outreach activity in a community, an agency must define the specific population to be served and determine their general needs. Based on this definition and determination, an agency can then decide appropriately *where* to conduct intervention efforts. Street and community outreach may be conducted anywhere from a street corner to a pool hall, from a parish hall to a school room. To determine the setting, an agency need only decide that the setting is easily, readily, and regularly accessed by the designated client population.

Outreach demonstrates an agency's willingness *to go* to the community rather than *wait* for the community *to come* to it. Often, agencies enlist and train peer educators to conduct the outreach activities. It is recommended that the content of the outreach activity be contingent upon the setting. The nature of activity varies in scope and intensity; the activity is best determined before an outreach team or individual educator goes out. Yet, flexibility is also very important. Remember, *everything is not appropriate everywhere all of the time.* A street corner may be an appropriate place to conduct a brief HIV risk assessment, but it is not an appropriate place to conduct HIV counseling and testing.

While street and community outreach can be complementary service components of a single agency, some agencies, based on needs assessment findings and staff capacity, may choose to provide one service and not the other. Street outreach and community outreach can also be stand-alone pieces.

Street Outreach

Street outreach commonly involves outreach specialists moving throughout a particular neighborhood or community to deliver risk reduction information and materials. The outreach specialists may set up an HIV/AIDS information table on a street corner. They may supply bleach to injecting drug users at shooting galleries and condoms to commercial sex workers and their customers at the hotels or locations that they frequent. The fundamental principle of street outreach is that the outreach specialist establishes face-to-face contact with the client to provide HIV/AIDS risk education information and services.

Effective street outreach staff

- know the target group's language
- have basic training and experience in health education
- are sensitive to community norms, values, cultural beliefs, and traditions
- have a shared identity with the population served, stemming from shared common personal experiences with the group
- are trusted by the group they serve

---

*Source: *Guidelines for Health Education and Risk Reduction Activities,* Centers for Disease Control and Prevention, Public Health Service, U.S. Department of Health and Human Services, 1995.

- act as role models to the clients they serve
- advocate for the population served
- act as liaisons between the community and the agency
- are informed about community resources and use them

Street outreach is not simply moving standard agency operations out onto the sidewalk. A number of specific issues are unique to the delivery of services through this type of outreach and must be considered before instituting a program of street outreach. These matters are usually addressed in an agency's street outreach program plan and include the following:

- regular contact among educators, outreach specialists, and supervisors
- observation of potential outreach areas to determine the locations, times of day, and the day of the week that are most productive for reaching the population to be served
- a written and comprehensive field safety protocol that is regularly updated (See box "Field Safety Protocol.")
- establishment of and adherence to regular and consistent schedules of activities, including times and locations (See box "Example of Weekly Outreach Schedule.")
- a mechanism for measuring the use of referral services
- creation and maintenance of a positive relationship between the agency and the local law enforcement authorities
- identification and development of collaborative relationships with gatekeepers (key informants) in the community
- activities for building and earning the trust and respect of the community
- descriptions of skills-building exercises relevant to stated program objectives
- establishment of mechanisms for maintaining client confidentiality

---

Field Safety Protocol

Field safety protocols are based on program activities and are intended to provide the staff and peer educators with guidance regarding their professional behavior.

- Carry picture identification (ID) at all times that includes name of the organization, name of the project, your name, and the purpose for your presence.
- Work in pairs and **always know where your partner is.**
- Establish a mechanism to keep your supervisor aware of your location and activities (e.g., carry a beeper, call telephone mailbox at a specified time).
- Establish contact with local police precincts in the area. Leave copy of ID with the commander. If appropriate for your program, maintain relations with the police and introduce the program and staff.
- Have contingency plans for worst case scenarios and share them with your partner.
- Make sure you have made contact with and have permission from a key person in the community before entering the setting in which you will conduct the intervention (e.g., shooting galleries, crack houses, or local high schools).
- Leave the area if tension or violence is observed or perceived.
- Avoid controversy and debate with clients and program participants.
- When you start your job as a peer educator in the field, get a TB skin test; you should be retested periodically thereafter.
- Be aware of weather conditions and be prepared for natural occurrences.
- Design and adhere to a schedule for outreach or peer education.
- Avoid drinking alcoholic beverages and buying, receiving, or sampling drugs while conducting outreach or peer education.

Example of Weekly Outreach Schedule

	8 AM–12 noon	1–5 PM	6–8 PM
Monday	no activity	no activity	no activity
Tuesday	office staff meeting	homeless shelter IDU outreach	methadone clinic client presentation
Wednesday	sexually transmitted disease clinic waiting room	city park IDU outreach	no activity
Thursday	office paperwork and data analysis	street work 10th and Vine IDU outreach	no activity
Friday	office materials development	motel alley sex worker/IDU outreach	shooting gallery outreach
Saturday	no activity IDU outreach	city park 10th and Vine IDU outreach	street work
Sunday	no activity	no activity	no activity

IDU = intravenous drug user

Community Outreach: Workshops and Presentations

Workshops and presentations are typical activities of community outreach. Because they usually follow lecture formats, they can be highly structured health education and risk reduction intervention efforts. While they supply important opportunities to disseminate HIV/AIDS prevention information, their impact on behavior change is limited because they are usually single-encounter experiences. Although they provide crucial technical information that raises awareness and increases knowledge and may be a critical first step in the change process, the information alone is usually inadequate to sustain behavior change.

To maximize their benefit, workshops and presentations should be planned carefully with knowledge goals and objectives specified before the individual sessions. To the extent possible, presenters should be informed about the setting where the workshop or presentation will take place, as well as the composition and knowledge level of the anticipated audience. The following are examples of issues the presenter might consider before conducting a presentation or workshop:

- Where will the workshop or presentation be held?
- What is the age range of the participants/audience?
- What is the language(s) of the participants/audience?
- What audiovisual equipment is available?

A well-planned, detailed outline, which allows flexibility, can prove useful and beneficial to the presenter and the participants/audience. Such an outline helps keep the presentation on track and focused. If a pretest evaluation is to be used, an outline can ensure that all relevant material will be covered in the lecture.

In a workshop or presentation, audience participation is to be strongly encouraged. Time must be allotted, usually at the end of the presentation, for a question and answer session. However, some questions may be so pressing, or some participants so persistent, that the presenter will have to address some questions and concerns during the presentation. The presenter should answer the questions succinctly and return to the original order of the presentation.

To increase the number of workshops and presentations they are able to provide, some agencies will elect to develop speaker's bureaus to augment their paid staff. Recruitment, training, and retention of volunteers present complex programmatic questions and are not to be undertaken lightly.

The points below are relevant to agencies providing workshops and presentations either by paid staff or by volunteers in a speaker's bureau. Effective presenters

- possess organizational and public speaking skills
- are well informed and comfortable talking about the subject
- ensure that the presentation is linguistically appropriate for the audience
- elicit and encourage audience participation
- are adaptable to logistics and audience needs
- are nonjudgmental
- assess the nature of questions to make appropriate responses, i.e., whether better answered in private
- seek accurate answers to difficult questions and provide information in a timely manner

A few items specifically are needed in a community outreach program plan.

- A comprehensive workshop/presentation curriculum.
- Assurance that curricula provide for discussion of related issues.
- Detailed workshop/presentation outlines.
- Logistical guidance for workshops/presentations (e.g., time and location, room arrangement, number of participants, number of facilitators).
- Methods to assure that the audience is informed about workshop/presentation goals and objectives and that discussion of subject matter is facilitated.
- Descriptions of skills-building exercises relevant to stated program objectives.
- Training in the operation of audiovisual equipment and the use of diverse forms of audiovisual equipment.
- Recruitment of staff with organizational and public speaking skills.

Peer Educators

Agencies that provide street and community outreach will frequently engage peer educators to conduct intervention activities. Peer education implies a role-model method of education in which trained, self-identified members of the client population provide HIV/AIDS education to their behavioral peers. This method provides an opportunity for individuals to perceive themselves as empowered by helping persons in their communities and social networks, thus supporting their own health enhancing practices. At the same time, the use of peer educators sustains intervention efforts in the community long after the professional service providers are gone.

Effective peer educators

- have a shared identity with the targeted community or group
- are within the same age range as the targeted community or group
- speak the same language as the community or group
- are familiar with the group's cultural nuances and are able to convey these norms and values to the agency
- act as an advocate, serving as a liaison between the agency and the targeted community or group

Peer education can be very powerful, if it is applied appropriately. The peer educator not only teaches a desired risk reduction practice but she or he also models it. Peer educators demonstrate behaviors that can influence the community norms in order to promote HIV/AIDS risk reduction within their networks. They are better able to inspire and encourage their peers to adopt health seeking behaviors because they are able to share common weaknesses, strengths, and experiences.

Agencies often recruit and train peer educators from among their client populations. However, not everyone is an educator. The model client does not necessarily make the model teacher, no matter how consistently she or he practices HIV/AIDS risk reduction or is liked by agency staff. Peer educators should be instinctive communicators. They should be empathetic and nonjudgmental. They should also be committed to client confidentiality.

Peer educators will not replace an agency's professional health educators, but they can complement the intervention team and enhance intervention efforts. Peer educators may act as support group leaders or street outreach volunteers who distribute materials to friends. They may be members of an agency's speaker's bureau and give workshop presentations. They may run shooting galleries, keeping bleach and clean water readily available to other intravenous drug users. They may be at-risk adolescents who model responsible sexual behaviors. The role of the peer educator is determined by the intervention need of the client population and the skill of the peer educator.

Although some agencies will hire peer educators as paid staff, others will not. As in the case of speaker's bureaus, engaging volunteer peer educators also involves issues of volunteer recruitment, training, and retention. In addition to the core elements identified for health education and risk reduction activities, an effective peer education program plan contains the following:

- a written and comprehensive field safety protocol (See box "Field Safety Protocol.")
- Establishment of and adherence to regular and consistent schedules of activities, including times and locations (See box "Example of Weekly Outreach Schedule.")
- A description of skills-building exercises relevant to the stated program objectives

Tobacco Use Questionnaire

1. Have you ever smoked cigarettes? Yes _____ No _____ (If no to this question, go to question 10.)
2. How old were you when you smoked your first cigarette? _____
3. Do you currently smoke cigarettes? Yes _____ No _____
4. Were you with someone when you smoked your first cigarette? Yes _____ No _____
5. Approximately how many cigarettes do you smoke each day? _____
6. Do you ever purchase cigarettes from a vending machine? Yes _____ No _____
7. Do you ever purchase cigarettes from a grocery store? Yes _____ No _____
    Convenience store? Yes _____ No _____
8. Usually are you asked for proof of age at the store where you purchased the
    cigarettes? Yes _____ No _____
9. Usually does someone else buy cigarettes for you? Yes _____ No _____
10. Do you use smokeless tobacco? Yes _____ No _____
11. If you have used smokeless tobacco, how old were you when you first tried tobacco? _____
12. Do the following people whom you know smoke?

Mother	Yes _____	No _____	Grandmother	Yes _____	No _____
Father	Yes _____	No _____	Grandfather	Yes _____	No _____
Brother	Yes _____	No _____	Aunt	Yes _____	No _____
Sister	Yes _____	No _____	Uncle	Yes _____	No _____
Friend	Yes _____	No _____	Teacher	Yes _____	No _____
Number of friends who smoke _____			Number of teachers _____		

13. Have you drank alcohol? Yes _____ No _____
    How old were you when you first consumed alcohol? _____
    How often do you use alcohol?
        Daily   Yes _____ No _____
        Weekly Yes _____ No _____
14. Have you smoked marijuana? Yes _____ No _____
    How old were you when you first tried marijuana? _____
    How often do you use marijuana?
        Daily   Yes _____ No _____
        Weekly Yes _____ No _____
15. How old are you? _____
16. Are you? Male _____ Female _____
17. What grade are you in? _____
18. How long have you attended this school? In years, _____
19. If you smoke, would you like to quit? Yes _____ No _____

Source: Bernard J. Healey, "Tobacco Use Questionnaire," *Inside Preventive Care*, Vol. 3, No. 1, Aspen Publishers, Inc., © April 1997.

Ten Steps To Improve Smoking Cessation Programs

Here are some tips hospitals, health plans, and employers can use to improve smoking cessation programs.

1. **Be flexible. One size does not fit all.**
   Offer a menu of choices for smokers who want to quit. Some smokers prefer to quit on their own, while others prefer a group approach. Some prefer nicotine patch supplements; others don't. So offerings should be flexible to meet individual needs.

2. **Assess how ready the smoker is to change.**
   There are five stages, ranging from "precontemplators" who are not ready to give up cigarettes to those who are ready to quit immediately. A smoking cessation program needs to determine which decisional phase smokers are going through and support them appropriately.

   For example, for smokers who have lost hope of finding the right way to quit, all of the lecturing in the world will not help them reframe their hopelessness. What is needed is to buddy them up with people who have been successful and help them find a way to quit smoking that addresses their concerns.

3. **Tie outcomes to what the smoker thinks is important.**
   Many smokers are not swayed by the fact that they have a much higher risk of lung cancer, emphysema, and heart disease. Instead, try to discover something that the smoker would like to be able to do better, such as playing sports with grandchildren, and suggest this as motivation.

   Helping people understand how they are going to feel better and be able to function at a higher level within several weeks of quitting smoking is more salient and important to people than lowering their risk over time, particularly if you can tie it to something the client thinks is important or wants to accomplish.

4. **Teach clients how to recognize warning signs.**
   If smokers are at high risk, it is very important

that they understand how to appropriately recognize the warning signals of problems such as lung and heart disease.

5. **Continually reassess the client.**
   Be ready to meet the quitter's needs at every step of the way. If quitters have any readiness at all, work with them to find a solution that will fit them and fit their preferences.

6. **Encourage the participation of supervisors.**
   A smoking cessation program will have more credibility if company executives and managers are active in promoting the program to employees.

7. **Urge employers to adopt a smoking policy.**
   It is important to create an environment that is going to support the behavior that you are trying to encourage. Employers should limit or ban smoking on the worksite to help workers trying to quit, she says. If a smoking policy in not in place, it sends a mixed message to employees. People are not going to take the offer of the smoking cessation program seriously if smoking is permitted.

8. **Communicate the program well.**
   Very often programs fall short because employers are not keeping the information out in front of employees.

9. **Integrate with demand management.**
   If telephone nursing support is offered to health plan beneficiaries, make sure that the nurse identifies smokers and refers them to smoking cessation programs.

   Employee assistance programs can also refer workers to smoking cessation programs. Health risk appraisals can give feedback to smokers about available programs, and so can any other fitness programs that employees have access to.

10. **Offer immediate access to programs.**
    Loyola University Medical Center near Chicago, for example, offers a group program at certain times of the year. However, the hospital found it needs to offer something for the person who doesn't want to wait for the next group clinic. So Loyola created individualized counseling sessions for immediate access.

Source: Steve Larose, "Hospitals and Health Plans Tailor Smoking Cessation Programs To Fit Individual Needs," *Inside Preventive Care*, Vol. 1:11, Aspen Publishers, Inc., © 1996.

Methods Used by Cessation Programs

PROGRAM PHASE	TYPICAL ELEMENTS
Preparation	Mobilizing client motivation and commitment • Refund of deposits contingent on attendance • Review reasons for quitting and benefits of stopping Self-monitoring; increase awareness of smoking patterns by keeping records[*] Setting target quit date 1 to 3 weeks ahead[*] Self-management training • Use self-monitoring to identify typical cues for smoking • Identify substitutes for smoking and alternative nonsmoking behaviors[*] • Stress management training; relaxation or exercise
Quitting (usually one of typical elements listed)	Aversive strategies • Pairing smoking with electric shock • Rapid smoking—inhaling every 6 to 8 seconds in the clinic until nausea is imminent or satiation—doubling or tripling at-home smoking Nonaversive strategies • Nicotine fading (switching successively to brands with increasingly lower nicotine content) • Target date contract Pharmacological—Using nicotine replacement methods (e.g., gum, patches) as a temporary substitute
Maintenance	Follow-up sessions or phone calls Coping skills training[*] • Transfer self-management skills to maintenance by avoiding cues to smoke and using substitutes (e.g., cinnamon sticks, water, deep breathing) • Cognitive behavioral coping: anticipating high-risk situations; planning coping strategies • Coping with slips or lapses; learning from mistakes Social support • Buddy systems • Involving significant others (e.g., spouse) Pharmacological—Continuing to use nicotine replacement to cope with withdrawal

[*]Found in most programs.

Source: National Cancer Institute, National Institutes of Health, U.S. Department of Health and Human Services.

Sample State and Local Strategies for Prevention and Cessation of Tobacco Use

RECOMMENDATION 1: INCREASE THE ABILITY OF CONCERNED AGENCIES AND COMMUNITY GROUPS TO REDUCE THE USE OF TOBACCO.

Strategy

- Establish a statewide coalition and local coalitions to assist in planning and implementing tobacco control plans.

Involved Agencies

Maryland Department of Health and Mental Hygiene
American Cancer Society—Maryland Division
American Lung Association—Maryland Unit
American Heart Association—Maryland Division
Medical and Chirurgical Faculty
University of Maryland, School of Medicine

RECOMMENDATION 2: REDUCE TOBACCO USE AMONG PREGNANT WOMEN.

Strategies

- Expand Smoking Cessation in Pregnancy (SCIP) intervention to all state-funded maternity, WIC, and family planning clinics.
- Increase training and materials available to currently practicing health professionals to enable them to counsel pregnant women in smoking cessation.

Involved Agencies

Maryland Department of Health and Mental Hygiene
American Cancer Society—Maryland Division
American Lung Association—Maryland Unit
American Heart Association—Maryland Division
Medical and Chirurgical Faculty
Johns Hopkins University
University of Maryland
National Cancer Institute
Office on Smoking and Health
Local Health Departments

continues

Sample State and Local Strategies continued

RECOMMENDATION 3: REDUCE TOBACCO USE AMONG MINORITIES.

Strategies

- Expand smoking cessation opportunities for minorities through established minority community networks.
- Increase training and materials available to currently practicing health professionals to enable them to counsel minorities in smoking cessation.

Involved Agencies

Maryland Department of Health and Mental Hygiene
American Cancer Society—Maryland Division
American Lung Association—Maryland Unit
American Heart Association—Maryland Division
Medical and Chirurgical Faculty
University of Maryland
National Cancer Institute
Office on Smoking and Health
Local Health Departments

RECOMMENDATION 4: REDUCE TOBACCO USE AMONG WOMEN.

Strategies

- Increase activities to encourage women smokers to quit.
- Increase activities to discourage smoking initiation among adolescent females.
- Increase counseling by health professionals for women obtaining mammograms and Pap smears.

Involved Agencies

Maryland Department of Health and Mental Hygiene
HSCRC-funded hospitals
American Cancer Society—Maryland Division
American Lung Association—Maryland Unit
American Heart Association—Maryland Division
Medical and Chirurgical Faculty
University of Maryland
Maryland Hospital Association

continues

Sample State and Local Strategies continued

RECOMMENDATION 5: REDUCE TOBACCO USE AMONG PEOPLE WITH LOW LEVELS OF EDUCATION AND INCOME.

Strategy

- For all high-risk groups (e.g., pregnant women) and channels for intervention (e.g., media) included in the recommendations, ensure that some portion of activities specifically targets low-education, low-income people.

Involved Agencies

Department of Health and Mental Hygiene
American Cancer Society—Maryland Division
American Lung Association—Maryland Unit
American Heart Association—Maryland Division
Medical Chirurgical Faculty
University of Maryland

RECOMMENDATION 6: REDUCE TOBACCO USE BY YOUTH.

Strategies

- Ensure that all Maryland children attending public and non-public schools receive tobacco resistance education at least twice between kindergarten and the 12th grade.
- Ensure that all Maryland public and non-public schools have policies that ban or severely restrict tobacco use on school property by students, staff, and visitors.
- Increase efforts to reduce tobacco use among out-of-school youth.
- Promote, support, and elicit support for state legislation to reduce access of minors to tobacco products.
- Sponsor anti-tobacco media campaigns that target youth.
- Increase efforts to target rural youth on the Eastern Shore with tobacco resistance education.

Involved Agencies

Maryland Department of Health and Mental Hygiene
Maryland Department of Education
Maryland Hospital Association
Medical and Chirurgical Faculty
National Cancer Institute
Office on Smoking and Health
Group Against Smoker's Pollution
American Cancer Society—Maryland Division
American Lung Association—Maryland Unit
American Heart Association—Maryland Division
University of Maryland

continues

Sample State and Local Strategies continued

RECOMMENDATION 7: INCREASE THE NUMBER OF HEALTH PROFESSIONALS ADVISING THEIR PATIENTS TO QUIT SMOKING.

Strategies

- Increase training and materials available to currently practicing health professionals to enable them to counsel clients in smoking cessation.
- Promote and standardize the use of model programs and policies in all channels.
- Promote the adoption of curricula by health professional preparation programs designed to enable health professionals to counsel clients in smoking cessation.
- Increase efforts to provide nurses with smoking cessation activities.

Involved Agencies

National Cancer Institute
Medical and Chirurgical Faculty
Maryland Department of Health and Mental Hygiene
Maryland Hospital Association
American Cancer Society—Maryland Division
American Lung Association—Maryland Unit
American Heart Association—Maryland Division
Office on Smoking and Health
University of Maryland

RECOMMENDATION 8: PROMOTE, SUPPORT AND ELICIT SUPPORT FOR LEGISLATION THAT WILL REDUCE EXPOSURE TO SECOND-HAND SMOKE AND REDUCE ACCESS TO TOBACCO PRODUCTS.

Strategies

- Promote, support, and elicit support for tobacco control legislation in the following areas:
  —legislation mandating smoke-free public places and worksites
  —reduction of access to tobacco products for minors
  —an increase in excise taxes on tobacco products
  —provision of economic incentives to health professionals to counsel patients in smoking cessation.

Involved Agencies

Medical and Chirurgical Faculty
American Cancer Society—Maryland Division
American Heart Association—Maryland Division
American Lung Association—Maryland Unit
Maryland Hospital Association
University of Maryland

continues

Sample State and Local Strategies continued

RECOMMENDATION 9: USE MARKETING STRATEGIES TO PROMOTE NON-SMOKING AS THE NORM.

Strategy

- Utilize Maryland media outlets for public education on tobacco issues.

Involved Agencies

Maryland Department of Health and Mental Hygiene
American Cancer Society—Maryland Division
American Lung Association—Maryland Unit
American Heart Association—Maryland Division
Medical and Chirurgical Faculty
Local Health Departments
National Cancer Institute
Office on Smoking and Health
University of Maryland

NOTES:

Courtesy of the Montgomery County Department of Health, Rockville, Maryland.

Developing a Tobacco-Free School Policy

1. Obtain the commitment of school administrators and the local school board for development of a comprehensive tobacco-free policy.
   a. Meet with the school administration and/or school board and request a review of the policy (or discuss the lack of one) and obtain board commitment for the development of a comprehensive tobacco-free policy.
   b. Recommend the formation of a board-based advisory committee to research and recommend a new policy.
   c. Obtain support of top management and suggest an active and visible role in the process.
2. Form a broad-based advisory committee for the purpose of reviewing the current policy, collecting relevant data, soliciting opinions, making recommendations, and constructing and submitting a final draft tobacco-free policy for approval.
   a. Form the advisory committee. Include a school board member, school administrator, teacher(s), drug-free schools coordinator, local D.A.R.E. officer, community members, etc.
   b. Review the current policy. Collect relevant data of the health, economic, and legal consequences of tobacco use in the school and make recommendations for deficient areas based upon supporting factual (quantitative) information.
   c. Research existing labor contracts to determine if employee (faculty) smoking rights are addressed.
   d. Develop and distribute a short survey instrument to faculty and to a random selection of students to collect opinion (qualitative) data.
   e. Discuss concerns of the local school board, administration, and interested others.
   f. Determine possible areas of conflict and provide anticipatory solutions or alternatives for inclusion within the structure of the proposed policy.
3. Develop the new tobacco-free policy.
   a. The new policy should be comprehensive in scope, simple, and specific in its delineation. For example, smoking and chewing tobacco should be given similar attention. Rationale for the various segments of the policy as well as benefits should be included.
   b. The new policy should be uniform in its application. Identify where and to whom the policy applies. For example, outbuildings on school property should be subject to the same provisions outlined in the policy as the main school building.
   c. Include violation and enforcement provisions within the policy. Invite local law enforcement to assist. Be creative here!
   d. Set a start date for the policy, such as the first day of the new school year.
4. Present the new policy to the school board.
   a. Make the necessary contacts to be placed on the school board meeting agenda.
   b. Assemble a small group of policy supporters to develop and provide a presentation to the board, providing information on the rationale for the policy, the content of the policy itself, and the implementation plan including enforcement, complaints, and possible conflicts.
   c. Provide a brief "fact sheet" and a copy of the draft policy to each board member. Use audiovisuals such as slides, overheads, or flip charts. Endorsement of the draft policy by a recognized community leader can also be beneficial. Also, community support and attendance at the meeting can be vital.
5. Implement the new tobacco-free policy.
   a. Allow sufficient time for people to prepare for implementation of the policy. Create an implementation timetable that allows for a smoother integration.
   b. Identify tobacco cessation resources available to tobacco users affected by the policy.
   c. Provide training to volunteer faculty members in policy enforcement, student/faculty

continues

Developing a Tobacco-Free School Policy continued

counseling, and conflict resolution. Focus on the use of tobacco, not the user.

d. Maintain absolute enforcement expectations, which will minimize problems.

e. Conduct a public relations and communication campaign announcing the new policy to faculty, students, parents, and the community.

6. Communicate a description of the new policy and its rationale, the benefits of a tobacco-free school, those who will be affected, the enactment date, enforcement procedures, how and where to obtain help with quitting tobacco use, and any other issues surrounding the new policy.

Three months in advance of the policy enactment date, administer a communications plan directed toward the *faculty, students, parents,* and the *community*.

FACULTY—

- Send each faculty member a copy of the policy with an explanation of why the policy is necessary.
- Discuss the new policy at a staff meeting.
- Include an article(s) in the staff newsletter.
- Distribute information in the staff lounge.
- Inform all potential employees of the policy.
- Post signs in all restrooms, lounges, meeting rooms, vehicles, and building foyers.

STUDENTS—PROVIDE INFORMATION THROUGH...

- student handbooks and orientation meetings
- student body organizations

- verbal and written announcements
- student-designed posters, banners, and signs
- school newspaper articles
- health and physical education classes

PARENTS—INFORM THEM BY...

- sending a letter to each parent explaining the new policy, providing an explanation of why the policy is needed, and asking for their support
- involving and requesting the support of parent organization groups from the beginning
- posting signs at the entrance of the school asking for their support and adherence to the policy
- publishing articles in the newspaper or stories on the radio and television news

COMMUNITY—INFORM THEM THROUGH...

- feature stories in the newspaper
- letters to the editor in the newspaper
- signs at all school entrances/foyers
- empowering students and staff to ask community members to refrain from using tobacco while at school
- announcements of the new policy at all athletic events, meetings, concerts, plays, and other public events
- a letter to those neighboring retailers and homeowners near the school to inform them about the policy and encourage their support
- widespread use of the "Tobacco-Free School" logo on letterhead, envelopes, student organization materials, school function programs, etc.

Courtesy of the Montana Office of Public Instruction, Helena, Montana.

Tips for Establishing Falls Prevention Programs

- Use data from hospital emergency departments to target your efforts. Find out how many elderly have been treated for fall-related injuries and where the highest rates are.
- Build a coalition of community resources your program can refer cases to.
- Identify agencies that may want to participate in the falls prevention program. Brainstorm with these organizations to set goals and objectives.
- Survey seniors to find out if they have fallen within the past three weeks. Survey data can serve as a baseline. After home visits have been made, survey seniors again to find out if the changes have resulted in fewer falls.

- Have a hospital legal department draw up a release consent form to protect your program against liability.
- Publicize your program in the news media. Invite reporters to do a walk-through, and show them typical safety problems a home assessment can eliminate.
- Choose someone who can speak to the elderly about the program. This individual should visit senior centers, hand out flyers, and talk about falls and how to prevent them. The message should be short and simple because the elderly often have short attention spans.

NOTES:

Source: Steve Larose, ed., "Elderly Avoid Slips with Dallas Injury Prevention Program," *Inside Preventive Care*, Vol. 2, No. 12, Aspen Publishers, Inc., © March 1997.

Tips for Establishing Injury Control Programs

- Aim for a long-term commitment from all parties involved. Injury prevention does not happen overnight. A systematic, communitywide approach needs to be a long-term commitment.
- Collect data on your community and find out what the issues are for your own environment.
- Get a group of interested community leaders together and prioritize the issues. Think beyond the walls of the hospitals and HMOs when looking for people who might be involved.
- Involve hospital CEOs in the effort by outlining how trauma affects young people for life.

- Use prevention literature to justify creating and financing a local program.
- Sell foundations on making a long-term investment in injury prevention. This concept, if packaged correctly in an application, is attractive to foundations that are interested in overall health issues and particularly prevention issues.
- Generate media coverage by looking for the human angle as the hook to the story. Go for non-obvious things, such as motorcycles, bikers, and Mothers Against Drunk Driving. Be careful not to bombard news and health reporters with too many ideas.

NOTES:

Source: Steve Larose, ed., "Tips for Establishing Injury Control Programs," *Inside Preventive Care*, Vol. 2, No. 3, Aspen Publishers, Inc., © June 1996.

Information To Consider When Profiling a Target Audience for Promoting Physical Activity

Demographic Data

- age range, age cohort
- gender
- ethnicity
- educational level
- employment status, occupation
- marital status
- presence and number of children in the home

Geographic Information

- What geographic places do members of your target audience share in common (e.g., residence, workplace, school, life path points, political boundary, county, state)?
- Can they be clustered within a defined geographic area, or are they scattered?

Current Behaviors and Lifestyle

- How would you characterize the lifestyle of people within your target audience? In what life stage (or stages) are they?
- How physically active are they on the job? At home? At school? During their leisure time?
- What do they do for recreation (e.g., watch television, read, take trips with the family, go to the movies)?
- What competes with the desired behavior (i.e., what are people doing instead of being physically active)?
- What other factors in their lifestyles will support or deter their efforts to be physically active (e.g., residence, occupation, income, tobacco use, social influences)?
- What other health- or physical activity-related messages and programs are currently being targeted at your own intended audience? What specific behaviors are these programs promoting? Do they complement or contradict your own program goals?

Values, Beliefs, Attitudes

- What would members of the target audience describe as their highest priorities (e.g., personal faith, time with family and friends, home life, work life, health, longevity, quality of lifestyle, financial security)?
- What would they describe as their greatest concerns or problems (e.g., lack of time, job security, child care, crime, finances)?
- What are the predominant needs and wants of your target audience?
- How can physical activity be linked to these overriding priorities, concerns, needs, or wants?
- How important to them is a healthy lifestyle? Do they believe that physical activity is an important or necessary component of a healthy lifestyle?
- Is looking good, feeling good about themselves, being energetic, or some other quality more important to them?
- Do they have a positive or negative self-image or body image?
- Do they see themselves as active, and are those perceptions accurate?
- If less than optimally active, do they intend to increase their physical activity in the foreseeable future?
- What is their level of readiness to change regarding physical activity-related behaviors?
- How physically active do they wish to be and how do their personal goals compare to nationally recommended levels of physical activity?
- Is being active the goal, or will being active simply help them accomplish a different goal, such as spending time with their families or getting a job done?
- What do they believe increased physical activity could do for them? Do they perceive those effects to be positive or negative?
- What is it that motivates them to be (or want to be) physically active?

continues

Promoting Physical Activity continued

- What are their personal barriers to physical activity (e.g., lack of time, money, safety, convenience, self-confidence, physical condition)?
- What activities do they believe are most enjoyable or would be fun?
- What does the target audience say would make physical activity less boring or more fun and enjoyable?

History

- What lessons could you learn from previous efforts to reach this target audience with health promotion, physical activity promotion, or other behavior-changing messages and services?

Awareness and Knowledge

- How aware is the target audience of the potential risks of a sedentary lifestyle?
- How aware are they of the benefits of moderate physical activity?
- How would they currently define physical activity or exercise? What comes to their minds when they hear those terms?
- When during the course of a day would members of the target audience be most open or receptive to information about physical activity? At what point during their day are they making decisions concerning physical activity?

Media Use

- What are the primary sources of health-related or physical activity-related information for members of your target audience?
- What media channels (e.g., radio, television, or print) do they routinely use?
- How accurate or appropriate is the health- or physical activity-related information that reaches the target audience via each of these channels?
- Considering a typical day, where would the target audience be most likely to see or hear your messages promoting physical activity?

Physical Health Status

- To what extent are other health-related factors present among members of the target audience (e.g., high blood pressure, high blood cholesterol, tobacco use, uncontrolled blood glucose, obesity, stress, pregnancy, arthritis)?
- Do members of the target audience have any physical conditions that would limit or alter their participation in a variety of physical activities?

Skill and Ability Level

- To what extent do people within the target audience possess the skills needed to successfully initiate and maintain a physically active lifestyle?

Level of Self-Efficacy

- How confident are members of your target audience in their ability to be regularly active?
- To what extent do they believe they can improve their levels of physical activity?

Cultural and Social Norms

- How does your target audience's social culture and climate support or deter being physically active?
- Do certain traditions, customs, folklore, or religious beliefs in your target audience either support or hinder men's, women's, or children's efforts to be physically active?
- How might supportive beliefs and traditions be reinforced while those that hinder physical activity be minimized?

Supportive and Reinforcing Social Network

- What social or peer pressures greatly influence the actions of people within your target audience?

continues

Promoting Physical Activity continued

- What do the people who are most important to members of the target audience think they should do in regard to physical activity?
- Who would support their efforts to be physically active and who would deter efforts to change? Consider those in authority over, under, and equal to the target audience (e.g., administrators, community leaders, supervisors, parents, teachers, clergy, health care providers, constituents, staff, clients, friends, family members, coworkers, peers).
- Who are their role models in general? Who are their role models for a physically active lifestyle in particular?
- Who are they most likely to turn to for information regarding health or physical activity?
- What organizations or groups do people within your target audience frequently join? Do any of these organizations have goals complementary to your own? Is there a potential for partnership with these organizations?

Physical Environment, Facilities, and Resources

- What natural resources are available in the local geographic area (e.g., rivers, lakes, trails)?
- What recreational resources are available to the target audience (e.g., safe sidewalks, bicycle paths, walking trails, playing fields, gymnasiums, showers and locker rooms, tennis courts,

community recreation centers, a local YMCA or YWCA)?
- Are existing resources accessible and affordable?
- Are current resources acceptable to your target audience (i.e., do members of your target audience feel welcomed and comfortable using these various resources)?
- Are recreational facilities and parks—including playground equipment; tennis, volleyball, or basketball nets and courts; soccer fields; swimming pools—safe, attractive, and well maintained (e.g., free of debris and broken glass, in good repair, well-lighted during early morning and evening hours, periodically patrolled by police or park security)?
- What untapped or underused resources are potentially available in your community or site (e.g., shopping malls closed to walkers, unlighted playing fields, vacant lots that could be converted to recreation space, or highway or transportation funds that could be used to construct bicycle paths)?

Political Environment

- What laws, policies, or regulations affecting the environment in which members of your target population live, work, or spend their leisure time either encourage or restrict their levels of physical activity (e.g., curfews, personnel policies, membership rules)?

Source: U.S. Department of Health and Human Services, Public Health Service, Centers for Disease Control and Prevention, National Center for Chronic Disease Prevention and Health Promotion, Division of Nutrition and Physical Activity, *Promoting Physical Activity: A Guide for Community Action*. Champaign, IL: Human Kinetics, 1999.

Ideas for Action in the Community To Promote a Physically Active Lifestyle

- Identify the skills that people need to make a change in their physical activity levels, then plan programs to teach those skills.
  - –increasing physical activity routinely throughout the day
  - –starting a walking or jogging program
  - –selecting the right shoes, clothing, or equipment
  - –using exercise or sports equipment properly and safely
  - –stretching, warm-up, and cool-down techniques
  - –exercising while sitting in a chair, standing, or watching television
  - –avoiding the risks of injury from exercise
  - –taking lessons of any kind (e.g., swimming, sailing, golf, or tennis)
  - –maintaining physical activity and preventing relapse to a sedentary lifestyle
- For groups of various ages or level of experience, work with physical education instructors, physical therapists, or exercise physiologists to design appropriate and quality instructional programs.
- Enhance the skills of gatekeepers who can successfully reach members of the target audience. Instruct physicians on effective techniques of assessment and counseling for physical activity.
- Develop or make available self-instructional materials, such as videotaped instruction, cassette tape instruction, computer-based instruction, how-to guides, manuals, and kits.
- Develop a community resource list so that people will know where to find courses or opportunities to develop skills.
- Provide formal and informal activity-oriented instructional programs, such as workshops, classes, seminars, demonstrations, lessons, and lectures.
- Provide individual assessment and counseling or personal trainers for a fee or as an incentive.
- Sponsor meet-the-expert events so community members can learn directly from those who have mastered various skills.
- Conduct demonstrations or small-group classes with active involvement by participants.
- Provide opportunities to try the desired behavior for just 1 day or for one event, such as
  - –community walking events
  - –using stairs instead of elevators for 1 day or 1 week
  - –bicycle-to-work day or other bicycling events
  - –periodic fun runs, such as the turkey trot (Thanksgiving), reindeer run (Christmas), and bunny hop (Easter)
  - –lunchtime walking groups at local businesses, schools, or shopping malls
  - –trial memberships and guest passes to use recreational facilities
- Reward each effort appropriately, praise success, and provide constructive feedback.

Source: U.S. Department of Health and Human Services, Public Health Service, Centers for Disease Control and Prevention, National Center for Chronic Disease Prevention and Health Promotion, Division of Nutrition and Physical Activity, *Promoting Physical Activity: A Guide for Community Action*. Champaign, IL: Human Kinetics, 1999.

Barriers To Being Active Quiz

Directions: Listed below are reasons that people give to describe why they do not get as much physical activity as they think they should. Please read each statement and indicate how likely you are to say each of the following statements:

How likely are you to say?	Very likely	Somewhat likely	Somewhat unlikely	Very unlikely
1. My day is so busy now, I just don't think I can make the time to include physical activity in my regular schedule.	3	2	1	0
2. None of my family members or friends like to do anything active, so I don't have a chance to exercise.	3	2	1	0
3. I'm just too tired after work to get any exercise.	3	2	1	0
4. I've been thinking about getting more exercise, but I just can't seem to get started.	3	2	1	0
5. I'm getting older so exercise can be risky.	3	2	1	0
6. I don't get enough exercise because I have never learned the skills for any sport.	3	2	1	0
7. I don't have access to jogging trails, swimming pools, bike paths, etc.	3	2	1	0
8. Physical activity takes too much time away from other commitments, like work, family, etc.	3	2	1	0
9. I'm embarrassed about how I will look when I exercise with others.	3	2	1	0
10. I don't get enough sleep as it is. I just couldn't get up early or stay up late to get some exercise.	3	2	1	0
11. It's easier for me to find excuses not to exercise than to go out and do something.	3	2	1	0
12. I know of too many people who have hurt themselves by overdoing it with exercise.	3	2	1	0
13. I really can't see learning a new sport at my age.	3	2	1	0
14. It's just too expensive. You have to take a class or join a club or buy the right equipment.	3	2	1	0
15. My free times during the day are too short to include exercise.	3	2	1	0
16. My usual social activities with family or friends do not include physical activity.	3	2	1	0
17. I'm too tired during the week and I need the weekend to catch up on my rest.	3	2	1	0

continues

Barriers to Being Active Quiz continued

How likely are you to say?	Very likely	Somewhat likely	Somewhat unlikely	Very unlikely
18. I want to get more exercise, but I just can't seem to make myself stick to anything.	3	2	1	0
19. I'm afraid I might injure myself or have a heart attack.	3	2	1	0
20. I'm not good enough at any physical activity to make it fun.	3	2	1	0
21. If we had exercise facilities and showers at work, then I would be more likely to exercise.	3	2	1	0

Follow these instructions to score yourself:

- Enter the circled number in the spaces provided, putting the number for statement 1 on line 1, statement 2 on line 2, and so on.
- Add the three scores on each line. Your barriers to physical activity fall into one or more of seven categories: lack of time, social influences, lack of energy, lack of will power, fear of injury, lack of skill, and lack of resources. A score of 5 or above in any category shows that this is an important barrier for you to overcome.

$$\underline{\quad}_{1} + \underline{\quad}_{8} + \underline{\quad}_{15} = \underline{\qquad} \text{lack of time}$$

$$\underline{\quad}_{2} + \underline{\quad}_{9} + \underline{\quad}_{16} = \underline{\qquad} \text{social influence}$$

$$\underline{\quad}_{3} + \underline{\quad}_{10} + \underline{\quad}_{17} = \underline{\qquad} \text{lack of energy}$$

$$\underline{\quad}_{4} + \underline{\quad}_{11} + \underline{\quad}_{18} = \underline{\qquad} \text{lack of willpower}$$

$$\underline{\quad}_{5} + \underline{\quad}_{12} + \underline{\quad}_{19} = \underline{\qquad} \text{fear of injury}$$

$$\underline{\quad}_{6} + \underline{\quad}_{13} + \underline{\quad}_{20} = \underline{\qquad} \text{lack of skill}$$

$$\underline{\quad}_{7} + \underline{\quad}_{14} + \underline{\quad}_{21} = \underline{\qquad} \text{lack of resources}$$

Source: U.S. Department of Health and Human Services, Public Health Service, Centers for Disease Control and Prevention, National Center for Chronic Disease Prevention and Health Promotion, Division of Nutrition and Physical Activity, *Promoting Physical Activity: A Guide for Community Action*. Champaign, IL: Human Kinetics, 1999; Division of Epidemiology, University of Minnesota.

IMMUNIZATION BARRIERS AND STRATEGIES

Barriers	Planned Strategies
Lack of knowledge about immunization	
How, when, where to get shots	Community outreach with fliers
When to return for shots	Speakers bureau
Immunizations are free	Hotline
	Local print media campaign
	Billboards, bus and taxi boards
	Immunization packet distribution
Difficulty accessing clinic	
Inconvenient hours and locations	Evening clinic hours
	Alternative and elementary school sites
Difficulty scheduling appointments	Walk-in system
Transportation and child care problems	Free bus tickets
	Community transport van
Environment that is not "family friendly"	Adopt-a-clinic program
	Parent incentives
	Suggestion boxes
	Staff training

Source: Frances D. Butterfoss et al., "Use of Focus Group Data for Strategic Planning by a Community-Based Immunization Coalition," *Family and Community Health*, Vol. 20:3, Aspen Publishers, Inc., © 1997.

WAYS TO DISSEMINATE IMMUNIZATION INFORMATION WITHOUT THE MEDIA*

Listed below are ways we can disseminate infant immunization facts to everyone during NIIW and increase the immunization rates of our children under two.

Events

- Sponsored run/walk for immunization
- Set up booths at different town/city events
- Parades—display chart or world map of the nation, showing county or city rank for immunization rate
- Employer-sponsored parental workshops
- Bingo using immunization facts/schedule
- Use local celebrities to be on reminder/recall phone banks or home visits
- State contest for "Best Immunization Coverage"—HMO, and other private practice with award ceremony and prizes

*Source: *Seven Days of Immunization: National Infant Immunization Week, Information and Organization Handbook* prepared by the Centers for Disease Control and Prevention, Public Health Service, U.S. Department of Health and Human Services, 1995.

- Display a chart with hypodermic as "thermometer" of immunization rate at town center (busy downtown location where it will be visible to many people)
- Conduct special immunization clinics, health fairs
- Press conference with elected officials or celebrities
- Special announcements at sporting events
- Talks at community centers
- Promotions at children's toy stores
- Special announcements at the circus
- Sponsorships at road races or bike races
- Phone banks to reach parents of the newly born
- Church bulletins
- Club newsletters
- Professional association newsletters

Mailing/Print/Posting

- Handbills
- Transit advertisement—inside buses and trains
- Bus shelters
- Wall posters
- Supermarket display
- Bodega/grocery store advertisements
- Chalk markings on the ground—"sidewalk art"
- Newsletters with facts/updates about immunization
- Flyers
- Value-pack coupons
- Fact sheet & immunization mailing schedule to parents of newborns
- Bookmarks
- Billboards
- Bus advertisement
- Bulletin boards
- Bench advertisement
- Insert information with utility bill
- Insert information with food stamps
- Have immunization information at the Department of Motor Vehicles
- Print immunization messages on prescription bottles
- Send an "Immunization Kit" gift to every legislator with fact sheets, information (if you have immunization products, T-shirts, mugs, posters, boots, lapel pins, pens, etc., send them with factual materials)
- Print payroll inserts for employees
- Co-op (printed napkins at restaurants)
- Labor unions leafleting
- On hospital bills for newborns
- On bank calendars/promotions
- On sports schedules
- Theaters/video stores

Merchandise

- Print information/informational phone number on baby bottles
- Print immunization slogans on grocery bags, milk cartons
- Print information/informational phone number on Frisbees
- Posters
- Bumper stickers
- Bookmarks
- "49%" buttons (or whatever 4:3:1 coverage level is in your state)
- Create T-shirts, bibs: "My kid is fully immunized, is yours?", "I have been immunized."
- Immunization magnets

Electronic

- E-mail
- Internet

Other

- Put immunization messages in kid's programming, soap operas, etc.
- Play immunization message video in emergency rooms
- Activities/information in:
    Hospital emergency rooms
    Day care centers
    Playgrounds
    Social service agencies

NOTES:

SOCIAL MARKETING OVERVIEW*

Social marketing is defined as the design, implementation, and control of programs developed to influence the social acceptability of a social idea or cause by a group. It has its roots in both commercial marketing and social reform campaigns, such as the abolition of slavery and campaigns for government regulation of the quality of food and drugs.

While social marketing campaigns often rely on the use of mass media channels, it is more than mass media advertising. It involves identifying the needs of a specific group of people, supplying information so people can make informed decisions, offering programs or services that meet real needs, and assessing how well those needs were met.

Social marketing can be used in a range of situations to give information to the public or encourage specific target groups to take specific actions. For example, a familiar campaign to reduce drinking and driving problems focused its message not on the drinking driver, but on others with its "Friends Don't Let Friends Drink and Drive" slogan. Using commercial marketing practices, social marketing makes the consumer, or in this case, the target audience, the focus of the program.

Marketing is the planned process of exercising influence on customer behavior. In the case of commercial product marketing, the desired behavior is, of course, the purchase of the product being marketed. Social marketing is more complex in that the product being promoted is more abstract, such as a change in behavior or belief to effect social change.

The following describes the differences between social marketing in the public health arena and product marketing campaigns:

- *Type of change expected*—Health campaigns aim to change fundamental behaviors, whereas much product advertising aims to mobilize an existing predisposition, as in switching brands. However, some product advertising does aim to create new markets.
- *Amount of change expected*—Health campaigns aim to change a large portion of the population. Product advertising is usually satisfied with small shifts in market share.
- *Time frame of expected benefits*—Health campaigns usually ask their target audience to wait for delayed statistical probabilities. Product advertisers promise immediate certainty.
- *Presentation of the product*—Product advertisers can dress up their product as much as they want or need to. Health campaigns do not, and probably cannot be seen to oversell benefits or the ease of their acquisition.
- *Available budgets*—Product advertisers have massive budgets. Health campaigners usually operate on relatively minuscule budgets.
- *Trustworthiness*—People often distrust advertising. Health campaigners cannot allow distrust to develop.

*Source: *Substance Abuse Prevention Primer*, Center for Substance Abuse, Public Health Service, U.S. Department of Health and Human Services.

- *Level of evaluation*—Product advertisers stress formative research: market research conducted before campaigns. Health campaigners tend to stress summative evaluation, conducted after the campaign, if they stress any evaluation at all.

In a society with heavy reliance on mass media and a crowded message environment, the art of social marketing can make a valuable contribution to prevention efforts.

SOCIAL MARKETING TUTORIAL*

Summary

Anchored in your broader health promotion program, social marketing serves as a tool within your overall strategy. Ideally, it should work in synergy with other programs.

Audience analyses are essential to the success of all social marketing plans. Furthermore, decisions relating to objectives, message positioning, and delivery are all based on your audience analysis.

Organizational and environmental considerations play an important role in the overall context of your plan. They also should have a strong influence on the partnerships you form.

Social marketing activities should include more than promotional activities. You may need to adjust your program, products, services, or the desired behavior to make it easier for audiences to change. As far as promotion activities are concerned, consider events and interpersonal communication in addition to media activities and promotional material. Remember to go where the traffic is because it's easier to go to your audience than have it come to you.

The more realistic and measurable your objectives, the more successful your plan will be. Objectives provide you with focus and simplify the evaluation stage of your social marketing plan. Since this is an introductory level tutorial, it does not include in-depth evaluation techniques.

Defining the Role of Social Marketing in Your Overall Health Promotion Program

This section will help you define the specific contribution of social marketing activities to your overall health promotion program. It will also clarify how social marketing relates to other program approaches, such as advocacy and community development. As part of this process, you will identify your audiences (who you need to reach) and the changes you seek in order to achieve your health promotion goals.

Social marketing is defined as "the application of commercial marketing technologies to the analysis, planning, execution, and evaluation of programs designed to influence the voluntary behavior of target audiences in order to improve their personal welfare and that of their society."**

So, what exactly are you expecting from social marketing?

What Are the Overall Goals of Your Health Promotion Program?

You may find this type of goal in the mission statement, purpose, or mandate of your organization or your program.

---

*Source: Reproduced from *Social Marketing Tutorial, Partnerships and Marketing Division*, Health Canada, 1999. © Minister of Public Works and Government Services Canada, 2001.

**A.R. Andreasen, *Marketing Social Change: Changing Behavior To Promote Health, Social Development and the Environment* (San Francisco: Jossey-Bass, 1995).

Which Factors Have You Identified To Explain the Current Situation? Which Factors Need To Change To Improve the Situation?

Key factors could include epidemiological descriptions, policy and environmental issues, lifestyle risks, and any number of other factors.

In Your Overall Health Promotion Program, What Approaches (Other Than Social Marketing) Are You Currently Using or Planning To Use To Achieve Your Overall Goals?

- policies
- community development/mobilization
- advocacy
- other approaches (specify):

Which Target Audiences Should You Attempt To Influence To Meet Your Objectives and Implement Your Advocacy or Community Development Initiatives?

Target audiences can be internal (employees, board members, committees, and volunteers) or external (population segments, decision-makers, policy-makers, partners, etc.). What do you want your target audiences to know, think, and do (adopt behaviors or policies, make donations or decisions, subscriptions, etc.)? Be specific about what you want them to do, since it is the most important component when analyzing target audiences.

Audience Analysis

This section will help you

- define the demographic, behavioral, and lifestyle profiles of your audiences. The analysis will also help differentiate between individuals or groups who have and who have not already adopted the desired behavior or action.
- identify the type of media and events, as well as the most influential individuals for effective interpersonal communication activities

Information Gathering

Market research may be required to complete this section. However, some community-based organizations may not have the resources or skills to conduct research. Regardless of whether or not you can afford market research, it would be worthwhile to conduct a thorough review of available materials as well as existing market research sponsored by other organizations. Potential sources include

- demographic data
- in-house membership databases (postal codes, current habits and behaviors, etc.)
- surveys (knowledge, attitudes, behaviors, perceptions, opinions, needs, satisfaction levels, media habits, etc.)
- focus groups or interviews
- audience and readership profiles for various media. Consider calling the sales departments of media outlets to identify which medium is most suitable for your audience based on demographics
- profiles of members who belong to specific organizations/groups, or participants at events

It is always advisable to consult market research experts for certain types of research activities, especially surveys. Even if you have insufficient funds, be sure to consult an expert to help you prepare your questionnaire and interpret responses. This will validate your research tools and ensure that results are objective. Determine the strategic information you need and the method you intend to use beforehand to avoid incurring unnecessary research costs.*

Developing Audience Profiles

Refer back to the section *"Which Target Audiences Should You Attempt To Influence. . . ."* Fill in the demographic, behavioral, and lifestyle profiles for each of your target audiences, along with the related behaviors and actions you seek.

Divide information between the two key segments in each audience.

- those who have already adopted the behaviors or actions
- those who have not. Some of these individuals may be against the idea. However, most of them are probably receptive, but face real or perceived barriers. Other people may not see the relevance of what you are suggesting. Understanding this population/audience segment (those who have not adopted the behavior or action) is essential to the rest of your plan. Social marketers do not assume that what worked with some people will work with everyone.
  – Audience:
  – Behavior(s)/action(s):

Demographic Profile		
	Those who have already adopted the behaviors or actions	Those who have not
Number of people in audience		
Age (specify age group)		
Sex (M/F)		
Level of education		
Family composition/marital status		
Household income		
Type of occupation(s)		
Urban/rural population		
Mother tongue, languages spoken, and other cultural characteristics		
Other defining characteristics		

*Recommended reading: D.B. Herron, *Marketing Nonprofit Programs and Services* (San Francisco: Jossey-Bass, 1997), 53–79.

Behavioral Profile		
	Those who have already adopted the behaviors or actions	**Those who have not**
Current behaviors		
Awareness levels		
Current attitudes		
Perceived benefits and consequences		
Factors that (would) predispose the audience to adopt specific behaviors		
Factors that are (or would be) barriers for individuals to adopt specific behaviors (time, access, as well as costs in monetary, psychological, and social terms, etc.)		
Belief in their personal ability to adopt the behaviors		
Others		

Lifestyle Profile		
	Those who have already adopted the behaviors or actions	**Those who have not**
Fundamental values and beliefs		
Influence and credibility of their networks (friends, family, colleagues, professionals, etc.) and your organization		
Types of organizations/groups to which they belong		
Lifestyle and interests		

continues

Lifestyle Profile continued

	Those who have already adopted the behaviors or actions	Those who have not
Media habits • TV • cable • radio • dailies • weeklies • magazines • newsletters • outdoor advertising • transit advertising • telephone • mail • e-mail/Internet • others		
Locations where the audience can be reached (specify) • schools (specify) • work (e.g., corporations, government offices, possible networks, full-time versus part-time employees) • malls • supermarkets • when consulting professionals • events they attend • other		

Summary and Implications

Summarize which components in the audience profiles distinguish the two segments.

Another approach would be to summarize the differences between the two segments in terms of

- benefits
- perceived or real (negative) consequences
- perceived or real barriers
- positive and negative influencers

For individuals who have adopted the behavior/action, your greatest challenge will most likely be to ensure that they maintain the behavior/action. For those who have not, your analysis should help you focus on barriers and/or relevance for the audience. You need to link the desired behavior or action to what is important to your audience.

You should already be planning what you could do to modify perceptions, eliminate barriers, and/or optimize positive influences, while neutralizing or minimizing negative ones. This may also mean altering some aspects of your program, and identifying the first step people should take to adopt the behavior or take the first step.

Context for Your Social Marketing Plan

A series of contextual considerations for your social marketing plan are listed below. These considerations will be important when choosing activities and seeking partners.

Organizational Considerations

Identify each organizational consideration you believe represents a strength or a weakness.

- current mission statement
- existing long-term social marketing plan
- personnel skills in the planning and delivery of social marketing activities
- approach to communications
- decision-making processes
- policies (e.g., partnerships/sponsorships)
- resources
  - human
  - material
  - financial
- current partners (list them)
- access to networks and channels (formal and informal access to audience/segment)
- production capacity and expertise
- other

Environmental Considerations

Identify environmental considerations that you feel represent an opportunity, threat, or constraint.

- Type of competition
  - Competition for attention
  - Opponents of the cause
  - Competition within your field
- Ethical issues (e.g., confidentiality)
- Legal issues (e.g., municipal by-laws)
- Social issues (e.g., poverty)
- Political issues (e.g., elections)
- Economic issues (e.g., closing of a major plant)
- Demographic issues (e.g., aging of population)
- Technological issues (e.g., nicotine patches)

Implications

Based on your observations, ask yourself the following four questions:

1. How can you build on your strengths?
2. How can you overcome your weaknesses?
3. How can you use the opportunities available to you?
4. How can you reduce outside threats?

Defining Measurable Objectives

Based on your audience analysis and context, you now have to define measurable and realistic objectives (awareness, attitudes, behaviors, and actions). Awareness can be achieved relatively quickly, but changes in attitude and behavior can take years, or even decades. You need to make behavior changes and actions achievable. Never assume that awareness alone can lead to changes in attitudes and behaviors. Focusing on barriers, perceptions, and key influencers may be more important.

Why Is It Important To Define Measurable and Realistic Social Marketing Objectives?

Defining measurable and realistic social marketing objectives is important because it brings focus to your plan. Objectives force you to identify priorities. They have a major influence on how you allocate resources and form the basis of your program monitoring and evaluation.

Try to limit the number of objectives to between three and five. Focus on key audience segments you may be able to reach and influence either directly or indirectly.

The basic formula for objectives is by (date), XX% of the (demographic or psychological segments) in (community) will (be aware of, believe that, do . . .) your goal for changed behavior.

Strategy and Tactics

At this point, you should establish the strategy and tactics to achieve your measurable objectives. This will include adjusting some aspects of your program (behavior, first step, products, services, etc.) before you consider promoting the program. You will then need to determine your positioning. This is followed by the message development and pre-testing phase through the channels you have identified. You may also consider forming partnerships with a number of organizations and individuals to enhance your credibility and increase your influence. Partners can increase your access to audiences and/or gather the resources you need for your social marketing and other health promotion activities.

Adjustments to Your Program

Some aspects of your program, such as the products, services, or the actual behaviors you want to promote, may need to be adjusted to make it easier for audiences to take action. This can include identifying the first step people should take to adopt the behavior. Consider making this first step the cornerstone of your promotion. Decide what you can do to make it easier for audiences to adopt the desired behavior or action steps by eliminating or showing people how to overcome barriers, changing policies or perceptions, increasing access to programs, or reducing the time required.

Positioning

A positioning statement should have a dual impact on your audience by sending a relevant message while informing them about your organization.

First of all, you need to determine if the behavior or your message is complementary with competing ideas in the daily life of your audience. It should be positioned according to your audience analysis (i.e., demographic profile and relevance). If your message is well positioned, the target audience will perceive it as being relevant. Focus on what is unique about the desired behavior and your organization. Be ready to back up your statements with facts. Then, you can be sure that your message will be more easily heard, understood, and taken to heart.

For example, Health Canada's Vitality program recognized that being active and having a positive self and body image are closely linked to healthy eating. The program targeted adults in the 25–45 age group with 9 to 13 years of education. The audience analysis found that

- they would like to spend more time with family and friends, which is their number one priority
- they are hard-working, no-nonsense Canadians who often feel too tired to exercise. Although they know they should eat nutritious meals, they feel that preparation time is too long and/or that nutritious food is too costly.

The Vitality program was developed and positioned with this audience profile in mind. The program demonstrated that it was easier than one would think to introduce special moments into a family setting that involve healthy eating, active living, and having fun. Parents were able to see how gratifying it can be to briefly forget their daily concerns and spend some quality time with their child(ren).

In addition to sending a relevant message, you need to inform the target audience about your organization. They should know how you are aligned with the issue at hand, and how you differ from competing organizations. Your approach should be based on the goal of your social marketing plan. For example, you might emphasize your organization's position if you were developing a fund-raising campaign. However, if your health message takes precedence, then you may only use a logo for your organization or for the larger program effort to maintain the focus on the message itself.

The following is an example of Health Canada's in-house positioning statement for the Vitality program: "To promote and support the ability of Canadians to strengthen and maintain their healthy eating practices by fostering and creating supportive environments and providing leadership in areas of policy, programs, knowledge development, education, and public awareness."

Delivering Your Message

What is the best method for getting your message across to your target audience? You need to look at their media habits, living environment, and the events they attend. Who or what has the most influence over them? This includes formal and informal networks, such as the media or family and friends. The answer is usually a combination of things, which is why you should choose a mix of communication methods (i.e., the media, interpersonal communication, and events) as well as people who are likely to have a lot of influence and credibility with the target audience. See the section titled "Developing Audience Profiles" for a list of potential media outlets, interpersonal communication activities, and events.

You may be considering using public service announcements (PSAs) to convey your message. Don't set your expectations too high. Nowadays, an increasing number of broadcasters and publishers require that you pay at least a portion of the advertising time and space. Otherwise, your message is likely to be broadcast during nonpeak hours or only used as a filler in print media.

Nevertheless, the following tips could prove useful:

- Use up-to-date, high-quality advertising.
- Humor and a positive tone can be very effective.
- The first audience of PSA material is the medium itself.
- Comply with media formats, procedures, and specifications.
- Maintaining personal contact with the media is very important.
- Avoid using the hard sell approach.
- Let the media know if it works.
- Ask for no charge invoices that show donated time or space to evaluate the value of donated time and space.

Message Development

This is the stage where you develop your messages (advertisements, speeches, scenarios for interpersonal exchanges, and so on) for each of your target audiences. Every message must involve some form of tangible action to answer the inevitable question, "Now what?" For example, it may be something as simple as calling a toll-free number, ordering a publication, visiting a Web site, or attending an event. Remember to consider possible barriers to adopting action immediately. Solve the problem or show people how to overcome barriers!

More importantly, you need to go beyond a simple list of benefits. Be sure that your messages answer the other question that a number of people in your target audience will be sure to ask: "So what?" Your answer will be crucial for showing the target audience that your message is relevant. Go beyond slogans.

You may want to get creative minds (volunteers or suppliers) involved. Another approach would be to have members of the target audience participate in the message development process. Try not to involve people who know too much about your program or the issue. Find people who know the audience. The idea is not to please your committee members but to reach an audience on its own terms.

After you have developed your messages, ask typical members of the target audience (who don't know you personally) to provide you with feedback. Make sure their reactions are consistent with your objectives. Ask the following questions about your positioning statement:

- Is it attention getting?
- Is it clear?
- Is it relevant?
- Is it persuasive?

- Is it credible?
- Is it generating the desired behavior/action?

Finding Partners and Sponsors

You are likely to seek the support of partners for one or more of the following reasons:

- reach—access to the audience. Partners can lead you directly to your audience. You can save a lot of time and effort by going to your audience instead of trying to have them come to you.

  Example: Your messages are aimed at children aged 5–11, so you form a partnership with the district school board to give you access to elementary schools.

- credibility—for greater audience impact. For one reason or another, your organization may not be perceived as credible by your target audience. If this is the case, your messages will not be meaningful to them. You need their acceptance and trust before you can successfully convey your messages.

  Example: Your organization is a community health clinic, and you are targeting teenagers and their sexual practices. Forming a partnership with a popular television music program would give your messages credibility.

- resources—financial, human, or material. You may not have all the resources to back the social marketing plan that your health promotion program needs. A partner can provide those resources for you. Of course, you need to present your situation and needs in a manner that will be relevant for a potential partner.

  Example: Your budget simply cannot accommodate the printing costs of your new publication. Form a partnership with a publishing company that can take care of that part of the project.

- support—to alleviate a previously identified weakness or threat. (See the section titled "Context for Your Social Marketing Plan.")

  There may be weaknesses in your social marketing plan or it could be subject to outside threats. Forming a partnership with an organization that has the resources and know-how to overcome these obstacles will in turn help you overcome your weaknesses and reduce outside threats.

  Example: Your organization lacks production expertise—an area in which your competition flourishes. Form a partnership with an advertising agency that is on the cutting edge of production.

  List the organizations (governments, foundations, private-sector companies, organizations, groups, clubs, institutions, etc.) you will need to contact for support. Specify the nature and the level of support you are seeking. Make sure you are realistic and that you have something to offer that is relevant and meaningful to them—without selling your soul!

  Example: Asking permission to hold an event in a school in return for having the school logo displayed on materials, and being included in the press release.

Example: Asking an organization to sponsor an event in exchange for visibility and the right to have a special discount for participants from the organization.

Monitoring and Evaluation

This section will help you determine if your plan

1. is well implemented
2. achieves the measurable objectives you have set
3. contributes to your overall health promotion program goals

Monitoring Implementation

In the Strategy and Tactics section, particularly the subsections Adjustments to Your Program, Delivering Your Message, and Finding Partners and Sponsors, you identified activities you are about to implement.

In each case, you should report

- if the action/activity was completed and when
- if it was on time and why (or why not)
- if it required the human, material, and financial resources allocated
- the number of individuals reached
- their profile versus the intended audience
- what was done well and less well
- what you have learned
- recommended adjustments to the activity and/or plan

You should consider monitoring implementation on an ongoing basis with brief progress reports on a monthly basis for the first few months.

Progress in Terms of Measurable Objectives

Your activities were strategically chosen to help achieve the measurable objectives you set in the section titled "Defining Measurable Objectives." During the first year, report at least twice on progress made. Progress reports will help reinforce the commitment of team members and partners. They also serve as a reminder of why you are involved in these activities. In some instances, progress reports may even lead you to reconsider your choice of activities and/or partners.

The methodologies outlined in the section titled "Audience Analysis" can be used to monitor progress in terms of measurable objectives. Use the statistics from your audience analysis as baseline data.

Progress in Terms of Health Promotion Program Goals

By engaging in social marketing, advocacy, community development, and/or other approaches, you have made the assumption that the combined results of your efforts would lead to significant change. Social marketing activities cannot easily be separated from all other initiatives and uncontrollable influences on your overall health promotion or behavior change goals. Although a separate evaluation of social marketing activities is possible, it would require sophisticated methodologies and significant budgets that are rarely available to local organizations. However, your evaluation reports should contain a section on the relative contribution of your social marketing activities to the overall program. Evaluations should also explain how other factors may have influenced outcomes, and may influence future social marketing activities.

Working Out Operational Details

Developing a Schedule

Set a date and assign a person to be responsible for the following tasks:

- finalizing audience analysis
- adjustments to program/products/services, etc.
- positioning and message development
- pre-testing positioning and messages
- finalizing message delivery
- forming partnerships
- implementation (planning and execution of each activity as well as production of materials)
- evaluation

Establishing a Budget

The following list will help you draw up a budget:

- Expenses
  - management/consultations/committees
  - research and evaluation
  - media activities
  - events
  - training of influencers
  - print or other material
  - mailing and distribution
  - other
  - contingencies (10% of the above)
  - applicable taxes
- Revenues
  - your organization
  - governments
  - nonprofit organizations
  - individual donations (employees, members, others)
  - foundations/service clubs
  - private-sector companies
  - other

GUIDELINES FOR DEVELOPING PUBLIC HEALTH FRAMES*

In developing frames, public health practitioners must identify how to define, position, and package an issue in ways that (1) present a unified, coherent core position; (2) evoke desired visual images; (3) employ recognizable catch phrases; (4) suggest appropriate metaphors; (5) attribute responsibility for the problem to society, rather than merely to the individual; and (6) imply as a solution the program or policy being marketed by the practitioner. The six objectives in developing a framing strategy for public health programs and policies are

1. Present unified, coherent core position on the policy or program that is consistent with the core values of target audience.
2. Evoke visual images that appeal to the core values.
3. Develop catch phrases (verbal images) that appeal to the core values.
4. Suggest appropriate metaphors that evoke themes and images that appeal to the core values.
5. Attribute responsibility for the public health problem to society (including government), not merely to individuals.
6. Imply as a solution the program or policy being marketed.

All of these individual objectives must work together effectively to reinforce the deeply ingrained, widely held principles and values of the target audience.

For example, consider the framing of a local ordinance to protect the health of restaurant workers by eliminating smoking in restaurants. To market such a policy, one might develop four frames based on widely held core values: freedom, independence, control, and fairness. Instead of defining the product of an anti-smoking ordinance campaign as a law to protect the health of nonsmokers and offering health for restaurant customers as a benefit, the product and benefits can be redefined as the freedom to work in an environment free of health hazards, the right to make a living without being involuntarily exposed to carcinogens, creating a level playing field for all workers by affording restaurant workers the same protection that is provided to almost all other workers, helping business by preventing huge liability risks for damages caused by secondhand smoke, preventing discrimination against blue-collar workers by extending to all workers the protection that almost all white-collar workers have from secondhand smoke, and protecting the livelihood of workers in small restaurants by ending the suffering they endure from exposure to a hazardous working environment (Table 3).

Similarly, instead of framing an initiative to increase the cigarette tax simply as a measure to reduce cigarette consumption and improve health, supporting the initiative could be framed as a way for voters to remain free of the tobacco industry's influence, raise their children independent of the pressure being placed on their children to smoke, maintain control of the health of their communities, and preserve the principles of democracy (see Table 1).

Programs to adopt such measures as stricter environmental regulations, needle exchange programs, mandatory seat belt laws, and screening and treatment programs

---

*Source: Michael Siegel and Lynne Doner, *Marketing Public Health: Strategies To Promote Social Change*, Aspen Publishers, Inc., © 1998.

Table 3 Core Values and Messages That Appeal to These Values for Several Public Health Policies

Public Health Policy	Core Value	Message
Eliminate smoking in restaurants	Freedom/Free enterprise	What could possibly be a more basic freedom to Americans than the freedom to make a living and support one's children without having to be exposed to dangerous working conditions? What is a more basic civil liberty than the right to work in a safe environment? Forcing employees to breathe in carcinogens in order to make a living is a violation of the free enterprise principle.
	Independence/Economic opportunity	Liability risks posed by allowing employees to be exposed to secondhand smoke (workers' compensation, disability, etc.) could hurt business owners. Illnesses and deaths will cause a loss of jobs, productivity, and sales.
	Control	How can workers pursue a livelihood and support children if they are too sick to work or suffer (can't breathe) at work?
	Fairness/Equality	Excluding restaurant workers from health protection that all other workers take for granted is not fair; it represents discrimination against a certain class of workers; this is a class issue. Excluding restaurant workers from protection is hardly a level playing field.
Increase cigarette tax	Freedom	Voting for the tax is a way to assert freedom from tobacco industry influence. Rejecting the tax is just playing into the hands of the industry and letting it dictate state policies.
	Independence	Without a higher tax, parents cannot effectively keep children from smoking, cannot effectively fight the tobacco industry's pressure on their children to smoke.
	Control	Voting for the tax allows you, not the tobacco industry, to decide the fate of your children's health.
	Democracy	Voting for the tax preserves the democratic ideal by keeping government in the hands of the people, not in the hands of a powerful, greedy, special-interest group that has intruded into our state.
Adopt stricter environmental regulations	Control	Regulations will allow society to retain control over the unknown consequences of environmental destruction.
	Economic opportunity	Regulations will help preserve livelihoods and economic opportunity by protecting tourism; rejecting the regulations will lead to economic devastation of the community.

continues

Table 3 continued

Public Health Policy	Core Value	Message
Adopt needle exchange program	Freedom	The program will allow society to remain free of the scourge of acquired immune deficiency syndrome (AIDS); without it, AIDS may spread from the drug-using population to the general population.
	Control	If AIDS spreads to the general population, the epidemic may soon be out of control.
Adopt mandatory seat belt law	Fairness	It is not fair for taxpayers to have to pay medical bills for people seriously injured because they were irresponsible and failed to wear seat belts.
	Economic livelihood	The medical costs of accidents involving individuals not wearing seat belts are wreaking havoc on the budget and the economy and increasing taxes for everyone. The law will create savings that will translate into lower taxes and increased economic livelihood.
Adopt tuberculosis (TB) screening and treatment program in drug treatment clinics	Freedom	The program will prevent the epidemic scourge of TB that threatens to affect all of us, as TB spreads from drug users into the general population.
	Control	The program will allow society to retain control over the unknown consequences of the spread of multidrug-resistant TB into the general population. The consequences are unknown, but could be devastating to society.

also could be framed to appeal to the core values of freedom, independence, economic opportunity, autonomy, control, fairness, and equality (see Table 3).

Reframing Public Health Issues

In addition to developing their own frames, public health practitioners must also learn to confront directly the frames developed by opponents of their proposed policies and programs.

How can public health advocates confront opposition framing? Two approaches are possible. Take, for example, the level playing field frame used by the tobacco industry in fighting local smoking regulations. First, advocates can simply ignore the opposition frame and emphasize that this is a health issue. The success of this approach depends on policy makers perceiving the policy's reinforcement of the value they place on fairness and equality. This approach may be successful, but only if advocates are able to make the public health frame the dominant one.

An alternative approach is to reframe the issue so that supporting the policy reinforces rather than conflicts with the core values being tapped by the opposition frame. In other words, public health advocates must develop a new frame that shows policy makers how a local restaurant smoking ordinance is necessary to preserve fairness and equality for the city's residents.

One way the issue could be reframed is to demonstrate how the exclusion of restaurant workers from the protection from secondhand smoke that we afford most other workers is unfair (Table 4). The real unlevel playing field is the singling out of restaurant workers as the one occupational group not deserving of basic public health protections that most other workers take for granted and consider to be their right.

A second way to reframe the issue might be to show how the failure to protect citizens in the city would perpetuate an unlevel playing field by denying citizens in that city a basic right guaranteed to the citizens of more than 200 cities throughout the country—the right to work in an environment free of hazards (Table 4).

In both frames, the core values are the same: fairness and equality. However, in the opposition frame, voting for the ordinance would conflict with these values, while in the proponent frame, voting for the ordinance would reinforce these values.

Table 4 The Level Playing Field Frame: Reframing for Use by Public Health Advocates in Promoting Local Smoke-Free Restaurant Ordinances

Frame	Level Playing Field—Reframe 1	Level Playing Field—Reframe 2
Core position	Singling out restaurant workers as the one occupational group not deserving basic health protection afforded to nearly all other workers creates an unlevel playing field for these workers.	Failing to protect citizens in this city from secondhand smoke when more than 200 cities nationwide have already afforded these protections to their workers creates an unlevel playing field for our residents.
Metaphor	An unlevel playing field in a sports event, favoring one team over another	An unlevel playing field in a sport's event, favoring one team over another
Images	An unlevel playing field in a sports event	An unlevel playing field in a sports event
Catch phrases	"Level playing field," "unfair," "disadvantage," "discrimination"	"Level playing field," "unfair," "disadvantage," "discrimination"
Attribution of responsibility for problem	Government, which is selectively protecting workers in typical offices, but excluding restaurant workers from protection	Government, which is selectively excluding our city's residents from protection that many residents in other cities have
Implied solution	Extend smoke-free working environment protections to all workers	Extend smoke-free working environment protections to workers in our city
Core values	Fairness Equality Justice Economic opportunity	Fairness Equality Justice Economic opportunity

HOW TO CONDUCT SPECIAL EVENTS: THE BASICS*

What Are Special Events?

Special events are defined as major activities whose primary purpose is to promote awareness, provide education, and conduct outreach. For nonprofit health organizations, special events provide an opportunity to promote services, conduct health education, encourage public involvement and commitment, strengthen community ties, recruit new volunteers, and establish a positive public image—all in one fell swoop.

One special event may consist of many subsidiary events, such as banquets, parades, contests, and speeches. Major forms of special events may include, but are not limited to:

- health fairs, featuring a variety of activities
- shows, displays, and exhibits
- road shows, moved from one location to another
- parades, pageants, and processions, such as a "walk for health"
- entertainment events, such as concerts, theater productions, puppet shows, and mime
- mass demonstrations
- athletic competitions
- stunts
- banquets, luncheons, and breakfast events
- events designed around special days or weeks, such as a "healthy heart day," the Great American Smokeout, and World Health Day
- conferences and conventions that attract important local, state, and/or national leaders and provide educational opportunities for participants

Special Events Are Publicity Events

To achieve positive results, a special event must generate good publicity. Special events achieve publicity in three ways:

1. They communicate directly to the audience in attendance.
2. They communicate to the community at large through the media.
3. They communicate to other local organizations and agencies.

Keys to a Successful Special Event

The keys to conducting a successful special event are careful planning, attention to detail, adequate staff and funding, creativity, and good publicity.

---

*Source: State of New York Department of Health, Albany, New York, © 1993.

The amount of work involved in planning, coordinating, and conducting a special event is substantial, possibly involving additional staff and time. The demands on the organization's resources—in personnel and money—must be considered when deciding whether a special event is feasible, and what type of special event to conduct. Organizations that are new to special events must be particularly careful not to plan events that are beyond their means.

Examples of Special Events

Exercise Events

Exercise events can attract a tremendous community response if they are designed as family-oriented fun. Plan a day of fitness activities that includes running events for all ages, a family walk, dancing, roller skating, and a variety of organized sports. Live music, hypertension screening, and nutrition counseling could also be provided throughout the day. Brochures and flyers are good ways to promote the event.

Conferences

Conferences can unite professionals and community organizations to participate in a program. They also may draw good media coverage if they feature major leaders or celebrities who support the program.

Contests

Contests provide a fun way for people who need incentives to stop smoking or lose weight. For example, your community could conduct a "community weigh-in," a contest for people to lose weight. People who attend the weigh-ins view a film about weight loss, are weighed, set weight-loss goals, receive a weight-loss kit, and pledge their own money toward their goals as an incentive. Blood pressure and blood cholesterol could also be checked. At the end of the contest, refund people's money in proportion to the extent that they reached their weight-loss goals.

Food Festivals

Food festivals are well attended, especially when the food is free. The Yonkers (New York) Healthy Heart Program, for example, launched its program with the "World's Largest International Salad Festival" held at a major raceway. Attended by 3,000, the festival featured free heart-healthy salads donated by restaurants and supermarkets. As a preliminary, the program conducted inservice courses in the preparation of heart-healthy salads to the chefs and staff of the restaurants. A local supermarket provided a refrigerator truck the day of the event and also donated a huge three-bean salad in the shape of a heart. A local food service donated an ice sculpture in the shape of a heart, which was placed at the entrance to the festival. Local businesses provided live music and composed several songs on the risk factors of heart disease. A local radio station provided live coverage of the event. Unused food was donated to a local homeless program.

Breakfast Events

Breakfast events are a good way to get community and business leaders together to tell them about your program. Invite business and media representatives, and encourage them to complete and return commitment forms, agreeing to participate in one or more suggested activities, such as cosponsoring a local healthy heart program or participating on a healthy heart marketing task force. Major follow-up may be required to respond to the commitment forms and organize corporate participation in your program.

Fairs

Fairs can be big events, with lots of activities, or small, with a single focus. For example, the New Orleans Health Department conducted a Nutrition Fair in cooperation with the local farmers market to promote increased use of the city's farmers market as a source of locally grown fresh fruits and vegetables. The produce was touted as healthy heart food low in calories, fat, sugar, and salt, but high in vitamins and roughage. The fair also featured human-sized costumed fruit and vegetable characters.

Special Event Planning Checklist

Preliminary Budget

Make a preliminary budget to act as a guide to the event's expenses. Start by choosing the best circumstances in which you would like to stage your event. Telephone each of the services, entertainers, and vendors you want to use and get precise prices for their goods and services. Build in a miscellaneous fund for last-minute items that inevitably crop up.

Event

☐ Create a theme.
☐ Identify a handicapped-accessible location.
☐ Establish a date and time.

Program

☐ Select and plan entertainment activities.
☐ Select and invite speakers and celebrities.
☐ Plan contests and make arrangements for judges.
☐ Select and invite exhibitors and vendors.
☐ Identify demonstrations.
☐ Identify other activities.
☐ Establish a schedule and invite a master of ceremonies.

Attendance

☐ Determine level of attendance desired that can be accommodated safely.

Budget

☐ Develop a realistic, line-item budget, based on sound estimates obtained for every aspect of the event.
☐ Evaluate in-kind contributions.

Materials

☐ Identify public relations and informational materials to be distributed before and during the event, such as brochures, printed invitations, flyers, program schedule, maps (if the event is a fair, parade, or walk) posters, pins, hats, T-shirts, etc. If any of these still need to be developed, start production.

Insurance

☐ Identify and obtain liability and other insurance needed to cover the event.

Food

☐ Determine food and beverages to be provided; make arrangements for caterers or vendors.

Security

☐ Determine security requirements and make arrangements with police or private security agency.

Fire Protection

☐ Determine fire protection needed and make arrangements.

Emergency Medical Services

☐ Determine type and level of services needed and make arrangements.

Parking

☐ Determine parking needs and make arrangements.

Restrooms

☐ Determine needs and make arrangements.

Special Permits

☐ Determine any permits needed from local, government and submit applications.

Accommodations

☐ Determine need for overnight lodging for any out-of-town guests and make arrangements.

Signs

☐ Determine necessary signs and banners needed and make arrangements.

Transportation

☐ Determine need for public transportation and make arrangements.

Decorations

☐ Determine decorations needed and make arrangements.

Credentials

☐ Design name-tag credentials for guests, media, staff, volunteers, entertainers, vendors, etc., as needed. Develop tags for children for "lost child" purposes. The tags should say: "I belong to:" to be filled out with the parent or guardian's name, not the child's name.

Event Set-up

☐ Identify who is responsible for setting up equipment, furniture, and props needed for the event.

Equipment

☐ Determine equipment needed, such as a sound system, microphones, phones, podiums, bleachers, FAX machine, tables and chairs, etc.

Publicity/News Coverage

☐ Press kits
☐ Press conference (if warranted)
☐ Radio public service announcements
☐ Radio talk shows
☐ Television public service announcements
☐ Television community affairs programs
☐ Newspaper news releases
☐ Newspaper advertising
☐ Photographs and speeches (copies for press)

Registration for Future Program Activities

☐ Develop a schedule for future or on-going activities, provide sign-up tables at the event, and promote the activities during the event.

Lost and Found

☐ Plan an easy-to-find area for lost children and objects. Mark the area clearly on maps, and identify the area at the event with flags, balloons, or banners. Make sure the area is staffed at all times during the event.

Contingency Plans

☐ Bad weather contingencies (If the site you select for the event is located partly or entirely outside, select an alternate site for bad weather and publicize the bad weather site in advance.)
☐ Program substitutions (Have one or two back-ups you can substitute in your program in the event one or more speakers or activities must cancel.)

Volunteer Help

☐ Recruitment of volunteers to help the day of the event. (Volunteers will be needed if your event will be large, with many activities. Develop specific job descriptions, and recruit help from civic organizations, churches, youth groups, etc. Assign a full-time staff person to coordinate volunteer efforts.)

Post-Event Activities

☐ Identify who is responsible for site clean-up, follow-up calls and reports to the media, thank you notes to guest speakers and volunteers, etc. Establish meeting dates for evaluation of the event.

Source: State of New York Department of Health, Albany, New York, © 1993.

PLANNING A HEALTH FAIR*

People have a natural curiosity about their health. They want to know everything they can about those big and little things that affect their everyday lives. One of the best ways they can get this information is through a health fair. And that makes a health fair a valuable tool your agency can use to reach large numbers of people.

A health fair should be conducted in an upbeat, easily digested format. It could focus on a single topic, such as smoking cessation, or on a single audience, such as the elderly; or it could cover many health-related issues for a number of audiences. Properly handled, a health fair is an ideal way for your organization to present health education and counseling, and allows you to communicate a wealth of information on a variety of health issues and services.

Health Fairs Come in All Sizes

A health fair is easier to organize than you may think. You are the one who controls the size and complexity of the health fair. It can be as simple as a table with posters and pamphlets, or it can be a three-day affair that fills the local park.

A health fair is anything you choose: exhibits, mini-workshops, displays, demonstrations, screenings, and more. The possibilities are endless—from eye tests to foot checkups. What matters is that it brings people and health professionals together.

Designing Your Health Fair

To organize a successful health fair, sit down with pencil and paper, define your audience, the message you want to deliver, and who could help you deliver that message.

Your audience could be the general public or a special interest group, such as senior citizens, women, or the poor. The location and hours will influence the type of audience. A health fair in a park or shopping center on a weekend will attract a different audience than an event at a business complex on a weekday.

The intended audience will determine the message. Different groups have different concerns; senior citizens and nutrition, middle-aged people and cholesterol, children and dental health, women and breast cancer, and so on.

Sponsors and Exhibitors

Local involvement is the key to a successful health fair. Your community has its share of potential sponsors, volunteers, and exhibitors. Draw up a resource list that includes health professionals, service organizations, community leaders, businesses, and labor groups. Do not neglect student groups from high schools, colleges, and universities—they are important sources of volunteer support. Help is also available from women's, neighborhood, and other advocacy groups.

In your search for a sponsor, approach the executive directors or managers of local organizations. Detail your plans and needs, and determine what an organization can supply in terms of personnel and materials. The organization may also have a public relations unit that could help you get the message out through daily and weekly

---

*Source: New York State Department of Health, Albany, New York, © 1992.

newspapers, radio and television stations, and the internal publications and newsletters that many businesses use to communicate with their employees. If this resource is not available, you will need to organize your own publicity program.

Spread the Word

The publicity coordinator will have one of the most important and demanding jobs. He or she will need to prepare press releases, feature stories, public service announcements or advertisements, editorials, posters, and hand-out materials, and organize a press conference or press kit. Important facts to include are site, date, time, selected activities, organizations involved as exhibitors, name(s) of organization(s) sponsoring the event, and a telephone number to call for more information. Posters and flyers should be creative. They should not only inform but motivate people to attend. Public service announcements to radio and television stations should be packaged as 10-, 20-, and 30-second spots.

What a Health Fair Provides

A model health fair can be divided into the areas of health education, screening, counseling and referral, and follow-up.

Health Education. Education is the most important facet of a health fair. Health education might include a poster or exhibit on nutrition or a nutritionist preparing a low-cholesterol meal. It could be a display on cancer risks or a computer health risk evaluation. When making choices, remember that passive displays of information will not attract large numbers. People like exhibits with which they can interact.

Screening. The longest lines at health fairs are for blood pressure and other screening tests. People want to know about themselves. The easiest screening tests to set up are height and weight, blood pressure, anemia, and vision acuity. Others, which may require more resources, are screenings for cancer, glaucoma, hearing, high blood cholesterol, and genetic disorders. Whenever laboratory tests are involved, consult the public health law for requirements that must be met.

Counseling and Referral. Counseling sessions allow a trained counselor to outline actions that need to be taken to eliminate poor health habits. Such counseling stops short of diagnosis. Counselors can encourage lifestyle changes in areas such as nutrition, stress, and smoking. Where indicated, the individual may be urged to see his or her usual health provider or be given information on local health care facilities or local health-related agencies and organizations.

Follow-Up. This can be done through mailings, by telephone, or through classes and other programs available in the community. Delivery of test results through follow-up mailings or telephone calls can motivate participants to take action. You can also call participants, three to six months after the health fair, as a reminder and an encouragement.

Your Checklist to Success

A health fair takes forethought. About four to six months' planning should be anticipated. Health professionals need plenty of advance notice. Other rules of thumb for a successful health fair include the following:

- **Site.** A one-day fair for 500 people will require an area of at least 2,500 square feet (25×100). Consider access roads, restroom facilities, lighting, parking, and accessibility for people with disabilities. Fairs have been held in churches, schools, community centers, shopping malls, and hospitals.
- **Layout.** Prepare a layout of the fair and plan for noise distractions, privacy, and people waiting in line. Separate learn-by-doing activities from each other. Be sure to clearly note areas assigned to exhibitors. Those with similar themes may be grouped together.
- **Materials.** Draw up a list of what you will need: electrical equipment, tables, chairs, easels, microphones, audiovisual equipment, pencils, and so on. These items are easily overlooked in the last-minute rush.
- **Registration.** Packets can be distributed at the registration. They can include a health fair map and list of activities, health fair carrying bag, health button, and nametag.
- **Timing.** Check the calendar before scheduling your event. Try not to conflict with other activities in the community that could affect attendance.
- **Permits.** Food service, sanitary, sign, structural, and other permits may be needed. The local municipal clerk should be able to give you information. Remember, there are several levels of government—city, county, and state—that may require various permits.
- **Exhibitors.** In selecting potential exhibitors, consider the organization's compatibility with the aims and objectives of the fair. Also consider the organization's commitment to staffing and its potential for capturing attention and stimulating audience participation.
- **Fees.** You may consider charging a fee for exhibitors to offset rental, heating and lighting, and other costs. Your decision on fees can be made by weighing such factors as whether the exhibitor is a nonprofit organization and whether it will reap a profit, directly or indirectly, as an exhibitor.
- **Giveaways.** Plastic bags with your logo and message are an inexpensive way to keep your name before the public. They also make it easier for people to carry publications gathered at the fair. Other possible giveaways are buttons, posters, rulers, and pencils. For information, look in the telephone book's yellow pages under "novelties."
- **Directions.** Avoid confusion by posting signs, arrows, and posters to direct participants to parking, exhibit areas, restrooms, mini-workshops, health fair entrance and/or registration, and so on.
- **Cleanup.** Make a firm agreement with the facility manager about when exhibits must be erected/dismantled, when the building will be cleaned, who will be responsible for cleaning, and how the furniture and equipment should be arranged.
- **Thanks.** As soon as the fair is over, thank everyone involved, *in writing*.

ORGANIZATIONAL STRATEGIES FOR YOUR HEALTH FAIR*

Goals and Objectives

Goals

Goals help the coordinator set specific objectives and assist in determining if procedures, methods, and results are according to plans. An example of a goal is as follows:

- To raise the health awareness of participants attending the health fair during Minority Health Month

Objectives

The objectives need to be measurable. Examples of measurable objectives are as follows:

- By the end of the health fair activity, 300 individuals will have received cholesterol, high blood pressure, and cancer screening.
- By the end of the health fair activity, organizations (hospitals, private institutions, or health professions) will have provided services/screenings at the health fair activity.

Organization of the Health Fair

The coordinator should organize activities to meet the goals and objectives. Each activity should clearly outline what procedures to follow and how they should be performed in order for expected outcomes to be realized. Listed below are examples of activities:

- Select a steering committee. Ideally, a good steering committee consists of health professionals and other interested persons.
- Send out a survey to determine the health needs of the targeted population.
- Review returned completed surveys.
- Invite qualified persons to participate in the health fair activity.
- Set a date for the health fair activity.
- Appoint a coordinator to be responsible for directing the goals and objectives.
- Choose a theme so that the health fair has a point of focus, for example: "Health Busters of the 20th Century."
- Develop a time frame for every activity.
- Once this information is assembled, select a committee to write a grant proposal that follows the guidelines contained in the funder's request for proposal.
- After receiving approval notification from the funder, reassess and reaffirm the goals and objectives.

---

*Source: *Health Fairs RX: A Prescription for Your Community,* Ephesus Seventh-Day Adventist Church, Columbus, Ohio, © 1992. Funded by the Ohio Commission on Minority Health.

- Determine ways to evaluate the progress of the health fair. Examples of evaluating tools are as follows:
  - Record the number of individuals attending the health fair activity.
  - Record the number of individuals attending the health fair activity from the target population.
  - Record the number of individuals receiving screening (if offered), and provide written feedback and explanation of outcomes to participants.
  - If screening identifies a participant in need of medical attention, a referral mechanism should be implemented.
- Assess the particular needs of the targeted population:
  - If the targeted population cannot get to the health fair, provide for transportation.
  - If the targeted population has a high rate of illiteracy or any type of language barrier, provide necessary personnel, such as tutors and/or translators, and/or use promotional or educational materials that emphasize visual rather than written communication.

Budget

The available funding will determine the number and extent of health fair activities envisioned in the overall program. Therefore, the committee will need to prioritize activities so that the available funds will meet those areas considered vital to the needs of the community. This procedure will determine expansiveness of the planned health fair activity.

Budgeting Tips

In outlining the budget, itemize in detail the costs of the anticipated expenditures. Such expenditures might include medical supplies, office and/or printing supplies, postage, advertising fees, and rental equipment fees.

All the expenditures should be appropriately justified in the proposal narrative. The amount requested from the funder must not exceed its maximum allowable limits unless the organization is willing to pay the difference. If questions arise, contact the funding source.

Contributions from Other Sources

To augment its resources, the organization may wish to contact businesses, health facilities, or other interested organizations and persons. Some contacts require as much as one year's prior notice to the scheduled date of the event. Personal, written, and telephone contacts are useful. All three modes of contact are very important. Contacts should be confirmed through written correspondence.

In-Kind Services

In-kind services represent any voluntary activity or service rendered by laypersons and/or professionals. These services greatly contribute toward the success of a health fair activity. In-kind services should be included separately in the state funding proposal.

Committees

The coordinator for the planned health fair activity needs to form a committee consisting of resourceful and energetic individuals who are willing to work. As suggested previously, a good committee will consist of health professionals and other interested persons.

The role for the main committee is to assist the coordinator in meeting deadlines and making decisions concerning the planning of the health fair activity.

Subcommittees can be helpful to accomplish the following tasks:

- Contact health fair participants.
- Write correspondence.
- Advertise the health fair.
- Reserve audiovisual equipment and other necessary equipment.
- Recruit volunteers to assist at the health fair.
- Form a cleanup crew.
- Develop a floor plan for the booths.
- Designate health fair personnel for booths.
- Strategically place educational materials and booths among the health screening booths.
- Clearly mark entrances and exits so that clients participate in the registration process on arrival and the exit interview on departure.
- Demonstrate foods. If foods will be a part of the health fair activity, the subcommittee should address the following questions:
  –Is the food economical?
  –Is the food nutritious?
  –Can the food be simply prepared?
  –Is the food attractive?
  –Are recipes available?
- Select appropriate promotional incentives.
- Write the final report. The funder may require a final written report that evaluates the effectiveness of the event (e.g., the number of people served, amount of referrals, etc.).

REMEMBER:
BE CREATIVE IN YOUR PLANNING.

NOTES:

Health Fair Committee Planning Sheet

Date To Be Completed	Assignment	Date Completed
_____	Set up steering committee	_____
_____	Complete grant proposal	_____
_____	Set up finance committee	_____
_____	Set up subcommittees:	_____
_____	• Contact committee	_____
_____	• Correspondence committee	_____
_____	• Food committee	_____
_____	• Advertising committee	_____
_____	• In-house volunteers	_____
_____	• Maintenance committee:	_____
_____	–Set-up	_____
_____	–Parking	_____
_____	–Clean-up	_____

NOTES:

Source: *Health Fairs RX: A Prescription for Your Community,* Ephesus Seventh-Day Adventist Church, Columbus, Ohio, © 1992. Funded by the Ohio Commission on Minority Health.

CHARACTERISTICS OF A GOOD SCREENING TEST*

There are five attributes of a good screening test: It should be simple, rapid, inexpensive, safe, and acceptable.

1. *Simple:* The test should be easy to learn and perform. One that can be administered by non-physician medical personnel will necessarily cost less than one that requires years of medical training to administer.
2. *Rapid:* The test should not take long to administer, and the results should be available soon. The amount of time required to screen an individual is directly related to the success of the program: If a screening test requires only 5 minutes out of a person's schedule, it is likely to be perceived as being more valuable than one that requires an hour or more. Furthermore, immediate feedback is better than a test in which results may not be available for weeks or months. Results of a blood pressure screening are usually known immediately; results of a screening for high cholesterol must await laboratory analysis.
3. *Inexpensive:* As discussed earlier, cost-benefit is an important criterion to consider in the evaluation of screening programs. The lower the cost of a screening test, the more likely it is that the overall program will be cost beneficial.
4. *Safe:* The screening test should not carry potential harm to screenees.
5. *Acceptable:* The test should be acceptable to the target group. An effective device has been developed to screen for testicular cancer, but acceptance rates among men have not been as high as for a similar procedure—mammography—among women.

NOTES:

---

*Source: Robert H. Friis and Thomas A. Sellars, *Epidemiology for Public Health Practice*, Aspen Publishers, Inc., © 1996.

PLANNING A BREAKFAST EVENT*

Why a Breakfast Event?

Many health problems communities face—acquired immune deficiency syndrome (AIDS), heart disease, teen pregnancy, and so on—are best addressed through communitywide approaches. However, short of holding dozens of individual meetings with health activists and opinion leaders, how can one enlist the support of all the appropriate players in such an effort?

Many organizations have discovered that "breakfast events" offer a time- and cost-efficient way to gathering representatives of a variety of groups together for a common purpose or goal. Breakfast events provide a great opportunity to gather all of a community's key people in one room and to enlist their support.

Breakfast events have a number of things going for them, not the least of which is that they are relatively "painless" for participants. First, breakfast events can be scheduled to begin before the start of the business day (7:30 or 8:00 AM) and end by 10:00 AM This holds special appeal for busy people who may not be able to find two hours in their schedules for a midday meeting or event, or who may not be able to sacrifice personal time in the evening.

Getting Started

If you think that a breakfast event could fill your organization's networking-building needs, there are things you will need to know. The following information and tips will help you organize and conduct a successful breakfast event, from the initial planning stages through valuable follow-up activities. First, ask yourself the following questions:

- Why is the event needed?
- What objective(s) do we wish to accomplish by getting various groups together?
- Who in the community will support the event?
- Is this an appropriate project for my organization?
- Is sponsorship, either corporate or foundation, available to assist in underwriting the event?
- Are the health goals of the community and possible funding sources consistent with the objective(s) of the breakfast event?
- What will make this event special or unique?
- Who should be invited?

Once you have established that your event will benefit the community, it can be effectively delivered by your organization, and it does not conflict with similar efforts of another agency, you can focus on logistics.

The size of the breakfast is one issue you should consider right away. Will it be a relatively small event (50–80 people) that you will be able to plan by yourself, or a larger event (150+ people) that will require the assistance of several people? If you decide that assistance will be necessary, organize a planning committee immediately.

---

*Source: State of New York Department of Health, Albany, New York, © 1992.

Initially, the planning committee should consist of responsible people from within your organization. Representatives from other organizations can be added as you recruit cosponsors. Your planning committee, no matter what its size or composition, must be a *working* committee. Delegate duties and responsibilities widely. Many hands really do make light work. And groups involved in planning will also have greater commitment to the project's success.

Set Goals and Objectives

The planning committee should establish the program's goals and objectives based on an assessment of specific needs and problems faced by your target audience or community. Goals and objectives should be defined as specifically as possible to allow for evaluation of the program's success. The following list presents examples of problems, along with possible goals and objectives:

- **Problem 1:** The risk of contracting human immunodeficiency virus (HIV) is much greater for black women than it is for white women. For every white woman who has AIDS in New York State, for example, there are three black women diagnosed.
  –Goal: To increase the number of black women being counseled and tested for HIV infection at county clinics.
  –Objective: To achieve a 30 percent increase in the number of black women referred for HIV antibody testing during the time period of _____ to _____.
- **Problem 2:** Smokers have a 300 percent greater chance of coronary heart disease (and smoking causes 85 percent of all lung cancer).
  –Goal: To increase the number of smoking clients receiving consultation on the hazards of smoking and obtaining materials that may help them stop the habit.
  –Objective: To achieve a 40 percent increase in the number of smoking clients receiving one-to-one consultation on quitting the habit in community health clinics during the year of _____.
- **Problem 3:** Although immunizations are not required until children go to school or day care, many parents and guardians fail to realize that a child's immunizations should start during the first year of life.
  –Goal: To increase the number of children receiving appropriate immunizations at the earliest recommended age.
  –Objective: To achieve a 50 percent increase in the number of child clients receiving appropriate vaccinations prior to 18 months of age.

Involve Other Groups and Agencies

When organizing your own breakfast event, it is important to determine if there are any organizations that would be interested in cosponsoring the event with you. Depending on the health issue you will be addressing, you may wish to contact:

- major employers
- health insurers
- service and fraternal organizations
- YMCA, YWCA
- YMHA, YWHA

- Boys Clubs, Girls Clubs
- Boy Scouts, Girl Scouts
- senior citizens' groups
- chamber of commerce
- cooperative extension services
- medical care providers (e.g., physicians, hospitals, health clinics, health maintenance organizations, rehabilitation centers, etc.)
- voluntary health organizations (e.g., American Lung Association, American Heart Association, American Cancer Society, March of Dimes, etc.)
- health/exercise clubs
- schools, universities, and colleges
- parent teacher associations
- church groups
- medical associations and specialty organizations
- advocacy groups (e.g., Children's Defense Fund, ACT-UP, N.Y.P.I.R.G., etc.)

Secure Help and Support

When contacting other agencies, try to identify any key people who may be interested in helping you. Meet with them to find out if they would be interested in cosponsoring the event, joining the planning committee, or supplying needed services or materials.

A great amount of community awareness and action can be achieved through these pre-event activities. Supply potential supporters with information (e.g., brochures, flyers, etc.) enabling them to learn about the event, the goals and objectives, and what may be expected of them and their organizations. The more prospective supporters know about the reasons for the event ahead of time, the better prepared they will be to participate actively.

There is "no free breakfast." Be prepared to pursue and obtain financial support, particularly if you intend to host a large event.

Remember, in-kind contributions (e.g., providing a location, copying, printing, providing mailing lists, donating volunteer staff, doing mailings, etc.) are as important as financial support. Many businesses are willing to support such efforts for tax purposes, to maintain good public relations, or to give something back to the community. Be sure to remind them of such advantages when asking for assistance.

Working with organizations or individuals outside your own agency is the best way to foster communitywide involvement. These agencies can help you by providing:

- access to a target audience
- increased credibility, if the target audience considers them to be trusted sources of information
- broader interest and participation
- additional resources (e.g., funding, volunteers, materials, etc.)
- added expertise

Although working with other organizations is essential, there are drawbacks that should be recognized:

- It can be time consuming (e.g., to coordinate meeting times, gain approvals, etc.).
- It can require changes in the event. (Each agency has different priorities, and compromises may be necessary to accommodate everyone's needs.)
- It can result in loss of "ownership" and control. (You will need to share planning functions and also give other groups partial credit for the success of the event.)

To help minimize problems, follow these steps:

- Select agencies that can reach and influence the target audience.
- Involve agencies you want to work with as early as possible in the program planning.
- Give agencies advance notice regarding program and schedule, and negotiate what will be expected of them.
- Ask them what they need to implement their part of the program.
- Remind them that they have responsibility for their part of the program. Help them do it, but do not do it for them. This is a collaborative effort.
- Provide them with a rationale, strategies, and messages that are consistent with the goals of the event.
- Do not give them too much to do at once. It is best to keep them busy with a series of short-term tasks.

Determine Size and Location

Once you have secured support, hold a meeting of the planning committee and cosponsors to discuss the event and to establish a budget. With a budget, you will be better able to determine the actual size of the guest list and the amount of space you will need. Do not fail to explore using a space donated by an organization wishing to be identified with or contributing to the event (e.g., a local school, museum, hospital, theater, business, etc.). Look for a site that is accessible to people with disabilities.

Select Keynote Speaker and Guest Host

It is best to limit a breakfast event to two hours. That way you can avoid interfering with the workday and better control the agenda. Keep speakers to a minimum. For an event this short, it is sufficient to schedule only one guest speaker. This person should be well known, knowledgeable, and charismatic. Contact your local university, hospital, or civic organizations for recommendations and referrals. Local agencies' speakers bureaus are possible sources. A well-known local radio or television personality can also lend interest and spark to your event. The host is not only a drawing card for attendance, but can introduce special guests, make announcements, and help the event run smoothly and according to schedule.

Make Catering and Seating Arrangements

Decide on a menu and arrange for catering. Depending on the space you have available, it is usually best to keep the menu simple: fruit, bagels, muffins, juices, and coffee. This approach is not as time consuming and confining as a traditional sit-down breakfast and will give your guests a chance to circulate and network.

Seating is very important. If one of your main objectives is to have your guests network and/or take part in round-table discussions, the physical setup of the room will be vital. You may want to find out if round tables (as opposed to long, rectangular tables) are available. These facilitate discussion and encourage group interaction. Decide how many people you want seated at each table. Round-table discussions flow most smoothly when there are eight or fewer people per table. Four to six people per table is appropriate if you want them to brainstorm ideas or to come up with a plan of action. Decide if a dais, podium, or head table will be needed and make the necessary arrangements.

Prior to the Event

Once you have dealt with the funding options, size and location, keynote speaker, and catering, you can proceed with the smaller but equally necessary tasks that will ensure a smooth-running event. Depending on the size of the event and the time frame with which you are dealing, these tasks may include any combination of the following:

- Use community resources to expand your mailing lists of possible guests (e.g., League of Women Voters, local professional and business clubs, Rotary clubs, parent teacher associations, etc.).
- Develop and print invitations. Always make certain that invitations cover all the vital information of who, what, why, where, and when. Consider including directions to the site or a small map of the area with the invitation. Invitations should be mailed no less than three weeks prior to the event to allow an adequate period for RSVPs. RSVPs are a must. You will not be able to confirm any information to the caterer, space coordinator, or other guests unless you know how many people will be attending.
- Consider stating on the invitation that the breakfast will begin at 7:59 AM (for example). This is a common marketing ploy indicating to your guests that the event will start promptly.
- Consider making invitations nontransferable or suggesting three or so "titles" that would be the most appropriate representatives of an organization to attend the event.
- Prepare a formal agenda of the morning's events: who will be speaking first, conducting the welcome, and so on.
- Prepare and distribute press releases, community calendar announcements, and so on, to promote the event in your target area(s). Be sure they go to all local news media as well as to business and organization newsletters.
- Meet with the facility's service manager. Check the microphone, lectern, any extra and/or special equipment a guest may need, and so on.
- Make copies of the program/agenda for each guest the morning of the event.
- Make name tags for those who will be attending. It may be easiest to do this as RSVPs are received.
- Invite all guests to bring their organization's pamphlets, brochures, handouts, and other materials for an information table.
- Get plenty of rest on the day before your event. You still have lots to do.

Obtain Commitments from Your Guests

The primary goal of the event is to inform your guests of a problem and get them to make a specific commitment to help with the solution. Since your guests will represent agencies of varying sizes and capabilities, the list of commitments should offer a wide range of tasks, from the simple to the more time consuming. Provide each guest with the list and request that, before leaving, he or she commit to accomplish at least one task.

The introduction to the commitment list should have a positive and helpful tone:

As a participant in the __(title of event)__, I agree to undertake one or more of the following activities. I understand that I will be contacted by a member of __(your agency or planning committee name)__ who will assist me and my organization with any or all activities that have been selected.

The form should include a section for the participant's name, title, organization name and address, telephone number, and signature.

Depending on the target audience, examples of commitments may include the following:

- plan an educational seminar for my employees/members
- provide information on the topic in my newsletter, with paychecks, and through employment assistance programs
- plan a special breakfast event for my colleagues and/or other groups with which I am involved
- distribute literature or put up posters about the problem in target neighborhoods or communities
- engage in letter-writing campaigns to urge local media to cover stories on the topic via editorials, public service announcements, and special features
- encourage a local celebrity to become a spokesperson for the topic
- incorporate messages on the topic into our advertising and promotional campaigns
- underwrite specific projects dealing with the topic
- lend an expert to a local program dealing with the topic, or offer to underwrite the cost of an expert
- donate equipment and provide appropriate training
- cosponsor a local program related to the topic; provide significant financial and/or in-kind services

Day of the Event

- Arrive at the breakfast site at least one hour in advance. Check to ensure that tables are in place and that equipment is in good working order.
- Set up the information table in a central location or high-traffic area, and organize all materials. Have a stack of 3- by 5-inch cards on which guests can write the names of others who may be interested in working with you.
- Assign a person to greet guests, hand out name tags, and provide any necessary materials.
- Assign a specific person to greet speaker(s) and provide any last-minute instructions.

- Assign a person to distribute and collect commitment forms from guests.
- Assign a person to greet and help reporters. This person should keep a list of all media representatives who attend.

Evaluate and Follow-Up

You can begin to evaluate the success of the event by asking yourself the following questions:

- Did the attendance level meet expectations?
- Did most guests complete commitment forms and express a willingness to become involved?
- Were you able to get key people to attend?
- How much overall publicity did the event generate?
- What media covered the event?
- Was the publicity positive?

Follow-up of every commitment received is essential to the overall success of your breakfast event. It is best to organize a subcommittee that will be accountable for contacting every person responsible for making a pledge. Written contacts should be made a week after the event. Send thank you notes to those who signed as a reminder of their pledges. Several weeks after the event, make renewed contact to offer help and check on the status of pledges. If the pledge has been completed, inquire as to its success. If the agency has yet to fulfill its pledge, ask if any assistance is needed and, if so, what exactly is needed to follow through on the pledge.

The follow-up subcommittee should keep a record of all pledges completed. An encouraging gesture is to send a report on all completed pledges to all who participated. This is not only a wonderful way in which to "close" your event, but will help to reinforce the accomplishments that were your goals in the first place.

Other follow-up activities may include the following:

- Call all media representatives who attended. Thank them and offer assistance in securing additional information, identifying people in photos, checking names and/or titles of guests who attended, and so on.
- Write thank you letters to all sponsor(s), guest speaker(s), guest host(s), and volunteers.
- Meet with all who helped to organize the event. Thank them and discuss what went well, what did not, any changes to be made for future reference, and so on.
- Discuss any comments, reactions, and/or feedback from guests:
  –Was the response generally positive?
  –What were the general reactions to time constraints?
  –Were the guest host(s) and keynote speaker(s) well received?
  –Was the event well organized; did things run smoothly?
  –Were materials and information timely, accurate, and relevant to your goals?
  –Were guests pleased with the other organizations invited?
  –Did guests feel enough networking time was available?

Final Tips

- Do not schedule more than two guest speakers. More than two for an event this short will be too time consuming and cut into networking time.
- Dissuade guest speaker(s) from using too many visual aids. They can distract from the speaker's message and make speeches run long.
- Start on time, despite latecomers. There is a lot to accomplish in a very short time.
- Make every effort to maintain new relationships and contact with fellow agencies. After all, that is why you did all this work.

NOTES:

Special Event Checklist

Date of event: _____ Main contact: _____

Phone #: _____

Event name: _____

Description: _____

Objective: _____

_____

PARTICIPANTS AND PROGRAM

Master of Ceremonies: _____ Phone: _____

Speaker #2: _____ Phone: _____

Speaker #3: _____ Phone: _____

Speaker #4: _____ Phone: _____

Speaker #5: _____ Phone: _____

___ Local officials/VIPs contacted   ___ Speeches/talking points drafted

___ Event script drafted/reviewed   ___ Agenda drafted

___ Participants briefed   ___ One-on-one interviews permitted?

___ Speakers' bios solicited/drafted   ___ Event content/message approved

SITE/PRESS LOGISTICS

___ Secure Site   Site contact _____

Phone #: _____

Address: _____

_____

Directions: _____

_____

What is/will be visual? _____

___ Rent or insurance required   ___ Parking and access OK
___ Wheelchair access OK   ___ Parking for TV trucks OK
___ Staging necessary or available   ___ Podium or lectern available
___ Location of electrical outlets   ___ Press risers necessary
___ Microphone/PA system   ___ Mult boxes (multi-line direct audio feed devices used by radio and TV) needed or available?

___ Press sign-in table   ___ Literature/handout table
___ Refreshments provided

continues

Special Event Checklist continued

MATERIALS

___ Media Advisory drafted/approved   ___ Q&A drafted

___ Source list drafted/okayed   ___ Charts, graphics, visuals created

___ Press release drafted/approved   ___ Flyers

___ Invitations   ___ Press packets assembled

MEDIA/TARGET AUDIENCE OUTREACH

___ Mail invitations sent (two weeks away)

___ Media advisory sent (one week away)

___ First follow-up calls made to press (one week away)

___ First follow-up calls made to invitees (one week away)

___ Reminder advisory sent (two days before)

___ Call and pitch story to key press (two days before)

___ Press materials ready

___ Press materials distributed

___ Any follow-up materials sent

___ Everyone thanked profusely

NOTES:

Source: *Seven Days of Immunizations: National Infant Immunization Week,* U.S. Department of Health and Human Services, Public Health Service, Centers for Disease Control and Prevention (CDC), Atlanta, Georgia 30333, 1995.

STATEN ISLAND COMMUNITY NUTRITION PROGRAM HELPS THOUSANDS IMPROVE THEIR DIET*

Staten Island University Hospital's booming Community Nutrition Program got its start about three years ago with a nutrition-related exhibit at an intermediate school. Students' and teachers' "overwhelming response" to a display of high-fat fast food, samples of healthy snacks, and a nutritional quiz convinced Linda Cupit, MS, MBA, senior vice president of community medicine and health, that the public was hungry for good dietary information.

In forums ranging from personal counseling sessions to group presentations, the Community Nutrition Program has since educated thousands of individuals in the hospital's Staten Island, N.Y., Brooklyn, and Manhattan market.

"This is very important to the community. Nutrition has such an impact on overall health care costs," Cupit notes.

The program initially expanded by offering free nutrition-related seminars to all Staten Island public schools, various churches and synagogues, and auxiliary organizations. Between 15 and 20 of the approximately 100 groups first contacted completed a return reply card or telephoned to arrange a seminar, according to Amy Olitsky, RD, community dietitian. More than 2,700 individuals have since attended group presentations.

The Community Nutrition Program also features:

- one-on-one counseling sessions that include body fat analysis and individual nutrition plan development
- hospital employee weight management guidance in association with the employee wellness program
- prenatal nutrition education for certain hospital patients
- development of heart-healthy menu items in collaboration with local restaurants
- participation in area schools' career days, highlighting the nutrition profession

Group presentations deal with topics such as basic nutrition, weight management, and meal preparation.

"We focus on how to eat healthy—like increasing calcium, healthy heart, and cancer prevention—and on low-fat cooking techniques. I review the food groups, the nutrients in each group, and [appropriate] portions. I bring models of food to show food group samples and size," Olitsky explains.

Olitsky also closely tracks media coverage of nutrition research and trends, and adjusts her presentations accordingly. "The media highlights different things and the public's interest follows," she explains. For example, she recently added a discussion about soy food products in response to publicized research suggesting a link between photo-estrogens and a lessening of certain menopause-related side effects.

Individual nutrition sessions, usually conducted at the hospital's Community Wellness Center, often help elderly or sick people address dietary problems such as food intolerance. Many consumers also seek weight management advice. In both

---

*Source: Gina Rollins, "Staten Island Community Nutrition Program Helps Thousands Improve Their Diet," *Inside Preventive Care*, Vol. 4:11, Aspen Publishers, Inc., © 1999.

cases, Olitsky focuses on the individual's food history and preferences, and designs a nutritional plan that ties in with their goals. Approximately 800 people have received nutritional counseling in the past three years, Cupit estimates.

Olitsky devotes about three days per week to the Community Nutrition Program, either making presentations in the community or manning the Wellness Center. She divides the remainder of her time between the hospital's prenatal program and working with Rama Koslowe, MD, at the hospital's outpatient nutrition center. An internist who specializes in nutrition, Koslowe also provides medical consultation to the Community Nutrition Program.

Olitsky's frequent presence at the hospital's Wellness Center led to the Community Nutrition Program's collaboration with area restaurants. The chefs of two facilities located near the Wellness Center in the Staten Island Mall approached her about working on heart-healthy menu items.

Once finalized, the collaborations will highlight the Community Nutrition Program to an even larger audience. The two restaurants plan to denote heart-healthy items with a menu icon and reference the hospital's participation, Cupit says.

The key to the program's popularity, according to Cupit, is Olitsky's ability to relate to people and to tailor nutrition education to their specific needs. "She talks in a way they can understand and makes it fun, interesting, and applicable to people's lives," says Cupit. For example, when meeting with women who work outside the home, Olitsky gives pointers on how to prepare an entire week's worth of nutritional meals in one day.

Olitsky also considers cultural differences among her audiences, and the impact of culture on their dietary habits. "You have to understand what food means to people before you can get them to change. You have to convince them to eat smaller amounts [of treasured foods]. You're whistling Dixie if you think you'll get them to stop," Cupit explains.

The program costs approximately $50,000 annually, including Olitsky's salary, materials, expenses, and an allocated portion of the Community Wellness Center lease, where most of the personal nutritional consultations take place.

Although "this could be turned into a business," the hospital provides it as a community service, Cupit says. "Our CEO [chief executive officer] and COO [chief operating officer] are very committed to community initiatives, especially for women and children. Dr. Andrew Passeri, our COO, has had a longstanding interest in nutrition and has encouraged us to pursue this program for the community."

Barring unforeseen economic circumstances, the facility has no plans to change the program's community service format. Still, Cupit and Olitsky minimize program expenses by obtaining free educational materials from associations and manufacturers and seeking grant funding for capital items. For example, the program will soon purchase a body fat analyzer with grant monies, according to Cupit.

The hospital measures the Community Nutrition Program's success by the number of participants in each aspect of the service. Cupit prepares an annual report that delineates overall program history, as well as year-to-year comparisons. Aside from weight loss reported by hospital employees receiving weight management counseling, the program does not formally track other clinical outcomes, Cupit reports.

For those considering a similar program, selecting a good dietitian is the most critical success factor, according to Cupit. "You need someone who is customer friendly, who has good interpersonal skills and can apply and integrate their knowledge in a practical way," she explains.

Once that certain dietitian is found, it is important to support his or her efforts both clinically and administratively, Cupit recommends. "They need a mentor to nurture and push them into new areas," she says. While Cupit works closely with Olitsky on program development, others have supported her clinical work. In addition to the ongoing clinical collaboration she has with Koslowe, Olitsky has collaborated and worked with other hospital dietitians.

In addition to a dynamic dietitian, a successful community nutrition program also needs an audience, so establishing a strong network is equally important. "You have to have good contacts in the community and good channels of distribution," Cupit suggests.

Olitsky agrees. "It's important to be very approachable and get to know the needs of the community," she explains. Doing so has helped her not only grow the Community Nutrition Program, but also tailor presentations to the needs and interests of her audiences.

The effort has been well worth it, according to Olitsky. "I really enjoy it. I see people making a lot of healthy changes in their diet and I like to know that I've had a part in it," she says.

CHILD HEALTH OUTREACH AND ENROLLMENT INITIATIVE GETS HIGH MARKS IN BROOKLYN*

Thanks to a child health outreach and enrollment initiative being conducted by the Sunset Park Family Health Center Network, children attending school in Brooklyn, N.Y., have better access to health care.

The School Health Outreach Project was formed in 1995 in response to the merging of several environmental forces that were impacting on the operations of the Sunset Park Family Health Center Network's School Health Program. There was clear indication of a growing number of uninsured children receiving care through school-based health centers. This was reinforced during routine discussions with school principals who found health needs to be a confusing issue for staff and parents alike.

The Sunset Park Family Health Center Network became a program site for the Community HealthCorps (CHC), an AmeriCorps national service project sponsored by the National Association of Community Health Centers.

Based on a community health worker model, the CHC recruits individuals, particularly from the neighborhood, who are interested in community health to fulfill a year of service in the framework of primary care health centers. All members are bilingual. They can speak one of the other major languages found in the community—Spanish, Cantonese/Mandarin, and Arabic.

Community responsiveness has long been a focus at the Sunset Park Family Health Center Network. The Network's governing board, the Health Council, consists of community residents, local business leaders, and health center clients.

The Health Council has continuously placed children's health, insurance coverage, and services for new immigrant populations as priorities. Historically a major proponent of the expansion and enhancement of the School Health Program, the Health Council is now a strong advocate for the CHC and its mission of community strengthening and member development.

The placement of CHC members in the school-based health centers addresses many community health needs. CHC members are community residents who speak the languages represented by the new immigrant population groups entering the neighborhood.

Because many HealthCorps members are members of these ethnic and cultural groups, there is a trust and comfort level established that serves to facilitate patient care. Members function as cultural brokers, helping patients understand the systems of care and assisting the school health staff to better understand the needs of the child and family.

Partnership Development

The School Health Program is staffed by a multidisciplinary team consisting of nurse practitioners, medical assistants, psychologists, social workers, board-certified pediatricians, doctors, a dental hygienist, dentists, and administrators.

The nurse practitioners, accompanied by a medical assistant, coordinate the on-site school health team with a permanent full-time assignment to a given school. Nurse

---

*Source: Orianne Sharir, "Child Health Outreach and Enrollment Initiative Gets High Marks in Brooklyn," *Inside Preventive Care*, Vol. 4:7, Aspen Publishers, Inc., © 1998.

practitioners, under the supervision of a board-certified pediatrician, provide medical care, health screening and assessments, first aid, management of acute and chronic conditions, and health education to more than 10,000 children who generate in excess of 34,000 visits per year to the School Health Program.

The mental health component is provided via a team of psychologists and social workers who rotate through the schools and provide on-site individual and group therapy for children who are at risk of school failure due to behavioral, emotional, or family problems. Dental health screenings at each elementary school are conducted annually by a dental hygienist working with teams of the network's dental residents.

Installation of computers at every school site has fully integrated the school health sites with the Sunset Park Family Health Center Network, permitting high-quality continuity of care throughout the network and enhanced identification of insurance and demographic information.

A second partnership exists with the Board of Education staff, both at the district and school levels, and the School Health Program.

The schools are committed to disseminating information regarding the availability of school health services and Child Health Plus. The schools have been key in reaching families. Further, child health center staff are active in scheduling health fairs and workshops for the participating schools. Principals, guidance counselors, and teach-

---

Tips on How To Duplicate This Program

The School Health Outreach Project's success has been achieved as a result of several factors that should be considered when creating your own program.

- It is imperative that the school-based health centers are located in areas of high need.
- The importance of community outreach needs to be recognized, and resources should be allocated to support it. A well-functioning HealthCorps program, or similar community service initiative, is key to the success of such a project.
- The establishment of an AmeriCorps program is a relatively costly proposition. There is federal monetary support for the program; however, there are significant costs to the sponsoring institution. Replicability, therefore, will require an initial period of development, followed by consistent evaluation and reassessment.
- Corps member development is key to this effort. Focus must be placed on providing the member with a challenging year of service. Attention must be paid to training at orientation and through ongoing inservice education. Consideration should be given to physical plant and space issues, both at the school-based health center and for the HealthCorps program specifically.
- As previously mentioned, program "buy-in" is absolutely key to the success of the School Health Outreach Project. Strong leadership from executive staff is important in two respects: first, in asserting that the school-based health centers must be more forceful in addressing sustainability issues; second, in asserting that the network is committed to the HealthCorps program and recognizing the unique talents of the members involved.

ers are the most vocal advocates on behalf of continued collaboration with the School Health Program.

The School Health Outreach Project is closely partnered with Health Plus, a major managed care organization in the community. Health Plus has, until very recently, been the only access point for Child Health Plus in southwest Brooklyn.

Its commitment has included working directly with school health staff and CHC members to "spread the word" about the availability of this product. The company has volunteered staff and resources to training members and actively sponsors community health events at School Health Program sites. Most recently, a Health Plus representative has been assigned to work full-time with the School Health Outreach Project to increase the number of children enrolled in Child Health Plus.

Community Benefits

Baseline data from 1995 showed that, program-wide, approximately 50 percent of children enrolled in the School Health Program were uninsured. Ten percent were enrolled in a Medicaid managed care plan and 24 percent were enrolled in traditional Medicaid fee-for-service.

Ten percent were enrolled in commercial or union plans, and the remaining six percent of children were already enrolled in Child Health Plus.

Data from 1997 have shown that, as a result of the School Health Outreach Project, there has been an increase in Child Health Plus participation from 6 percent to 17 percent. Another finding is that the percentage of uninsured children has decreased to 30 percent, and Medicaid coverage has expanded to approximately 45 percent.

Although it is unlikely that such significant results are directly the result of the School Health Outreach Project, it is our belief that the ability of CHC members to interact with non-English-speaking and new immigrant families has improved the process of insurance information collection at the school-based health centers.

Members are spending a significant amount of time providing medical interpretation and translating written materials. They are also performing many case management functions, including patient follow-up and referrals to social service agencies. To date, members have interpreted approximately 90 medical visits.

The School Health Program conducts quarterly parent and patient satisfaction surveys to determine its success in meeting key goals. Components of these surveys include questions on the parent understanding of the nurse practitioner's instructions and whether specific needs were met. This manner of accountability is used as a quality assurance tool and is updated on a quarterly basis.

An additional benefit has been the success of the School Health Outreach Project in generating interest in community health work on the part of CHC members. In the last program year, 50 percent of members have gone on to work in community health organizations.

COMMUNITY COLLABORATION PRODUCES CANCER VIDEO FOR IMMIGRANT POPULATION*

Nancy Grandt, RN, MS, AOCN, and her colleagues at HealthEast St. Joseph's Hospital in St. Paul, Minn., had noticed a troubling pattern among cancer patients from the area's Hmong immigrant population. They often refused to accept treatment.

"Several times, Hmong people received a diagnosis of cancer. Interpreters were used to communicate information about the illness and its treatment. After careful explanations from physicians and staff, Hmong people left the hospital and did not return," she says.

As the oncology care management specialist, Grandt was asked by her staff to find a way to make a connection to the Hmong people that would convince them to accept help from Western medicine.

Grandt turned to the Hmong community to get its participation in addressing the problem. As she discovered more about the history and culture of the people, she realized that there was a great deal of mutual learning needed.

Hmong History and Culture

Prior to the Vietnam War, the Hmong lived a somewhat isolated and nomadic existence in rural hill areas of Laos. During the Vietnam War, the Hmong assisted the United States Armed Forces in the war effort.

Following the departure of the United States from fighting territories, Hmong people found themselves persecuted by the Communists and their supporters. They were eventually granted special immigration status to come to the United States.

It is estimated that more than 150,000 Hmong people currently live in the United States, with many living in California and Minnesota. An estimated 50,000 live in the Minneapolis/St. Paul area.

The cultural adaptation required to live in the United States was significant. This farming people had little familiarity with the technology and lifestyle of the United States. Their social structure was based on a system of clans that was quite foreign to their American neighbors. Developing new job skills was a challenge, given the difficulty in communication.

The Hmong communication pattern was based on verbal interaction involving several dialects. There was little written language—in fact, many elders did not read, simply because the written language was developed after their youth.

Cultural differences in the area of health care were significant. The Hmong perspective placed great emphasis on wholeness and spiritual aspects of healing. Shamans played an important role in achieving health. Western technology was completely foreign to their understanding.

A Communication Partnership

The size of the communication challenge became clearer when Grandt and her colleagues discovered that there was no word in the Hmong language for "cancer." Related words such as "cell," "metastasis," and "chemotherapy" also had no Hmong

---

*Source: Bill Solberg, "Community Collaboration Produces Cancer Video for Immigrant Population," *Inside Preventive Care*, Vol. 3:10, Aspen Publishers, Inc., © 1998.

equivalent. "Radiation therapy" was translated as "we are putting fire inside of you." It was no wonder that Hmong people did not return to the hospital.

Grandt initiated a proposal to collaborate with the Hmong community to develop a communication strategy. She presented the proposal to the HealthEast Foundation.

"I was amazed at the result," Grandt says. "We not only were well-received, the Foundation understood the importance of the issue and the scope of the problem. The HealthEast Foundation allocated twice the amount of money we requested."

Christyne Stolpestad, associate director for public relations at HealthEast Foundation says, "The project met our criteria for having significant impact in a health treatment area. It was particularly attractive since it built in early involvement of the Hmong people and it encouraged collaboration with other providers."

As the project developed, The American Cancer Society, the Alma Foundation (representing another Minneapolis/St. Paul health system), the Medtronic Foundation, and the Green Tree Financial Foundation were other funding partners.

As a volunteer for American Cancer Society (ACS), Grandt discussed the project with ACS staff. ACS queried its members across the nation to see if any communication strategy or program existed. The response was consistent—nothing existed, but there was great need in communities across the country. The ACS was committed to being an active partner in the development of a communication tool.

Hmong Community Involvement

The Hmong community participated in the development of a communication strategy through the use of focus groups.

"A well-respected elder was a key member in the early development of focus groups," Grandt says. "Health professionals from American backgrounds and Hmong backgrounds participated. There were many lay people from the Hmong community as well. In all, over 40 different people participated in the two year focus group process."

Early on, the focus group decided that because the Hmong language was based on verbal expression, the communication had to be delivered through the spoken word. Audiovisual communication was the method of choice of the focus group.

Fortunately, the partnership of the foundations provided sufficient financial resources to do the job well. A video production entitled *Cancer: What You Should Know* began to gain momentum.

Video Production

The project was able to hire Foung Heu, an independent Hmong videographer with a national reputation. Heu set to work to develop a video by and for Hmong people.

He adopted the focus groups as his advisory board and used them to decide the best way to communicate the varied issues related to cancer diagnosis and treatment. For example, two focus group sessions were needed to decide how to communicate about radiation therapy. Finally the group decided to describe it as, "a beam of good sunlight shining on you—it can't be seen or felt, but it still helps you."

The foundations were pleased that Heu used a production strategy that funneled money back to the Hmong community.

"Heu not only used Hmong actors from the community, he went so far as to use the production to train Hmong people as technical support," Stolpestad explains. "They learned how to provide lighting and sound system support while earning money and producing a valuable community product."

Video Content

The final product took more than two years to complete, but it was applauded by all. The video opens showing a woman newly diagnosed with cancer. She wishes to accept treatment from an herbalist and shaman, but is not interested in Western medicine. Her husband convinces her to explore the treatment possibilities.

The video uses the spoken Hmong language with English subtitles to describe cancer, its diagnosis, and its treatment. Each of the treatment modalities is described by Hmong professionals in a manner that can be understood and accepted by Hmong people.

Throughout the video, other Hmongs describe their successful treatment using Western medicine as part of their healing. The video concludes with a dramatic statement by a Hmong shaman that occurs without subtitles. The shaman says in effect, "I am here to treat your soul and spirit. You need Western medicine to treat your body. We can be partners in healing."

Overcoming the Language Barrier

There are no words in Hmong language for "cancer," "cell," "metastasis," "chemotherapy," and other related words.

As a Hmong videographer developed *Cancer: What You Should Know*, a focus group advised him on translations. For example, the group decided to describe radiation therapy as "a beam of good sunlight shining on you—it can't be seen or felt, but it still helps you."

Outcomes

There were several positive outcomes from the process. Of primary importance was the development of a dramatic video that has already had an impact on people's lives.

"There have been two cases already in which the video helped to change people's minds," Grandt says. "One situation involved a woman with abdominal disease needing radiation therapy. Another involved a woman with ovarian cancer who needed surgery. Each initially refused Western medicine, but changed her mind after seeing the video."

The foundations have benefited from the funding partnerships they developed. "We were able to substitute cooperation for competition and collaboratively meet the health care needs of our community. Projects like this will dominate the future work of the foundation," says Linda Kay Smith, executive director of the HealthEast Foundation.

Hmong people were an integral part of the planning and development. Some benefited financially from their involvement as actors and technicians. New job skills were learned.

The project received the 1997 Community Health Award of the Minnesota Hospital and Healthcare Partnership in recognition of its collaborative effort.

DIABETES SUNDAY PROGRAM HELPS REACH THE AFRICAN AMERICAN COMMUNITY*

Diabetes Risk

- Almost 10 percent of Americans with diabetes are African American.
- Nearly 6 percent of African American men and 8 percent of African American women have diabetes.
- One in four African American women over the age of 55 has diabetes.

A proverb from the African nation of Cameroon states succinctly, "Knowledge is better than riches."

This wisdom is particularly important when it pertains to diabetes, the incidence of which has tripled in African Americans during the last 30 years. The American Diabetes Association (ADA) has developed an African American program to bring valuable information to a community that is significantly at risk.

Diabetes Risk

The ADA reports the following statistics concerning African Americans and diabetes:

- Almost 10 percent of Americans with diabetes are African American.
- Nearly 6 percent of African American men and 8 percent of African American women have the disease. A third of those with diabetes are not aware of their diagnosis.
- One in four African American women over the age of 55 has diabetes.
- African Americans experience disproportionately higher rates of serious diabetic complications, including blindness, amputation, and kidney failure.

Regarding the prevalence of diabetes, Kenneth Inchausti of the ADA says that "the old adage 'Everyone knows someone with diabetes' is quite true today, particularly in the African American community."

These statistics made it clear to the ADA that the magnitude of the health issue required focused attention.

African American Program

Developed in 1996, the African American program provides a variety of health education resources to support local ADA offices in their outreach to African American people.

"The African American program is fluid and flexible to support the efforts of local offices to meet the needs of their communities," says Shelly Heath-Watson, associate director of programs and cultural diversity for the ADA. "Communities may use Diabetes Sundays, Healthy Eating programs, an exercise module called 'Get Up & Go,' and focused educational materials which are specifically targeted to the African American community."

---

*Source: Bill Solberg, "Diabetes Sunday Program Helps Reach the African-American Community," *Inside Preventive Care*, Vol. 4:3, Aspen Publishers, Inc., © 1998.

Diabetes Sunday symbolizes the ADA's strategy of partnership with grass-roots organizations that have significant impact in peoples' lives.

"Churches play a key role in the African American community—providing leadership, exhibiting a genuine concern for physical and spiritual health of members, and serving as a link between church members and the wider community," says Heath-Watson.

The ADA prepared a packet of information that was sent to local chapters that suggested "Diabetes Sunday" partnerships with local churches. "Because of their strong leadership in the community, the pastors' support is key to the success of Diabetes Sunday," says Heath-Watson.

The goals of Diabetes Sunday are simple: to create an awareness that diabetes is a serious disease, to inform the congregation that African Americans are at high risk for developing diabetes, and to increase awareness that diagnosis and treatment can make a significant difference in overall health.

On Diabetes Sunday, pastors or their designees are asked to deliver a five- to seven-minute presentation consistent with their own preaching style and religious beliefs. Local offices of the ADA support the pastors with educational materials and statistics, as well as with examples of presentations that have been given by other pastors.

Following the service, all congregation members are provided with culturally appropriate information regarding diabetes and risk factors.

Included in the information is a brief risk assessment questionnaire, as well as information about signs and symptoms of diabetes. Congregation members are encouraged to call the ADA at 800/DIABETES for more information if they or a loved one has diabetes or is at risk for developing the disease.

Local offices may use Diabetes Sunday as a springboard to get residents into the ADA's Healthy Eating workshop and exercise programs. They can also be referred to educational presentations by health professionals.

Congregation members are always encouraged to communicate with their physicians about concerns or questions. In fact, the function of Diabetes Sunday is primarily to awaken the interest in congregation members in discussing their risk factors and health status with their physicians.

The Gospel singing greats, The Clark Sisters, have served as honorary spokespersons for "Diabetes Sunday." The message of the Clark Sisters is especially dramatic since the death of their mother to diabetes-related complications. The encouragement and example of the Clark Sisters helped spread the Diabetes Sunday message to more than 300,000 people in community churches in 1997.

Nutritional Information

The ADA is also involved in activities to help African Americans revise many traditional African American and Southern recipes to be more consistent with a healthy diabetic diet.

The Healthy Eating workshop is an hour-long interactive session for those who have been diagnosed with diabetes or who are at high risk for the disease.

The goals of the workshop are to impress the participants with the importance of healthy eating and to provide two or three specific strategies that can be used in their cooking. A traditional meal may be prepared using the healthy cooking ideas.

Another strategy has been the development of a sampler of five recipes that were created through the efforts of African American nutritionists. The recipe sampler has been described in *Ebony Magazine* and is available by calling the ADA's toll free number.

Web Site

The African American program maintains a Web site to support education and program information for local offices of the ADA as well as for the general public. The site includes information regarding the African American program, as well as statistical information regarding the impact of diabetes on African Americans.

The Diabetes Risk Test is also available at the Web site. People taking the test online enter their gender, age, height, weight, family history of diabetes, and the level of activity they usually maintain. Their risk score is computed immediately and they are provided with information about the disease.

The site also contains more detailed information about initiating Diabetes Sunday programs and Get Up and Move programs through local offices of the ADA. The African American program page will soon have examples of culturally appropriate public information that will be available for distribution through local offices.

Perhaps in agreement that "knowledge is better than riches," the American Society of Association Executives awarded the African American program of the ADA its Associations Advance America Award of Excellence in 1996.

HAIRCUTS AND HEALTH PROMOTION*

One example is found in an unusual and nontraditional clinical practice site. In early 1995, Bernardine M. Lacey, Director of the Western Michigan University School of Nursing, conceptualized the idea of health promotion activities in a beauty shop. Not only do people get a haircut and manicure, but they also receive blood-pressure screening and health care information that is specially geared to African Americans.

This program is a women's health care initiative sponsored by Western Michigan University, the Black Nurses Association, and the Mane Attraction, a beauty salon in Kalamazoo, Michigan. With the support from the salon patrons and publicity gained from an article printed in *The Western News,* a Kalamazoo newspaper, the salon initiative received a grant of $10,000 from the John E. Fetzer Institute of Kalamazoo. These funds were allocated to special workshops and development of culturally sensitive health promotion materials.

Lacey and the faculty observed that unlike conventional clinical settings, the beauty shop is a warm, friendly, nonthreatening environment. In such a setting, the women were more receptive to health care information. These women were willing to share with their beauticians some of their most private thoughts. Historically, it has been a place for women to talk about their joys and sorrows, pains and sufferings, so it appeared to be a natural place to introduce, promote, and educate individuals about health care.

The program added educational information on breast self-examination, CPR training, stress reduction, and healthy cooking and eating. Once a month, low-fat recipes featuring traditional African American fare are prepared for clients to sample.

Most of the health care services and information is provided by area nurses or WMU nursing students who are offered opportunities to establish relationships with the clients. This in turn meets program objectives of facilitating partnerships that improve health in families, populations, and communities. In reply to requests made by the women at the beauty salon, several other professional groups share their expertise and provide additional pertinent health information.

The faculty underscores the fact that this approach "is not prescriptive, but rather oriented towards health and wellness promotion . . . Clients are continually surveyed to make sure the programs offered meet their specific needs." Information is recorded and maintained on how clients view and manage their health care, allowing health providers to assist clients more effectively.

The positive community impact of using the beauty salon as a clinical site has been useful as a referral base that strengthens ties to primary care physicians, local hospitals, and other available resources. Course objectives were accomplished by students as they became engaged in partnerships with a community having urgent health care needs.

*Source: Bernardine M. Lacey and Jewel Moseley-Howard, "Haircuts and Health Promotion," *The Outcomes Mandate: Case Management in Health Care Today,* E. Cohen and V. DeBack, eds., Mosby, Inc., © 1999.

NUTRITION: STRATEGIES THAT WORKED*

Setting the Stage

Situation: In the Harlem community, there was concern about the high prevalence of cardiovascular disease, hypertension, and obesity.

Strategy: To provide a comfortable and familiar setting for nutrition and health education for the entire family, enlist assistance from churches in the community.

Action: A health festival was planned, with the church setting the stage. For several weeks, the minister gave sermons leading up to the festival, which focused on mental and physical health, the family unit, and achievement.

Result: The church implemented several health-related measures: (1) Smoking was prohibited in the church; (2) meals served at the church were planned to be low in fat and sodium; and (3) walking clubs and exercise classes were started.

At Work in the Community

Situation: A nutritionist at a local health department tried to have nutrition classes for migrant farm workers at the health department, but nobody came. The health department tried extending its hours so that the clients could be seen after they came in from the fields, but that did not work either.

Strategy: Use a community-based approach. Let the client group determine the appropriate time and place for communicating food and nutrition information, and let them choose the content.

Action: Since the farm workers and their whole families gathered every Sunday afternoon in the city park to picnic, the nutritionist set up information booths in the town square and took the message to the people, who were already in an environment where food was the focal point.

Result: The nutritionist found that the people were relaxed and interested in talking about the foods they were eating, many of which were tied to their culture.

Teaching Food Safety and Sanitation

Situation: A Head Start nutritionist identified the need to teach parents the importance of sanitation and food safety.

Strategy: She decided to model safe food practices at a parent meeting set up for another purpose.

Action: She asked the parents to bring in food representing their culture. As they brought the food in, the nutritionist talked about not letting hot foods cool before serving them and the importance of keeping cold foods cold so that germs would not grow. Cold food was set in a large container of crushed ice to keep it cold. Hot food was kept above 140° F by heating it in the oven or on the range until right before serving. The nutritionist showed parents how to make sure their children's hands were clean before they sat down to eat.

Result: The danger of food-borne illness was minimized, and the families learned the importance of food safety and sanitation.

---

*Source: Graves DE, Suitor CW, 1998. *Celebrating Diversity: Approaching Families through Their Food* (rev. ed.). Arlington, VA: National Center for Education in Maternal and Child Health.

Using Food To Teach English

Situation: Because California is home to many recent immigrants who do not speak English and who do not read or write in their primary language, the WIC nutrition educators were not able to communicate effectively with them. The number of languages spoken by bilingual WIC staff members was limited, and it was discovered that WIC participants were often not excited about the WIC classes on nutrition and health. The greatest perceived need among non-English-speaking WIC participants was learning English.

Strategy: To meet this need, the San Bernardino County WIC Program established a nutrition and English as a Second Language (ESL) program. Health and nutrition were the subject content, and ESL was the vehicle for content delivery. Nutrition education was provided in the same way as low-literacy adult education ESL, where recent immigrants are taught survival skills such as going to the doctor and applying for a job. In the WIC/ESL pilot project, the theme of the curriculum was making good choices at the grocery store.

Action: The pilot WIC/ESL classes were designed to accommodate a variety of students who spoke different languages and whose levels of English comprehension were not the same. Only English was spoken in these 25-minute classes. No translation was used. Cooperative learning was encouraged so that those who had a better understanding of English could help those who had less.

The curriculum incorporated some of the most recent advances in ESL teaching:

- Environment—WIC/ESL classes are dynamic, visual, participatory, and fun. Learning is enhanced by the stimulation of the five senses.
- Realia—Visual aids such as food models, photographs, and illustrations are used to define English/nutrition words and concepts.
- Total physical response (TPR)—This is the students' physical response to commands given by the teacher, such as "stand up," "sit down," and "stretch." (In this setting, TPR was extended to include the use of body language to help define words and concepts such as "sick" and "healthy."
- Comprehensible input—Language is acquired through listening in this method. Students are not expected or pressured to speak until they are ready.

Result: The WIC participants received the nutrition education positively because their perceived need to learn English was met. The curriculum was designed so that learning was active and fun. Additionally, all participants were referred to low-cost community ESL classes in their neighborhood so that they could continue to learn English.

IMMUNIZATION COALITIONS THAT WORK: TRAINING FOR PUBLIC HEALTH PROFESSIONALS*

The year 2000 Health Objectives for the United States program has as its goal the completion of the basic immunization series in at least 90 percent of children under two years of age.[1] Despite this, National Immunization Survey (NIS) data indicate that approximately 30 percent of two-year-old children in the United States are underimmunized for the four diphtheria, tetanus, pertussis (DTP); three oral polio-myelitis vaccine (OPV); and one measles-mumps-rubella (MMR) vaccine series.[2] Given the degree of underimmunization of this nation's children, innovative approaches are required to mobilize communities in ways that will help increase immunization rates.[3] A coalition approach to underimmunization is an appropriate strategy because underimmunization is a multi-faceted health problem that involves multiple levels and sectors of communities.[4,5] While coalitions are a recent development in the promotion of immunization, they have been used successfully to build community capacity around other health issues such as alcohol, tobacco, and other drug abuse and chronic disease prevention.[6-8] Underimmunization is similar to other health problems that involve lack of education as well as access to care or delivery of services.

Coalition development was established as a national goal by President Clinton's Childhood Immunization Initiative, which mandated that all states, territories, and major municipalities produce an immunization action plan (IAP).[9] Each IAP site was encouraged to develop a local immunization coalition; rudimentary technical assistance in coalition development was offered on a regional basis. However, experience on a national level suggests that many state and local health departments are either unprepared or struggling with the difficulty of coalition work.[10]

The Need for Training

Research has shown that regardless of the health issue being addressed, coalition leaders and staff need more training and technical assistance in coalition development, community planning, and program implementation.[11-15] In response to these needs, several national agencies have sponsored ongoing training and technical assistance for coalition efforts, including: National Institutes of Health (COMMIT and ASSIST Tobacco Control Coalitions); the Center for Substance Abuse Prevention (Community Partnership Programs); the Knight Foundation (National Immunization Initiative); Robert Wood Johnson Foundation (Fighting Back Substance Abuse Prevention Coalitions); and the Centers for Disease Control and Prevention (Five-a-Day Nutrition Coalitions, HIV Community Planning Prevention Coalitions, Breast and Cervical Cancer Control Coalitions, IMPACT Tobacco Control Coalitions). Immunization coalitions appear to experience the same overall problems as other health promotion coalitions.[16] If immunization coalitions are to succeed, they need training and technical assistance that promote coalition development and collaborative needs assessments.

Based on these identified needs, the Center for Pediatric Research in Norfolk, Virginia, was awarded a grant to establish an Immunization Coalition Training

*Source: Frances D. Butterfoss et al., "Immunization Coalitions That Work: Training for Public Health Professionals," *Journal of Public Health Management and Practice*, Vol. 4:6, Aspen Publishers, Inc., © 1998.

Institute (Institute) in October 1995. The Association of Teachers of Preventive Medicine (ATPM) and the Centers for Disease Control and Prevention (CDC) National Immunization Program sponsored the collaborative, three-year program. The Center for Pediatric Research received the program grant because of its successful management of the Consortium for the Immunization of Norfolk's Children (CINCH), a three-year, CDC-funded demonstration project that used a local coalition to improve the rate of infant immunizations.[16,17] The purpose of this article is to describe the Institute, report the results of its national immunization coalition needs assessment, and evaluate the three sessions conducted in its first year.

Immunization Coalition Training Institute

The Institute trains key health agency staff and others who are responsible for development and implementation of immunization coalitions in 87 state, territorial, and urban sites that have CDC-funded IAPs. Each Institute includes representatives from 10 sites that are selected according to a set of criteria that includes geographic location, population density, coalition and needs assessment status, immunization rate, and site preference. Each site may send three representatives who should include: (1) the IAP coordinator or staff member responsible for community outreach; (2) an epidemiologist or staff member responsible for assessment of immunization status and data management; and (3) a community partnership representative. Representatives attend the three-day Institute in Norfolk, Virginia, with all expenses covered by the grant. The Institute program is based on the premise that coalitions can effectively improve immunization rates when they involve multiple levels and diverse members of the community; are well informed of community needs; and utilize data for planning, implementation, and evaluation. IAP staff and coalition coordinators are taught how to perform needs assessments, use data to drive planning, plan comprehensive and feasible strategies, and evaluate the coalition process and its outcomes. The Institute curriculum is based on training needs identified by a national survey of immunization coalitions, on approaches that have demonstrated effectiveness, and on evaluation of the training provided by the Institute.

The Institute focuses on two main content areas: the art of building and maintaining effective coalitions, and conducting community needs assessments. The Institute maintains that coalitions must be developed as organizationally competent entities. Participants are encouraged to develop and maintain coalitions that are culturally sensitive, responsive to their members, structurally effective, and attentive to group process. Participants are taught how to develop mission statements and goals; work groups; job descriptions for staff, members, and leaders; and bylaws and operating procedures. Research has established that coalitions that pay attention to these factors are more likely to endure over time and have members who are more satisfied, committed, and participative.[15,16,18,19] Coalitions take time and resources to develop; collaborative decision making is difficult. However, when coalitions are functioning effectively, they may be able to develop and maintain more effective interventions more effectively than public health institutions working alone.

Research and experience indicate that to be effective, coalitions should undertake needs assessment and evaluation. The needs assessment process generally occurs during the formation and implementation stages of coalition development. Coalitions that do not begin their work with a needs assessment can proceed to maintenance and institutionalization—the last two stages of development. However, these same coalitions frequently return to the implementation stage to complete the needs assessment task when they realize that they lack the data to guide and evaluate their intervention plans.[20] Experience demonstrates that coalitions generally require technical assistance and support in order to conduct needs assessments as well as to interpret and utilize the data required for planning and evaluation.[11–16]

The Institute guides participants through the process of rapid needs assessment (RNA). In the context of immunization, RNA is a comprehensive but rapid approach to gathering information that helps communities diagnose the causes of underimmunization in the community. It also helps communities plan and coordinate immunization services and/or educational programs to improve the immunization status of their populations.[16,21] Coalition members help design and carry out the RNA, and then help review and use the data as the foundation of a community IAP.

Because most immunization coalitions were formed after 1993, the evaluation of their impact on immunization rates is premature. It usually takes one to two years for coalitions to coalesce and effectively initiate strategies in their communities. Thus, the two-year-old immunization rates for the cohort of children born *after* these strategies were implemented will be determined in the near future. A CDC-funded demonstration coalition in Norfolk, Virginia, found a 17% improvement in its post-intervention immunization rate.[17] However, immunization rates are not the only outcome measure of importance for coalitions. Coalitions also measure improving access to care; linking with other social service programs [such as the Women, Infants and Children's (WIC) program]; and improving the knowledge, attitudes, and practices of health care providers and parents.[17] Related benefits reported by immunization coalitions include increased citizen participation and collaboration; development of community skills, resources, and capacities; and increased support for legislative change and advocacy.[16] In addition, a coalition that begins with a narrow focus on immunization may develop the competency to address broader child health issues later.[22]

The Institute is presented as a train-the-trainer experience to be replicated in the participants' communities. Institute sessions are varied by style of presentation and are highly interactive and rich in materials and examples. The Institute's curriculum addresses the six priority training areas identified by the Joint Council of Governmental Public Health Agencies' Work Group on Human Resources Development. These training areas are:

1. emphasizing cultural competency
2. promoting healthful behaviors
3. building leadership capacity
4. enhancing public health managers' competency to manage programs
5. training in community assessment
6. emphasizing community organization, outreach, and development[22]

The Joint Council also identified 15 characteristics of effective public health training. Of these characteristics, 12 appear to be strengths of the Coalition Training Institute. The Institute is:

1. linked with academia
2. has the capacity to reach a wide audience by its train-the-trainer focus
3. may be replicated in other sites

4. can adapt its curriculum at each session to respond to emerging issues
5. is adaptable among regions, states, and over time
6. is a planned approach to training based on a needs assessment
7. has culturally sensitive course materials
8. provides incentive for participation, i.e., expenses are paid by Institute
9. has a dynamic presentation style and quality
10. has a setting conducive to learning
11. has a strong evaluation component
12. has a potential for self-study

The Institute does not meet three characteristics deemed important by the Joint Council: (1) it is not as cost effective as larger training seminars or teleconferences; (2) it is not open to all interested participants; and (3) it is not presented as a training series.

Prior to the Institute: National Needs Assessment

A national needs assessment survey was conducted prior to the first Institute session. Surveys were mailed to the IAP coordinator or immunization program director for each of the 87 IAP sites. Follow-up phone calls and re-mails of questionnaires to non-responders were used to maximize the response rate. Questionnaires were received from 84 of 87 sites (a response rate of 97 percent), with two urban sites and one territorial site not responding.

Respondent Characteristics

Respondents held a number of different jobs; most were immunization program directors (55%), followed by IAP coordinators (15%). Respondents were asked to list up to three main areas of job responsibility related to immunization. The most common responses were outreach development (70%), program operations (54%), contract and grants administration (27%), IAP coordination (23%), and vaccine-preventable disease surveillance and assessment (17%).

Coalition Profile

Fifty-eight sites (69%) reported having an active immunization coalition. Twenty-four of the 27 (89%) respondents from urban sites reported having active coalitions, compared with 34 of 57 (60%) state and territorial sites. This difference between urban and state or territorial sites was significant ($p < 0.05$, Fisher's Exact test for two proportions). The number of members in coalitions varied highly, ranging from 12 to 300 with a mean of 74 members. All of the coalitions were formed between 1990 and 1995, with 32 (56%) initiated from 1992–1993. Most coalitions (93%) were reported to have a combination of grass-roots and professional members. As for the formality of the coalitions, 81 percent had a written mission statement and goals, 70 percent had a formal committee structure, and 57 percent had written roles for members. Fewer coalitions had bylaws (16%) or elected leadership (17%).

Nearly all of the coalitions (98%) claimed to have an information and resource sharing function, while most considered advocacy (88%) and planning (83%) as part of their role. Only 55 percent provided training and technical assistance. Most sites reported having either partial (40%) or no funding (44%) for their coalition efforts. Only 16 percent of the coalitions were fully funded. Most of the funding for these coalitions came from a combination of federal, state, and private foundation grants and member contributions.

Coalition Accomplishments and Challenges

As shown in Table 5, the major accomplishment reported by the majority of sites was public awareness and education activities. Immunization events (33%) and collaborating with other agencies (19%) were the next accomplishments most frequently reported. Table 1 also illustrates the major challenges reported, which include maintaining momentum (54%), obtaining adequate funding (32%), evaluating progress (32%), obtaining member participation (30%), implementing strategies (29%), and recruiting a diverse membership (27%).

Conducting Needs Assessments

Excluding the 1995 National Immunization Survey that was conducted by CDC, 46 (55%) of the sites reported conducting an immunization needs assessment. Eleven of 27 (41%) urban sites reported having conducted needs assessments, compared with 36 of 57 (61%) state and territorial sites. However, this difference was not significant ($p = 0.14$, Fisher's Exact test for two proportions). Further, no significant association was found between sites that developed coalitions and sites that conducted needs assessments ($p = 0.3$, chi square). To accomplish needs assessments, respondents reported relying primarily on health department staff (84%), epidemiologists (49%), statisticians (31%), and academic consultants (27%). Table 6 documents the primary problems that were experienced, including accessing existing immunization data (50%), deciding what data were needed (47%), survey and other data collection design (44%), deciding on data collection methods (36%), and analyzing data (33%).

Table 5 Major Accomplishments and Challenges Reported about Immunization Coalitions (n = 56)

Major Accomplishments	n	%
Public awareness and education	42	81
Immunization events	17	33
Collaboration with other agencies	10	19
Planning	10	19
Legislative action	9	17

Major Challenges	n	%
Maintaining momentum	30	54
Obtaining adequate funding	18	32
Evaluating progress	18	32
Obtaining member participation	17	30
Implementing strategies	16	29
Recruiting diverse membership	15	27
Planning and goal setting	13	23
Obtaining effective leaders	12	21

Table 6 Experience Regarding Immunization Needs Assessments

Problems Experienced	n	%
Accessing existing data	18	50
Deciding what data are needed	17	47
Designing surveys, interviews, focus groups	16	44
Deciding on data collection methods	13	36
Analyzing data	12	33
Using data to plan strategies	9	25
Presenting data to community	9	25

Respondent Preferences

The three persons most often designated to attend the Institute training were the survey respondent (79%), the IAP coordinator (80%), and the local coalition member (68%). Most respondents (72%) opted to attend the three early sessions of the Institute (1996 sessions). The topics that respondents were most interested in having included in the training Institute were: social marketing and media advocacy (75%); coalition structures (71%); evaluation of coalition effectiveness (65%) and outcomes (61%); planning a needs assessment (64%); using data to plan strategies (59%); analyzing, interpreting, and presenting data (55%); team building (50%); the art of coalition building (49%); and coalition funding (49%). Most members agreed that networking among participants (89%), lunch roundtable discussions (60%), and guest speakers (82%) would be valuable learning experiences. Directed group discussions (88%) and mini-lectures with visuals (79%) were the learning formats reported to be the most desired by potential attendees.

Implications of Survey Results for Curriculum Development and Planning

The high response rate for this survey, the number of respondents who selected an early Institute date, and the nature of the written comments attested to the need for the Institute. Sixty-nine percent of sites report having an active coalition, and analysis showed that urban sites were more likely to have immunization coalitions than state sites. The experience of members at the Institute revealed that grass-roots development and ongoing maintenance of coalitions were more easily accomplished in smaller geographic areas and within local and familiar networks.

However, the effectiveness of these coalitions remains to be determined. The high number of participating organizations and the lack of basic structural elements reported by respondents leave the efficacy of such coalitions in doubt. Because most of the coalitions are either partially funded or not funded at all, the question is whether they are able to fulfill roles other than information and resource sharing. This is supported by the fact that most coalitions reported public awareness education, immunization events, and collaboration as their main accomplishments. If coalitions fulfilled the roles of community planning, advocacy, and training, one would expect to find reports of achievement of strategies that matched these roles. The major challenges experienced by the coalitions mirror national trends. The topics selected for training by respondents related to coalition development and maintenance correspond to these challenges.

Although more than half of the sites reported conducting a needs assessment, again, the quality and comprehensiveness were not assessed. The challenges in this area were of the most basic nature—deciding what data to use and how to collect, analyze, and present it to the community—and were verified by the topics of training that were requested. No association was found concerning whether sites that conducted needs assessments were more likely to develop coalitions.

The survey provided a profile of potential Institute participants and helped staff select a roster for each session that represented diversity in terms of geography, training, and experience. Participant expectations were useful in determining the emphasis of each element of the curriculum. The challenges that respondents reported in coalition building and needs assessments were reassessed in course evaluations to make sure that training objectives were met. Likewise, suggestions for course improvement were incorporated into a curriculum redesign.

The Coalition Training Institute

The Institute conducted three sessions for 85 IAP site representatives in 16 states, 13 urban areas, and two territories during 1996. Each Institute session consisted of eight modules that included: The Art of Coalition Building; Empowerment Evaluation; Coalitions and Advocacy; Rapid Needs Assessment (RNA); Clinic Assessment Software Application (CASA) and Methodology; RNA and Community Planning; From Planning to Action; and Funding Your Coalition. An evaluation was completed by participants, faculty, and staff at the conclusion of each Institute session that included an extensive, written participant evaluation and a faculty and staff "out-briefing." The cumulative results of the first-year evaluation follow.

Post-Institute: Participant Evaluation

The participant survey measured participants' opinions on module content and format, quality of teaching, course administration/facilities, and overall satisfaction with the Institute. In addition, several participants wrote comments and addressed concerns related to the Institute. Surveys collected from 78 of 85 (92%) participants demonstrated that the overall stated goal to "provide training and technical transfer to IAP staff and coalition facilitators in order to enhance the effectiveness of LAP coalitions" was met.

Course Content and Outcomes

Participants were asked to rate each module (see Table 7). Ratings for all modules were combined to obtain mean values. Participants reported very favorable responses about the usefulness of the course, with 94 percent agreeing that they would be able to apply the information and skills learned in the course to their coalition activities. Ninety-three percent of the respondents were satisfied with the course and 93 percent would recommend the course to their colleagues. Participants' overall comments pointed out that the course was "organized," "professional," "interesting," "beneficial," and "one of the best workshops I ever attended."

According to Table 3, participants' perceived ability to apply information and skills learned to their coalition activities ranged from 85 percent (CASA Assessment/Methodology module) to 96 percent (Art of Coalition Building, RNA and Community

Table 7 Participant Evaluation of Institute Modules

Module	n	Can Apply Information/ Skills Learned in Course (%)	Satisfied with Course (%)	Would Recommend Course to Colleagues (%)
Art of Coalition Building	78	96	99	99
Empower. Evaluation	77	95	91	90
Coalitions and Advocacy	78	94	90	91
RNA Methods	77	95	97	96
CASA Assessment	76	85	87	86
RNA and Planning	77	96	92	92
From Planning to Action	73	95	95	99
Coalition Funding	66	95	94	92
Mean Response		94	93	93

Planning modules). Reported levels of satisfaction ranged from 87 percent (CASA Assessment and Methodology module) to 99 percent (Art of Coalition Building module). The intention to recommend specific modules to colleagues ranged from 86 percent (CASA Assessment and Methodology module) to 99 percent (Art of Coalition Building, From Planning to Action modules).

The survey also solicited comments from participants about course content that were mostly favorable: "*very* helpful for understanding application of principles," "very useful foundation," "great suggestions and activities to bring back to our coalition," "exceeded my expectations," "information provided in manual and hand-outs was excellent," "amazing amount of information overall," "inspiring," "some activities were superb, especially research round-tables," "common sense, practical information that could be applied effectively," and "appreciated having the coalition volunteers participate." Many participants commented that the content of the Institute was too ambitious for the time allowed: "needed to structure in more time for discussion and interaction" and "frustrated that sessions were packed with too much information." Other constructive criticism included: "needed clearer instructions for some activities," "more emphasis on advocacy," "too much emphasis on staffed coalition model and one that has easy access to professional staff and support," and "would like speakers from coalitions in other localities."

Faculty

Participants rated each instructor and their ratings were combined to obtain mean values. Institute faculty and guest presenters received excellent overall evaluations. Ninety-five percent of the participants stated that faculty presented the material in an understandable fashion and 96 percent stated that faculty demonstrated a thorough knowledge of the subject. Ninety-three percent of the participants reported that faculty invited and stimulated participation. Participants commented that faculty were "organized," and "enthusiastic and knowledgeable." Teaching styles that were highly interactive and structured with exercises were rated more favorably than didactic presentations; roundtable presentations were preferred over lecture format. Specific suggestions to improve the presentations included decreasing the amount of material being presented and allowing more discussion and participant interaction.

Administration and Social Activities

Participants reported that the Institute was "well organized and staffed." Ninety-four percent of respondents found reading materials and other correspondence received prior to their arrival helpful. Seventy-three participants (86%) attended evening social activities and 94 percent highly recommended them for future Institutes.

Faculty and Staff "Out-briefing"

Immediately following the Institute sessions, faculty and staff discussed specific issues related to scheduling, curriculum content, and the training manual. The recommended changes included streamlining modules, eliminating several activities, allowing participants more time to present their coalition successes and challenges, developing concurrent sessions to accommodate the diversity of coalitions and needs assessment experiences, and using CINCH members as facilitators during more modules. These recommendations and survey results help faculty and staff continually prepare for upcoming Institutes.

In addition, a follow-up survey was mailed to participants four months after the Institute to determine the impact of the training on technology transfer as well as coalition development and effectiveness. The survey was modeled after Ottoson's work on applying innovations learned in continuing education programs for the Center for Substance Abuse Prevention (CSAP).[23] Ottoson reported that such programs must spend as much time preparing participants for application as in helping them to understand the innovation itself. "Limited resources, responses of others, the nature of the participant's job and organizational structure, taken separately or in combination, have the potential to influence application."[23] In innovations as complex as coalition development and needs assessment, these and other factors may influence whether or not assessments are actually done and whether coalitions succeed.

Conclusion

The Institute completed its first year successfully. Seven other sessions will have been completed by 1998. Final results from course evaluation follow-up surveys and focus groups of participants will be forthcoming. The Institute is based on the premise that building and maintaining coalitions is difficult; but when established, coalitions offer a creative, citizen-based resource to solve health problems. Training focuses on needs assessment, coalition development, community planning, and implementation and evaluation of strategies to improve immunization education, access, and delivery. The sessions model the work of successful local and statewide coalitions, while promoting community capacity-building and empowerment. Because the issues facing state coalitions differ from those facing local coalitions, the Institute faculty focus on those differences and tailor the training to meet the unique needs of participants.

Even though the focus of this training is on immunization coalitions, participants are expected to apply the primary lessons learned to other coalition efforts. Underimmunization is a case example of a problem that can be solved by using a coalition as an innovative public health approach. After a community coalition develops the competency to address a single health problem, it may focus on multiple issues or even broaden its geographic scope.

The Institute has answered the call to provide timely, practical training that creates viable public and private partnerships. This training responds to the Joint Council of Governmental Public Health Agencies' recommendation for "community organization, outreach, and development, as well as an emphasis on empowerment and coalition building, which together will help keep communitywide approaches to improved health at the forefront of the public health agenda."[22(p.65)]

REFERENCES

1. Public Health Service. *Healthy People 2000: National Health Promotion and Disease Prevention Objectives.* DHHS Publication No. PHS91-50213.Washington, D.C.: U.S. Department of Health and Human Services, 1991.

2. Centers for Disease Control and Prevention. National, State and Urban Area Vaccination Coverage Levels among Children Aged 19–35 Months—United States, April 1994–March 1995. *Morbidity and Mortality Weekly Report* 45, no. 7 (1996): 145–150.

3. Bernier, R. Toward a More Population-Based Approach to Immunization: Fostering Private- and Public-Sector Collaboration. *American Journal of Health Promotion* 84 (1994): 1,567–1,568.

4. McLeroy, K., et al. An Ecological Perspective on Health Promotion Programs. *Health Education Quarterly* 15 (1988): 351–377.

5. Winett, R.A. A Framework for Health Promotion and Disease Prevention Programs. *American Psychologist* 50 (1995): 341–350.

6. Butterfoss, F.D., et al. Community Coalitions for Health Promotion and Disease Prevention. *Health Education Res: Theory and Practice* 8, no. 3 (1993): 315–330.

7. Pentz, M., et al. A Multi-Community Trial for Primary Prevention of Adolescent Drug Abuse: Effects on Drug Use Prevalence. *JAMA* 261 (1989): 3,259–3,266.

8. Mittelmark, M.B., et al. Realistic Outcomes: Lessons from Community-Based Research and Demonstration Programs for the Prevention of Cardiovascular Diseases. *Journal of Public Health Policy* 14 (1993): 437–462.

9. National Immunization Program (NIP), Centers for Disease Control. U.S. Childhood Immunization Initiative Accelerates Goals. *Immunize Action News,* December 27 (1993): 1–2.

10. Kaye, G., and Wolff, T. *From the Ground Up: A Workbook on Coalition Building and Community Development.* Amherst, MA: AHEC Community Partners, 1995.

11. Florin, P., et al. Identifying Technical Assistance Needs in Community Coalitions. *Health Education Res: Theory and Practice* 8, no. 3 (1993): 417–432.

12. Goodman, R.M., et al. A Critique of Contemporary Community Health Promotion Approaches: Based on a Qualitative Review of Six Programs in Maine. *American Journal of Health Promotion* 7, no. 3 (1993): 208–221.

13. Goodman, R.M., and Wandersman, A. Forecast: A Formative Approach to Evaluating Community Coalitions and Community-Based Initiatives. *American Journal of Community Psychology,* Monograph Series, CSAP special issue (1994): 6–25.

14. Butterfoss, F.D., et al. The Plan Quality Index: A Consultation and Feedback Tool for Improving the Quality of Community Plans. In *Empowerment Evaluation: Knowledge and Tools for Self-Assessment and Accountability,* eds. Fetterman, D., et al. Thousand Oaks, CA: Sage Publications, Inc., 1995.

15. Butterfoss, F.D., et al. Community Coalitions for Prevention and Health Promotion: Factors Predicting Satisfaction, Participation and Planning. *Health Education Quarterly* 23, no. 1 (1996): 65–79.

16. Butterfoss, F.D., et al. CINCH: An Urban Coalition for Empowerment and Action. *Health Education and Health Behavior* 25, no. 2 (1998): 212–225.

17. Morrow, A., et al. A Population-Based Study of Access Barriers to Immunization among Urban Virginia Children Served by Public, Private, and Military Health Care Systems. *Pediatrics,* 1998: 101–102.

18. McLeroy, K.R., et al. Community Coalitions for Health Promotion: Summary and Further Reflections. *Health Education Res: Theory and Practice* 8, no. 3 (1994): 417–432.

19. Florin, P., et al. A Systems Approach to Understanding and Enhancing Grassroots Organizations: The Block Booster Project. In *Analysis of Dynamic Psychological Systems. Vol. 2: Methods and Applications,* eds. Levine, R.L., and Fitzgerald, H.E. New York: Plenum Press, 1987.

20. Butterfoss, F.D., et al. Coalition Development: A Tale of Two Cities. Unpublished manuscript.

21. Hlady, W.G., et al. Use of Modified Cluster Sampling Method To Perform Rapid Needs Assessment after Hurricane Andrew. *Annals of Emergency Medicine* 23 (1994): 719–725.

22. Weisner, P.J., et al. Taking Training Seriously: A Policy Statement on Public Health Training by the Joint Council of Governmental Public Health Agencies. *Journal of Public Health Management Practice* 1, no. 4 (1995): 60–69.

23. Ottoson, J.M. After the Applause: Exploring Multiple Influences on Application Following an Adult Education Program. *Adult Education Quarterly* 47, no. 2 (1997): 92–107.

RECOMMENDATIONS FOR COMMUNITY-BASED EFFORTS TO REDUCE YOUTH VIOLENCE IN LOW-INCOME URBAN COMMUNITIES*

The following recommendations are based on data gathered from young people in the South Bronx, a poor urban community in New York City. Sources of data include a street survey, five focus groups, interviews with incarcerated young males, and observations of several youth programs.

The recommendations are drawn from the comments of young people in the focus groups, the suggestions of the community advisory board based on its review of the study findings, and the researchers' experience in developing and evaluating youth programs. The recommendations can best be seen as hypotheses that require further testing by intervention research. In addition, since the objective of this work was to understand youth violence in the South Bronx, those in other areas will need to investigate the specific dynamics of violence in their communities.

Violence Prevention Programs Need To Strengthen the Specific Protective Factors and Reduce the Specific Risk Factors for Violence That Young People Identify in Their Own Communities

The young people in these studies identified several factors that they believe protect them against violence and other factors that increase their vulnerability. These are summarized in Table 4.

It is noteworthy that many of the major influences in their lives—family, peers, school, and neighborhood—were described as both protective and risk factors. This dual character of what should be the stable foundations of adolescent life making coming of age in low-income urban neighborhoods especially difficult. Other elements such as gangs, weapons, and the police played both positive and negative roles in relation to violence, further complicating the task of safely reaching adulthood.

Most interventions to reduce youth violence fall into two categories: (1) hard approaches, such as more police, stiffer sentences for juveniles, and curfews, and (2) soft interventions, such as conflict resolution, after-school programs, sports and recreation programs, and support groups for victims of violence. While each of these approaches has a role to play in reducing violence, none seems to adequately address the complexity or pervasiveness of violence described by young people themselves.

Moreover, existing programs do not always adequately assess the protective mechanisms young people describe using themselves, nor do they develop specific strategies to reduce the risks they identify (e.g., abusive parents, violent or disrespectful police, a popular culture that sometimes celebrates male violence against women). One solution may lie in helping young people to find safe yet realistic alternatives to the protection that a gang or an accessible weapon is perceived to offer.

The participants in these studies identified ways that adults and institutions failed to protect them adequately. Parents warned them against strangers instead of family members or friends, schools taught conflict resolution skills that did not address the scope or magnitude of violence in their lives, community organizations could not always provide them with safe space or consistent adult relationships. If vio-

Table 8 Protective and Risk Factors for Violence Identified by Young People

Factor	Protective Mechanisms	Risk Mechanisms
Family/parents	Provide support, encouragement, and safety, and set limits	Abuse or neglect children, fail to protect against real threats, overprotect leading to dangerous rebellion, overwhelmed by other responsibilities
Friends/peers	Provide emotional support, offer safety against other youth	Tease and taunt leading to fights, pull into turf or other battles
Youth programs	Offer safer places, relationships with caring adults, and opportunities to try new activities	Fail to ensure safe place, fail to provide skills needed to avoid violence
Schools	Provide safer space	Fail to provide skills needed to avoid violence, fail to engage youth, leading to involvement in risk behavior and risk environments
Gangs	Provide protection	Attack some young people, media hype on gangs leads schools and police to overreact provoking disrespect of youth and possible violence
Mass media	Expose young people to ideas and images outside their own community	Reinforce disrespect for females, portrays young men of color as enemy, making them possible targets of violence, reinforce images of romance that increase young women's vulnerability
Drugs and Alcohol		Increase parental abuse or neglect, can lead to sexual victimization, create violence through drug trade, elicit police response threatening community safety
Police	Help to reduce crime and violence	Harass or assault young people, making victims reluctant to report crime because of fear they will be harassed or response will be excessive
Weapons	Provide feeling of safety, protect against violence	Increase threat of retaliation from others, increase risk of serious criminal charges

lence prevention programs are to achieve sustainable reductions in violence, they must address the real threats that young people experience, not those imagined by adults.

Develop Interventions That Address Both the Shared and the Gender-Specific Needs of Adolescent Males and Females

Practitioners in the field now realize that young women need youth programs that address their specific needs and create safe spaces for them. Other work has focused on the importance of helping young men to develop attitudes and behaviors that support both positive male identities and gender justice.

These findings suggest that young men and women share certain important characteristics with respect to violence: high rates of exposure, victimization, and perpetration of various forms of violence; negative attitudes toward the police and school-based violence prevention programs, and feelings of not being respected by adult authorities. However, male and female adolescents experience violence differently: Violence against young women is more associated with intimate relationships than it is for young men, and young women's concepts of romance and heterosexual relationships play a role in their vulnerability to violence.

For young people, violence is not a single phenomenon but rather a continuum of behaviors and attitudes. Effective violence prevention programs need to deconstruct the meaning of different forms of violence and address the gender-specific dimensions of each form, sometimes separately for young women and men, at other times integrating the two.

In one agency, for example, the goal may be to reduce sexual harassment of young women so they can participate fully in existing activities, whereas in another agency, the goal may be to create specific programs to attract girls. All violence prevention programs need to help young men and women analyze the role of the media in shaping attitudes on gender and violence and to combat messages that encourage violence against women.

Analyze the Specific Causes and Consequences of Different Forms of Violence in the Lives of the Young People Served by a Youth Program in Order To Address Each Adequately

Violence was a regular refrain in the lives of most young people who participated in these studies, but it played different roles in the lives of different groups of young people. In our studies, age, gender, and family issues played out differently in different settings.

For some of the incarcerated young men, for example, parental drug or alcohol use made it difficult or unsafe for them to return home after release from jail, increasing the chances that they would be exposed to violence on the streets. Parental drug treatment or safe transitional housing may be the best protection against additional violence for this group.

Young women in the focus groups reported that they sometimes turned to older male partners to avoid the immaturity of their male peers. Providing access to older female role models may help these young women to assess the risks and benefits of older partners more carefully.

Assessing experiences by setting, category of violence, and types of perpetrators and victims can help program planners to map the ecology of youth violence in the specific communities where they work. This approach may help to ground interventions in the circumstances of a particular population or neighborhood and to make them more effective in achieving their objectives.

Assist Youth Programs To Offer Young People Meaningful Relationships with Adults Who Care, a Safe Space To Explore Options, and Opportunities To Connect with a Wider World

Focus group participants articulated what they wanted from a youth program: stable and caring adults, a safe place to explore new ideas and activities, and opportunities to investigate the world outside their community. Each confirms basic principles of youth development; put together, they provide for a youth program in which young people can begin to gain the skills and confidence needed to reduce their risk of violence in the home, school, and community.

Some young people find the resources to help them reach adulthood safely within their family or school but, as our data show, others do not. Youth programs have the potential to offer such support to young people. However, a variety of factors made it difficult for some youth programs to achieve this basic goal. In one setting, for example, the lack of structured activities provided few alternatives to the teasing, bullying, and play fighting. Limited resources, changing priorities on the part of public and private funders, and the resulting high staff turnover can make it difficult for youth agencies in low-income urban communities to respond to young people's needs effectively.

Public health professionals can help community-based agencies to strengthen their programs for youth by helping to develop structured, comprehensive interventions, create and sustain an environment in which violence and harassment are not accepted; and establish linkages with other health-promoting organizations inside and outside the community. Equally important, public health workers can help youth organizations to create or join coalitions to advocate for the public resources needed to protect youth from violence. These include support for comprehensive youth programs, job training, and preparation for and access to quality secondary and higher education.

Finally, we believe that these studies suggest alternative approaches to working with communities to analyze and address problems such as youth violence. Some of the methods we used were as follows:

- creating forums in which young people and staff of youth organizations can articulate their perspectives on violence
- involving youth and community residents in planning and interpreting studies
- selecting targeted samples that provide information about various aspects of violence and young people
- analyzing data collected for other purposes to shed light on the topic of interest
- using long-term relationships with the community to gain access to the variety of settings in which youth can be found
- designing several low-cost, short-term studies to produce useful results within a reasonable time frame

Research of this type is not a substitute for more systematic or longitudinal studies. It does, however, offer the opportunity to understand a problem from the perspectives of those it affects and to engage key stakeholders in creating solutions to one of the most pressing social problems facing low-income urban communities.

6

Creating and Tailoring Effective Materials

Considerations for Material Development

Message Construction 444
Educational Materials Review Form 446
Sizing Up Program Resources for Material
   Development 448
Promotion Options: Action-Oriented
   Exercises 449
Promotion Options: Visual Materials 451
Promotion Options: Audiovisual
   Materials 452

Material Adaptation and Production

Adapting Existing Materials 453
How To Make Print Materials Easier To
   Read 459
How To Choose the Right Reading Level
   for Educational Materials 460
Rapid Estimate of Adult Literacy in
   Medicine 461
REALM Word List 465
Checklist for Health Education Methods
   and Materials for Low-Literacy
   Patients 466
Ten Tips on Graphics, Design, and
   Color 467
How To Reprint Camera-Ready
   Materials 468
How To Write a Brochure 469
How To Design and Produce a
   Newsletter 472

How To Write a Discussion Guide 478
Sample Discussion Guide 482
Tips for Web Site Design 483

Pretesting

Six Methods of Pretesting 486
Applicability of Pretesting Methods 489
What Pretesting Can and Cannot Do 490

Reaching Low-Literate Audiences

Getting To Know Your Low-Literate
   Audience 492
How To Write for Adults with Limited
   Reading Skills 493
Developing Low-Literacy Materials:
   Questions and Answers 504
Checklist: Key Principles of Effective
   Low-Literacy Print Materials 508
Pretesting Low-Literacy Materials 509

Sample Program Materials

Heart-Healthy Eating Self-Contract 515
Check Your Healthy Heart IQ 516
Check Your Weight and Heart
   Disease IQ 519
Check Your High Blood Pressure
   Prevention IQ 521

On the Teen Scene: Preventing STDs 523

STD Facts 525

How To Use a Condom 526

Condom Labels 527

Community-Based Immunization Clinic
Supplies Checklist 528

Screening Questionnaire for Child and
Teen Immunization 530

Understanding the Screening
Questionnaire for Child and Teen
Immunization 531

Vaccine Administration Record for
Children and Teens 533

Immunizations for Babies 534

After the Shots...What To Do If Your
Child Has Discomfort 535

Questions Parents Ask about Baby
Shots 537

Screening Questionnaire for Adult
Immunization 539

Understanding the Screening Questionnaire
for Adult Immunization 540

Vaccine Administration Record for
Adults 542

4-Month Baby Shots 543

6-Month Baby Shots 544

12- and 15-Month Baby Shots 545

18-Month Baby Shots 546

Chapter 6

Creating and Tailoring Effective Materials

OBJECTIVES

At the completion of this chapter, the reader will

- understand the development of health education and promotion materials
- be able to adapt and produce health education materials
- be knowledgeable about pretesting methods
- appreciate the need to reach low-literate audiences
- be aware of the techniques used to develop low-literacy materials

INTRODUCTION

This chapter examines creating and tailoring materials for your community health program. It begins with an overview of those considerations that must be addressed before material development. You may want to adapt or produce your own materials and this too is explained. If you choose to produce your own or to adapt already developed material, pretesting is essential. The chapter includes a section on not only pretesting for applicability to your audience, but also an in-depth discussion for reaching low-literate audiences. Finally, sample program materials are made available to you.

Handouts, pamphlets, and brochures are the main method of communicating with your clients. When little time is available to talk with them or explain the contents of a handout, it is essential that the material be tailored to the audience you seek to impress with your message. The materials you use not only reflect on your agency and you, but they also convey your message in a short period of time. Therefore, your message must be compact and at a grade level that your clients can understand. This chapter provides numerous examples of materials that have been tested in agencies and can be used by your agency. It also supplies the principles supporting their use or to support the development of your own materials. The chapter will meet the needs of both the expert health educator and the novice looking for concrete guidelines about creating and adapting effective materials.

MESSAGE CONSTRUCTION*

Both the channel and the purpose of communicating health information influence message design. Information may be designed to convey new facts, alter attitudes, change behavior, or encourage participation in decision making. Some of these purposes overlap; often they are progressive. That is, for persuasion to work, the public must first receive information, then understand it, believe it, agree with it, and then act upon it. Regardless of the purpose, messages must be developed with consideration of the desired outcome. Factors that help determine public acceptance include:

- **Clarity**—Messages must clearly convey information to ensure the public's understanding and to limit the chances for misunderstanding or inappropriate action. Clear messages contain as few technical/scientific/bureaucratic terms as possible and eliminate information that the audience does not need in order to make necessary decisions (such as unnecessarily detailed explanations). Readability tests can help determine the reading level required to understand drafted material and help writers to be conscientious about the careful selection of words and phrases.
- **Consistency**—In an ideal world there would be scientific consensus on the meaning of new health findings, and all messages on a particular topic would be consistent. Unfortunately, consistency is sometimes elusive. Experts tend to interpret new health data differently, making consensus among government, industry, health institutions, and public interest groups difficult.
- **Main points**—The main points should be stressed, repeated, and never hidden within less strategically important information.
- **Tone and appeal**—A message should be reassuring, alarming, challenging, or straightforward, depending on the desired impact and the target audience. Messages should also be truthful, honest, and as complete as possible.
- **Credibility**—The spokesperson and source of the information should be believable and trustworthy.
- **Public need**—For a message to break through the "information clutter" of society, messages should be based on what the target audience perceives as most important to them, what they want to know, and not what is most important to or most interesting to the originating agency.

---

*Source: *Making Health Communication Programs Work: A Planner's Guide*, NIH Publication #92-1493, U.S. Department of Health and Human Services, Public Health Service, National Institutes of Health, Office of Cancer Communications, National Cancer Institute, April 1992.

Health messages should be drafted with consideration of these factors. Prior to final production, messages should be pretested with the target audiences (and in some cases with channel "gatekeepers") to ensure public understanding and other intended responses.

NOTES:

Educational Materials Review Form

```
Accession No.:
_____

Date:
_____

Screener:
_____
```

I. PRODUCT DESCRIPTION

Title of Product _____   Publication Date _____

Producer/Author _____   Contact _____

Organization _____

Address _____

_____   Phone _____

Other Sponsors/Endorsers _____

Format:

__ Fact Sheet   __ PSA
__ Brochure   __ Magazine
__ Booklet   __ Article
__ Book   __ Performance
__ Poster   __ Taped Message
__ Print Ad   __ Newsletter
__ ¾" Video   __ Contest
__ VHS Video   __ Workbook
__ 16mm Film   __ Curriculum
__ Slides   __ Classroom
__ Audiotape   Material
__ Script   __ Comic Book
__ Information Package
__ Software
__ Other (describe):

_____

Length: _____

Context(s): (Check all that apply)

__ Part of a Program (describe):

_____

__ With Other Materials
__ Stands Alone
__ Has Training Component
   (please enclose)

Topic(s): (check all that apply)
__ Alcohol
__ Drugs
__ Drug (specify) _____
__ Both Alcohol and Drugs
__ Awareness
__ Prevention
__ Intervention
__ Treatment
__ General Health/Safety
__ Other (describe)

_____

Mode(s) of Delivery:
   (check all that apply)
__ Individual
__ Group
__ Instructor-led
__ Mass Media
__ Self-Instructional

Setting(s): (check all that apply)
__ Home
__ School
__ Community
__ Health/Mental Health Care
__ Worksite
__ Justice System
__ Social Services System
__ Mass Media
__ Other (describe):

_____

Target Audience(s):
   (check all that apply)

__ General Public
__ Parents
   (specify age of child) _____
__ Blacks
__ Hispanics
__ Native Americans
__ Asian and Pacific Islanders
__ Health Care Providers
   (specify specialty)

_____

__ High-Risk Families/Youth
__ Policymakers/Administrators
__ Youth (specify ages)
__ Young Adults (18–25 years)
__ Educators
   (specify grade[s]) _____
__ A/D Treatment Professionals
__ A/D Prevention Professionals
__ Employers
__ Scientists and Researchers
__ Other (describe):

_____

Language(s): (check all that apply)

__ English
__ Spanish
__ Bilingual (specify) _____
__ Other (indicate) _____

continues

Educational Materials Review Form continued

Readability:
__ Low Literacy (grade level 3–5)
__ Very Easy (grade level 6–7)
__ Easy (8)
__ Average (9–10)
__ Fairly Difficult (11–13)
__ Difficult (14–16)
__ N/A

Pretested/Evaluated:

__ Yes   __ Unknown
__ No
(If yes, describe and include copy of
report if possible) _____
_____

Current Scope:

__ National: _____
__ Regional: _____
__ State: _____
__ Local: _____

Availability:

__ Unknown
__ Restrictions on Use:
__ Permission Required to
   Reproduce
__ Citation Required
__ Available Free

__ Negatives Available on Loan
__ Payment Required
__ Price $_____
__ Available through Free A-V
   Loan Program
Source (if different from above)
_____
_____
_____
_____
_____
_____
_____
_____

Description: (Please describe the product in two-three sentences.)

_____
_____
_____
_____
_____

Comments: _____
_____
_____
_____
_____
_____

Source: *Making Health Communication Programs Work: A Planner's Guide*, NIH Publication #92-1493, U.S. Department of Health and Human Services, Public Health Service, National Institutes of Health, Office of Cancer Communications, National Cancer Institute, April 1992. Courtesy of the Office for Substance Abuse Prevention, ADAMHA.

Sizing Up Program Resources for Material Development

The checklist below describes some resource considerations for developing original materials, which includes examining existing materials to make sure they cannot be made more appropriate. Although financial resources are listed first, they are not necessarily the most important. A program may have very little money but may have talented and dedicated staff and community members who can create materials.

FINANCIAL

☐ What program funds are available for materials development?

☐ Are there other sources of money (i.e., grants, donations, other programs)?

EXISTING MATERIALS

☐ What publications, videos, fact sheets, or other materials are available that would be appropriate?

☐ What materials have been developed by others that would be appropriate?

☐ What materials can be adapted for the intended audience?

STAFF

☐ Who on the staff has actually developed materials?

☐ Who are the creative people on the staff?

☐ Who is artistic?

☐ Who writes well and appropriately?

☐ Who is interested in working on the project?

☐ Who can devote the time to materials development?

MEMBERS OF THE INTENDED AUDIENCE

☐ Who has experience in developing materials?

☐ Who can help develop design, layout, artwork, and wording?

☐ Who is artistic and is able to design appropriate artwork?

☐ Who writes well and appropriately?

☐ Who is interested?

☐ Who has time to work on the project?

COMMUNITY CONTACTS

☐ What other community resources would be helpful?

☐ Are there agencies that will illustrate, print, or produce the materials?

☐ Do members of the staff or intended audience know who to contact at each community resource or agency?

Source: AMC Cancer Research Center, *Beyond the Brochure: Alternative Approaches to Effective Health Communication*, U.S. Department of Health and Human Services, Public Health Service, Centers for Disease Control and Prevention (CDC), Atlanta, Georgia 30333, 1994.

Promotion Options: Action-Oriented Exercises

Type	Benefits	Limitations
Role play	<ul><li>Can bring learning close to real life.</li><li>Requires few props or special objects. Learners can represent objects through pantomime.</li><li>Useful for developing practical and social skills.</li><li>Requires learners to combine a range of skills and understanding.</li><li>Stimulates discussions.</li></ul>	<ul><li>Used exclusively in a group session. More than one person takes part in the role play itself, and an audience group watches the role play and participates in the discussion.</li><li>Requires a well-trained facilitator.</li><li>May become too real and too emotional for participants, and as such, becomes a barrier to participation.</li><li>Requires audience participation in a group activity. Audience members must feel comfortable being in front of a group.</li></ul>
Theater	<ul><li>Brings people together, including those who do not typically go to meetings or health talks.</li><li>Provides entertainment. Holds people's attention and makes them think.</li><li>Realistic if based on true, personal stories and experiences.</li><li>Presents information and encourages discussion about sensitive issues. Learners watch others who are "just like us" perform on stage and discuss topics that are not typically discussed in the community.</li><li>Draws people's emotions, which can motivate behavior change. Real people are up on stage, talking about and acting out real experiences and feelings.</li></ul>	<ul><li>Requires rehearsals and thus a large time commitment.</li><li>Keeping the theater troupe together and managing it can be difficult and time intensive. Theater productions are often performed more than once by the same group of actors.</li><li>Recruitment of community participants may be difficult. Acting requires performing in front of groups, and this may be uncomfortable for some people.</li></ul>
Song	<ul><li>Easy for most people to remember songs and rhymes.</li><li>Can be very up-beat and positive.</li><li>Does not require reading or writing skills.</li><li>Requires few resources to develop.</li><li>Effective for reaching communities with oral traditions.</li></ul>	<ul><li>Requires someone skilled in song writing to write lyrics and music.</li><li>Requires recording equipment if song is to be recorded for broadcasting.</li><li>Requires someone willing and able to lead a group in song if it is to be learned by the audience.</li></ul>
Storytelling	<ul><li>May take less preparation time than other forms of action-oriented exercises. Learners can tell their own stories that are related to the topic of discussion.</li><li>Can teach lessons through the use of parables. Parables are often used as traditional methods of learning among communities that have a strong oral tradition.</li><li>Avoids confronting learners with inadequate knowledge. Allows learners to identify with story characters who find solutions to the similar personal problems.</li><li>Can be used by learners to gain confidence in themselves and pride in their own culture.</li></ul>	<ul><li>Requires a group setting and a trained facilitator.</li><li>Can be time consuming. It takes time to develop and describe characters, problems, actions, and solutions.</li><li>Requires a storyteller who is sensitive to and aware of community patterns, customs, beliefs, and traditions.</li></ul>

continues

Promotion Options: Action-Oriented Exercises continued

Type	Benefits	Limitations
Games	• Provide entertainment. • Encourage interaction among the learners, providing peer support. • Can involve a group of participants of different ages.	• Use of symbols must be handled carefully. Symbols often have specific meanings in different cultures. • Require audience participation.

NOTES:

Source: AMC Cancer Research Center, *Beyond the Brochure: Alternative Approaches to Effective Health Communication,* U.S. Department of Health and Human Services, Public Health Service, Centers for Disease Control and Prevention (CDC), Atlanta, Georgia 30333, 1994.

Promotion Options: Visual Materials

Type	Benefits	Limitations
Poster	Stands alone. May be distributed and posted in a variety of settings.	Typically informational and does not generally influence behavior change.
Flipchart	Tells a story or teaches skills in a step-by-step manner. May be used as a guide for presentations by trained facilitators.	Requires a trained facilitator. Not appropriate for larger audiences.
Talk board	Enables learners to share experiences through the telling of a story.	Requires a trained facilitator. Can be time intensive because of the experiential-based interaction that use creates.
Real objects and models	Make concepts and ideas easy to understand.	Require creativity to make objects, funding to buy objects.
Display board	Involves the learner.	Transport can be cumbersome.
Fotonovela	Entertaining, often shared with family members. Portrays real-life situations and emotional, sensitive, and private subjects.	Not appropriate for large-group presentations. Individuals should read the booklet on their own. Group discussions can be conducted based on the story presented.

NOTES:

Source: AMC Cancer Research Center, *Beyond the Brochure: Alternative Approaches to Effective Health Communication*, U.S. Department of Health and Human Services, Public Health Service, Centers for Disease Control and Prevention (CDC), Atlanta, Georgia 30333, 1994.

Promotion Options: Audiovisual Materials

Type	Benefits	Limitations
Videotapes	• Can include issues and topics that are culturally acceptable to the intended audience. The language, dialect, characters, and scenery used in a videotape can help the viewer to identify with the message or story being conveyed. • Can be used in group settings when appropriate equipment is available. • Distribution may be simplified because of common access to videocassette recorders (VCRs) in homes, schools, and libraries. • Can be used as "triggers" for group discussion. • Can help viewers to feel comfortable stating their feelings on topics without personalizing their comments.	• Are expensive to produce. Many learners are exposed to high-quality video media, which places a demand for high-quality videotapes. • Require production equipment. • Require VCR and monitor to use. Videotapes are appropriate only in certain environments where the viewer has time to watch the video and perhaps discuss it with a facilitator. • Can be "tuned-out" by viewer. Continuously running videotapes are sometimes ignored by clients in waiting rooms. • Collaboration with production companies can be difficult. They may have a different agenda than that of a health professional. • Require a trained facilitator if used as a "trigger" for discussion.
Slide-tape programs	• Appeal to both hearing and visual senses. • Do not rely on the printed word to get message across. • Can be used in conjunction with workbooks. • Can use sound effects to enhance message. • Can use local language, dialects, accents, and references that enhance the listener's ability to identify with the message contained on the tape. • Use of visuals can be specific to the intended audience to enhance viewers' identification with the message. • Can be stopped periodically to allow viewer time to absorb information presented or for discussion opportunities. • Can be used in a group setting or as a stand-alone.	• Are less sophisticated than videotapes, so audiences may be less satisfied with them. • Require an automatic advance slide projector and screen. • Use still photography and therefore are not as engaging as videotapes. • Updating can be time consuming if both slides and audio portions of the slide-tape program must be changed. • Can be "tuned-out" by viewer.
Interactive multimedia programs	• Can be fun to use. Learners may feel they are receiving computer training as they use the program. • Provide learner opportunity to choose topics or receive responses to questions, which enhances thought processing and motivation to continue with the lesson. • Are usually self-instructional, and require minimal staff support. • Can incorporate new technology: graphics, photographs, movies, and music, which are likely to entice users to investigate the program.	• Require self-motivated learners to approach and use the program. • Require some computer literacy on the user's part. • May not provide the help the learner needs if placed in an unstaffed kiosk or station. • Can be damaged by inappropriate use. • Require technical skills in development. • Require a secure location to prevent theft.

Source: AMC Cancer Research Center, *Beyond the Brochure: Alternative Approaches to Effective Health Communication*, U.S. Department of Health and Human Services, Public Health Service, Centers for Disease Control and Prevention (CDC), Atlanta, Georgia 30333, 1994.

ADAPTING EXISTING MATERIALS*

Public health initiatives generate massive quantities and types of materials. Many agencies have accumulated stockpiles, and most professionals can readily tap someone else's cache by picking up the telephone.

Most new program initiatives thus begin with vows to "not reinvent the wheel" and to use or adapt existing materials—only to conclude along the way that nothing in existence will quite do, for any number of reasons. To colleagues outside the program, some of these reasons seem quite sound, but usually it is unclear why new material was needed.

In fact, though, few materials have been designed for low-literate or oral-culture audiences, and the truth may be that nothing available is quite right for a specific audience and locale in this category. Decision making then turns to adapting an existing piece of material versus starting from scratch.

Adaptation generally requires less time and fewer resources than starting from the beginning. Often, a piece of the material contains some useful information but is not written at an appropriate reading level or contains too many concepts. Or it may contain suitable visuals or graphics, or a unique approach to presentation, without the appropriate message. The hard work that went into developing such materials can be enhanced by adapting them to meet the needs of a new audience.

When considering adaptation of all or parts of a piece of educational material, the following questions may be useful:

- Do the concepts and messages help meet the program's learning objectives?
- Does the material fit the audience's learning style (i.e., oral, written, visual, audiovisual)?
- Is the content limited to a few concepts that help identify the key messages?
- Are concepts presented simply in an organized manner?
- Are appropriate culturally specific values and beliefs represented in the messages?
- Are visuals, photographs, and images culturally relevant?
- Do visuals, photographs, and images correspond with the message in a way that is clear to the audience?
- Is text written or narrated at an appropriate reading/comprehension level?

As always, members of the intended audience can help answer these questions and ensure that materials and strategies will work. Audience members already working with the program can provide input; broader input from the intended audience should also be obtained.

When incorporating text or visuals from copyrighted material, permission must be obtained from the original authors or artists. A small fee may be required, but many artists and authors will grant permission to nonprofit organizations free of charge if they receive appropriate credit. Be sure to obtain permission in writing.

---

*Source: AMC Cancer Research Center, *Beyond the Brochure: Alternative Approaches to Effective Health Communication*, U.S. Department of Health and Human Services, Public Health Service, Centers for Disease Control and Prevention (CDC), Atlanta, Georgia 30333, 1994.

Government documents and materials are in the public domain and have no copyright.

Materials and activities generally include three components:

- **Text, Narrative, Captions**—written or spoken language that provides information or instruction about the topic or the use of the material/activity. Some materials contain only the written word (e.g., brochures) or narrative (e.g., audiotapes), and some contain both (e.g., games, videotapes).
- **Visuals**—photographs, cartoons, drawings, images, graphics, and other representations of people, places, and things that communicate a message or action to the viewer.
- **Format**—the style and amount of "white space" (or empty space) in a piece of material; the sequence of events and length of time of an activity.

The following guidelines may be useful in adapting materials to become appropriate for a program and its audience. The questions can help identify specific areas that need modification. (These questions are provided as examples of issues to be explored through focus groups, in-depth interviews, or other pretesting methods.)

Text, Narrative, Captions

1. *Examine the Messages or Content*

Determine whether the material contains too many concepts. Each paragraph should contain just one message or action. Consider the following:

- Are the concepts accurate?
- Do the messages provide too little, too much, or adequate information?
- Are the concepts presented in logical order?
- Are the concepts and their sequence appropriate for the audience?

Include only a few concepts and only information that enables the user to follow the message.

2. *Examine How the Text or Narrative Is Written*

Text or script should be written with the intended audience in mind. Keep it simple and understandable. Perform a readability test (e.g., SMOG, Fry). Consider the following:

- Is the reading level understandable to the intended audience?
- Does the information use appropriate local idioms?
- Are statements made in an active voice?
- Are statements community specific?
- Is the audience's preferred language used?

Use short sentences and words. Use active language. Use words and phrases familiar to the audience. In narratives, be sure the pace and intonation are appropriate.

3. *Determine Whether Text or Narrative Matches or Corresponds to Visuals*

Visuals should complement, not compete with, text or narrative. They should enhance the message being delivered. Consider the following:

- Does the text/narrative/caption describe what occurs in the visual?
- Do the visuals compete with what is written or spoken?

Use visuals that reinforce text and/or narrative. Visuals should make sense to the audience. Visuals and text should be clearly related.

4. *Determine Whether the Message Is Believable/Credible to the Audience*

When adapting material, the audience's preferences should be known and considered in the selection of the channel used for message delivery. The message source should be known and credible to the audience. Consider the following:

- Is the narrator a respected peer or credible community member?
- Will the audience view the message as believable?
- Is the message suggesting a behavior change that is possible for the audience?

Quote credible spokespeople in written text. Make messages believable and practical. Promote behaviors that are appropriate in the cultural, social, and economic environment.

Inexpensive Options for Adapting Text/Narrative

- Ask some members of the intended audience to write the text/script. Test the results by asking other audience members what they think the main points are and how to make the text and visuals more appropriate and easier to understand.
- When recording a new narrative for a video or radio piece, find a quiet room with good acoustics. Interview a few members of the intended audience with good reading abilities and dramatic skills. Use rented or donated sound equipment. University students, college or local radio stations, drama clubs, or local actors may make good narrators. A university communications laboratory or local radio station may dub in the new soundtrack at little or no cost.

Visuals

1. *Decide Whether Visuals Correspond with Text/Narrative*

Visuals must be culturally appropriate and should enhance the message being delivered, not compete with it. Consider the following:

- Do the visuals correspond to the text without being abstract or cluttered?
- Do the visuals provide additional information about how to adhere to the message being delivered?

Choose photographs, images, or drawings that are clear and easy to understand. Use visuals that show specific examples of the behavior described. Cartoons and drawings should be life-like. Avoid diagrams, graphs, and other complicated visuals. Illustrate only the desired behaviors, not those to be avoided.

2. Illustrate the Important Points

Visuals should highlight only the most important points made in the text, so as not to confuse the learner. Consider the following:

- Do the graphics or photographs illustrate the most important concepts?
- Do the visuals enhance rather than confuse the message?

Limit the number of visuals to emphasize the most important points, and place them in an order that the learner would understand.

3. Represent the Intended Audience and Its Culture

Members of the intended audience must be able to identify with the message. Visuals can assist in this process by reflecting culture and ethnicity. Consider the following:

- Do images of people look like members of the intended audience?
- Do geography and setting represent where the audience lives, works, and plays?
- Are people shown doing things that are realistic in the lives of the audience?
- Are the images familiar and acceptable to members of the audience?

Illustrations should reflect the ethnic and cultural background of the intended audience. Place the people in everyday settings, using familiar belongings and wearing familiar clothes. Show the full body of a person illustrating a behavior. Use symbols that are appropriate and understandable to the audience.

Inexpensive Options for Adapting Visuals

- Ask an artistic member of the intended audience to draw visuals or take photographs. Offer to compensate the person for his or her time and effort.
- Ask advertising or marketing firms to donate photographs or illustrations. Give them credit on the material.
- Seek donated time from local art institutes, university or high school photography or art classes, or local art galleries. Give them credit.
- Use several members of the intended audience, rather than formal focus groups, to determine acceptability of a mock-up with visuals (e.g., find people in a natural gathering place in their community and ask them to review the visual).

Format

1. Make Materials Inviting, Visually Appealing, and Easy To Follow

If the text appears too dense, members of the intended audience are less likely to read it. Visuals and format are also very important in making material appealing. Consider the following:

- Are text and/or visuals clear and easy to read?
- Is the type big enough to be easily read?
- Is the typeface appropriate for the reader?
- Are colors attractive?
- Are people and situations represented realistically for the intended audience?

Use only a few concepts and pages. Leave enough space between text and visuals to allow the eye to move easily from one to the other. Place related messages and illustrations together. Use large type for written text. Typeface with serifs, such as Times Roman and Century Schoolbook, is generally considered easier to read. Use colors appropriate and acceptable to the audience. Use everyday people or situations that represent the audience.

2. Use Quality Materials When Possible

- Are photographs, drawings, or images accurate, up-to-date, and realistic?
- Are props or models realistic?
- Is the weight of paper heavy enough for repeated use?

Use a paper that is thick enough to withstand repeated use (i.e., 20–60 pound bonded paper). Use current and realistic visuals. Incorporate props/models that are used in everyday life.

Inexpensive Options for Adapting Format

- Choose production materials that may be discontinued but for which sufficient stock is available. Order bulk quantities for lower prices.
- Ask local printers, art supply stores, university art departments, university computer departments, or local photography shops to donate or discount supplies.
- Contact high schools, universities, churches, and civic or social organizations for individuals who might be willing to be photographed.
- Ask appropriate organizations or businesses for donated props or models.

Pretesting Adapted Material

Pretesting should be conducted at several stages: planning and strategy selection, concept development, draft review, materials comparison, and final production. Mock-ups (cut and paste) and storyboards are good ways to pretest ideas before creating an expensive final version. Focus groups, in-depth interviews, theater testing, and gatekeeper reviews can also help determine whether the material is acceptable to the intended audience, the general community, and individuals charged with using or distributing the material.

The following case studies illustrate how materials were pretested and adapted to meet the needs of two breast cancer programs.

Case Study #1

In adapting materials for participants in its breast and cervical cancer control program, a state health department started with a low-literacy flyer developed by another organization. The flyer had been pretested using one-on-one interviews and found to be written at an appropriate grade level. However, staff noted that women in the breast and cervical cancer program folded the flyers to fit them in their purses, and many women left the flyers behind in the clinic.

The department adapted the low-literacy flyer by modifying its format but keeping the original text, producing a low-literacy brochure that easily fit into a woman's purse.

Case Study #2

A state health department found that educational print materials were written at too high a reading level and were not culturally appropriate for the older, low-income African American women in its target community. Focus groups were used to identify appropriate communication channels, credible information sources, and the acceptability of breast cancer materials among the target audience. One piece of material reviewed by the focus group was a shower-card illustrating how to do breast self-examination.

Women in the focus groups felt the shower card illustration of a young woman did not represent them, and the wording was too complex. A professional graphic artist was hired to create illustrations of older African American women, and text was simplified. After adaptation, the shower card was acceptable to women in the community.

NOTES:

How To Make Print Materials Easier To Read

Writing about health often requires the use of some technical language. However, the way the message is presented—the writing style, vocabulary, typography, layout, graphics, and color—can favorably affect whether it is read and understood.

Text

Text should be:

- [ ] introduced, stating the purpose to orient the reader
- [ ] summarized at the end to review major points
- [ ] presented in short sentences, short paragraphs
- [ ] broken up with visuals placed to emphasize key points, text as "bullets," and titles or subtitles to reinforce important points
- [ ] written in the active, not passive, voice
- [ ] underlined, boldfaced, or boxed for reinforcement
- [ ] clarified with the use of examples
- [ ] tested for readability
- [ ] tested with the audience
- [ ] explained, if necessary, in a glossary (with key words defined within the sentence)

Try to avoid:

- [ ] jargon and technical terms or phrases
- [ ] abbreviations and acronyms

Graphics

Just as necessary as clear writing is presentation: text that is easy to read and graphics that help the reader understand and remember the text.
Graphics should be:

- [ ] immediately identifiable
- [ ] relevant to the subject matter and reader
- [ ] simple, uncluttered
- [ ] used to reinforce, not compete with the text

Try to avoid:

- [ ] small type (less than 10-point)
- [ ] lines of type that are too long or too short
- [ ] large blocks of print
- [ ] justified right margins
- [ ] photographs that do not reproduce well
- [ ] less than professional-quality drawings (which could make the text appear less credible)
- [ ] technical diagrams

NOTES:

Source: *Making Health Communication Programs Work: A Planner's Guide*, NIH Publication #92-1493, U.S. Department of Health and Human Services, Public Health Service, National Institutes of Health, Office of Cancer Communications, National Cancer Institute, April 1992.

HOW TO CHOOSE THE RIGHT READING LEVEL FOR EDUCATIONAL MATERIALS*

For the general public, writing at the sixth-grade reading level is usually safe. You can check if you're on target by using a readability test such as the SMOG, the Fog-Gunning Index, or the Fry Readability Formula. To determine the approximate reading level of a publication, you need a passage with 30 sentences. Choose 10 consecutive sentences at the beginning, middle, and end of the piece. Count all the words containing three or more syllables (polysyllabic) including repetitions. Then use the SMOG Conversion Chart below to determine the approximate reading level.

Computer programs also are available to measure reading levels. Whichever method you choose, let your professional judgment rather than the test guide your word choices. For example, while a polysyllabic word like "alcohol" increases the readability score of a document, it is familiar and understandable to most people. Conversely, the two-syllable word "triage" is scored as an easy word, although it will be unfamiliar to many readers. Health-related materials often require long, complex words. To keep materials comprehensible, choose simpler words where possible and explain complex words in the test or consider a simple glossary of unfamiliar terms.

SMOG Conversion Chart*

Polysyllabic Word Count	Grade Level	Polysyllabic Word Count	Grade Level
0–2	4	57–72	11
3–6	5	73–90	12
7–12	6	91–110	13
13–20	7	111–132	14
21–30	8	133–156	15
31–42	9	157–182	16
43–56	10	183–210	17
		211–240	18

*Predicts the grade-level difficulty within 1.5 grades, plus or minus.

NOTES:

*Source: Center for Substance Abuse, "Technical Assistance Bulletin: You Can Prepare Easy-To-Read Materials," U.S. Department of Health and Human Services, Public Health Service, Substance Abuse and Mental Health Services Administration, Washington, D.C., September 1994.

Rapid Estimate of Adult Literacy in Medicine

The Rapid Estimate of Adult Literacy in Medicine (REALM) is a screening instrument to assess an adult patient's ability to read common medical words and lay terms for body parts and illnesses. It is designed to assist medical professionals in estimating a patient's literacy level so that the appropriate level of patient education materials or oral instructions may be used. The test takes 2 to 3 minutes to administer and score. The REALM has been correlated with other standardized tests.

	Correlation of REALM with SORT, PIAT-R, and WRAT-R		
	PIAT-R Recognition	SORT	WRAT-R
Correlation Coefficient	.97	.96	.88
p Value	*p*<.0001	*p*<.0001	*p*<.0001

Reliability Studies	
Test-Retest	Inter-Rater
(n = 100)	(n = 20)
.99	.99

ADMINISTRATION AND SCORING

1. Give the patient the laminated copy of the REALM word list. Attach the examiner record form to the clipboard. Hold the clipboard at an angle such that the patient is not distracted by your scoring procedure.

In your own words, introduce the REALM to the patient:

In a research setting or for research purposes:

"It would be helpful for us to get an idea of what medical words you are familiar with. What I need you to do is look at this list of words, beginning here [point to first word with pencil]. Say all of the words you know. If you come to a word you don't know, you can sound it out or just skip it and go on." If the patient stops, say, "Look down this list [point] and say the other words you know."

In a clinical setting:

"Sometimes in this office, we may use medical words that patients aren't familiar with. We would like you to take a look at this list of words to help us get an idea of what medical words you are familiar with. It will help us know what kinds of patient education to give you. Start with the first

continues

Rapid Estimate of Adult Literacy in Medicine continued

word [point to 1st word with pencil], please say all of the words you know. If you come to a word you do not know, you can sound it out or just skip it and go on." If patient stops, do as above.

**Special Note: Do not use the words "read" and "test" when introducing and administering the REALM. These words may make patients feel uncomfortable and unwilling to participate.

"Please <u>say</u> these words for me."

2. If the patient takes more than 5 seconds on a word, encourage the patient to move along by saying,

"Let's try the next word."

If the patient begins to miss every word or appears to be struggling or frustrated, tell the patient,

"Just look down the list and say the words you know."

3. Count as an error any word that is not attempted or mispronounced (see "Special Considerations" for pronunciation/scoring guidelines).

4. Scoring options:

- Place a check mark (√) in the box next to each word the patient pronounces correctly.

OR

- Place an X in the box next to each word the patient does not attempt or mispronounces.

RAPID ESTIMATE OF ADULT LITERACY IN MEDICINE (REALM)©

Terry Davis, PhD • Michael Crouch, MD • Sandy Long, PhD

Reading Level _____

Patient name
Subject # _____   Date of birth _____   Grade completed _____

Date _____   Clinic _____   Examiner _____

List 1	List 2	List 3
√ fat	☐ fatigue	☐ allergic
√ flu	☐ pelvic	X menstrual
☐ pill	☐ jaundice	☐ testicle
☐ dose	☐ infection	X colitis
√ eye	☐ exercise	X emergency
☐ stress	☐ behavior	☐ medication

continues

Rapid Estimate of Adult Literacy in Medicine continued

Scoring should be strict, but take into consideration any problems that could be related to dialect or articulation difficulties. Use the dictionary if in doubt. Count as correct any self-corrected word.

5. Count the number of correct words in each list and record the number in the blank. Total the numbers and record the total score in the "Raw Score" blank. Match the total raw score with its grade equivalent found in the table on the following page.

SPECIAL CONSIDERATIONS FOR ADMINISTRATION AND SCORING

Examiner Sensitivity

Many low literate patients will attempt to hide their deficiency. Ensure that you approach each patient with respect and compassion. You may need to provide encouragement and reassurance.

A positive, respectful attitude is essential for all examiners. (Remember, many people with low literacy feel ashamed.) Be sensitive.

Visual Acuity

If the patient wears glasses, ask him/her to put them on for this test. The REALM is designed to be read by persons with 20/100 vision or better. A large print version of the REALM is available for persons with 20/200 vision, the level of legal blindness.

Pronunciation

Dictionary pronunciation is the scoring standard.

continues

Rapid Estimate of Adult Literacy in Medicine continued

	GRADE EQUIVALENT
Raw Score	**Grade Range**
0–18	3rd Grade and Below Will not be able to read most low-literacy materials; will need repeated oral instructions, materials composed primarily of illustrations, or audio- or videotapes.
19–44	4th to 6th Grade Will need low-literacy materials; may not be able to read prescription labels.
45–60	7th to 8th Grade Will struggle with most patient education materials; will not be offended by low-literacy materials.
61–66	High School Will be able to read most patient education materials.

The REALM KIT is available for $50.00 and includes the REALM manual, 20 Examiner sheets (which may be photocopied), and 4 laminated patient word lists. Materials can also be purchased separately; 4 laminated patient word lists (regular or large print) are $15.00; one tablet of 20 Examiner sheets is $15.00; and the REALM manual is $20.00. Prices are subject to change. If you wish to purchase these items, you may send a request to Terry C. Davis, PhD, LSU Health Science Center, 1501 Kings Highway, Shreveport, LA 71130-3932 or you may call (318) 675-4585.

Source: T. Davis, M. Crouch, S. Long, and K. Green, *Rapid Estimate of Adult Literacy in Medicine: Administration Manual,* © Louisiana State University Medical Center, Shreveport, Louisiana.

REALM Word List

1	2	3
fat	fatigue	allergic
flu	pelvic	menstrual
pill	jaundice	testicle
dose	infection	colitis
eye	exercise	emergency
stress	behavior	medication
smear	prescription	occupation
nerves	notify	sexually
germs	gallbladder	alcoholism
meals	calories	irritation
disease	depression	constipation
cancer	miscarriage	gonorrhea
caffeine	pregnancy	inflammatory
attack	arthritis	diabetes
kidney	nutrition	hepatitis
hormones	menopause	antibiotics
herpes	appendix	diagnosis
seizure	abnormal	potassium
bowel	syphilis	anemia
asthma	hemorrhoids	obesity
rectal	nausea	osteoporosis
incest	directed	impetigo

Source: T. Davis, M. Crouch, S. Long, K. Green, *Rapid Estimate of Adult Literacy in Medicine Administration Manual*, Louisiana State University Health Sciences Center, School of Medicine in Shreveport, Louisiana, © 1993.

Checklist for Health Education Methods and Materials for Low-Literacy Patients

1. Set realistic objective(s).
   - Limit the objective to what the majority of the target population needs now.
   - Use a planning sheet to write down the objective and key points.
2. To change health behaviors, focus on behaviors and skills.
   - Emphasize behaviors and skills rather than facts.
   - Consider placing the key points first and last.
3. Present context first (before giving new information).
   - State the purpose or use for new content information before presenting it.
   - Relate new information to the context of patients' lives.
4. Break down complex instructions.
   - Break instruction into easy-to-understand parts.
   - Provide opportunities for small successes.
5. Make it interactive.
   - Consider including an interaction after each key topic. The patient must write, tell, show, demonstrate, select, or solve a problem.

NOTES:

Source: Cecelia Conrath Doak, Leonard G. Doak, and Jane H. Root, *Teaching Patients with Low Literacy Skills*, ed. 2, Lippincott Williams & Wilkins, © 1996.

Ten Tips on Graphics, Design, and Color

1. Project a consistent image.
   Your marketing materials (flyers, brochures, magnets, posters) should have the same "look." A hodge-podge of materials in different styles and colors will not do much to inspire confidence from your prospects.

2. Avoid trendy graphics.
   Graphics are as fickle as fashion. What's "in" today is "out" tomorrow. Stick to a traditional style that will serve you for 5 years instead of 5 months.

3. A picture is worth more than 1,000 words.
   Not only do we remember pictures longer than copy itself, but we comprehend information better when pictures are used with copy, as they call attention to important points. We also learn faster when pictures are combined with copy. Moral: Use pictures to illustrate your copy.

4. Show off your staff.
   In your promotional materials, consider using photos and mini-biographies of your clinic or outreach staff. Knowing what they look like, what languages they speak, and what they do will make first-time visitors feel more comfortable.

5. When in doubt, don't.
   Rather than use poor photos or illustrations, don't use any.

6. Which images?
   Select your images carefully. Images of women, families, and children attract female readers. Photos of men attract male readers. Also, consider the cultural appropriateness of the images you present. Will they be appealing? Will they offend any other group? Are they realistic? Consider some preliminary test marketing.

7. No logo ego.
   When you create a brochure or poster, resist the urge to make the name of the program the biggest element on the page. An overbearing logo detracts from your message.

8. Use a professional graphic designer.
   If you're going to print outreach materials, don't skimp on the artwork. The best printer in the world can't salvage a badly designed piece. And since printing generally costs more than artwork, it makes sense to begin with good art. If you can, hire a professional graphic artist. If not, contact your local community college regarding student designers or the possibility of getting an intern to create some artwork.

9. Color catches the eye.
   Readers clearly prefer pages with color to those in black-and-white. If you can't print in color, invest in some colored paper.

10. No purple people, please!
    If you print a brochure, print your photos in either full color or black-and-white. Photos printed in red, purple, green, or other ink colors usually look terrible—especially if there are people in the picture.

Source: *Public Relations & Community Outreach Guide for Site Coordinators: Kids Care Fair*, Founding Kids Care Fair Office, American Red Cross, © 1995.

How To Reprint Camera-Ready Materials

Some nonprofit organizations and federal agencies may be willing to provide camera-ready copy or permit you to reproduce materials they have already developed. All materials produced by the federal government are in the public domain. That is, they are not copyrighted and may be reproduced without permission. However, many other organizations do copyright their materials. You should be sure to check with the producer about any materials you would like to use.

Sometimes it may be cheaper for you to make your own copies than to purchase them. When you think about printing, consider other organizations that may want copies. Because printing larger quantities will reduce the cost per copy, you will save money if you can combine orders.

What Are the Ways Materials Can Be Duplicated?

Two simple options are available for reprinting materials: photocopying and printing.

What Factors Affect Printing Costs?

Five variables are involved:

1. **Quantity.** The greatest expense in printing is making the printing plates. Thus, unlike photocopying costs, which remain constant per item, printing costs per unit go down as quantities go up. And up to 50,000 copies, the more you print, the more you save. For example, a one-sided, black and white flyer might cost:
   - $40 for 1,000 copies ($.04 per copy)
   - $53 for 2,000 copies ($.026 per copy)
   - $85 for 4,000 copies ($.021 per copy)
2. **Printer.** Every printer prices work differently, and a single printer's price for similar work may vary. Always get several cost estimates, and discuss any special requirements. Printing quality can also vary. To find a reliable printer, ask your colleagues for their recommendations. Look at samples of different printers' work, and check their references.
3. **Paper quality.** Once you have chosen a printer, he or she will show you paper samples in different weights, colors, and finishes. There are papers for all budgets. If the initial estimate seems high, ask about using a more modest paper stock.
4. **Ink color.** Materials that use only one ink color will be the most economical. For quantities under 10,000, black ink will be the cheapest choice. Prices increase with each different color ink you add.
5. **Artwork.** Printers charge more for materials with drawings or photographs than they do for materials with type alone, but these fees are generally small.

Can I Customize or Adapt Camera-Ready Materials?

Yes, with permission from the producer and a little help from a graphic artist. For example, you can do the following:

- ☐ Add your organization's name, contact information, and logo.
- ☐ Combine parts of existing materials to make a new piece. A graphic artist can "cut and paste" for printing or photocopying.
- ☐ Combine the best components you can find—graphics from one source to accompany the text from another.

Source: *Making Health Communication Programs Work: A Planner's Guide*, NIH Publication #92-1493, U.S. Department of Health and Human Services, Public Health Service, National Institutes of Health, Office of Cancer Communications, National Cancer Institute, April 1992.

HOW TO WRITE A BROCHURE*

An informative and interesting brochure can be an effective means of communicating important information. It has many advantages over other media: It is relatively permanent; it can be used for detailed information; it can be targeted at a selected audience; it can be easily transported and distributed; and it can reach a wide audience, as one reader passes it on to another.

If you are a first-time brochure writer, do not be intimidated. A lack of confidence can be your greatest enemy. The information that follows will help you avoid the pitfalls that plague many new writers and guide you through the process of brochure writing—from planning to revision.

Planning

Before you write your first sentence, think things through. What are your goals and expectations? Draw up a list of the points you want to cover. Key questions to be answered include: What new information do you want to give to your reader? What concerns of the reader do you want to address? What misconceptions do you want to correct? What are the selling points of your message?

Once you have clarified these, develop an outline of what you want to say. Make sure the outline clearly reflects your goals. Review the outline to see if you will arouse interest or influence attitudes, provide new or important information, or encourage your readers to take action.

Do not try to present more than your audience can absorb in one sitting. An effective brochure should have a single theme. Delete all material that detracts from that theme or makes the brochure complicated.

Break your topic into parts, and arrange those segments in a logical sequence. As you read the outline, do your thoughts move easily from one idea to the next? If your brochure is to be effective, it must be organized. Each part should prepare the reader for what is to follow.

Be familiar with your audience. Educational and cultural experiences vary widely among different groups—urban, rural, poor, middle class, native born, immigrant. Groups also may have different attitudes toward such concepts as good nutrition and preventive medicine. On the other hand, persons with a particular illness or disease are more likely to be familiar with that health problem and will find a fairly detailed brochure on the topic easy to understand.

Make sure you thoroughly research the topic before you start to write. To your future readers, you will be an expert, and you owe it to them to become one. One note of caution: Do not let your new-found knowledge impose on your writing. Write to inform, not to impress.

Sources of information on your topic may include state, county, and local health departments; professional and private health organizations; local hospitals and clinics; health advocacy groups; and your local public library. Medical periodicals are good sources of up-to-date information in their articles, editorials, display ads, and even classified advertising.

*Source: State of New York Department of Health, Albany, New York, © 1992.

Writing

Your first priority in writing a brochure is to communicate. To do this well, you must write clearly and concisely. People are easily turned off when they read boring or difficult material. Make sure your writing is readable. Follow the example of many periodicals: Direct your writing to the sixth to eighth grade reading level.

A simple readability test has been devised by writing authority Rudolf Flesch. The Flesch test includes a count of the number of sentences and syllables in a 100-word sample of the written material. The test offers a seven-step rating system—from very difficult, to standard, to very easy. It is available in Flesch's book, *The Art of Readable Writing*.

Each time you write a sentence, ask yourself if its meaning is clear. Your readers must be certain of your intent. Select words and phrases that convey your meaning and that have only one interpretation.

On the average, sentences should contain 17 or fewer words. However, sentence length should vary so as not to appear choppy and monotonous.

Other stumbling blocks include the following:

- **Jargon and technical terms.** Just because you understand a term, do not assume your readers can grasp its meaning. Health professionals have a vocabulary that is not easily understood by the general public. Use shorter, more familiar words whenever possible. For example, replace "mandated" and "to network" with "required" and "to meet."
- **Cliches.** They are generally trite and interrupt the flow of your message. Forget about "tip of the iceberg" and "one minute to midnight." The same applies to phrases such as "health is your most important possession" and fad expressions such as "top gun" and "Where's the beef?"
- **Redundancy.** Avoid using a word that is similar to one just written. "Polio is a disease that has been largely eliminated" is better written as "Polio has been largely eliminated." Another example of redundancy is the double modifier, such as "true facts" or "future plan."
- **Spelling.** Use correct spelling. There are no such words as "nite" or "thru." Also beware of words having similar spellings and meanings. "Affect" is a verb. "Effect" is generally a noun. "Farther" indicates distance. "Further" denotes quantity or degree. "Last" means final, while "latest" means most recent.
- **Abstract nouns.** The sentences "The incidence of AIDS is increasing" and "Diseases of a serious nature were recorded" are burdened with unnecessary abstract nouns. It's better to say "AIDS is increasing" and "Serious diseases were recorded."
- **Passive voice.** Avoid the passive voice whenever possible. For example, "it is estimated by the Health Department" is less effective than "the Health Department estimates."

The key is to keep it simple.

Present all the facts in a positive, honest, and sincere tone. This allows your readers to feel that they are making their own decisions. Use the present tense throughout. It lends an air of permanence.

For a more complete guide to writing style and concise language, a number of style books are available in bookstores and libraries. Those most often recommended include *The Art of Readable Writing* by Rudolf Flesch and *The Elements of Style* by William Strunk, Jr., and E.B. White.

Revising

Revising the draft is probably the most important step in writing. If possible, put your draft aside for a day or two, and then reread it. You may find that the meaning is not what you intended or as clear as you had thought.

Carefully review the content. Have you achieved your original intent? Is it based on sound, easy-to-understand reasoning, or is it vague? Have you confused your readers with jargon or complicated reasoning?

Check all spelling, mathematics, graphs, and charts for accuracy. Are there any misleading statements or unanswered questions? Do not do it alone. Ask others to read it for comprehension. Your draft should be reviewed by experts on the topic, as well. You can rely on their judgment for accuracy, but not necessarily for style.

Review all material for wordiness. You can always cut excess material in subsequent drafts. Typical examples of verbosity include "in the event that" when "if" will do as well. "Demonstrates that there is" is the wrong way of saying "shows." "There are many things that will affect health" is better said as "Many things affect health."

Once you have incorporated any suggestions from your experts and are satisfied with your draft, it is time to proofread the materials. Nothing can hurt the credibility of an otherwise excellent brochure as much as misspelled words or poor punctuation.

Layout

When you are ready to prepare your brochure for printing, you will need the help of people with experience in the field. Fortunately, there are many. They include local printers, artists, photographers, journalists, public relations people, and students and teachers from high school and college journalism departments. They can offer guidance on choices of artwork, typefaces, paper, and the other aspects of preparing your brochure for printing.

A Final Word

By now, you should have a general understanding of how to write a brochure. The task is not as involved as you may have thought. It can be even easier if you have fun with your writing. Do not be afraid to brainstorm with others or to try something new. If you feel good about the final product, your readers probably will, too; and you will have created an effective and informative means of communicating an important message.

HOW TO DESIGN AND PRODUCE A NEWSLETTER*

Does your organization, program, or facility produce a newsletter? If not, you are missing out on one of the most effective tools for internal and/or external communications. A newsletter is the best way to keep your management team, staff, board of directors, volunteers, clients, community leaders, and the general public informed about your organization and its services to the community.

Any organization, no matter what its size or scope of activities, can use a newsletter as a vehicle to build employee morale, pride, and loyalty. A newsletter also can be used to reach audiences served by the agency, to promote philosophies, or to solicit support for a program. To be successful, a newsletter has to be read. To be read, it must be a quality package of news and human interest stories that will attract and hold the interest of readers.

Every organization generates news—current events, future plans, new policies, and so on. Human interest covers a wider field, but all human interest stories have the appeal of providing a unique look at the human condition. They can be about anything, from an unusual hobby to the reunion of long-lost siblings.

A good newsletter emulates its commercial counterparts. News coverage should be complete, factual, objective, and well balanced. Like a daily newspaper, the newsletter must conform to the laws governing libel, copyright, and confidentiality.

At the same time, you must weigh everything that goes into your newsletter in light of the fact that it is a "house organ," which means it must reflect the interests of the organization. It is good policy to review editorial content with administrators. It may be time consuming, but the effort will help to avoid mistakes, encourage cooperation, and promote executive support for your efforts.

Before you can start a newsletter, however, you need five things: an audience, some news, a staff, production support, and money.

Audience

As noted above, a newsletter can have a variety of audiences. The size and composition of the audience will determine what the newsletter contains and how it will be distributed.

If the target audience is staff only, staff activities and personal news items need to be emphasized. Employees want to know about new policies, coworkers who have been recognized for exceptional service, and changes in benefits.

When the audience includes clients, their activities and accomplishments become newsworthy. Stories about successful treatments and clarification of how policy changes affect clients must be included.

If the audience includes the board of directors, volunteers, or the community at large, more general, agency-oriented articles should be used. These might include: What are the effects of rising medical costs? How well is the organization achieving long-range goals? What is the organization's budget and how is it being distributed within the agency and community?

---

*Source: State of New York Department of Health, Albany, New York, © 1991.

News

What Is News?

News is the who, what, where, when, why, and how of things that affect your readers.

In general, there is "hard" news, "soft" news, and "feature" news. For example, the announcement of a new continuing education class is hard news. A review of the continuing education program is soft news. A story about a person's exceptional success in the continuing education program is human interest or feature news.

Where and How To Get News

To find interesting stories about people and events, you must regularly visit all program areas of your organization. Make visits often enough to keep abreast of activities and plans. Get to know the people and let them know how they can contact you.

Establish a network of contacts. Look for people who can be relied upon to keep you informed. Ideally, some could write stories for you. Even if you have to edit or rewrite contributed stories, they will make your job much easier. Encourage people to write for you by using bylines (the author's names) whenever possible.

People like being recognized. If your organization has a sports team, ask someone to keep track of scores and write about player achievements. If someone participates in a conference, ask him or her to write about it.

Condense official announcements, program reports, policy statements, study outcomes, and the like. You can focus on key points, clarify them, and give them wide distribution.

The organization's management team will ultimately be held responsible by the board of directors and the public for the content of your newsletter. Give them the opportunity to thoroughly review it before publication. It is especially important to obtain executive clearance on any complex or potentially controversial material.

How To Present the News

The easiest approach for an inexperienced editor is to read other newsletters and use those that are attractive as models. Newsletters can be any size or shape. Yours can be as simple as two sides of an 8½" × 11" sheet of paper. Or you can start with a 17" × 11" sheet that, when folded in half, becomes four 8½" × 11" pages.

It is not difficult to fill four pages. About one-fifth of the front page is filled with the "banner" or "flag," which is the name of the newsletter and other relevant information, such as the name of the organization and date of publication. A feature story about an exceptional staff member or activity and a news story (e.g., a new department policy, upcoming event, award, etc.) should occupy the front page. A third, smaller story, perhaps set off in a box or shaded area, will break up the copy and add variety. You may also consider a front page box as a "teaser" to draw readers into the newsletter.

Any of a variety of regular features can appear on the next three pages: a director's column or department columns on employee relations or promotions and awards; a calendar of upcoming events; or a "people in the news" column, featuring one- or two-paragraph items of human interest. Whenever you find short, unique items, save and use them as "filler." Short humorous pieces and one- or two-line items add a light, personal touch to a newsletter.

If you include photos (called "halftones" when prepared for printing) in your publication, do not forget to correctly identify everyone, using a caption that is short and to the point.

Finally, a newsletter will have a "masthead." This is an information box listing the name and address of the sponsoring organization, publication schedule, and a list of key individuals responsible for production. Other masthead elements could include subscription costs, ordering information, and a copyright advisory, if these are applicable.

You may choose to publish quarterly, monthly, or weekly. The decision will depend on such factors as staff, budget, amount of available news, and the objectives of your newsletter.

A monthly publication schedule is a common choice because it is frequent enough to have a sense of continuity, while not as much of a burden on the budget and staff

time as a weekly. However, if your readers need to be kept abreast of a fluid situation, they might be better served by a weekly publication.

The advantage of a quarterly publication is that it may provide the time and budget to produce a high-quality product with long-term value.

Staff

Ideally, a four-page monthly newsletter can be put together by a single person. Someone with experience in broadcasting, photography, or journalism would be a natural editor. Barring such in-house miracles, potential editors may be found by checking on hobbies (photography, writing, etc.) or education (art or English).

With new desktop publishing or word processing equipment, a single individual can produce professional-looking material.

Also, if contributors from different departments are encouraged to submit material on a regular basis, there will be less need for staff.

A photographer or artist can serve an important role. Photographs, cartoons, graphs, and other artwork break up the print, catch the reader's eye, and inform or entertain.

The Newsletter

Published monthly by the New York State Health Department Bureau of Community Relations, 1084 Corning Tower, ESP, Albany, NY 12237.

Mario M. Cuomo
Governor

Joseph Smith
Editor

Mary Jones
John Doe
Staff

Richard Brown
Technical Advisor

The Newsletter is distributed free of charge to all employees of the New York State Health Department. To submit items of interest, call (518) 666-6666.

Second class postage paid at Albany, NY POSTMASTER: Send address changes to: Community Relations, 1084 Corning Tower, Albany, NY 12237

But even these are not essential. You can solicit photos from individuals mentioned in stories, and you can buy books of "clip art" at an art supply store. Clip art is line art (black and white artwork, both illustrations and graphs, without gray tones) and camera-ready photographs that can be used to illustrate your stories.

Production Support

To be reproduced, your material must be neatly typed or typeset and then arranged and laid out in a form that can be photographed. It is then camera-ready.

Desktop publishing is becoming the most viable method to prepare camera-ready material. It is a simple, fast, and flexible way to produce all newsletter elements, including columns, graphs, screens, borders, and other artwork.

Desktop publishing requires access to a personal computer, a laser printer, and page layout program. Anyone who can operate a personal computer has the potential to do desktop publishing. And an investment in software will be relatively small compared to the cost of layout and typesetting services from a commercial printer.

If you do not have access to the equipment, desktop publishing services can be purchased. Camera-ready material is then prepared either from typewritten manuscript or a word processor disk. You will have a wide choice of typefaces.

If you opt to use a print shop to produce your newsletter, you should provide the printer with a "layout sheet," also called a "dummy," that shows the location of all elements. It could be as simple as a rough outline of the position of stories, photos, and other artwork.

A clean, double-spaced, corrected manuscript should accompany the layout sheet.

If you have access to a typesetting machine, you could have the written material typeset and paste it in place. You could make arrangements for your printer to typeset material, or you might hire a typesetting service.

If your budget permits, do not overlook using a local weekly newspaper, pennysaver (free weekly buyers' guide), or shopping guide in your production efforts. These publishers should have the capability to typeset your material, make halftones, prepare camera-ready material, and print your newsletter at a reasonable cost.

If you have little money or equipment but have the time, you may choose to type your own copy and prepare camera-ready material that can be reproduced on an office high-speed copier or taken to a "quick print" shop.

In this case, your finished product will consist of typed material, headlines, and line art. You will not be able to use photographs with high-speed reproduction.

Budget

Your newsletter will be shaped by its budget as much as by any other factor.

Draw up estimates of expenses. They will help you anticipate and control costs and make decisions on methods of production and the scope of your newsletter.

You may anticipate expenses for printing, paper, ink, halftones, clip art, postage, computer software, and, possibly, overtime by staff members assigned to the newsletter.

Printers' fees will vary widely, so consult with several different printers. Ask about price breaks for volume. Seek recommendations from others who use similar services.

For volume discounts and availability, it is best to choose one combination of ink and paper stock and use it consistently.

If you choose to mail, expenses will include the fee for a bulk mailing permit, postage, labels, and, perhaps, envelopes or wrappers. Be prepared for possible postage rate hikes and such miscellaneous costs as charges for material returned or forwarded.

Postal regulations are detailed and strictly enforced, so check carefully with the post office to ensure that your newsletter complies with them.

Your postage choices include precancelled stamps, a postage meter, or a third class, bulk mail permit.

While bulk mail is the least expensive choice, it may be inappropriate for you. A bulk mail permit has annual fees, and you may have to pay an additional initial fee with your first mailing. You must mail at least 200 pieces, or 50 pounds, sorted in ZIP code order. You will have to set aside a portion of the bottom back page for the address and the bulk mail permit information.

Note to Editors

Prepare a list of your organization's long- and short-term objectives. Then develop a strategy whereby your newsletter contributes to their achievement.

Your newsletter must be relevant to the goals and needs of your organization and its readers. Through trial and error, you will develop the blend of news, features, and artwork that works best for you.

Be aware of the issues of interest to your readers, and address them to the best of your ability. Stay attuned to your readers by encouraging their comments. If you have the space and authorization, consider a "letters to the editor" column. If that is not possible, you could insert a "suggestion box" with an address and telephone number.

From the very first issue, work to establish a good reputation and protect the good name of your newsletter and organization.

Whether the newsletter will be a weekly, monthly, or quarterly, you need to set a schedule and meet all publication dates. The reliability of your newsletter will help ensure the loyalty of your audience.

It is just as important to keep staff and columnists informed about deadlines so they can submit material on time. Remember to give ample warning of early deadlines due to holidays or special events.

Periodically review your distribution procedures. As changes take place within your organization, you may want to shift methods of distribution to more effectively reach readers.

Mailing lists should also be regularly reviewed. Employees leave and other readers move. Your lists can be outdated within a few months.

A final word of caution: **proofread all copy** that is prepared by you or your printer before it is printed and distributed. A misspelled name is embarrassing and hurts the credibility of your newsletter. Other errors are more serious. An incorrect telephone number or the wrong time for a scheduled event may result in great aggravation for you, your readers, and your organization.

Enjoy Your Newsletter

If you are the editor of your organization's newsletter, consider yourself privileged. You have been given a creative assignment. It will allow you to present your organization in a favorable manner and encourage employee and public support for its goals and programs.

Take advantage of this opportunity and have fun with it. Be creative and open to new ideas and approaches to issues. Your newsletter will come to reflect the way you feel about it. Work to expand your skills and create something of which you and your organization can be proud.

HOW TO WRITE A DISCUSSION GUIDE*

An educational film, video, play, or other product is only the beginning of a learning experience. A lot more learning takes place during the discussion that follows.

Use discussion guides for:
• films
• videotapes
• puppet shows
• plays
• skits

Discussion helps the audience digest and analyze a film's lessons and talk about those lessons in terms of their own experiences. A discussion guide should help the audience relate characters and events to their own families and communities.

A discussion guide is a brief outline of information and talking points or discussion questions related to a film or other product. They help discussion leaders by

- highlighting major themes and messages
- providing background information on issues dealt with, including scientific facts and data when appropriate
- listing problem-solving or conflict-resolution steps
- suggesting discussion questions
- suggesting related activities
- listing resources for more information

Whether you are making a film or other product from scratch or using one from another source, consider writing a discussion guide to accompany it. For the sake of discussion, the following guidelines refer to films; however, the guidelines can be applied to plays, puppet shows, skits, and other kinds of audiovisual products and presentations.

Provide Background Information

Discussion leaders need to know the film's major purpose, its intended audience, and why the film's themes are important for that audience. They may also need to know how it will help them with their jobs—for example, by meeting learning objectives for an alcohol, tobacco, and other drug (ATOD) curriculum or module.

Background information may include the following:

- summary of the plot or content
- major themes and messages
- intended audiences
- suggested settings for showing the film
- information about the audience, such as what was learned during formative research, including the audience's knowledge and attitudes about alcohol, tobacco, and other drugs
- pointers on sensitive subjects that may arise, such as parental abuse of alcohol or other drugs
- information about the broader program or curriculum, if the film is part of one, to explain how the film will meet learning objectives

*Source: Center for Substance Abuse, "Technical Assistance Bulletin: A Discussion Guide Can Enhance Your Presentation," U.S. Department of Health and Human Services, Public Health Service, Substance Abuse and Mental Health Services Administration, Washington, D.C., September 1994.

Use Open-Ended Questions

Questions that call for a simple "Yes" or "No" answer do not lead to discussion. So avoid questions that begin "Do you think . . . ?" "Can teachers help . . . ?" "Should friends try . . . ?" Instead, use open-ended questions, such as the following:

- "What do you think about . . . ?"
- "Where would you go if . . . ?"
- "How can friends help?"
- "How does your neighborhood . . . ?"
- "How would you tell your brother or sister about . . . ?"

Begin with Objective Questions

Questions about the content of the film are nonthreatening, help viewers remember themes and situations, and lead into more thought-provoking questions. For a film about drinking, for 8- to 12-year-olds, some early questions in the discussion guide could be

- "What did Tom do to show that he did not want the wine cooler?"
- "What did Tom and Janet do outside of school to have fun?"

Ask for Reactions to Specific Characters and Situations

A good way to stimulate discussion is to ask participants to share their thoughts and feelings about what happens in the film. For example

- "How do you think Teresa felt while her grandmother and mother were arguing?"
- "Why do you think Tony hesitated when Bob asked him to play basketball?"
- "What is Carla's mother like? What things did you see her do to show her love for her children?"

Ask Questions about the Participants' Own Experiences

The next step is to ask the audience how they might feel, think, or act in similar circumstances, or how the film relates to their own community. For example

- "What kinds of problems do drugs cause in your community?"
- "Who could you talk to if you had a problem like Adrienne's?"

Suggest Ways To Close the Discussion

Closing questions stimulate the audience to summarize the film's lessons and think ahead to next steps. For example

- "What are some slogans that would tell other people what this film is about?"
- "What are some different ways you, as a group, could create a drug-free school/ community?"

Suggest Related Activities

These may be short-term or long-term activities. If your film or video is intended primarily for school children, activities that can fit into various parts of the curriculum are most useful to teachers. Also, using related activities over several days or weeks will allow teachers to reinforce the lessons. For example

- Have participants scan magazines and newspapers for alcohol advertisements aimed at audiences from particular ethnic/racial groups.

Parts of a Discussion Guide

Here's a typical table of contents:
I.   Background information
II. Questions
III. Related activities
IV. Resources

- Have participants write and perform some possible commercials or public service announcements about the themes in the film.
- Have students design posters illustrating the video's message.

Format: Make It User-Friendly

One pitfall in writing a discussion guide is the temptation to write too much. Remember that it is intended to be a practical, on-the-job tool. So keep your guide brief and easy to use.

- Highlight major themes using bold type or bullets.
- Avoid lengthy blocks of text.
- Use clear, large subheads to label each section.
- Use a type size large enough to be read easily during discussion.
- Use graphics.

Give Tips for Handling the Discussion

These may include ways to introduce the film itself, so that participants know what to look for. The discussion guide could suggest points at which the film might be stopped for some preliminary discussion. You may also want to alert discussion leaders to the sensitivity of certain subjects, such as ethnic and racial issues or parental alcoholism. For example

"Children from families in which alcohol is abused may be used to denying the problem and may find it difficult to discuss the scene in the Jones's living room. These children may need reassurance that (1) the children in the film did not cause the disease, (2) they cannot cure it, and (3) any child can talk about such problems with a teacher or school counselor."

For some questions, it can help the discussion leader to know what sort of responses to expect (or encourage). Sample responses should be listed briefly, and preferably in a different typeface, immediately after the questions. For example:

"What is self-esteem?"

Sample responses: *"Standing up for yourself; not letting others push you into doing things you don't want to; making up your own mind."*

Consider Arranging Questions around Key Themes

You may want to group questions according to the different themes or messages of the film. Each set of questions, like the overall guide, can have learning objectives and background information. Begin with general, objective questions and proceed to more subjective ones.

Obtain Feedback on What You Have Written

It's a good idea to have your discussion guide pretested with its audience, along with the film. Also be sure to have it reviewed by several different people who work with the intended audience—perhaps classroom teachers or community group leaders. Help reviewers give you useful feedback by asking questions like these:

- "Would the background information be clear to someone who had not yet seen the film?"
- "Do you think these suggested activities will appeal to urban seventh graders?"
- "Are these activities feasible for elementary school teachers?"
- "Are there other resources that should be listed?"

NOTES:

Sample Discussion Guide

BE SMART! DON'T START!

This federal campaign included a music video for preteens. There is a sample page adapted from its *Music Video Discussion Guide*.

FITTING IN AND BELONGING

Goals for Discussion

- Children will learn about positive and negative peer pressure.
- Children will be able to demonstrate three ways of saying "No."

Overview for Discussion Leader

A major reason that preteens (and adolescents) give for drinking is to "fit in"—to belong and to be accepted by a peer group. When young people begin to seek important friendships outside the home, their need to belong is increased. They are trying out new behaviors away from home, and acceptance becomes extremely important. They will go to great lengths to avoid being different. If they believe that most kids are drinking, they will want to drink, too.

Discussion Suggestions

Scene in Film

- Group at concert appears to be self-confident, comfortable with one another, excited to see one another, not drinking, and happy.

Questions

- What is the group like?
- Why are they excited?
- What's your peer group like and what does it get excited about doing?
- How are the people in the film like people you know?
- How does it feel if you feel like you don't belong?

Suggested Activities

- Role play the refusal scene.
- Role play positive peer pressure.

NOTES:

Source: Center for Substance Abuse, "Technical Assistance Bulletin: A Discussion Guide Can Enhance Your Presentation," U.S. Department of Health and Human Services, Public Health Service, Substance Abuse and Mental Health Services Administration, Washington, D.C., September 1994.

TIPS FOR WEB SITE DESIGN*

An Internet Web site often forms the core of an organization's on-line identity. The site can serve a variety of functions. It can provide information on a social change initiative and the steps visitors can take in support of the initiative. It can serve as a distribution channel, providing a means of downloading materials that can then be printed or used in other ways (e.g., brochures, presentations). It can be a gateway to other information by including links to other relevant sites or a system for ordering materials.

Earlier in this chapter we recommended establishing a graphic identity and graphic standards for an initiative's printed materials. The same recommendations hold true for Web sites: Paying some up-front attention to site design can improve readability and use, as well as speed approval of additions to the site. A Web site's graphic identity can be established by using the same colors, fonts, backgrounds, and signature icons throughout the site.

Color, Fonts, and Backgrounds

To reduce eye fatigue (which occurs when the eyes have to refocus constantly), experts recommend limiting screens to four nonneutral colors and avoiding complementary colors and red-blue combinations. When assigning colors to various screen elements, keep in mind that users assume objects of the same color are related. Dark type (black or dark blue) on plain, light-colored backgrounds is easiest to read. In general, blue, red, and purple should not be used for text other than hyperlinks (otherwise those text elements may be confused with default hyperlinks). Selecting one or two font families and sticking with them provides a consistent look without creating clutter. As with printed publications, type in all capital letters is more difficult to read. Finally, although background patterns are a popular way to establish a site's identity, care should be taken in their use because strong background patterns can render text unreadable.

Site Layout

The best layout for a particular site depends on its content. However, there are some technical aspects of site design that can determine the degree to which the site is friendly (or unfriendly) to use. For example, including a search capability or index on the home page is a good way to help users locate the information they want. Such a feature is particularly helpful on large sites that include many different topics.

Organizing the site contents in a user-friendly manner is critical. In particular, sites that regularly add menu items run the risk of becoming disorganized and unwieldy over time. A general rule of thumb is to limit lists to seven choices, breaking longer lists into smaller groups. Frequent visitors will appreciate a "last updated" date next to menu items; this feature lets them avoid waiting for a screen to load only to discover there is no new information. Adding hyperlinks to partner sites and resources provides site users with access to more information and increases the perceived value of your site.

---

*Source: Michael Siegel and Lynne Doner, *Marketing Public Health: Strategies To Promote Social Change*, Aspen Publishers, Inc., © 1998.

Including a means to contact the organization sponsoring the site is also important. People may have comments on the site itself (ensuring that each Web page has a clear, brief title will help them comment and help you understand what they are talking about), or they may have questions about the initiative or want to know if more information is available on a particular topic. It is a good idea to provide both electronic and traditional addresses and telephone numbers, because some people will access the site to find out how to contact the organization through traditional means. Similarly, if the site includes suggestions on actions to take (such as contacting a policy maker), information should be provided on how to contact the appropriate parties (e.g., name, address, phone number).

Images and Photos

Part of the Web's appeal is the ability to bring ideas to life and simplify complex information using illustrations and photographs. Adding many images to Web pages is tempting because it is an opportunity to use all those full-color images an organization could never afford to print. However, they have their own hefty price in response time. Every image added to a Web page increases the time it takes for the page to appear on someone's screen. While a target audience member is waiting for your organization's page to appear, he or she may get bored and decide to go somewhere else.

By using images sparingly and paying attention to how they are constructed, you can harness the visual power of the Web while minimizing response time. In general, Web designers recommend that graphic elements be kept small and that animation be avoided unless it is truly necessary, because continuous animation tires the eyes.

Testing the Site

One of the most important steps in Web site design is testing the site after it is constructed. Sites are often built and tested using state-of-the-art setups: large monitors, the most current versions of software, and, most important, the fastest modes of access. If your site is intended to provide information to members of the public, looking at it through their eyes (and their computers) can help you make sure it does its job as effectively as possible. Some aspects of the site to consider when testing it out include the following:

- *How long do pages take to load using a slow modem over a dial-up line?* Users are typically unwilling to wait more than 20 or 30 seconds. Putting up brief descriptions that users can click on to proceed before the images load is another way to retain user interest and let them make progress—and to let them know what is on the screen if they have graphics turned off.
- *What do pages look like when viewed with different browsers or lower end graphics settings?* For example, do the pages still make sense if they are viewed with a text-only browser or one with deactivated graphics? What happens if the monitor is set to 16 or 256 colors rather than millions of colors (if the monitor cannot display some of the colors used, whatever is in those colors can disappear) or if the screen resolution differs from that of the screen the site was developed on?

- *How user-friendly is the menu structure?* The goal is to strike a balance: If users have to wade through huge lists, they may get frustrated and quit looking before they find what they need. On the other hand, if they have to navigate through a series of menus, each with two or three choices, they may also get frustrated and stop before they reach their destination. Every screen they have to wait through increases the chance that they will get bored and go elsewhere.
- *If your pages are part of a larger site, what steps would users have to take in order to find the pages relevant to the initiative?* Most look for content, not departments. Many large organizations create Web sites that are arranged according to their organizational structure. This schema may work for their employees, but it has the effect of burying information on social change initiatives unless a search option is part of the site's home page.

SIX METHODS OF PRETESTING*

Pretests show what works with a particular audience. The slogan that seems persuasive to an adult may be confusing to a sixth grader. A poster that captures the attention of teenagers in one community may alienate or seem boring to those in another.

Pretesting can prevent problems like these. It helps ensure that materials convey a clear and effective message to a program's target audience. Specifically, pretesting can help program managers:

- select message concepts—styles, formats, spokesperson, and appeals (such as fear, humor, compassion)
- guide creative work
- fine-tune wording and visual images
- guide revisions (before spending time and money on the finished product)

Several issues should be considered before pretesting begins:

- Pretesting is just one step in the communications process. Before the organization plans materials and messages, it must define its target audience, determine audience needs, and define organizational goals and objectives.
- It can help to find out what other materials exist for the target audience and whether they have been pretested. One call to a resource center may turn up this kind of information.
- As valuable as pretesting is, it has the limitations of *qualitative research*; that is, it provides insights and ideas. It usually cannot provide statistically valid conclusions about an entire audience because not enough people are involved, and they have not been randomly selected. *Quantitative research*, such as polls and surveys, can be used to obtain statistically valid data.

Pretesting is valuable at several stages of message and material development. Some methods can be used in the early stages to test concepts or general issues and to spark ideas; other methods are more useful when materials are in close-to-final form.

Factors to consider in selecting a pretest method include, in addition to the stage of development of the materials, the kind of audience at which the materials are aimed (e.g., professional, rural); the sensitivity and complexity of the materials; and the resources available. The following overview summarizes the purposes, requirements, pros, and cons of six pretest methods.

Focus Groups

Focus groups are small gatherings of eight to twelve people who meet with a trained moderator to talk about ideas and materials. This pretesting method is especially useful to answer questions in the early stages of a project: What kind of spokesperson could convince sixth graders that drugs are not the path to popularity? What kind of

---

*Source: *The Fact Is . . .*, U.S. Department of Health and Human Services, Public Health Service, Alcohol, Drug Abuse, and Mental Health Administration, Office for Substance Abuse Prevention, February 1992.

format would parents prefer for information about alcohol and other drugs? Focus groups are also used to generate new ideas and insights through group interaction.

- **Use to pretest:** program themes and images, general issues, materials in early stage of development
- **Minimum number of respondents:** 8 to 12 per group; at least two groups per type of respondent
- **Resources needed:** trained moderator, discussion outline, list of respondents, fees or incentives to participate, meeting room, recording equipment, audiovisual (AV) equipment if pretesting audiovisuals, analysis expertise
- **Pros:** group interaction stimulates responses; can cover many topics
- **Cons:** individual responses may be swayed by group response; can provide misleading information if not skillfully managed; cannot probe sensitive or complex questions

Individual Interviews

Individual interviews elicit reactions to sensitive issues or complex materials and permit lengthy discussion of draft materials. Interviews are worth the extra time and expense when the response of an individual, free of group pressure, is important, and when long, confidential conversations may provide special insights.

- **Purpose:** to explore individuals' responses, feelings, and concerns
- **Use to pretest:** program themes and images, sensitive images, complex materials
- **Minimum number of respondents:** 10 per type of respondent
- **Resources needed:** list of potential respondents, fees or incentives (optional), trained interviewer, telephone or quiet room, tape recorder (optional), analysis expertise
- **Pros:** can reach hard-to-reach audiences, people with limited reading and writing skills; can explore emotional or complex issues
- **Cons:** time consuming to conduct and analyze; may yield no patterns in responses, especially if number of interviews is limited

Central Location Intercept Interviews

Intercept interviews take place in spots, such as shopping malls and schools, where many members of a target audience congregate. Intercept interviewers use questionnaires designed for quick answers, so that each interview is short and the results can be tabulated easily. Use intercept interviews when the stimulus of a group interaction is not important.

- **Purpose:** to obtain many individual reactions
- **Use to pretest:** print and audiovisual materials, program themes, and images
- **Minimum number of respondents:** 60 to 100 per target audience
- **Resources needed:** trained interviewer, structured questionnaire, access to central location (e.g., school, laundromat, mall), quiet spot for interview, AV equipment if pretesting audiovisuals, analysis expertise
- **Pros:** quick; can be inexpensive; can be designed to obtain quantitative data
- **Cons:** short; cannot probe sensitive or complex questions

Theater Testing

These pretests gather large numbers of people together to view messages embedded in other programming. This method simulates actual viewing conditions. Theater testing can help you learn how and whether your message stands out among the clutter of other messages broadcast each day.

- **Purpose:** to obtain many responses at once; to measure recall under conditions that simulate actual viewing
- **Use to pretest:** audiovisual materials; can be adapted to print materials, e.g., posters displayed with other wall hangings in a clinic
- **Minimum number of respondents:** 60 to 100 per target audience
- **Resources needed:** list of potential respondents, fees or incentives to participate, large room, AV equipment, questionnaire, analysis expertise
- **Pros:** can simulate natural exposure to materials and help gauge how they compete with other messages; responses can be analyzed quickly
- **Cons:** time consuming to arrange; can be expensive

Self-Administered Questionnaires

Mailed or personally delivered, questionnaires accompany draft materials and elicit brief, individual responses. Questionnaires can be useful in reaching audiences who are widely dispersed, do not congregate in public spots, and are not likely to attend focus groups, such as professionals and people living in rural areas.

- **Purpose:** to obtain many individuals' reactions to materials
- **Use to pretest:** print and audiovisual materials
- **Minimum number of respondents:** 20 (100 to 200 is ideal)
- **Resources needed:** list of potential respondents, questionnaire, postage if mailed, AV equipment if pretesting audiovisuals, analysis expertise
- **Pros:** inexpensive; can reach homebound, rural, or other dispersed audiences easily
- **Cons:** response rate may be low (if mailed); may require follow-up; may take a long time to receive responses; exposure to materials is not controlled

Readability Testing

If most members of the audience read at the ninth-grade level, written materials should be about this level. Readability formulas provide a rough indication of the grade level needed to understand text. It is important to use judgment when applying reading formulas. Some multisyllable words—such as *alcohol*—are easy to understand but artificially raise the reading level score. Also remember that other factors, such as graphics and type size, influence readability.

- **Purpose:** to gauge the reading level of materials
- **Use to pretest:** all print materials
- **Number of respondents:** none
- **Resources needed:** a readability formula
- **Pros:** fast, inexpensive
- **Cons:** provides only a rough indication; does not obtain audience reaction

Applicability of Pretesting Methods

	Nonparticipatory	Qualitative		Qualitative or Quantitative			
	Readability Tests	Focus Groups	Self-Tests	Individual Interviews	Central Location Interviews	Mail Questionnaires	Theater Tests
1. Concept development		X		X	X		
2. Poster	X	X			X		
3. Flyer	X	X	X	X	X	X	
4. Booklet	X	X	X	X	X	X	
5. Notification letter	X	X	X	X	X	X	
6. Storyboard		X			X		
7. Radio public service announcement (PSA)		X			X		X
8. TV PSA		X			X		X
9. Videotape		X					X

NOTES:

Source: *Making Health Communication Programs Work: A Planner's Guide*, NIH Publication #92-1493, U.S. Department of Health and Human Services, Public Health Service, National Institutes of Health, Office of Cancer Communications, National Cancer Institute, April 1992.

What Pretesting Can and Cannot Do

Use Pretesting for . . .

Assessing Comprehension

Understanding of health messages and materials is essential as a prior condition to acceptance. For example, by pretesting a slide-tape presentation on breast cancer, it was learned that the presentation was considered clear and informative, but the narration needed to be slowed down so that all of the information could be better understood.

Assessing Attention and Recall

Television and radio public service announcements (PSAs) and posters must first attract audience attention to work. These messages are rarely seen or heard in an isolated environment, and they must compete (e.g., with advertisements, news, and entertainment) for attention. For example, after pretesting two different versions of television PSAs to promote exercise, program planners learned that the message showing runners talking about their own exercise experiences was remembered more often. A second message, which used special visual techniques and a voice-over announcer, was not effective in attracting the attention of pretest respondents.

Identifying Strong and Weak Points

This means making sure that all elements of the materials (e.g., message, format, style) are likely to work with the target audience. For example, a booklet on health risk appraisal contained a self-test for readers to complete. The pretest indicated that the booklet was considered interesting and informative. However, the instructions for scoring the test were confusing. Respondents needed clear directions to calculate their scores.

Determining Personal Relevance

For the message to take effect, audience members must understand the problem, accept its importance in their lives, and agree with the value of the solution for them. For example, pretest results of a booklet on high blood pressure among hypertensives and a general audience revealed several important differences in the responses of these two groups. Hypertensives recalled and understood more specific points related to high blood pressure control than did the general audience group. Further, when asked whom the booklet was for, a higher proportion of hypertensives felt the booklet was "talking to someone like me."

Gauging Sensitive or Controversial Elements

Questions about audience sensitivity to subject matter often arise in developing health messages. Pretesting can help predict whether messages may alienate or offend target audiences. For example, would a televised demonstration of breast self-examination on a live model be an affront to viewers? Pretest results of such a PSA indicated that respondents held a range of views about the propery of this demonstration.

Pretesting Limitations

Given the qualitative nature of most pretesting research, it is important to recognize its limitations:

- Pretesting cannot absolutely predict or guarantee learning, persuasion, behavior change, or other measures of communication effectiveness.
- Pretesting in health communication is seldom designed to quantitatively measure small differences among large samples; it is not statistically precise. It will not reveal that booklet A is 2.5 percent better than booklet B. (Presumably, pretests of such precision could be applied, but the cost of obtaining such data would be high, and the findings may be no more useful than the diagnostic information from more affordable approaches.)
- Pretesting is not a substitute for experienced judgment. Rather, it can provide additional information from which to make sound decisions.

continues

What Pretesting Can and Cannot Do continued

It is important to avoid misuse of pretest results. Perhaps the most common error is to overgeneralize. Qualitative, diagnostic pretest methods should not be used to estimate broad-scale results. If five of the ten respondents in a focus group interview do not understand portions of a pamphlet, it does not necessarily mean that 50 percent of the total target population will be confused. The lack of understanding among those pretest respondents suggests, however, that the pamphlet may need to be revised to improve comprehension. In sum, pretesting is indicative, not predictive.

Another problem that arises in health communication pretesting concerns interpretation of respondent reactions to a sensitive or emotional subject such as breast cancer or acquired immune deficiency syndrome (AIDS). Respondents may become unusually rational when reacting to such pretest materials, and cover up their true concerns, feelings, and behavior. As a result, the pretester must examine and interpret responses carefully.

NOTES:

Source: *Making Health Communication Programs Work: A Planner's Guide*, NIH Publication #92-1493, U.S. Department of Health and Human Services, Public Health Service, National Institutes of Health, Office of Cancer Communications, National Cancer Institute, April 1992.

Getting To Know Your Low-Literate Audience

There are several things to look for when getting to know a low-literate or oral-culture audience:

- **cultural health beliefs** specific to the problem being addressed

- **treatments, remedies**, or other ways the audience deals with the health issue (i.e., whether there are treatments, remedies, and local mores that differ from the health messages the professionals want to provide)

- **environmental circumstances** (i.e., social and home environments) that may influence health-related behaviors and beliefs

- **potential barriers** to personal involvement in the program (e.g., cost, transportation, child care, issues related to privacy, other obligations)

- **perceived benefits** of particular health behaviors

- **preferred learning styles** (i.e., traditional versus nontraditional, written versus oral, visual, action-oriented, or audiovisual)

- **community impressions of similar programs** (i.e., why they succeeded or failed, their motives, their inclusion of community members during development)

- **opinion leaders and organizational gatekeepers** (i.e., who they are and how they can be reached)

NOTES:

Source: AMC Cancer Research Center, *Beyond the Brochure: Alternative Approaches to Effective Health Communication*, U.S. Department of Health and Human Services, Public Health Service, Centers for Disease Control and Prevention (CDC), Atlanta, Georgia 30333, 1994.

HOW TO WRITE FOR ADULTS WITH LIMITED READING SKILLS*

Know the Audience

To be effective in writing for adults with limited reading skills, one must understand some of their characteristics and keep in mind one basic point: The lack of good reading and comprehension skills is not an indication of readers' intelligence. The writing style should be simple and direct without "talking down" to readers.

Characteristics of Individuals with Limited Reading Skills

- The individual reads at a level at least one to two school grades below the highest grade completed. Anyone with a reading level below the fifth grade does not have enough language fluency to make good use of written materials.
- The individual has a short attention span. The message should be direct, short, and specific.
- The individual depends on visual cues to clarify and interpret words. Appropriate pictures, illustrations, and graphics must work in conjunction with words.
- The individual has difficulty understanding complex ideas. The message must be broken down into basic points with supporting information.
- The individual lacks a broad set of inferences other than personal experiences from which to draw when reading. Personally involving readers by applying the material to their lifestyle makes it more meaningful.

Defining and Organizing the Message

Ask yourself what the reader needs to know about the subject. List the ideas or concepts you want to convey and refine them to their simplest forms. Then organize the presentation of your message:

- Be consistent in presenting and organizing the information, from idea to idea and from page to page. Consistency provides continuity to help the reader follow the points you want to make.
- Put important information either first or last. Even good readers have a tendency to forget or skip over information between the introductory and summary sections.
- Summarize or repeat ideas or information often to refresh a reader's memory, particularly when preparing materials in a series.
- Present one idea on a single page (or two pages if they are face to face). This allows the reader to complete an idea without the distraction of having to turn pages. Simple ideas should not need more than two facing pages.
- Stay with one idea at a time, presenting only the most relevant information. Avoid going off on tangents.
- Be specific, concise, and accurate so the reader has only the most essential information to think about or decisions to make while reading. Break complex ideas down into subideas.

---

*Source: Nancy Gaston and Patricia Daniels, *Guidelines: Writing for Adults with Limited Reading Skills*, United States Department of Agriculture, Food and Nutrition Service, Office of Information, February 1988.

- Start with the completed idea you want understood, then provide an explanation or give "how to" information.
- Sequence information logically. The following are all good sequencing techniques:
  –step by step (1, 2, 3)
  –chronological (a timeline)
  –topical (using main topics and subtopics)

Writing the Message

To the unskilled reader, all the physical elements of the written message are important. Words, sentences, and paragraphs should all work together to make reading easier, more enjoyable, and more easily comprehended. The goal is to keep the "story" or message moving so it does not get boring.

Tips on Using Words

- Choose and use your words carefully. That does not necessarily mean using *fewer* words to explain an idea. Unskilled readers can become frustrated and disinterested in the material if they do not understand or relate to the words on a page.
- Choose frequently used written words when writing. Words appropriate to the cultural and environmental backgrounds of the readers can be added.
- Avoid using abstract words or phrases. If you must use them, help the reader understand them through examples and pictures. For example:

    Avoid: "Labels let you in on the inside."
    Better: "Food labels can tell you a lot about the food inside the package."

- Use short, nontechnical words of two syllables or less. Hyphenated words are counted as one polysyllabic word.
- Use live, active **verbs** and strong, concrete <u>nouns</u> to add strength and emphasis to sentences. Avoid adjectives and adverbs. For example:

    Keep your own <u>yard</u> and <u>street</u> clean.
    Pick up <u>trash</u> around your <u>home</u>.
    Put <u>trash</u> in the proper <u>container</u>.
    Work with your <u>neighbor</u> to clean up <u>areas</u> in your <u>neighborhood</u> and to keep them clean.

- Use words and expressions familiar to the reader. If you must introduce unfamiliar words, explain them through simple definition, word/picture associations, or by example. Repeat new words at short intervals to make them familiar. For example:

  Aquaculture

  Many farmers raise catfish and other fish in ponds on their farms. This kind of farming is called aquaculture.

  Aquaculture farming works this way: Farmers buy small fish called fingerlings and feed them in the farm ponds. The fish grow to weigh about one or two pounds. Then they are caught and sold to grocery stores and restaurants.

  A lot of catfish can be raised in a pond. Aquaculture is a good way to raise a lot of food in a small space. Aquaculture is a good way for some farmers to make money.

- Avoid sentences with double negatives. Use of negative words may not be objectionable, but positive statements are more motivating. For example:

Avoid:	"Do not eat nonnutritious snacks."
Better:	"Choose snack foods that are high in nutrients."

- Avoid a writing style that uses abbreviations (unless commonly recognizable, e.g., USA), contractions, acronyms, unfamiliar spelling of words, or quotation marks. People with limited reading skills may not understand these elements, and, more importantly, their eyes may not read over them smoothly.
- Avoid statistics. Often they are extraneous and difficult for unskilled readers to interpret.
- Use words with single meanings. Based on how they are used, words, like pictures, can mean different things to different people. For example:

  "Poor readers" (unskilled)
  "Poor readers" (limited income)

Tips on Writing Sentences

- Control the three key elements of a sentence (length, punctuation, and structure). These elements work together to provide sentence rhythm. Their use or misuse influences the clarity and comprehension of a sentence and the reader's attention. To keep the reader's attention, vary sentence rhythm:
  - *Sentence length.* Short sentences averaging eight to ten words are ideal. Longer ones tend to contain multiple ideas. They probably should be made into two sentences. To keep sentences short, avoid unnecessary words, descriptive phrases and clauses, and parenthetical expressions (clarifying or explanatory remarks put in parentheses).
  - *Sentence punctuation.* Asking questions to emphasize a point is a good technique, wouldn't you say? Exclamation points are good for emphasizing your message, too! But, they can be get misused through overuse! So watch it!

—Sentence structure. Usually the subject precedes the verb in a sentence. But sometimes, to vary sentence structure, try putting the verb in front of the noun. For example:

"The use of exclamation points should be minimized."
"Minimize the use of exclamation points."

- Write generally in the active voice. Active sentences place "doers" before "action," clearly showing the doer doing the action. Active sentences present concise, logical, and more direct information to readers and make a stronger statement than passive sentences. Passive sentences have a form of the verb "to be" (am, is, are, was, were, be, being, been) plus a main verb ending in "en" or "ed." Often passive sentences are wordy and roundabout. The receiver of the verb's action comes before the verb, and the doer comes after. For example:

Active: "Jane identified a variety of trees."
          (doer) (verb)   (receiver)
Passive: "A variety of trees were identified by Jane."
          (receiver)   (verb)   (doer)

Tips on Writing Paragraphs

- Tell readers only what they need to know. Excess information can be confusing and distracting. For example:

Excessive:

There are many ways to keep food safe to eat. One way to help keep food safe is to always wash your hands before getting food ready to eat. Other things that touch the food should be clean, too, such as pans, knives, spoons, countertops, mixing bowls, and dishes. This is very important if you plan to eat the food raw, such as in green salads. You can pick up bacteria on your hands from things you touch during the day. The bacteria can get on the food you are preparing. There are many kinds of bacteria. Some bacteria will not hurt you, but some of the bacteria can cause you to be ill. Every year many people get ill from eating foods that were prepared by someone who did not keep their hands or cooking tools clean.

Better:

Always wash your hands before getting food ready to eat. Make sure the pans, knives, bowls, spoons, cutting boards, and other cooking tools are clean before you use them. Keeping your hands and cooking tools clean is VERY important if you plan to eat the food raw, such as in a green salad.

- Sequence information logically. Build connections between what the reader already knows and any new information presented. For example:

You may know someone who was sick from eating food that was spoiled. Sometimes spoiled food does not look or taste spoiled. Here are some rules that can help you keep food safe to eat:

> Keep food clean.
> Keep hot foods hot.
> Keep cold foods cold.

- Use short paragraphs.

Tips on Headings

Headings are useful organizational tools. They give an ordered look to the material, help readers locate information quickly, and give cues about the message content. There are several characteristics of effective headings:

- Short explanatory headings are more instructional than single words, which tend to be abstract. Abstract words are not specific enough. If readers must decipher words, they may lose attention.
- Visuals with headings allow readers to react before more detailed information is given, particularly if the information is new.
- Headings are most effective when used with long paragraphs, but for unskilled readers headings are also appropriate for shorter messages.
- Captions or headings should summarize and emphasize important information.

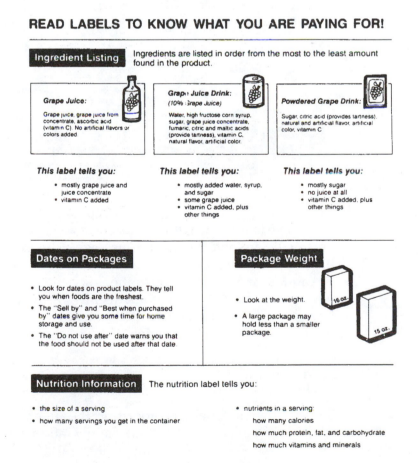

READ LABELS TO KNOW WHAT YOU ARE PAYING FOR!

Ingredient Listing   Ingredients are listed in order from the most to the least amount found in the product.

Grape Juice:
Grape juice, grape juice from concentrate, ascorbic acid (vitamin C). No artificial flavors or colors added.

Grape Juice Drink:
(10% Grape Juice)
Water, high fructose corn syrup, sugar, grape juice concentrate, fumaric, citric and malic acids (provide tartness), vitamin C, natural flavor, artificial color.

Powdered Grape Drink:
Sugar, citric acid (provides tartness), natural and artificial flavor, artificial color, vitamin C

This label tells you:
- mostly grape juice and juice concentrate
- vitamin C added

This label tells you:
- mostly added water, syrup, and sugar
- some grape juice
- vitamin C added, plus other things

This label tells you:
- mostly sugar
- no juice at all
- vitamin C added, plus other things

Dates on Packages
- Look for dates on product labels. They tell you when foods are the freshest.
- The "Sell by" and "Best when purchased by" dates give you some time for home storage and use.
- The "Do not use after" date warns you that the food should not be used after that date.

Package Weight
- Look at the weight.
- A large package may hold less than a smaller package.

Nutrition Information   The nutrition label tells you:

- the size of a serving
- how many servings you get in the container

- nutrients in a serving:
  how many calories
  how much protein, fat, and carbohydrate
  how much vitamins and minerals

Using Illustrations To Support the Message

Photographs and line art attract and keep a reader's interest and are often remembered longer than words. Properly chosen and placed illustrations make the text more meaningful and reduce the burden of details in the text.

Illustrations should be used with a specific informational purpose in mind, not just as decoration. They should emphasize, explain, or summarize the text.

Some guidelines for using illustrations are as follows:

- Place illustrations, along with any captions, next to the related text.
- Use captions or text that tell readers what to look for in the illustration. People see different things in the same picture, based on their experiences and knowledge.
- Keep illustrations simple by removing unneeded background or extraneous detail. Each variation in types of lines, shapes, textures, and spacial arrangements adds to the complexity of the illustration. Remove extraneous detail, as shown below:

- Use realistic pictures of people or activities with which a reader can identify. By being able to identify with characters or action in a picture, a reader may feel more personally involved with the message. Choose full-face pictures of people or illustrations that show definite actions that are easy to understand.
- Be cautious in using two illustrations showing wanted versus unwanted behavior or action. If the difference is not distinct, the reader may get the wrong message.
- Use illustrations to get the reader's attention and complement the message, not to dominate the reader's attention.

Formatting To Get Attention

If the written material does not attract the attention of its audience, chances are the message will never be read. Both the overall visual presentation and the written message are important in developing useful and effective materials. The format should be a simple, uncluttered, and balanced layout of text, illustrations, and design features. Once you have finished formatting, try the upside-down test. If you turn the finished layout upside down, it should look as good and be as appealing as when it is right-side up.

Tips on Design and Layout

- Balance illustrations and words with background space. Lots of white space and wide margins will make your work seem simple and uncluttered.
- Start the message in the upper left corner or upper middle of the page.
- Put text and illustrations of greatest interest around the center square of a page (marked by Xs in the figure below), as if the page was divided into thirds both horizontally and vertically. For example:

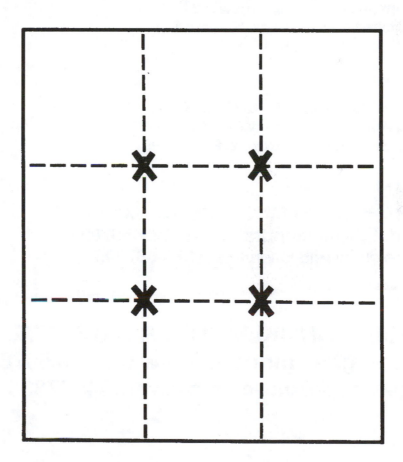

- Number frames of sequential or grouped information. Numbering leads a reader logically through the message.
- Avoid lengthy lists. Unskilled readers have trouble remembering items on a list. Also, like most of us, they get bored reading lists.

Tips on Lettering

- Select a style and size of typeface (lettering) that is easy to look at and read.
- A simple typeface without italic, serif, or curls is good. Handwriting (script) is difficult for unskilled readers to read. A good range of typeface sizes would be from 10 to 14 points.
- Mix upper- and lowercase lettering together. They are easier to read than LETTERING IN ALL CAPITALS.
- Avoid crowded letters. Rely on what is pleasing to the eye. Try mixing both mechanical and optical spacing techniques:
  - *Mechanical spacing* is equal distance between letters without regard to letter shape.
  - *Optical spacing* allows shapes of letters to determine spacing between them.

---

10 POINT

ABCDEFGHIJKLMNOPQRSTUVWXYZ
abcdefghijklmnopqrstuvwxyz1234567890
ABCDEFGHIJKLMNOPQRSTUVWXYZ1234567890

12 POINT

ABCDEFGHIJKLMNOPQRSTUVWXYZ
abcdefghijklmnopqrstuvwxyz1234567890
ABCDEFGHIJKLMNOPQRSTUVWXYZ1234567890

14 POINT

ABCDEFGHIJKLMNOPQRSTUVWXYZ
abcdefghijklmnopqrstuvwxyz1234567890
ABCDEFGHIJKLMNOPQRSTUVWXYZ1234567890

18 POINT

ABCDEFGHIJKLMNOPQRSTUVWXYZ
abcdefghijklmnopqrstuvwxyz1234567890
ABCDEFGHIJKLMNOPQRSTUVWXYZ1234567890

24 POINT

ABCDEFGHIJKLMNOPQRSTUVWXYZ
abcdefghijklmnopqrstuvwxyz1234567890
ABCDEFGHIJKLMNOPQRSTUVWXYZ1234567890

- Contrast lettering color with background color. The best ink and paper combinations for reading are those that provide good contrast. Dark ink colors, particularly black, dark blue, and brown, on white or off-white paper are very legible. If photocopies of the material are sharp and clear, the contrast is good.
- Thin, dark lettering on a light background is best. If light-colored lettering on a dark background is used, the lettering should be a thicker typeface to facilitate reading. For example:

| **Ingredient Listing** | Ingredients are listed in order from the most to the least amount found in the product. |

Tips on Visual Design

Every element of a publication's design should serve a purpose. Heading, visual devices, and spacing help to attract and keep the reader's attention, organize the information, and keep the "story" moving.

Visual devices. Visual devices draw the reader's attention to the most important places on a page. However, their overuse could be distracting:

- Use arrows, color, and other highlighting techniques to lead the reader's eye sequentially from one piece of information to the next.
- Box in concepts that belong together or stress common similarities or differences. For example:

Sugar: The Basic Facts

What Is Sugar?

To most people, "sugar" means white table sugar. In the Dietary Guidelines, "sugar" means all forms of caloric sweeteners, including white sugar, brown sugar, raw sugar, corn syrup, honey, and molasses.

Table sugar, or sucrose, is the most commonly used sugar. Corn-based sweeteners are also used in large amounts in food processing.

Sugars are simple carbohydrates. Another type of carbohydrate, complex carbohydrate, includes starch and dietary fiber.

How Much Sugar Is in the Foods You Eat?

The trade-offs below are equations that show approximately how much sugar is added to some popular foods. Foods on each side of the equation provide about the same amount of nutrients. For example, milk- and grain-based desserts provide the same nutrients as the enriched flour or milk from which they are made, but they also provide much more sugar and fat.

Sugary Foods	
1 tsp. jam or jelly	= 1 tsp. sugar, syrup, or molasses
1-ounce chocolate bar	= 2 tsp. fat + 5 tsp. sugar
12 ounces fruit drink, ade, or punch	= 12 tsp. sugar
12 ounces cola	= 9 tsp. sugar

Spacing. Generally, the size of the page dictates an appropriate column width, typeface style and size, spacing between lines, and the placement of visuals. Maintaining consistency in spacing through the publication is important.

Margins. If possible, make margins wider at the bottom than at the top of the page, and equalize side margins. Also, use an unjustified right margin. Justifying makes inconsistent spacing within and between words and can confuse an unskilled reader. For example:

Justified	**Unjustified**
A justified right-hand margin will have each line end at exactly the same place on the right margin and be the same length. The spacing will be uneven between words. Newspaper columns are good examples of justified margins.	An unjustified right-hand margin will have each line end at different places on the right margin. Like this example, each line will be a different length. No irregularity can be seen with the spacing between words.

Columns. Use narrow columns, not full-page wide text. They are easier to read. A column of 40 to 45 characters is recommended.

Paragraphs. When paragraphs are short, do not indent. When text is complex, start each sentence of a paragraph on a new line. Double space between paragraphs; single space between a heading and the first paragraph.

Words. Avoid putting the first word of a sentence as the last word on a line.

Pretesting before Production

Pretesting allows an opportunity to evaluate and reassess the material for appropriateness with the target audience. Results of a pretest should give feedback on five basic components of effective communication: attractiveness, comprehension, acceptability, self-involvement, and persuasion:

- *Attractiveness* is visual appeal. Its role is to motivate readers to pick up the material and read it. Visual appeal includes elements such as overall design, title, color, and illustrations.
- *Comprehension* is how well the ideas are understood and retained. Elements that affect comprehension include repetition of key words or concepts, sentence structure, word usage, highlighting techniques, and appropriate reading level. One element the writer cannot control, but which strongly influences comprehension, is the extent to which a reader's background knowledge and experiences can be applied to make the material meaningful.
- *Acceptability* is a condition (state) of favorable approval or belief. Some elements that make written materials acceptable include culturally appropriate illustrations and words, credibility of the author, and legibility of typeface.
- *Self-involvement* is the degree to which readers can apply what they read to their own lifestyle. Elements that contribute to self-involvement are action-oriented

illustrations that incorporate the reader's point of view, text with personal references, and words common to the reader's vocabulary.

- *Persuasion* is the ability to convince the reader to undertake a desired behavior or accept new information. Persuasion can be achieved through identifying and presenting topics relative to the reader's concerns, logically sequencing information, and being a credible author in the eyes of the reader or quoting a well-known, reliable source.

Checklist for Written Materials

Check how your materials meet some of the basic techniques on writing for adults with limited reading skills:

- ☐ *Need* for information is established.
- ☐ *Information* is useful without being extraneous.
- ☐ *Target audience* is identified. Its characteristics are understood and not forgotten as the primary receiver of the information.
- ☐ *Audience* is made to feel personally involved and motivated to read the material.
- ☐ *Sentences* are simple, short, specific, and mostly in the active voice.
- ☐ *Ideas* are clear and logically sequenced, and each idea is limited to one page or two pages, face to face. Important points are highlighted and summarized.
- ☐ *Illustrations* are relevant to text, meaningful to the audience, and appropriately located.
- ☐ *Words* are familiar to the reader. Any new words are clearly defined. None, or very few, are three syllables or more.
- ☐ *Readability level* is determined to be close to fifth grade level.
- ☐ *Layout* balances white space with words and illustrations.

NOTES:

DEVELOPING LOW-LITERACY MATERIALS: QUESTIONS AND ANSWERS*

Defining the Audience

Question: How do I decide whether I need to develop a low-literacy product versus a regular publication at a lower reading level?

Answer: The key criterion is a need to reach individuals with very poor or marginal written communication skills. These groups are distinct from general public audiences who may profit from materials written in simple language but who probably do not *need* special low-literacy readers' aids and educational devices to comprehend a message.

A variety of factors can suggest a need to focus specifically on low-literate readers. One planner based her decision to target this group on an analysis of public knowledge of her topic, cancer prevention. Surveys repeated at three-year intervals showed little to no gain in knowledge among some audiences despite ambitious public information campaigns designed at the ninth and tenth grade reading level. "That said to me that messages directed to the general public weren't getting through to all of the target audience," this program professional explained. "We decided to develop a prevention message specially targeted to low-literate Americans because demographic profiles and our experience had shown that this was a group our earlier campaigns could well have missed."

Another cancer prevention project also used available data to help identify its target audience. In this case, data showing that hard-core smokers were more likely to have lower educational levels argued for conveying a stop-smoking message in low-literacy format.

Once you decide that you need to reach readers with limited-literacy skills, then you can define that audience more specifically in relation to your messages.

Question: Can I communicate effectively to people with average or good reading skills by using a low-literacy format?

Answer: Testing your product with the audience is the only way to find out. The experiences and opinions of those in the field vary on this point. Some have found that better-educated information seekers will not even pick up a product that clearly is aimed at a basic level. Others say that all readers appreciate a message conveyed simply and clearly and that those readers who want more detail can be directed to sources of more in-depth information.

Question: Must I use these research methods to develop an effective low-literacy product? I do not always have the time or the budget to do new audience research.

Answer: Many product developers echo this concern. While formal research methods can provide invaluable insights, many projects will not be able to make use of them due to a variety of practical constraints. The best approach is to make audience research a routine part of your product development process for audiences of all literacy levels; then the time and budget for research will be built in automatically.

What are the alternatives to formal research? Product developers commonly use two other methods to get needed information about their target audience: (1) seeking

*Source: *Clear and Simple: Developing Effective Print Materials for Low-Literate Readers*, NIH Publication #95-3594, U.S. Department of Health and Human Services, Public Health Service, National Institutes of Health, National Cancer Institute, December 1994.

input from target audience members who agree to serve on an advisory board or (2) seeking input from individuals who have close working contacts with the target audience.

"I've worked with this audience for 20 years," notes one writer, "and I have gained lots of insights. I feel confident in using this knowledge as a starting point. But I supplement it with advisory board guidance when I can't conduct formal research. And even when I can't do all the up-front research I would prefer, I know that pretesting will supplement what I've learned earlier and ensure that the product is on target."

When you rely on indirect information sources, such as asking health professionals what they believe their clients think, feel, or do, it is especially important to pretest the product with members of the audience themselves.

A low-literacy educator stresses that "it's critical to get direct audience involvement at some point. No matter how well you or others think you know your target group, only someone with limited-literacy skills can provide a true test of your materials' comprehensibility and appropriateness. Programs that rely only on secondary or gatekeeper opinions can make big mistakes."

Question: If I do audience research before I develop my concept, how can I get information that is specific to my product?

Answer: The steps suggested here need not be completed in strict chronological order. In many cases, audience research occurs in several stages as product developers have need for new or different information.

Often before a concept statement is fully developed, you will have certain fundamental ideas in mind that could be tested during audience research. For example, you may have a key message line that you have always used in your products. Will it work with this audience? In producing a booklet on food safety, the Food and Drug Administration found that their traditional message, "keep hot foods hot, keep cold foods cold," did not communicate to low-literate readers. While the words are simple, they did not convey safety concepts clearly.

Another example might be the planning of a campaign or a product that includes a celebrity. In the initial research stage, you could determine whether the celebrities you have in mind are credible—or known—to this audience. One writer recalls the results of not taking this step. "I used to staff exhibits where we offered our products to health organizations with low-literate clients. Numerous program directors and nurses commented on one of our posters that used gambling odds-maker 'Jimmy the Greek' to convey a health message. They told us that their clients did not understand the concept at all. The target audience's response to the poster was 'Who's he?' or 'What does he have to do with health?' The program directors said the only way they could use the poster was to turn it over and write their own message on the blank side."

Content Development

Question: Technical terms raise the reading level of a publication. Do low-literate readers need to know them? Will they understand them?

Answer: There is no absolute answer to this question. When technical terms are used in the reader's daily life, they can be as familiar as any other words. For example, an older American will know the term "Social Security benefits," and a person with diabetes will be accustomed to technical words such as "insulin" and "reaction."

When a text does include technical terms, some writers suggest putting a simple explanation next to the term. They believe a glossary approach may add to the low-literate reader's difficulty in getting through the text. People may not realize that unfamiliar words are defined in a separate section.

Many practitioners feel that the "need to know" criterion is an important one to apply to this decision. "If my objective is to increase the use of mammography, I have to use that term," one writer says. "But if I'm asking people with HIV to takes AIDS-delaying actions, does the audience need to know the term 'opportunistic infection'? I chose to avoid the term, and pretesting showed that the audience understood what they needed to do to avoid infections without learning it."

Question: How can I keep material on technical topics simple throughout an expert and/or organizational review process?

Answer: This is a common concern. The simplicity of effective low-literacy products is startling to many reviewers, especially those accustomed to scientific or technical publications. They often are unfamiliar with low-literacy techniques and may be concerned that a product written at a low reading level may reflect poorly on the expertise of an agency or organization.

Several writers suggested ways to work constructively with reviewers on this issue. Ideas include the following:

- Educate reviewers about the need and scientific foundation for low-literate writing techniques.
- Involve reviewers at the concept development stage so that they are not surprised at the draft they receive.
- Make sure that all simple explanations are accurate. Do not distort the scientific or technical facts as you pare away the details.
- Work personally with the reviewers. If a suggested change is inappropriate, discuss your concerns and work cooperatively toward a solution.
- Test reviewer-inserted concepts, specifically during prepublication evaluations. If the reviewer's idea does not work with the audience, you will have a firm basis for change.

Question: Are pictorial signs, symbols, and charts more effective than words for a low-literate reader?

Answer: Not necessarily. Some experts suggest that "universal" symbols, such as a stop sign, an arrow, or a big black "X" usually test well with this audience. When a pictorial representation is open to interpretation, however, it can fail to communicate with any audience. Likewise, while a simple chart may work well, a large matrix or visually busy schema are likely to confuse. For example, functionally illiterate individuals have trouble using a bus schedule.

Question: I know that low-literacy products should focus only on a few key concepts. How do I handle a complex topic with eight or ten important messages when I can only afford to do one low-literacy publication?

Answer: A strong grouping of main and subpoints is a common solution to this problem. When individual sections are sequenced effectively and each can stand alone, readers can approach the text at their own pace.

Question: I cannot afford to do separate low-literacy publications for all of our organization's publications. Is there an effective way to adapt higher level reading materials for low-literacy populations?

Answer: For many years, the only products available to professionals who work with low-literate groups were written at a high reading level. These professionals became adept at picking out the key concepts and highlighting them for their clients—using underlining, circles, stars, or arrows that meant "pay special attention to this." Although the experts would not call this approach ideal, it does meet the readers' needs better than untailored higher level material.

Writers also attempt to meet the needs of both audiences by using headlines and subheads to carry key messages points, in logical order. Low-literate readers—and others who only skim written materials—can skip the details that the accompanying text provides.

Question: All of my products need to be photocopied and that means I cannot use color. Sometimes my budget will not allow for illustration either. Can I still design an effective low-literacy product?

Answer: Although color is a powerful communication tool, strong format, good use of white space, and alternative highlighting devices can help a black-and-white product convey its message.

Low-literacy products do not always need illustrations to break up the text. Boxes, lines, and white space can keep a design from being too copy dense.

Pictures that illustrate an action or a key point are valuable, however, and they do not have to be expensive to produce. In fact, simple line drawings usually are preferable to detailed pictures for this audience. Even off-the-shelf computer clip art can be effective if it fits the message and tests well with the audience.

Checklist: Key Principles of Effective Low-Literacy Print Materials

CONTENT/STYLE

☐ The material is interactive and allows for audience involvement.

☐ The material presents "how-to" information.

☐ Peer language is used whenever appropriate to increase personal identification and improve readability.

☐ Words are familiar to the reader. Any new words are defined clearly.

☐ Sentences are simple, specific, direct, and written in the active voice.

☐ Each idea is clear and logically sequenced (according to audience logic).

☐ The number of concepts is limited per piece.

☐ The material uses concrete examples rather than abstract concepts.

☐ The text highlights and summarizes important points.

LAYOUT

☐ The material uses advance organizers or headers.

☐ Headers are simple and close to text.

☐ Layout balances white space with words and illustrations.

☐ Text uses upper- and lowercase letters.

☐ Underlining or bold type, rather than all caps, gives emphasis.

☐ Type style and size of print are easy to read; type is at least 12 point.

VISUALS

☐ Visuals are relevant to text, meaningful to the audience, and appropriately located.

☐ Illustrations and photographs are simple and free from clutter and distraction.

☐ Visuals use adult rather than childlike images.

☐ Illustrations show familiar images that reflect cultural context.

☐ Visuals have captions. Each visual illustrates and is directly related to one message.

☐ Different styles, such as photographs without background detail, shaded line drawings, or simple line drawings, are pretested with the audience to determine which is understood best.

☐ Cues, such as circles or arrows, point out key information.

☐ Colors used are appealing to the audience (as determined by pretesting).

READABILITY

☐ Readability analysis is done to determine reading level.

NOTES:

Source: *Clear and Simple: Developing Effective Print Materials for Low-Literate Readers*, NIH Publication #95-3594, U.S. Department of Health and Human Services, Public Health Service, National Institutes of Health, National Cancer Institute, December 1994.

PRETESTING LOW-LITERACY MATERIALS*

Pretesting is a qualitative measure of audience response to a product. It is critical to pretest draft messages and visuals with members of the intended audience. Pretesting helps ensure that materials are well understood, responsive to audience needs and concerns, and culturally sensitive. It is a tool for identifying elements in a communication that need to be changed to make it more appropriate for the intended audience.

Although funds may not be available for extensive pretesting, some pretesting is essential to ensure that materials are culturally relevant and understandable to the target audience.

Pretesting is an important step in developing materials for any audience. There are special requirements, however, for pretesting low-literacy materials.

Pretesting Variables: What To Test For

The basic purpose of pretesting materials with low-literate audiences is to find out whether the readers understand the messages. In addition to comprehension, three other factors are important: audience members' attraction to the product, its acceptability to them, and their personal involvement with the material. In discussing materials with participants, key issues to probe for include the following.

Comprehension

Does the respondent understand what the material is recommending and how and when to do it? Is anything clear, confusing, or hard to believe? What meaning does the respondent attach to key words? to symbols and abbreviations? to visuals? Important aspects include:

- *Suitability of the words used*: "What does the educational piece mean when it says to eat *balanced* meals? How do you do that?"
- *Distinguishing key details*: "Which vegetables have lots of fiber?"
- *Meaning or relationship of visuals to text*: "Looking at this picture, how will you cut down on fat in your soups or stocks when cooking?"

Attraction

What kind of feelings does the material generate—enthusiasm? just OK? or a "turnoff"? The respondent could be asked, for example, "Are the people in the material attractive to you? Is there anything you don't like about the people (or pictures) in this material? How about the color and the layout of the material?"

Acceptability

Is the material compatible with local culture? Is it realistic? Would it offend people in any way? Are the hairstyles, clothing, and so forth, appropriate?

- *Suitability for both sexes and all ages*: "Is this mostly for men (women)?"
- *Supportive of ethnic practices*: "Do you think your friends and neighbors would be willing to cook their foods this way?"

---

*Source: *Clear and Simple: Developing Effective Print Materials for Low-Literate Readers*, NIH Publication #95-3594, U.S. Department of Health and Human Services, Public Health Services, National Institutes of Health, National Cancer Institute, December 1994.

- *Personal involvement or relevance:* "Can you see yourself carrying out the actions called for in the materials?"

Not every word, picture, or idea has to be tested. The most important points to verify are that the reader understands what he or she should do and how to do it. Comprehension often depends on understanding fundamental vocabulary terms and visuals. For example, the word *diet* may be understood by different people to mean different things; applying the wrong definition could lead to the wrong behavior. When key content is conveyed in word/picture associations of tables and lists, it is critical to test comprehension of these formats and to ensure that the reader has the skills needed to use them.

Organizing a Pretest

Pretesting with low-literate audiences involves some unique logistical considerations. This section discusses some issues to keep in mind while organizing the pretest.

When To Pretest

Pretesting is done at either or both of these stages of product development:

- rough draft of copy and graphic concepts using a manuscript of the product, with a few examples of potential illustrations
- preliminary typeset, laid-out version of the product with rough graphics in place

Where To Pretest

Pretesting can be done in:

- clinic/hospital waiting rooms
- physicians' offices
- clients' homes
- community facilities (e.g., church, senior center)
- adult basic education and English as a second language classes
- agency/organization's facilities (e.g., Social Security office, job training centers)

Environment

Some researchers believe it is best to test a product in the same type of environment in which a reader will be using the material. For example, if a client will be reading a fact sheet in a noisy, busy clinic, be sure that test readers have the same distractions.

Methods

- Individual interviews (10–20 minutes each)
  - *Advantages:* Provide "cleanest" results; less chance of one respondent biasing another; good for short materials.
  - *Disadvantages:* Scheduling may not allow speedy completion.

- Group interviews (eight to ten people, 30–60 minutes)
  - *Advantages:* Better for longer pieces (booklets, kits); group discussion may elicit valuable information not contained in interview questions.
  - *Disadvantages:* Need to organize in advance; need a trained group facilitator to conduct. Session must be paced to maintain attention.

Number of Participants

Ideally, at least 25 to 50 members of the intended audience should review the product. If time or budget is limited, however, it is far better to test the material with 5 to 10 people than not to test it at all.

Fewer participants are needed if the product is:

- very simple
- very short, needing only a brief attention span to complete
- directed at one homogeneous target group

More participants are needed if the product is relatively:

- complex
- long, demanding a sustained attention span
- culturally diverse

Determining the Reading Level of Pretest Participants

Are you pretesting your materials with the right readers? Having pretest participants who have the same characteristics as the low-literate audience you are trying to reach is critical to the validity of your pretest results. Recruiting participants through groups or settings that include people with limited-literacy skills is a logical starting point. But the only way to be sure your pretest volunteers read at the same level as your intended audience is to test their reading skills. The Wide Range Achievement Test (WRAT) is used to measure reading levels, and the Cloze technique is used to measure comprehension. To avoid offending or causing discomfort to those whose reading ability you are testing, you can integrate a WRAT or a Cloze test into the pretest interview. For example, in a recent pretest conducted by the National Cancer Institute, the interviewers introduced the WRAT test as the last part of the pretest. They stated, "Thank you for helping with the questions on the chemotherapy booklet. We need your help with one last part—a word list. This will take only a few minutes. The word list will help us know how difficult the words are in the chemotherapy booklet." This integrated approach spared the participant the pressure or potential embarrassment of "failing a reading test."

The Wide Range Achievement Test

The Wide Range Achievement Test is based on word recognition and does not measure comprehension or vocabulary. An efficient way to determine reading levels, it takes only a short time to administer.

The WRAT has the reader look at a written word and say that word out loud. Pronouncing the word correctly shows that the reader recognizes the word. The

WRAT focuses on recognition because, at the most basic level, if a person does not recognize a word, comprehension is impossible.

The test involves listening to the participant read from a prepared list of words, arranged in increasing order of difficulty. The test is over after the reader mispronounces 10 words, and the test administrator notes the level at which the last mispronunciation occurred. The "stop" level equates to a grade level of reading skills. This level can be compared with the reading level of the intended audience to see if pretest readers are a good representative match.

The Cloze Technique

This procedure measures the reader's ability to comprehend a written passage. Because it requires readers to process information, it may take up to 30 minutes to administer.

In a Cloze test, text appears with every fifth word omitted. The reader tries to fill in the blanks. This task demonstrates how well the reader understands the text. The reader's ability to identify the correct word also reflects his or her familiarity with sentence structure.

Conducting Pretest Interviews: Special Considerations

Just as effective low-literacy products are designed to meet audience needs, effective pretesting also must be tailored to participants with limited reading skills. Those experienced in pretesting with a low-literate audience offer the following suggestions:

- Give only one product to each individual or group, even if you are testing a series of publications. This ensures the respondent's maximum concentration level for each product.
- Distance yourself from the product and assure participants that you want their honest assessment. "If you don't," one pretester explains, "this audience is more likely than higher-level readers to avoid criticizing. Perhaps it's because they aren't sure they understand or perhaps they aren't comfortable explaining negative responses."
- Make sure participants understand that *they* are not being tested; the materials are. Explain this clearly when you introduce the materials and the participant's role. People concerned about their literacy skills need this reassurance.
- Pay attention to audience interest in the proceedings. Change the pace, if necessary, to maintain attention levels. When attention was waning in a large group discussing product text, for example, the facilitator split the group in half to allow more one-to-one interaction and switched the focus to illustrations.
- Choose people who are culturally sensitive and who have good social skills to recruit and interview pretest participants. Unless potential participants feel at ease with the interviewing staff, they may not agree to take part.

Using Pretest Results To Revise Materials

Pretest results, usually in the form of a report with recommendations, are not a blueprint for revisions. They raise issues and point out problems; the solutions are up to you. Common issues about low-literacy products include the following.

Question: Should the product be scrapped and begun again when pretesting raises concerns?

Answer: Much of the time, simple to extensive revisions can fix problems that pretesting uncovers. You should start over only when the majority of responses indicate *fundamental* problems, such as the following:

- Most readers were completely lost and could not identify the key behavioral actions the material was designed to convey.
- The medium interferes with the message (e.g., a large chart poster is too complicated to understand).
- The format is altogether unappealing or off target (e.g., readers do not want a booklet; they want a video. A tip sheet gives only "how-to" information, but readers really want background information).
- The product is culturally inappropriate, with no relevance to the audience.

Question: If one or only a few respondents raise a concern, are revisions necessary?

Answer: This is a judgment call. Your answer will depend on two factors:

- *How many respondents you had.* If you only tested the material with 10 people, each response needs to be considered seriously; with 50 participants, percentages can be relied on more comfortably.
- *The nature of the comment.* Any remark that shows lack of understanding of a key concept should receive careful attention. If one person did not grasp a point, others may have problems as well. Idiosyncratic comments about a product's appeal or personal relevance are less of a concern, however. No format will please everyone in *any* audience.

Question: Should respondents' suggestions for reviewing a product be followed?

Answer: Pretest participants are experts in what they can understand and accept in a product; they are not experts in the material's design. Most of the time, professional judgment is needed to devise an effective way to address reader concerns.

Many writers like to attend pretest group sessions or read interview questionnaires themselves rather than relying only on the pretest report. To get the most useful results, writers often contribute to questionnaire development as well. That way, they can draw special attention to specific wording or format choices they want an audience to validate.

Questions about Pretesting

Question: My time frame is very tight. How can I fit pretesting into the schedule?

Answer: Pretesting need not be an elaborate, time-consuming research project. How long it takes depends on how quickly you work, how elaborate your internal review process is, how large your test group sample is, and the schedules of the sites or organizations involved. The best approach is to include time for pretesting in the initial product development schedule. If time is short, plan a small-scale test and begin the preparatory steps right away. Much of the preliminary work in pretesting can be completed long before the actual testing period. For example, arranging with a group or site to get access to audience representatives can begin during concept development. You can begin to draft your questionnaire while a product is still going through internal review, with any needed modifications made later.

"At first I had to educate my organization about the critical role pretesting plays in low-literacy product development," one writer remembers. "Now that everyone has seen how valuable it is, pretesting is no longer a 'refinement' we consider using in special circumstances. We make time for it in every low-literacy product development process."

Question: How can I get access to people from the target audience for pretesting?

Answer: Many agencies work with literacy organizations. State directors of adult basic education and English as a second language programs often are good sources.

You also can cooperate with groups that represent your particular target audience. In pretesting booklets about human immunodeficiency virus (HIV) and acquired immune deficiency syndrome (AIDS), for example, the National Institute for Allergy and Infectious Diseases (NIAID) worked with organizations such as People With AIDS and community clinics that are part of NIAID's research network. Several professionals interviewed for this guide suggested that offering incentives, such as small cash payments or reduced waiting time for an appointment, can help motivate individual participation. Overworked and underfunded literacy programs also are more able to provide timely assistance if your agency can compensate them for their recruiting time.

Question: Professional intermediaries distribute our pamphlets to their clients. Should they be part of pretesting?

Answer: Professional intermediaries and advisory groups can be an important source of insights about your product's utility. Product developers interviewed for this guide cautioned, however, that responses of audience members should take precedence over professional views if you receive conflicting opinions. It also is important not to rely on professional review alone; no matter how close professionals are to their clients, they are not low-literate themselves.

Heart-Healthy Eating Self-Contract

I, _____, agree with the following small steps to reduce my fat intake.

☐ I pledge to use the Food Guide Pyramid *twice a week* to choose foods to make a healthy meal.

☐ I pledge to eat a fruit or vegetable for a snack *every day*.

☐ I pledge to select low-fat foods *more often* & my favorite high-fat food, _____, only *once a week*.

Within the next 4 weeks, by _____, I'll be following these pledges *regularly*.

If I do, I will reward myself with/by _____

_____

If I do not, I will *revise the contract and start over*.

_____
Signature   Date

_____
Witness   Date

NOTES:

Source: Gail C. Frank-Spohrer, *Community Nutrition: Applying Epidemiology to Contemporary Practice*, Aspen Publishers, Inc., © 1996.

Check Your Healthy Heart IQ

Answer "true" or "false" to the following questions to test your knowledge of heart disease and its risk factors. Be sure to check the answers and explanation on the following pages to see how well you do.

1. The risk factors for heart disease that you *can do something about* are high blood pressure, high blood cholesterol, smoking, obesity, and physical inactivity.   T F

2. A stroke is often the first symptom of high blood pressure, and a heart attack is often the first symptom of high blood cholesterol.   T F

3. A blood pressure greater than or equal to 140/90 mm Hg is generally considered to be high.   T F

4. High blood pressure affects the same number of Blacks as it does Whites.   T F

5. The best ways to treat and control high blood pressure are to control your weight, exercise, eat less salt (sodium), restrict your intake of alcohol, and take your high blood pressure medicine, if prescribed by your doctor.   T F

6. A blood cholesterol level of 240 mg/dL is desirable for adults.   T F

7. The most effective dietary way to lower the level of your blood cholesterol is to eat foods low in cholesterol.   T F

8. Lowering blood cholesterol levels can help people who have already had a heart attack.   T F

9. Only children from families at high risk of heart disease need to have their blood cholesterol levels checked.   T F

10. Smoking is a major risk factor for four of the five leading causes of death including heart attack, stroke, cancer, and lung diseases such as emphysema and bronchitis.   T F

11. If you have had a heart attack, quitting smoking can help reduce your chances of having a second attack.   T F

12. Someone who has smoked for 30 to 40 years probably will not be able to quit smoking.   T F

13. The best way to lose weight is to increase physical activity and eat fewer calories.   T F

14. Heart disease is the leading killer of men *and* women in the United States.   T F

continues

Healthy Heart IQ continued

1. **TRUE** High blood pressure, smoking, and high blood cholesterol are the three most important risk factors for heart disease. On the average, each one doubles your chance of developing heart disease. So, a person who has all three of these risk factors is 8 times more likely to develop heart disease than someone who has none. Obesity increases the likelihood of developing high blood cholesterol and high blood pressure, which increase your risk for heart disease. Physical inactivity increases your risk of heart attack. Regular exercise and good nutrition are essential to reducing high blood pressure, high blood cholesterol, and overweight. People who exercise are also more likely to cut down or stop smoking.

2. **TRUE** A person with high blood pressure or high blood cholesterol may feel fine and look great; there are often no signs that anything is wrong until a stroke or heart attack occurs. To find out if you have high blood pressure or high blood cholesterol, you should be tested by a doctor, nurse, or other health professional.

3. **TRUE** A blood pressure of 140/90 mm Hg or greater is generally classified as high blood pressure. However, blood pressures that fall below 140/90 mm Hg can sometimes be a problem. If the diastolic pressure, the second or lower number, is between 85–89, a person is at increased risk for heart disease or stroke and should have his or her blood pressure checked at least once a year by a health professional. The higher your blood pressure, the greater your risk of developing heart disease or stroke. Controlling high blood pressure reduces your risk.

4. **FALSE** High blood pressure is more common in Blacks than in Whites. It affects 29 out of every 100 Black adults compared to 26 out of every 100 White adults. Also, with aging, high blood pressure is generally more severe among Blacks than among Whites and therefore causes more strokes, heart disease, and kidney failure.

5. **TRUE** Recent studies show that lifestyle changes can help keep blood pressure levels normal even into advanced age and are important in treating and preventing high blood pressure. Limit high-salt foods, which include many snack foods, such as potato chips, salted pretzels, and salted crackers; processed foods, such as canned soups; and condiments, such as ketchup and soy sauce. Also, it is extremely important to take blood pressure medication, if prescribed by your doctor, to make sure your blood pressure stays under control.

6. **FALSE** A total blood cholesterol level of under 200 mg/dL is *desirable* and usually puts you at a lower risk for heart disease. A blood cholesterol level of 240 mg/dL or above is *high* and increases your risk of heart disease. If your cholesterol level is high, your doctor will want to check your levels of LDL-cholesterol ("bad" cholesterol) and HDL-cholesterol ("good" cholesterol). A HIGH level of LDL-cholesterol increases your risk of heart disease, as does a LOW level of HDL-cholesterol. A cholesterol level of 200–239 mg/dL is considered borderline-high and usually increases your risk for heart disease. If your cholesterol is borderline-high, you should speak to your doctor to see if additional cholesterol tests are needed. All adults 20 years of age or older should have their blood cholesterol level checked at least once every 5 years.

7. **FALSE** Reducing the amount of cholesterol in your diet is important; however, eating foods low in saturated fat is the most effective dietary way to lower blood cholesterol levels, along with eating less total fat and cholesterol. Choose low-saturated fat foods, such as grains, fruits, and vegetables; low-fat or skim milk and milk products; lean cuts of meat; fish; and chicken. Trim fat from meat before cooking; bake or broil meat rather than fry; use less fat and oil; and take the skin off chicken and turkey. Reducing overweight will also help lower your level of LDL-cholesterol as well as increase your level of HDL-cholesterol.

8. **TRUE** People who have had one heart attack are at much higher risk for a second attack. Reducing blood cholesterol levels can greatly slow down (and, in some people, even reserve) the buildup of cholesterol and fat in the walls of the coronary arteries and significantly reduce the chances of a second heart attack.

9. **TRUE** Children from "high risk" families, in which a parent has high blood cholesterol (240 mg/dL or above) or in which a parent or grandparent has had heart disease at an early age (at 55 years of age or younger), should have their cholesterol levels tested. If a child from such a family has a cholesterol level that is high, it should be lowered under medical supervision, primarily with diet, to reduce the risk of developing heart disease as an adult. For most children, who are not from high-risk families, the best way to reduce the risk of adult heart disease is to follow a low-saturated fat, low cholesterol eating pattern. All children over the age of 2 years and all adults should adopt a heart-healthy eating pattern as a principal way of reducing coronary heart disease.

10. **TRUE** Heavy smokers are two to four times more likely to have a heart attack than nonsmokers, and the heart attack death rate among all smokers is 70 percent greater than that of non-smokers. Older male smokers are also nearly twice as likely to die from stroke than older men who do not smoke, and these odds are nearly as high for older female smokers. Further, the risk of dying of lung cancer is 22 times higher for male smokers than male nonsmokers and 12 times higher for female smokers than female nonsmokers. Finally, 80 percent of all deaths from emphysema and bronchitis are directly due to smoking.

11. **TRUE** One year after quitting, ex-smokers cut their extra risk for heart attack by about half or more, and eventually the risk will return to normal in healthy ex-smokers. Even if you have already had a heart attack, you can reduce your chances of having a second

continues

Healthy Heart IQ continued

attack if you quit smoking. Ex-smokers can also reduce their risk of stroke and cancer, improve blood flow and lung function, and help stop diseases like emphysema and bronchitis from getting worse.

12. **FALSE** Older smokers are more likely to succeed at quitting smoking than younger smokers. Quitting helps relieve smoking-related symptoms like shortness of breath, coughing, and chest pain. Many quit to avoid further health problems and take control of their lives.

13. **TRUE** Weight control is a question of balance. You get calories from the food you eat. You burn off calories by exercising. Cutting down on calories, especially calories from fat, is key to losing weight. Combining this with a regular physical activity, like walking, cycling, jogging, or swimming, not only can help in losing weight but also in maintaining weight loss. A steady weight loss of ½ to 1 pounds a week is safe for most adults, and the weight is more likely to stay off over the long run. Losing weight, if you

are overweight, may also help reduce your blood pressure, lower your LDL-cholesterol, and raise your HDL-cholesterol. Being physically active and eating fewer calories will also help you control your weight if you quit smoking.

14. **TRUE** Coronary heart disease is the Number One killer in the United States. Approximately 489,000 Americans died of coronary heart disease in 1990, and approximately half of those deaths were women.

Source: *Check Your Weight and Heart Disease IQ*. National Heart, Lung, and Blood Institute, National Institutes of Health, Publication No. 93-3034, May 1993.

Check Your Weight and Heart Disease IQ

The following statements are either true or false. The statements test your knowledge of overweight and heart disease. The correct answers can be found on the next page.

1. Being overweight puts you at risk for heart disease.   T   F

2. If you are overweight, losing weight helps lower your high blood cholesterol and high blood pressure.   T   F

3. Quitting smoking is healthy, but it commonly leads to excessive weight gain, which increases your risk for heart disease.   T   F

4. An overweight person with high blood pressure should pay more attention to a low-sodium diet than to weight reduction.   T   F

5. A reduced intake of sodium or salt does not always lower high blood pressure to normal.   T   F

6. The best way to lose weight is to eat fewer calories and exercise.   T   F

7. Skipping meals is a good way to cut down on calories.   T   F

8. Foods high in complex carbohydrates (starch and fiber) are good choices when you are trying to lose weight.   T   F

9. The single most important change most people can make to lose weight is to avoid sugar.   T   F

10. Polyunsaturated fat has the same number of calories as saturated fat.   T   F

11. Overweight children are very likely to become overweight adults.   T   F

YOUR SCORE: How many correct answers did you make?

10–11 correct = Congratulations! You know a lot about weight and heart disease. Share this information with your family and friends.

8–9 correct = Very good.

Fewer than 8 = Go over the answers and try to learn more about weight and heart disease.

continues

Check Your Weight and Heart Disease IQ continued

1. **TRUE**   Being overweight increases your risk for high blood cholesterol and high blood pressure, two of the major risk factors for coronary heart disease. Even if you do not have high blood cholesterol or high blood pressure, being overweight may increase your risk for heart disease. Where you carry your extra weight may affect your risk too. Weight carried at your waist or above seems to be associated with an increased risk for heart disease in many people. In addition, being overweight increases your risk for diabetes, gallbladder disease, and some types of cancer.

2. **TRUE**   If you are overweight, even moderate reductions in weight, such as 5 to 10 percent, can produce substantial reductions in blood pressure. You may also be able to reduce your LDL-cholesterol ("bad" cholesterol) and triglycerides and increase your HDL-cholesterol ("good" cholesterol).

3. **FALSE** The average weight gain after quitting smoking is 5 pounds. The proportion of ex-smokers who gain large amounts of weight (greater than 20 pounds) is relatively small. Even if you gain weight when you stop smoking, change your eating and exercise habits to lose weight rather than starting to smoke again. Smokers who quit smoking decrease their risk for heart disease by about 50 percent compared to those people who do not quit.

4. **FALSE** Weight loss, if you are overweight, may reduce your blood pressure even if you don't reduce the amount of sodium you eat. Weight loss is recommended for all overweight people who have high blood pressure. Even if weight loss does not reduce your blood pressure to normal, it may help you cut back on your blood pressure medications. Also, losing weight if you are overweight may help you reduce your risk for or control other health problems.

5. **TRUE**   Even though a high sodium or salt intake plays a key role in maintaining high blood pressure in some people, there is no easy way to determine who will benefit from eating less sodium and salt. Also, a high intake may limit how well certain high blood pressure medications work. Eating a diet with less sodium may help some people reduce their risk of developing high blood pressure. Most Americans eat more salt and other sources of sodium than they need. Therefore, it is prudent for most people to reduce their sodium intake.

6. **TRUE**   Eating fewer calories and exercising more are the best ways to lose weight and keep it off. Weight control is a question of balance. You get calories from the food you eat. You burn off calories by exercising. Cutting down on calories, especially calories from fat, is key to losing weight. Combining this with a regular exercise program, like walking, bicycling, jogging, or swimming, not only can help in losing weight but also in maintaining the weight loss. A steady weight loss of 1 to 2 pounds a week is safe for most adults, and the weight is more likely to stay off over the long run. Losing weight, if you are overweight, may also help reduce your blood pressure and raise your HDL-cholesterol, the "good" cholesterol.

7. **FALSE** To cut calories, some people regularly skip meals and have no snacks or caloric drinks in between. If you do this, your body thinks that it is starving even if your intake of calories is not reduced to a very low amount. Your body will try to save energy by slowing its metabolism, that is decreasing the rate at which it burns calories. This makes losing weight even harder and may even add body fat. Try to avoid long periods without eating. Five or six small meals are often preferred to the usual three meals a day for some individuals trying to lose weight.

8. **TRUE**   Contrary to popular belief, foods high in complex carbohydrates (like pasta, rice, potatoes, breads, cereals, grains, dried beans, and peas) are lower in calories than foods high in fat.

In addition, they are good sources of vitamins, minerals, and fiber. What adds calories to these foods is the addition of butter, rich sauces, whole milk, cheese, or cream, which are high in fat.

9. **FALSE** Sugar has not been found to cause obesity; however, many foods high in sugar are also high in fat. Fat has more than twice the calories as the same amount of protein or carbohydrates (sugar and starch). Thus, foods that are high in fat are high in calories. High-sugar foods, like cakes, cookies, candies, and ice cream, are high in fat and calories and low in vitamins, minerals, and protein.

10. **TRUE**   All fats—polyunsaturated, monounsaturated, and saturated—have the same number of calories. All calories count whether they come from saturated or unsaturated fats. Because fats are the richest sources of calories, eating less total fat will help reduce the number of calories you eat every day. It will also help you reduce your intake of saturated fat. Particular attention to reducing saturated fat is important in lowering your blood cholesterol level.

11. **FALSE** Obesity in childhood does increase the likelihood of adult obesity, but most overweight children will not become obese. Several factors influence whether or not an overweight child becomes an overweight adult: (1) the age the child becomes overweight, (2) how overweight the child is, (3) the family history of overweight, and (4) dietary and activity habits. Getting to the right weight is desirable, but children's needs for calories and other nutrients are different from the needs of adults. Dietary plans for weight control must allow for this. Eating habits, like so many other habits, are often formed during childhood, so it is important to develop good ones.

For more information, write:
NHLBI Obesity Education Initiative
P.O. Box 30105
Bethesda, MD 20824-0105

Source: *Check Your Weight and Heart Disease IQ*. National Heart, Lung, and Blood Institute, National Institutes of Health, Publication No. 93-3034, May 1993.

Check Your High Blood Pressure Prevention IQ

Test your knowledge of high blood pressure with the following questions. Circle each true or false. The answers are given on the next page.

1. There is nothing you can do to prevent high blood pressure.   T   F

2. If your mother or father has high blood pressure, you'll get it.   T   F

3. Young adults don't get high blood pressure.   T   F

4. High blood pressure has no symptoms.   T   F

5. Stress causes high blood pressure.   T   F

6. High blood pressure is not life threatening.   T   F

7. Blood pressure is high when it's at or over 140/90 mm Hg.   T   F

8. If you're overweight, you are two to six times more likely to develop high blood pressure.   T   F

9. You have to exercise vigorously every day to improve your blood pressure and heart health.   T   F

10. Americans eat two to three times more salt and sodium than they need.   T   F

11. Drinking alcohol lowers blood pressure.   T   F

12. High blood pressure has no cure.   T   F

NOTES:

continues

High Blood Pressure Prevention continued

Answers to the High Blood Pressure Prevention IQ Quiz

1. FALSE High blood pressure can be prevented with four steps: keep a healthy weight; become physically acute; limit your salt and sodium use; and, if you drink alcoholic beverages, do so in moderation.

2. FALSE You are more likely to get high blood pressure if it runs in your family, but that doesn't mean you must get it. Your chance of getting high blood pressure is also greater if you're older or an African American. But high blood pressure is NOT an inevitable part of aging, and everyone can take steps to prevent the disease—the steps are given in answer 1.

3. FALSE About 15 percent of those ages 18 to 39 are among the 50 million Americans with high blood pressure. Once you have high blood pressure, you have it for the rest of your life. So start now to prevent it.

4. TRUE High blood pressure, or "hypertension," usually has no symptoms. In fact, it is often called the "silent killer." You can have high blood pressure and feel fine. That's why it's important to have your blood pressure checked—it's a simple test.

5. FALSE Stress does make blood pressure go up, but only temporarily. Ups and downs in blood pressure are normal. Run for a bus and your pressure rises; sleep and it drops. Blood pressure is the force of blood against the walls of arteries. Blood pressure becomes dangerous when it's always high. That harms your heart and blood vessels. So what does cause high blood pressure? In the vast majority of cases, a single cause is never found.

6. FALSE High blood pressure is the main cause of stroke and a factor in the development of heart disease and kidney failure.

7. TRUE But even blood pressures slightly under 140/90 mm Hg can increase your risk of heart disease or stroke.

8. TRUE As weight increases, so does blood pressure. It's important to stay at a healthy weight. If you need to reduce, try to lose ½ to 1 pound a week. Choose foods low in fat (especially saturated fat), since fat is high in calories. Even if you're at a good weight, the healthiest way to eat is low fat, low cholesterol.

9. FALSE Studies show that even a little physical activity helps prevent high blood pressure and strengthens your heart. Even among the overweight, those who are active have lower blood pressures than those who aren't. It's best to do some activity for 30 minutes, most days. Walk, garden, or bowl. If you don't have a 30-minute period, do something for 15 minutes, twice a day. Every bit helps—so make activity part of your daily routine.

10. TRUE Americans eat way too much salt and sodium. And some people, such as many African Americans, are especially sensitive to salt. Salt is made of sodium and chloride, and it's mostly the sodium that affects blood pressure. Salt is only one form of sodium—there are others. So you need to watch your use of both salt and sodium. That includes what's added to foods at the table and in cooking, and what's already in processed foods and snacks. Americans, especially people with high blood pressure, should eat no more than about 6 grams of salt a day, which equals about 2,400 milligrams of sodium.

11. FALSE Drinking too much alcohol can raise blood pressure. If you drink, have no more than two drinks a day. The "Dietary Guidelines" recommend that for overall health, women should limit their alcohol to no more than one drink a day. A drink would be 1.5 ounces of 80 proof whiskey, or 5 ounces of wine, or 12 ounces of beer.

12. TRUE But high blood pressure can be treated and controlled. Treatment usually includes lifestyle changes—losing weight, if overweight; becoming physically active; limiting salt and sodium; and avoiding drinking excess alcohol—and, if needed, medication. But the best way to avoid the dangers of high blood pressure is to prevent the condition.

For more information on high blood pressure, call 1-800-575-WELL, or write to the National Heart, Lung, and Blood Institute Information Center, P.O. Box 30105, Bethesda, MD 20824-0105.

National High Blood Pressure Education Program National Heart, Lung, and Blood Institute

U.S. Department of Health and Human Services Public Health Service National Institutes of Health NIH Publication No. 94-3671 September 1994

Source: *Check Your High Blood Pressure Prevention IQ,* National Heart, Lung, and Blood Institute, National Institutes of Health, Publication No. 94-3671, September 1994.

On the Teen Scene: Preventing STDs

You don't have to be a genius to figure out that the only sure way to avoid getting sexually transmitted diseases (STDs) is to not have sex.

But in today's age of AIDS, it's smart to also know ways to lower the risk of getting STDs, including HIV, the virus that causes AIDS.

Infection with HIV, which stands for human immunodeficiency virus, is spreading among teenagers. According to the Centers for Disease Control and Prevention (CDC), as of June 30, 1997, 2,953 people had been diagnosed with HIV or AIDS when they were in their teens and 107,281 when in their twenties. Because it can be many years from the time a person becomes infected to when the person develops symptoms and is diagnosed with HIV infection, many people diagnosed in their 20s likely contracted HIV in their teens.

You may have heard that birth control can also help prevent AIDS and other STDs. This is only partly true. The whole story is that only one form of birth control currently on the market—latex condoms (thin rubber sheaths used to cover the penis)—is highly effective in reducing the transmission (spread) of HIV and many other STDs.

The Food and Drug Administration has approved the marketing of male condoms made of polyurethane for people allergic to latex. Reality Female Condom, another form of birth control made of polyurethane, may give limited protection against STDs, but it is not as effective as male latex condoms.

So people who use other kinds of birth control, such as the pill, diaphragm, Norplant, Depo-Provera, cervical cap, or IUD, also need to use condoms to help prevent STDs.

Here's why: Latex condoms work against STDs by keeping blood, a man's semen, and a woman's vaginal fluids—all of which can carry bacteria and viruses—from passing from one person to another. For many years, scientists have known that male condoms (also called safes, rubbers, or prophylactics) can help prevent STDs transmitted by bacteria, such as syphilis and gonorrhea, because the bacteria can't get through the condom. More recently, researchers discovered that latex condoms can also reduce the risk of getting STDs caused by viruses, such as HIV, herpes, and hepatitis B, even though viruses are much smaller than bacteria or sperm.

After this discovery, FDA, which regulates condoms as medical devices, worked with manufacturers to develop labeling for latex condoms. The labeling tells consumers that although latex condoms cannot entirely eliminate the risk of STDs, when used properly and consistently they are highly effective in preventing STDs. FDA also provided a sample set of instructions and requested that all condoms include adequate instructions.

MAKE THE RIGHT CHOICE

Male condoms now sold in the United States are made either of latex (rubber), polyurethane, or natural membrane (called "lambskin," but actually made of sheep intestine). Scientists found that natural skin condoms are not as effective as latex condoms in reducing the risk of STDs because natural skin condoms have naturally occurring tiny holes or pores that viruses may be able to get through. Only latex condoms labeled for protection against STDs should be used for disease protection, unless one of the partners is allergic to latex. In that case, a polyurethane condom can be used.

Some condoms have lubricants added and some have spermicide (a chemical that kills sperm) added. The package labeling tells whether either of these has been added to the condom.

continues

On the Teen Scene continued

Lubricants may help prevent condoms from breaking and may help prevent irritation. But lubricants do not give any added disease protection. If an unlubricated condom is used, a water-based lubricant (such as K-Y Jelly), available over-the-counter (without prescription) in drugstores, can be used but is not required for the proper use of the condom. Do not use petroleum-based jelly (such as Vaseline), baby oil, lotions, cooking oils, or cold creams because these products can weaken latex and cause the condom to tear easily.

Some condoms have added spermicide; an active chemical in spermicides, nonoxynol-9, kills sperm. But spermicides alone (as sold in creams and jellies over-the-counter in drugstores) and spermicides used with the diaphragm or cervical cap do not give adequate protection against HIV and other STDs. For the best disease protection, a latex condom should be used from start to finish every time a person has sex.

FDA requires condoms to be labeled with an expiration date. Condoms should be stored in a cool, dry place out of direct sunlight. Closets and drawers usually make good storage places. Because of possible exposure to extreme heat and cold, glove compartments of cars are not a good place to store condoms. For the same reason, condoms shouldn't be kept in a pocket, wallet, or purse for more than a few hours at a time. Condoms should not be used after the expiration date, usually abbreviated EXP and followed by the date.

Condoms are available in almost all drugstores, many supermarkets, and other stores. They are also available from vending machines. When purchasing condoms from vending machines, as from any source, be sure they are latex, labeled for disease prevention, and are not past their expiration date. Don't buy a condom from a vending machine located where it may be exposed to extreme heat or cold or to direct sunlight.

NOTES:

Source: *On the Teen Scene: Preventing STD's,* FDA Publication No. (FDA) 98-1210.

STD Facts

- Sexually transmitted diseases affect more than 12 million Americans each year, many of whom are teenagers or young adults.
- Using drugs and alcohol increases your chances of getting STDs because these substances can interfere with your judgment and your ability to use a condom properly.
- Intravenous drug use puts a person at higher risk for HIV and hepatitis B because IV drug users usually share needles.
- The more partners you have, the higher your chance of being exposed to HIV or other STDs. This is because it is difficult to know whether a person is infected, or has had sex with people who are more likely to be infected due to intravenous drug use or other risk factors.
- Sometimes, early in infection, there may be no symptoms, or symptoms may be confused with other illnesses.
- You cannot tell by looking at someone whether he or she is infected with HIV or another STD.

STDs Can Cause:

- pelvic inflammatory disease (PID), which can damage a woman's fallopian tubes and result in pelvic pain and sterility
- tubal pregnancies (where the fetus grows in the fallopian tube instead of the womb), sometimes fatal to the mother and always fatal to the fetus
- cancer of the cervix in women
- sterility—the inability to have children—in both men and women
- damage to major organs, such as the heart, kidney and brain, if STDs go untreated
- death, especially with HIV infection

See a Doctor If You Have Any of These STD Symptoms:

- discharge from vagina, penis, or rectum
- pain or burning during urination or intercourse
- pain in the abdomen (women), testicles (men), or buttocks and legs (both)
- blisters, open sores, warts, rash, or swelling in the genital or anal areas or mouth
- persistent flu-like symptoms—including fever, headache, aching muscles, or swollen glands—which may precede STD symptoms

Source: *On the Teen Scene: Preventing STD's*, FDA Publication No. (FDA) 98-1210.

How To Use a Condom

- Use a new condom for every act of vaginal, anal, and oral (penis-mouth contact) sex. Do not unroll the condom before placing it on the penis.

- Put the condom on after the penis is erect and before any contact is made between the penis and any part of the partner's body.

- If the condom does not have a reservoir top, pinch the tip enough to leave a half-inch space for semen to collect. Always make sure to eliminate any air in the tip to help keep the condom from breaking.

- Holding the condom rim (and pinching a half inch space if necessary), place the condom on the top of the penis. Then, continuing to hold it by the rim, unroll it all the way to the base of the penis. If you are also using water-based lubricant, you can put more on the outside of the condom.

- If you feel the condom break, stop immediately, withdraw, and put on a new condom.

- After ejaculation and before the penis gets soft, grip the rim of the condom and carefully withdraw.

- To remove the condom, gently pull it off the penis, being careful that semen doesn't spill out.

- Wrap the condom in a tissue and throw it in the trash where others won't handle it. (Don't flush condoms down the toilet because they may cause sewer problems.) Afterwards, wash your hands with soap and water.

Latex condoms are the only form of contraception now available that human studies have shown to be highly effective in protecting against the transmission of HIV and other STDs. They give good disease protection for vaginal sex and should also reduce the risk of disease transmission in oral and anal sex. But latex condoms may not be 100 percent effective, and a lot depends on knowing the right way to buy, store, and use them.

Source: *On the Teen Scene: Preventing STD's*, FDA Publication No. (FDA) 98-1210.

Condom Labels

Information about whether a birth control product also helps protect against sexually transmitted diseases (STDs), including HIV infection, is emphasized on the labeling of these products, because a product that is highly effective in preventing pregnancy will not necessarily protect against sexually transmitted diseases.

Labels on birth control pills, implants such as Norplant, injectable contraceptives such as Depo-Provera, intrauterine devices (IUDs), and natural skin condoms will state that the products are intended to prevent pregnancy and do not protect against STDs, including HIV infection (which leads to AIDS). Labeling of natural skin condoms will also state that consumers should use a latex condom to help reduce risk of many STDs, including HIV infection.

Laboratory tests show that organisms as small as sperm and the HIV virus cannot pass through polyurethane condoms. But the risks of STDs, including HIV infection, have not been well studied in actual use with polyurethane condoms. So unless one or both partners is allergic to latex, latex condoms should be used.

Labeling for latex condoms states that if used properly, latex condoms help reduce risk of HIV transmission and many other STDs. This statement, a modification from previous labeling, now appears on individual condom wrappers, on the box, and in consumer information.

Besides highlighting statements concerning sexually transmitted diseases and AIDS on the consumer packaging, manufacturers will add a similar statement to patient and physician leaflets provided with the products.

FDA may take action against any products that don't carry the new information.

FDA is currently reviewing whether similar action is necessary for the labeling of spermicide, cervical caps, and diaphragms.

LOOKING AT A CONDOM LABEL

Like other drugs and medical devices, FDA requires condom packages to contain certain labeling information. When buying condoms, look on the package label to make sure the condoms are:

- made of latex
- labeled for disease prevention
- not past their expiration date (EXP followed by the date)

Source: *On the Teen Scene: Preventing STD's*, FDA Publication No. (FDA) 98-1210.

Community-Based Immunization Clinic Supplies Checklist

VACCINES TO BRING

___ DTaP
___ Td
___ IPV
___ Hib
___ Pneumococcal conjugate (PCV7)
___ MMR
___ Varicella
___ Hepatitis B
___ Hepatitis A
___ Pneumococcal polysaccharide (PPV23)
___ Influenza—in season

Storage Notes:
- *Put one layer of ice on bottom of cooler, then one layer of ice on top of vaccines.*
- *No bottles should directly touch ice because they could freeze.*
- *Keep vaccines in their original boxes when stored in the cooler.*
- *When varicella vaccine is taken to community-based clinics, pack it in dry ice.*

VACCINE SUPPLIES

___ 2 "Sharps Away" containers
___ 1 box of 3cc syringes with 1", 25-gauge needles
___ 25-gauge needles
    ___ 5/8"
    ___ 1"
    ___ 1 ½"
___ 1 box of latex gloves
___ alcohol wipes
___ spot bandaids
___ rectangle bandaids
___ rectal thermometer
___ oral thermometer
___ probe covers for thermometer
___ 3 table pads and clean paper to cover table for work site
___ one cloth towel
___ paper towels
___ bleach solution

___ spray bottle for bleach solution
___ acetaminophen elixir samples
___ acetaminophen drops samples
___ acetaminophen children's chewables (80 mg)
___ acetaminophen adult tablets

EMERGENCY KIT

___ Standing orders for emergencies
___ 2 ampules epinephrine 1:1000 SQ
___ 2 ampules diphenhydramine (Benadryl) 50 mg IM
___ two 3cc syringes with 1", 25-gauge needles
___ two 1 ½" needles
___ 2 tuberculin syringes with 5/8" needle, for epinephrine
___ alcohol swabs
___ 2 tongue depressors
___ pediatric pocket mask with one-way valve
___ adult pocket mask with one-way valve
___ pediatric airway
___ adult airway
___ tourniquet
___ flashlight

VACCINE INFORMATION STATEMENTS (VISs)

___ DTaP   ___ Var
___ Td   ___ Hep B
___ IPV   ___ Hep A
___ Hib   ___ PPV23
___ PCV7   ___ Influenza
___ MMR

PAPERWORK AND OFFICE SUPPLIES

___ immunization clinic standing orders and protocols
___ this materials checklist
___ "Summary of rules for childhood immunization"
___ "Summary of recommendations for adult immunization"

continues

Community-Based Immunization Clinic Supplies Checklist continued

____ "Screening questionnaire for childhood immunization"
____ "Screening questionnaire for adult immunization"
____ billing forms
____ clinic vaccination administration record
____ personal immunization record cards
____ notification letters to other clinics
____ release of information forms
____ child and adult vaccination schedules
____ pre-stamped acetaminophen prescription blanks
    ____ elixir
    ____ drops
    ____ children's chewables
    ____ adult tablets
____ prescription blanks
____ dosage schedules to hand out to patients (Spanish also)
____ Vaccine Adverse Events Reporting forms
____ list of clinics, phone numbers, and other referral resources
____ calendar
____ tiny "Post-its" for return appointment times
____ extra pens

____ envelopes
____ rubber bands
____ tape
____ paper clips
____ stapler/staples
____ scissors
____ telephone

MISCELLANEOUS MATERIALS

____ toys
____ stickers
____ other: _____
____ other: _____

CLINICIAN ITEMS

____ otoscope
____ stethoscope
____ good light source
____ tongue depressors
____ container of clean ear specula, different sizes
____ professional cards

Courtesy of the Immunization Action Coalition, 1573 Selby Avenue, St. Paul, Minnesota 55104. 651-647-9009. admin@immunize.org. Web site: www.immunize.org.

Screening Questionnaire for Child and Teen Immunization

For parents and guardians: The following questions will help us determine which vaccines may be given today. If a question is not clear, please ask the nurse or doctor to explain it.

Patient name: _____

Date of birth: mo _____   day _____   year _____

Today's date: mo _____   day _____   year _____

	Yes	No	Don't Know
1. Is the child sick today?	☐	☐	☐
2. Does the child have allergies to medications, food, or any vaccines?	☐	☐	☐
3. Has the child had a serious reaction to a vaccine in the past?	☐	☐	☐
4. Has the child had a seizure or a brain problem?	☐	☐	☐
5. Does the child have cancer, leukemia, AIDS, or any other immune system problem?	☐	☐	☐
6. Has the child taken cortisone, prednisone, other steroids, or anticancer drugs, or had x-ray treatments in the past 3 months?	☐	☐	☐
7. Has the child received a transfusion of blood or blood products, or been given a medicine called immune (gamma) globulin in the past year?	☐	☐	☐
8. Is the child / teen pregnant or is there a chance she could become pregnant in the next 3 months?	☐	☐	☐
9. Has the child received any vaccinations in the past 4 weeks?	☐	☐	☐

Form completed by: _____   Date: _____

Did you bring your child's immunization record card with you?   yes ☐   no ☐

It is important to have a personal record of your child's vaccinations. If you don't have a record card, ask the child's health care provider to give you one! Bring this record with you every time you seek medical care for your child. Make sure your health care provider records all your child's vaccinations on it. Your child will need this card to enter daycare, kindergarten, junior high, etc.

Courtesy of the Immunization Action Coalition, 1573 Selby Avenue, St. Paul, Minnesota 55104. 651-647-9009. admin@immunize.org. Web site: www.immunize.org.

Understanding the Screening Questionnaire for Child and Teen Immunization

1. **Is the child sick today?**
   There is no evidence that acute illness reduces vaccine efficacy or increases vaccine adverse events (1, 2). However, with moderate or severe acute illness, all vaccines should be delayed until the illness has improved. Mild illnesses (such as otitis media, upper respiratory infections, and diarrhea) are NOT contraindications to vaccination. Do not withhold vaccination if a person is taking antibiotics.

2. **Does the child have allergies to medications, food, or any vaccine?**
   History of anaphylactic reaction such as hives (urticaria), wheezing or difficulty breathing, or circulatory collapse or shock (not fainting) from a previous dose of vaccine or vaccine component is a contraindication for further doses. For example, if a person experiences anaphylaxis after eating eggs, do not administer influenza vaccine, or if a person has anaphylaxis after eating gelatin, do not administer MMR or varicella vaccine. Local reactions (e.g., a red eye following instillation of ophthalmic solution) are not contraindications. For an extensive table of vaccine components, see reference 3.

3. **Has the child had a serious reaction to a vaccine in the past?**
   History of anaphylactic reaction (see question 2) to a previous dose of vaccine or vaccine component is a contraindication for subsequent doses. History of encephalopathy within 7 days following DTP/DTaP is a contraindication for further doses of pertussis-containing vaccine. Precautions to pertussis-containing vaccines include the following: (a) seizure within 3 days of a dose, (b) pale or limp episode or collapse within 48 hours of a dose, (c) continuous crying for 3 hours within 48 hours of a dose, and (d) fever of 105°F (40°C) within 48 hours of a previous dose. There are other serious reactions to vaccines that constitute contraindications or precautions (4). Under normal circumstances, vaccines are deferred when a precaution is present. However, situations may arise when the benefit outweighs the risk (e.g., community pertussis outbreak).

4. **Has the child had a seizure or a brain problem?**
   DTaP is contraindicated in children who have a history of encephalopathy within 7 days following DTP/DTaP. An unstable progressive neurologic problem is a precaution to the use of DTP/DTaP. For children with stable neurologic disorders (including seizures) unrelated to vaccination, or for children with a family history of seizure, vaccinate as usual but consider the use of acetaminophen or ibuprofen to minimize fever.

5. **Does the child have cancer, leukemia, AIDS, or any other immune system problem?**
   Live virus vaccines (e.g., MMR, varicella) are usually contraindicated in immunocompromised children. However, there are exceptions. For example, MMR and varicella vaccines are recommended for asymptomatic HIV-infected children who do not have evidence of severe immunosuppression. For details, consult the ACIP recommendations (5, 6).

6. **Has the child taken cortisone, prednisone, other steroids, or anticancer drugs, or had x-ray treatments in the past 3 months?**
   Live virus vaccines (e.g., MMR, varicella) should be postponed until after chemotherapy or long-term high-dose steroid therapy has ended. For details and length of time to postpone, consult the ACIP statement (1). To find specific vaccination schedules for stem cell transplant (bone marrow transplant) patients, see reference 7.

continues

Understanding the Screening Questionnaire for Child and Teen Immunization continued

7. **Has the child received a transfusion of blood or blood products, or been given a medicine called immune (gamma) globulin in the past year?**

Live virus vaccines (e.g., MMR, varicella) may need to be deferred, depending on several variables. Consult the *2000 Red Book,* p. 390 (2), for the most current information on intervals between immune globulin or blood product administration and MMR or varicella vaccination.

8. **Is the child/teen pregnant or is there a chance she could become pregnant in the next 3 months?**

Live virus vaccines (e.g., MMR, varicella) are contraindicated prior to and during pregnancy due to the theoretical risk of virus transmission to the fetus. Sexually active young women who receive MMR or varicella vaccination should be instructed to practice careful contraception for 3 months following MMR vaccination and for one month following varicella vaccination (5, 8). Different inactivated vaccines may be given to a pregnant woman whenever indicated.

9. **Has the child received any vaccinations in the past 4 weeks?**

If two live virus vaccines (e.g., MMR, varicella) are not given on the same day, the doses must be separated by at least 28 days. Different inactivated vaccines may be given at any spacing interval if they are not administered simultaneously.

1. CDC. General recommendations on immunization. *MMWR* 1994; 34 (RR-I).

2. AAP. *2000 Red Book: Report of the Committee on Infectious Diseases.* 25th ed. Elk Grove Village, IL: AAP, 2000.

3. Visit the website: www.cdc.gov/nip/publications/pink/vaxcont.pdf

4. CDC. Guide to contraindications to childhood vaccinations. Oct. 2000. Available online at: www.cdc.gov/nip/recs/contraindications.pdf

5. CDC. Measles, mumps, and rubella—vaccine use and strategies for elimination of measles, rubella, and congenital rubella syndrome and control of mumps. *MMWR* 1998; 47 (RR-8).

6. CDC. Prevention of varicella: updated recommendations of the ACIP. *MMWR* 1999; 48 (RR-6).

7. CDC. Guidelines for preventing opportunistic infections among hematopoietic stem cell transplant recipients. *MMWR* 2000; 49 (RR-10).

8. CDC. Prevention of varicella. *MMWR* 1996:45 (RR- 11).

Source: Adapted from CDC's *Guide to Contraindications to Childhood Vaccinations,* Oct. 2000, and *Epidemiology & Prevention of Vaccine-Preventable Diseases,* WL Atkinson et al., editors, CDC, 6th edition, Jan. 2000.

Vaccine Administration Record for Children and Teens

Vaccine administrator: Make sure you give the parent/guardian all appropriate Vaccine Information Statements (VIS) and an updated shot record at every visit.

Patient name: _____

Birthdate: _____

Clinic chart number: _____

Vaccine and route (circle type given)	Date given	Site given (LA, RA, LT, RT)	Vaccine lot number	Vaccine manufacturer	VIS date*	Signature or initials of vaccine administrator	Comments
Hepatitis B—1 ___mcg (IM)							
Hepatitis B—2 ___mcg (IM)							
Hepatitis B—3 ___mcg (IM)							
DTaP ● DT ● Td—1 (IM)							
DTaP ● DT ● Td—2 (IM)							
DTaP ● DT ● Td—3 (IM)							
DTaP ● DT ● Td—4 (IM)							
DTaP ● DT ● Td—5 (IM)							
DTaP/Hib—4 (IM)							
Td booster (IM)							
Td booster (IM)							
Hib—1 (IM)							
Hib—2 (IM)							
Hib—3 (IM)							
Hib—4 (IM)							
Hib/Hep B—1 (IM)							
Hib/Hep B—2 (IM)							
Hib/Hep B—3 (IM)							
Polio—1 (SQ●IM)							
Polio—2 (SQ●IM)							
Polio—3 (SQ●IM)							
Polio—4 (SQ●IM)							
Pneum conj (PCV)—1 (IM)							
Pneum conj (PCV)—2 (IM)							
Pneum conj (PCV)—3 (IM)							
Pneum conj (PCV)—4 (IM)							
MMR—1 (SQ)							
MMR—2 (SQ)							
Varicella—1 (SQ)							
Varicella—2 (SQ)							
Hepatitis A—1 (IM)							
Hepatitis A—2 (IM)							
Other†							
Other†							
Other†							
Other†							
Other†							

*Each VIS is identified by a date at the bottom. Record the VIS identification date in this column.
†Influenza, pneumococcal polysaccharide (PPV23), meningococcal, and/or Lyme disease vaccines are recommended for certain high-risk children.

Courtesy of the Immunization Action Coalition, 1573 Selby Avenue, St. Paul, Minnesota 55104. 651-647-9009. admin@immunize.org. Web site: www.immunize.org.

Immunizations for Babies

A Guide for Parents

These are the vaccinations your baby needs!

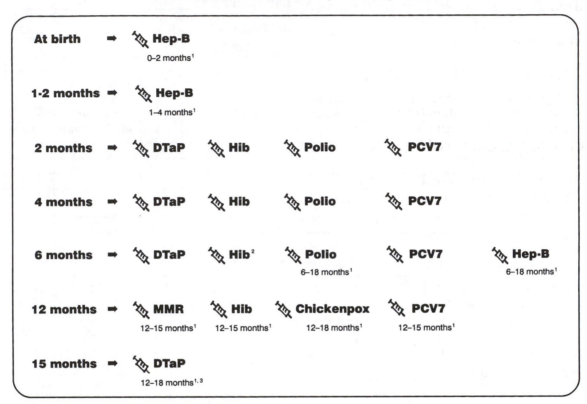

Check with your doctor or nurse to make sure your baby is getting immunized on time. Also make sure you ask your doctor or nurse to give you a record card with all the dates of your baby's shots and be sure to bring it to every visit.

Hep-B: protects against hepatitis B, a serious liver disease
DTaP: protects against diphtheria, tetanus (lockjaw), and pertussis (whooping cough)
Hib: protects against *Haemophilus influenzae* type b
Polio: inactivated (injected) vaccine (IPV) protects against polio
PCV7:   pneumococcal conjugate vaccine protects against serious pneumococcal infections
MMR: protects against measles, mumps, and rubella (German measles)
Chickenpox: varicella zoster vaccine protects against chickenpox

1. This is the age range in which this vaccine should be given.
2. Depending on the brand of Hib vaccine used for the 1st and 2nd doses, a dose at 6 months of age may not be needed.
3. DTaP may be given as early as 12 months if 6 months have elapsed since the previous dose and if the child might not return by 18 months of age.

Courtesy of the Immunization Action Coalition, 1573 Selby Avenue, St. Paul, Minnesota 55104. 651-647-9009. admin@immunize.org. Web site: www.immunize.org.

After the Shots... What To Do If Your Child Has Discomfort

Your child may need extra love and care after getting immunized. Many of the shots that protect children from serious diseases can also cause discomfort for a while. Here are answers to questions many parents have about the fussiness, fever, and pain their children may experience after they have been immunized. If you don't find the answers to your questions, call the clinic!

My clinic phone number: [   ]

My child has been fussy since you immunized him/her. What should I do?

After immunization, children may be fussy due to pain and/or fever. You may want to give your child acetaminophen, a medicine that helps to reduce pain and fever. Some examples of acetaminophen are Tylenol, Panadol, and Tempra. DO NOT GIVE ASPIRIN. See chart below. If the fussiness lasts for more than 24 hours, you should call the clinic.

My child's arm (or leg) is swollen, hot, and red. What should I do?

- A clean, cool washcloth may be applied over the sore area as needed for comfort.
- If there is increasing redness or tenderness after 24 hours, call the clinic.
- For pain, give acetaminophen. See chart below. DO NOT GIVE ASPIRIN.

I think my child has a fever. What should I do?

Check your child's temperature to find out if there is a fever. The most accurate way to do this is by taking a rectal temperature. (Be sure to use a lubricant, such as petroleum jelly, when doing so.) If your child's fever is 105°F or higher by rectum, you need to call the clinic.

If you take the temperature by mouth (for an older child) or under the arm, these temperatures are generally lower and may be less accurate. Call your clinic if you are concerned about these temperatures.

Here are some things you can do to reduce fever:

- Give your child plenty to drink.
- Clothe your child lightly. Do _not_ cover or wrap your child tightly!
- Give your child acetaminophen. DO NOT USE ASPIRIN.
- Sponge your child in a few inches of lukewarm (not cold!) bath water.

My child seems really sick. Should I call the doctor?

If you are worried AT ALL about how your child looks or feels, please call the clinic!

Call the clinic if you answer "yes" to any of the following questions:

- Does your child have a rectal temperature of 105°F or higher?
  (Remember, a temperature taken under the arm or by mouth usually registers lower than a rectal temperature. You should call the clinic if you are concerned about these temperatures.)
- Is your child pale or limp?
- Has your child been crying for over 3 hours and just won't quit?
- Does your child have a strange cry that isn't normal (a high-pitched cry)?
- Is your child's body shaking, twitching, or jerking?

---

continues

After the Shots continued

How much fever-reducing medicine (acetaminophen) should I give my child?

Dose of acetaminophen to be given every 4–6 hours, by age or by weight				
1–3 months 6–11 lbs.	4–11 months 12–17 lbs.	12–23 months 18–23 lbs.	2–3 years 24–35 lbs.	4–5 years 36–47 lbs.
1/2 dropperful infant drops*	1 dropperful infant drops*	1 1/2 droppersful infant drops*	2 chewable (80mg) tablets*	3 chewable (80 mg) tablets*
	or 1/2 teaspoon children's liquid*	or 3/4 teaspoon children's liquid*	or 1 teaspoon* children's liquid	or 1 1/2 teaspoons children's liquid*

NOTES:

Questions Parents Ask about Baby Shots

What are vaccinations?

Vaccinations protect your child against serious diseases. Most vaccinations are given in a shot. The words "vaccination" and "immunization" mean the same thing.

What diseases do vaccines protect against?

Vaccines protect against measles, mumps, rubella, hepatitis B, polio, diphtheria, tetanus, pertussis (whooping cough), Hib disease, and chickenpox, and pneumococcal disease. Vaccines can't prevent children from getting minor illnesses like colds, but they can keep children safe from many serious diseases. Without vaccinations, your child could get very sick.

Isn't all this talk about diseases just a way to scare parents so they'll bring their children in for shots?

No. Many of these diseases still kill people. From 1989 through 1991, more than 150 people in the United States died from measles and thousands more were permanently damaged. Children in the United States also continue to die from chickenpox. When children get measles, chickenpox, and other diseases that vaccines could have prevented, they can also suffer from brain damage, hearing loss, heart problems, and lung damage.

I don't know anybody who has had mumps or rubella. Why does my baby need these shots?

You might not think that these diseases are a serious threat today because you don't see or hear much about them, but they are still around. If we stop vaccinating against these diseases, many more people will become infected. Vaccinating your child will keep him or her safe.

Are vaccinations safe?

Most vaccines cause only minor side effects, such as soreness where the shot was given or a slight fever. These side effects do not last long and are treatable. Serious reactions are very rare. Remember, if your child gets one of these dangerous childhood diseases, the risks of the disease are far greater than the risk of a serious vaccine reaction. If you have concerns, talk to your doctor or nurse.

What if my child has a cold, a fever, or is taking antibiotics? Can he or she still get vaccinated?

Yes. Your child can be vaccinated if he or she has a mild illness such as a cold, a slight fever, or is taking antibiotics. Talk to your doctor or nurse if you have questions.

continues

Questions Parents Ask about Baby Shots continued

How many times do I need to take my baby in for vaccinations?

A lot! Your baby needs at least five visits to the doctor for vaccinations before he or she is two years old. All these visits are necessary because there are eleven diseases your baby needs to be protected against and most require several doses for full protection. Your child will also need vaccinations between the ages of 4 and 6, and then again when he or she is 11–12.

How do I know when to take my baby in for shots?

If you are not sure, call your clinic or your local health department to find out when the next shots are due. Every time your child gets vaccinated, make sure you know when to bring him or her back for the next set of shots.

How do I keep track of my baby's shots?

You need a personal record card of your child's immunizations. This card should be brought with you to all medical appointments. Whenever your child receives vaccinations, make sure your clinic updates your child's shot record.

What if I miss an appointment? Does my baby have to get the shots all over again?

No. If your baby misses some vaccinations, it's not necessary to start over. Your clinic will continue the shots from where they left off.

What if my child is older than two? Is it too late to get him or her vaccinated?

No. Although it's best to have your child vaccinated as a baby, it's never too late to start. If your baby did not receive his or her shots, now is the time to start.

What if I can't afford to get my child vaccinated?

Vaccinations are usually free for children when families can't afford them. You can call (800) 232-2522 or your local or state health department to find out where you can go for vaccinations. Your child's health depends on it!

And here's a friendly reminder for parents:

Adults need shots, too! Call your clinic or health department to find out what shots you need or when your next shots are due! Your baby is counting on you!

Courtesy of the Immunization Action Coalition, 1573 Selby Avenue, St. Paul, Minnesota 55104. 651-647-9009. admin@immunize.org. Web site: www.immunize.org.

Screening Questionnaire for Adult Immunization

For patients: The following questions will help us determine which vaccines may be given today. If the question is not clear, please ask your health care provider to explain it.

Your name: _____

Date of birth: mo _____ day _____ year _____

Today's date: mo _____ day _____ year _____

	Yes	No	Don't Know
1. Are you sick today?	☐	☐	☐
2. Do you have allergies to medications, food, or any vaccine?	☐	☐	☐
3. Have you ever had a serious reaction after receiving a vaccine?	☐	☐	☐
4. Do you have cancer, leukemia, AIDS, or any other immune system problem?	☐	☐	☐
5. Do you take cortisone, prednisone, other steroids, or anticancer drugs, or have you had x-ray treatments?	☐	☐	☐
6. During the past year have you received a transfusion of blood or blood products, or been given a medicine called immune (gamma) globulin?	☐	☐	☐
7. For women: Are you pregnant or is there a chance you could become pregnant in the next three months?	☐	☐	☐
8. Have you received any vaccinations in the past 4 weeks?	☐	☐	☐

Form completed by: _____   Date: _____

Did you bring your immunization record card with you?   yes ☐   no ☐

It is important for you to have a personal record of your vaccinations. If you don't have a record card, ask your health care provider to give you one! Bring this record with you every time you seek medical care. Make sure your health care provider records all your vaccinations on it.

Courtesy of the Immunization Action Coalition, 1573 Selby Avenue, St. Paul, Minnesota 55104. 651-647-9009. admin@immunize.org. Web site: www.immunize.org.

Understanding the Screening Questionnaire for Adult Immunization

1. **Are you sick today?**

   There is no evidence that acute illness reduces vaccine efficacy or increases vaccine adverse events (1, 2). However, with moderate or severe acute illness, all vaccines should be delayed until the illness has improved. Mild illnesses (such as upper respiratory infections or diarrhea) are NOT contraindications to vaccination. Do not withhold vaccination if a person is taking antibiotics.

2. **Do you have allergies to medications, food, or any vaccine?**

   History of anaphylactic reaction such as hives (urticaria), wheezing or difficulty breathing, or circulatory collapse or shock (not fainting) from a previous dose of vaccine or vaccine component is a contraindication for further doses. For example, if a person experiences anaphylaxis after eating eggs, do not administer influenza vaccine, or if a person has anaphylaxis after eating gelatin, do not administer MMR or varicella vaccine. Local reactions (e.g., a red eye following instillation of ophthalmic solution) are not contraindications. For an extensive table of vaccine components, see reference 3.

3. **Have you ever had a serious reaction after receiving a vaccination?**

   History of anaphylactic reaction (see question 2) to a previous dose of vaccine or vaccine component is a contraindication for subsequent doses (4). Under normal circumstances, vaccines are deferred when a precaution is present. However, situations may arise when the benefit outweighs the risk (e.g., community measles outbreak).

4. **Do you have cancer, leukemia, AIDS, or any other immune system problem?**

   Live virus vaccines (e.g., MMR, varicella) are usually contraindicated in immunocompromised people. However, there are exceptions. For example, MMR is recommended for asymptomatic HIV-infected individuals who do not have evidence of severe immunosuppression. For details, consult the ACIP recommendations (5, 6).

5. **Do you take cortisone, prednisone, other steroids, or anticancer drugs, or have you had x-ray treatments?**

   Live virus vaccines (e.g., MMR, varicella) should be postponed until after chemotherapy or long-term high-dose steroid therapy has ended. For details and length of time to postpone, consult the ACIP statement (1). To find specific vaccination schedules for stem cell transplant (bone marrow transplant) patients, see reference 7.

6. **During the past year, have you received a transfusion of blood or blood products, or been given a medicine called immune (gamma) globulin?**

   Live virus vaccines (e.g., MMR, varicella) may need to be deferred, depending on several variables. Consult the ACIP Statement "General Recommendations on Immunization" (1) or *2000 Red Book*, p. 390 (2), for the most current information on intervals between immune globulin or blood product administration and MMR or varicella vaccination.

7. **For women: Are you pregnant or is there a chance you could become pregnant in the next 3 months?**

   Live virus vaccines (e.g., MMR, varicella) are contraindicated prior to and during pregnancy due to the theoretical risk of virus transmission to the fetus. Sexually active women in their child-bearing years who receive MMR or varicella vaccination should be instructed to practice careful contraception for 3 months following MMR vaccination and for one month following varicella vaccination (5, 8). Inactivated vaccines may be given to a pregnant woman whenever indicated.

continues

Understanding the Screening Questionnaire for Adult Immunization continued

8. **Have you received any vaccinations in the past 4 weeks?**

   If two live virus vaccines (e.g., MMR, varicella, yellow fever) are not given on the same day, the doses must be separated by at least 28 days. Inactivated vaccines may be given at any spacing interval if they are not administered simultaneously. (For travelers, consult the Yellow Book (9).)

1. CDC. General recommendations on immunization. *MMWR* 1994; 34 (RR-l).

2. AAP. *2000 Red Book: Report of the Committee on Infectious Diseases.* 25th ed. Elk Grove Village, IL: AAR, 2000.

3. Visit the Web site: www.cdc.gov/nip/publications/pink/vaxcont.pdf

4. CDC. Guide to contraindications to childhood vaccinations. Oct. 2000. Available online at: www.cdc.gov/nip/recs/contraindications.pdf

5. CDC. Measles, mumps, and rubella—vaccine use and strategies for elimination of measles, rubella, and congenital rubella syndrome and control of mumps. *MMWR* 1998; 47(RR-8).

6. CDC. Prevention of varicella: updated recommendations of the ACIP. *MMWR* 1999; 48 (RR-6).

7. CDC. Guidelines for preventing opportunistic infections among hematopoietic stem cell transplant recipients. *MMWR* 2000; 49 (RR-10).

8. CDC. Prevention of varicella. *MMWR* 1996; 45 (RR-11).

9. CDC. Health Information for International Travel, 1999–2000, DHHS, Atlanta, GA.

Source: Adapted from *Epidemiology & Prevention of Vaccine-Preventable Diseases*, WL Atkinson et al., editors, CDC, 6th edition, Jan. 2000, and CDC's *Guide to Contraindications to Childhood Vaccinations*, Oct. 2000.

Vaccine Administration Record for Adults

Before administering any vaccines, give the patient copies of all pertinent Vaccine Information Statements (VISs) and make sure he/she understands the risks and benefits of the vaccine(s). Give the patient an updated immunization record card whenever you administer vaccine.

Patient name: _____

Birthdate: _____

Clinic chart number: _____

Vaccine and route	Date given	Site given (RA, LA, RT, LT)	Vaccine lot number	Vaccine manufacturer	VIS date*	Signature or initials of vaccine administrator	Comments
Tetanus/diphtheria—1 (IM)							
Tetanus/diphtheria—2 (IM)							
Tetanus/diphtheria—3 (IM)							
Td booster (IM)							
Td booster (IM)							
Td booster (IM)							
Td booster (IM)							
Hepatitis B—1 ___mcg (IM)							
Hepatitis B—2 ___mcg (IM)							
Hepatitis B—3 ___mcg (IM)							
Hepatitis A—1 (IM)							
Hepatitis A—2 (IM)							
MMR—1 (SQ)							
MMR—2 (SQ)							
Varicella—1 (SQ)							
Varicella—2 (SQ)							
Influenza (IM)							
Influenza (IM)							
Influenza (IM)							
Influenza (IM)							
Influenza (IM)							
Influenza (IM)							
Influenza (IM)							
Influenza (IM)							
Influenza (IM)							
Pneum poly (PPV23)(IM•SQ)							
Other†							
Other†							
Other†							
Other†							

*A date is printed at the end of each Vaccine Information Statement (VIS). Record this date. According to federal law, VISs must be given to patients before administering each dose of Td, MMR, varicella, or hepatitis B vaccine.

†Meningococcal and/or Lyme disease vaccines are recommended for certain high-risk patients. Some high-risk patients may need a one-time revaccination with pneumococcal polysaccharide vaccine (PPV23).

Courtesy of the Immunization Action Coalition, 1573 Selby Avenue, St. Paul, Minnesota 55104. 651-647-9009. admin@immunize.org. Web site: www.immunize.org.

4-Month Baby Shots

At the 4-month checkup, your baby will get these immunizations:

Date My Baby Received Shot

DTP #2 _____

OPV #2 _____

Hib #2 _____

- Fill in the date when your baby receives these shots. It will help you keep track of what shots your baby still needs.

- Remember to write down any questions you have about shots to bring with you to the doctor.

- If you think your baby had a reaction last time he or she got shots, be sure to discuss this with your doctor.

- Your baby can get shots even if he or she has a mild cold or minor illness.

- Have infant drops of acetaminophen (Tylenol) at home to give to your baby if a fever develops.

- Review the 2-month baby shot page before your baby's 4-month visit. If your baby is missing some shots, be sure to tell your doctor.

Questions I have about shots:

_____

_____

_____

NOTES:

Source: Lisa R. Cohen et al., *Child Development, Health, and Safety*, Aspen Publishers, Inc., © 1996.

6-Month Baby Shots

At the 6-month checkup, your baby will get these immunizations:

Date My Baby Received Shot

DTP #3 _____

Hib #3 _____

HepB #3 _____

- Your baby will have most of his or her baby shots by six months, but there are still some left. Be sure to record the date next to the shot so you can keep track of the shots.

- Review the 2- and 4-month baby shot pages before your 6-month visit. If any shots are missing, be sure to tell your doctor.

- Don't forget to check your supply of infant acetaminophen (Tylenol) at home. The correct dose for my baby is: _____.

- Don't forget that your baby will still need several shots when he or she is 12–15 months old and again at 18 months.

- Many doctors will want to see your baby for a 9-month checkup.

Questions I have about shots:

_____

_____

_____

NOTES:

Source: Lisa R. Cohen et al., *Child Development, Health, and Safety*, Aspen Publishers, Inc., © 1996.

12- and 15-Month Baby Shots

When your baby sees the doctor for a checkup at 12 months of age and 15 months of age, he or she will get the shots listed below. Some doctors will give these shots at one visit while others will split them between two visits.

Date My Baby Received Shot

MMR #1 _____

HepB #3 _____

Hib #4 _____

Varicella _____

- Record the date when your baby receives these shots, so you will know when your baby is up-to-date.

- Check your baby's shot record before your baby's 12- and 15-month checkups. If any shots are missing, be sure to tell the doctor so your baby can get any missing shots.

- Remember to have some acetaminophen (Tylenol) at home in case your baby develops a fever. The correct dose of acetaminophen for my baby is _____.

- Don't forget, your baby can safely get shots even if he or she has a mild cold, a low-grade fever, or other minor illness.

- If you have questions about shots, ask your doctor or home visitor.

- Your baby has only a few more shots to go!

Questions I have about shots:

_____

_____

_____

NOTES:

Source: Lisa R. Cohen et al., *Child Development, Health, and Safety*, Aspen Publishers, Inc., © 1996.

18-Month Baby Shots

At the 18-month checkup, your baby will get these immunizations:

Date My Baby Received Shot

OPV #3 _____

DTP #4 _____

- Once again, it will be helpful if you record the date next to the shot after your baby gets the shot.

- Be sure to discuss anything you thought was a shot reaction with your doctor.

- Don't forget to ask your doctor or nurse what the correct dose of acetaminophen is for your baby.

- Remember, if your baby has a mild cold or other illness, it is safe for him or her to get a shot.

- Check your baby's records before this 18-month visit to see if your baby is missing any shots. Be sure to tell your doctor if your baby is missing any shots.

- Your baby will need only two or three more shots before entering school. The final shots your baby needs are DTP#5, OPV#4, and MMR#2. Children usually get these shots when they are between four and six years old.

Congratulations on keeping your baby up-to-date on shots!

NOTES:

Source: Lisa R. Cohen et al., *Child Development, Health, and Safety*, Aspen Publishers, Inc., © 1996.

7

Publicizing Your Program

Using the Media

How To Generate Local Media
  Coverage 550
Characteristics of Mass Media
  Channels 552
Who To Contact in the Media 553
Working with the Media 555

Public Service Announcements

Standard PSA Pretest Questions 563
Writing Public Service Announcements .. 565

Tips for Developing TV PSAs 569

Publicity Campaigns

Conducting a Special Event Publicity
  Campaign 570
How To Select an Advertising Agency ... 573
Using Celebrity Spokespersons 574
Hiring Agencies, Contractors, and
  Consultants 575
Screening Questions To Identify Potential
  Communication Firms 578
Tips on Working with Contractors 579

Chapter 7

Publicizing Your Program

OBJECTIVES

At the completion of this chapter, the reader will

- know how to generate local media coverage
- write a Public Service Announcement (PSA)
- understand how to conduct a special event publicity campaign
- understand the process of hiring advertising agencies, consultants, and contractors

---

INTRODUCTION

This chapter describes very practical approaches to publicizing a health education or community health program. It begins with ways to generate local media and mass media coverage, and ways to work with the media. Public Service Announcements (PSAs) are detailed with tips for writing them and developing them for TV. Finally, methods are outlined for publicity campaigns including how to conduct a publicity event, selecting an advertising agency, and screening, interviewing, and evaluating potential contractors. Tips for working with the chosen contractor are included.

Publicity is difficult to obtain without an interesting, focused, and captivating message. This chapter details methods for either creating an attention-grabbing message or for hiring an agency to create a contemporary message or image for a project. Without this information, the health professional wishing to publicize a health promotion activity will have an intimidating learning curve. With the information, he or she will become a relative expert within a short time. Background information about how to publicize a program is essential and seldom found in community health texts. This chapter provides this essential but seldom found information.

HOW TO GENERATE LOCAL MEDIA COVERAGE*

Step 1: Get Organized

- Designate a media relations coordinator. (This person is usually not the spokesperson.)
- Develop your media contact list. Include names and titles, mailing addresses, and telephone numbers. (Make sure the names are spelled correctly.)
- Develop a media call sheet to fill out if you receive unsolicited calls from reporters; this will help document the actual numbers of calls that come in.
- Become familiar with editorial deadlines. For example, weekly newspapers published on Wednesday often have a Monday afternoon news deadline. News received after the deadline seldom gets published. Likewise, know when radio and TV stations air their newscasts. Never call them when they are working on deadlines.
- Segment your media list by topic or audience. Business reporters will be interested in different "angles" than will medical writers, for example. Segment your media list, and you can target your story.

Step 2: Get Prepared

- Develop a local fact sheet on your health promotion program.
- Create a source list that contains the telephone numbers of a few good people you can trust to stay "on message" for quotes or background, and who would be willing to be available to reporters. These people also provide a range of perspectives.
- Develop a question and answer sheet. By creating a document that poses—and then answers—your most frequently asked questions, you can be poised to deliver "home run" answers to the media.
- Put together a press briefing packet. A press briefing packet is a folder full of the documents you want reporters to have within reach when they cover your issue. Starting with a simple, pocketed folder with your logo affixed to the front (or attached inside), the contents of your press packet could include the following:
  –letter of introduction
  –fact sheet
  –source list
  –calendar of upcoming events
  –your business card
  –positive and informative articles or editorials
  –brochures and flyers
  –charts or graphics, color slides (if available)

---

*Source: *Seven Days of Immunizations: National Infant Immunization Week*, U.S. Department of Health and Human Services, Public Health Service, Centers for Disease Control and Prevention (CDC), Atlanta, Georgia 30333, 1995.

Step 3: Establish Contact

- Even if you already have relationships with key editors and reporters in your community, arrange introductory meetings.
- Contact them by telephone, and schedule a time to stop by to introduce yourself and/or the campaign. Provide background information (media kit) and offer assistance.
- Let editors and news directors know you will contact them periodically with news items, and that you are a resource for information.
- Inform radio and television talk show producers that you can access state and local experts for interviews and/or segments on their programs.
- Ask public service directors if they can help raise awareness by producing and/or airing public service announcements (PSAs); assist them in every way possible.
- Make a note of any unique needs or interests of media you have contacted. Then be responsive to those needs and interests in all future contacts.

Step 4: Maintain Contact

- Contact editors and reporters only when you have something newsworthy, local, and important to report. Do not wear out your welcome by repeatedly requesting coverage on non-news stories.
- How you contact the media will depend on the story, the needs of the particular media outlet, and what you hope to accomplish.
- Send a news release when you have an announcement to make.
- Send a query letter when you have a specific story idea for a particular media outlet.
- Send a media advisory when you want to invite media coverage of an event (e.g., a news conference).
- Always follow up by telephone after you send a news release, query letter, or media advisory. Ask the reporters if they received your material, if they have any questions, and if you can assist them in any way.

Step 5: Be Professional

- Keep your promises and you will gain media trust. When you say you will do something, do it. If you do not have the information they want, or you cannot do what they ask, then say so. This way you can avoid burning bridges with the media.
- Always present and package your story professionally, and think about why the media and the public would care about the story.
- Respond to inquiries and informational requests you receive from reporters as quickly as possible. Do not wait too long to return calls; reporters have to meet deadlines. If you miss their deadlines, chances are your message will not be included in their reports.
- Be aware of how you present yourself to reporters. Are you a spokesperson or just providing background information? If you are providing background, make sure you say that early in the conversation. You will not be quoted specifically. If you do not want any affiliation, say that your comments are off the record. Even then, expect to be quoted. When you are at all uncertain, do not say anything.

Characteristics of Mass Media Channels

Television	Radio	Magazines	Newspapers
Potentially largest/widest range of audiences, but not always at times when PSAs are most likely to be broadcast.	Various formats offer potential for more audience targeting than television (e.g., teenagers via rock stations). May reach fewer people than TV.	Can more specifically target to segments of public (young women, people with an interest in health).	Can reach broad audiences rapidly.
Deregulation ended government oversight of stations' broadcast of PSAs, public affairs programming.	Deregulation ended government oversight of stations' broadcast of PSAs, public affairs programming.	No requirement for PSA use; PSAs more difficult to place.	PSAs virtually nonexistent.
Opportunity to include health messages via news broadcasts, public affairs/interview shows, dramatic programming.	Opportunity for direct audience involvement via call-in shows.	Can explain more complex health issues, behaviors.	Can convey health news/breakthroughs more thoroughly than TV or radio and faster than magazines. Feature placement possible.
Visual as well as audio make emotional appeals possible. Easier to demonstrate a behavior.	Audio alone may make messages less intrusive.	Print may lend itself to more factual, detailed, rational message delivery.	
Can reach low-income and other audiences not as likely to turn to health sources for help.	Can reach audiences who do not use the health care system.	Audience has chance to clip, reread, contemplate material.	Easy audience access to in-depth issue coverage is possible.
Passive consumption by viewer; viewers must be present when message is aired; less than full attention likely. Message may be obscured by commercial "clutter."	Generally passive consumption; exchange with audience possible, but target audience must be there when aired.	Permits active consultation. May pass on. Read at reader's convenience.	Short life of newspaper limits rereading, sharing with others.
PSAs can be expensive to produce and distribute. Feature placement requires contacts and may be time consuming.	Live copy is very flexible and inexpensive; PSAs must fit station format. Feature placement requires contacts and may be time consuming.	Public service ads are inexpensive to produce; ad or article placement may be time consuming.	Small papers may take public service ads; coverage demands a newsworthy item.

NOTES:

Source: *Making Health Communication Programs Work: A Planner's Guide*, NIH Publication #92-1493, U.S. Department of Health and Human Services, Public Health Service, National Institutes of Health, Office of Cancer Communications, National Cancer Institute, April 1992.

WHO TO CONTACT IN THE MEDIA*

To spread the word about your health promotion program, you have a number of different media options. When looking at targeted media, consider what audience you are trying to reach, and what kind of station or publication would find your health issues the most important.

It is also helpful to look at different angles of your health issue depending on what media and what department you will be approaching with stories. For example, talking about money saved through immunization would be a good angle for the business editor. For the children's issue reporter, a story about a local child stricken by a preventable disease would be effective. Some suggestions for contact are:

- **Daily newspapers:**
  –city editor
  –health care/medical reporter or editor
  –parenting/children's issue reporters
  –photo editor
  –business editor
  –community calendar ("What's Happening")
  –columnist

- **Weekly newspaper:**
  –news editors
  –columnists

- **Special interest publication** (seniors, business, etc.):
  –news editor

- **Television stations:**
  –news assignment editor
  –health/medical reporter
  –talk show producers/hosts
  –public service directors

- **Radio stations:**
  –news directors
  –talk show producers/hosts
  –public service directors
  –community relations director (for sponsorships, corporate partnerships)

What the Media Can Do To Help

Once you have targeted the specific media that you think are most likely to run your story, it is important to have several suggestions for them regarding your story. Keep

---

*Source: *Seven Days of Immunizations: National Infant Immunization Week*, U.S. Department of Health and Human Services, Public Health Service, Centers for Disease Control and Prevention (CDC), Atlanta, Georgia 30333, 1995.

in mind that you need to sell your story and make it compelling for them to cover. Depending on the publication or station and their interest level, they might be able to provide several services. You also need to prioritize which services would reach the target audience most directly. The media can:

- increase news coverage of health issues in your community by:
  −running stories from news releases distributed by the department of health, your local health department, and/or your local coalition
  −publicizing local special events in advance to promote public awareness
  −assigning reporters to attend and cover local events

- produce and air public service announcements by using recorded or live announcer-read copy

- publish "filler stats" in local newspapers by printing educational information on a space-available basis

Why the Media May Be Interested in the Story

Newspapers and television and radio newscasts provide information of interest to readers, viewers, and/or listeners. It is important to make the story attention-getting and substantive when preparing a story for the media. You have to sell your story. Editors are inclined to cover stories that meet one or more of the following criteria:

- The story is newsworthy. It has the qualities of news; it is timely and interesting.

- The story is local. It relates to the community directly; it has a local news angle that warrants local media attention.

- The story is important. It is something the community should be aware of; the public needs to know, and may benefit from having the information.

NOTES:

WORKING WITH THE MEDIA*

For any public health program to be successful, it must be able to reach the public. Whether you want to promote a walking club, warn people about a measles outbreak, encourage parents to have their children immunized, or increase general knowledge of nutrition, you have to find a way to communicate with your target audience.

Often the quickest, most reliable and effective way to do this is via the local news media—daily and weekly newspapers, radio, and television.

But whether you write a news release, hold a news conference, or give an interview, your efforts could be wasted if you do not know the media in your community, which reporters are responsible for health issues, or even the form a news release should take. The following guidelines provide health professionals, who have little or no experience in dealing with the news media, with the basic information needed to do so successfully.

Getting To Know the Local Media

The first step is to get to know the people who can help you. Start by making a list of all daily and weekly newspapers, pennysavers, and radio and television stations that serve your community, even if you are physically located elsewhere. For newspapers, include the name of the managing, city, and lifestyle editors; health and science reporters; and general assignment reporters who cover your city, county, or region. For pennysavers (weekly, free shoppers' guides), you will need the names of the publishers; and for radio and television, the names of health reporters/editors, public service and program directors, and assignment editors. Remember to include their addresses, telephone numbers, and fax numbers.

You can get this information simply by calling the newspaper office or station, and asking. Once you have a list, you can start contacting the people on it. Introduce yourself and your organization or project. Keep in mind that news people are busy people who work on deadlines. Their time is limited. So, you want to keep these initial contacts brief and to the point. Find out their deadlines and how much lead time is needed for articles, calendar listings, or news releases. Do this twice a year, and update your list to reflect any changes. This will save you postage and embarrassment and eliminate any duplication of effort.

Working with the Local Media

Newspapers

Daily newspapers are essential to communicating with residents of large urban communities. In small towns and villages, this role is played by weekly newspapers. The city editor (dailies) or editor (weekly) is the key person on a newspaper's staff. He or she is the one who will decide if your story gets told. Some of the ways to use newspapers to reach your public include meetings with editorial boards, "op-ed" pieces, feature articles, letters to the editor, and news releases.

---

*Source: State of New York Department of Health, Albany, New York, © 1993.

Radio

Radio can get your message to the largest number of people when you have an urgent message to convey that requires immediate action. Since most radio stations have a specific format (country, jazz, classical, rock, etc.), it is important to understand their different audiences and tailor your messages accordingly.

Television

Television has the largest audience of all the media, as it reaches all segments of the population. On the average, a person spends more than seven hours a day watching television. While it reaches a great number of people, television is also visual. Therefore, you must present something interesting for the camera to show.

Television news usually reduces complex stories to 30- to 60-second segments. When preparing materials for the news, your contact should be the news director or assignment editor. For talk shows, it is the host or producer of the show. For public service programming, it is the public service director.

Ways To Get Media Attention

Editorial Boards

A daily newspaper's editorial board consists of editors and/or reporters who research issues and determine the paper's position on them. If an issue is of great significance to the community and your organization, or you want to explain an important policy change, you may ask to meet with a newspaper's editorial board. This meeting will enable you to help the paper formulate its stand on the topic.

To schedule a meeting, make contact by telephone or letter with the editorial page editor to outline the issue and suggest a meeting. If a meeting is scheduled, confirm the date, time, and place in a letter and include any relevant background information. Before the meeting, research the issue in depth from both the local and national perspectives. Be familiar with any previous news coverage of the issue and who has been covering it locally (this reporter may be at the meeting). Bring information on the problem, supported by local statistics and quotes from community leaders, if possible.

Choose no more than two or three succinct messages you want to communicate. Research the facts to support your position. Write them down to ensure that they make sense and that everything representing the organization agrees.

Make sure you understand and can address the opposition's viewpoint, if any. Focus on the local angle and those points that will make the strongest impression. If you can obtain local statistics, you will be able to make a stronger point.

Op-Ed Page

Another way to express your opinion in a daily newspaper is to submit what is called an op-ed piece, as it will usually appear opposite the editorial page. You may be able to get the newspaper to accept an op-ed piece if the issue is relevant or important to the community. An op-ed piece is best used to persuade readers to adopt or support an organization's viewpoint on an issue. It should be relatively short (800 words is ideal) and authored by the head of your organization.

Feature Articles

Newspapers like stories that have human interest, that is, stories that deal with who people are, what they do, and why they do it. Feature articles are most commonly used to expand on a news story, to add color or background, or to present a particular slant or point of view. Features are designed for special reader appeal and impact. Radio and television stations are less likely to use feature stories as they are not considered "hard news."

Letters to the Editor

A letter is an excellent way to respond to a newspaper when it has run a story or an editorial on an issue of concern to your organization. Save letters for important issues; if you send them too often, they will lose their impact and will not be printed.

A letter to the editor should be short, no more than 400 words. The shorter a letter is, the more likely it is to be printed without being edited. Make your most important point in the first paragraph or two. If your letter responds to a particular article, editorial, or another letter, refer to the title, date, and author of the original piece in your opening sentence. Letters to the editor should be signed by an officer of the organization.

News Releases

You should submit news releases when you have something important to talk about, for example, the start of a new program, a change in an existing program that will affect many people, or the results of a program or study. Whenever possible, include local statistics and quotes from specialists. To be sure that your story gets into the proper hands, it is best to have your news release hand delivered or faxed to the editor. To ensure that your release gets read, you must follow the proper format. Editors can (and often do) dispose of news releases, regardless of content, simply because they are prepared incorrectly. (See box on following page for an example of guidelines.)

Be sure to send news releases to the news directors of local radio and television stations. Immediate news or information about an upcoming event or possible feature story can be telephoned to the news director, assignment editor, or reporter. Remember, television is a visual medium, so the event or setting must have "eye appeal."

After speaking with the assignment editor or reporter, follow up with a letter and a press kit that includes additional information on the event and your organization and its efforts. If appropriate, provide a list of specialists who can be contacted regarding the story.

If a piece is considered inappropriate for a radio news segment, it could be used in another format, such as an event announcement. Or the program director could decide to use it as the basis for a caller participation show, community service show, or talk show. Do not try to tell the stations where or how to use your information. Let them decide.

For more information, contact:

(name)

(telephone number)

FOR IMMEDIATE RELEASE:

Suggested guidelines for writing and submitting successful news releases.

News releases should be cleanly typed (double-spaced) or photocopied on 8½" × 11" paper. They should be hand delivered or faxed to the designated media, including radio and television stations, weekly and daily newspapers, and wire services.

Other guidelines are as follows:

Identification: Your organization should be plainly identified. Use your letterhead or printed news release forms. The name and telephone number of a contact person for additional information must appear at the top of the page.

Release date: Most releases should be "immediate" or "for release on (date)." Stipulate a release time only when there is a good reason, such as an important speech by your organization's chief official.

Margins: Leave wide margins and space at the top so that editors can edit.

Headline: Give your release a title that captures its essence. While the title will not likely be used for a headline, it tells the editor about the contents of the release.

Length: Do not use more than one page unless you must, and never more than two.

Style: Summarize all critical information in the first paragraph or two (the lead), using the five Ws: who, what, when, where, why (and sometimes how). Write in a conversational tone; keep it simple and short. Keep paragraphs short and focused, only two to four sentences each. Do not editorialize; state facts, not opinions, unless you are quoting someone. Do not hyphenate words at the end of lines or split a paragraph from the first to second page.

Avoid: Fancy words. Use plain, simple English.

Check: Names, titles, dates, spelling, numbers, and grammar. Then double-check them and proofread the release carefully.

Delivery: Your news release should be in the hands of editors within 24 hours before and after any event or activity. You should know in advance where to deliver your news release. General news goes to the city desk or assignment editor; specialized news should be given directly to reporters or departments, especially if they know you.

Photos: If you have photos of an event, they can be submitted with your news release. Photos should be submitted only as 5 × 7 or 8 × 10 black-and-white glossies. Do not submit color photos or Polaroids. On the back of the photo, use a china marker ("grease pencil") or soft-lead pencil to identify any people (list them left to right). Also, write a caption that identifies the event and any people pictured (again, left to right). Tape the caption to the back of the photo.

At bottom of the first page: Put -more-.

At end: Put -30-.

Public Service Announcements

Daily newspapers rarely, if ever, carry advertisements on a public service basis. They just do not have the space. Weekly newspapers are more likely to do so, and pennysavers (weekly, free shoppers' guides) offer the best forums for public service print ads. If you have designed a poster or flyer about a special program or event, it can be easily adapted to serve as a print ad.

Both radio and television are excellent outlets for public service announcements (PSAs). For information on writing, producing, or delivering radio and television PSAs, see the New York State Department of Health publication, "Writing Public Service Announcements."

Interviews

If a reporter or editor asks for an interview on your organization's efforts or an issue on which your organization is an expert, you must select an appropriate spokesperson. A program spokesperson should:

- be willing to work with the media (and not see reporters as "the enemy")
- have good listening skills
- be spontaneous
- have a working knowledge of the situation
- be a quick study
- view the opportunity as a good way to get your message across
- have experience with all media (newspapers, television, and radio)

Beforehand, ask the reporter/interviewer about the questions or areas that will be covered during the interview. Using this information, draw up a list of all the questions you think will be asked. Prepare the answers and practice answering. Also, you can give a reporter a list of questions you would like to have asked. Be aware, however, that the reporter may not use your questions.

Usually, a person will have 15–20 seconds to respond to a reporter's question during a radio or television interview. Therefore, he or she must be able to relate the entire message in very short sentences, in an interesting and appealing way. It is best to use simple, easily understood words and avoid jargon and technical terms, whenever possible. Remember that long, convoluted sentences and complex concepts increase the chances of being misquoted. If you do not know the answer to a question, say so— do not try to bluff. Tell the reporter that you will look into the matter and get back with an answer; then do so.

Because reporters often need to respond quickly to breaking news, much of their work is done over the telephone rather than in person. Reporters may be gathering information for an in-depth story or just looking for a brief comment. Give a summary of your position on the issue and then be prepared to answer specific questions.

A telephone interview may or may not be taped. In the case of radio or television, it may or may not be live. Determine the situation at the outset. Remember, you can decline to be aired live or taped, yet still cooperate with the reporter by providing the information needed for the story. If you agree to be aired live or taped, you need to make your point in one short, declarative sentence, two at the most.

Studio interviews are used for live talk shows, which sometimes have listener call-in options. They may also be used for community service programs. Keep in mind that listeners cannot see you or any gesture you may use to explain or emphasize your point. Keep sentences short and easy to understand. Deliver your key message in as clear a manner as possible.

Be poised, speak clearly, and keep eye contact with the reporter. Shifting or glancing about and jumbling your words will make a very poor impression on camera and distract viewers from what you are saying. Do not lean into the microphone; let the reporter position it. If you gesture, do so slowly and with purpose.

Television gives you the option of using slides or videotape to illustrate your organization's needs, relevant data, or anticipated results. Make sure to preview your slides or video prior to the date of your interview. Also, let the interviewer know that you plan to use visuals. The interviewer or production staff may want to preview your materials for format, quality, or to determine how best to use them.

Dress in soft, medium, or pastel colors. Avoid very dark or light clothing and contrasting patterns and stripes. Women should not wear noisy bracelets or bright, sparkling jewelry.

Use these interviewing tips for radio and television:

- Be prepared. You will be more confident and comfortable and be able to tell your story clearly to those who count most—the viewers or listeners.
- Before the interview, make sure you and the reporter agree on the topics to be covered. This way you or your spokesperson can prepare specific answers.
- Concentrate on how to communicate ideas and feelings, not just words.
- Give the reporter a list of the questions you would like to be asked.
- Be early, especially if it is a taped program. Studios are heavily booked, and punctuality is essential.
- Do not try to adjust the placement of the microphone or its volume. That is what the sound technician is paid to do.
- If a response is not short (8–15 seconds) and to the point, it will not be used on the air. Formulate concise answers to expected questions in advance.
- There may be only 30 seconds to present your organization's message. Focus on the essential points.

News Conferences

Always remember that a news conference should be a special event. Do not hold too many. You may want to hold a news conference to introduce your organization, its project, or plans. Then hold conferences only to announce new programs, major improvements, or important changes in your organization's activities. A news release would be more appropriate than a news conference when publicizing your organization's background or viewpoint, your role in the community, or an upcoming event. Three days prior to the news conference, send a media advisory to all newspapers and radio and television stations. A media advisory outlines the five Ws and gives a contact name and telephone number for information. (See box on following page.) On the day before, call the radio and television assignment editors to remind them of the event. This will help you determine attendance, as well. On the day of the news conference, have on hand extra copies of releases, press kits, and speeches (if applicable).

MEDIA ADVISORY
A paragraph explaining your organization's
goals, activities.

What:
When: } Logistics of event
Where:

Who: Speakers, guests, etc.

For more information contact _____.

Use the following tips for holding a news conference:

- To boost media attendance and get better coverage, try to schedule news conferences between 10:00 AM and 11:00 AM and in the middle of the week (Tuesday, Wednesday, Thursday). Do not hold a news conference on a weekend, and avoid Fridays—the story will get lost in the weekend news.
- Select a location that is convenient for the media. Avoid rooms with mirrors and undraped windows, as both can cause problems for television cameras. The room must be large enough to accommodate all the media and their equipment, including television cameras. The room should have an ample supply of two- and three-prong electrical outlets for cameras, lights, and tape recorders.
- Post signs to help people find the site.
- Place a table outside the room or just inside for media sign-in. Have someone greet attendees and hand out news releases or press kits.
- Provide a lectern with a microphone for speakers and space for reporters' microphones.
- Begin the news conference on time. Limit it to 30 minutes, including time for a question-and-answer period.
- Conduct a question-and-answer period after speakers' remarks.
- After the news conference, send copies of the news release to those reporters who were unable to attend. Continue to update reporters on your project's successes, and provide statistics, if applicable.

Media Kits

Your organization should have a standard set of background and informational materials that can be compiled to form a media kit. These are helpful for news conferences. Media kits can include news releases about the program, 5" by 7" or 8" by 10" glossy photographs, biography of speakers or specialists, history of your organization, fact sheets, and any clippings or articles regarding your organization or project.

Dealing with Bad News

The time to prepare for a crisis is before it happens. Crises are inevitable in any large organization, so you should be prepared with a plan that is thoughtfully drafted and regularly rehearsed.

When faced with a crisis, respond quickly and with authority. If you provide the facts quickly and accurately, the press will appreciate your help. Your openness can lead to a closer working relationship in the future.

Tell the public what happened and why. Then say what you are going to do to make sure it does not happen again.

Keeping in Touch

No matter if the story is good news or bad, always say thank you. Continue to update reporters on the successes of your project, and provide statistics on any changes in your community's health that can be traced to your program.

Remember, achieving good coverage for your organization and generating interest in its activities requires time, imagination, attention to detail, and a certain amount of perseverance. With these, you can ensure that your efforts will be successful.

NOTES:

Standard PSA Pretest Questions

1. **Main Idea Communication/Comprehension**
   What was the main idea this message was trying to get across to you?

   _____

   _____

   What does this message ask you to do?

   _____

   _____

   What action, if any, is the message recommending that people take?

   _____

   _____

   In your opinion, was there anything in the message that was confusing?

   _____

   _____

   Which of these phrases best describes the message?
   _____ Easy to understand
   _____ Hard to understand

2. **Likes/Dislikes**
   In your opinion, was there anything in particular that was worth remembering about the message?

   _____

   _____

   What, if anything, did you particularly like about the message?

   _____

   _____

   Was there anything in the message that you particularly disliked or that bothered you? If yes, what?

   _____

   _____

3. **Believability**
   In your opinion, was there anything in the message that was hard to believe? If yes, what?

   _____

   _____

   Which of these words or phrases best describes how you feel about the message?
   _____ Believable
   _____ Not believable

4. **Personal Relevance/Interest**
   In your opinion, what type of person was this message talking to?
   _____ Someone like me
   _____ Someone else, not me

continues

Standard PSA Pretest Questions continued

In your opinion, which of these groups was the message talking to?
_____ All people
_____ All people, but especially (the target audience)
_____ Only (the target audience)

Which of these words or phrases best describes how you feel about the message?
_____ Interesting
_____ Not interesting

_____ Informative
_____ Not informative

Did you learn anything new about (health subject) from the message? If yes, what?
_____
_____

5. **Other Target Audience Reactions**
(Target audience reactions to messages can be assumed using pairs of words or phrases or using a five-point scale. The following is an example of how this is done.)

Listed below are several pairs of words or phrases with the numbers 1 to 5 between them. Indicate which number best describes how you feel about the message. The higher the number, the more you think the phrase on the right describes it. The lower the number, the more you think the phrase on the left describes it. You could also pick any number in between. Look at each set of words and circle the number that best describes your reaction to the message.

Too Short	1	2	3	4	5	Too Long
Discouraging	1	2	3	4	5	Encouraging
Comforting	1	2	3	4	5	Alarming
Well Done	1	2	3	4	5	Poorly Done
Not Informative	1	2	3	4	5	Informative

Is there anything in the message that would bother or offend people you know?
_____
_____

6. **Impressions of Announcer**
Please select the one answer from each pair of phrases that describes your feelings about the announcer.
_____ Believable
_____ Not believable

_____ Appropriate to the message
_____ Not appropriate to the message

_____ Gets the message across
_____ Doesn't get the message across

Source: *Making Health Communication Programs Work: A Planner's Guide*, NIH Publication #92-1493, U.S. Department of Health and Human Services, Public Health Service, National Institutes of Health, Office of Cancer Communications, National Cancer Institute, April 1992.

WRITING PUBLIC SERVICE ANNOUNCEMENTS*

If you want to quickly communicate an important health message to a wide and diverse audience, or if you want to get a message to a specific population whose members are not likely to be influenced by other media or community activities, consider using radio or television.

Commercial advertisers have long recognized this fact, as have national and regional public service organizations and charities. Local nonprofit organizations can have access to the audiences of these powerful communications media as well, through public service announcements (PSAs).

Public service announcements are messages from bona fide community agencies that stations air during unsold blocks of advertising time or station identification breaks. Station managers and public service directors are always looking for PSAs that are well-written, that carry messages of importance to their audiences, and that represent an opportunity for stations to perform a public service for their communities.

Writing for Radio

Radio is the portable broadcast medium. Your message must compete with many distractions. People listen to radio at the same time that they drive, work, study, or read. So, you must grab the listeners' attention and hold it.

The first step is to make sure that your PSA reflects a single, basic idea. This is one of the most important elements of good advertising: Decide exactly what you want to sell, then sell *it*, and *only* it.

Start your PSA with short, punchy sentences that are directed at the individual listener. You want to get his or her attention. Here are two examples:

- "Exercise. It may be just what you need. With a good exercise program you can improve your heart and lungs, relieve emotional and nervous tension, and help control your weight."
- "Did you know that you have a right to know? There's a right-to-know law in New York State that can protect you from toxic hazards at work."

Avoid the tendency to shift from second to third person. It is difficult to follow. For example, "Are you taking steps to control your high blood pressure? Many people wait until it's too late," is better written, "Are you taking steps to control your high blood pressure? Don't wait until it's too late."

You must write for the ear instead of the eye. Your writing should reflect the way you talk—clear, uncomplicated, and informal.

If possible, use the present tense or active voice. It lends immediacy to your message.

Vary the lengths of sentences to create a flow or rhythm that makes it pleasant to your listeners. A series of short sentences read aloud often creates a choppy, monotonous cadence that makes listening a chore.

Words should be chosen for descriptive color and precise meaning. Factual clarity, conversational tones, and sentence brevity are the cornerstones of good broadcast

---

*Source: State of New York Department of Health, Albany, New York, © 1988.

writing. An example of wordy writing is the phrase "in order to" (which means "to"). Others are "due to the fact that" (because) and "prior to" (before).

Remember that the ear cannot easily take in large blocks of information. It has to be presented in easily digested portions. Avoid long, rambling sentences, alliteration, awkward sounds, and proper names. Select only the most essential facts and information. When possible, do not use medical, legal, or scientific terms.

Because someone not familiar with your organization will be reading your PSA, indicate how an unusual name or word is pronounced. You can use phonetic symbols or simply spell the word as it sounds. For example, "Edward D. Lynde (pronounced (Lined)" or "Edward D. Lynde (rhymes with signed)."

Whenever an address or telephone number is part of your PSA, try to mention it a second time, preferably at the end, to help your audience remember it.

Other rules to keep in mind are the following: Do not use abbreviations, unless they are appropriate and very well known. Use contractions to give a conversational tone. Spell out fractions. Round off numbers (use "about," "nearly," "approximately," "more than," etc.). Avoid symbols. Use titles before names (such as Doctor, Reverend, etc., but not Mr., Mrs., Miss, or Ms.). Avoid cliches, meaningless phrases, and overmodifications.

Writing for Television

All of the rules that apply to radio writing should be followed when writing for television as well. The only difference is that, with television, you add sight to sound.

Television PSAs can be prepared either as produced videotaped spots or as slide/announcer copy spots. Produced videotaped spots deliver action, together with a soundtrack. But, because they are complex and expensive to produce, a discussion of produced spots is beyond the scope of this chapter.

Slide/announcer spots are easy to produce and relatively low cost. The elements of slide/announcer copy spots are copy written to be read by an announcer (sound), along with 35-mm slides (sight). Many local agencies have prepared excellent and effective slide/announcer copy PSAs.

Do not allow yourself to be influenced by the apparent emphasis on the visual aspect of television. The visual and the spoken material must be treated equally. Ideally, each communicates the central message as clearly as possible. One should enhance and reinforce the other. The purpose of the spoken message is to explain. The purpose of the visual message is to demonstrate, emphasize, or set a tone.

PSA Formats

A balanced package of radio public service announcements includes spots that are 10-, 20-, and 30-seconds long. The same is true for television, except that you can add a 15-second PSA to your package. Do not try a 60-second public service announcement. It is hard to sustain an audience's interest for that long, and it is very unlikely that you will find a broadcaster willing to donate 60 seconds of free air time.

When writing a PSA, be aware that broadcasters generally speak at the rate of 155 words per minute. Always time your copy by reading it aloud to yourself, at a natural speaking pace, to ensure that it fits the word-total requirement.

Use the following as a guide when writing PSAs:

10-second PSA . . . . 20–25 words
15-second PSA . . . . 30–35 words
20-second PSA . . . . 40–50 words
30-second PSA . . . . 60–75 words

When writing for television, keep the announcer copy shorter (8-, 13-, 18-, and 28-seconds). This ensures that your spots will fit any station's programming slot and that you will avoid having your message accidentally cut off or mistimed.

Type your PSA copy with one spot to a sheet. Make sure that it is double- or triple-spaced, and never split words at the end of lines. In addition to the information that normally appears on your letterhead, include the length of the announcement and the period of time during which you want it to be used, for example, "FOR USE: September 25–October 15" or "IMMEDIATE: TFN" (till further notice).

The following are examples of how your radio and television PSAs should look:

Radio PSA

Program Material:	**Spot announcement**	Time: **20 seconds**
Log:	**PSA**	
Subject:	**New York State Health Department— AIDS Does Not Discriminate (Giveaway)**	
Use:	**TFN**	

AIDS does not discriminate. Anyone can get AIDS . . . through sexual contact or by sharing a needle with an infected person. The New York State Health Department says AIDS can be prevented. To get all the facts, write: AIDS Does Not Discriminate, Box 2000, Albany, New York 12220.

Television PSA

Program Material:	**Voice-over TV spot**	Time: **10 seconds**
Log:	**PSA**	
Subject:	**New York State Health Department—Child Safety Caps**	
Use:	**February 1–February 28**	

Slide: Health Department logo (Enclosed)	Parents, help safeguard your children by using safety caps on medications in your home. A safety tip from this station and the New York State Health Department.

If you are working with 35-mm slides and announcer copy for television, you will need one slide for a 10-second spot, two for 15 seconds, and three for 30 seconds. Have your slides plastic mounted so that they will not jam a station's slide chain.

Slides must be horizontal so the image properly fits within the shape of a television screen. The subject matter of the slide should be well centered, allowing for a marginal loss of the picture when viewed on the screen. The aspect ratio of the standard 2 × 2-inch slide is 2:3, not the 3:4 aspect ratio of the television screen. A certain amount of picture area will be lost on all sides when the slide is projected on television. The illustration on the left shows a message that crowds the slide's horizontal margins; and on the right, what is lost when that slide is used on television:

Broadcast Media Relations

Before your spot is heard or seen by anyone, you will have to overcome the stiff competition for air time. Stations receive hundreds of requests from national, state, and local nonprofit groups who want access to a limited amount of public service air time. Your strongest advantage is that your promotional campaign is local and vital to the community that the station serves.

One way to emphasize the importance and local nature of your campaign is to personally deliver your PSAs to the stations' public service directors. Make appointments and deliver the PSAs to each station at least ten days before they are to be used. Include a cover letter, fact sheet, brochure, or other information material about your organization and its program. Also provide the PSA director with your telephone number. Let him or her know that you will call in about two weeks to see if the spots are being aired and how often.

Make a straightforward appeal for support, but do not go farther. An offer of favorable treatment by your group, such as exclusive news or future paid advertising, would be seen as both unethical and insulting.

Be sure to acknowledge the support that local stations give your organization. A certificate of appreciation, or a letter of thanks from your chief executive officer, will go far toward cementing good relations.

A final word of caution: Understand the limits of PSAs. By their nature, as free spots aired when paid advertising is not available, PSAs are likely to be used late at night and at other less desirable times. There is little you can do to influence this.

On the other hand, PSAs offer you access to mass audiences and thousands of dollars worth of free advertising. For a small investment of time, PSAs yield important benefits. It is in the best interests of local, nonprofit organizations to take full advantage of this valuable communications tool.

Tips for Developing TV PSAs

☐ Keep messages short and simple—just one or two key points.

☐ Be sure *every word* works.

☐ Repeat the main message as many times as possible.

☐ Identify the main message in the first ten seconds in an attention-getting way.

☐ Summarize or repeat the main point/message at the close.

☐ Superimpose the main point on the screen to reinforce the oral message.

☐ Recommend a specific action.

☐ Demonstrate the health problem, behavior, or skills (if relevant).

☐ Provide new, accurate, straightforward information.

☐ Present the facts in a straightforward manner.

☐ Use a memorable slogan or theme, music, or sound effects to aid recall.

☐ Be sure that the message presenter is seen as a credible source of information, whether an authority, celebrity, or target audience representative.

☐ Use only a few characters.

☐ Select an appropriate approach (e.g., testimonial, demonstration, or slice-of-life format).

☐ Make the message understandable from the visual portrayal alone.

☐ Use positive rather than negative appeals.

☐ Emphasize the solution as well as the problem.

☐ Use a light, humorous approach, if appropriate, but pretest to be sure it works—and does not offend the audience.

☐ Avoid high degrees of fear arousal, unless the fear is easily resolved and the message carefully tested.

☐ Be sure the message, language, and style are considered relevant by the intended audience.

☐ Use 30- or 60-second spots to present and repeat the complete message; use 10-second spots only for reminders.

☐ If the action is to call or write, show the telephone number or address on the screen for at least five seconds, and reinforce orally (telephone calls require less effort than writing for most people).

☐ Check for consistency with campaign messages in other media formats.

☐ Use language and style appropriate for the target audience.

☐ **Pretest prior to final production.** Remember that the most careful message planning does not replace the need for creativity.

NOTES:

Source: *Making Health Communication Programs Work: A Planner's Guide*, NIH Publication #92-1493, U.S. Department of Health and Human Services, Public Health Service, National Institutes of Health, Office of Cancer Communications, National Cancer Institute, April 1992.

CONDUCTING A SPECIAL EVENT PUBLICITY CAMPAIGN*

Effective publicity efforts conducted before and during a special event are essential to its success. All publicity must be planned well in advance of the event and coordinated by someone with expertise in working with the media. If you do not have an expert on staff, consider hiring a freelance writer or contracting with an ad agency for publicity services.

Your publicity efforts should be designed to:

- Create awareness about your agency and program.
- Attract spectators/participants to the event.
- Persuade the media to provide news and feature coverage of the event and your program.

Use a Media Mix

Most experts agree that the most successful publicity efforts use a combination of media (newspapers, radio, and television) and involve both free and paid media reports. The free reports may consist of news and feature coverage provided by the media, news releases, and radio and TV public service announcements. Paid reports may include newspaper ads and radio and TV commercials.

Programs in suburban or rural communities, and in distinct neighborhoods within large urban areas, may find that nontraditional community-based channels are more effective in reaching their target audience than the mass media. These channels include school and church newsletters; posters placed in stores, schools, and recreational facilities and in halls operated by the local Grange, American Legion, Knights of Columbus, or other organizations; flyers sent home with school children or stuffed in grocery store bags; news releases and ads in weekly commercial newspapers (pennysavers); paycheck or bill stuffers, such as a notice sent out with the community water and sewer bills. Also, consider placing banners announcing the event across the main business street (a permit is required for this).

Find out which channels of communication your target audience uses most to get information about the community. Then use those channels.

Be Creative

Some nonprofit organizations have effectively used a pre-event activity to obtain publicity about their special events. These have included:

- making arrangements for the media to interview the star of the event's main attraction three days to a week before the event (over the telephone, if necessary)
- having a representative talk about the event on a local radio or TV talk show
- making arrangements for a plane to trail a banner about the event as it flies over the community

---

*Source: State of New York Department of Health, Albany, New York, © 1993.

- having a hot-air balloon land on a school athletic field, with the balloonist distributing flyers, free admission tickets, or discount coupons for the event
- having a person dressed in a character costume (such as a "Healthy Heart") visit the downtown section, a mall, or the schools to talk about the event and hand out balloons containing a message about the event
- holding a fun pre-event race or parade

If you want to conduct a pre-event activity to publicize your main event, make sure it is one that will convey the theme and atmosphere of the main event. If you have designed your main event to be fun, exciting, and family oriented, make sure your pre-event conveys those qualities. Notify the media about the pre-event several days in advance and make reminder calls to the media the day before the pre-event.

Getting Good News Coverage

The extent and quality of media coverage you are able to obtain for your event and your program depend on some things you can influence and some things, unfortunately, you cannot. The things you can influence have to do with making your event newsworthy—and persuading the media that it is newsworthy. In planning your event, consider the factors that enter into the media's decision on how much time or space, if any, to devote to covering an event:

- Is the event really special—something fresh and exciting for their readers and viewers?
- How important is the program or service to the community?
- How colorful (action oriented) is the event? Will there be opportunities to take interesting photos for newspapers and to obtain good video footage for TV and good audio for radio?
- Are there any major local or national celebrities attending? (*Note:* If your headliner is a local media celebrity, such as a news or sports broadcaster, competing stations will reduce their coverage.)
- Are major community, county, or state leaders attending?
- How many different organizations and businesses are participating?
- How strong is audience interest in the subject?

Circumstances affecting media coverage that generally are beyond your control include other local, national, and world activities that may occur on the same day as your event. A newspaper or a radio or television station may make plans for extensive coverage of your event, only to shift its coverage at the last minute to some unexpected hard news event. The best you can do is to schedule your event on what should be a slow news day for the media, such as a weekend or holiday, when government offices, banks, schools, and many businesses are closed. Check with community calendars maintained by the local chamber of commerce and other organizations to make sure you do not select a date that is already earmarked for another major event.

To persuade the media that your event is newsworthy, ask to meet with newspaper editorial boards and radio and television news managers to talk about your program and upcoming events. Find out what news coverage they are willing to provide.

Make Things Easy for the Media

If you want good media coverage, make things as easy as possible for the media. Become familiar with their deadlines. Morning newspapers prefer events conducted in the afternoon and early evening for next-day reporting. Evening television news programs prefer events conducted in late-morning or early-afternoon hours. If they are very interested in your event, some stations might broadcast "live" from the event if it is going on during their news broadcast times. Peak listening hours for radio are morning and evening rush hours. Radio also can be enticed to broadcast live from the event site.

Keep the Media Informed

Do not rely on letters or news releases delivered by mail to keep the media informed of your program's activities. Hand deliver your news releases and public service announcements. Know the editors, reporters, and broadcasters by name and ask to speak with them. Contact them by telephone about any new developments. In addition to these ongoing efforts, contact all the media three days before the event to remind them about the event and advise them of any special arrangements made for them at the event.

Assist the Media at the Event

Find out ahead of time what special assistance and equipment the media would like you to provide for them at the event. On the day of the event, have a special check-in site for the media. Provide them with press kits containing a program schedule; brief biographies of the main speakers and stars of the event; a map (if the event is a fair, parade, or walk); news releases and public service announcements about your organization (including names of key administrators), your organization's program, and the event; 8½" by 11" black-and-white photos of headline speakers, stars, or entertainers at the event; copies of major speeches to be given during the event; and samples of promotional and educational materials (brochures, buttons, flyers, posters, etc.). Have at least one person available through the day to assist the media in obtaining answers to their questions (be prepared to give an estimate of attendance) and in obtaining access to major speakers and entertainers for interviews. If your event is spread over a large area, such as a fair, you will need several people to escort media representatives and to point out the important activities. For speeches and award ceremonies, provide special seating for the media in the front. If your event runs over a period of hours, reporters and camera crews will arrive at varying times. Keep in mind that you must approach the reporter who arrives five minutes before the end of the event with the same enthusiasm you displayed to those who arrived early. On the day following the event, send press kits to any media that did not attend the event.

How To Select an Advertising Agency

If you decide to develop a media campaign, you may want the help of an advertising agency. Although you do not have to be an advertising expert yourself, you need to have a basic understanding of the process and know what you want in order to direct the agency staff. Remember that you are hiring them for their advertising expertise. You understand the health problem and may understand how the public reacts to health messages better than agency staff. Agency and program staff should respect each other's areas of expertise. Consider these questions to decide whether you are prepared to hire an ad agency:

☐ **Do you have a clear strategy statement?**
Unless you have a clear picture of what you want, an agency will have difficulty responding to your requests.

☐ **Have you developed a list of ad agencies to contact?**
Be alert to good health-related work you have seen and find out who did it. Ask other health program managers for recommendations or call a local advertising club. *Check references.*

☐ **Do you have a good idea of what works and what does not?**
If you are not sure you can separate *effective* (not necessarily the advertising that merely looks good) from ineffective advertising, try to learn more (by talking with others and reading the articles or books referenced in this guide) before you select an agency.

☐ **Do you have a budget?**
Sometimes advertising agencies will be interested in working on a health topic and may provide you with more commitment and effort than could be expected for small health campaign budgets. However, do not ask for more work than you can afford. If the agency feels obligated to deliver more than your budget can reasonably support, the quality of the work may suffer.

☐ **Have you thought about selection criteria?**
Make a list of the services you will need (e.g., creative strategy development, market research, materials production, help with planning message dissemination or materials placement), and ask several agencies to tell you how they have handled these services for other clients. Do not require creative work on your campaign as a part of the selection process. It is expensive for the agency and it may not accurately reflect what the agency would produce for you after more careful consideration. However, you should look at work the agency has done for other clients. Guard against quick or easy answers from a potential agency. Health messages are usually more complex to design than those for commercial products, and certainly they are *different* from commercial messages.

☐ **Are you prepared to work with the agency?**
Developing an effective health campaign demands close cooperation between you (the health expert) and the agency (the advertising/marketing expert). Visit agencies you are seriously considering hiring; make sure you feel comfortable with the staff with whom you will work. Be prepared to be a good client: Be supportive of good work, and clearly indicate what you do not like (and tell them why); be consistent; simplify the approval system as much as you can; and trust agency staff to know how to do their work.

Source: *Making Health Communication Programs Work: A Planner's Guide*, NIH Publication #92-1493, U.S. Department of Health and Human Services, Public Health Service, National Institutes of Health, Office of Cancer Communications, National Cancer Institute, April 1992.

Using Celebrity Spokespersons

Using the right celebrity to represent your campaign can be an exciting proposition. The following are a few considerations to think about as you make your decision:

☐ Celebrities can be effective *if they are directly associated* with your message by the audience (e.g., an ex-cancer patient, a pregnant woman, an ex-smoker).

☐ Celebrities speak for themselves and their image. Have a firm agreement about their role and what they will—and will not—say.

☐ Celebrities can increase attention to your message from audiences and gatekeepers.

☐ The appearance of a celebrity may compete with your message for attention.

☐ Some audiences may not react favorably to some celebrities.

☐ A network may not use a top star from a rival network's show.

☐ Production schedules will be built around the celebrity's schedule, which could result in production delays or a need to reschedule, increasing production time and costs.

☐ Be sure that the celebrity does not practice health habits or hold health-related opinions that could later contradict your own messages (e.g., a spokesperson for eating well during pregnancy who is known to have bulimia).

☐ Remember that celebrities live in the public eye. A change in their popularity or personal lifestyle could affect the acceptability of your message.

☐ A local celebrity or well-known person may be more credible for some audiences than a national figure.

NOTES:

Source: *Making Health Communication Programs Work: A Planner's Guide*, NIH Publication #92-1493, U.S. Department of Health and Human Services, Public Health Service, National Institutes of Health, Office of Cancer Communications, National Cancer Institute, April 1992.

HIRING AGENCIES, CONTRACTORS, AND CONSULTANTS*

The following information is designed to provide guidance on (1) determining when to go outside your organization for assistance in developing, implementing, or assessing social change interventions; (2) assessing the options to ensure a good fit between the organization and the agency, consultant, or contractor once the decision has been made; and (3) working with outside firms or consultants. Many of the specific examples are oriented toward selecting firms for marketing communication tasks (usually advertising or public relations agencies) because their services are often used in social change interventions. However, many of the tips would apply when hiring firms for other activities.

When Is Outside Assistance Needed?

Social change interventions can include such diverse components as grass-roots advocacy, advertising, special events, media advocacy, continuing medical education modules, train-the-trainer courses, curriculum development, and direct service provision. Organizations rarely have in-house staff trained in all the disciplines that can help develop and implement a social change intervention. Public health organizations turn to outside help for one or more of the following reasons:

- to obtain specialized skills not available internally. For example, few public health organizations employ staff with advertising copywriting and production skills.
- to handle work overflow. Sometimes in-house staff have the necessary skills, but the intervention creates more work than they can handle.
- to obtain an outside viewpoint. Evaluation is most often contracted out for this reason, but outside viewpoints also can be very helpful with strategic planning and message development. And in some situations, the opinions of "outsiders" may have more credibility than the opinions of staff who are trying to get an intervention funded.

Tips on Selecting Agencies, Consultants, and Other Contractors

Every organization has unique constraints on hiring outside contractors. The process outlined can be modified to fit your organization's requirements.

- Determine what in-house staff can do—based on skills and time available—versus what should be contracted out.
- Group the tasks that must be contracted out based on skills required to perform them—for example, market research, evaluation, advertising, media relations, grass-roots advocacy.
- Determine how many contractors you will need. Be careful about assuming that one contractor can handle many tasks—or about believing those who say they can. For example, organizing grass-roots advocacy is very different from producing advertising or handling media relations; most firms do not have staff that can handle all of these assignments equally well. If your organization's staff does not

---

*Source: Michael Siegel and Lynne Doner, *Marketing Public Health: Strategies To Promote Social Change*, Aspen Publishers, Inc., © 1998.

have the expertise to assess the types of contractors needed, it may help to convene a search committee that includes in-house staff and outside consultants.

- Identify potential contractors (firms or independent consultants). Ask colleagues for recommendations, and find out who did work that you think is outstanding. A good next step is to send a short questionnaire to each firm (or consultant) to assess its interest and capabilities.

- Request written proposals or presentations from the firms of interest to you. Make the request in writing, and be clear about what you want done. Convey, at a minimum

    –basic facts about the program, including goals and objectives

    –specific services that will be needed

    –details regarding compensation

    Giving bidders a ballpark budget helps them tailor their response to your resources.

- Protect yourself. As part of your initial request or, at the latest, before a contract is signed

    –*ask what percentage of time proposed staff are committed to other projects.* Some contractors are notorious for the bait and switch: they bid staff that have the capabilities you are looking for even though they know they are committed to other projects. Then when they win the contract, they substitute other, less experienced staff.

    –*include a key personnel clause.* This clause states that the contractor cannot remove anyone designated key personnel from your project without notifying you first, and that you must approve any key personnel replacements.

    –*ask for unit pricing and cost assumptions* (including any additional tasks or materials needed to complete the project that are not in the budget). Both pieces of information help you compare contractor costs. Also, sometimes organizations forget to include particular items in their request (or don't realize they should be included). Scrupulous contractors then find themselves in a quandary: Should they include the necessary steps in their budget, thereby increasing their costs (and possibly causing them to lose the business), or should they assume that the organization will handle the other tasks some other way? (Unscrupulous contractors just ignore the other tasks and materials, wait until the contract is signed, and then bring them up as modifications.) If the contract is for publications or reports that could go through many revisions, ask for the number of anticipated revisions to be noted in the assumptions.

    –*ask for budgets in terms of labor hours as well as dollars.* This information will help you (1) assess whether the contractor understands the scope of work and (2) compare the level of effort each contractor is proposing (i.e., the total dollar amount might be the same but might buy you vastly different quantities of professional time).

    –*ask for examples of past work done by proposed staff.* Ask that each example be accompanied by a description of the role each staff member played in it. When you hire a contractor, particularly for creative products, you are really buying the expertise of the individuals who work on your project. Asking for examples of their work (rather than the firm's) helps ensure that you get what you think was proposed.

    –*always get multiple bids or proposals.* Doing so not only helps you compare prices, it helps you assess how clear you were in your instructions—if all bidders have radically different proposals and prices, your scope of work may not have been clear.

—stipulate that the contractor will incorporate your revisions before finalizing the product. While most contractors want you to be happy with the final product, it is safest to have all approval points written into the contract.

- Evaluate the prospects.
  The following are some thoughts to keep in mind as you assess each candidate:
  - *Excellent skills are more important than content knowledge in most cases.* Successful contractors get that way by being fast learners. You can teach them what they need to know about your problem, but you can't teach them their discipline. For example, if you have to choose between an advertising agency with great creative abilities but little knowledge of your particular topic and an agency with mediocre creative abilities but lots of content knowledge, go with the former, with one caveat: Agencies that have no experience working with public health organizations often have difficulty working within the scientific constraints imposed by the field and the levels of approval required. Evaluate such agencies carefully to see how willing they are to work within your parameters.
  - *Make sure they tell you how they will apply their experience to your problem.* They may have done some great work in the past, but if they can't apply it to your needs, who cares?
  - *Did they follow your instructions?* Contractors are on their best behavior when they are pursuing a business opportunity. If they don't listen to you now, they never will.
  - *Don't penalize them if they didn't provide something you didn't ask for.* One contractor may include a great idea that is not part of the services you requested. It is unfair to penalize the others for not proposing the same thing.
  - *Make yourself available for questions.* If possible, meet with the candidates before you ask for proposals. You're hiring contractors for their expertise. They may recommend a totally different approach after hearing a little bit about the issue.
  - *How's the chemistry?* Do you want to work with them? Contracting relationships are often fraught with tension due to project demands. If you aren't comfortable with the organization, you won't have a good working relationship with that organization, and the project will suffer.

Screening Questions To Identify Potential Communication Firms

GENERAL INFORMATION

- What were the total annual billings of your firm for each of the last 5 years?
- List your firm's three largest clients and the percentage of total current agency billings each represents.
- List three average-sized clients and the percentage of billings each represents.
- List the accounts your firm has won and lost over the past 2 years and the total billings for each account. Why were the accounts lost or resigned?
- Describe any experience that your firm and executives have with [SOCIAL CHANGE TOPIC].
- What experience has your firm had that is pertinent to the marketing, merchandising, and advertising of [SOCIAL CHANGE TOPIC]?
- (For advertising agencies) Approximately what percentage of your last year's billings went into the following media? (List TV, radio, newspaper, magazines, outdoor, other.)
- Describe your approach to developing communication messages and materials.

ORGANIZATION AND PERSONNEL

- What is the total number of people employed full time by your agency? Provide a breakdown by department or function.
- Describe the organization and philosophy of your creative department. What are the agency's capabilities regarding the creation and production of TV, radio, and print advertising?

- Who is your creative director, and how long has this individual been employed by you? What other agencies has he or she worked for?
- (For Advertising Agencies) What is the organization of your media planning staff? Describe how they function.

RESEARCH

- If applicable, describe the organization and capabilities of your research department.
- How would you describe effective communications?
- Have you measured the effectiveness of your work for clients?
- What methods do you use to measure communication effectiveness pre- and post-production?

ADDITIONAL INFORMATION

- Provide a functional organizational chart of your firm.
- Furnish biographical information on the people who will work on the account.
- List your current accounts, approximate billings, and length of time they have been with the firm.
- Assuming you have no objection, please provide the names, addresses, and telephone numbers of several of your clients and principal contacts, preferably at least one large account and one medium-sized account.
- List any new products or services you have introduced for clients during the past 3 years.
- In a paragraph or two, describe the attributes of your agency vis-à-vis other agencies in [NAME OF CITY/STATE].

Source: Reprinted with permission from D. Zucker, *The Advertising Agency: Your Partner in Communications,* © 1992, The Academy for Educational Development.

Tips on Working with Contractors

Once you have selected a contractor

- make sure you understand how the contractor charges (i.e., hourly, retainer, per project, commission, or some combination) and what the contractor will charge for, including incidentals (such as local travel and phone). Find out how much the contractor charges for services such as photocopying and faxing—these are often money makers for the firm and can send your bill much higher than you anticipated. For example, faxing at $2 per page can add up very quickly. Ask if the contractor marks up out-of-pocket costs, and if so, how much (charging 15 percent or more is not unusual and can add up fast on major expenditures, such as research and production).
- remember that for most contractors time equals money. Don't waste your money by wasting your contractor's time, and don't expect the contractor to give you lots of time for free. Contract staff who bill hourly face enormous pressure to bill as many hours as possible.
- make sure everyone involved understands who is responsible for each aspect of the project. Make sure you understand who your point of contact is for each aspect.
- limit contractor staff at meetings to those who absolutely need to be there (every body is usually costing you money). But make sure that everyone who needs to be there is.
- always give as much direction as possible up front, and be consistent. It usually costs you a lot of money if contractors have to go back to the drawing board, plus it demoralizes them, so future work may not be as good.
- establish a timeline that includes regular meetings and milestones for you to review the work. Waiting to review a project until it is finished is almost always a bad idea because there are too many opportunities for the contractor to go off strategy. But, particularly for creative products, keep the approval process simple and the number of people who must approve small. Good creative products almost never emerge from a committee.
- ask for estimates of hours for all tasks, and ask for monthly progress reports that account for all hours and expenditures. Monitor them carefully, and discuss any significant discrepancies between estimated and actual costs with the contractor immediately. You don't need to find out halfway through a project that you're out of money.

NOTES:

Source: Michael Siegel and Lynne Doner, *Marketing Public Health: Strategies To Promote Social Change*, Aspen Publishers, Inc., © 1998.

8

Program Evaluation

Evaluation Basics

Types of Evaluation 584
Evaluation Options Based on Available
   Resources 586
Choosing Your Evaluation 587
Elements of an Evaluation Design 589
Writing an Evaluation Report 590
Outline of an Evaluation Report 592
Revising Your Program 593

Evaluation Pitfalls

Assessing the Accuracy of Data
   Measurements and Subject
   Classification in Screening Programs ... 594

The Importance of Adequate Control
   Groups in the Evaluation of Worksite
   Health Promotion Programs 596

Evaluation Tools and Resources

Worksheet Evaluating Printed
   Materials 599
Worksheet Evaluating Posters and
   Charts 600
Worksheet Evaluating Audiovisual
   Aids 601
Worksheet Evaluating Exhibits 602

Chapter 8

Program Evaluation

OBJECTIVES

At the completion of this chapter, the reader will

- understand the different types of evaluation
- write an evaluation report
- appreciate the pitfalls of evaluating health education and promotion programs
- understand the need for adequate control groups when evaluating health education and promotion programs
- appreciate the control of confounding factors in evaluation research

---

INTRODUCTION

This chapter begins with the evaluation basics for determining the cost-effectiveness of any community program. The basics include the types of evaluation, choosing an evaluation, designing an evaluation, and how to write the final report. Evaluation pitfalls are emphasized. Sample evaluation forms are included for evaluating printed materials, posters and charts, audiovisual aids, and exhibits.

Evaluation is both the most essential and the most technical aspect of program development. Evaluation methodology ought to be carefully planned and controlled. For this reason, the chapter emphasizes control of confounding factors in evaluation research. This chapter describes the process as manageable and important to the success of any program.

TYPES OF EVALUATION*

This guide describes four types of evaluation. Some of the concepts and definitions used here conform to standard textbook terminology; others do not.

These types of evaluation are designed to predict the results of a program, measure the results, or help determine why certain results occur. Examining *why* specific effects happen helps determine which strategies or tasks work well and provides direction for improving the functions of a program.

Although there are many barriers to undertaking formal evaluation projects, it is important to consider using evaluation tools to assess work performed.

Four types of evaluation are discussed below: formative, process, outcome, and impact.

Formative

Formative evaluation, including pretesting, is designed to assess the strengths and weaknesses of materials or campaign strategies before implementation. It permits necessary revisions before the full effort goes forward. Its basic purpose is to maximize the chance for program success before the communication activity starts.

Process

Process evaluation examines the procedures and tasks involved in implementing a program. This type of evaluation also can look at the administrative and organizational aspects of the program.

Outcome

Outcome evaluation is used to obtain descriptive data on a project and to document short-term results. Task-focused results are those that describe the output of the activity (e.g., the number of public inquiries received as a result of a public service announcement). Short-term results describe the immediate effects of the project on the target audience (e.g., percentage of the target audience showing increased awareness of the subject). Information that can result from an outcome evaluation includes:

- knowledge and attitude changes
- expressed intentions of the target audience
- short-term or intermediate behavior shifts (e.g., purchasing a sunscreen)
- policies initiated or other institutional changes made

---

*Source: *Making Health Communication Programs Work: A Planner's Guide*, NIH Publication #92-1493, U.S. Department of Health and Human Services, Public Health Service, National Institutes of Health, Office of Cancer Communications, National Cancer Institute, April 1992.

Impact

Impact evaluation is the most comprehensive of the four evaluation types. It is desirable because it focuses on the long-range results of the program and changes or improvements in health status as a result. Impact evaluations are rarely possible because they are frequently costly, involve extended commitment, and may depend on other strategies in addition to communication. Also, the results often cannot be directly related to the effects of an activity or program because of other (external) influences on the target audience that occur over time. Information obtained from an impact study may include:

- changes in morbidity and mortality
- changes in absenteeism from work
- long-term maintenance of desired behavior
- rates of recidivism

NOTES:

Evaluation Options Based on Available Resources

Type of Evaluation	Program Levels		
	Minimal Resources	**Modest Resources**	**Substantial Resources**
Formative	Readability test	Central location intercept interviews	Focus groups, individual in-depth interviews
Process	Recordkeeping (e.g., monitoring activity timetables)	Program checklist (e.g., review of adherence to program plans)	Management audit (e.g., external management review of activities)
Outcome	Activity assessments (e.g., numbers of health screenings and outcomes, or program attendance and audience response)	Progress in attaining objectives monitored (e.g., periodic calculation of percentage of target audience aware, referred, participating)	Assessment of target audience for knowledge gain (e.g., pretest and post-test of change in audience knowledge)
Impact	Print media review (e.g., monitoring of content of articles appearing in newspapers)	Public surveys (e.g., telephone surveys of self-reported behavior)	Studies of public behavior/health change (e.g., data on physician visits, or changes in public's health status)

NOTES:

Source: *Making Health Communication Programs Work: A Planner's Guide*, NIH Publication #92-1493, U.S. Department of Health and Human Services, Public Health Service, National Institutes of Health, Office of Cancer Communications, National Cancer Institute, April 1992.

CHOOSING YOUR EVALUATION*

Limited resources may force you to choose between process evaluation and outcome evaluation. Neither, independently, will provide you with a complete picture of what happened. Some experts say that if you must choose, you could choose outcome evaluation—the only way to certify that you accomplished your objectives. However, process evaluation can help you understand *why* you did or did not accomplish your objectives. Therefore, others will advise that process measures are more important—to allow you to manage your program well.

Every program planner faces constraints to undertaking evaluation tasks, just as there are constraints to designing other aspects of a communication program. These constraints may include:

- limited funds
- limited staff time and capabilities
- length of time allotted to the program
- limited access to computer facilities
- agency restrictions to hiring consultants or contractors
- policies limiting the ability to gather information from the public
- management perceptions regarding the value of evaluation
- levels of management support for well-designed evaluation activities
- difficulties in defining the objectives of the program or in establishing agency consensus
- difficulties in designing appropriate measures for communication programs
- difficulties in separating the effects of program influences from other influences on the target audience in real-world situations

These constraints make it necessary to accommodate to existing limitations as well as the requirements of a specific program. However, it is *not* true that "something is better than nothing." If evaluation design, data collection, or analysis must be compromised to fit limitations, the program *must* make a decision regarding:

- whether the required compromises will make the evaluation results invalid
- whether an evaluation strategy is essential for the particular situation, compared with other compelling uses for existing resources

These are some of the questions you should consider before deciding what kind of evaluation will be best for your program:

- How long will your program last? Will the implementation phase be long enough to permit measurement of significant effects and periodic adjustment?
- Do you want to repeat or continue your program?
- Are your objectives measurable in the foreseeable future?
- Which program components are most important to you?
- Is there management support or public demand for program accountability?

---

*Source: *Making Health Communication Programs Work: A Planner's Guide,* NIH Publication #92-1493, U.S. Department of Health and Human Services, Public Health Service, National Institutes of Health, Office of Cancer Communications, National Cancer Institute, April 1992.

- What aspects of the program fit best with your agency's priorities?
- Will an evaluation report help competition for future program funding?

A frequent response to "What kind of evaluation measures are you planning?" is "I don't have enough money for evaluation." Rarely does anyone have access to resources for an ideal health communication program, much less an ideal evaluation component. Nevertheless, there are practical benefits to including evaluation as a part of your work: to tell you whether your program is on track and how well it worked. With a little creative thinking, you will find that you can include *some* form of evaluation for almost any size of budget.

NOTES:

Elements of an Evaluation Design

Every formal design, whether formative, process, outcome, impact, or a combination, must contain certain basic elements. These include the following:

- **A statement of objectives.** Unless there is an adequate definition of desired achievements, evaluation cannot measure them. Evaluators need clear and definite objectives to measure program effects.

- **Definition of data to be collected.** This is the determination of what is to be measured in relation to the objectives.

- **Methodology.** A study design is formulated to permit measurement in a valid and reliable manner.

- **Instrumentation.** Data collection instruments are designed and pretested. These instruments range from simple tally sheets for counting public inquiries to complex survey and interview forms.

- **Data collection.** This is the actual process of gathering data.

- **Data processing.** The data are put into usable form for analysis.

- **Data analysis.** Statistical techniques are applied to the data to discover significant relationships.

- **Reporting.** Evaluation results are compiled and reported. These results rarely pronounce a program a complete success or failure. To some extent all programs have good elements and bad. It is important to appreciate that lessons can be learned from both if results are properly analyzed. These lessons should be applied to altering the existing program or as a guide to planning new efforts.

NOTES:

Source: *Making Health Communication Programs Work: A Planner's Guide*, NIH Publication #92-1493, U.S. Department of Health and Human Services, Public Health Service, National Institutes of Health, Office of Cancer Communications, National Cancer Institute, April 1992.

WRITING AN EVALUATION REPORT*

Taking the time to write a report about a pretest or other evaluation task that you have conducted is essential for several reasons. The report can provide:

- the discipline to help you critically analyze the results of the evaluation and think about any changes you should make as a result
- a tangible product for your agency
- evidence that your program or materials have been carefully developed—to be used as a sales tool with gatekeepers (e.g., television station public service directors)
- a record of your activities for use in planning future programs
- assistance to others who may be interested in developing similar programs or materials
- a foundation for evaluation activities in the future (e.g., it is easier to design a new questionnaire based on one you have previously used than to start anew)

Careful Analysis

Most frequently, evaluation tasks are added on to other responsibilities that already represent full-time commitments. Therefore, there is seldom sufficient time to think about the meaning of evaluation findings. If you are conducting or observing a pretest or another evaluation task, it may be easy to develop conclusions about the effectiveness of your materials or program during the time the tasks are being conducted. You may want to avoid this temptation and take the time to review all of the findings before you conclude how well your program or materials work, or what changes should be made.

It is important to consider the subtleties or absences demonstrated in the evaluation (e.g., an absence of discussion or a lukewarm vote of support), as well as what may have been directly stated. Writing a report can provide the opportunity to consider everything that happened in the course of the evaluation, how these events relate to the purpose of the evaluation, and any recommendations or modification to improve your materials or program.

A Tangible Product

Pretesting and other evaluation tasks require a considerable investment of scarce program time and funds. Presenting your agency with a product may be particularly useful if there is a lack of support for evaluation. It can help others not only to see that something was received for their investment, but also to understand why the evaluation was valuable.

*Source: *Making Health Communication Programs Work: A Planner's Guide*, NIH Publication #92-1493, U.S. Department of Health and Human Services, Public Health Service, National Institutes of Health, Office of Cancer Communications, National Cancer Institute, April 1992.

Evidence of Effectiveness

If you want intermediaries (e.g., a television station, clinic, school, organization, or employer) to use your material or program, you may have to convince them of its value. An evaluation report offers proof that the materials and program were carefully developed. This evidence can help you explain why your materials or program may be better than others.

A Formal Record

What you learned in conducting an evaluation, both the process and the results, may be applicable to future programs to be planned by you or others. Staff may change and your memory may fade; an evaluation report is assurance that lessons learned are available for future application.

Help for Others

Sharing your evaluation report with peers who may be considering the development of similar programs may help them to design their programs more effectively, convince them to use (or modify) your program instead, and establish your reputation for good program design.

A Foundation for Future Evaluation Efforts

It is much easier to design an evaluation based on former experience than to start from scratch. A report outlining what you did and why, as well as what worked and what should be altered in the future provides a solid base from which to plan a new pretest or evaluation. Be sure to include any questionnaire or other instruments you used in your report so that you can find and review them later.

Report Outline

Consider including these sections in your report:

- *Background:* purpose and objectives of the program
- *Description:* what was evaluated
- *Purpose:* why the evaluation was conducted
- *Methodology:* how it was conducted (with whom, when, how many, which instruments used)
- *Obstacles:* problems in designing or conducting the evaluation
- *Results:* what you found out, and what application it has to the program (program recommendations)

Although the report should provide a clear record of what you did, it should not be any longer or more formal than needed. Keep it short and easy to read. Attach any questionnaires, tally sheets, or other instruments you used as appendixes instead of describing them in narrative form. Do not make it any harder than necessary.

Finally, make sure to share it with those who might find it useful, as well as program implementers who provided feedback. The best report is of no value if it is filed unread.

Outline of an Evaluation Report

Summary

- What were your goals?
- What were your objectives?
- How did you evaluate your program?
- What were the major results of your evaluation?

Background of Program

- Why was this program done?
- Who were you trying to reach?
- How long did your program run?
- What did you do that was very important or unique?

Description of the Evaluation

- What was your evaluation design?
- How did you collect data?

NOTES:

- How did you select people from the community to participate in your evaluations?

Program Results

- What were your results (for each objective)?
- Do you have any interesting quotes or stories about people who participated in your program?

Discussion of Results

- How do you interpret or explain your findings?
- What have you learned from this experience?

Conclusions and Recommendations

- What do you recommend regarding changes in the program or your activities, or issues for the community to consider?

Source: *Restoring Balance*, Health Promotion Resource Center, Stanford Center for Research in Disease Prevention (and the Indian Health Service), Stanford University, 1000 Welch Road, Palo Alto, California 94304-1885. Phone: (415) 723-0003. Fax: (415) 725-6906, © 1992.

Revising Your Program

If your program is continuing or you have an opportunity to advise others who may plan similar programs, take the time to apply what you have learned:

- Reassess goals and objectives:
  –Has anything changed (e.g., with the target audience, the community, or your agency's mission) to require revisions in the original goals and objectives?
  –Is there new information about the health issue that should be incorporated into the program messages or design?

- Determine areas where additional effort is needed:
  –Are there objectives that are not being met? Why?
  –Are there strategies or activities that did not succeed? Are more resources required? Do you need to review why they did not work and what can be done to correct any problems?

- Identify effective activities or strategies:
  –Have some objectives been met as a result of successful activities?
  –Should these be continued and strengthened because they appear to work well?
  –Should they be considered successful and completed?
  –Can they be expanded to apply to other audiences or situations?

- Compare costs and results of different activities:
  –What were the relative costs (including staff time) and results of different aspects of your program?
  –Are there some activities that appear to work as well but cost less than others?

- Reaffirm support for the program:
  –Have you shared the results of your activities with the leadership of your agency?
  –Did you remember to share this information with the individuals and organizations outside your agency who contributed and with community participants, if appropriate?
  –Do you have evidence of program effectiveness and continued need to convince your agency to continue your program?
  –Do you have new or continuing activities that suggest the involvement of additional organizations?

- Determine to end a program that did not work.

NOTES:

Source: *Making Health Communication Programs Work: A Planner's Guide*, NIH Publication #92-1493, U.S. Department of Health and Human Services, Public Health Service, National Institutes of Health, Office of Cancer Communications, National Cancer Institute, April 1992.

ASSESSING THE ACCURACY OF DATA MEASUREMENTS AND SUBJECT CLASSIFICATION IN SCREENING PROGRAMS*

Although medical technology has provided exceptional methods for assessing the physiology of the human body, our attempts to glimpse its inner workings are not always exact. Anytime we perform a screening test to identify abnormal function or early disease, there are opportunities for misclassifying participants. This occurs for several reasons.

Natural Variation

First, there is considerable variability in the day-to-day functioning of human systems. Blood pressure, serum cholesterol, and lung function are good examples. Any single determination of each of these represents only an estimate of an individual's usual value. Blood pressure changes over the course of the day. It rises during moments of exertion or stress and is lower when one is resting. Even the anxiety of having blood pressure measured during an examination may cause an elevation in some individuals. Cholesterol levels vary with the time of day, the season, and the relationship to the last meal. Lung function measures follow substantial circadian cycles and are subject to the level of effort exerted by the person being tested as well as the technician performing the test.

Measurement Error

Second, in addition to these natural fluctuations, there is variation due to measurement error. Blood pressure readings are notoriously susceptible to observers' digit preferences, rounding errors, and bias. Cholesterol determinations on a single specimen have been shown to range over 40 percent among presumably proficient laboratories. Researchers have found that even experienced mammography readers vary considerably in their interpretations when reading the same radiographs. Lung function is commonly estimated using one of a variety of available measurement devices. Each has its own range of internal variability for repeated measures, as well as differences when compared to other devices.

Misclassifications

All this means that anytime a screening program is conducted, there is a chance that some participants will be misclassified. Some individuals who have an abnormality will be missed, while others who are free of the disease or condition will be identified as abnormal. The first of these misclassification problems causes *false negatives* and the second causes *false positives*. In the case of blood pressure or cholesterol screening, the misclassification may not represent a serious problem. Repeat determinations can be made and the screened participant reclassified into a lower risk category. A false-positive screen for cancer, on the other hand, may lead to invasive examinations and unnecessary surgery.

---

*Source: Stephen H. Gehlbach and Kenneth A. Mundt, "Evaluating Worksite Health Programs," *Journal of Ambulatory Care Management*, Vol. 17, No. 2, Aspen Publishers, Inc., © 1994.

The Gold Standard

Ideally, screening techniques are validated quantitatively against a known measure of high quality, frequently referred to as the *gold standard*. Standards are often created by combining information obtained through more invasive tests such as biopsies, endoscopies, catheterizations, and the like. Or, they may be constructed from combinations of clinical and pathological findings. Gold standards represent our closest approximation of "the truth." The relationship between the screening test result and the standard is expressed through two common and intuitive concepts known as *sensitivity* and *specificity*. Sensitivity is the proportion of all true cases correctly identified by the screening test. For instance, if, out of an employee population of chromium chemical manufacturers, there were truly 10 cases of chrome nasal sores, but the screening clinic only identified 7, then we would say that this method has a 70 percent sensitivity.

Specificity is the proportion of all individuals without the condition for whom the screening test is negative. This can also be described as the true negative rate among those *without* the condition. Suppose that of 100 chrome chemical workers without nasal lesions, 15 were identified as positive, possibly due to upper respiratory infections. Specificity of the screening test would be 85 percent, as 85 out of 100 were correctly screened as negative.

Careful attention must be paid to maximizing accuracy in screening programs. In general, tests that have a sensitivity much below 85 to 90 percent should be viewed with circumspection. Somewhat lower levels of specificity can be accepted if the measures required to correctly classify false positives (the result of reduced specificity) are not too expensive or invasive (a second blood test rather than an open biopsy).

Necessary Precautions

It is important that only well-trained individuals conduct screening and that only proven, quality-controlled laboratory tests are used. Supervision by medical staff who are familiar with the limitations of the screening techniques is essential. Because fluctuations in measurements are likely to occur for a variety of reasons, repeated determinations may be necessary to improve the estimate of an employee's result. As a general rule, characteristics that fluctuate more widely (e.g., blood pressure) require more frequent repeated measures in order to understand better the true state of an individual, and those that are more constant or take longer to change (e.g., weight) may be measured less frequently without a loss of general accuracy (provided the scale is accurate). While the caveats concerning measurements and classification may seem obvious, they are frequently overlooked in the course of practice. Equally important, if less intuitive, are issues surrounding the methodology for evaluating program effectiveness.

THE IMPORTANCE OF ADEQUATE CONTROL GROUPS IN THE EVALUATION OF WORKSITE HEALTH PROMOTION PROGRAMS*

Too often, when programs are introduced and changes in behavior such as decreased smoking or fewer work-related absences are observed, results are assumed to be due to the programs. This may or may not be true. Human behavior, like physiology, is complex, At any given moment, some smokers are trying to kick the habit. Many of those who quit do so of their own accord, without benefit of an organized program. In other words, there is always a background level of behavior change that is occurring. To demonstrate the effect of any health intervention, one must have some idea of the background or base rate of behavior change. A comparison or control group is required.

Control Group Subjects

Comparison groups may be obtained from nonparticipants at places where programs are introduced or from other plants or worksites. But several important caveats apply. First, comparison subjects must be as similar to those receiving the program or intervention as possible. It makes little sense, for example, to use plant managers as a comparison for assembly line workers who are participating in a health promotion program. Differences in age, education, and socioeconomic conditions are likely to mean that baseline risks among these groups are dissimilar.

It is similarly hazardous to use those who decline participation in a program as a control group. People who are reluctant to participate in an exercise program or have their cholesterol and blood pressure checked are likely to be at different health risks from those who volunteer for such programs. They may, for example, decline participation because they already have health problems or other risk factors.

Workplace fitness centers commonly attract those who are already fit. Employees may join company centers because of the convenience and low cost of these facilities, and their participation signifies a change in exercise venue rather than a change in health-related behavior. Thus, the temptation to compare health outcomes between center utilizers and nonutilizers should be avoided. The role of the center in any differences discovered would likely be overestimated. Managers of such workplace fitness centers must be aware of the obstacles preventing those who need the services most from fully utilizing them. For example, some who have never exercised regularly might not know how to begin, some might have a poor self-image and be reluctant to exercise alongside the company athlete, and others may simply require some extra support and encouragement. Similarly, older female employees who would potentially benefit most from a mammography program may believe, for a number of reasons, that certain aspects of health (specifically the health of the breasts) are not the proper concern of an employer.

Using plants that volunteer for a program as intervention sites and those that are nonparticipants for comparison is an alternative strategy that seems appealing but is also unwise. There may be important differences in workers' health habits or management's attitudes between the groups that can influence program acceptance

*Source: Stephen H. Gehlbach and Kenneth A. Mundt, "Evaluating Worksite Health Programs," *Journal of Ambulatory Care Management*, Vol. 17, No. 2, Aspen Publishers, Inc., © 1994.

and results. Contrasting the effect of a healthy back training program in one plant where the program was requested with a control representing a plant that rejected an offer of such a program or did not request one may lead to erroneous conclusions. The plant requesting the program might have experienced some work-related back injuries and now might have greater motivation to implement the recommendations made in the program. In contrast, a plant less interested in the healthy back training course might have fewer or no known back complaints.

Selection Bias

These problems represent a phenomenon known as *selection bias*. This bias is a well-known bane to evaluators and can occur anytime when groups being compared have been assembled by subject choice or evaluator allocation. Without proper precautions, characteristics of subjects that may influence outcomes can be unequally proportioned between groups and create the spurious appearance of a program effect. Weight reduction and exercise levels improve at the intervention sites not because of the educational activities or new health club, but because the plants that opted for the programs had a younger, more health-conscious work force at the start.

Random Allocation

One of the best ways to avoid selection bias when evaluating a program is to *randomly allocate* individuals to various groups (i.e., those participating in the program and those who are not). In this way, each individual has an equal probability of being assigned to any of the groups in the study, and, on average, each group should receive a similar proportion of individuals with relevant risk characteristics. Thus, bias is eliminated and the likelihood of imbalance among groups with respect to attributes that might influence the success or failure rate of the program is greatly reduced. For example, if all individuals interested in improving fitness are randomly assigned to one of three programs (preferably including a control group that receives no intervention), the three groups should contain equal proportions of young and old, men and women, smokers and nonsmokers, and those most motivated as well as those least motivated.

It is possible, however, that, despite randomization, the comparison groups end up unbalanced for one or more attributes, simply due to chance or bad luck. It is recommended that program groups be compared on several demographic attributes (i.e., age, gender, employment category) to verify that the randomization was successful.

In many cases, random allocation of individuals is not practical. Evaluation of a plant's safety awareness program, for example, by educating a randomly selected group of workers while not instructing others who may work in the same units presents difficulties. Contact and conversations among workers would likely spread the intervention information to the control group and invalidate the comparison. Randomly allocating the program to one or more plants may represent a reasonable way to make a difficult management decision, but this does not achieve the same benefit as randomly allocating individuals to program groups; the group of individuals at one plant may still be very different from those at another plant. If the program can be randomly allocated to units smaller than plants—such as departments or offices—then some of the benefits of random allocation might be achieved. However, there must be a relatively large number of these smaller units so that differences in the groups of individuals constituting these units can be evenly distributed.

Control for Confounding Factors

Randomization of any kind may be impossible if the program being evaluated has already been implemented. For such situations, other methods must be used to identify and temper factors (known as *controlling for confounding factors*) that might spuriously create the appearance of program success or failure. Programs in which plants or other relatively large groups (rather than individuals) are randomly allocated run the risk of having unbalanced groups, but they can also benefit from post hoc adjustment techniques. These have been borrowed from the field of epidemiology, which is almost always dependent on nonrandom allocation of the risk factors of interest. For example, in comparing the fitness level of individuals in a fitness program with those in a control group, one must consider other important factors that might differ by group and also influence the outcome (fitness, in this case), such as level of conditioning at the beginning of the program, age, gender, level of physical demand on the job, and so forth. Because randomization of individuals is not possible, statistical control of these potential confounders must be performed in order to validly identify any effect of the program.

The techniques for statistically controlling for confounding have become highly sophisticated and often quite complicated. The simplest means of controlling for a factor is to divide the analysis into parts according to levels of the potential confounder. For example, if it were thought that gender were a potential confounder for some program, one might compare those in the program group with those in the control group separately by gender (i.e., males with males and females with females). All techniques that control for confounding in the analysis require that the potential confounder be accurately measured on each individual.

While this might seem straightforward regarding gender, measurement of other common confounders may require collection of additional data. For example, valid evaluation of a blood pressure control program would require consideration of factors other than the interventions that are known to influence blood pressure: weight, smoking, alcohol consumption, exercise, and possible diet. Information on most of these is available only from the individual participants. This underscores the importance of considering evaluation of planned programs before they are implemented so that adequate information on potential confounders is obtained. As a general rule, data on any known risk factor for a targeted health problem should be captured so that statistical control for confounding is possible.

NOTES:

Worksheet Evaluating Printed Materials

Title: _____

Publisher: _____

Cost: _____ Date of publication: _____ Language used: _____

Purpose or theme: _____

For what groups is this material most appropriate? (Check all appropriate.)

___ Men ___ Women ___ Children ___ Geriatric

Cultural _____

Occupational _____

Language _____

Literacy level _____

A	B	C	D	Audience appeal: Does it get attention, lead the reader on, keep attention?
A	B	C	D	Accuracy: Is the health and clinical information accurate and up-to-date?
A	B	C	D	Approach: Does it agree with the emphasis and approach used locally?
A	B	C	D	Organization: Is it logical, clearly developed, easy to follow, believable?
A	B	C	D	Completeness: Is there sufficient detail? Too much detail?
A	B	C	D	Tone: Is the message personal, supportive, positive, honest?
A	B	C	D	Physical properties: Are the layout, print, illustrations, and color appropriate for the intended group? Is the piece attractive?
A	B	C	D	Graphics: Are the graphics simple and clear?
A	B	C	D	Vocabulary: Is the vocabulary familiar or explained for readers?
A	B	C	D	Readability: Are the sentences short? Has jargon been avoided?

Grade Level: _____

Strengths:

Weaknesses:

Recommendation:

Signed: _____

Date: _____

Source: Donald J. Breckon et al., *Community Health Education: Settings, Roles, and Skills for the 21st Century*, ed. 3, Aspen Publishers, Inc., © 1994.

Worksheet Evaluating Posters and Charts

Title: _____

Publisher: _____

Cost: _____ Approximate size: _____ Language: _____

Purpose or theme: _____

For what group is this material most appropriate? (Check all that apply.)

___ Men ___ Women ___ Pediatric ___ Geriatric

Specific cultural groups _____

Specific occupational groups _____

Language _____

Literacy level _____

A   B   C   D   Appeal: Does it get attention quickly; hold attention?

A   B   C   D   Physical properties: Artwork, lettering, color, etc.

A   B   C   D   Accuracy: Accurate clinically, culturally? Contemporary?

A   B   C   D   Balance: Not symmetrical, but size and color are compensated for.

A   B   C   D   Movement: Center of interest not centered; flows in sequence.

A   B   C   D   Unity: Close together or tied together so as to appear a whole.

A   B   C   D   Simplicity: Only necessary elements; small elements grouped so as to reduce their apparent number.

A   B   C   D   Clarity: Good lettering, enough contrast; understood at a glance.

A   B   C   D   Color intensity: Attention-getting colors are yellow, orange, red, green, blue, indigo, violet. Colors read most easily at a distance are dark blue on white, black on yellow, white on red, green on white, blue on white.

A   B   C   D   Color appropriateness: Red, orange, and yellow attract and excite; green, blue, and purple are soothing, cool, and restful; light colors appear to increase the size of objects while dark colors appear to decrease size. Blue, green, and red are the most generally preferred colors.

Strengths:

Weaknesses:

Recommendation:

Signed: _____

Date: _____

Worksheet Evaluating Audiovisual Aids

Title: _____

Subject: _____ Date: _____

Publisher: _____

Purchase price: _____ Rental: _____

Type of media:
___ Videodisc
___ 35-mm slides
___ Videotape
___ Audiotape
___ Slide tape program
___ Transparencies
___ Other
___ Color ___ Sound ___ Time

Purpose or theme: _____

For what group is this material most appropriate? (Check all that apply.)

___ Men ___ Women ___ Pediatric ___ Geriatric

Specific cultural groups _____

Specific occupational groups _____

Language _____

Literacy level _____

A B C D   Appeal: Does it get and hold attention?
A B C D   Physical properties: Photography and sound?
A B C D   Accuracy: Accurate, up-to-date?
A B C D   Approach: Does it agree with approach used locally?
A B C D   Organization: Logical, easy to follow?
A B C D   Completeness: Sufficient detail; too much detail?

Strengths:

Weaknesses:

Recommendations:

Signed: _____

Date: _____

Source: Reprinted from *Hospital Health Education: A Guide to Program Development* by D.J. Breckon, p. 111, Aspen Publishers, Inc., © 1982 Donald J. Breckon.

Worksheet Evaluating Exhibits

Conference: _____

Sponsor: _____

Address: _____

_____

Contact person: _____

Phone no.: _____

A   B   C   D   Is it physically possible to read the exhibit from the point of observation?

A   B   C   D   Will all graphs, charts, and diagrams be understood by the intended audience? Has the use of statistical presentations been kept to a minimum?

A   B   C   D   Are the vocabulary and style of writing such that the intended audience can comfortably follow and understand the exhibit?

A   B   C   D   Does the exhibit sustain interest long enough to be read completely?

A   B   C   D   Does the exhibit employ supplementary items (qualified attendant present, visual aids used, visitor-operated devices used and contributing to exhibit, literature supporting the exhibit objectives)?

A   B   C   D   Does the exhibit impart the desired message?

A   B   C   D   Does the exhibit tie in with the visitors' interests?

A   B   C   D   Does the exhibit offer visitors a chance to participate in satisfying a personal purpose?

Strengths:

Weaknesses:

Recommendation:

Signed: _____

Date: _____

Source: Donald J. Breckon et al., *Community Health Education: Settings, Roles, and Skills for the 21st Century*, ed. 3, Aspen Publishers, Inc., © 1994.

9

Adapting to Diverse Audiences in Different Settings

Health Promotion at Work

How To Locate Worksite Health
Promotion Program Resources 606
Wellness Outreach at Work: What Works
and What Doesn't 613
Reaching Blue-Collar Workers: Keys to
Success 614

How To Create a Healthy Work
Environment 615

Health Promotion in Schools

Establishing a Successful School-Based
Health Center 622

603

Chapter 9

Adapting to Diverse Audiences in Different Settings

OBJECTIVES

At the completion of this chapter, the reader will

- locate worksite health promotion program resources
- identify health promotion activities at work and in schools
- understand how to successfully reach blue-collar workers with health messages
- understand how to create a healthy work environment

INTRODUCTION

This chapter describes how to adapt health promotion programs to diverse audiences and settings. It contains specific information about health promotion programs with suggestions for adapting them to the worksite and school. Health promotion motivational methods for reaching the blue-collar worker and students in schools are suggested. Many innovative and creative ideas for advancing health promotion programs, with the help of coworkers in the workplace, are described.

Health promotion is the basis for community health education. As such, it is essential for community health practice. Yet, much of health promotion requires interpretation for diverse individuals and groups. This chapter applies health promotion principles to various groups at work and in school. Specific means and methods are delineated for developing the motivation to change health and the support necessary to both achieve and maintain health promotion gains. This systematic approach to planning health promotion programs for diverse audiences is an excellent starting point for both the novice health educator and the seasoned community health planner. The content of the chapter will appeal to health promotion novices and experts in various settings.

HOW TO LOCATE WORKSITE HEALTH PROMOTION PROGRAM RESOURCES*

Find Resources at Your Own Worksite

Often the best place to start looking for resources for a health promotion program is right in your own worksite. The most active collaboration and cooperation usually come from individuals you already know. They can be valuable links to the network of organizations that are already active in your community. In addition, your worksite may already sponsor activities that can provide the starting point of a health promotion program. Talk with the following people:

- managers
- labor union officials
- human resource managers
- occupational health nurses and physicians
- industrial hygienists
- employee assistance program staff
- personnel administrators
- employee benefits staff
- safety and health staff
- food service directors
- fitness directors
- health educators
- interested volunteers from the employees at large

Employee Committees

The most successful worksite programs include an advisory or coordinating committee composed of employees from various levels and departments. This committee can offer advice to the professional staff and help plan wellness activities. They will feel ownership for the program from the start and help to keep it going.

Health Insurance Carrier

Many health insurance carriers offer information on and assistance in establishing health promotion programs. They may be able to tell you where your health care dollars are being spent. Some companies, including many Blue Cross and Blue Shield plans, can actually help you set up a program. Also, contact your health maintenance organization (HMO) for health promotion programs and services they offer to your employees.

---

*Source: *Finding Resources for Healthy Heart Programs at Work*, NIH Publication #92-737, U.S. Department of Health and Human Services, Public Health Service, National Institutes of Health, National Heart, Lung, and Blood Institute, October 1992.

Check Basic Resources in Your Community

After you have checked the resources available at your own worksite, look for health promotion resources in your local community by starting with these basic sources of help.

Telephone Directory

Check the white pages of the telephone directory for addresses and telephone numbers of organizations listed in this guide. Also, look in the yellow pages under appropriate listings, such as hospitals, HMOs, dietitians, nutritionists, weight control services, health and fitness program consultants, health clubs, and libraries.

Local Information and Referral Service

Local governments, the United Way, health and welfare councils, or similar organizations often establish information and referral services in communities. Many produce directories for locating health and social services in addition to responding to telephone or written requests for information.

Public Library

The reference room, the information desk, or a special section on health or consumer resources may provide listings of local services, programs, and organizations for health promotion. In addition, find healthy heart cookbooks, health and nutrition magazines, and similar publications.

Locate the "Healthy" Organizations in Your Town

The following agencies and organizations may offer programs, materials, staff expertise, volunteers, facilities, or equipment to help you set up or expand a worksite program. Some offer help at no cost, while others charge fees. They may conduct wellness screenings, train your employees in blood pressure measurement, or offer follow-up counseling for employees with high blood pressure or cholesterol. Well-coordinated and efficient community resources will be especially helpful to small worksites.

Wellness Councils

Wellness councils are local groups of businesses and other employers interested in promoting worksite wellness. Ask your local chamber of commerce if there is a wellness council in your community. Or call or write the Wellness Councils of America (WELCOA), the national organization of wellness councils, to obtain a local contact. WELCOA is dedicated to providing direction and support services to community-based wellness councils. It also offers detailed reports on programs under way in local councils and a newsletter. WELCOA offers manuals and videotapes on health promotion topics. Contact WELCOA for an order form for current resources.

Business/Health Coalitions

Business/health coalitions are groups of businesses organized to find solutions to the rising cost of employer-paid health care. One of their interests is health promotion. Ask your local chamber of commerce whether there is a local coalition nearby.

City and County Public Health Departments

> Check with these units of your local health department: chronic disease control, community health nursing, health promotion, nutrition, preventive health, disease prevention, or adult health. One or more of these units may offer materials, protocols, staff assistance, training, or suggestions about other resources. Some local health departments may have special initiatives to reach out into local businesses to promote health among the employees.

Local Recreation Departments

> City and county departments of recreation often offer a wide range of exercise, fitness, and sports activities, including team sports and walking clubs.

Public School Systems or Education Departments of Counties and Towns

> For healthy heart cooking classes, weight control courses, and other health programs, contact the adult education or evening education departments in your local government. Consult the government blue pages in the telephone book under education or schools.

Community and County Colleges and Universities

> Contact these departments: health education, recreation, physical education, adult education, home economics, nutrition, food sciences, dietetics, human ecology, and nursing and medical schools. Both faculty and students may offer training in cholesterol and blood pressure measurement, assistance in developing healthy heart courses and other education activities, protocols for screening and follow-up, and many other services.

Voluntary Health Agencies and Professional Associations

> Contact your local units of voluntary health groups, professional associations, and other community organizations. They may offer services and assistance at the local level, such as materials, programs, training, professional advice, and technical assistance. Several major groups that are likely to have local units are highlighted below.
>
> **American Association of Occupational Health Nurses (AAOHN).** This national professional membership organization for occupational health nurses provides educational opportunities through traditional continuing education activities, self-instructional modular materials, an annual national conference with workshops on various risk factors for developing cardiovascular disease, and a comprehensive reference library. Publications include the monthly refereed *AAOHN Journal*, a monthly newsletter, and special manuals, brochures, and guides. Local and state AAOHN chapters can provide referrals to local occupational health nurse experts. They can also offer information on developing and maintaining wellness programs in local business and industry and resources for carrying out a program.
>
> **The American Dietetic Association (ADA).** The ADA offers publications on food and good nutrition for worksite program planners, health professionals, and employees and their families. The ADA sponsors National Nutrition Month in March and a Nutrition InfoCenter.

Employees and their families can get answers to their nutrition questions by calling the ADA toll-free consumer hotline. To reach a registered dietitian in person, callers can dial (800) 366-1655 Monday through Friday from 10 AM to 5 PM (Eastern time). Taped messages about nutrition are available 24 hours a day in English and Spanish.

Officers in state ADA affiliates can help identify local dietitians who will accept employees for nutrition counseling. Local nutrition councils may also offer classes or have nutrition hotlines staffed by dietitians. Through state and local dietetic associations, the ADA also provides technical assistance and speakers to outside groups.

American Heart Association (AHA). The AHA provides materials, conducts programs and training, and offers support to individuals and groups. Materials include catalogs, fact sheets, brochures, and audiovisual materials on topics such as heart disease, exercise, high blood pressure, cholesterol, smoking, and nutrition. Contact the corporate health account executive at the national center to receive information on the American Heart Association nearest you or to conduct national worksite wellness programs.

American Lung Association (ALA). The ALA offers materials and programs on such topics as quitting smoking, occupational health, lung diseases, and air conservation. The ALA offers a catalog of all its publications. Fees are determined by local affiliates. Contact your local ALA unit or the national office to find one near you.

United Way. The United Way in many communities offers a worksite presence program that includes activities such as lunchtime seminars, health fairs, community service directories, and referral services. Contact your local United Way for more information on programs available in your area.

YMCA of the USA. The Corporate Health and Fitness Program provides services to worksites, ranging from YMCA membership as an employee benefit to full-scale health and fitness programs for employees. The YMCA also offers educational materials and seminars, fitness and health testing, health monitoring, and program management. Program topics include nutrition education, weight management, exercise, quitting smoking, and stress management, along with traditional sports such as swimming and aerobics. Participation is open to men and women. Fees are determined by local YMCAs. Contact your local YMCA or the associate director for health and fitness, program services division, at the national office for further information.

Other Groups. There are many other groups that may be able to help you establish your wellness program. You may want to contract for services with individuals who are members of these professional groups. Or staff people at voluntary health groups can sometimes offer their time and talents for a modest fee or for free. In addition, they may have established programs that can be used at the worksite. Look for local units of these organizations:

- American Cancer Society
- American College of Occupational and Environmental Medicine
- American Red Cross
- National Kidney Foundation
- Society for Nutrition Education

- Society for Public Health Education
- YWCA

Hospitals and HMOs

Contact local hospitals and HMOs for classes on healthy heart topics such as cholesterol control, high blood pressure education, stop-smoking programs, and weight control. Consider the health promotion offerings of local HMOs when choosing future health care providers for your employees.

Occupational Health Clinics and Other Health Promotion Providers

In industrial and well-populated areas, businesses have been established to provide traditional occupational health services and the newer health promotion services to local employers. Look in the yellow pages of your telephone book under health and fitness program consultants, health promotion programs, and occupational health services.

Nutritionists, Including Registered Dietitians and Other Qualified Nutrition Professionals

Nutritionists sometimes work as consultants in developing worksite nutrition programs. In addition, employees may need individualized nutrition counseling, and you will want to refer them to qualified nutritionists. The American Dietetic Association (ADA) maintains a roster of dietitians and will respond to written requests for assistance in locating registered dietitians in your state. In addition, officers in state ADA affiliates could help identify local dietitians who will accept employees for nutrition counseling.

Visiting Nurse Associations

Visiting nurse associations (VNAs) offer a wide range of community-based health care services, including those associated with worksite wellness programs, such as nutrition counseling and blood pressure screening. The Visiting Nurse Associations of America maintains a toll-free telephone number, (800) 426-2547, for client referral and other public information. Call to obtain the name, address, and telephone number of a local VNA.

Labor Unions

Local community services committees—composed of labor union members with special training—help meet the health needs of their fellow union members and their families. Contact your shop steward, local president, or central labor council officers to find out how organized labor can help in your worksite.

USDA Cooperative Extension Service

The Extension Services has a network of professionals across the country ready to deliver food and nutrition education programs to the public. In cooperation with the land-grant universities, they share nutrition information with people in every state and 3,150 counties in the United States. To find a local office, consult the county or state government section of the white telephone pages under Cooperative Extension or Extension.

Check Your State Health Department

Publications, services, and other resources offered by state health departments vary. Check with these units of your state health department: chronic disease control, community health nursing, health promotion, nutrition, preventive health, disease prevention, family health, or adult health. One or more of these units may offer materials, screening procedures and standards, staff assistance, training, or suggestions about other resources. Check to see whether your state offers resources that are tailored to specific groups and reading levels.

Contact your state health department to find out the resources available to you. These contacts may also be able to put you in touch with someone in your local health department or other agency.

Get Help from National Groups

Many national organizations offer health promotion materials, programs, and services to worksites. The following national information centers are good places to start in your search for health promotion materials and other resources.

NHLBI Information Center

The National Heart, Lung, and Blood Institute (NHLBI) Information Center is the source of a wide variety of information and materials on high blood pressure, high blood cholesterol, smoking, obesity, nutrition, and general heart health. The Information Center offers materials for planning wellness programs aimed at employees and their families.

**Special Help for Minority
Employers and Employees**

The Office of Minority Health Resource Center, U.S. Department of Health and Human Services, responds to requests for information on minority health, locates sources of technical assistance through the Resource Persons Network, and refers requesters to relevant organizations. Activities concentrate on areas with priority for minority health. Bilingual staff members are available to serve Spanish-speaking requesters.

Other materials include those developed for health professionals, such as guidelines for the detection and evaluation of high blood pressure and cholesterol. NHLBI also has numerous brochures, booklets, and posters for employees and their families. A kit, designed to help carry out awareness activities in communities, includes many short, reproducible handouts on high blood pressure, cholesterol, and smoking. The Information Center publishes the newsletter HEART*MEMO*, which contains information on NHLBI activities and resources. Most materials are available in limited quantities and are free.

National Resource Center on Worksite Health Promotion

This resource center provides information for employers on worksite health promotion programs currently in place in U.S. corporations and other worksites. The information is contained in a database that includes information related to worksite health promotion programs, evaluation, research, and supporting organizations. The resource center also gathers experts to discuss emerging issues in worksite health promotion and publishes materials on topics such as small business and health promotion, cost savings from worksite programs, and integration of health promotion with employee benefits. Publications include *Healthy People 2000 at Work: Strategies for Employers, Directory of Worksite Health Promotion Resources*, and *Directory of State Health Promotion Resources for Employers*. Call for a publications order form.

ODPHP National Health Information Center

The ODPHP (Office of Disease Prevention and Health Promotion) National Health Information Center offers information and referral services on all health-related topics. Most inquiries concern the availability of publications and referrals to other organizations. When possible, the center directly answers inquiries from health professionals and the general public. Otherwise, callers are referred to other special federal information centers and private organizations. The DIRLINE, maintained by the center, is a database of 1,200 health-related organizations with descriptions of their publications and services. The center produces Healthfinders, a series of publications on a variety of topics, including a directory of federal health information resources, a list of toll-free numbers for health information, and a list of national health observances.

NOTES:

Wellness Outreach at Work: What Works and What Doesn't

The Task	What Works	What Doesn't Work
1. Assessing employees' health needs	In-person, one-to-one wellness screening. Measuring blood pressure and cholesterol. Asking for health risk information regarding smoking, weight, exercise, etc. Surveying employees about their interest in wellness programs.	Self-administered health risk appraisals filled out by the employee without professional help. Using only self-reported estimates of blood pressure and cholesterol. Lack of an immediate opportunity for employees to enroll in appropriate wellness activities.
2. Recruiting eager employees	Signing up employees "on the spot" for wellness activities during their screening. Making follow-up telephone calls to alert them to the time and place of the activities.	Depending only on the media and individual mailings to the homes of employees to publicize and promote wellness activities.
3. Recruiting reluctant employees	Persistent outreach and follow-up with at-risk employees via telephone calls and personal visits.	Continued use of the media and mailings to the homes of employees.
4. Enrolling employees in programs	Offering choices to employees (the "menu approach"): Guided self-help, mini-groups, and classes on smoking cessation, weight loss, nutrition, stress management, etc.	Offering health improvement interventions only through classes. There may not always be enough participation to make up a full class. Many people lose interest if they have to wait, and some people don't like classes.
5. Helping employees change their health risks	Continued outreach and follow-up with at-risk employees. Using "engagement" strategies tailored to the individual. Making follow-up contacts to prevent relapse.	Continued dependence on classes, with little or no personalized follow-up or "engagement" strategies. Little activity to prevent false starts or relapse.
6. Changing corporate culture to support wellness	First implementing follow-up and health improvement programs, then using the momentum from these programs to introduce health-related changes in the work environment.	Attempting to introduce changes in the work environment before launching health improvement activities and allowing time for the program to work.

Source: John C. Erfurt et al., *The Wellness Outreach at Work Program: A Step-by-Step Guide*, NIH Publication #95-3043, U.S. Department of Health and Human Services, Public Health Service, National Institutes of Health, National Heart, Lung, and Blood Institute, August 1995.

Reaching Blue-Collar Workers: Keys to Success

- **Target blue-collar workers.** Involve blue-collar workers in planning and running the program from the start. Many programs simply overlook blue-collar workers. Make sure the wellness committee includes workers from all levels, including union members. If the worksite does not have a union, identify rank-and-file employees whom other workers respect.

- **Reach out to blue-collar workers by offering programs where they work and at times when they can participate.** Set up screening stations where large numbers of blue-collar employees work—in the production area, the lunchroom, or off-site. Consider setting up a temporary wellness office near the workers, making screening free to workers, giving workers many chances to be screened and counseled, and planning programs during work hours and for each shift.

- **Offer choices and options.** Blue-collar employees participate less often in formal classes to reduce specific health risks. Offering other options, such as one-on-one counseling and guided self-help, may be especially important for these workers. Be sure that they can easily read any written materials given to them and that the wellness counselor goes over the materials with them.

- **Staff the program with people who work well with all types of employees.** Program staff must be able to reach out to people and to be comfortable in any kind of setting. Try to find staff with the same range of backgrounds as the work force.

- **Follow up and offer long-term support.** Counselors should make routine contact with workers at least every six months for as long as the workers can be reached. One-to-one follow-up counseling, not simply sending a letter, is crucial to the success of wellness programs. A personal verbal message can increase the chances that a worker will stick with a new behavior.

- **Target both the workers and their place of work.** Besides helping workers change, a comprehensive program should help change the worksite. This involves reviewing the worksite's services, policies, and social climate, or "corporate culture." For example, food vendors should provide healthy choices in cafeterias and vending machines.

It is possible to involve blue-collar workers in wellness programs. But to do so, the program needs to address their space and time constraints. In addition, the program staff need to treat them with the same dignity and consideration they offer management.

NOTES:

Source: John C. Erfurt et al., *The Wellness Outreach at Work Program: A Step-by-Step Guide*, NIH Publication #95-3043, U.S. Department of Health and Human Services, Public Health Service, National Institutes of Health, National Heart, Lung, and Blood Institute, August 1995.

HOW TO CREATE A HEALTHY WORK ENVIRONMENT*

Essential to comprehensive worksite wellness programs are worksite-wide activities and policies that promote a healthy environment. A healthy worksite environment will help employees maintain changes and reduce their risks. It can also help prevent health risks from developing. Finally, it can enhance overall health among all employees, including those who do not have any identified health risks.

Organizing the worksite begins with individuals, then involves groups, and then addresses broader organizational changes. During follow-up counseling you can encourage individual employees to think about what they can do to make the work environment healthier or to help others improve their health. This is why the Wellness Outreach at Work Program begins with screening and follow-up. These activities involve one-to-one conversations, first with all employees (at screening) and then with those employees who are most likely to be interested in health improvement (at follow-up with those with health risks). By working with individuals, you build understanding and support for what you want to do, and you develop the skills and resources to get it done. These individuals then begin working within their own groups. These groups can then make changes in the organization as a whole. You can take the following steps to create a healthy worksite environment with the Wellness Outreach at Work Program.

Step 1: Enlist the Support of Key Employees

A small number of individuals will be involved in the wellness program from the very beginning. These are the people on the wellness committee. But some of them may come to the committee with their own objectives. Some may be there only because they were assigned to come by their supervisor. Some may want to protect their own department or group. Others may not have enough time to give or may lack talents that the program needs. You will want to develop supporters from outside the committee as well as inside.

Every workplace has key people who can endorse the program, interest others in it, and help carry it out. These include people in positions of power, as well as people who are influential. Try to identify these individuals and enlist their support:

- members of the wellness committee, such as key managers, labor leaders, occupational health staff, health and safety people, and employee assistance program staff
- people whose jobs take them around the worksite, such as relief operators, in-plant truck drivers, messengers, maintenance workers, health and safety staff, and union officers
- people at central communication points within a worksite, such as secretaries, dispatchers, and supervisors who have broad responsibilities
- interested employees, who may express great interest in the wellness program at the time of screening and offer to help with it

Some employees in these roles will not be inclined to help spread news and interest about wellness activities. Try to identify those who will become involved in the program and believe in it. Try to enlist the support of people who are well liked.

---

*Source: John C. Erfurt et al., *The Wellness Outreach at Work Program: A Step-by-Step Guide*, NIH Publication #95-3043, U.S. Department of Health and Human Services, Public Health Service, National Institutes of Health, National Heart, Lung, and Blood Institute, August 1995.

People who are in these roles and also have health risks should be among the first people that the wellness counselors contact for follow-up. Working with them on their own health risks can cultivate their interest in helping with the larger wellness program.

Case Study #1

In one industrial plant the union shop chairman was overweight. He took part in a one-to-one nutrition program and a guided, self-help exercise program. He gradually, but steadily, lost weight. As he moved throughout the plant, many workers commented on his weight loss and increased fitness. He became a strong and vocal supporter of the program and organized a committee to improve the quality of food offered in the cafeteria and vending machines. Soon low-fat, low-cholesterol items were available.

Make Personal Contact with New Wellness Committee Members

As people are transferred or promoted, new people may be assigned to the wellness committee. Each time a member of the committee leaves, the wellness counselor should start personal health counseling with his or her replacement. This makes it easier to introduce the new member to the wellness program and its potential.

As these changes occur, it may be important to reassign some roles within the wellness committee to take advantage of new members and their interests.

Step 2: Include Key Employees When Planning Activities

Planning and scheduling follow-up counseling is the task of the wellness counselors. The wellness committee does not decide which employees should be contacted or when. But the wellness committee and other key individuals should be involved in planning activities that are more public in nature. These may include media promotions, special health-related events, and health improvement programs.

Scheduling Classes and Other Events

The wellness committee can provide important assistance in deciding when to schedule classes and other events. Classes in each of the risk areas should take place as soon as possible after screening. The level of participation in these first classes can help you decide how soon to schedule them again. Ask the wellness committee about the customs and policies of your workplace when scheduling classes. In some worksites many employees will not come early or stay after work to attend classes; in other worksites they will. In some worksites the lunch hour is not a good time to schedule interventions; in other worksites it is the best time. Some jobs have scheduled break times during which employees can participate in wellness activities; other worksites do not.

Solving Problems and Generating New Ideas

The wellness committee and program staff should also monitor levels of participation in programs so they can identify problems or barriers to participation and find new program ideas.

Case Study #2

An aerobic fitness program that used martial arts was offered to 1,500 mostly male employees in a somewhat aging work force. A small group of employees was enthusiastic in the beginning, but their numbers dwindled after a while. Other more traditional aerobics classes were scheduled, but they also failed to attract participants. The wellness committee concluded that the employees were not interested in aerobic exercise in groups. They had to try a different approach. They decided to develop a walking route within the worksite that passed near most of the employees' work stations, thus providing easy and convenient access to exercise that they could do at their own convenience. And finally, the program sponsored a walking contest to introduce the walking route and gain participation from the start. This was highly successful.

Case Study #3

A wellness program offered two health improvement interventions that required employees to see their own physicians. One was a stop-smoking program built around the use of nicotine chewing gum that smokers had to get from a physician. The other was a high-level exercise program that required approval from a physician. No employees took part in either program. Employees did not see the need to visit their physician to get an okay to use gum or to exercise. So the staff redesigned both programs. The smoking program no longer required the use of the gum, and the exercise program was lowered to a moderate level so that no one was placed at risk while doing it. Both programs then attracted participants.

In each of the two cases described above, the wellness committee helped identify the problem as well as the solution by talking with their fellow employees about the programs.

Preparing Committee Members To Tackle Difficult Issues

Including the wellness committee in program discussions and decisions encourages them to take responsibility for wellness and prepares them to address some more difficult issues that may require attention by other decision makers in the worksite. For example, smoking cessation programs may trigger worker concerns about airborne contaminants. The wellness committee may need to address these concerns when it plans smoking cessation programs. Stress management is another example. Unfortunately, most stress management programs focus on how to adjust to stress and pay little attention to how to remove the causes of stress. But the wellness committee can work with the stress management instructors to plan a program that includes attention to stress-related issues at the worksite.

Step 3: Organize Group Activities Focused on Health

Group activities can grab employees' attention and get them involved with each other and with health promotion. Encourage employees to choose activities that will work best for them. Examples of group activities are:

- informal buddy systems
- formal activities to develop mutual support
- special events that focus attention on a health issue

Informally Organized Buddy Systems

Informal buddy systems occur when two or more friends who are trying to make health improvements "sponsor" each other as they try to break old habits and develop new ones. This practice helps create a supportive, friendly climate that encourages other workers to think about making their own changes. Wellness counselors assist in developing these buddy systems by encouraging the employees they counsel to find a coworker who is interested in improving his or her health. They need not be making the same change. The important thing is that they like each other and can support each other.

Formal Activities To Develop Mutual Support

Formal methods can also be used to develop these types of support. People who have already succeeded in making major health changes can organize formal events with coworkers who are trying to make similar changes.

Case Study #4

At one worksite, employees who were ex-smokers adopted coworker friends who still smoked, encouraged them to quit, and helped them as they tried. To help get things started, ex-smokers wore buttons identifying themselves as successful quitters. The buttons, part of a formal stop-smoking campaign, were a way to involve large numbers of employees (ex-smokers) with very little effort by the wellness staff.

Special Events To Focus Attention on a Specific Aspect of Health

A major part of the planning done by the wellness committee is the planning of worksite-wide events. Special activities that involve the whole work force can help keep employees focused on improving their health. The wellness committee should consider sponsoring a special activity every one to three months, depending on how much planning and energy is required for the activity selected. The committee can plan a variety of activities, for example, a media blitz, a smoke-out, and a contest.

A media blitz about health issues might be conducted in the fall and describe how to get through the November–December holiday season without gaining weight or raising one's cholesterol level.

Events such as smoke-free days include many activities dealing with a single health risk and take place within a short period of time. These events are based on the premise that even if one fails once or twice, the more one tries to make a behavioral change (such as quitting smoking), the closer one comes to succeeding. Smoke-outs encourage people to go "cold turkey" for a day—and longer, if possible—or to reduce the number of cigarettes they smoke. Immediate follow-up counseling with participants can encourage them to continue their efforts for longer periods. Special campaigns can be used for risks besides smoking. Weight loss or cholesterol reduction campaigns might be addressed in a similar way.

Health improvement contests are another type of special event. Those with many winners often create high interest. Units or locations can compete with each other, or the contests can be based on informal friendship groups. Walking contests can be particularly successful when they are organized so that everyone can participate and when participants are given incentives that keep them involved.

Case Study #5

One company set up a walking route throughout the worksite, but soon found that only a few employees were using it. To attract attention, members of the wellness committee and the wellness counselors organized a parade—with balloons, whistles, music, and so on. They marched through the plant, answering questions as they went. After that, they began a contest for three-person teams. This established a cooperative (as well as a competitive) situation in which team members supported each other in using the walking route. T-shirts were given to teams as incentives after they had walked a certain number of miles. This contest succeeded in involving many more employees—more than ten percent of the plant population.

Held during lunch hour or work breaks, walking contests encourage people to socialize and get exercise. They give them an energy boost for the afternoon. They also help people control their weight and have immediate benefits that encourage some people to make more changes. Most important, a walking contest is a fitness activity that almost anyone is willing to try.

Think Long Term, Even for One-Time Events

Competitions can be developed around virtually any health risk. The rules of the competition should be designed to foster long-term risk reduction. Weight-loss competitions, for example, should be structured to encourage gradual, long-term weight loss rather than fast weight loss. This suggests a longer rather than a shorter competition time period, and perhaps a prize structure based on the number of people in the team who lose weight, rather than on the number of pounds each person loses.

Social Events Can Be Fun as Well as Effective

Worksite-wide events can provide opportunities for socializing as well as improving health. They can reinforce the benefits of one-to-one counseling and cut down on individual relapse. These events should be planned after a good proportion of the employees have been contacted through one-to-one outreach. These contacts will identify employees interested in helping with special events. And, when events occur, many employees will recognize the program and be reminded of their own health goals.

Step 4: Review Services and Policies To Help Change the Corporate Culture

The final step in the process of organizing the worksite for wellness is making changes at the organizational level. This involves helping the organization to review its services, policies, and the general social environment—often referred to as the "corporate culture." The corporate culture includes all the habits, routines, and conditions that characterize the workplace and work environment.

Examples of Changes

Below are some examples of possible changes to make in the worksite environment:

- Introduce low-fat, heart-healthy foods in the cafeteria and vending machines.
- Remove cigarette vending machines.
- Bring fitness facilities and wellness activities together.
- Establish a company smoking policy.
- Introduce incentives for health.
- Reduce worksite health and safety hazards by enforcing safety regulations, training employees to recognize unsafe situations, and improving safety practices.
- Introduce new management approaches and programs that reduce stress on individuals and groups.

While each of these examples involves employee health, in each case the wellness program itself probably does not have the authority or resources to take on the whole task. In changing the corporate culture, the wellness program staff can act in two ways. They can be consultants to the organization regarding issues that affect employee health and well-being. They can also act as catalysts to empower individual employees, work groups, or departments to take actions toward their goals.

In making changes in cafeteria menus and vending machine items, the program may need to work with dietitians and financial staff who handle revenue from those services. Changes in corporate policy are made at various levels, often outside the jurisdiction of the wellness program. However, the wellness program staff may recommend and encourage the implementation of health promotion policies in consultation with the appropriate individuals in management, labor, and their legal department.

Turning Fitness Centers into Wellness Centers

Wellness counselors can recruit more employees into walking contests and other simple forms of exercise than highly equipped exercise facilities can. Unless they provide methods for drawing in the average employee, fitness centers attract mostly people who would exercise on their own anyway. They may have even less impact on cardiovascular risks than exercise programs that do not rely on equipment.

Case Study #6

Two very different exercise programs had equally different results. One worksite bought a couple of exercise bicycles and rowing machines, put in a walking path, and sponsored a walking contest—all at a cost of $1,300. A nearby plant invested $88,000 in a fitness facility. Staffing costs per employee were similar at the two sites. But employees at the plant with the complete fitness equipment and athletic trainers showed little improvement in blood pressure levels and had an overall weight gain. The plant that had the walking contest showed both lower blood pressure levels and moderate, lasting weight loss for most overweight employees in the plant. In addition, many more of its employees exercised regularly. About 45 percent exercised at least three times a week, compared with only 30 percent at the site with a fitness facility.

On the other hand, a fitness facility can become a much greater resource when it is made part of a program that provides the outreach to bring people in and the follow-up to keep them involved. Fitness facilities are very popular with employees. They represent tangible evidence that the company cares, even when the employees do not use the facility much. When the staff of the fitness facility are properly trained in both the use of the equipment and counseling about the broad array of health risks, the fitness center becomes a wellness center. The true value of the facility can then be realized.

Case Study #7

A large corporation is considering combining the fitness centers at each of its locations with the Wellness Outreach at Work Program. Each wellness/fitness center would be staffed with at least one exercise physiologist and one registered nurse. All staff members would receive training in the proper use of the center's exercise equipment and in outreach and follow-up counseling for a variety of health risks.

Reducing Worksite Health and Safety Hazards

The health risks addressed by worksite wellness programs are mostly risks that employees bring with them to the worksite (high blood pressure, cigarette smoking, etc.). But the worksite itself may pose health risks to employees. Most industrial worksites have health and safety programs that deal with these issues. The wellness program should not interfere with or attempt to take on those tasks.

But the wellness staff members will talk with large numbers of employees, so they may receive information that is of concern to the health and safety department (or other operating units, such as the cafeteria, the medical department, and human services). It is important that the wellness staff work with these groups so they can share information without overstepping boundaries.

If the workplace does not have an office or person responsible for health and safety, the wellness committee can promote discussion about the work environment, its effect on the health and safety of employees, and the ways in which it can be improved. This is especially important if employees believe that there are health and safety hazards in the environment that are not being properly addressed. It may be hard for them to believe the company's offer of wellness when they see health hazards ignored.

The wellness program can provide a forum for raising these issues, and it can encourage employees to voice their concerns through appropriate channels. The wellness program should not accept responsibility for dealing with workplace health and safety issues. Identifying and addressing environmental hazards requires a different set of skills and expertise than those needed for wellness promotion. The tasks of each program should be clearly defined.

ESTABLISHING A SUCCESSFUL SCHOOL-BASED HEALTH CENTER*

School-based health centers provide an opportunity to educate youths about healthy lifestyle choices. Health education, along with knowing when and how to access care, can reduce emergency department visits for youths and facilitate the managed care goals of continuity, quality, and cost-efficiency. The guidelines that follow were developed while planning and implementing a high school health center serving a diverse ethnic population of students. Although the center is owned by San Francisco State University, the link among the university, the community, and the hospital has been beneficial for all involved.

Models

Health centers are essentially divided into two types: school linked and school based. School-linked health centers may be located at a particular campus but offer service to additional schools that are close by. School-based health centers (SBHCs) are usually located at one school and offer services only to students at that campus. School health centers are school based and are usually located in urban areas where there is poverty, a high percentage of minority individuals who are under- or noninsured, and alarmingly low access to care. The low health-seeking behavior of adolescents is the most compelling reason to place these centers in schools.

Services

The problems that children and adolescents bring to school are complex and are closely related to the economic conditions surrounding these youths. To be effective, the services provided at school must match the needs of the students. Not all services may be delivered by the health center itself. In fact, other community resources may be more appropriate and will increase students' knowledge of and familiarity with local resources. What is necessary is the development of collaboration between school clinics and community sites, along with referral protocols that facilitate access to care. When youths are referred to hospital clinics, continuity of care is enhanced, and students with more complex problems can be managed in a more cost-efficient and high-quality manner.

The primary care services provided in school clinics may include routine physical examinations, sport physicals, laboratory services, treatment for minor injuries, prescriptions, immunizations, pregnancy testing, screening for sexually transmitted diseases, and the treatment of chronic illnesses such as asthma and allergies. Services also should meet the needs of special education students.

Some centers provide prenatal care and testing for the human immunodeficiency virus (HIV). Services are usually consistent with the needs of a particular age group and are developmentally appropriate. For example, eye and audiometric examinations along with immunizations are provided more often in elementary and middle schools. However, in high schools, particularly those with high immigrant populations, screening for immunizations, tuberculosis, and hepatitis may be offered.

---

*Source: Charlotte Ferretti, "School-Based and School-Linked Health Centers: Core Issues for Nurse Executives," *Aspen's Advisor for Nurse Executives*, Vol. 10, No. 5, Aspen Publishers, Inc., © February 1995.

Mental health services are critical to providing comprehensive care to students. The student who arrives at the clinic with a headache or stomachache may be referred to a counselor for depression or anxiety stemming from anything from a dysfunctional family to a fear of gang violence.

Staffing

Staffing for a school clinic should include a pediatric or adolescent physician specialist, a pediatric or family nurse practitioner experienced in family planning, a registered nurse with experience in case management, a licensed clinical social worker, a director, and a health educator. In addition, a cross-trained health intake coordinator who has skills not only in filing, data entry, and scheduling, but also in some medical tasks such as taking vital signs and drawing blood for laboratory work is helpful. A core of consistent staff is important to build trust between providers and students and ensure convenience and confidentiality.

Three Hints for Successful Performance

1. *Hire staff who are team players.* The school clinic environment is hectic and requires collaboration and coordination. Staff members must be able to work as an interdisciplinary team. They must know their own limitations, be familiar with each other's expertise, and know when to refer to an appropriate colleague.
2. *Ensure that staff members have experience with and knowledge about the age groups to which they are providing services.* Knowledge of the target population's growth and development, values, fears, issues, and pressures is imperative. When working with an ethnically diverse population, staff members must also be aware of their own issues, values, biases, and beliefs to be culturally sensitive and competent in providing services to youth.
3. *Ensure that staff members collaborate and are sensitive to the culture of the school itself.* Successful clinics have developed strong relationships with administration and faculty, reflected in good communication, a shared commitment to youth, and the personal qualities brought to the job.

Hospitals and School Health Centers

In the early 1970s, the innovative models of school health were linked closely with hospitals. Currently, many school health centers are operated by hospitals. In some cases, hospitals are looking for improved ways to meet their commitment to their communities. For example, Healthy Communities, a collaboration between businesses and local hospitals, is looking at ways to improve the health of community residents and has identified school health centers as one strategy for meeting this goal.

The planning, development, and implementation of school health centers are far easier for hospitals than for organizations starting from ground zero. Frequently, the hospital already has formal and informal agreements with local health care resources. Credibility in the community is usually strong. A needs assessment identifying morbidity and mortality rates for adolescents, teenage pregnancy rate, rate of low-birth-weight infants, and number of emergency department visits by adolescents can be easily compiled from hospital records.

Making the Decision

The decision to implement a school health center and provide selected services depends on the resources of the hospital and the restrictions put forth by school boards or local school districts. For example, many states do not allow testing for HIV or reproductive services at schools. There is more freedom for service delivery in such situations if the health center is located off campus. For nonprofit hospitals, school health centers provide opportunities to meet community service objectives. In this era of managed care, outreach to schools can reduce the potential for costly emergency visits.

There is strong support for nurse executives to take the lead in the development of school health centers. Since the early 1990s, the American Medical Association and many other major health and social organizations have supported community entities such as school health programs. The Office of Technology Assessment, in its review of adolescent health issues, recommended that comprehensive health centers be established in schools and communities. The National Board of State Boards of Education strongly supports the establishment of health centers in schools. Now, more than ever, hospitals, school districts, and community organizations must come together to enhance both the health and the education outcomes of today's youth.

NOTES:

Appendixes

Appendix A—Professional Organizations for the Health Educator 627
Appendix B—The Internet and Other Resources 633
Appendix C—*Healthy People 2010:* Summary of Goals and Objectives 641

Professional Organizations for the Health Educator

American College Health Association

The American College Health Association (ACHA) is made up of professionals and institutions of higher education dealing with health problems and issues in academic communities. It promotes continuing education, research, and program development related to educational institutions. With the increased amount of health education programming in college and university health services, ACHA has become an important forum for health educators functioning in those settings. For additional information, contact ACHA at P.O. Box 28937, Baltimore, MD 21240-8937; ph #: 410-859-1500, fax: 410-859-1510; Web: www.acha.org; e-mail: contact@acha.org

American Public Health Association

The American Public Health Association (APHA) is the largest and oldest professional health organization in the United States. It represents the major disciplines and specialists related to public health from community health planning and dental health to statistics and veterinary public health. APHA has two primary sections of interest to health educators: the Public Health Education and Health Promotion Section and the School Health Education and Services Section.

The Public Health Education and Health Promotion Section has more than 2,000 members and is one of the largest sections of APHA. It is concerned with providing input on public health education concerns to the overall APHA organization and its various sections and state affiliates. It is a major sponsor of scientific papers related to health education during the APHA annual meetings.

The School Health Education and Services Section, like the Public Health Education and Health Promotion Section, provides input to the APHA organization on matters related to comprehensive school health. Such input includes the traditional areas of school health education, school health services, and healthful school environment. This section also sponsors major scientific papers on school health during annual meetings of APHA. For further information, contact APHA at 800 I Street, NW, Washington, DC 20001-3710; ph #: 202-777-APHA; fax: 202-777-2534; Web: www.apha.org; e-mail: comments@apha.org

American School Health Association

The American School Health Association (ASHA) is the primary professional organization concerned with issues related to school-age children. School health services, healthful school environment, and comprehensive school health education are key areas of concern. ASHA provides the major forum for discussing school health issues through annual, regional, and local affiliate meetings as well as through publications and journals. ASHA provides leadership in professional preparation and practice standards for school health educators, school nurses, physicians, and dental personnel. For further information, contact ASHA at 7263 State Route 43, P.O. Box 708, Kent, OH 44240-0708; ph #: 330-678-1601; fax: 330-678-4526; Web: www.ashaweb.org; e-mail: asha@ashaweb.org

American Society for Health Care Education and Training

The American Society for Health Care Education and Training (ASHET) is a membership organization representing a diversity of health care and educational organizations for the purpose of promoting awareness of the educational needs common to all health care personnel, facilitating continuation of professional development in management, and encouraging participation in national health care issues. Health educators in medical care settings find this organization particularly helpful. Local chapters in large cities present programs for professional development. The organization also is linked to the American Hospital Association. ASHET can be reached at 1 North Franklin, Chicago, IL 60606-3421; ph #: 312-422-3000; Web: www.aha.org

Association for the Advancement of Health Education

The Association for the Advancement of Health Education (AAHE) is part of the larger American Alliance for Health, Physical Education, Recreation, and Dance, which comprises more than 43,000 professionals in sports, dance, safety education, physical education, recreation, and health education. The association has a membership of more than 6,500 professionals from schools, universities, community health agencies, and voluntary agencies. It promotes comprehensive health education programming in schools, colleges, and community settings. AAHE's full-time staff maintain close contact with federal legislative issues. For further information, contact AAHE at 1900 Association Drive, Reston, VA 22191-1599; ph #: 703-476-3437 or 1-800-213-7193; fax: 703-476-6638; Web: www.aahperd.org/aahe/aahe_main.html; e-mail: aahe@aahperd.org

Association for Worksite Health Promotion

The Association for Worksite Health Promotion (AWHP), formerly the Association of Fitness in Business, exists to advance the profession of worksite health promotion and the career development of its practitioners and to improve the performance of the programs they administer. AWHP has over 3,000 members and provides a newsletter, job bureau, publications, and guidelines. The AWHP journal is the *American Journal of Health Promotion*. For further information, contact the Association for Worksite Health Promotion at 60 Revere Drive, Suite 500, Northbrook, IL 60062; ph #: 847-480-9574, fax: 847-480-9282; Web: www.awhp.org; e-mail: awhp@awhp.org

Association of State and Territorial Directors of Health Promotion and Public Health Education

The Association of State and Territorial Directors of Health Promotion and Public Health Education (ASTDHPPHE) membership is made up of directors of health education in official state and territorial departments of public health. The association is primarily concerned with developing standards of health education programming at the state level and encouraging other state health education staff. It has been quite active in developing communication mechanisms on health education between state health departments and the federal government. The association is an affiliate of the Association of State and Territorial Health Officials. For further information, contact ASTDHPPHE at 750 First St., NE, Suite 1050, Washington, DC 20002; ph #: 202-312-6460; fax: 202-336-6012; Web: www.astdhpphe.org; e-mail: director@astdhpphe.org

The Health Project

The Health Project is a private-public organization formed to seek out, evaluate, promote, and distribute programs with demonstrated effectiveness in influencing personal health habits and the cost-effective use of health care services. The project has a Worksite Programs Task Force and Community Programs Task Force. In 1992, the project recognized what it considered the top worksite health promotion programs in the United States with the first annual C. Everett Koop Award. For further information, contact the Health Project, 1166 Avenue of the Americas, 43rd Floor, New York, NY 10036; ph #: 212-345-7336, fax: 212-345-5999; Web: www.healthproject.stanford.edu; e-mail: healthproject@stanford.edu

International Union for Health Promotion and Education

Although not a member of the coalition, the International Union for Health Promotion and Education (IUHPE), formerly the International Union for Health Education, is an international professional organization committed to development of health education around the world and bears special mention. The union cooperates closely with the World Health Organization and the United Nations Education, Scientific, and Cultural Organization (UNESCO) in a variety of international forums. IUHPE has four major objectives aimed at improving health through education:

1. establishing an effective link between organizations and people working in the field of health education in various countries of the world and enabling them to pool their experience and knowledge
2. facilitating worldwide exchanges of information and experiences on all matters relating to health education, including programs, professional preparation, research, methods and techniques, communication media, and so on
3. promoting scientific research and improving professional preparation in health education
4. promoting the development of an informed public opinion on matters related to healthful living

The union has constituent, institution, and individual memberships and meets every three years for international conferences. Its journal, the *Hygie International Journal of Health Education*, is printed as a three-language edition (English, French, and German), as are other technical publications. For further information on the union, write the North American Regional Office, University of North Texas, Health Science Center, School of Public Health, 3500 Camp Bowie Blvd., Fort Worth, TX 76107.

National Coordinating Committee on Worksite Health Promotion

Composed of national organizations representing employers and employee groups, the National Coordinating Committee on Worksite Health Promotion (NCCWHP) serves as a forum for networking and problem solving for the business and labor community. The NCCWHP includes federal liaisons from multiple departments and agencies. It examines emerging trends in worksite health promotion and identifies barriers and strategies to encourage implementation of worksite activities to achieve the goals and objectives of *Healthy People 2000*. For further information, contact the Office of Disease Prevention and Health Promotion at Public Health and Science, Office of the Secretary, Room 738G, 200 Independence Ave., SW, Washington, DC 20201; ph #: 202-401-6295; fax: 202-205-9478.

National Council for the Education of Health Professionals in Health Promotion

Another organization that warrants attention, but does not strictly constitute a professional organization for health educators in the context of others described here, is the National Council for the Education of Health Professionals in Health Promotion. Staffed by the American College of Preventive Medicine, its mission is to "assure that all health professionals are adequately prepared to make health promotion and disease prevention part of their routine practice." As such, the council is working with academic institutions that prepare allied health, public health, and primary care professionals to enhance health promotion and disease prevention components in their curricula, accreditation, certification, licensure, and continuing education. For further information, write the American College of Preventive Medicine, 1660 L Street, NW, Suite 206, Washington, DC 20036-5603; ph #: 202-466-2044; fax: 202-466-2662.

Society for Public Health Education, Inc.

Founded in 1950, the Society for Public Health Education, Inc. (SOPHE), has represented a major leadership role in public health education, both nationally and internationally, and is the only independent, free-standing health education organization. The society was formed to promote, encourage, and contribute to the advancement of health for all people by encouraging research, standards of professional preparation and practice, and continuing education. SOPHE has local chapters throughout the United States. It has an approval process for baccalaureate-level programs in community health education and a code of ethics that is widely used in health education. For further information, contact SOPHE at 750 First Street, NE, Suite 910, Washington, DC 20002-4242; ph #: 202-408-9804; fax: 202-408-9815; Web: www.sophe.org

Society of State Directors of Health, Physical Education, and Recreation

The Society of State Directors of Health, Physical Education, and Recreation (SSDHPER) membership comprises directors of school health, physical education, and recreation in state agencies. Its goal is to promote comprehensive statewide programs of school health, physical education, recreation, and safety. The society works closely with the American Alliance for Health, Physical Education, Recreation, and Dance and the other members of the coalition. For further information, contact SSDHPER at 1900 Association Drive, Reston VA 20191-1599; ph #: 703-476-3402; fax: 703-476-0988; Web: www.thesociety.org; e-mail: info@thesociety.org

Wellness Councils of America

Wellness Councils of America (WELCOA) is a national nonprofit organization dedicated to promoting healthier lifestyles for all Americans, especially through health promotion activities at the worksite. It has a nationwide network of locally affiliated wellness councils serving corporate members and their employees. WELCOA also acts as a national clearinghouse and information center on corporate health promotion. For further information, contact the Wellness Councils of America at 9802 Nichols Street, Suite 315, Omaha, NE 68114; ph #: 402-872-3590; fax: 402-872-3594; Web: www.welcoa.org; e-mail: welcoa@welcoa.org

The Internet and Other Resources

The resources in this appendix are numerous. All addresses, telephone numbers, FAX numbers, e-mail addresses, and Web addresses are current as of publication. These resources include professional organizations for the health educator, governmental granting bodies, several resources for health education materials related to minority health concerns, and various community nursing organizations. These addresses can be used to access a variety of health education and health promotion materials for patient education, grant applications, money to support health education programs, and professional development of the community health professional.

The Internet is a relatively new phenomenon that can be very useful for community health delivery. Much of community health involves making referrals and finding resources, educational materials, grant funding, and other professional services for programs or patients. The Internet can be an invaluable tool for connecting with organizations that supply these resources. Many times the necessary resources have already been discovered by another agency and can be shared on the Web. A combination of sharing resources, developing relationships with other community health practitioners, and staying current with professional educational materials makes the Internet unrivaled as a resource. Within hours one can find a plethora of current resources and educational materials by browsing the Web.

Caution is advised, however. Because the Internet is an unregulated resource, what is found ought to be critically evaluated before sharing it with patients or other professionals. Many times one can tell that educational material is current by noting the date on which the Web page was last changed. The book, *Internet Resources for Nurses* by editors Joyce J. Fitzpatrick and Kristin S. Montgomery, is recommended.[1] Lists of Internet resources under general categories are suggested by nurse experts in each area. These include government sites, professional organizations, and patient education sites. In this text, Romano, Hinegardner, and Phyillaier also discuss how to evaluate Web sites.[2] They suggest that the source or authority of the source be evaluated, that the objectivity and purpose of the site be considered, that the informational content be assessed, and that the currency of the site be critically analyzed. In addition, the design of the Web site is recommended as an evaluation criterion. According to the authors, these five criteria were those most often discussed in the literature. This text does not supply mailing addresses or telephone numbers, but does offer Web sites and a summary of the purpose of the site. There is also a chapter provided about "Evaluating Health Care Information on the Internet."[3] This chapter suggests several evaluation taxonomies proposed by various organizations—some health care oriented and others generally interested in the integrity of the information found on the Internet.

The following resources are a beginning for the health educator or community health professional. By accessing these resources, other similar organizations may be discovered in the search. Searching the Web is not only fun but also important to the goals of community health. As with other professional responsibilities, however, care is recommended.

REFERENCES

1. Fitzpatrick, J.J., and Montgomery, K.S., eds. *Internet Resources for Nurses.* New York: Springer Publishing Co., Inc., 2000.

2. Romano, C.A., Hinegardner, P.G., and Phyillaier, C.R. Some guidelines for browsing the Internet. In *Internet Resources for Nurses,* eds. Fitzpatrick, J.J., and Montgomery, K.S. New York: Springer Publishing Co., Inc., 2000:15–17.

3. Holloway et al. Evaluating health care information on the Internet. In *Internet Resources for Nurses,* eds. Fitzpatrick, J.J., and Montgomery, K.S. New York: Springer Publishing Co., Inc., 2000:197–213.

GENERAL HEALTH EDUCATION AND PROMOTION INFORMATION

Agency for Health Care Policy and Research (AHCPR)
2101 East Jefferson Street
Rockville, MD 20852
301-594-1364
FAX: 301-594-3212
Web: www.ahcpr.gov
e-mail: info@ahrg.gov

AHCPR Clearinghouse
P.O. Box 8547
Silver Spring, MD 20907-8547
410-381-3150
800-358-9295
FAX: 301-594-2800

American Association of Occupational Health Nurses
  (AAOHN)
2920 Brandywine Road, Suite 100
Atlanta, GA 30341
770-455-7757
FAX: 770-455-7271
Web: www.aaohn.org
e-mail: aaohn@aaohn.org

American Medical Association
515 North State Street
Chicago, IL 60610
312-464-5000
FAX: 312-464-4184
Web: www.ama-assn.org

Association of Schools of Public Health
1101 15th Street, NW, Suite 910
Washington, DC 20005
202-296-1099
FAX: 202-296-1252
Web: www.asph.org
e-mail: info@asph.org

Centers for Disease Control and Prevention (CDC)
Public Inquiries
1600 Clifton Road, NE
Mailstop E72
Atlanta, GA 30333
404-639-3534
800-311-3435
FAX: 404-639-1537
Web: www.cdc.gov

Council on Education for Public Health (CEPH)
800 I Street, NW, Suite 202
Washington, DC 20001-3710
202-789-1050
FAX: 202-789-1895
Web: www.ceph.org

Institute of Medicine
Division of Health Promotion & Disease
National Academy of Sciences
2101 Constitution Avenue, NW
Washington, DC 20418
202-334-2000
FAX: 202-334-1412
Web: www.iom.edu
e-mail: iomwww@nas.edu

National Association of Community Health Centers
1330 New Hampshire Avenue, Suite 122
Washington, DC 20036
202-659-8008
FAX: 202-659-8519
Web: www.nachc.com

National Association of County & City Health
 Officials (NACCHO)
1100 17th Street, NW, Second Floor
Washington, DC 20036
202-783-5550
FAX: 202-783-1583
Web: naccho.org
e-mail: info@naccho.org

National Commission for Health Education
 Credentialing, Inc.
944 Marcon Blvd., Suite 310
Allentown, PA 18109
610-264-8200
800-624-3428
FAX: 800-813-0727
Web: www.nchec.org

National Health Information Center (NHIC)
 (a national health referral agency)
P.O. Box 1133
Washington, DC 20013-1133
800-336-4797
FAX: 301-984-4256
Web: health.gov/nhic
e-mail: nhicinfo@health.org

National Wellness Institute
1300 College Court
P.O. Box 827
Stevens Point, WI 54481-0827
715-342-2969
800-243-8694
FAX: 715-342-2979
Web: nationalwellness.org
e-mail: nwi@wellnessnwi.org

AGING

American Association of Retired Persons (AARP)
601 E Street, NW
Washington, DC 20049
202-424-3410
Web: www.aarp.org

National Council on the Aging, Inc. (NCOA)
409 Third Street, SW, Suite 200
Washington, DC 20024
202-479-1200
FAX: 202-479-0735
Web: www.ncoa.org
e-mail: info@ncoa.org

National Institute on Aging
Public Information Office
Building 31, Room 5C-27
31 Center Drive, MSC 2292
Bethesda, MD 20892
301-496-1752
800-222-2225 (publications)
FAX: 301-496-1072
Web: www.nih.gov/nia

ALCOHOL AND OTHER DRUG ABUSE

Alcoholics Anonymous (AA) World Services
475 Riverside Drive, 11th Floor
New York, NY 10115
Mailing address:
Alcoholics Anonymous (AA) World Services
Grand Central Station
P.O. Box 459
New York, NY 10163
212-870-3400
FAX: 212-870-3003
Web: www.alcoholics-anonymous.org

National Clearinghouse for Alcohol and Drug
  Information
P.O. Box 2345
Rockville, MD 20847-2345
800-729-6686
FAX: 301-468-6433
Web: www.health.org
e-mail: info@health.org

CANCER

American Cancer Society (ACS)
1875 Connecticut Ave, NW, Suite 730
Washington, DC 20009
800-ACS-2345
202-483-2600
FAX: 202-483-1174
Web: www.cancer.org

National Institutes of Health
National Cancer Institute
Cancer Information Service
Building 31, Room 10A-31
31 Center Drive, MSC 2580
Bethesda, MD 20892-3100
800-4-CANCER
301-435-3848
FAX 301-402-2594
Web: www.nci.nih.gov

CARDIOVASCULAR DISEASE/SMOKING CESSATION

American Heart Association
National Center
7272 Greenville Avenue
Dallas, TX 75231
214-373-6300
800-AHA-USA1
Web: www.americanheart.org

American Lung Association
1740 Broadway
New York, NY 10019
212-315-8700
800-LUNG-USA
Web: www.lungusa.org
e-mail: info@lungusa.org

Centers for Disease Control and Prevention (CDC)
Office on Smoking and Health
4770 Buford Highway, NE
Mailstop K50
Atlanta, GA 30341
800-CDC-1311
FAX: 888-CDC-FAXX
Web: www.cdc.gov
e-mail: tobacco@cdc.org

National Heart, Lung, and Blood Institute
Education Programs Information Center
P.O. Box 30105
Bethesda, MD 20824-0105
301-592-8573
FAX: 301-592-8563
Web: www.nhlbi.nih.gov
e-mail: NHLBIinfo@rover.nhlbi.nih.gov

National Stroke Association
9707 E. Easter Lane
Englewood, CO 80112
303-649-9299
800-STROKES
FAX: 303-649-1328
Web: www.stroke.org

CHRONIC DISEASES

American Association of Diabetes Educators
444 North Michigan Avenue, Suite 1240
Chicago, IL 60611
312-644-2233
800-338-3633
FAX: 312-644-4411
Web: www.aadenet.org
e-mail: aade@aadenet.org

American Diabetes Association
1710 North Beauregard Street
Alexandria, VA 22311
703-439-1500
800-DIABETE
e-mail: customerservice@diabetes.org

Centers for Disease Control and Prevention (CDC)
National Center for Chronic Disease Prevention and
  Health Promotion
4770 Buford Highway NE
Mailstop K13
Atlanta, GA 30341
800-311-3435
Web: www.cdc.gov

National Diabetes Information Clearinghouse
1 Information Way
Bethesda, MD 20892-3560
301-654-3327
800-860-8747
FAX: 301-907-8906
Web: www.niddk.nih.gov/health/diabetes/ndic.htm

HIV INFECTION/AIDS

AIDS Education Office
American Red Cross
8111 Gatehouse Road
Falls Church, VA 22042
703-206-7120
FAX: 703-206-7754
Web: www.redcross.org

American Foundation for AIDS Research (AmFAR)
120 Wall Street, 13th Floor
New York, NY 10005-3902
212-806-1600
800-39-AMFAR
FAX: 202-806-1601
Web: www.afmar.org

National AIDS Hotline
24 hours a day, 7 days a week
800-342-AIDS (2437)

National Prevention Information Network
P.O. Box 60003
Rockville, MD 20849-6003
202-387-1950
800-458-5231
FAX: 888-282-7681
Web: www.cdcnpin.org

National Minority AIDS Council
1931 13th Street, NW
Washington, DC 20009
202-483-6622
FAX: 202-483-1135
Web: www.nmac.org
e-mail: info@nmac.org

MATERNAL AND CHILD HEALTH

American Academy of Pediatrics
141 Northwest Point Blvd.
Elk Grove Village, IL 60007-1098
800-433-9016
847-434-4000
FAX: 847-434-8000
Web: www.aap.org

American College of Obstetricians and Gynecologists
409 12th Street, SW
P.O. Box 96920
Washington, DC 20090-6920
202-863-2518
FAX: 202-484-5107
Web: www.acog.org

Association of Maternal and Child Health Programs
1350 Connecticut Avenue, NW, Suite 803
Washington, DC 20036
202-775-0436
FAX: 202-775-0061
Web: www.amchp1.org

Maternal and Child Health Bureau
Health Resources and Services Administration
1805 Parklawn Building
5600 Fishers Lane
Rockville, MD 20857
301-443-2170
FAX: 301-443-1797
Web: www.mchb.hrsa.gov

National Center for Education in Maternal & Child Health
2000 15th Street North, Suite 701
Arlington, VA 22201-2617
703-524-7802
FAX: 703-524-9335
Web: www.ncemch.org
e-mail: info@ncemch.org

National Maternal and Child Health Clearinghouse
2070 Chain Bridge Road, Suite 450
Vienna, VA 22182
703-356-1964
888-434-4MCH
FAX: 703-821-2098
Web: www.nmchc.org
e-mail: nmchc@circsol.com

MULTICULTURAL HEALTH PROMOTION

AT&T Language Line
Provides 24-hour access to interpreters who speak over 140 languages
800-752-0093

Office of Minority Health
Resource Center
P.O. Box 37337
Washington, DC 20013-7337
800-444-6472
FAX: 301-230-7199
Web: www.omhrc.gov
e-mail: info@omhrc.gov

Ohio Commission on Minority Health
77 South High Street, Suite 745
Columbus, OH 43266-0377
614-466-4000
FAX: 614-752-9049
Web: www.state.oh.us/mih

African Americans

Black Womens' Health Council
P.O. Box 31089
Capitol Heights, MD 20743-0089
301-808-0786
FAX: 301-808-0963

Health Promotion Council
260 South Broad Street
Philadelphia, PA 19102
215-731-6150
FAX: 215-731-6199
Web: www.hpcpa.org

National Association for the Advancement of
    Colored People (NAACP)
4805 St. Hope Drive
Baltimore, MD 21215
410-521-4939
Web: www.naacp.org
e-mail: communications@naacp.org

National Black Women's Health Project
600 Pennsylvania Ave., SE, Suite 310
Washington, DC 20003
202-543-9311
FAX: 202-543-9743
Web: www.nbwhp.org
e-mail: nbwhp@nbwhp.org

National Urban League, Inc. (NUL)
120 Wall Street
New York, NY 10005
212-558-5300
Web: www.nul.org
e-mail: info@nul.org

Asian Americans

Asian Health Project
T.H.E. Clinic
3860 West Martin Luther King Boulevard
Los Angeles, CA 90008
213-295-6571
FAX: 213-295-6577

Asian Health Services
818 Webster Street
Oakland, CA 94607
510-986-6830
FAX: 510-986-8696
Web: www.ahschc.org

Asian and Pacific Islander American Health
    Forum, Inc.
942 Market Street, Suite 200
San Francisco, CA 94102
415-954-9988
FAX: 415-954-9999
Web: www.apiahf.org
e-mail: hforum@apiahf.org

Asian Resource Center
635 North Erie, Room 104
Toledo, OH 43624
419-841-7542
FAX: 419-841-7542

Association of Asian/Pacific Community Health
    Organizations
439 23rd Street
Oakland, CA 94612
510-272-9536
FAX: 510-272-0817
Web: www.aapcho.org

Japanese American Citizens League
National Headquarters
1765 Sutter Street
San Francisco, CA 94115
415-921-5225
Web: www.jacl.org
e-mail: jacl@jacl.org

Korean Health Education, Information and Research
    Center
545 South Gramercy Place
Los Angeles, CA 90020
213-427-4000
FAX: 213-427-4008
Web: www.koreanhealth.org/english
e-mail: info@koreanhealth.org

Organization of Chinese Americans
1001 Connecticut Ave, NW, Suite 707
Washington, DC 20036
202-223-5500
FAX: 202-296-0540
Web: www.ocanatl.org
e-mail: oca@ocanatl.org

Hispanic/Latino Americans

Hispanic Health Education Center
Southwest Regional Educational Laboratory
4665 Lampson Avenue
Los Alamitos, CA 90720
310-598-7661
FAX: 301-985-9635

National Coalition of Hispanic Health and Human
  Services Organizations (COSSMHO)
1501 16th Street, NW
Washington, DC 20036-1401
202-387-5000
FAX: 202-797-4353
Web: www.hispanichealth.org
e-mail: alliance@hispanichealth.org

National Council of La Raza
1111 19th Street, NW, Suite 1000
Washington, DC 20036
202-785-1670
FAX: 202-785-0851
Web: www.nclr.org

Native Americans

Indian Health Service (IHS)
Communications Office
Health Resources and Services Administration
Department of Health and Human Services
Parklawn Building, Room 6A-35
5600 Fishers Lane
Rockville, MD 20857
301-443-3593
FAX: 301-443-0507
Web: www.ihs.gov

National Indian Health Board
1385 South Colorado Boulevard, Suite A-707
Denver, CO 80222
303-759-3075
FAX: 303-759-3674
Web: www.nihb.org
e-mail: nihb@nihb.aol.com

Native American Research and Training Center
University of Arizona
1642 East Helen Street
Tucson, AZ 85719
520-621-5075
FAX: 520-621-9802
Web: www.ahsc.arizona.edu/nartc
e-mail: lclore@u.arizona.edu

Zuni Wellness Center
P.O. Box 308
Zuni, NM 87327
505-782-2665
FAX: 505-782-2232
Web: www.healthytribes.com/zuni
www.zuni.kiz.nm.us/tribe/programs/wellness.html

NUTRITION/PHYSICAL FITNESS

American Dietetic Association
216 West Jackson Boulevard, Suite 800
Chicago, IL 60606-6995
312-899-0040
800-877-1600 (Consumer Nutrition Hotline)
FAX: 312-899-1758
Web: www.adaf.org

Food and Drug Administration
Office of Consumer Affairs
5600 Fishers Lane, Room 16-75
Rockville, MD 20857
301-827-4420
888-INFO-FDA
800-532-4440
FAX: 301-443-9767
Web: www.fda.gov

President's Council on Physical Fitness and Sports
200 Independence Avenue, SW
Humphrey Building, Room 738-H
Washington, DC 20201
202-690-9000
FAX: 202-690-5211
Web: www.fitness.gov

SEXUALLY TRANSMITTED DISEASES

American Social Health Association
P.O. Box 13827
Research Triangle Park, NC 27709
919-361-8400
FAX: 919-361-8425
Web: www.ashastd.org

Sexuality Information and Education Council of the
  United States (SIECUS)
130 West 42nd Street, Suite 350
New York, NY 10036-7802
212-819-9770
FAX: 202-819-9776
Web: www.siecus.org
e-mail: siecus@siecus.org

WOMEN'S HEALTH

National Resource Center on Women and AIDS
Center for Women Policy Studies
1211 Connecticut Avenue, NW, Suite 312
Washington, DC 20036
202-872-1770
FAX: 202-296-8962
Web: www.centerwomenpolicy.org
e-mail: cwps@centerwomenpolicy.org

National Women's Health Network
514 10th Street, NW, Suite 400
Washington, DC 20004
202-347-1140
FAX: 202-347-1168
Web: www.womenshealthnetwork.org

National Women's Health Resource Center, Inc.
120 Albany Street, Suite 820
New Brunswick, NJ 08901
877-986-9472
FAX: 732-249-4671
Web: www.healthywomen.org

WORKSITE HEALTH PROMOTION

Association for Worksite Health Promotion
60 Revere Drive, Suite 500
Northbrook, IL 60062
847-480-9574
FAX: 847-480-9282
Web: www.awhp.org
e-mail: awhp@awhp.org

Wellness Councils of America (WELCOA)
9802 Nichols Street, Suite 315
Omaha, NE 68114
402-872-3590
FAX: 402-872-3594
Web: www.welcoa.org
e-mail: welcoa@welcoa.org

Healthy People 2010—Summary of Goals and Objectives

ACCESS TO QUALITY HEALTH SERVICES

Goal: Improve access to comprehensive, high-quality health care services.

Number   Objective

Clinical Preventive Care

1-1	Persons with health insurance
1-2	Health insurance coverage for clinical preventive services
1-3	Counseling about health behaviors

Primary Care

1-4	Source of ongoing care
1-5	Usual primary care provider
1-6	Difficulties or delays in obtaining needed health care
1-7	Core competencies in health provider training
1-8	Racial and ethnic representation in health professions
1-9	Hospitalization for ambulatory-care-sensitive conditions

Emergency Services

1-10	Delay or difficulty in getting emergency care
1-11	Rapid prehospital emergency care
1-12	Single toll-free number for poison control centers
1-13	Trauma care systems
1-14	Special needs of children

Long-Term Care and Rehabilitative Services

1-15	Long-term care services
1-16	Pressure ulcers among nursing home residents

Source: *Healthy People 2010* (Conference Edition, in Two Volumes), U.S. Department of Health and Human Services, November 2000. For more information, access *Healthy People 2010* online, www.health.gov/healthypeople or call 1-800-367-4725.

ARTHRITIS, OSTEOPOROSIS, AND CHRONIC BACK CONDITIONS

Goal: Prevent illness and disability related to arthritis and other rheumatic conditions, osteoporosis, and chronic back conditions.

Number	Objective

Arthritis and Other Rheumatic Conditions

Number	Objective
2-1	Mean days without severe pain
2-2	Activity limitations due to arthritis
2-3	Personal care limitations
2-4	Help in coping
2-5	Employment rates
2-6	Racial differences in total knee replacement
2-7	Seeing a health care provider
2-8	Arthritis education

Osteoporosis

Number	Objective
2-9	Cases of osteoporosis
2-10	Hospitalization for vertebral fracture

Chronic Back Conditions

Number	Objective
2-11	Activity limitations due to chronic back conditions

CANCER

Goal: Reduce the number of new cancer cases as well as the illness, disability, and death caused by cancer.

Number	Objective
3-1	Cancer deaths
3-2	Lung cancer deaths
3-3	Breast cancer deaths
3-4	Cervical cancer deaths
3-5	Colorectal cancer deaths
3-6	Oropharyngeal cancer deaths
3-7	Prostate cancer deaths
3-8	Melanoma cancer deaths
3-9	Sun exposure
3-10	Provider counseling about preventive measures
3-11	Pap tests
3-12	Colorectal cancer screening
3-13	Mammograms
3-14	Statewide cancer registries
3-15	Cancer survival

CHRONIC KIDNEY DISEASE

Goal: Reduce new cases of chronic kidney disease and its complications, disability, death, and economic costs.

Number	Objective
4-1	End-stage renal disease
4-2	Cardiovascular disease deaths in persons with chronic kidney failure
4-3	Counseling for chronic kidney failure care
4-4	Use of arteriovenous fistulas
4-5	Registration for kidney transplantation
4-6	Waiting time for transplantation
4-7	Kidney failure due to diabetes
4-8	Medical therapy for persons with diabetes and proteinuria

DIABETES

Goal: Through prevention programs, reduce the disease and economic burden of diabetes, and improve the quality of life for all persons who have or are at risk for diabetes.

Number	Objective
5-1	Diabetes education
5-2	Prevent diabetes
5-3	Reduce diabetes
5-4	Diagnosis of diabetes
5-5	Diabetes deaths
5-6	Diabetes-related deaths
5-7	Cardiovascular deaths in persons with diabetes
5-8	Gestational diabetes
5-9	Foot ulcers
5-10	Lower extremity amputations
5-11	Annual urinary microalbumin measurement
5-12	Annual glycosylated hemoglobin measurement
5-13	Annual dilated eye examinations

Number	Objective
5-14	Annual foot examinations
5-15	Annual dental examinations
5-16	Aspirin therapy
5-17	Self-blood glucose monitoring

DISABILITY AND SECONDARY CONDITIONS

Goal: Promote the health of people with disabilities, prevent secondary conditions, and eliminate disparities between people with and without disabilities in the U.S. population.

Number	Objective
6-1	Standard definition of people with disabilities in data sets
6-2	Feelings and depression among children with disabilities
6-3	Feelings and depression interfering with activities among adults with disabilities
6-4	Social participation among adults with disabilities
6-5	Sufficient emotional support among adults with disabilities
6-6	Satisfaction with life among adults with disabilities
6-7	Congregate care of children and adults with disabilities
6-8	Employment parity
6-9	Children and youth with disabilities included in regular education programs
6-10	Accessibility of health and wellness programs
6-11	Assistive devices and technology
6-12	Environmental barriers affecting participation
6-13	Surveillance and health promotion programs

EDUCATIONAL AND COMMUNITY-BASED PROGRAMS

Goal: Increase the quality, availability, and effectiveness of educational and community-based programs designed to prevent disease and improve health and quality of life.

Number	Objective

School Setting

Number	Objective
7-1	High-school completion
7-2	School health education
7-3	Health-risk behavior information for college and university students
7-4	School nurse-to-student ratio

Worksite Setting

7-5	Worksite health promotion programs
7-6	Older adult participation in employer-sponsored health promotion activities

Health Care Setting

7-7	Patient and family education
7-8	Satisfaction with patient education
7-9	Health care organization sponsorship of community health promotion activities

Community Setting and Select Populations

7-10	Community health promotion programs
7-11	Culturally appropriate community health promotion programs
7-12	Older adult participation in community health promotion activities

ENVIRONMENTAL HEALTH

Goal: Promote health for all through a healthy environment.

Number	Objective

Outdoor Air Quality

8-1	Harmful air pollutants
8-2	Alternative modes of transportation
8-3	Cleaner alternative fuels
8-4	Airborne toxins

Water Quality

8-5	Safe drinking water
8-6	Waterborne disease outbreaks
8-7	Water conservation

8-8	Surface water health risks
8-9	Beach closings
8-10	Fish contamination

Toxics and Waste

8-11	Elevated blood lead levels in children
8-12	Cleanup of hazardous sites
8-13	Pesticide exposures
8-14	Toxic pollutants
8-15	Recycled municipal solid waste

Healthy Homes and Healthy Communities

8-16	Indoor allergens
8-17	Office building air quality
8-18	Homes tested for radon
8-19	Radon resistant new home construction
8-20	School policies to protect against environmental hazards
8-21	Disaster preparedness plans and protocols
8-22	Lead-based paint testing
8-23	Substandard housing

FAMILY PLANNING

Goal: Improve pregnancy planning and spacing and prevent unintended pregnancy.

Number	Objective
9-1	Intended pregnancy
9-2	Birth spacing
9-3	Contraceptive use
9-4	Contraceptive failure
9-5	Emergency contraception
9-6	Male involvement
9-7	Adolescent pregnancy
9-8	Abstinence before age 15 years
9-9	Abstinence among adolescents aged 15 to 17 years
9-10	Pregnancy prevention and sexually transmitted disease (STD) protection
9-11	Pregnancy prevention education
9-12	Problems in becoming pregnant and maintaining a pregnancy
9-13	Insurance coverage for contraceptive supplies and services

FOOD SAFETY

Goal: Reduce foodborne illnesses.

Number	Objective
10-1	Foodborne infections
10-2	Outbreaks of foodborne infections
10-3	Antimicrobial resistance of *Salmonella* species
10-4	Food allergy deaths
10-5	Consumer food safety practices
10-6	Safe food preparation practices in retail establishments
10-7	Organophosphate pesticide exposure

HEALTH COMMUNICATION

Goal: Use communication strategically to improve health.

Number	Objective
11-1	Households with Internet access
11-2	Health literacy
11-3	Research and evaluation of communication programs
11-4	Quality of Internet health information sources
11-5	Centers for excellence
11-6	Satisfaction with providers' communication skills

HEART DISEASE AND STROKE

Goal: Improve cardiovascular health and quality of life through the prevention, detection, and treatment of risk factors; early identification and treatment of heart attacks and strokes; and prevention of recurrent cardiovascular events.

Number	Objective

Heart Disease

12-1	Coronary heart disease (CHD) deaths
12-2	Knowledge of symptoms of heart attack and importance of dialing 911

12-3 Artery-opening therapy

12-4 Bystander response to cardiac arrest

12-5 Out-of-hospital emergency care

12-6 Heart failure hospitalizations

Stroke

12-7 Stroke deaths

12-8 Knowledge of early warning symptoms of stroke

Blood Pressure

12-9 High blood pressure

12-10 High blood pressure control

12-11 Action to help control blood pressure

12-12 Blood pressure monitoring

Cholesterol

12-13 Mean total blood cholesterol levels

12-14 High blood cholesterol levels

12-15 Blood cholesterol screening

12-16 Low-density lipoprotein cholesterol level in CHD patients

HIV

Goal: Prevent HIV infection and its related illness and death.

Number	Objective
13-1	New Acquired Immune Deficiency Syndrome (AIDS) cases
13-2	AIDS among men who have sex with men
13-3	AIDS among persons who inject drugs
13-4	AIDS among men who have sex with men and who inject drugs
13-5	New Human Immunodeficiency Virus (HIV) cases
13-6	Condom use
13-7	Knowledge of serostatus
13-8	HIV counseling and education for persons in substance abuse treatment
13-9	HIV/AIDS, sexually transmitted diseases (STD), and tuberculosis (TB) education in state prisons

13-10 HIV counseling and testing in state prisons

13-11 HIV testing in TB patients

13-12 Screening for STDs and immunization for hepatitis B

13-13 Treatment according to guidelines

13-14 HIV-infection deaths

13-15 Interval between HIV infection and AIDS diagnosis

13-16 Interval between AIDS diagnosis and death from AIDS

13-17 Perinatally acquired HIV infection

IMMUNIZATION AND INFECTIOUS DISEASES

Goal: Prevent disease, disability, and death from infectious diseases, including vaccine-preventable diseases.

Number	Objective

Diseases Preventable through Universal Vaccination

14-1 Vaccine-preventable diseases

14-2 Hepatitis B in infants and young children

14-3 Hepatitis B in adults and high-risk groups

14-4 Bacterial meningitis in young children

14-5 Invasive pneumococcal infections

Diseases Preventable through Targeted Vaccination

14-6 Hepatitis A

14-7 Meningococcal disease

14-8 Lyme disease

Infectious Diseases and Emerging Antimicrobial Resistance

14-9 Hepatitis C

14-10 Identification of persons with chronic hepatitis C

14-11 Tuberculosis

14-12 Curative therapy for tuberculosis

14-13 Treatment for high-risk persons with latent tuberculosis infection

14-14	Timely laboratory confirmation of tuberculosis cases
14-15	Prevention services for international travelers
14-16	Invasive early-onset group B streptococcal disease
14-17	Peptic ulcer hospitalizations
14-18	Antibiotics prescribed for ear infections
14-19	Antibiotics prescribed for colds
14-20	Hospital-acquired infections
14-21	Antimicrobial use in intensive care units

INJURY AND VIOLENCE PREVENTION

Goal: Reduce disabilities, injuries, and deaths due to unintentional injuries and violence.

Number   Objective

Injury Prevention

15-1	Nonfatal head injuries
15-2	Nonfatal spinal cord injuries
15-3	Firearm-related deaths
15-4	Proper firearm storage in homes
15-5	Nonfatal firearm-related injuries
15-6	Child fatality review
15-7	Nonfatal poisonings
15-8	Deaths from poisoning
15-9	Deaths from suffocation
15-10	Emergency department surveillance systems
15-11	Hospital discharge surveillance systems
15-12	Emergency department visits

Unintentional Injury Prevention

15-13	Deaths from unintentional injuries
15-14	Nonfatal unintentional injuries
15-15	Deaths from motor vehicle crashes
15-16	Pedestrian deaths
15-17	Nonfatal motor vehicle injuries
15-18	Nonfatal pedestrian injuries
15-19	Safety belts
15-20	Child restraints
15-21	Motorcycle helmet use

15-22	Graduated driver licensing
15-23	Bicycle helmet use
15-24	Bicycle helmet laws
15-25	Residential fire deaths

MATERNAL, INFANT, AND CHILD HEALTH

Goal: Improve the health and well-being of women, infants, children, and families.

Number   Objective

Fetal, Infant, and Child Deaths

16-1	Fetal and infant deaths
16-2	Child deaths
16-3	Adolescent and young adult deaths

Maternal Death and Illness

| 16-4 | Maternal deaths |
| 16-5 | Maternal illness and complications due to pregnancy |

Prenatal Care

| 16-6 | Prenatal care |
| 16-7 | Childbirth classes |

Obstetrical Care

| 16-8 | Very low birth weight infants born at Level III hospitals |
| 16-9 | Caesarean deliveries |

Risk Factors

16-10	Low birth weight and very low birth weight
16-11	Preterm birth
16-12	Weight gain during pregnancy
16-13	Infants put to sleep on their backs

Developmental Disabilities and Neural Tube Defects

| 16-14 | Developmental disabilities |
| 16-15 | Spina bifida and other neural tube defects |

16-16   Optimum folic acid

Prenatal Substance Exposure

16-17   Prenatal substance exposure

16-18   Fetal alcohol syndrome

Breastfeeding, Newborn Screening, and Service Systems

16-19   Breastfeeding

16-20   Newborn bloodspot screening

16-21   Sepsis among infants with sickle cell disease

16-22   Medical home for children with special health care needs

16-23   Service systems for children with special health care needs

MEDICAL PRODUCT SAFETY

Goal: Ensure the safe and effective use of medical products.

Number	Objective
17-1	Monitoring of adverse medical events
17-2	Linked, automated information systems
17-3	Provider review of medications taken by patients
17-4	Receipt of useful information from pharmacies
17-5	Receipt of oral counseling from pre-scribers and dispensers
17-6	Blood donations

MENTAL HEALTH AND MENTAL DISORDERS

Goal: Improve mental health and ensure access to appropriate, quality mental health services

Number	Objective

Mental Health Status Improvement

18-1   Suicide

18-2   Adolescent suicide attempts

18-3   Serious mental illness (SMI) among homeless adults

18-4   Employment of persons with SMI

18-5   Eating disorder relapses

Treatment Expansion

18-6   Primary care screening and assessment

18-7   Treatment for children with mental health problems

18-8   Juvenile justice facility screening

18-9   Treatment for adults with mental disorders

18-10   Treatment for co-occurring disorders

18-11   Adult jail diversion

State Activities

18-12   State tracking of consumer satisfaction

18-13   State plans addressing cultural compe-tence

18-14   State plans addressing elderly persons

NUTRITION AND OVERWEIGHT

Goal: Promote health and reduce chronic disease associated with diet and weight.

Number	Objective

Weight Status and Growth

19-1   Healthy weight in adults

19-2   Obesity in adults

19-3   Overweight or obesity in children and adolescents

19-4   Growth retardation in children

Food and Nutrient Consumption

19-5   Fruit intake

19-6   Vegetable intake

19-7   Grain product intake

19-8   Saturated fat intake

19-9   Total fat intake

19-10   Sodium intake

19-11   Calcium intake

Iron Deficiency and Anemia

19-12   Iron deficiency in young children and in females of childbearing age

19-13 Anemia in low-income pregnant females

19-14 Iron deficiency in pregnant females

Schools, Worksites, and Nutrition Counseling

19-15 Meals and snacks at school

19-16 Worksite promotion of nutrition education and weight management

19-17 Nutrition counseling for medical conditions

Food Security

19-18 Food security

OCCUPATIONAL SAFETY AND HEALTH

Goal: Promote the health and safety of people at work through prevention and early intervention.

Number	Objective
20-1	Work-related injury deaths
20-2	Work-related injuries
20-3	Overexertion or repetitive motion
20-4	Pneumoconiosis deaths
20-5	Work-related homicides
20-6	Work-related assault
20-7	Elevated blood lead levels from work exposure
20-8	Occupational skin diseases or disorders
20-9	Worksite stress reduction programs
20-10	Needlestick injuries
20-11	Work-related, noise-induced hearing loss

ORAL HEALTH

Goal: Prevent and control oral and craniofacial diseases, conditions, and injuries and improve access to related services.

Number	Objective
21-1	Dental caries experience
21-2	Untreated dental decay
21-3	No permanent tooth loss
21-4	Complete tooth loss
21-5	Periodontal diseases
21-6	Early detection of oral and pharyngeal cancer
21-7	Annual examinations for oral and pharyngeal cancer
21-8	Dental sealants
21-9	Community water fluoridation
21-10	Use of oral health care system
21-11	Use of oral health care system by residents in long-term care facilities
21-12	Dental services for low-income children
21-13	School-based health centers with oral health component
21-14	Health centers with oral health service components
21-15	Referral for cleft lip or palate
21-16	State-based surveillance system
21-17	Tribal, state, and local dental programs

PHYSICAL ACTIVITY AND FITNESS

Goal: Improve health, fitness, and quality of life through daily physical activity.

Number	Objective

Physical Activity in Adults

22-1	No leisure-time physical activity
22-2	Moderate physical activity
22-3	Vigorous physical activity

Muscular Strength/Endurance and Flexibility

22-4	Muscular strength and endurance
22-5	Flexibility

Physical Activity in Children and Adolescents

22-6	Moderate physical activity in adolescents
22-7	Vigorous physical activity in adolescents
22-8	Physical education requirement in schools
22-9	Daily physical education in schools
22-10	Physical activity in physical education class
22-11	Television viewing

Access

22-12   School physical activity facilities
22-13   Worksite physical activity and fitness
22-14   Community walking
22-15   Community bicycling

PUBLIC HEALTH INFRASTRUCTURE

Goal: Ensure that federal, tribal, state, and local health agencies have the infrastructure to provide essential public health services effectively.

Number   Objective

Data and Information Systems

23-1   Public health employee access to Internet
23-2   Public access to information and surveillance data
23-3   Use of geocoding in health data systems
23-4   Data for all population groups
23-5   Data for leading health indicators, health status indicators, and priority data needs at tribal, state, and local levels
23-6   National tracking of Healthy People 2010 objectives
23-7   Timely release of data on objectives

Workforce

23-8   Competencies for public health workers
23-9   Training in essential public health services
23-10   Continuing education and training by public health agencies

Public Health Organizations

23-11   Performance standards for essential public health services
23-12   Health improvement plans
23-13   Access to public health laboratory services
23-14   Access to epidemiology services

23-15   Model statutes related to essential public health services

Resources

23-16   Data on public health expenditures

Prevention Research

23-17   Prevention research

RESPIRATORY DISEASES

Goal: Promote respiratory health through better prevention, detection, treatment, and education.

Number   Objective

Asthma

24-1   Deaths from asthma
24-2   Hospitalizations for asthma
24-3   Hospital emergency department visits for asthma
24-4   Activity limitations
24-5   School or work days lost
24-6   Patient education
24-7   Appropriate asthma care
24-8   Surveillance systems

Chronic Obstructive Pulmonary Disease (COPD)

24-9   Activity limitations due to chronic lung and breathing problems
24-10   Deaths from COPD

Obstructive Sleep Apnea (OSA)

24-11   Medical evaluation and follow-up
24-12   Vehicular crashes related to excessive sleepiness

SEXUALLY TRANSMITTED DISEASES

Goal: Promote responsible sexual behaviors, strengthen community capacity, and increase access to quality services to prevent sexually transmitted diseases (STDs) and their complications.

Number   Objective

Bacterial STD Illness and Disability

25-1   Chlamydia
25-2   Gonorrhea
25-3   Primary and secondary syphilis

Viral STD Illness and Disability

25-4   Genital herpes
25-5   Human papillomavirus infection

STD Complications Affecting Females

25-6   Pelvic inflammatory disease (PID)
25-7   Fertility problems
25-8   Heterosexually transmitted HIV infection in women

STD Complications Affecting the Fetus and Newborn

25-9   Congenital syphilis
25-10   Neonatal STDs

Personal Behaviors

25-11   Responsible adolescent sexual behavior
25-12   Responsible sexual behavior messages on television

Community Protection Infrastructure

25-13   Hepatitis B vaccine services in STD clinics
25-14   Screening in youth detention facilities and jails
25-15   Contracts to treat nonplan partners of STD patients

Personal Health Services

25-16   Annual screening for genital chlamydia
25-17   Screening of pregnant women
25-18   Compliance with recognized STD treatment standards
24-19   Provider referral services for sex partners

SUBSTANCE ABUSE

Goal: Reduce substance abuse to protect the health, safety, and quality of life for all, especially children.

Number   Objective

Adverse Consequences of Substance Use and Abuse

26-1   Motor vehicle crash deaths and injuries
26-2   Cirrhosis deaths
26-3   Drug-induced deaths
26-4   Drug-related hospital emergency department visits
26-5   Alcohol-related hospital emergency department visits
26-6   Adolescents riding with a driver who has been drinking
26-7   Alcohol- and drug-related violence
26-8   Lost productivity

Substance Use and Abuse

26-9   Substance-free youth
26-10   Adolescent and adult use of illicit substances
26-11   Binge drinking
26-12   Average annual alcohol consumption
26-13   Low-risk drinking among adults
26-14   Steroid use among adolescents
26-15   Inhalant use among adolescents

Risk of Substance Use and Abuse

26-16   Peer disapproval of substance abuse
26-17   Perception of risk associated with substance abuse

Treatment for Substance Abuse

26-18   Treatment gap for illicit drugs
26-19   Treatment in correctional institutions
26-20   Treatment for injection drug use
26-21   Treatment gap for problem alcohol use

State and Local Efforts

26-22	Hospital emergency department referrals
26-23	Community partnerships and coalitions
26-24	Administrative license revocation laws
26-25	Blood alcohol concentration (BAC) levels for motor vehicle drivers

TOBACCO USE

Goal: Reduce illness, disability, and death related to tobacco use and exposure to secondhand smoke.

Number   Objective

Tobacco Use in Population Groups

27-1	Adult tobacco use
27-2	Adolescent tobacco use
27-3	Initiation of tobacco use
27-4	Age at first tobacco use

Cessation and Treatment

27-5	Smoking cessation by adults
27-6	Smoking cessation during pregnancy
27-7	Smoking cessation by adolescents

27-8	Insurance coverage of cessation treatment

Exposure to Secondhand Smoke

27-9	Exposure to tobacco smoke at home among children
27-10	Exposure to environmental tobacco smoke
27-11	Smoke-free and tobacco-free schools
27-12	Worksite smoking policies
27-13	Smoke-free indoor air laws

Social and Environmental Changes

27-14	Enforcement of illegal tobacco sales to minors laws
27-15	Retail license suspension for sales to minors
27-16	Tobacco advertising and promotion targeting adolescents and young adults
27-17	Adolescent disapproval of smoking
27-18	Tobacco control programs
27-19	Preemptive tobacco control laws
27-20	Tobacco product regulation
27-21	Tobacco tax

Index

A

Abstract, 64
Abstract nouns, 470
Abusive behavior, 22
Acceptability, 502, 509–510
Access, 167–168
Action
  failure of, 172
  orientation, 164
Action plan, immunization, 425–435
Activities coordination, 152
Activity level, membership, 165–166
Adolescent
  sexually transmitted disease
    intervention, 331–339
  women, reproductive pathways, 326
Adult
  education principles, 286–287
  immunization, 38
Advertising agency selection, 572
Advisory committees, 144
African American
  health education, 248–250
  issues, 244–245
    Diabetes Sunday program, 419–421
    parenting, 246–247
  resources, 637
Agency
  screening questions, 578
  selection, 575–577

Agenda, 168
Aging focus group guide, 125–126
Aid to Families with Dependent
  Children, 315
AIDS, 34–37. *See also* HIV / AIDS
  education worksheet, 115
Alcohol abuse
  resources, 635–636
  risk reduction, 21
Alliances, 144
Alzheimer's Disease focus group
  guide, 125–126
American Alliance for Health,
  Physical Education, Recreation and
  Dance, 631
American Association of Occupational
  Health Nurses, 608
American College Health Association,
  627
American College of Preventive
  Medicine, 630
American Diabetes Association,
  419–421
American Dietetic Association, 609,
  610
American Heart Association, 609
American Lung Association, 609
American Public Health Association,
  627–628
American School Health Association,
  628

American Society for Health Care
  Education and Training, 628
Amputations, lower extremity, 34
Appeal, 443
Applicant agency description, 69
Asian American resources
  issues, 251–252
  program for Hmong, 416–418
  resources, 638
Association for the Advancement of
  Health Education, 628
Association of State and Territorial
  Directors of Health Promotion and
  Public Health Education, 629
Association for Worksite Health
  Promotion, 629
Assurances, 71
Attractiveness, 502, 509
Audience
  analysis, 373–377
  health messages and, 82–83
  information about, 78
  knowledge of, 180
  learning about, 79–81
  low-literacy, 491, 492
Audiovisual materials, 452, 601

B

Background, 64

Behavioral profile, 375
Bilingual/bicultural providers, health workers, 217
Bisexual issues, 278–280
Boards of education, 93
Body language, 211
Body mass index, 33
Breakfast event, 390
    activities prior to, 404
    catering, seating arrangements, 403–404
    day of, 405–406
    evaluation, follow up, 406
    goals, objectives, 401
    guest commitments, 405
    help and support, 402–403
    keynote speaker, guest host, 403
    organizing, 400–401
    other groups, agencies involvement, 401–402
    size, location, 403
    why use, 400
Breast cancer screening, 32
Brochure
    layout, 471
    planning, 469
    revising, 471
    writing, 470–471
Budget, 64, 70, 117, 383, 396
Business/health coalitions, 608

C

Camera-ready materials, 468
Cancer
    resources, 636
    risk reduction, 23
    screening, management, 31–32
    video, 416–418
Captions, 454–455
Cardiovascular disease, 32–34. See also Heart health
    resources, 635
Catalog of Federal Domestic Assistance, 68
Catering, 403–404
Celebrity spokespersons, 574
Census data, 84
Center for Applied Linguistics, 222
Centers for Disease Control and Prevention, 297, 298–299, 314, 317, 318, 425
Center for Substance Abuse Prevention, 425
Certified health education specialist, 4
    responsibilities of, 12
Cervical cancer screening, 32
Chairperson, 144

Chambers of commerce, 93
Chemical dependency, African American, 250
Child health
    outreach, enrollment initiative, 413–415
    resources, 637
Childhood immunization, 37–38
Children
    focus group guide for, 127
    tips for working with, 128
Children's Aid Society, 322–323
Cholesterol, serum, 33
Chronic diseases resources, 636–637
Church partnerships, 192–193, 423
Citizens role, 166
Clarity, 443
Cleanup, 394
Clearinghouse, 203
Clerical staff, 152
Clichés, 470
Clinical preventive services, 24
Cloze test, 512
Coalitions
    advantages of, 145–146
    building effective, 146–161
    convening, 151
    defined, 144–145
    difficulties, 157–159
    leadership, 158, 162–164
    life expectancy, 153
    lobbying, 182–188
    membership, 165–166
    multisectoral, multicultural, 166
    overcoming barriers, 171–175
    program objectives and, 146–148
    public relations plan, 179–181
    resident activities in, 167–170
    resources for, 151–153
    school-community partnerships, 176–178
Code of Ethics, 15–17
Collaborating group inventory, 190
Colleagues, 12–13
College health program, 7, 93, 608
Colloquialisms, 262–263
Commissions, 144
Common vision, 173–174
Communication
    African American, 245
    culturally sensitive, 210–214
    Hispanic, Latin American, 254
    Native Americans, 267
    patient does not speak English, 215–216
    skills, 162
Community, 4

assessment, 75–76
    capacity, 4
    defined, 84
    demographic data worksheet, 97–98
    demographics, 79
    health assessment program tips, 110
    health indicators, 103–104
    health issue concerns, 112
    health status dataset, 87–92
    mapping needs, 105–106
    morbidity data, 93
        worksheet, 94–95
    nature of, 76
    needs assessment, 100
        checklist, 102
        data sources for, 101
    organization, 4
    prioritizing problems, 111
    profile, 84
        worksheet, 85–86
    representation, 235
    structures, 76–77
Community-based programs, 22
Community group
    first meeting, 58
    leader checklist, 59
    process evaluation, 60
Community health advisor
    competency, 289–291
    roles of, 288–289
Community health education, 4
Community health plan, 109
Community health problems
    analysis, 107
    worksheet, 108
Community involvement, 136–137
    checklist, 141
    follow-up contact sheet, 143
    resource inventory survey, 142
Community links, 174–175
Community partners
    guidelines, 138
    potential, 139–140
    reduce tobacco use in children, 191
Community preventive services program, 313
Competition, 171
Complimentary and alternative health practices, 5
Comprehension, 502, 509
Comprehensive school health education, 5
Condom
    labels, 527
    use, 526
Conferences, 389
Conflict resolution skills, 163

Confounding factors control, 598
Consistency, 443
Consortia, 144
Consultant selection, 575–577
Contests, 389
Continuing education, 203
Contractor selection, 575–577
  working tips, 579
Contracts, 61
Coordinated school health program, 5
Corporate culture, 619–621
Corporate grants, 62
Cost, 168–169
Counseling, 393
Credibility, 443
Crisis management, 561–562
Criticism, 163
Cultural barriers, overcoming, 217–219
Cultural characteristics, Native
  Americans, 266
Cultural competence, 5
  assessment, 234–243
Culturally competent program,
  201–202
  adaptation for, 206–207
  checklist, 236–239
  diversity worksheet, 209
  health promotion checklist, 240
  language barriers, 204
  partnerships for, 204–205
  resources, 637–639
  special needs children, 241–243
  training, 203, 208
Culturally sensitive communication,
  210–214
Cultural values, 198–199

D

Data collection instruments, 120, 130
Data measurement
  error, 594
  misclassifications, 594
  natural variation, 594
Data planning, 293
Decision-making process, 155–156
Delegation, 163
Demographic data worksheet, 97–98
Demographic profile, 374
Department of Agriculture Extension
  Service, 610–611
Department of Health and Human
  Services, 41, 316, 317, 321
Determinants of health, 5
Diabetes, 34–35
  risk reduction, 24
Diabetes Sunday program, 419–421

Diabetic retinopathy, 34
Dietitians, 610
Discussion guide
  background information for, 478
  character, situation reactions, 479
  feedback, 481
  questions in, 479
  related activities, 480
  sample, 482
  suggestions to close, 479
  theme, 481
  tips for handling discussion, 480–481
Disease prevention, 5
Distance, 210
Diversity worksheet, 209
Drug abuse assessment, 113
  data request form, 114
  resources, 635–636
Drugs risk reduction, 21

E

Editorial boards, 556
Educational materials
  adapting existing, 453–458
  audiovisual aids evaluation, 601
  exhibits evaluation, 602
  format, 455–456
  graphics, design, color, 467
  low-literacy. *See* Low-literacy
    materials
  posters, charts evaluation, 600
  pretesting, 456–457
  printed, evaluation, 599
  readability, 459
  reprinting camera-ready, 468
  resources for, 448
  review form, 446–447
  text, narrative, captions, 454–455
  visuals, 455–456
Education department, 608
Electronic immunization, 369
Emotional expression, 211
Employee
  committees, 606
  language bank, 218
  selection, 46–47
Employers, 13, 93
Employment application form, 46,
  48–51
End-stage renal disease, 34
Energy, 163
English, as second language, 212–213
Environment, 180
Environmental health risk reduction,
  22
Ethics

areas of responsibility, 12–13
  code of, 15–17
  nature of, 11–12
Evaluation, 13, 70
  choosing, 587–588
  cultural competence, 235
  elements of, 589
  improvements through, 159–160
  options, 586
  plan, 64
  planning, 296
  posters, charts, 600
  printed materials, 599
  program revision, 593
  progress, 178
  public relations plan, 181
  report
    outline, 592
    writing 590–591
  social marketing, 382–383
  types of, 584–585
Events, 618–619
  immunization, 367–368
Evidence-based health education, 6
Exercise events, 389
Exhibitors, 392–393, 394
Exhibits evaluation, 602
Experience, 169
Eye contact, 210

F

Facilitation skills, 162
Facilitator, 144–145
Fact gathering, 152
Fairs, 390
Falls prevention programs, 359
Family involvement, 177
Family planning, 21
Family relationships
  African American, 244
  Asian, Pacific American, 251
  Hispanic, Latin American, 253
Feature articles, 557
Federal Register, 68
Fees, 394
Field safety protocol, 345
Financial resources, 153
Fitness, 20
Fitness centers, 620–621
Flesch test, 470
Focus group, 81
  benefits, 117
  conducting, 120–122
  methodology, 118–122
  moderator's guide, 125–126, 127
  planning, 116–117

pretesting methods, 485–486
results analysis, 122
self-administered survey of, 336
specific issues, 334–335
study design, 119–120
topic guide, 124
when to use, 135
Follow-up, 393
contact sheet, 143
Food and drug safety, 22
Food festivals, 390
Food safety, sanitation, 423
Formality, 211–212
Formative evaluation, 584, 586
Foundation Center, 65
Foundation Directory, The, 65
Foundation, 153
grants, 62
proposal for, 65–67
Frames, 384–387
Fund-raising, 152
mission and, 305

G

Gatekeepers, 445
Gay issues, 278–280
Giveaways, 394
Goals, 64
Gold standard, 595
Gonorrhea intervention, 331–339
Government grants, 62–64
Grant developer checklist, 72
Grant money, lobbying and, 183
Grants, 61, 62
Group leader, 117
Guest host, 403
Guidelines, 27

H

Haircuts, health promotion and, 422
Hazard reduction, 621
Headings use, 497
Health advocacy, 6
Health assessment program tips, 110
Health behavior, 79
Health beliefs, 79, 199–200
Health Canada, 379
Health communications program
organizations, activities to consider, 312
outline, 310
planning, implementation, 311
Health departments, 93
Health education, 6, 393
African American, 248

development of, 3–4
ethical, legal issues, 11–14
field, 6
health promotion outcomes and, 6
program, criteria for development of, 9–10
promotion resources, 634–635
terminology, 4–8
Health education materials, 235. *See also* Education materials
Hispanic, Latin American, 259–265
in other languages, 221–222
special audiences, 220
translation procedure, 223
Health educator, 6
Health fair
committees, 397
planning sheet, 398
organizational strategies, 395–397
planning, 392–394
Health indicators, community, 103–104
Health informatics, 6
Health information, 6
Health insurance carrier, 606–607
Health issue concerns, 112
Health literacy, 7
Health maintenance organizations, 610
Health messages, public perception of, 82–83
Health opinion, Zuni community, 276
Health outcome, 7, 26
Health plan, sample, 109
Health problems analysis, 107
worksheet, 108
Health Project, The, 629
Health promotion, 7
cross-cultural, 240
funds, 61–64
haircuts and, 422
program
criteria for development of, 9–10
social marketing of, 372–373
providers, 610
worksheet, 309
worksite, 596–598
resources, 606–612
Health resources, African American, 248
Health risk, teen pregnancy, 319–320
Health status dataset, 87–92
Healthy Communities 2000, 3
model standards in use, 27
model standards principles, 26–27
overview, 76–77
Healthy lifestyle, 7
Healthy People 2000, 3, 4, 629
goals, 294–295

midcourse review of, 18–19
priority areas and governmental agencies, 25
risk reduction objectives from, 20–24
Healthy People 2010, 3, 4
defined, 39
disparity elimination for, 29–38
focus areas of, 40–41
goals, objectives, 39, 40, 641–651
leading health indicators, 41
proposed framework, 28
state and community health objectives of, 39
Heart disease, 23
weight and, 519–520
Heart-healthy
eating contract, 515
IQ, 516–518
High blood pressure, 32
prevention IQ, 521–522
Highway safety departments, 93
Hispanic American
audience materials, 259–265
issues, sociocultural, 253–254
natural support systems, 255–258
resources, 639
HIV/AIDS, 24, 34–37
education
gay, bisexual men, 278, 279
Native Americans, 268–275
hotline, 341–343
prevention, outreach program, 344–348
resources, 637
Home health hazards, African American, 248–249
Hope, 163
Hospitals, 93, 610, 623
Hotline
criteria for, 341–342
establishing, 341
quality assurance, 341
staff characteristics for, 342–343
Human sexuality, African American, 249
Hygie International Journal of Health Education, 630

I

Images, 484
Immunization, 24
adult record, 542
adult screening, 539
understanding, 540–541
baby shots, 534
18-month. 546

4-month, 543
6-month, 544
12 and 15-month, 545
barriers, 367
child discomfort after, 535–536
clinic supplies checklist, 528–529
coalitions, 425–435
information, 367–369
parents' questions, 537–538
rates, 37–38
screening questionnaire, 530
understanding, 531–532
vaccine administration record, 533
Immunization Coalition Training
need for, 425–426
needs assessment, 428–431
post-institute evaluation, 431–433
Immunization Coalition Training
Institute, 426–428, 431, 433–434
Impact evaluation, 585, 586
Implementation, culturally competent
program, 235
Indian Health Care Improvement Act,
40
Individual member, 145, 148
Infant
health, 23
mortality rates, 29–30
Infectious disease reduction, 24
Informal conversations, 80
Information, 169
acquisition, 214
gathering, 373–374
Injury control programs, 360
In-kind services, 396
International Union for Health
Promotion and Education, 629–630
Internet, 222, 633–634
Interpreters, 213, 215, 216, 218–219
Intervention strategies, 314–315
Interview, 47
in-depth, 80–81, 130–131
when to use, 135
individual, 487
intercept, 487
media, 559–560
report, 52
respondent description, 133

J–K

Jargon, 470
Jealousy, 163
Job descriptions, 53
Key messages, 223
Keynote speaker, 403
Knight Foundation, 425

L

Labor unions, 610
Language, 235
Language barrier, 204, 212–213
food and, 424
Hmong, 418
Latin American
audience materials, 259–265
issues, sociocultural, 253–254
natural support systems, 255–258
resources, 638
Lead agency, 145, 152
Lead poisoning, 248–249
Leadership, 158, 162–164, 174
checklist, 59
development, 164
Leading health indicators, 41
Learning principles, 284–285
action-oriented exercises, 449–450
audiovisual materials, 452
visual materials, 451
Legislation, introducing, 187–188
Legislative committee role, 185–186
Legislative process, 184, 185
Legislator education, 189
Lesbian substance abuse, 280
Letter of transmittal, 69
Letters to the editor, 557
Letter-writing campaigns, 187
Liability issues, 13–14
Library resources, 607
Lifestyle profile, 375–376
Lifestyles, 79
Literature reviews, 79–80
Lobbying
defined, 182–183
nuts, bolts of, 185–188
preparation, 184
working with legislature, 184–185
Local service clubs, 153
Low-literacy materials
audience, 491, 492
definition, 504–505
checklist, 503
content development, 505–507
format, 498–502
illustrations, 498
key principles, 508
message
organization, 493–494
writing, 494–497
pretesting, 502–503, 509–514

M

Mailing, immunization, 368

Management
plan, 64
tool, mission, 305
March of Dimes, 319, 320
Marketing, nonsmoking as norm, 356
Matching funds, 71
Materials adaptation, 137
Maternal and Child Health Block
Grant, 40
Maternal health, 23
resources, 636
Measurement error, 594
Media, 54, 153
channel
characteristics, 552
Hispanic, Latin American, 264
editorial boards, 556
feature articles, 557
interviews, 559–560
kits, 561
knowing local, 555
letters to editor, 557
news conferences, 560–561
news releases, 557, 558
op-ed page, 556
Public Service Announcements, 559
relationship, 181
strategy, 179–180
tools, 180
working with, 555–556
Media relations
broadcast, 568
contacting, 553–554
contacts, 551
handling bad news, 561–562
organization, 550
preparation, 550
professionalism, 551
Medical beliefs, practices, Asian,
Pacific American, 252
Meetings, 152, 154
effective, 57
first with community group, 58
participation between, 156–157
structure, 156
Member organization, 145, 148
Membership
coalitions, 165–166
parameters, 153–154
recruitment, 152, 158–159
Mental health/disorders, 21
Merchandise, immunization, 369
Message
construction, 444–445
delivery, 379–380
development, 380–381
Minority

recruitment, 203
smoking cessation, 353
Misclassifications, 594
Mission statement, 302, 303
use of, 304–305
visibility of, 304
Monitoring, social marketing, 382–383
Morbidity data, 93
worksheet, 94–95
Mortality data, contributors to leading causes of death, 96
Multicultural populations, serving, 203–205

N

Narrative, 454–455
National Campaign to Prevent Teen Pregnancy, 316, 317–318, 321
National Center for Health Statistics, 19
National Commission for Health Education Credentialing, 4, 12
National Committee on Quality Assurance, 40
National Coordinating Committee on Worksite Health Promotion, 630
National Council for the Education of Health Professionals in Health Promotion, 630
National Health Information Center, 612
National Heart, Lung, and Blood Institute, 611
National Immunization Survey data, 425
National Institutes of Health, 425
National Resource Center on Worksite Health Promotion, 612
National Survey of Family Growth, 317
Native American
issues, 266–276
resources, 639
Natural support system
background information form, 258
defined, 255
identifying, accessing, 256–257
rationale, 255
Natural variation, 594
Need, 64
Needs assessment, 53, 100
data sources for, 101
Immunization Coalition Training, 428–431
Negotiation, 26
Networks, 144
News conferences, 560–561

Newsletter, 54
audience, 472
budget, 476–477
editorial notes, 477
news aspects of, 473–475
production support, 476
staff, 475
Newsletters, 54
Newspaper media, 555
News releases, 557, 558
Non-governmental organization, 7
Nutrition, 20
African American, 249
program, Staten Island, 410–412
resources, 639
strategies that worked, 423–424
Nutritionists, 610

O

Objectives, 64, 70
coalition, 149–151
writing, 307
Observations, 80
Obstacle worksheet, 308
Occupational health clinics, 610
Occupational safety and health, 22
Office of Disease Prevention and Health Promotion, 612
Office of Minority Health, 19
Older Americans, reaching, 277
Op-ed page, 556
Opinion data, 129
Opinion leader, 129
survey, 134
Opinion survey, 132
Oral communication, 211
Oral health, 22–23
Outcome evaluation, 584–585, 586
Outcome measurement, 294–295
Hmong video program, 418
Outreach methods, 263–264
Outreach program
child health initiative, 413–415
peer educators, 347–348
schedule, 346
street, 344–345
wellness, 613
workshops, presentations, 346–347
Outside assistance, 575–577

P

Pacific American issues, 251–252
Paragraph elements, 496–497
Parenting
African American, 246–247, 248–250

involvement, 177
Partners, 381–382
Brooklyn program, 413–415
Passive voice, 470
PATCH program, 297, 298–299
critical elements of, 298–299
defined, 298
goal of, 298
process, 300–301
Peer educators, 347–348
People planning, 293
Performance planning, 293–294
Permits, 394
Personal interviews, 47
Personnel management, 45–46
Person-to-person contact, 54
Persuasion, 503
Philosophy writing, 306
Photos, 485
Physical activity, 20
barriers to, 365–366
promoting lifestyle, 364
target audience, 361–363
Physical fitness resources, 638
Picnic atmosphere, 423
Planned Parenthood, 316
Planning
brochure, 469
principles, 292–296
team, 176
Points, 443
Policy makers, 186–187, 189
Population-based health education, 8
Positioning statement, 379
Post-secondary health program, 7
Posting, immunization, 368
Pregnant women, smoking cessation, 352
Prenatal care, 320–321
Presentations, 346–347
Press plan, 180
Preterm birth, 30
Pretesting
educational materials, 502–503, 509–514
methods
advantages, limitations of, 490–491
applicability of, 489
focus groups, 486–487
interviews, 487
readability, 488
self-administered questionnaires, 488
theater, 488
Prevention, 7
Preventive Health and Health Services Block Grant, 40

Printed material, immunization, 368
Priorities planning, 294
Privacy, 253
Private funds, 61
Procedures, 70
Process evaluation, 584, 586
Professional associations, 608–610
Professional development, 8
Professional dominance, 173
Professional preparation, 8
Professionalism, 169
Profiles, 374–376
Program Evaluation and Review
    Techniques, 292
Program revision, 593
Proposal, 63–64
    defined, 68
    elements of, 69–71
    foundations, 65–67
    organization of, 65–66
    preparation, 63
    state or federal agency, 68–71
    submitting, 67
    writing, 66
Public funds, 61
Public health department, 608, 611
Public health grants, 384–387
Public health policies, 385–387
Public Health Service, 18
Publicity, 549–550. *See also* Media
    relations; specific media
    generating coverage, 550–551
    special event, 570–572
Public information, 152
Public need, 443
Public relations, 152
    plan, 179–181
Public school system, 608
Public Service Announcements, 549,
    559
    formats, 566–568
    pretest questions, 563–564
    radio writing, 565–566
    television writing, 566
    tips, 569
Public welfare, 12

Q–R

Quality assurance, hotline, 341
Questionnaires, 488
Radio media, 556
Radio writing, 565–566
Random allocation, 597–598
Rapid Estimate of Adult Literacy in
    Medicine (REALM), 461–464 word
    list, 465

Rapport, 212
Readability, 262, 458
    pretesting, 488
Reading level
    determination, 511–512
    selection, 460
Recording, 117
Recreation department, 608
Recruitment, coalition, 148–149
Redundancy, 470
Reference check, 46–47
Referral, 393
Referral services, 607
Registration, 394
Religious attitudes, beliefs
    African American, 244–245
    Hispanic, Latin American, 253–254
    Native American, 267
Representatives, 145
Reproductive pathways, adolescent
    women, 326
Request for application, 62, 63
Request for proposal, 62, 63
Research, 13, 152, 180
Residual guarantor, 26
Resource inventory survey, 142
Resources, 633–640
Respondent description, 133
Risk factors, youth violence, 437
Risk reduction, 8
Robert Wood Johnson Foundation, 425

S

Schedule development, 383
Scheduling, 168
School-based health center
    hospitals and, 623
    implementation decision, 624
    models, 622
    performance, 623
    services, 622–623
    staffing, 8, 623
School-community partnerships,
    176–178
    sexual risk reduction, 340
School health coordinator, 8
School policy, tobacco free, 357–358
Screening, 393
    data measurements in, 594
    gold standard, 595
    precautions, 595
    subject classification in, 594
    test characteristics, 399
Seating arrangements, 403–404
Second-hand smoke reduction, 355
Self-involvement, 502–503

Sentence elements, 495–496
Sexually transmitted disease, 24
    condom
        labels, 527
        use, 526
    facts, 525
    hotline, 341–343
    intervention, 331–339
    prevention, 523–524
    resources, 639
    risk reduction, 340
Silence, 210
Skills, 169
Skill testing, 47
SMOG conversion chart, 460
Smoke-free restaurant ordinances, 387
Smoking cessation, 33
    advice, 355
    methods, 351
    program steps, 350
    resources, 636
    strategies, 352–356
Social demographics, 79
Social marketing, 8
    audience analysis, 373–377
    content, 377–378
    measurable objectives, 378
    monitoring, evaluation, 382–383
    operational details, 383
    overview, 370–371
    role of, 372–373
    strategy, tactics, 378–382
Social service departments, 93
Society for Public Health Education,
    Inc., 631
Society of State Directors of Health,
    Physical Education, and Recreation,
    631
Sociocultural issues
    African American, 244–250
    Asian, Pacific Americans, 251–252
    gay, bisexual, lesbian, 278–280
    Hispanic, Latin American, 253–265
    Native American, 266–276
    smoking cessation, 354
Special event
    checklist, 408–409
    defined, 388
    examples, 389–390
    planning, 391
    publicity, 388, 569–571
    successful, 388–389
Special needs children, cultural
    diversity and, 241–243
Special populations, 19
Spelling, 470
Spirituality, African American, 250

Sponsors, 381–382, 392–393
Staff
  motivator, mission, 305
  paid, 164
  school-based health center, 623
Staffing, 145, 152
  cultural competence, 234
  hotline, 342–343
Standards, 27
Staten Island nutrition program, 410–412
Steering committee, 145
Street outreach programs, 344–345
Stress, African American, 250
Stroke risk reduction, 23
Students, 13, 153
Subject matter, 212
Substance abuse campaign, gay, lesbian, 280
Success, celebration of, 178
Sudden infant death syndrome, 30
Surgeon General, Workshop on Hispanic/Latino Health, 19
Survey, 80, 129, 134
  resource inventory, 142

T

Table of contents, 69
Target audience, 64, 69–70
  ethnic minorities, 220
  physical activity, 361–363
  track record of, 234
Task forces, 144
Technical assistance, 177
Technical terms, 470
Teen pregnancy
  factors, 325
  prevention
    battling, 316–318
    community pulse on, 329–330
    health risk assessment, 319–320
    myths, 318–319
    prenatal care, 320–321
    prevalence of pregnancies, 315–316
    principles, 324
    programs, 321–323
    steering committee, 327–328
Telephone calls, 187
Telephone director, 607
Television media, 556
Television writing, 566
  tips, 569
Text, 454–455

Theater pretests, 488
Timeline, 223, 224
Tobacco. *See also* Smoking cessation
  free school policy, 357–358
  reduction, in children, 191
  risk reduction, 20–21
  use
    prevention strategies, 352–356
    questionnaire, 349
Tone, 443
Trainees, 153
Training
  cultural competence, 234
  cultural sensitivity, 203, 208
Translation
  checker guidelines, 229–231
  checking, health staff, 232–233
  checklist, 228
  health education materials, 221
  materials, 219
  procedure, 223
    model, 226–227
  process, steps in, 223–225
Translator selection, 224–225
Transportation, 117
Tribal healing practices, 267
Trust, 163
Turf, 145, 171
Typeface, 500

U

United Nations Education, Scientific and Cultural Organization, 629
United Way, 609
Universities, 93, 608

V

Vaccine administration record, 533
  adult, 542
Video program, 416–418
Violence reduction, youth, 436–439
Violent behavior, 22
Visiting nurse associations, 610
Visual materials, 451, 454–455, 501–502
Vital statistic comparisons, 99
Voluntary health agencies, 93, 608–610
Volunteer, 153
  interviewing, 55
  recruitment
    mission and, 305
    training, 53–55
  retaining, 55

rewards for, 54
supervision, 55

W

Web site
  design
    color, fonts, backgrounds, 483
    images, photos, 484
    layout, 483–484
    testing, 484–485
  Diabetes Sunday, 421
Weight, heart disease and, 519–520
Welcoming stance, 162
Welfare reform, 316
Wellness, 8
  centers, 620–621
  outreach, 613
Wellness Councils of America, 607, 631
Wide Range Achievement Test, 511–512
Women
  health resources, 640
  smoking cessation, 353
Women's health resources, 640
Word
  list, 465
  use, 494–495
Work climate, positive, 56
Workshops, 346–347
Worksite health promotion, 8
  blue-collar workers and, 614
  confounding factors control, 598
  control group subjects, 596–597
  corporate culture and, 619–621
  group activities, 617–619
  key employees in, 615–616
  planning activities in, 616–617
  random allocation, 597–598
  resources, 606–612, 640
  selection bias, 597
  wellness outreach, 613
World Health Organization, 629
Writing, 177
  brochure, 470–471
  low-literacy materials, 494–497

Y

Yin-yang, 252
YMCA of the USA, 609
Youth
  smoking cessation, 354
  violence reduction, 436–439